SO-AFD-751

Code Listings

Linux Apache Web Server Administration

Charles Aulds

SYBEX

San Francisco Paris Düsseldorf Soest London

Associate Publisher: Neil Edde
Contracts and Licensing Manager: Kristine O'Callaghan
Acquisitions and Developmental Editor: Maureen Adams
Editor: James A. Compton
Production Editor: Dennis Fitzgerald
Technical Editor: Will Deutsch
Book Designer: Bill Gibson
Graphic Illustrator: Eric Houts, epic
Electronic Publishing Specialist: Franz Baumhackl
Proofreaders: Erika Donald, Nathan Whiteside
Indexer: Jack Lewis
Cover Designer: Ingalls & Associates
Cover Illustrator/Photographer: Ingalls & Associates

Library of Congress Card Number: 00-106196

ISBN: 0-7821-2734-7

SYBEX and the SYBEX logo are either registered trademarks or trademarks of SYBEX Inc. in the United States and/or other countries.

Screen reproductions produced with FullShot 99. FullShot 99 © 1991-1999 Inbit Incorporated. All rights reserved.
FullShot is a trademark of Inbit Incorporated.

Netscape Communications, the Netscape Communications logo, Netscape, and Netscape Navigator are trademarks of Netscape Communications Corporation.
Netscape Communications Corporation has not authorized, sponsored, endorsed, or approved this publication and is not responsible for its content. Netscape and the Netscape Communications Corporate Logos are trademarks and trade names of Netscape Communications Corporation. All other product names and/or logos are trademarks of their respective owners.

TRADEMARKS: SYBEX has attempted throughout this book to distinguish proprietary trademarks from descriptive terms by following the capitalization style used by the manufacturer.

The author and publisher have made their best efforts to prepare this book, and the content is based upon final release software whenever possible. Portions of the manuscript may be based upon pre-release versions supplied by software manufacturer(s). The author and the publisher make no representation or warranties of any kind with regard to the completeness or accuracy of the contents herein and accept no liability of any kind including but not limited to performance, merchantability, fitness for any particular purpose, or any losses or damages of any kind caused or alleged to be caused directly or indirectly from this book.

Manufactured in the United States of America

10 9 8 7 6 5 4

Foreword

Linux and open-source software are synonymous in the minds of most people. Many corporations fear Linux and reject it for mission-critical applications because it is open source. They mistakenly believe that it will be less secure or less reliable because the code is openly available and the system has been developed by a diverse collection of groups and individuals from around the world. Yet those same organizations depend on open-source systems every day, often without being aware of it.

The Internet is a system built on open-source software. From the very beginning, when the U.S. government placed the source code of the Internet Protocol in the public domain, open-source software has led the way in the development of the Internet. To this day, the Internet and the applications that run on it depend on open-source software.

One of the greatest success stories of the Internet is the World Wide Web—the Internet's killer application. The leading Web server software is Apache, an open source product. No library of Linux system administration books could be complete without a book on Apache configuration and administration.

Linux and Apache are a natural combination—two reliable, powerful, open source products that combine to create a great Web server!

Craig Hunt

September 2000

Acknowledgments

If I ever believed that a technical book was the work of a single author, I no longer hold that belief. In this short section, I would like to personally acknowledge a few of the many people who participated in writing this book. A lot of credit goes to the Sybex production and editing team, most of whom I didn't work with directly and will never know.

Craig Hunt, editor of this series, read all of the material and helped organize the book, giving it a continuity and structure that brings together all of the many pieces of the Apache puzzle. Before I met Craig, however, I knew Maureen Adams, the acquisition editor who recommended me for this book. Her confidence in my ability to accomplish this gave me the resolve to go further than simply saying, "I believe that some day I might write a book." Associate Publisher Neil Edde's can-do attitude and problem-solving skills also helped the project over a few bumps in the road.

Also part of the Sybex team, production editor Dennis Fitzgerald kept the project on schedule. Many times, prioritizing a long list of things that needed to be done is the first step toward their accomplishment. Jim Compton, editor, provided invaluable editing assistance, and often surprised me with his keen grasp of the technical material, many times suggesting changes that went far beyond the merely syntactic or grammatical. Will Deutsch was the technical editor for this book, and his research background and experience filled in more than a few gaps in my own store of knowledge.

Electronic publishing specialist Franz Baumhackl handled the typesetting and layout promptly and skillfully, as usual.

I must thank my employer, Epic Data — Connectware Products Group, for allowing me the freedom to work on this book. Particular thanks go to Linda Matthews, who was my supervisor during most of the project.

I also appreciate the time my keen engineering friend, Carl Sewell, spent reviewing all of the material I'd written, and I thank my Epic colleague Robert Schaap, whose knowledge of Apache and comments on the use of the `mod_rewrite` module proved quite valuable.

Last, but certainly most of all, I want to thank my dear wife, Andrea, for her unwavering support during what turned out to be a much harder endeavor than I anticipated. Finding time to devote to this project was the biggest challenge I had to overcome, and she found ways to give me that, taking on many of the household and outdoor chores that had been my responsibility.

Contents at a Glance

Contents

Part 3   Advanced Configuration Options   171

Introduction

The first Internet Web servers were experimental implementations of the concepts, protocols, and standards that underlie the World Wide Web. Originally a performance-oriented alternative to these early Web servers, Apache has been under active development by a large cadre of programmers around the world. Apache is the most widely used Web server for commercial Web sites and it is considered by many Webmasters to be superior to commercial Web server software.

Like Linux, Apache owes much of its incredible success to the fact that it has always been distributed as open-source software. Apache is freely available under a nonrestrictive license (which I'll discuss in Chapter 1) and distributed in the form of source code, which can be examined or modified. There's nothing up the developers' sleeves. While the sharing of intellectual property has always appealed to those who program computers primarily for the sheer love of it, until quite recently the motivations of the open-source community were lost on the business world, which understood only the bottom line on the balance sheet.

Today, however, the situation is much different from what it was when Apache and Linux were first introduced, and many companies now see open-source in terms of cost savings or as a way of leveraging technology without having to develop it from scratch. The open source software model seems to be with us to stay, and many companies have been structured to profit from it, by offering solutions and services based on computer programs they didn't create. While recent security and performance enhancements to its commercial rivals have left Apache's technical superiority in question, there is no doubt that Apache is a robust product in the same class as commercial Web engines costing far more. Apache is free, which enables anyone willing to make a moderate investment in inexpensive computing equipment to host Web services with all the features of a world-class site.

Who Should Read This Book?

This book is intended for the owner or administrator of one or more Linux workstations or servers who is interested in using the open-source Apache Web server software. A familiarity with Linux is assumed, and the book is ideal for the Linux administrator who needs to learn about Apache. The typical reader has access to a Linux system (and may have personally installed Linux on that system) and is anxious to know how to make use of the Apache software that came with the Linux distribution. This book will provide a valuable companion reference for anyone administering a Web server for a small to medium-sized company. While the book is not a professional programmer's reference, it provides an introduction to all aspects of programming for the Web, with useful examples of Web-based programs and server-side Web page parsing.

Linux is an excellent platform upon which to run a Web server. A review of Web server engines by *Network Computing* magazine made the point that, while some commercial applications now (surprisingly) exhibit performance superior to that of Apache, the underlying operating system plays a critical role in determining the overall reliability, security, and availability of a Web server. This is particularly true in e-commerce applications. Apache was given high marks when coupled with the robustness provided by the Linux operating system. While Apache is now available for non-Unix/Linux platforms, the real value of Apache is realized on Unix-like operating systems. To an increasing number of businesses today that means using Linux, with its unparalleled ability to compete on a price/performance basis.

Whenever Linux is used to provide commercial-quality Web services, Apache is the first and best choice of web server software. The intended reader of this book is someone who is using both Apache and Linux for the same reasons: quality, reliability, features, and price.

How This Book Is Organized

The chapters of this book are grouped into four parts: How Things Work, Essential Configuration, Advanced Configuration Options, and Maintaining a Healthy Server.

You can read this book either as a whole, from beginning to end, or by using the index and table of contents to find the topics you currently need to learn about. We start with foundation material that explains the basics of the World Wide Web and the architecture of Apache. The book then describes installation and basic configuration of the Apache software. The next group of chapters describes the advanced features used to create a dynamic, interactive server. The book concludes with a section that describes the day-to-day tasks of a Web administrator. A reader who understands the fundamentals of the Web and the Apache architecture can jump to the Essential Configuration section. An experienced administrator who understands all of the basics of Apache configuration can jump to the Advanced Configuration Options part of the book. However, most Web administrators will benefit from reading the entire text.

Many of the topics involved in Apache administration are closely related to each other; for example, you can't adequately discuss request redirection without assuming some familiarity with virtual hosting. Throughout the book I've used cross-references to help you trace these relationships without wading through too much repetition.

Part 1: How Things Work

Part 1 provides the introductory information the reader will need to understand what the Apache Web server does, how it is designed and how it compares to alternative software that performs the same tasks.

Chapter 1: An Overview of the World Wide Web

Chapter 1 provides a brief history of the World Wide Web, how it came to exist, and why. The chapter describes how the Web works, with a discussion of the network mechanisms and protocols used (IP, HTTP, HTML, etc).

Chapter 2: Apache and Other Servers

Chapter 2 provides an overview of the features and architecture of an Apache server, explaining the process swarm and other fundamentals of the Apache design. This chapter also surveys the various Web servers that compete with Apache, both free and commercial. As you'll see, Apache compares quite favorably to most of them.

Part 2: Essential Configuration

Part 2 details the compilation, installation, and configuration of a working Apache server. The chapters here cover the basics to get your server up and running.

Chapter 3: Installing Apache

To install Apache, you can either download and compile it yourself or use a precompiled binary distribution. This chapter first helps you decide between these options and then demonstrates each method, step by step.

Chapter 4: The Apache Directive

Directives are the administrator's primary tools for configuring Apache and controlling its operation. Chapter 4 discusses the basic concepts underlying the use of directives, including the essential topic of directive scope, and then summarizes the most important directives.

Chapter 5: Apache Modules

All of Apache's directives are grouped into modules. Chapter 5 discusses the Apache core module and the most important add-on modules.

Chapter 6: Virtual Hosting

Chapter 6 describes how to use virtual hosting to make your server function as if it were actually several different servers. Virtual hosting is used extensively by Web hosting services and ISPs to give clients their own (virtual) Web server, often hosting a number of these virtual sites on a single Web server.

Part 3: Advanced Configuration Options

The chapters in Part 3 discuss configuration options that are eventually required by a professional Webmaster. These options extend beyond the requirements of a basic Web server that provides only static documents.

Chapter 7: Server-Side Includes

Server-Side Includes (SSI), also known as server-parsed HTML, offer the simplest way to add dynamic content to a Web page. This technique embeds commands to the server directly in HTML content. Chapter 7 shows how to configure Apache to work with SSI and presents the most important SSI commands, known as *tags*.

Chapter 8: Scripting/Programming with CGI and Perl

Today, interactivity is a requirement for any commercial Web site. The ability to script or program a Web server greatly extends its value. The first of two chapters on scripting, Chapter 8 shows how to work with CGI, FastCGI, and Perl. The focus of this chapter and the next is on configuring Apache to work with these scripting tools.

Chapter 9: Other Apache Scripting/Programming Tools

Continuing the discussion of scripting and programming, Chapter 9 covers the most important newer scripting tools, including PHP, Active Server Pages, and various Java-related tools such as Apache JServ, Java Server Pages, and Resin. Again the focus is on installing these tools in Apache and configuring the server to work with them.

Chapter 10: Aliasing and Redirection

Nearly every Apache administrator needs to know how to implement the *aliasing* and *redirection* of client requests for resources that may not always be located where the server expects to find them. Chapter 10 first describes the capabilities provided by the standard mod_alias module and then provides a path through the complexities of the powerful third-party URL rewriting tool mod_rewrite.

Chapter 11: Controlling Apache

Chapter 11 is a quick look at starting and stopping the server both manually and programmatically, along with Apache's built-in monitoring tools and some third-party GUI configuration tools.

Part 4: Maintaining a Healthy Server

Part 4 is an administrator's handbook that covers the day-to-day activities of managing an Apache server, updating the information that is available from it, and ensuring that the server and the information that resides on it are secure.

Chapter 12: Apache Logging

The Apache log files provide the information you need to understand who is using your server and how they are using it. Chapter 14 discusses the basics of logging, including the standard log formats. It describes how logs can be customized using the mod_log_config Apache module. This chapter discusses techniques for interpreting the Apache logs, finding information in them, and rotating logs, and it also discusses the programs available for summarizing logs.

Chapter 13: Proxying and Performance Tuning

Once you have a working Apache Web server, you will want to tune the server to optimize its performance—minimizing the delay experienced by users in retrieving resources from your server and maximizing the number of requests you can respond to in a given time. Apache is already highly optimized and offers the administrator only a few performance directives. Chapter 13 discusses these directives and then examines one of the most important tools you can use to minimize document retrieval times on a local area network, Web caching using Apache as a proxy server.

Chapter 14: Basic Security for Your Web Server

Security is an essential topic for administrators of both Internet-connected and intranet servers. Web servers are particularly attractive targets for purveyors of mayhem on the Internet and crackers who want to compromise system security and steal information such as credit card numbers. The first of two chapters on security, Chapter 14 shows how to implement basic access control through authorization and authentication.

Chapter 15: Secure Sockets Layer

For sites that need to go beyond the basic security techniques discussed in Chapter 14, this chapter shows how to implement Netscape's Secure Sockets Layer technology and explains how it works.

Chapter 16: Metainformation and Content Negotiation

In order to do its job and deliver the optimum content acceptable to each client, Apache needs to know as much as possible about each resource that it serves. Metainformation not only tells the server how to process the data, it also instructs the client browser how to handle the data, determining which application to pass the data to if the browser is incapable of dealing with it directly. Chapter 16 shows how to work with metainformation in Apache.

Appendices

Four appendices present essential reference information about various aspects of Apache administration.

Appendix A: Apache Directives

Appendix A is a table listing all the directives included in the standard Apache distribution, summarizing each directive's context, overrides, module, and any default value.

Appendix B: Online References

Apache and Web services are complex topics. The Web itself is a great source of information to shed light on these topics. This appendix provides an extensive list of pointers to online information that can help you learn more about Apache and the Web.

Appendix C: Transferring Files to Apache

Appendix C shows how files are uploaded and placed on the Apache server. The discussion covers tools specifically designed for this purpose, like the PUT handlers used to accept uploads from products like Netscape Composer and Apache modules like the one for Microsoft Front Page Extensions. The chapter also covers the use of FTP, the most common means of updating files on a Linux Apache Web server.

Appendix D: Using Apache Documentation Effectively

Perhaps the most important reference information about Apache is provided by its own documentation. This appendix is a quick guide to getting the most out of the help system.

Conventions

This book uses the following typographical conventions:

`Program Font` is used to identify the Linux and Apache commands and directives, file and path names, and URLs that occur within the body of the text and in listings and examples.

Bold is used to indicate something that must be typed in as shown, such as command-line input in listings.

Italic is used in directive or command syntax to indicate a variable for which you must provide a value. For example,

    UserDir enabled *usernames*

means that in entering the `UserDir` directive with the `enabled` option, you would need to supply real user names.

[ ] in a directive's syntax enclose an item that is optional.

| is a vertical bar that means you should choose one keyword or another in a directive's syntax.

Help Us Help You

Things change. In the world of computers, things change rapidly. Information presented in this book, although it's current now, will become invalid over time. When that happens, we need your help locating the necessary changes. In addition, a 600-page book is bound to have typographical errors. Let us know when you spot one. Send your improvements, fixes, and other corrections to `support@sybex.com`.

Part 1

How Things Work

Featuring:

- A brief history of the World Wide Web and Apache
- How the HyperText Transfer Protocol (HTTP) works
- HTTP/1.0 response codes and other headers
- Apache's importance in the marketplace
- Other Web servers: free and commercial alternatives to Apache
- Major features of Apache
- Features planned for Apache version 2.0

1

An Overview of the World Wide Web

No book written about Apache, the most widely used Web server software on the Internet today, would be complete without a discussion of the World Wide Web (WWW) itself—how it came into existence, and how it works. Understanding the underlying technology is a key part of mastering any technical topic, and the technology that underlies Apache is the World Wide Web. This chapter is an introductory overview of a vast subject. The chapter begins with a history of the World Wide Web, introducing the Apache Web server, and then moves through an explanation of how the Web works, with a short introductory tour to the inner workings of the HyperText Markup Language (HTML) and the HyperText Transfer Protocol (HTTP). We'll look at new features of the HTTP/1.1 version of the protocol and use three common tools to observe the protocols in action.

A Brief History of the WWW

The World Wide Web (referred to throughout this book simply as *the Web*) is the result of years of evolutionary change. No one person or group can be credited with its creation. Indeed, it is unlikely that the original designers had notions as grand as the eventual reality of their accomplishment. Although based on the concept of embedded links between documents, called *hypertext,* which has its beginnings in the mid-Forties, the Web is generally considered the idea of one man, Tim Berners-Lee. In 1989, Berners-Lee submitted a proposal for a research project to CERN (*Conseil Europeen pour la Recherche Nucleaire*) in Geneva, Switzerland. Berners-Lee's proposal outlined a hypertext-based system that we would all recognize as today's Web, but it didn't discuss the technical foundation of that system, and didn't address the need to develop network protocols to support the system. The paper basically proposed extending the HyperCard system that was available for the Apple Macintosh computer to a local network-based system. The Web actually has a very humble beginning; the proposal does not, for example, foresee the expansion of the proposed system to global proportions.

The following year, 1990, a NeXT Cube workstation was purchased by CERN, and work began on the first graphical hypertext delivery system—the first Web *browser*. The CERN labs also distributed technical details that allowed developers to create their own Web servers. The first Web sites were initially set up as experimental, or "proof of principle" sites, mostly by academic and research institutions with the resources to develop them. Most of these were very simple servers, consisting of a few hundred lines of C code, based on source code obtained from CERN. In November 1992, the CERN list of "reasonably reliable servers" consisted of only 26 servers, at sites around the world.

All that changed in 1993. CERN was making available its own "reasonably reliable" server, with instructions on how to port and compile it to different types of hardware. In the United States, the National Center for Supercomputing Applications (NCSA), located at the University of Illinois at Urbana-Champaign, released NCSA Mosaic. The development and free distribution of the Mosaic browser was the catalyst that caused a sudden and sustained increase in the proliferation of Web servers on the Internet. NCSA also offered its own version of a Web server that was freely downloadable and relatively easy to install. The NCSA server was more widely adopted than the CERN server and lead the way with the addition of new features.

By 1994 the most widely used Web server software in the world was NCSA `httpd`. NCSA also had the lead in the development of the HTTP client portion with the Mosaic browser. The Web looked like it belonged to NCSA—a *nonprofit* organization, something that is almost inconceivable from our viewpoint a mere six years later. Progress on the NCSA server project stalled when its developer, Rob McCool, left NCSA in mid-1994. Since the source code for the NCSA server was widely available, many developers were already working on improvements and bug fixes. This trend toward decentralized, uncoordinated development continued into 1995, the year in which the Apache server was born.

The Apache server was assembled and released in early 1995 as a set of patches to the NCSA `httpd` 1.3 Web server. The name Apache is derived directly from this beginning as *a patchy server*. Get it? Numerous individual programmers, loosely bound into a consortium initially called the Apache Group, contributed the original source code patches that made up the first Apache server. In the true spirit and style of what is best about the Internet and open-source development, they collaborated by sharing ideas, criticism, encouragement, and camaraderie via e-mail and Usenet newsgroups.

Less than a year after the Apache group was formed, the Apache server replaced NCSA httpd as the most-used Web server. There are several reasons why Apache was so rapidly accepted and widely installed so soon after its initial availability. First and foremost, Apache was functionally identical to, and administered exactly like, NCSA httpd. With virtually no alterations to the file system, or configuration files, Apache could be plugged in as a replacement for NCSA. And there were good reasons to do so: Apache was faster, it was more reliable, it enjoyed wide support—and it was cool. Apache administrators immediately became part of a development effort that was on the leading edge of a new technology that was changing every facet of computing. Later developments only increased the superiority of Apache over the noncommercial, freely distributed servers available at the time. The most significant change was probably its support for add-on modules; this was achieved by exposing the internal workings of the server engine to third-party programs through a set of Application Programming Interfaces (APIs). This allows anyone, anywhere, to customize Apache to meet their own specific needs, but more important, it has led to the development of modules that can be freely obtained and added to the server to extend its capabilities. Many of these modules have been adopted for inclusion as part of the Apache distribution, though the use of most is optional.

With the decline in use of the two most prominent HTTP servers of the mid-90s (new development for both CERN and NCSA HTTP servers has been completely abandoned), Apache grew to become the most widely used Web server software on the Internet. As shown on the timeline in Figure 1.1, it achieved this status in April 1996, according to the Netcraft Web Survey (www.netcraft.com), and has held this position continuously since. Today most competing servers are commercially developed and supported, predominately those from Netscape and Microsoft. The growth of commercial servers doesn't reflect superiority over Apache as much as it points to the increasing use of the Web for commercial purposes. Many large companies, integrating their Web commerce engines with legacy databases and enterprise resource planning (ERP) systems, insist on using only commercial software. Traditionally, noncommercial software has been seen as experimental and not production-ready, incapable of performance and reliability equal to software developed for commercial resale. It's also possible to sue a commercial software vendor, even if it's difficult to win such a lawsuit. But Apache has overcome corporate prejudice. Linux, and software servers like Apache that use Linux, have made major inroads in changing industry perception of noncommercial open source software. As PCs did in the early 80s, Apache is steadily filtering into Fortune 1000 firms.

Figure 1.1 A Timeline of the Web and Apache

March 1989
Tim Berners-Lee proposes
a hypertext-based computer system.

October 1990
Work begins on the project that Berners-Lee
names World Wide Web.

March 1991
The National Science Foundation lifts restrictions
on the commercial use of the Internet.

January 1992
First version of line-mode browser released
to public.

February 1993
NCSA releases first version of Mosaic
for X Window System.

October 1993
Number of known HTTP servers exceeds 200.

March 1994
Marc Andreessen, et al. form Mosaic
Communications (later renamed Netscape).

February 1995
Apache Group (later renamed the Apache
Software Foundation) founded.

April 1995
First version of Apache released.

August 1995
Netcraft survey shows 18,957 HTTP servers.

January 1996
Netcraft survey shows 74,709 HTTP servers.

April 1996
Apache is the most widely used Web server
on the Internet.

April 1997
The number of HTTP servers exceeds 1 million.

The Apache License

What does it mean to describe Apache as open-source software? Open-source soft-ware is often associated with the GNU Public License (GPL), mainly because the GPL is the licensing agreement used by Linux and many applications written for Linux. Apache does not use the GPL and has a special license of its own. The Apache License, which can be retrieved from `http://www.apache.org/LICENSE.txt`, doesn't specifically prohibit any use of Apache and, unlike the GPL, does not require that modifications to Apache be made public. The Apache license exists mainly to limit the liability of the Apache Software Foundation (formerly known as the Apache Group) for damages or loss resulting from the use of Apache software. It also requires that the Foundation is properly credited in any commercial use of Apache or products based on the Apache server.

The Apache License *(continued)*

The essential thing to remember about the Apache license is that it expresses a copyright held by the Foundation for the Apache source code. Apache is not in the public domain. Control of the Apache source code remains ultimately in the hands of the Apache Software Foundation. Although it is possible that the Foundation could suddenly decide to pull the rug out from under hundreds of thousands of site administrators by requiring licensing or even prohibiting use of the software for commercial purposes, the likelihood of that happening is extremely remote. You'll find more precedents of commercial software vendors suddenly deciding to change their corporate practices or policies to the detriment of their clients; deciding, for example, that it is no longer economically feasible to support particular software. How many times has a software support technician told you, "You need to buy an upgrade to fix that problem"? Using open-source software can often protect your company from the vagaries of software vendors in a ruthless marketplace.

How the Web Works

The rapid adoption of the Web can be largely attributed to the accessibility of its technology. From the very first, Web browsers have been freely distributed, and it is highly unlikely that use of the Web would have exploded in the mid-90s had the situation been any different. The Web provides an interface to information that is simple and intuitive, providing links to millions of site around the world. We now have access to vast repositories of information, and it's all free for the taking. Was it our relentless search for intellectual self-improvement that enticed most of us into downloading our first Web browser onto our PCs, or an insatiable need for information to help us do our jobs more efficiently? Hardly. The truth is that the character of the early Web sites had a lot to do with the Web's instant popularity. What Web user wasn't first attracted by the interesting new combinations of text and color graphics (not to mention the fact that the personal computer gave a sense of security that the boss didn't know what we were *really* doing with our computers on company time)?

We were checking out something cool and always looking for something even cooler. It's not surprising that time spent using the new information distribution system became known by a simple nontechnical term: "browsing" the Web. The system of hyperlinks that allows one page to reference others, each of which leads to other (hopefully related) pages is what opened the Web to a vast, mostly nontechnical, audience. The Web was an astounding success because, even on a 14-inch monitor with a pixel resolution that is a joke by today's standards, nearly everyone said the same thing when they saw their first

Web page: "Cool!" No competing scheme for exchanging information that ignored the "cool" factor stood a chance against the Web.

At the heart of the design of the Web is the concept of the hyperlink. The clickable links on a Web page can point to resources located anywhere in the world. The designers of the first hypertext information system started with this concept. For this concept to work on a major scale, three pieces of the Web had to be invented. First, there had to be a universally accepted method of uniquely defining each Web resource. This naming scheme is the Uniform Resource Locator (URL), described in the accompanying sidebar. The second piece was a scheme for formatting Web-delivered documents so that a named resource could become a clickable link in another document. This formatting scheme is the Hyper-Text Markup Language (HTML). The third piece of the Web is some means to bring everything together into one huge information system. That piece of the puzzle is the network communication protocol that links any client workstation to any of millions of web servers: the HyperText Transfer Protocol (HTTP)

A hyperlink embedded in HTML-formatted page is only one way to use a URL, but it is the hyperlink that gave rise to the Web. If we had to resort to exchanging URLs by hand-writing them on napkins, there would be no Web. Most of us think of the Web in terms of visiting Web sites, but the mechanism is not one of going somewhere, it is one of retrieving a resource (usually a Web page) across a network using the unique identifier for the resource: its URL.

URLs can also be manually entered into a text box provided for that purpose in a Web browser, or saved as a *bookmark* for later point-and-click retrieval. Most e-mail programs today allow URLs to be included in the message body so that the recipient can simply click on them to retrieve the named resource. Some e-mail packages allow you to embed images in the message body using URLs. When the message is read, the image is retrieved separately; it could reside on any Internet server, not necessarily the sender's machine.

What is a URL?

A Uniform Resource Locator (or URL) is a means of identifying a resource that is accessible through the Internet. Although the distinction is academic, a URL is a special case of a Uniform Resource Identifier (URI) that is understood by Web servers. A URI is any string that uniquely identifies an Internet resource.

What is a URL? *(continued)*

Each URL is composed of three parts, a mechanism (or *protocol*) for retrieving the resource, the hostname of a server that can provide the resource, and a name for the resource. The resource name is usually a filename preceded by a partial path, which in Apache is relative to the path defined as the DocumentRoot. Here's an example of a URL:

    http://www.apache.org/docs/misc/FAQ.html

This URL identifies a resource on a server whose Internet name is www.apache.org. The resource has the filename FAQ.html and probably resides in a directory named misc, which is a subdirectory of docs, a subdirectory of the directory the server knows as DocumentRoot, although as we'll see later, there are ways to redirect requests to other parts of the file system. The URL also identifies the Hypertext Transfer Protocol (HTTP) as the protocol to be used to retrieve the files. The http:// protocol is so widely used that it is the default if nothing is entered for the protocol. The only other common retrieval method you're likely to see in a URL is ftp://, although your particular browser probably supports a few others, including news:// and gopher://.

A URL can also invoke a program such as a CGI script written in Perl, which might look like this:

    http://jackal.hiwaay.net/cgi-bin/comments.cgi

It was the Web browser, with its ability to render attractive screens from HTML-formatted documents, that initially caught the eye of the public. Beneath the pretty graphical interface of the browser, however, the Web is an information-delivery system consisting of client and server software components that communicate over a network. These components communicate using the HyperText Transfer Protocol (HTTP). The following sections describe this client/server relationship and the HTTP protocol used to move Web data around the world. This provides an introduction to the subject of the book, Apache, which is the foremost implementation of the HTTP server component.

What Is a Web Server?

Essentially, a Web server is a software application that listens for client connections on a specific network port. When a connection is made, the Web server then waits for a request from the client application. The client is usually a Web browser, but it could also be a Web site indexing utility, or perhaps an interactive telnet session. The resource request, usually a request to send the contents of a file stored on the server, is always phrased in some version of the Hypertext Transfer Protocol (HTTP).

Although the Web server's primary purpose is to distribute information from a central computer, modern Web servers perform other tasks as well. Before the file transfer, most modern Web servers send descriptive information about the requested resource, instructing the client how to interpret or format the resource. Many Web servers perform user authentication and data encryption to permit applications like online credit card purchasing. Another common feature of Web servers is that they provide database access on behalf of the client, eliminating the need for the client to use a full-featured database client application. Apache provides all of these features.

The HTTP Protocol

The Web consists of all the Web servers on the Internet and the millions of client systems that are capable of establishing temporary connections to them. The essential glue that holds the Web together is the set of interoperability standards that permit these clients and servers to exchange information across the Internet. These defined standard methods of communicating across a network are called *protocols*. To understand the Web, it is important to understand the protocols that establish and define it.

What is a protocol? Traditionally, the word refers to the rules of social behavior followed by dignitaries and heads of states. In computer networking, the term also refers to rules of behavior—those that apply to the two sides of a network connection. In this sense, the HTTP protocol defines the behavior expected of the client (browser) and server components of an HTTP connection. A browser can be written only if it knows what to expect from the servers it connects to, and that behavior is defined by the protocol specification (HTTP).

Generally, when an HTTP/1.1 server like Apache receives a request from a client browser, it will perform one of two actions. It will either respond to the request by sending a document (either static or dynamically generated by a program) or refuse to respond to the request, sending instead a numeric status code indicating why. If the numeric status code is in the range 300–399, it indicates to the browser that the server is redirecting the request to an alternate location.

A Web server cannot *force* a browser to retrieve a resource from another location. It sends a status code showing that the server couldn't respond to the browser's requests, along with a `Location:` directive indicating an alternate location for the resource. The browser is politely asked to redirect its request to this alternate location. The important thing to keep in mind is that the server does not direct the browser's behavior, but suggests or requests a certain action. That's the essence of a protocol, which is simply a codification of the acceptable (proper) and expected behavior of the components of a system.

The one protocol that all Web servers and browsers must support is the Hypertext Transfer Protocol, or HTTP. HTTP is actually not very complex as protocols go. The first version of HTTP (now referred to as version 0.9, or HTTP/0.9, although at the time there was no official versioning of the protocol) was extremely simple, designed only to transfer raw data across the Internet. The early Web servers that implemented this now-obsolete version of HTTP responded to simple requests like:

```
GET /welcome.html
```

Upon receiving this request, a server responds by sending a document stored in the file `welcome.html`, if it exists in the server's defined `DocumentRoot` directory, or an error response if it does not. Today's Web servers still respond to HTTP/0.9 requests, but only the very oldest browsers in existence still form their requests in that manner. HTTP/0.9 was officially laid to rest in May 1996 with the release of Request for Comments (RFC) 1945 ("Hypertext Transfer Protocol—HTTP/1.0"), which formally defined HTTP version 1.0. The most important addition to the HTTP protocol in version 1.0 was the use of *headers* that describe the data being transferred. It is these headers that instruct the browser how to treat the data. The most common header used on the Web is certainly this one:

```
Content-Type: text/html
```

This header instructs the browser to treat the data that follows it as text formatted using the HyperText Markup Language (HTML). HTML formatting codes embedded in the text describe how the browser will render the page. Most people think of HTML when they think of the Web. We're all familiar with how an HTML document appears in a browser, with its tables, images, clickable buttons and, most importantly, clickable links to other locations. The use of HTML is not limited to applications written for the Web. The most popular electronic mail clients in use today all support the formatting of message bodies in HTML.

The important thing to remember is that the Web's most commonly used formatting specification (HTML) and the network transfer protocol used by all Web servers and browsers (HTTP) are independent. Neither relies exclusively on the other or insists on its use. Of the two, HTTP is the specification most tightly associated with the Web and needs to be part of all World Wide Web server and browser software.

NOTE The operation of the Web is standardized by a number of documents called Requests for Comments (RFCs). While many of these are considered "informational" documents and have no status as standards or specifications, those that have been accepted by the Internet Engineering Task Force (IETF) are the accepted specifications that are used in the development of network applications. While RFCs are available from a number of sites, probably the best source is www.rfc-editor.org, which is funded by the Internet Society.

New Features in HTTP/1.1

The current version of HTTP is version 1.1, which is described and defined by RFC 2616 ("Hypertext Transfer Protocol – HTTP/1.1"). The official date of this document is June 1999, but work on the specification has been ongoing for years, and features embodied in the specification slowly found their way into mainstream servers and clients during that time. Version 1.1 includes several important new features that have been requested for years. You can expect HTTP/1.1 to be fully supported in all versions of Apache starting with version 1.3.4.

Most of the changes to HTTP in version 1.1 were made to the way HTTP client and server programs communicate and are designed primarily to enhance performance, especially using caching proxies (Chapter 13). Most features of HTTP/1.1 operate almost unchanged from HTTP/1.0, but some of the changes are quite visible and important to the Web site administrator.

One of the features of HTTP/1.1, hostname identification, is a way for the server to determine which of several virtual hosts should receive the request. In Chapter 6, we'll see how this eliminates the need for Web site hosting services to reserve unique IP addresses for each virtual Web site on a single host server. Hostname identification was one of the most requested changes in HTTP/1.1.

HTTP/1.1 supports a feature called *content negotiation*, in which an exchange of new HTTP/1.1 headers allows the browser and server to negotiate a common set of settings. This is useful, for example, in cases where a Web server provides resources in several versions (called *representations* or *variants*). The content negotiation feature of HTTP/1.1 allows the browser to automatically indicate a preferred language for the requested resource, or perhaps an alternate format for a document like PDF or Post-Script. Content negotiation is covered in Chapter 16, "Metainformation and Content Negotiation."

Four new request methods, described in detail in the next section, were added to HTTP/ 1.1: OPTIONS, TRACE, DELETE, and PUT (Table 1.1). Ever encounter a Web site that lets you upload a file from your Web browser? Probably not. That feature isn't seen more often because it requires that both server and browser support the PUT request method introduced in HTTP/1.1. (Actually, it is possible to upload files to a Web server using the POST method and CGI in earlier versions of HTTP, but HTTP/1.1 is the first to support two-way file transfers). Few Web site administrators are willing to rely on a new feature that would exclude a significant number of potential customers who are using outdated browsers. Soon, most browsers in use on the Internet will support HTTP/1.1. Increased server support for HTTP/1.1 has been introduced in each new release of Apache since work began on the specification several years ago.

The shakeout in the Web browser market, reducing the field of major competitors to just Netscape Communicator and Internet Explorer, has had one effect at least. Regardless of the browser you choose, ensuring compatibility with the very latest release has become almost essential. Although I had to have my fingers pried from Netscape Navigator 3.04 (I am using Netscape Communicator 4.7 now), I will never again use a Web browser even a few revisions old, in order to have the latest features of most modern browsers.

HTTP Request Methods

All HTTP requests begin with a header that specifies the request *method*. The most common method is the one used to request a resource from the server. This is the GET method. It is used to retrieve a resource from a Web server whenever you type a URL in the text box of your browser. The GET method is also used to invoke scripts, and it has provision for parameters to be appended to the method to allow data to be sent to the server. The primary use of the GET method is resource retrieval.

Table 1.1 shows the eight methods supported by HTTP/1.1. With the exception of the first three, GET, HEAD, and POST, all of these methods were added in HTTP/1.1 and are not part of HTTP/1.0 and earlier. Not all of these are retrieval methods; the PUT and POST methods are used to send data from the client to the server.

Table 1.1   HTTP 1.1 Methods

Method	Purpose
GET	Retrieves the resource identified in the request URL.
HEAD	Identical to GET except that the server does not return a message body to the client. Essentially, this returns only the HTTP header information.
POST	Instructs the server to receive information from the client; used most often to receive information entered into Web forms.
PUT	Allows the client to send the resource identified in the request URL to the server. The server, if it will accept the PUT, opens a file into which it saves the information it receives from the client.
OPTIONS	Used to request information about the communication options provided by the server. This allows the client to negotiate a suitable set of communication parameters with the server.

Table 1.1   HTTP 1.1 Methods *(continued)*

Method	Purpose
TRACE	Initiates a loopback of the request message for testing purposes, allowing the client to see exactly what is being seen by the server.
DELETE	Requests that the server delete the resource identified in the request URL.
CONNECT	Instructs a Web proxy to tunnel a connection from the client to the server, rather than proxying the request.

Observing the HTTP Protocol in Action

The quickest path to understanding how a basic HTTP retrieval works is to connect directly to a Web server and enter the HTTP request manually. Observing the protocol interactions between a client and server or manually requesting a resource and observing the server's response to your request shows the full range of HTTP protocol interactions. You can do this with a few different tools:

lwp-request   A Perl tool that allows you to control an HTTP connection manually.

HttpSniffer.pl   A Perl tool you can use to observe the HTTP connection between a client and server.

telnet   Allows you to connect directly to a remote server's HTTP port in order to manually control an HTTP connection.

Using lwp-request

If you've installed the collection of Perl modules and utility scripts collectively known as libwww-perl, you can use the lwp-request script that comes with that package to test HTTP connections. With this script, you can specify different request methods and display options. The following example illustrates the use of the -e argument to display response headers (more on headers shortly) with the -d argument to suppress the content in the response:

```
# lwp-request -e -d http://jackal.hiwaay.net/
Cache-Control: max-age=604800
Connection: close
Date: Wed, 21 Jun 2000 14:17:36 GMT
Accept-Ranges: bytes
Server: Apache/1.3.12 (Unix) mod_perl/1.24
Content-Length: 3942
Content-Type: text/html
```

```
ETag: "34062-f66-392bdcf1"
Expires: Wed, 28 Jun 2000 14:17:36 GMT
Last-Modified: Wed, 24 May 2000 13:45:21 GMT
Client-Date: Wed, 21 Jun 2000 14:17:37 GMT
Client-Peer: 127.0.0.1:80
Title: Charles Aulds's Home Page
```

Be sure to explore the other options available for `lwp-request`. For example, you can use the -H option to specify arbitrary request headers. This can be especially useful when experimenting with HTTP. For example, you can add `Referer:` and `Host:` headers to your request with this command:

```
lwp-request -H 'Referer: http://another.url.com/' \
    -H 'Host: vhost1.hiwaay.net' http://jackal.hiwaay.net/
```

`libwww-perl` consists of several scripts, supported by the following standard Perl modules (available separately, although most easily installed as part of the `libwww-perl` bundle):

URI   Support for Uniform Resource Identifiers

Net::FTP   Support for the FTP protocol

MIME::Base64   Required for authentication headers

Digest::MD5   Required for Digest authentication

HTML::HeadParser   Support for HTML headers

Even though you may not actually use the functionality of one of these modules, they must be properly installed on your machine to use the utility scripts provided with `libwww-perl`. Use the following commands to install all things at once, on a Linux system on which you have the `CPAN.pm` module:

```
# cpan
cpan> install Bundle::LWP
```

Among the utilities provided with `libwww-perl`, the most important (and the one most useful for examining the exchange of headers in an HTTP transaction) is `lwp-request`. Another that I find very useful, however, is `lwp-download`, which can be used to retrieve a resource from a remote server. Note that besides the HTTP shown in this example, you can use FTP:

```
# lwp-download http://jackal.hiwaay.net
Saving to 'index.html'...
3.85 KB received
```

CPAN

The best way to maintain the latest versions of all Perl modules is to use the CPAN.pm module. This powerful module is designed to ensure that you have the latest available versions of Perl modules registered with the *Comprehensive Perl Archive Network* or CPAN (http://cpan.org). CPAN archives virtually everything that has to do with Perl, including software as source code and binary ports, along with documentation, code samples, and newsgroup postings. The CPAN site is mirrored at over 100 sites around the world, for speed and reliability. You generally choose one nearest you geographically.

The CPAN.pm Perl module completely automates the processes of comparing your installed modules against the latest available in the CPAN archives, downloading modules, building modules (using the enclosed makefiles) and installing them. The module is intelligent enough to connect to any one of the CPAN mirror sites and (using FTP) can download lists of the latest modules for comparison against your local system to see whether you have modules installed that need upgrading. Once you install it, CPAN.pm even updates itself! Not only does the module automate the process of updating and installing modules, it makes the process almost bulletproof. I have never experienced problems with the module.

Another powerful Perl tool for observing the HTTP protocol is HttpSniffer.pl. Although not as convenient as lwp-request, because it does require setup and a separate client component (usually a Web browser), HttpSniffer.pl allows you to "snoop" on a real-world HTTP exchange, and it is more useful when you need to examine header exchanges with a browser (during content negotiation, for example).

Using HttpSniffer.pl

If you are using a fairly up-to-date version of Perl (at least version 5.004), you should consider a utility called HttpSniffer.pl to monitor the headers that are exchanged between a client browser and a Web server. HttpSniffer.pl acts as an HTTP tunnel, connecting directly to a remote server, and forwarding connections from client browsers, displaying the headers (or writing them to a log file) exchanged between the client and server.

Download HttpSniffer.pl directly from its author's Web site at www.schmerg.com. You can run the program on any platform running Perl 5.004 (or later). Figure 1.2 shows a typical session. The command window in the foreground shows how I invoked HttpSniffer.pl, pointing it at my Web server, jackal.hiwaay.net, with the -r argument. HttpSniffer.pl, by default, receives connections on TCP port 8080, and forwards them to the specified remote host. The browser in the background (running on the same computer as HttpSniffer.pl) is pointed at the URL http://localhost:8080. It appears to receive a page directly from jackal.hiwaay.net, but the connection is actually made by HttpSniffer.pl, which displays both the client request HTTP headers and the server response HTTP headers. The pages retrieved from jackal.hiwaay.net by HttpSniffer .pl are returned to the requesting browser.

Figure 1.2   HttpSniffer.pl at work

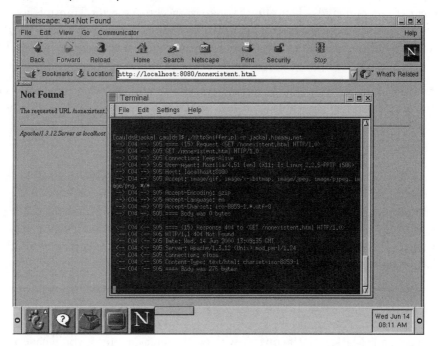

HttpSniffer.pl is not only an invaluable debugging tool, it is also the best way to learn the purpose of HTTP headers, by watching the actual headers that are part of an HTTP exchange. If you have access to a proxy server, on a remote server, or through Apache's mod_proxy (discussed in Chapter 13), you can point HttpSniffer.pl at the proxy, and then configure your client browser to connect to HttpSniffer.pl as an HTTP proxy server. That way, you can use your browser to connect to any remote host, as you normally would, and all requests will be redirected (or *proxied*) by HttpSniffer.pl. Be prepared for lots of output, though. Generally, you should invoke HttpSniffer.pl with a line like the following (the -l argument causes all of the output from the command to be written into the text file specified):

```
# HttpSniffer.pl -r jackal.hiwaay.net -l /tmp/httpheaders.txt
```

The only problem with `HttpSniffer.pl` and `lwp-request` is that they are not available on every Linux system. But `telnet` is. I use `telnet` in all of the following examples because every Linux administrator has access to it and can duplicate these examples. However, if you have `HttpSniffer.pl` or `lwp-request`, I encourage you to use them for testing.

Using `telnet`

You can connect directly to a Web server and enter the HTTP request manually with the Linux `telnet` command, which allows you to connect to a specific Transmission Control Protocol (TCP) port on the remote system. Not only will this allow you to see the complete exchange of messages between the client and server, it also gives you complete control of the session and provides a valuable tool for troubleshooting your Web server.

Enter the following `telnet` command at the shell prompt, replacing `somehost.com` with the name of any server accessible from your workstation and known to be running a Web server:

```
telnet somehost.com 80
```

This command instructs `telnet` to connect to TCP port 80, which is the well-known port reserved for HTTP connections. You should receive some confirmation of a successful connection, but you will not receive data immediately from the remote server. If the process listening on Port 80 of the remote system is an HTTP server (as it should be), it sends nothing upon receiving a connection, because it is waiting for data from the client. This behavior is defined by the HTTP specification.

The examples that follow are actual traces from my Linux server, which hosts a fully operational Apache server. I `telnet` to *localhost*, which is a special reserved hostname for the local system. You can do the same, if the system on which you are executing `telnet` also hosts an HTTP server. (If you stay with me through Chapter 5, you'll have a working system on which to test these commands.) Until then, you can connect to any Web server on the Internet to perform these tests.

```
$ telnet localhost 80
Trying 127.0.0.1...
Connected to localhost.
Escape character is '^]'.
```

At this point, `telnet` has an open connection to the remote HTTP server, which is waiting for a valid HTTP request. The simplest request you can enter is

```
GET /
```

This requests the default Web page for the directory defined as the server root. A properly configured HTTP server should respond with a valid page. Our request, which makes no mention of the HTTP version we wish to use, will cause the server to assume we are using HTTP/0.9. This should cause no problem with any server, but it is considered an obsolete form. All requests in HTTP/1.0 and subsequent versions should contain the HTTP version of the requester (or browser software).

```
$ telnet localhost 80
Trying 127.0.0.1...
Connected to localhost.
Escape character is '^]'.
GET /
<HTML>
<HEAD>
<TITLE>Charles Aulds's Home Page</TITLE>
</HEAD>
<BODY>

    Many Lines Deleted

</BODY>
</HTML>
```

The server, which assumes you are a client that understands only HTTP/0.9, simply sends the requested resource (in this case, the default page for my Web site). In the following example, I've issued the same request, but this time my GET line specifies HTTP/1.0 as the version of HTTP I'm using. Notice this time that the server will not respond as soon you type the request and press Enter. It waits for additional information (this is normal HTTP/1.0 behavior). Two carriage-return/line-feed character pairs are required to indicate the end of an HTTP/1.0 request.

Listing 1.1   Testing Apache with `telnet`

```
$ telnet localhost 80
Trying 127.0.0.1...
Connected to localhost.
Escape character is '^]'.
GET / HTTP/1.0

HTTP/1.1 200 OK
Date: Thu, 16 Dec 1999 08:56:36 GMT
Server: Apache/1.3.9 (Unix) mod_perl/1.19
```

```
Last-Modified: Tue, 14 Dec 1999 17:19:11 GMT
ETag: "dd857-ea1-38567c0f"
Accept-Ranges: bytes
Content-Length: 3745
Connection: close
Content-Type: text/html

<HTML>
<HEAD>
<TITLE>Charles Aulds's Home Page</TITLE>

    Deleted Lines

</HTML>
```

The Response Code Header

Notice that HTTP/1.0 sends a group of headers before sending the requested resource. The first header identifies the version of HTTP supported by the server and gives a request response code. The response code is in two parts, a number and a comment. 200 is the response code for a fully successful request, the OK is the comment provided as a convenience for human viewers only.

In Listing 1.1, the server replies with the response code 200, indicating that everything went well. Of course, that is not always the case. HTTP response codes fall into five categories, with a range of codes for each category:

Code Range	Response Category
100–199	Informational
200–299	Client request successful
300–399	Client request redirected
400–499	Client request incomplete
500–599	Server errors

The response categories contain more than 40 individual response codes. Each is accompanied by a short comment that is intended to make the code understandable to the user. To see a full list of these codes, go to the HTML Writers Guild at www.hwg.org/lists/hwg-servers/response_codes.html.

When using `telnet` to test an HTTP connection, it is best to replace the GET request method with HEAD. This prevents the server from actually sending the requested resource; it sends only the headers in reply. The resource is best viewed with a real browser. For `telnet` tests, the headers are what you're interested in. All of the following tests use HEAD instead of GET.

The request shown in Listing 1.2, specifying HTTP/1.1, has a very different result from the first test:

Listing 1.2 The headers in a failed test

```
$ telnet localhost 80
Trying 127.0.0.1...
Connected to localhost.
Escape character is '^]'.
GET / HTTP/1.1

HTTP/1.1 400 Bad Request
Date: Thu, 16 Dec 1999 08:57:30 GMT
Server: Apache/1.3.9 (Unix) mod_perl/1.19
Connection: close
Transfer-Encoding: chunked
Content-Type: text/html

177
<!DOCTYPE HTML PUBLIC "-//IETF//DTD HTML 2.0//EN">
<HTML><HEAD>
<TITLE>400 Bad Request</TITLE>
</HEAD><BODY>
<H1>Bad Request</H1>
Your browser sent a request that this server could not understand.<P>
client sent HTTP/1.1 request without hostname (see RFC2068 section 9, and
14.23>
<HR>
<ADDRESS>Apache/1.3.9 Server at Jackal.hiwaay.net Port 80</ADDRESS>
</BODY></HTML>
```

The response code header clearly indicates that our request failed. This is because HTTP/1.1 requires the client browser to furnish a hostname if it chooses to use HTTP/1.1. Note that the choice of HTTP version is always the client's. This hostname will usually be the same as the hostname of the Web server. (Chapter 6 discusses *virtual hosting*, in which a single Web server answers requests for multiple hostnames.)

In addition to warning the client about a failed request, the server makes note of all request failures in its own log file. The failed request in Listing 1.2 causes the following error to be logged by the server:

```
[Wed May 14 04:58:18 2000] [client 192.168.1.2] client sent HTTP/1.1 request
without hostname (see RFC2068 section 9, and 14.23): /
```

NOTE Logging is an important topic that is covered extensively later in the book. Chapter 12 is a complete discussion of connection and error logging in Apache. The path and filename of the log are defined in the Apache configuration, as we'll see in Chapter 4.

Request redirection is an essential technique for many Web servers, as resources are moved or retired. (Chapter 10 shows how to use Apache's tools for aliasing and redirection.) Listing 1.3 illustrates a redirected request.

Listing 1.3   A redirected request

```
# telnet localhost 80
Trying 127.0.0.1...
Connected to localhost.
Escape character is '^]'.
GET /~caulds HTTP/1.0

HTTP/1.1 301 Moved Permanently
Date: Wed, 21 Jun 2000 01:40:37 GMT
Server: Apache/1.3.12 (Unix) mod_perl/1.24
Location: http://jackal.hiwaay.net/~caulds/
Connection: close
Content-Type: text/html; charset=iso-8859-1

<!DOCTYPE HTML PUBLIC "-//IETF//DTD HTML 2.0//EN">
<HTML><HEAD>
<TITLE>301 Moved Permanently</TITLE>
</HEAD><BODY>
<H1>Moved Permanently</H1>
The document has moved <A HREF="http://jackal.hiwaay.net/~caulds/">here</
A>.<P>
```

```
<HR>
<ADDRESS>Apache/1.3.12 Server at jackal.hiwaay.net Port 80</ADDRESS>
</BODY></HTML>
Connection closed by foreign host.
```

If the browser specifies HTTP/1.1 in the request line, the very next line *must* identify a hostname for the request, as in Listing 1.4.

Listing 1.4   Using the HTTP 1.1 Host command

```
# telnet localhost 80
Trying 127.0.0.1...
Connected to localhost.
Escape character is '^]'.
GET / HTTP/1.1
Host: www.jackal.hiwaay.net

HTTP/1.1 200 OK
Date: Thu, 16 Dec 1999 11:03:20 GMT
Server: Apache/1.3.9 (Unix) mod_perl/1.19
Last-Modified: Tue, 14 Dec 1999 17:19:11 GMT
ETag: "dd857-ea1-38567c0f"
Accept-Ranges: bytes
Content-Length: 3745
Content-Type: text/html

<HTML>
<HEAD>
<TITLE>Charles Aulds's Home Page</TITLE>

        Deleted Lines
```

If our server answers requests for several virtual hosts, the Host: header of the request would identify the virtual host that should respond to the request. Better support for virtual site hosting is one of the major enhancements to the HTTP protocol in version 1.1.

The Other Headers

The response code header is always the first header sent by the server, and is usually followed by a number of additional headers that convey additional information about the HTTP message or the resource it contains (usually referred to as the *message body*). For example, the test shown in Listing 1.4 produced seven additional headers after the response code header: Date, Server, Last Modified, ETag, Accept-Ranges, Content-Length, and Content-Type. The following sections briefly outline these and other HTTP headers.

General Headers   Headers that carry information about the messages being transmitted between client and server are lumped into the category of general headers. These headers do not provide information about the content of the messages being transmitted between the client and server. Instead, they carry information that applies to the entire session and to both client request and server response portions of the transaction.

Cache-Control   Specifies directives to proxy servers (Chapter 13).

Connection   Allows the sender to specify options for this network connection.

Date   Standard representation of the date and time the message was sent.

Pragma   Used to convey non-HTTP information to any recipient that understands the contents of the header. The contents are not part of HTTP.

Trailer   Indicates a set of header fields that can be found in the trailer of a multiple-part message.

Transfer-Encoding   Indicates any transformations that have been applied to the message body in order to correctly transfer it.

Upgrade   Used by the client to specify additional communication protocols it supports and would like to use if the server permits.

Via   Tacked onto the message by proxies or gateways to show that they handled the message.

Warning   Specifies additional information about the status or transformation of a message which might not be reflected in the message itself.

Request Headers   Request headers are used to pass information from HTTP client to server; these headers always follow the one mandatory line in a request, which contains the URI of the request itself. Request headers act as modifiers for the actual request, allowing the client to include additional information that qualifies the request, usually specifying what constitutes an acceptable response.

Accept   Lists all MIME media types the client is capable of accepting.

Accept-Charset   Lists all character set the client is capable of accepting.

Accept-Encoding   Lists all encodings (particularly compression schemes) the client is capable of accepting.

Accept-Language   Lists all languages the client is willing to accept.

`Authorization` Provides the user's credentials to access the requested resource (usually a username/password pair).

`Expect` Indicates server behaviors that are required by the client.

`From` An Internet e-mail address for the person controlling the requesting user agent (browser).

`Host` Indicates an Internet hostname and port number for the resource being requested. Used by HTTP/1.1 clients to specify a single virtual host among many on a server.

`If-Match` A client that has one or more resources previously obtained from the server can verify that one of those resources is current by including a list of their associated tags in this header.

`If-Modified-Since` Specifies a date received in a previously received entity to check it for currency.

`If-None-Match` Similar to the `If-Match:` header but used to verify that none of the previously received resources is current.

`If-Range` If a client has a partial copy of a resource in its cache, it can use this header to retrieve the rest of the resource if it hasn't been modified.

`If-Unmodified-Since` Used by caching engines to specify that the resource should be sent only if not modified since a specified date.

`Max-Forwards` Specifies the number of times this client request can be forwarded by proxies and gateways.

`Proxy-Authorization` Supplies the credentials that the client must supply to use a proxy server.

`Range` Specifies the retrieval of a portion of a resource, usually specified as a range of bytes.

`Refererer` Specifies the URI of the resource from which the request URI was obtained (usually from a hyperlink in another Web page).

`TE` Indicates what transfer encodings the client is willing to accept and whether it will accept headers in trailer fields in chunked transfer-coding.

`User-Agent` Contains information about the user agent (browser) originating the request.

Response Headers The server uses response headers to pass information in addition to the request response to the requesting client. Response headers usually provide information about the response message itself, and not necessarily about the resource being sent to satisfy a client request. Increasingly, response headers serve to provide information used by caching gateways or proxy server engines. The response headers will be an important part of the discussion on proxy caching (Chapter 13).

Accept-Ranges   Specifies units (usually bytes) in which the server will accept range requests.

Age   The server's estimated time (in seconds) required to fulfill this request.

Etag   Contains the current value of the requested entity tag.

Location   Contains a URI to which the client request should be redirected.

Proxy-Authenticate   Indicates the authentication schema and parameters applicable to the proxy for this request.

Retry-After   Used by the server to indicate how long a URI is expected to be unavailable.

Server   Contains information about the software used by the origin server to handle the request. Apache identifies itself using this header. In Listing 1.4, notice that the server describes the version of Perl supported.

Vary   Indicates that the resource has multiple sources that may vary according to the supplied list of request headers.

WWW-Authenticate   Used with a 401-Unauthorized response code to indicate that the requested URI needs authentication and specifies the authorization scheme required (usually a username/password pair) and the name of the authorization realm.

Entity Headers   Entity headers contain information directly related to the resource being provided to the client in fulfillment of the request, in other words, the response message content or body. This information is used by the client to determine how to render the resource or which application to invoke to handle it (for example, the Adobe Acrobat reader). Entity headers contain *metainformation* (or information about information), the subject of Chapter 16.

Allow   Informs the client of valid methods associated with the resource.

Content-Encoding   Indicates the encoding (usually compression) scheme applied to the contents.

Content-Language   Indicates the natural language of the contents.

Content-Length   Contains the size of the body of the HTTP message.

Content-Location   Supplies the resource location for the resource in the message body, usually used when the resource should be requested using another URI.

Content-MD5   Contains the MD5 digest of the message body, used to verify the integrity of the resource.

Content-Range   Sent with a partial body to specify where in the complete resource this portion fits.

Content-Type   Describes the MIME media type of the contents.

Expires   Specifies a date and time after which the resource should be considered obsolete.

Last-Modified   Specifies the date and time at which the original document or resource was last modified.

NOTE   More details about these and other headers are available in the HTTP specification RFC 2616.

In Sum

This chapter looked at the World Wide Web, its origins and history, and described briefly how it functions. An essential part of the design of the Web is the standard set of protocols that allow applications to interoperate with any of the millions of other systems that make up the Web. The essential protocol that enables the Web to exist is the HyperText Transfer Protocol (HTTP), which defines how data is communicated between Web clients and servers. I demonstrated a couple of ways to view HTTP headers and listed those headers that are defined by the HTTP specification (or RFC). The chapter concluded with a discussion of the important enhancements to the HTTP protocol that were added in its current version, HTTP/1.1. This information provides the foundation for understanding what Apache does and how it does it.

Although Apache is quite well established as the leading Web server on the Internet, it is by no means the only Web server to compete for that status. The next chapter provides a brief look at the most important of its competitors, in order to place Apache in its proper context as it stands out as the best of the breed, even among champion contenders. I'll also discuss the important changes that are being made to Apache for the upcoming 2.0 commercial release. These changes will help Apache maintain its dominance of the Internet Web server market.

2

Apache and Other Servers

Chapter 1 presented a brief historical overview of the World Wide Web and the technologies that make it possible. Fast-forward to the present, and there are a number of good servers for the Web. This chapter provides a very brief description of the best of those and compares their architectures to the architecture used by Apache.

I generally don't like one-size-fits-all systems, and I try to avoid products that are marketed as the best solution for everyone's needs. Apache is an exception to this rule, largely because it is easily customized by design. While Apache runs well on commercial Unix platforms and Microsoft Windows NT, it truly shines on the open-source Unix variants. Apache is the number one choice for a Web server for both Linux and FreeBSD, and in this chapter, I'll tell you why.

The first part of the chapter takes a look at the major Web servers in use on the Internet. The chapter continues with a look at the present state of Apache, including its current feature set and features planned for the next release, and ends with a discussion of why Apache is an excellent and exciting choice to run an Internet Web site.

Who Are the Major Players?

Since a Web server can be any software used to implement HTTP, there are far too many different types of Web servers in use for me to describe them all. Some are completely homegrown solutions unique to their developers, but most are recognizable and identifiable by a specific name and version. Despite the large number of different HTTP server engines available, a small field of competitors handles the majority of HTTP traffic on the Internet.

In determining what Web servers are currently in use on the Internet, and in what relative numbers, I first turned to two respected surveys from the consulting firms Netcraft (www.netcraft.com) and SecuritySpace.com (www.securityspace.com). Both surveys are widely accepted as objective, and neither seems to be controlled by commercial interests. The companies don't attempt to profit from the surveys, which they publish to lend credibility to their consulting services. These surveys tend to agree pretty closely, which lends credibility to both.

I also ran my own survey, using an HTTP 1.1 HEAD request (see Chapter 1) incorporated into a simple Perl script that I ran on my Netscape bookmarks list, which consists of 338 sites, mostly of a technical orientation. I got the results summarized below, along with the May 2000 survey results from Netcraft and SecuritySpace:

Server	Aulds Survey	Netcraft	SecuritySpace
Apache	59.8%	60.4%	56.7%
Microsoft	21.6%	21.1%	27.8%
Netscape	11.5%	7.2%	4.7%
Other	7.1%	11.3%	10.8%
Total	100.0%	100.0%	100.0%

Looking at my data, I noticed that a large percentage of my Apache sites are running the binary versions of Apache provided with a canned Linux distribution (mostly Red Hat and Debian). I concluded that the majority of Internet Web sites today are hosted on Intel Pentium systems running either Apache on Linux or Microsoft IIS 4.0 on NT, and Apache holds the lion's share of the spoils.

Alternatives to Apache

The surveys say that while Apache leads the pack, it is not the only server in widespread use. This section examines the features and architectures of several other Web servers.

The Free Servers

Some of the best Web server software available is free software. Apache itself is free, open-source software. The roots of the Web—its protocols, browsers, and servers— spring from a free and open academic environment. The free CERN and NCSA servers started the Web revolution, and while neither is currently a viable choice, several choices of server software maintain that free tradition to this day.

thttpd

One of the most interesting free HTTP servers is a product called simply thttpd. The thttpd server is the work of one man, Jef Poskanzer, a Berkeley, California-area consultant, who distributes freeware through a nonprofit site called ACME Laboratories (www.acme.com).

Thttpd is one of two HTTP servers I'll mention that are designed to be extremely fast, with small memory footprints, simple to install and manage, highly secure—and almost feature-free. In most environments, thttpd will perform comparably to any other Web server. Under extreme loads, however, thttpd will run away from the pack.

It is unlikely that your Internet server has a data pipe large enough to flood a single Web server with such a large number of requests that a server like thttpd is needed. If your company has an internal server, attached to the network with a Gigabit Ethernet link, you might find you need a super-fast server; the problem is that on an intranet server, you'll almost certainly need features that aren't found in thttpd. High-performance servers like thttpd are a little like Formula-1 racecars: our highways aren't built for them, and they aren't designed to carry payload.

Mathopd

Minimization is taken to the extreme with Mathopd (available from its author at http://mathop.diva.nl/). The number of options and features in Mathopd is deliberately small. The server is made available only for Unix and Linux operating systems.

Why would anyone want to run Mathopd? The code is designed to handle a very large number of simultaneous connections. Like the thttpd server, Mathopd uses the select() system call in Unix, rather than spawning a number of processes or threads to handle multiple client connections. The result is a very fast Web server, designed to handle the basic functions required by HTTP/1.1 and occupying a very small memory footprint on a Unix machine.

A cinch to install and configure, and optimized for the maximum possible speed in serving static documents to a large number of connecting clients, Mathopd at first seemed a very attractive alternative to Apache. However Mathopd offers no user authentication, secure connections, or support for programming. Upon reflection, I realized that the server was too limiting for most administrators, without the ability to add functionality, and almost no one has data pipes sufficiently large to require the speed of Mathopd. What it does, though, it does better than anyone.

Boa

The last server I'll mention in the free software category is Boa (`www.boa.org`), a respectable alternative to Apache for those administrators who are looking for greater speed and system security and are willing to sacrifice some functionality to get it. Boa is another of the nonforking single-process servers that use the `select()` system call to multitask I/O.

Boa turns in very good numbers for CGI scripts; probably some of the best numbers (measured in transactions handled per second) that you'll get on a Linux Web server. The performance gain apparently comes from that fact that output from CGI scripts spawned by Boa is sent directly to the client. This is unlike most Web servers, which receive data output from CGI programs and send it to the Web client (browser).

The Commercial Variety

Commercial Web servers are in demand by a certain type of organization. Some organizations have a difficult time accepting that open-source software can have better quality and support than commercial software. These organizations demand commercial software, and several companies have responded to this demand by creating commercial Web server software. Here are several of the best commercial products.

Stronghold

For those sites that require strong security based on the Secure Sockets Layer (SSL), using a commercial server often seems an attractive alternative to open-source Apache. There are good reasons for these e-commerce Web sites to use commercial software. Probably the best reason to choose a commercial solution is for the support offered by the vendor. If you go the commercial route, you should take full advantage of that product support. You are paying not so much for the product as for that company's expertise in setting up an SSL Web site. You should expect all the handholding necessary from these companies in getting your site up and running. Another advantage of a commercial SSL product is that most include a license to use the cryptographic technology patented to RSA Security, Inc. The patent that requires licensing of RSA technology applies only in the United States, and expires in September 2000, so this may be of no relevance to you. If, however, you are maintaining a Web site in the U.S. and wish to use SSL, you may need to secure such a license, and purchasing a commercial SSL product is one way to do that. There are alternatives, though, that I'll discuss in detail in Chapter 15.

If you are seriously considering a commercial SSL Web product, Stronghold should be near the top of your list.

Many commercial Web products are derived from open-source software, and Stronghold is no exception. Stronghold is Apache server software, specially modified to include strong SSL support, and sold as a ready-to-install product, supported by the vendor. There's absolutely nothing wrong with this, and the value added to open-source Apache may be exactly what you need. What you're buying, however, is essentially what you can put together through lots of sweat, trial and error, and time spent in books like this one. You may well decide that the effort required to "roll your own" pays off rich dividends in education and familiarity with your system. If so, Chapter 15 is all about Secure Sockets Layer. And since Stronghold is Apache, nearly everything in this book is directly relevant to a Stronghold server.

For information on Stronghold, visit C2Net at `www.c2.net`.

iPlanet (formerly Netscape Enterprise)

Probably the best commercial server available for high-end multiprocessing hardware is iPlanet Web Server (formerly known as Netscape Enterprise Server), a product from the Sun-Netscape Alliance. iPlanet is well suited for large sites, with large development staffs that aren't afraid to program in Java. Make no mistake about it, iPlanet is made for Java, and you won't get much mileage from it if you aren't willing to work in that language.

iPlanet is available for a wide variety of operating systems including Linux. iPlanet for Linux version 4.1 is a fairly new, but strong product, and bears a price tag of $1500 per CPU. The product includes add-ons that are not standard with Apache (such as SSL and support for the Java Servlets 2.2 specification and Java Server Pages 1.1). However, these can be added to Apache (as I'll show in Chapter 9).

> **NOTE** America Online, Inc. (which owns Netscape Communications) and Sun Microsystems, Inc. formed the Sun-Netscape Alliance, which now sells Netscape Enterprise Server as the iPlanet Enterprise Server, Enterprise Edition (`www.iplanet.com`). A rose by another name?

Many IT managers in the past liked Netscape Enterprise Server because it is backed by Netscape Communications, and the support offered by the company can be valuable. In my opinion, however, the odds of finding documentation that addresses your problem, or a savvy techie who's willing to offer truly useful advice, or better still, someone who has overcome the problem before, are much better with an open-source application like Apache. Online resources (like those listed in Appendix C) are often every bit as valuable as technical support for commercial software. As attractive as these commercial servers are, for Linux, Apache should be the first server you evaluate.

Roxen

Roxen is actually not a single Web server product; the name is used to refer to a line of Internet server products offered by Idonex AB of Linköping, Sweden (`www.roxen.com`). Roxen Challenger is the Web server and is available for free download. Roxen Challenger, however, is part of a larger set of integrated Web site development tools called Roxen Platform. Roxen SiteBuilder is a workgroup environment that lets a group of Web site developers collaborate in designing a Web site. Like most modern development systems, SiteBuilder concentrates on separating site display and content.

At a cost of $11,800, Roxen Platform requires a serious financial commitment even though the Challenger Web server is free. Without the costly developer's tools, Roxen Challenger offers no advantages over Apache, which is far more widely used and, as a result, better supported.

Zeus

The Zeus Web server from Zeus Technology of Cambridge, England (`www.zeus.co.uk`) is an excellent commercial Web server for Linux. Zeus consistently turns in superlative numbers in benchmark tests (like the SPECWeb96 Web server benchmarks published by the Standard Performance Evaluation Corporation, `www.spec.org/osg/web96`).

The original version of Zeus was designed for raw speed, with a minimum of overhead (features and functions). That version of Zeus is still available as version 1.0. Subsequent releases of the product include a full list of advanced functions expected in a modern e-commerce Web server. Zeus competes well with Apache in nearly every area, including speed, functionality, configurability, and scalability. The one area in which Zeus cannot best Apache is cost. Zeus Web Server version 3 currently costs $1699, with a discounted price to qualified academic and charitable organizations of $85.

Two features of Zeus that have traditionally appealed to Web server administrators are its Apache/NCSA `httpd` compatibility (support for `.htaccess` files, for example) and the fact that it can be completely configured from a Web browser. Zeus is especially popular with Web hosting services and ISPs that host customer Web sites, and the company increasingly targets this market. Zeus is available for Unix and Linux platforms.

IBM

Most of the Web servers discovered in my survey that did not fall into one of the big three (Apache, Microsoft, Netscape) were running on some type of IBM hardware, indicated by Lotus-Domino. Most of them are really running a special version of Apache. Several years ago, IBM stunned the computing world by announcing their intention to support Apache as a Web server included with their Internet Commerce solutions. They have since brought Apache to market as IBM HTTP Server, which is bundled with their e-commerce solutions like the IBM WebSphere Application Server. IBM markets their server as being "powered by Apache." IBM HTTP Server only runs on IBM hardware.

Microsoft IIS

Microsoft's Internet Information Server (IIS) Version 4.0 is listed here with the commercial servers, because, although it is provided free as part of the NT Option Pack 4, you must purchase NT Server or NT Workstation in order to use it. The Option Pack can be downloaded from www.microsoft.com, or if you're a subscriber to the Microsoft Technet, you'll find it on one of your subscription CDs.

The performance of IIS 4.0 will surprise you. IIS stands as an exception to the oversized, often underpowered, applications that often seem to hog all the resources on an NT system and cry for more. Microsoft seems to be quite serious about the Web, and for shops that are heavy users of NT, IIS is a very respectable platform for Web site development. IIS, however, does not run on Linux. Using IIS forces you to run NT.

The Features of Apache

OK, I've said good things about all of the Web servers that compete with Apache for mindshare among Internet Web site developers and administrators. I even said nice things about Microsoft's IIS. Any one of these servers is capable of adequately supporting a production Web server. So why is Apache the most widely used Web server on the Internet? This section outlines the most important features.

Standards Compliance Apache offers full compliance with the HTTP/1.1 standard (RFC 2616). Apache has strong support for all the improvements made to the HTTP protocol in version 1.1, such as support for virtual hosts, persistent connections, client file uploading, enhanced error reporting, and resource caching (in proxy or gateway servers).

Apache also supports sophisticated content negotiation by HTTP/1.1 browsers, allowing multiple formats for a single resource to be served to meet the requirements of different clients. Multiple natural language support is a good example of how this is commonly used. Chapter 16, "Metainformation and Content Negotiation," discusses content negotiation.

Scalability   Apache provides support for large numbers of Web sites on a single machine. Virtual hosting is the subject of Chapter 6 and is of particular interest to anyone who needs to host several Web sites on a single server. Many commercial Web hosting services take full advantage of Apache's low cost and strong support for virtual hosting.

Dynamic Shared Objects   Apache also supports Dynamic Shared Objects (DSOs). This permits loading of extension modules at runtime. Features can be added or removed without recompiling the server engine. Throughout the book, when explaining how to install a module, I will demonstrate how to compile it as a DSO and enable it for use when Apache is started. There are a few modules that cannot be dynamically linked to Apache and must be compiled into the Apache runtime, but not many. The DSO mechanism will be preserved in future releases of Apache, and learning to compile and use DSO modules is a critical skill for Apache administrators.

Customizability   Apache can be fully customized by writing modules using the Apache module API. Currently, these can be written in C or Perl. The code to implement a minimal module is far smaller than one might think. Source code is completely available for examination, or alteration. The Apache license permits almost any use, private or commercial.

Another important feature is customizable logging, including the ability to write to multiple logs from different virtual servers. Apache logging is the subject of Chapter 12.

Also customizable in Apache are HTTP response headers for cache control and error reporting to the client browser. See Chapter 13 on enhancing Apache performance for a discussion of mod_header.

Programmability   Apache provides support for server programming using a variety of languages and integration techniques, including PHP, Perl, Java servlets, Java Server Pages, Active Server Pages, CGI, FastCGI, and Server-Side Includes. Chapters 8 and 9 discuss the scripting/programming tools available for Apache.

Potential Use as a Caching Proxy Server   Apache is not designed for general proxy use, but by using a module called mod_proxy, you can make it a very efficient caching proxy server. In other words, Apache can cache files received from remote servers and serve them directly to clients who request these resources, without downloading them again from the origin server. Caching for multiple clients (on a local area network, for example) can greatly speed up Web retrieval for clients of the proxy server, and reduce the traffic on an Internet connection. Chapter 13, "Enhancing the Performance of Apache," discusses the use of mod_proxy.

Security   Apache's security features are the subject of Chapters 14 and 15. They include support for user authentication and the SSL protocol:

- Support for DBM (and other databases such as Oracle or MySQL) for user authentication allows very large lists of authorized users to be searched efficiently. In Chapter 14, I'll demonstrate two methods of user authentication against databases.

- Support for SSL allows the exchange of digital certificates and encryption of data crossing the Internet. Secure Sockets Layer is already a critical component of any Internet-based Web server used for commercial purposes. In future years, expect to see reliable server and user authentication becoming more widely used on the Internet. Apache will always support the leading security mechanisms. In Chapter 15, I show how to set up Secure Sockets Layer in Apache and configure it to use server certificates that are either self-generated or issued by a well-known certificate authority like VeriSign.

Further Benefits

None of the major features outlined for the current Apache release is unique to Apache. The feature set alone, while impressive, is not enough to justify a decision to choose Apache over other excellent alternatives. There are, however, other benefits to Apache.

Apache has been ranked (by Netcraft) the number one Web server on the Internet since April 1996, and as this book goes to press, Apache powers an estimated 60% of all Web sites reachable through the Internet. While its popularity alone doesn't indicate its superiority, it does say that a lot of successful, high-volume sites have been built using Apache. That represents a huge vote of confidence in the software. It also means Apache is thoroughly tested. Its security, reliability, and overall performance are demonstrated, documented, and unquestionable.

Apache has unparalleled support from a tremendous group of individuals. Some are programmers; most are end users and administrators. For a software system as widely used as Apache, regardless of the nature of your problems, the odds are that someone, somewhere has encountered it and can offer some insight into its resolution. While it might seem logical to assume that support for no-cost software will necessarily be inferior to that provided by commercial software vendors, I haven't found that to be true at all. As a professional network administrator, the most difficult problems I've had to solve were nearly all related to commercial software (for which I usually paid dearly) and often involved licensing servers and product keys. The usual answer from Tech Support is "you need to upgrade to the next revision level." Trust me, you won't have these problems with Apache.

Apache is under intense active development at all times, and yet many Web sites continue to operate just fine with Apache engines many revisions behind the current release. I believe it is the not-for-profit motivation of its developers that is responsible for this degree of dependability in each revision. There is simply no reason for Apache developers to rush to market with incomplete, bug-ridden releases. The result is a tremendous benefit to administrators who are already stressed trying to roll out product upgrades on an almost continuous basis.

The most compelling reason to use the Apache Web server is that, by design, Apache is highly configurable and extensible by virtue of its support for add-on modules. The Apache Application Program Interface (API) gives programmers access to Apache data structures and the ability to write routines to extend the Apache core functionality. It is possible, of course, to write modifications to any server for which the source code is freely available, but only Apache makes this easy with a well-documented API that doesn't require a module programmer to understand the Apache core source code. The upshot of all of this is that there are a wide variety of third-party modules available for Apache. You'll learn about the most important of these in relevant chapters throughout this book. From these modules, you can pick and choose the ones you need and forget the rest. Most of the standard modules provided with the basic server as distributed by the Apache Software Foundation are optional and can be removed from the server core if statically linked, or simply not used if they are compiled separately as dynamically loadable modules. It's a great alternative to programs bloated with functions that are never used.

The Architecture of Apache

I'll admit, when I first saw benchmarks showing that some HTTP servers were significantly faster than Apache, at first I doubted the test results and then wondered why anyone would choose Apache over one of these speed-demon Web servers.

Many of these servers do, indeed, outperform Apache at serving static resources to clients, both in response time and in the number of simultaneous clients they can handle. A closer examination of what these super-fast servers are capable of revealed that much of their speed is achieved by stripping them of most of the functionality that is standard in Apache.

Most of the fast, small servers handle all client connections from a single process that is written to use nonblocking synchronous I/O multiplexing. That sounds impressive, doesn't it? Essentially, it means they make use of a call to a function called `select()`, which is available in operating systems like Linux. The `select()` function allows the calling process to be notified of an incoming connection on one or more sockets. In other words, the process is not blocked waiting for connections but can be performing other tasks rather than sitting in a listening state. Using `select()` also allows data to be written and read on multiple sockets (I/O multiplexing); it notifies the calling process of which socket has data waiting in buffers to be written or read.

Apache is an example of a *preforking* server. This means that the main server starts a pool of processes to handle client requests, rather than forking a new process for each incoming request. Having the pooled processes already online and waiting (idle) greatly speeds up the process of serving requests. I find this model more robust than the single-process model using multiplexed I/O, because the main Apache server process is protected (it doesn't talk to any client) and is always available to restart child processes that misbehave or die unexpectedly. In fact, the default behavior of Apache is to kill and restart each client process after it has answered an arbitrary (user-configurable) number of requests. This eliminates the possibility that a small memory leak in any process will grow into a big problem if that process is allowed to run for many days, weeks, or even months.

Apache's use of a preforked process pool rather than a single process making use of `select()` is not a bad design decision, and especially not one that leads to less than adequate performance. Perhaps a more valid criticism of Apache is that it uses a pool, or *swarm*, of multiple processes rather than *threads* to handle requests. Apache provides the administrator with some control over the Apache process storm (see Chapter 13, "Enhancing the Performance of Apache"). However, the benefits that can be achieved from these optimization options are small even in the best cases.

Unix systems traditionally schedule CPU time by process, and Apache has definite Unix roots. Threads, however, are less demanding of resources than processes, and are generally much faster to schedule, especially on multiprocessing operating systems with multiple processors that are capable of running multiple threads simultaneously. A move to fully threaded code in Apache should result in significant performance enhancements without sacrificing functionality and versatility. Apache 1.3 for NT is multithreaded (and runs as a single process or *task*, which is an NT service that creates multiple threads to handle connections). A major new feature of Apache Version 2.0 (previewed later in this chapter) is the use of *multiple-processing modules* to allow work to be performed on the thread/process scheduling layer independently of the Apache core code.

The important thing to keep in mind about speed and Apache is just how unimportant raw speed is on most Web servers. In fact, most Web servers function with less than 10Mbps of bandwidth, and most Internet Web servers are at the end of links no faster than a T1 line, which is 1.544Mbps. Apache, on a low-end Pentium workstation running Linux with only 64MB of RAM, can easily fill these data pipes. Anything faster is simply unnecessary, and every administrator needs to balance speed against limited functionality in many of the super-fast servers. A number of criteria should be used to determine the applicability of Web server software to the needs of the business, and speed is only one of these.

New Features of Apache Version 2.0

As of mid-year 2000, new development efforts for Apache are being applied to a Beta version of Apache 2.0. Version 2.0 is primarily of interest to programmers, and shouldn't significantly change the way Apache is installed, configured, and administered. Everything in this book is accurate for version 2.0. The feature set of version 2.0 is nailed down, and I'll describe the major changes that can be expected. Soon 2.0 will be a production release, and will contain the features described in this section.

The most significant changes to Apache that will emerge in version 2.0 are designed to increase the portability of Apache, enhance the already strong support for add-on modules, and to increase the performance of Apache on all platforms. The first of these changes involves moving the multi-processing capability of Apache (currently implemented in Unix by one server process per client connection, and in Win32 as one "thread" per client) into *Multiple-Processing Modules (MPMs)*. These are responsible for mapping client requests to either a thread or a process, making it possible for one set of Apache code to work on multiple platforms. Initially, version 2.0 will include MPMs for several different process-forking schemes in Unix, and MPMs for NT and OS/2. On Unix systems that support POSIX-compliant threads, there is a new mode of operation for Apache called a *hybrid* mode. This enhancement is designed to improve the scalability of Apache, not necessarily the performance or stability of the server, and will make no difference at the majority of installed Apache sites.

The second change is also intended for programmers, and is designed to increase the cross-platform portability of code written to support Apache. Apache 2.0 will be packaged with an Application Program Interface (API) implemented in an Apache Portable Run-Time (APR) layer. The APR completely masks fundamental differences in the way platforms handle things like process forking and socket connections. Programmers working on Apache 2.0 and later versions will only need to ensure that they program to the APR to ensure that their programs, or modules, run on all supported platforms. For example, using the Apache Run-Time, a programmer will not really have to know the details of how processes are forked in both Unix and NT, where the system calls are quite different. The programmer will need to learn only how to spawn or fork a process in the Apache Run-Time to produce code that works identically on both platforms.

The third change to Apache in version 2.0, and the one that most affects us as system administrators, is in the way that Apache modules register *callbacks*, or functions, with the Apache server. Here again, while the details of the changes in 2.0 are germane only to the Apache programmer, the implications of this change directly affect all Apache server administrators because modules written for Apache 1.3 will not work with 2.0 without modification. Before moving your site to Apache 2.0, carefully ensure that you have 2.0 versions of all the Apache modules you'll require. Ports of the core modules will probably be released along with version 2.0, but third-party modules may not be modified immediately.

Apache 2.0 incorporates changes that the Apache Software Foundation and the principal Apache developers consider essential to maintaining the viability of the Apache server in an increasingly commercial Internet. A move to Apache 2.0 will be essential to any Apache site that wants to remain leading edge. The question is *when would be the best time to upgrade to Apache 2.0?* As with all software in production use, the answer to that question is determined by the features that will improve your site with added capabilities, or increased performance. Simply upgrading to have the very latest version is a time-consuming, frustrating, never-ending exercise. Consider all the angles before making your decision to update.

In Sum

In this chapter, we looked at what Web server software powers the Internet and determined that 60 percent of all Internet-accessible Web servers are running Apache. Only on the very largest Internet sites does Apache yield prominence to commercial engines, for reasons that probably have less to do with the suitability of Apache than with the fact that many large firms are still reluctant to rely on open-source software (an attitude that is rapidly eroding). The major Web servers that compete with Apache have some strong features but the features of Apache show why Apache is dominant.

These first two chapters have served as an extended introduction to Apache and its foundations. Beginning in the next chapter, we'll (metaphorically) roll up our sleeves and start getting our fingernails dirty—that is, we'll install the server on a Linux system. Then, in succeeding chapters, we'll move on to various aspects of configuring Apache.

Part 2

Essential Configuration

Featuring:

- Downloading, compiling, and installing Apache from source code
- Installing precompiled Apache binary files
- The role of Apache directives in the `httpd.conf` file
- General server directives
- Container directives
- Setting up user home directories
- How modules work
- Linking modules statically or as dynamic shared objects
- Using apxs
- IP-based virtual hosting
- Name-based virtual hosting
- Virtual hosting guidelines

3

Installing Apache

The previous two chapters presented an overview of the Web and its history, and they introduced Apache as well as other Web servers commonly used on the Internet. The topics of installing, configuring, and administering Apache begin here, in this chapter.

One of the important things to realize about installing Apache is that there are two completely different ways to do it. You can choose to download the source code and compile it on your own machine, or you can take the easier route and download binary files that have already been compiled for your machine and operating system.

Both methods of installation have merit, and both are discussed in this chapter, with step-by-step examples of the procedures that you should use on your own Linux system. The installation of a basic Apache server is a straightforward process. Follow the instructions in this chapter, regardless of which method of installation you choose, and soon you'll have a working Apache server, ready to configure.

The Decision to Compile

Before proceeding, determine whether it makes sense to compile the Apache code yourself. There are some very good reasons to start with the source code to create your own copy of Apache.

One of the reasons most often cited for the success of open-source software like Apache and Linux is that the source code is available for inspection and custom modification. That's certainly an enticement for C code hackers and for companies with the programming resources to customize the code. The vast majority of us, however, don't write customized Apache code. Instead, we benefit from the code improvements made by others.

Compiling Apache from the source code makes it possible to add user-written modifications (or *patches*) to the code. Patches are essentially files that contain changes to a source code base and are usually created by "*diffing*" modified source to the original; in other words, comparing the modified and original source files and saving the differences in a file distributed as a *patch*. Another user acquires the patch, applies it to the same source code base to reproduce the modifications, and then compiles the altered source.

Patches make it possible for nonprogrammers to make (often quite sophisticated) changes to source code and then compile it themselves. Without the ability to patch the source and compile it yourself, you need to search for precompiled binaries that already include the necessary patches. Depending on your particular platform, it might be difficult to locate binaries that include the patches you require.

Another reason to compile from source code is that it allows you to take advantage of compiler optimizations for your hardware platform and operating system. This consideration is by no means as important as it was once, because chances are you can easily find binaries for your particular system. Figure 3.1 shows the binary distributions of Apache available from the Apache Project Web site for a variety of platforms. In the unlikely circumstance that your operating system is missing from this list, you can always download and compile the Apache source yourself.

It is not necessary to compile source code on your own hardware to optimize the resulting binary. Most binaries are already optimized for a given type of hardware. For example, to run on an Intel 486 or Pentium system, download an i386 binary, or an i686 binary for the Pentium II or Pentium III processor. A compiler designed to optimize code to run on an Intel processor was probably used to create the binary. It is unlikely that your compiler will produce code that performs significantly better. Some companies offer Linux distributions that are optimized for performance on Pentium-class Intel processors (Mandrake Linux is one such distribution: www.linux-mandrake.com). If the fastest possible system performance is your goal, you should consider such a Linux distribution teamed with more or faster hardware.

One word of warning about using binaries is in order. Often, the available binaries lag behind new releases. If you want to stay on the "bleeding edge" of changes, you must use source code distributions, which is not always the best decision for production servers.

In sum:

- Use an Apache binary distribution when you need a basic Apache server with the Apache modules included in that distribution. All standard Apache modules are included with these binary distributions, compiled separately from the server as DSO modules. You can pick and choose the ones you want, using only those that you require, and disabling the others to conserve the memory required to run

Apache. If all the functionality you require is available in the set of standard Apache modules, and your operating system is supported, you have nothing to lose by installing one of these. Even if you require a few modules not included with the binary distribution, most of these are easily compiled separately from the Apache server itself, without requiring the Apache source. A few, however, require that the Apache source be patched, and will require that you have the source code available on your system. A good example is mod_ssl, which is discussed in Chapter 15. It is impossible to install these modules without the Apache source code; you won't find them in an Apache binary distribution.

- Compile the Apache server source code whenever you need functionality that requires patching the original source code (Secure Sockets Layer, or SSL, is an example of such a module or server extension). You will also need to compile the Apache source if you intend to write your own modules.

Figure 3.1   Apache binary distributions

Essential Configuration

PART 2

If you can work with precompiled binaries, feel free to skip the material on compiling Apache. It will always be here if you need it in the future. If you have decided to compile the Apache source code, take a look at the next section; otherwise, you can jump ahead to the "Installing the Apache Binaries" section.

Downloading Apache Source

Download the source code for Apache by pointing your Web browser at www.apache .org/dist or one of its mirror sites (see Figure 3.2). Download the latest Apache, which will be in Unix tar format, compressed with the GNU Zip (gzip, or simply gz) utility. The latest Apache source code archive is named apache_1.3.12.tar.Z.

Figure 3.2   The Apache source code distribution site

Change directory to the location where you intend to unpack the Apache source code and compile the server. A common location for source code on Linux systems is the

/usr/local/src directory, and that's a pretty logical choice. If you want to place the Apache source in a subdirectory of /usr/local/src, do the following:

```
# cd /usr/local/src
```

From this directory, invoke the Linux tar utility to decompress the archive and extract the files. Tar will automatically create the necessary directories. When the operation is finished, you will have the Apache source saved in the directory /usr/local/src/apache_1.3.12:

```
# tar xvzf /home/caulds/apache_1.3.12.tar.gz
apache_1.3.12/
apache_1.3.12/src/
apache_1.3.12/src/ap/
apache_1.3.12/src/ap/.indent.pro
apache_1.3.12/src/ap/Makefile.tmpl
apache_1.3.12/src/ap/ap.dsp
apache_1.3.12/src/ap/ap.mak
   … many files extracted
```

The top-level Apache source directory is /usr/local/src/apache_1.3.12, and I'll refer to this as the Apache source directory frequently in the book. If you install Apache from source, you'll return frequently to this directory, to make changes to your Apache installation. This directory is distinct from the Apache installation directory, where you'll install Apache and from where you'll run it.

Compiling Apache

Old (pre-1.3) versions of Apache could only be compiled the old-fashioned way: by manually editing the Configuration.tmpl file, running the ./configure command, and then running the make utility. An editor was used to customize the compiler flags (EXTRA_CFLAGS, LIBS, LDFLAGS, INCLUDES) stored in the template as needed for a given system. Thank goodness there is now a better way.

All recent versions of Apache include the APACI configuration utility. Although some administrators insist that configuring the Apache compilation manually gives them better control over the compiler switches and installation options, I disagree. APACI is the installation method preferred by the Apache development team; it is the easiest way to compile Apache, and it is the best way to maintain your Apache source code, especially if you've altered it by applying source patches and a number of third-party modules (Chapter 5). It is probably best to learn only one way to configure Apache compilation options. If you're going to learn only one method, it is best to learn the APACI installation method.

Using APACI

With Apache version 1.3, a new configuration module was introduced with the Apache source distribution. The APache AutoConf-style Interface (APACI) is a configuration utility similar to the GNU Autoconf package, although it is not based on that popular GNU utility. APACI provides an easy way to configure the Apache source prior to compilation in order to specify certain compiler options and the inclusion (or exclusion) of Apache modules. Like GNU Autoconf, APACI also performs a number of tests in order to ascertain details about your system hardware and operating system that are relevant to the Apache source compilation.

APACI does not compile the Apache source; its purpose is to create the files that specify how that compilation is performed. Its most important task is to create the *makefiles* that are used by the Linux make utility to direct the C compiler how to proceed, and also where to place the compiled programs when make is instructed to perform an install.

The Need for ANSI-C

The Apache source code is written in C language compliant with the specifications codified by the American National Standards Institute, or ANSI-C. For that reason, you will need an ANSI-C–compliant compiler to complete the install. This is not a big deal, because your Linux distribution includes the GNU C compiler (gcc), which is the ANSI-C compiler recommended by the Apache Software Foundation. If APACI is unable to locate a suitable compiler, you will be notified, and the configuration will abort. You can then install gcc from your Linux CD-ROM or from www.gnu.org. The Free Software Foundation makes binary distributions available for Linux and a large number of Unix platforms or you can download and compile the source code yourself, although compiling gcc can turn into a time-consuming exercise. Binary distributions of gcc are well optimized so it is unlikely that you can build a more efficient C compiler.

The configure Script

The heart of APACI is a shell script named configure, which you'll find in the top-level Apache source directory. This script does not compile the Apache server; its function is to examine your system to identify its capabilities and locate the supporting files it needs. The configure script may warn you that it can't build Apache and give instructions on how to correct problems it finds. On most systems running a fairly recent version of Linux, this will not occur. Once `configure` determines that it can build Apache on your system, it then identifies the best possible combination of options for that system. The information it gathers and the decisions it makes about configuring Apache for your system are written into a special file that you'll find stored in `src/Configuration.apaci`. In this file it stores information specific to your system (including build options you specify to `configure`).

The last step that the `configure` script takes is to run a second script, which you'll find as `src/Configure`. This script takes the information from `src/Configuration.apaci` and uses it to create a set of files that control the actual compilation and installation of Apache (using the `make` utility on your Linux system). You'll find these makefiles created in a number of the Apache source directories.

You will usually run `configure` with a number of options (command-line arguments) to customize your Apache configuration. In fact, if you run `configure` with no command-line arguments, it will report, "Warning: Configuring Apache with default settings. This is probably not what you really want," and it probably isn't. The next few sections will show you how to specify additional options to `configure`, or override its default values. This is a procedure you'll return to many times, whenever you need alter your Apache configuration or change its functionality by adding new modules. The following `configure` statement compiles Apache version 1.3.12. Note that this is a single Linux command with three arguments; the backslash (\) character is used to continue the command on a new line. It's a handy trick for manually entering long command lines, and can also be used to improve the readability of shell script files.

```
# ./configure --prefix=/usr/local/apache \
> --enable-module=most \
> --disable-module=auth_dbm \  > --enable-shared=max
```

The `--prefix` argument in the example above tells Apache to install itself in the directory `/usr/local/apache`. (This is the default installation location for Apache, so in this case the option is unnecessary.) However, there are many times you may want to install into an alternate directory—for example, if you do not want to install a second Apache version alongside one that already exists (I have five versions of Apache on my server for testing purposes). Another reason you may want to install Apache into an alternate directory is to preserve the default locations used by a Linux distribution. For example, assume the version of Apache that comes with your Linux distribution is installed in `/etc/apache` instead of the default `/usr/local/apache` directory. Use `--prefix` to install Apache in the `/etc/apache` directory. (For standard file location layouts, see the discussion on the `config.layout` file below.)

Linux systems can use `--enable-module=all` to enable all modules in the standard distribution. The `--enable-module=most` option enables all the standard modules in the Apache distribution that are usable on all platforms supported by Apache. Table 3.1 lists the modules that are not installed when you specify `--enable-module=most`, along with the reason they are not used. Red Hat Linux 7.0 users will not be able to compile Apache with `mod_auth_dbm` and should use the `--disable-module=auth_dbm` directive to disable use of that module. Users of other Linux distributions (or earlier Red Hat distributions) who wish to use the module can omit the directive. The `mod_auth_dbm` module is discussed in detail in Chapter 14. Table 3.2 later in this chapter lists all of the standard modules included in the 1.3.12 release of Apache.

Table 3.1   Apache Modules Omitted by `--enable-module=most`

Module	Reason for omitting
mod_auth_db	Some platforms may not support Berkeley DB.
mod_mmap_static	Some platforms do not support memory-mapped files.
mod_so=no	Some platforms do not support dynamic loading of modules.
mod_example	This module is only for programmers and isn't required on production servers.
mod_auth_digest	This module conflicts with mod_digest.
mod_log_agent	This module has been replaced by mod_log_config.
mod_log_referer	This module has been replaced by mod_log_config.

On Linux systems, I recommend specifying `--enable-module=most`, and then manually adding any modules from Table 3.1 that you require. To enable support for DSOs, for example, add the `--enable-shared=max` option, which causes Apache to build all modules as *dynamic shared objects*, or *DSOs*, with the exception of two, `http_core` and `mod_so`, both of which must be statically linked into the Apache kernel. The `http_core` module provides core directives for managing the Apache server, and `mod_so` enables the server to use DSO modules.

Throughout the book, as I discuss adding additional modules, I'll describe how to use additional arguments to `configure` to alter the way Apache is built. For Linux systems, I consider the following command line sufficient to build a suitable Apache system:

```
./configure --enable-module=most --enable-shared=max"
```

Why use DSOs?

The extension of Apache Server through the use of modules has always been part of its design, but it wasn't until release 1.3 that Apache supported dynamic loadable modules. These dynamic shared objects are available in Apache on Linux and other operating systems that support the necessary system functions for a program to load a module into its address space with a system call. This is similar to the way dynamic link library (or DLL) files work in Microsoft Windows; in fact, DLLs are used to provide this functionality in the Windows version of Apache.

The use of DSO modules in Apache has several advantages. First, the server can be far more flexible because modules can be enabled or disabled at runtime, without the need to relink the Apache kernel. The exclusion of unnecessary modules reduces the size of the Apache executable, which can be a factor when many server instances are run in a limited memory space.

On Linux systems, the only significant disadvantage to the use of DSO modules is that the server is approximately 20 percent slower to load at startup time, because of the system overhead of resolving the symbol table for the dynamic links. This is not generally a factor unless Apache is run in inetd mode (see Chapter 4), where a new instance of httpd is spawned to handle each incoming client connection.

In most cases, Linux administrators should build their Apache server to make maximum use of DSO modules.

A Sample configure Run

Using the configure command described above, the compilation will proceed as shown in Listing 3.1. (The output is far too long to reproduce here, and much of it is repetitive, so it has been edited to suit this text.)

Listing 3.1   Compiling Apache with the configure Command

```
# ./configure --prefix=/usr/local/apache \
> --enable-module=most \
> --disable-module=auth_dbm \
> --enable-shared=max
Configuring for Apache, Version 1.3.9
 + using installation path layout: Apache (config.layout)
```

```
Creating Makefile
Creating Configuration.apaci in src
 + enabling mod_so for DSO support
Creating Makefile in src
 + configured for Linux platform
 + setting C compiler to gcc
 + setting C pre-processor to gcc -E
 + checking for system header files
 + adding selected modules
     o rewrite_module uses ConfigStart/End
 + using -lndbm for DBM support
       enabling DBM support for mod_rewrite
     o dbm_auth_module uses ConfigStart/End

-- Many deleted lines --

make[2]: Leaving directory `/usr/local/src/apache_1.3.9/src/support'
<=== src/support
make[1]: Leaving directory `/usr/local/src/apache_1.3.9'
<=== src
```

The configure script essentially creates a set of instructions to the compiler for compiling the source files into a working system. It uses information you provide, along with other information about the capabilities of your system, such as what function libraries are available. The result is primarily a set of makefiles, which instruct the Linux make utility how to compile source files, link them to required function libraries, and install them in their proper locations.

The config.status File

Whenever you run the configure script, it creates a file with the name config.status in the Apache source directory (or overwrites the file if it already exists). This file is actually a shell script that contains the last command line used to successfully run configure and typically looks like the one in Listing 3.2.

Listing 3.2   A Typical config.status File

```
# cat config.status
#!/bin/sh
##
##  config.status -- APACI auto-generated configuration restore script
##
##  Use this shell script to re-run the APACI configure script for
##  restoring your configuration. Additional parameters can be supplied.
##

SSL_BASE="/usr/local/src/openssl-0.9.5" \
./configure \
"--with-layout=Apache" \
"--prefix=/usr/local/apache" \
"--enable-module=most" \
"--disable-module=auth_dbm" \
"--enable-module=ssl" \
"--activate-module=src/modules/extra/mod_define.c" \
"--enable-shared=max" \
"$@"
```

There are a few lines here that have been added since I showed the minimal set of options required to compile a full working Apache server. The SSL_BASE line, which actually precedes the invocation of the configure utility, sets an environment variable that points to the OpenSSL source. This environment variable will be used later by the Secure Sockets Layer (SSL) module, which is enabled by the line --enable-module=ssl. This will be covered in full detail in Chapter 15. The --activate-module line is used to compile a third-party module and statically link it into Apache from a source file previously placed in the location designated for these "extra" modules. You can also use another option, --add-module, to copy a module source file into this directory before compiling and statically linking it to the server. This option saves you only the copy step, however, so it isn't terribly useful:

```
--add-module=/home/caulds/mod_include/mod_include.c
```

A great benefit of the config.status file is that it saves your hard-won knowledge.

You can rerun the last configure command at any time, simply by ensuring that this file is executable by its owner (probably root), and invoking it as follows:

```
# chmod u+x config.status
# ./config.status
```

Although the `config.status` file contains many lines, all of them (except for comments and the last line) end in a backslash character, which indicates that the lines should be concatenated and passed as a single command to the shell interpreter. The last line, `"$@"`, concatenates to the end of the command line any argument passed to `config.status` when it is executed. You might run `config.status`, for example, with an additional option:

```
# ./config.status "--activate-module=src/modules/auth_mysql/libauth_mysql.a"
```

In this case, the portion of the command line enclosed in quotes is substituted for `$@` in the `config.status` script and concatenated to the command line passed to `/bin/sh` for processing.

You can modify `config.status` and rerun it to add, remove, or change the order of the arguments. This order is often significant. For example, I discovered that, to use the **--enable-shared** option (which specifies compilation of modules as Dynamic Shared Objects), you must include this option after all `--enable-module` and `--activate-module` arguments. I learned this the hard way. But once I did learn how to do it right, I had the `config.status` file to retain that information for later use. Unfortunately, determining the precedence of `configure` options is largely a matter of trial and error.

I prefer to copy the `config.status` file to another filename. This ensures that the file I use to configure Apache won't be accidentally overwritten if I choose to run `configure` to test other options. After running `configure`, you may wish to do something like the following:

```
# cp config.status build.sh
# chmod u+x build.sh
```

This creates a brand-new file (a shell script), named `build.sh`, which can be edited and then executed to reconfigure Apache. I have used the same `build.sh` over and over again during the course of writing this book, with several versions of Apache, modifying it as needed to enable or disable modules or install locations.

The `config.layout` File

The paths that Apache uses to locate files during compilation and to determine where to move files during the installation are stored in a special configuration file named `config.layout`, which you will find in the Apache source directory. This file contains collections of directory paths to be used as defaults on different types of systems. Each of these collections is identified by a system name, and so they are called *named layouts*. When you run `configure`, Apache attempts to guess the operating system using a helper script, `src/helpers/GuessOS`. If its best guess matches the name of one of the named layouts, it uses that layout to determine the correct path information. Otherwise, it uses the Apache default setup, which is defined in `config.layout` as layout "Apache." The Apache layout is shown in Listing 3.3.

Listing 3.3   The Apache Path Layout in `config.layout`

```
#   Classical Apache path layout.
<Layout Apache>
    prefix:        /usr/local/apache
    exec_prefix:   $prefix
    bindir:        $exec_prefix/bin
    sbindir:       $exec_prefix/bin
    libexecdir:    $exec_prefix/libexec
    mandir:        $prefix/man
    sysconfdir:    $prefix/conf
    datadir:       $prefix
    iconsdir:      $datadir/icons
    htdocsdir:     $datadir/htdocs
    cgidir:        $datadir/cgi-bin
    includedir:    $prefix/include
    localstatedir: $prefix
    runtimedir:    $localstatedir/logs
    logfiledir:    $localstatedir/logs
    proxycachedir: $localstatedir/proxy
</Layout>
```

Each line of `config.layout` defines a directory pathname. Some of the paths are derived from others previously defined in the file. You might note from this layout that all the paths are derived from the one identified as `prefix`. Therefore, simply by running `configure` with the `--prefix` argument to change this location, you automatically change *all* of the default paths for the Apache installation.

You can specify a named layout when running `configure` by using the `--with-layout` argument. For example, if you chose to use the same file locations that Red Hat Linux uses, specify `configure` with the `--with-layout=RedHat` argument:

```
# ./configure --with-layout=RedHat
```

It's important to realize that `config.layout` is a convenience and is used to provide a single location in which a number of directory paths are set. Apache will store data in these directories (or expect to find it there).

You can modify `config.layout` creating a custom layout as described later, if you want to change any of these paths, or you can override and change any default with a separate `configure` option. Table 3.2 lists all of the `configure` options used to set Apache's paths.

Table 3.2   configure Options to Set Apache's Paths

Option	Specifies Location For
`--bindir=DIR`	User executables
`--sbindir=DIR`	System executables
`--libexecdir=DIR`	Supporting libraries (DSO modules)
`--mandir=DIR`	Apache manual (man) pages
`--sysconfdir=DIR`	Configuration files (httpd.conf)
`--datadir=DIR`	Read-only data files
`--iconsdir=DIR`	Image files used by Apache
`--htdocsdir=DIR`	Read-only document files
`--cgidir=DIR`	Read-only CGI files
`--includedir=DIR`	Includes files
`--localstatedir=DIR`	Writeable data files
`--runtimedir=DIR`	Runtime data
`--logfiledir=DIR`	Apache log files
`--proxycachedir=DIR`	Proxy cache data

The following example uses path variables as `configure` arguments to install all of Apache's user executables in `/usr/bin` and all system executables in `/usr/sbin`, which is where the Red Hat layout puts them. All other layout options are read from the Apache layout in `config.layout`. The following command accomplishes the same thing as the custom layout shown later, in Listing 3.5:

```
# ./configure --bindir=/usr/bin --sbindir=/usr/sbin
```

For those readers who are using the Red Hat Linux distribution, the Apache that is provided as a Red Hat Package (RPM) uses a layout that looks like this:

```
#   RedHat 5.x layout
<Layout RedHat>
    prefix:        /usr
```

```
        exec_prefix:    $prefix
        bindir:         $prefix/bin
        sbindir:        $prefix/sbin
        libexecdir:     $prefix/lib/apache
        mandir:         $prefix/man
        sysconfdir:     /etc/httpd/conf
        datadir:        /home/httpd
        iconsdir:       $datadir/icons
        htdocsdir:      $datadir/html
        cgidir:         $datadir/cgi-bin
        includedir:     $prefix/include/apache
        localstatedir:  /var
        runtimedir:     $localstatedir/run
        logfiledir:     $localstatedir/log/httpd
        proxycachedir:  $localstatedir/cache/httpd
</Layout>
```

Note that, since the Red Hat layout modifies the Apache `prefix` variable, all paths are altered, because all depend on `prefix`. The Red Hat layout actually tries to put files into more standard directories. Rather than storing Apache binaries in a special directory (like `/usr/local/apache/bin`), Red Hat places them in the Linux directories that are actually reserved for them, `/usr/bin` and `/usr/sbin`. Likewise, Red Hat prefers to keep Apache configuration files under `/etc`, a directory in which you'll find configuration files for a large number of other Linux utilities, such as FTP, DNS, sendmail, and others.

Viewing the Layout `configure` Will Use

If you're planning to alter the paths that `configure` will use, you'll want to see which layout `configure` will choose and then either make a copy of that layout to edit and rename or simply edit that layout in `config.layout`. Running `configure` with the `--show-layout` argument prints the layout that `configure` intends to use and the paths it reads from that layout. Listing 3.4 shows typical output.

Listing 3.4   Using `--show-layout` with the configure Command

```
# ./configure --show-layout
Configuring for Apache, Version 1.3.9
 + using installation path layout: Apache (config.layout)

Installation paths:
            prefix: /usr/local/apache
       exec_prefix: /usr/local/apache
```

```
             bindir: /usr/local/apache/bin
            sbindir: /usr/local/apache/bin
         libexecdir: /usr/local/apache/libexec
             mandir: /usr/local/apache/man
         sysconfdir: /usr/local/apache/conf
            datadir: /usr/local/apache
           iconsdir: /usr/local/apache/icons
          htdocsdir: /usr/local/apache/htdocs
             cgidir: /usr/local/apache/cgi-bin
         includedir: /usr/local/apache/include
       localstatedir: /usr/local/apache
         runtimedir: /usr/local/apache/logs
         logfiledir: /usr/local/apache/logs
       proxycachedir: /usr/local/apache/proxy

Compilation paths:
           HTTPD_ROOT: /usr/local/apache
      SHARED_CORE_DIR: /usr/local/apache/libexec
       DEFAULT_PIDLOG: logs/httpd.pid
   DEFAULT_SCOREBOARD: logs/httpd.scoreboard
     DEFAULT_LOCKFILE: logs/httpd.lock
      DEFAULT_XFERLOG: logs/access_log
     DEFAULT_ERRORLOG: logs/error_log
     TYPES_CONFIG_FILE: conf/mime.types
    SERVER_CONFIG_FILE: conf/httpd.conf
    ACCESS_CONFIG_FILE: conf/access.conf
  RESOURCE_CONFIG_FILE: conf/srm.conf
  SSL_CERTIFICATE_FILE: conf/ssl.crt/server.crt
```

At the very least, --show-layout is a convenient way to find out where Apache puts all the files. Because it expands variables, it is more readable than looking directly in the file. Whether you should use it to modify default settings directly is debatable. Many administrators consider it safer to use the information displayed by --show-layout to build a new layout as described in the next section. But whether you work with the default layout or a copy, editing a named layout has the advantage that you can change the default path values that configure uses without specifying your changes as arguments to the configure command. All the settings are visible in one place, and since you modify only those you want to change in a given layout, you don't have to do a lot of work in most cases.

Creating and Using a Custom Layout

The best way to modify an Apache layout is to create a custom layout of your own, copying another layout, renaming it, and making your modifications to a custom layout that you will use during the Apache compilation by calling it with a name of your own choosing. This what I recommend, and Listing 3.5 shows a custom layout that I have used, named MyLayout. I modified the standard Apache layout and made two changes, to put the Apache executables in the same locations as the Red Hat layout shown above. I'm running a Red Hat system, and this places them where Red Hat's startup files expect to find them.

As noted, many administrators consider it inherently risky to edit the default layout directly; they prefer to leave the original layout values intact and work on a copy. Apache's use of named layouts makes it easy to follow this approach. You might add a layout to config.layout like the one shown in Listing 3.5.

Listing 3.5   A Custom Path Layout

```
<Layout MyLayout>
    prefix:        /usr/local/apache
    exec_prefix:   $prefix
# Use all Apache layout options,
# but install user and system
# executables as Red Hat does
    bindir:        /usr/bin
    sbindir:       /usr/sbin
# end of changes from Apache layout
    libexecdir:    $exec_prefix/libexec
    mandir:        $prefix/man
    sysconfdir:    $prefix/conf
    datadir:       $prefix
    iconsdir:      $datadir/icons
    htdocsdir:     $datadir/htdocs
    cgidir:        $datadir/cgi-bin
    includedir:    $prefix/include
    localstatedir: $prefix
    runtimedir:    $localstatedir/logs
    logfiledir:    $localstatedir/logs
    proxycachedir: $localstatedir/proxy
</Layout>
```

Essential Configuration

PART 2

To use the new custom layout, run `configure` with the `--with-layout` argument, and compile:

```
# ./configure --with-layout=MyLayout
```

The Other `configure` Command Options

You can get a complete list of all `configure` options by running the command with its `--help` argument. All of the variables that are used as named layout options are available, as well as all of the configuration options discussed earlier. The options I've shown are probably the only `configure` options that you'll ever need to use, but there are several others with far more specific purposes. For example, the `--enable-rule` option is used to enable certain compiler rules to enable Apache to compile on certain systems (Linux users will never need this). There are also a number of options that deal with suEXEC (which is discussed in Chapter 4).

Making Apache

Upon completion of the configuration phase, you have constructed a set of makefiles in various places within your Apache source tree. The `make` command is used to begin the actual compilation phase of the install:

```
# make
===> src
make[1]: Entering directory `/usr/local/src/apache_1.3.9'
make[2]: Entering directory `/usr/local/src/apache_1.3.9/src'

-- Many lines deleted --
```

The final step of the install is to call `make` again, this time with the `install` argument, which moves all the compiled binaries and support files to their default locations (or locations you specified in the configuration step above). Most files are copied into directories relative to the Apache root directory that you specified with the `--prefix` argument:

```
# make install
make[1]: Entering directory `/usr/local/src/apache_1.3.9'
===> [mktree: Creating Apache installation tree]

-- Lines deleted --
```

```
+---------------------------------------------------------+
| You now have successfully built and installed the       |
| Apache 1.3 HTTP server. To verify that Apache actually   |
| works correctly you now should first check the          |
| (initially created or preserved) configuration files    |
|                                                          |
|   /usr/local/apache/conf/httpd.conf                     |
|                                                          |
| and then you should be able to immediately fire up      |
| Apache the first time by running:                       |
|                                                          |
|   /usr/local/apache/bin/apachectl start                 |
|                                                          |
| Thanks for using Apache.              The Apache Group   |
|                                       http://www.apache.org/ |
+---------------------------------------------------------+
```

With the appearance of the message above, you have installed an Apache system that should run after making a few simple changes to its configuration file.

An optional step you can take is to reduce the size of the Apache executable using the Linux `strip` command. This command removes symbolic information that is used only by debuggers and other developer tools. For a production version of the Apache kernel, this information can be stripped to reduce the memory required by the server. The reduction is slight, but if you are running a number of Apache processes, the savings do add up. Running `strip` on a freshly compiled Apache 1.3.9 executable reduced its size by about 14 percent. Be aware that once you `strip` symbol information from a binary file, you can no longer run debugging tools if you have problems running that program.

```
# ls -al httpd
-rwxr-xr-x   1 root      root         461015 Dec  6 11:23 httpd
# strip httpd
# ls -al httpd
-rwxr-xr-x   1 root      root         395516 Dec  6 11:46 httpd
```

If you compile Apache from source code feel free to skip down to the section "Running the Server." That's where you'll learn to start the server.

Installing the Apache Binaries

Compiling Apache from source code is so easy, especially for Linux, that it should be your choice of installation method if you plan to make any alterations to the out-of-the-box Apache configuration. If you plan to add third-party modules that are not compiled as DSO objects or if you plan to modify your server to support SSL, you have no choice; you *must* work with the Apache source code and compile it yourself.

On the other hand, if you need only a simple server, which is used primarily to distribute static HTML pages or other documents and has little if any user input or server-side programming, there are two much quicker ways to get up and running. If you are not concerned with implementing specialized modules that aren't among those provided with the standard Apache distribution, consider using one of two alternatives to compiling Apache. The first of these is to install Apache precompiled binaries using a Linux package manager; the second method is to download binary distributions from a trustworthy source like the Apache Software Foundation. Both methods are described below.

Which Modules Are Included?

In deciding whether to install from the RPM or source distribution, you'll probably want to know which modules each one includes. Table 3.3 lists the Apache modules that are provided with the RPM and those included the binary distribution for Linux made available on the Apache Web site (www.apache.org/dist/binaries/linux). The first column lists all the standard modules; the second and third columns indicate which of these are enabled as dynamically loadable modules by default when you install Apache. The Red Hat RPM and the Apache binary distribution differ slightly, probably because of differing ideas about what is important to Red Hat Linux users. This list is based on release 1.3.12.

Note that if you install Apache with Red Hat Linux, you'll get some freebies—the last three listed modules are installed from separate RPMs and provide PHP and Perl programming support for your Web server. PHP and Perl are discussed in detail in Chapter 8, although we'll compile and install them from source code, rather than from an RPM.

Table 3.3   Apache Modules Provided with the Red Hat RPM and with the Apache Binary Distribution

Module	1.3.12 RPM	1.3.12 Binary
Libproxy.so	X	X
Mod_access	X	X
Mod_actions	X	X

Table 3.3   Apache Modules Provided with the Red Hat RPM and with the Apache Binary Distribution *(continued)*

Module	1.3.12 RPM	1.3.12 Binary
Mod_alias	X	X
Mod_asis	X	X
Mod_auth	X	X
Mod_auth_anon	X	X
Mod_auth_db	X	
mod_auth_dbm		X
mod_auth_digest	X	
mod_autoindex	X	X
mod_bandwidth	X	
mod_cern_meta	X	X
mod_cgi	X	X
mod_digest	X	X
mod_dir	X	X
mod_env	X	X
mod_example	X	
mod_expires	X	X
mod_headers	X	X
mod_imap	X	X
mod_include	X	X
mod_info	X	X
mod_log_agent	X	

Essential Configuration

PART 2

Table 3.3 Apache Modules Provided with the Red Hat RPM and with the Apache Binary Distribution *(continued)*

Module	1.3.12 RPM	1.3.12 Binary
mod_log_config	X	X
mod_log_referer	X	
mod_mime	X	X
mod_mime_magic	X	X
mod_mmap_static	X	
mod_negotiation	X	X
Mod_put	X	
Mod_rewrite	X	X
Mod_setenvif	X	X
Mod_speling	X	X
Mod_status	X	X
Mod_throttle	X	
Mod_unique_id	X	X
Mod_userdir	X	X
Mod_usertrack	X	X
Mod_vhost_alias	X	X
Mod_php	*	Not incl
Mod_php3	*	Not incl
Mod_perl	*	Not incl

* installed from separate RPMs by the Red Hat Linux installation program

Red Hat Package Manager

For Linux users, there is probably no better way to install already-compiled programs than a package manager. The most widely used of these is RPM. RPM is an abbreviation for Red Hat Package Manager, and it was originally developed by Red Hat (`www.redhat.com`) for inclusion in its Linux distribution. RPM packs a set of files into a single package, usually a file with the `.RPM` extension. This file can then be transferred to any other system and unpacked to reproduce the files in the exact location where they were found on the source system, creating directories where necessary. Traditionally, this is done with `tar` in the Unix world, and most source code is still distributed in so-called *tarballs*. But RPM is better. It can manage all the packages installed on your system, it can use newer packages to upgrade those already installed, it can cleanly uninstall packages, and it can even verify the installed files against the RPM database. Verification is useful because it detects changes that might have been made accidentally or deliberately by an intruder.

True to the spirit of open-source software, Red Hat donated RPM to the public domain, and many other Linux distributions have the ability to load RPM files. Red Hat, SuSE, Mandrake, TurboLinux, and Caldera OpenLinux are all "RPM Linux Distributions." Although other package managers exist for Linux, RPM is the most widely used, and more packages are available as RPMs than any other format.

> **NOTE**   If your Linux doesn't support RPM, you can add that support yourself. In keeping with the spirit of open source, and as a way of encouraging other Linux developers to use the RPM package manager, the source is no longer distributed by Red Hat (although you may be able to find it on their Web site). The source files are available from the `www.rpm.org` FTP server, `ftp://ftp.rpm.org/pub/rpm`. This site also contains a wealth of information about using the Red Hat Package manager. You'll find not only the source for all versions of RPM ever released, but also precompiled binary distributions for Intel 386 and Sparc platforms. For most versions of Linux, adding your own RPM support will not be necessary.

The best source for RPMs that I've ever found is the RPM repository on rpmfind.net (`http://rufus.w3.org/linux/RPM`). Figure 3.3 illustrates the RPM site after we've chosen the option to view the index by name. There are numerous packages for Apache 1.3.12, so to make a choice we need more information about them. Figure 3.4 shows the detailed display for `apache-1_3_12-2_i386.rpm`.

Figure 3.3 A sampling from the `rpmfind.net` RPM repository

Figure 3.4 The `rpmfind.net` display for Apache 1.3.12

Before installing the Apache 1.3.12 RPM on my Linux system, I removed the existing Apache RPM that was installed when I loaded the Red Hat distribution. Run rpm with the -qa argument, which says "query all installed packages," to determine which Apache RPMs are installed. Pipe the output to grep to display only those lines containing the string apache:

```
# rpm -qa |grep apache
apache-1.3.6-7
apache-devel-1.3.6-7
```

The -e argument to rpm erases an RPM package. It removes all files installed with the RPM package, unless those files have been modified. Uninstalling an RPM also removes all directories created when installing the RPM, unless those directories are not empty after the RPM files are removed.

In this example, removing the installed RPMs failed. The error warns that other packages were installed after, and are dependent on, the Apache RPM:

```
# rpm -e apache-1.3.6-7
error: removing these packages would break dependencies:
        webserver is needed by mod_perl-1.19-2
        webserver is needed by mod_php-2.0.1-9
        webserver is needed by mod_php3-3.0.7-4
```

To remove the Apache-1.3.6-7 RPM, it is necessary to first remove the three RPMs listed as dependent on that RPM, which I did with the following commands (if the package removal happens without error, the rpm command returns no output):

```
# rpm -e mod_perl-1.19-2
# rpm -e mod_php-2.0.1-9
# rpm -e mod_php3-3.0.7-4
# rpm -e apache-1.3.6-7
```

Once all the RPMs are removed, install the new Apache RPM using rpm with the –i argument in the following manner:

```
# ls -al apache*.rpm
-rw-r--r--   1 caulds    caulds     833084 Jan 17 09:41 apache-1_3_12-2_
i386.rpm
# rpm -i apache-1_3_12-2_i386.rpm
```

This RPM is designed to install Apache in the /home/httpd and /etc/httpd directories, which is where you'll find it on standard Red Hat systems. The RPM installs all the required configuration files, with values that allow the server to start:

```
# cd /home/httpd
# ls
cgi-bin html icons
```

Essential Configuration

PART 2

The RPM even provides a default HTML page in the default DocumentRoot directory (/home/httpd/html). This page allows your server to be accessed immediately after installation:

```
# ls html
index.html  manual  poweredby.gif
```

A listing of the /home/httpd/html directory shows two files and a subdirectory. The index.html file contains the HTML page the newly installed server will display by default; it is a special filename used to indicate the default HTML page in a directory. The poweredby.gif file is a graphic the server displays on the default page. The directory manual contains HTML documentation for the new Apache server. Access the manual from a Web browser using http://localhost/manual.

The Apache configuration files, logs, and loadable modules are all found elsewhere on the file system (in /etc/httpd):

```
# cd /etc/httpd
# ls
conf  logs  modules
# ls conf
access.conf  httpd.conf  magic  srm.conf
# ls modules
httpd.exp          mod_bandwidth.so   mod_include.so     mod_setenvif.so
libproxy.so        mod_cern_meta.so   mod_info.so        mod_speling.so
mod_access.so      mod_cgi.so         mod_log_agent.so   mod_status.so
mod_actions.so     mod_digest.so      mod_log_config.so  mod_unique_id.so
mod_alias.so       mod_dir.so         mod_log_referer.so mod_userdir.so
mod_asis.so        mod_env.so         mod_mime.so        mod_usertrack.so
mod_auth.so        mod_example.so     mod_mime_magic.so  mod_vhost_alias.so
mod_auth_anon.so   mod_expires.so     mod_mmap_static.so
mod_auth_db.so     mod_headers.so     mod_negotiation.so
mod_autoindex.so   mod_imap.so        mod_rewrite.so
```

The RPM also writes the Apache executable httpd into a directory reserved for system executable binaries:

```
# ls -al /usr/sbin/httpd
-rwxr-xr-x  1 root  root  282324 Sep 21 09:46 /usr/sbin/httpd
```

Binary Distributions

The last means of installing Apache is almost as easy as the RPM method. Binary distributions of Apache, compiled for a large number of operating systems and hardware platforms, are available from the Apache Software Foundation and can be downloaded from www.apache.org/dist/binaries/linux. You may need to look elsewhere if your hardware or OS is quite old (an old Linux kernel on a 486, for example). The page listing Apache for Linux distributions is shown in Figure 3.5.

Figure 3.5   Linux binary distributions on the www.apache.org site

When downloading binary distributions for Intel microprocessors, you need to make sure you download a version that was compiled to run on your specific processor family. For example, the i686 family includes the Pentium II, PII Xeon, Pentium III and PIII Xeon, as well as the Celeron processors. The i586 family includes the Pentium and Pentium with MMX CPUs, and i386 generally indicates the 80486 family. A binary compiled for the i386 family will run on any of the processors mentioned above, including the latest Pentium CPUs, but it will not be as fast as code compiled specifically for a processor generation. If you are downloading a binary distribution for a Pentium II or Pentium III, look for an i686 distribution; if you are downloading for an 80486, you must get the i386 binaries.

There is a handy Linux utility that will query the system's processor and return its hardware family type. Enter /bin/uname -m to obtain this information (the m is for *machine type*). When run on my server machine, which has an old Pentium 200 MMX chip, I got this result:

```
# uname -m
i586
```

For a Pentium PC running Linux, use the following steps:

1. Download the file apache_1.3.12-i686-whatever-linux2.tar.gz, which is the binary tarball, compressed with gzip. This long filename indicates the version of Apache (1.3.9), the CPU for which it was compiled (Intel 686 family), the operating system version (in this case, any Linux 2.*x* kernel).

NOTE For every binary package on the Web site, there is a README file to accompany it. You can view or download this file for information about the binary distribution; for example, who compiled it and when, as well as what compiler options and default locations for files were built into the Apache executable.

2. Make sure you are in the directory where you downloaded the binary distribution (or move the downloaded file elsewhere and change to that directory). After the installation process is complete, you will probably want to delete the directory that was created to hold the installation files. All the files you need to run Apache from the binary are moved from that directory to their intended locations:

```
# cd /home/caulds
# pwd
/home/caulds
# ls apache*
apache_1_3_9-i686-whatever-linux2_tar.gz
```

3. Uncompress and extract the distribution with tar to create a new directory tree containing all the files from the distribution:

```
# tar xvzf apache_1_3_12-i686-whatever-linux2_tar.gz
```

4. Change the working directory to the directory you just created:

```
# cd apache_1.3.12
# ls
ABOUT_APACHE    Makefile.tmpl    build.log    icons
```

```
Announcement      README           cgi-bin          install-bindist.sh
INSTALL           README.NT        conf             logs
INSTALL.bindist   README.bindist   config.layout    src
KEYS              README.configure config.status
LICENSE           WARNING-NT.TXT   configure
Makefile          bindist          htdocs
```

```
# ls bindist
bin  cgi-bin  conf  htdocs  icons  include  libexec  logs  man  proxy
```

```
# ls bindist/bin
ab          apxs       htdigest  httpd        rotatelogs
apachectl   dbmmanage  htpasswd  logresolve
```

5. The binary distribution includes a shell script for installing the files in their proper locations (the locations that the Apache daemon expects to find them). Run the shell script as follows to create the Apache folders. After it runs, you should find everything neatly installed under **/usr/local/apache**:

```
# ./install-bindist.sh
Installing binary distribution for platform i686-whatever-linux2
into directory /usr/local/apache ...
[Preserving existing configuration files.]
[Preserving existing htdocs directory.]
Ready.
   +--------------------------------------------------------+
   | You now have successfully installed the Apache 1.3.12  |
   | HTTP server. To verify that Apache actually works      |
   | correctly you should first check the (initially        |
   | created or preserved) configuration files:             |
   |                                                        |
   |    /usr/local/apache/conf/httpd.conf                   |
   |                                                        |
   | You should then be able to immediately fire up         |
   | Apache the first time by running:                      |
   |                                                        |
   |    /usr/local/apache/bin/apachectl start               |
   |                                                        |
   | Thanks for using Apache.            The Apache Group   |
   |                                     http://www.apache.org/ |
   +--------------------------------------------------------+
```

You can actually start the Apache server from the httpd file in the bin directory (the last listing above), but it has been compiled with default values that will not allow it to operate from this location. You can verify that it is operational, though, by entering a command such as the following, which will cause httpd to start, display its version information, and quit:

```
# ./bindist/bin/httpd -v
Server version: Apache/1.3.12 (Unix)
Server built:   Feb 27 2000 19:52:12
```

Running the Server

The Apache daemon is started from a single executable file (httpd), which is usually supported by a number of modules that are loaded by the server after it reads its configuration files. The Apache server is started when httpd is invoked, either manually at the command line, or more commonly as part of a startup script. Chapter 11, "Controlling Apache," discusses common ways of invoking httpd and controlling its behavior.

The normal behavior of httpd is to run as a system daemon, or listening server process, waiting for HTTP client connections on one or more sockets, bound to one or more of the system's network interfaces. The httpd file can also be invoked with several arguments that cause it to run, display some information, and quit immediately without going into daemon mode. A few of those arguments are demonstrated below; you can use this to test your Apache executable and display its running environment. In each case, I am invoking httpd from its standard location, although it could be placed anywhere on your file system without affecting it's operation. On my systems, I usually choose to place the file in a protected location reserved for system binaries (/usr/sbin/).

I've already demonstrated the -v argument, which displays the version number and compile date of the httpd file.

The -V (uppercase) option provides the same information, and also displays all the default values compiled into httpd. The most useful information is the default locations in which the Apache server looks for its supporting files and writes its directories. Most of these locations can be overridden at runtime by special directives in httpd.conf, but this is rarely necessary.

```
# /usr/local/apache/bin/httpd -V
Server version: Apache/1.3.12 (Unix)
Server built:   Jun 11 2000 16:51:03
Server's Module Magic Number: 19990320:7
Server compiled with....
 -D EAPI
 -D HAVE_MMAP
```

```
-D HAVE_SHMGET
-D USE_SHMGET_SCOREBOARD
-D USE_MMAP_FILES
-D USE_FCNTL_SERIALIZED_ACCEPT
-D HTTPD_ROOT="/usr/local/apache1_3_12"
-D SUEXEC_BIN="/usr/local/apache1_3_12/bin/suexec"
-D DEFAULT_PIDLOG="logs/httpd.pid"
-D DEFAULT_SCOREBOARD="logs/httpd.scoreboard"
-D DEFAULT_LOCKFILE="logs/httpd.lock"
-D DEFAULT_XFERLOG="logs/access_log"
-D DEFAULT_ERRORLOG="logs/error_log"
-D TYPES_CONFIG_FILE="conf/mime.types"
-D SERVER_CONFIG_FILE="conf/httpd.conf"
-D ACCESS_CONFIG_FILE="conf/access.conf"
-D RESOURCE_CONFIG_FILE="conf/srm.conf"
```

The -l argument displays the modules that are compiled into httpd (also referred to as *statically linked*). One module, httpd_core, is always statically linked into httpd. A second module (the shared object module, mod_so) is statically linked when dynamic loading of modules is required. For this server, all other modules are available to the server only if dynamically loaded at runtime:

```
# /usr/local/apache/bin/httpd -l
Compiled-in modules:
  http_core.c
  mod_so.c
```

The –t option runs a syntax test on configuration files but does not start the server. This test can be very useful, because it indicates the line number of any directive in the httpd.conf file that is improperly specified:

```
# /usr/local/apache/bin/httpd -t
Syntax OK
```

Every configuration option for a basic Apache server is stored in a single file. On most standard Apache systems, you'll find the configuration file stored as /usr/local/apache/conf/httpd.conf. If you have Apache loaded from a Red Hat Linux distribution CD or an RPM distribution, you'll find the file in an alternate location preferred by Red Hat, /etc/apache/conf/httpd.conf. When Apache is compiled, this location is one of the configurable values that are hard-coded into it. Unless explicitly told to load its configuration from another file or directory, Apache will attempt to load the file from its compiled-in path and filename.

This compiled-in value can be overridden by invoking the Apache executable with the -f option, as shown in Chapter 4. This can be handy for testing alternate configuration files, or for running more than one server on the system, each of which loads its own unique configuration.

Finally, you can run httpd with no arguments to start the server as a system daemon. Some simple modifications will probably have to be made to the default httpd.conf provided when you install Apache, although only very minor changes are actually required to start the server. In all likelihood, the first time you start Apache, you'll receive some error telling you the reason that Apache can't be started. The most common error new users see is this:

```
httpd: cannot determine local host name.
Use the ServerName directive to set it manually.
```

If you get an error when starting Apache the first time, don't panic; it is almost always fixed by making one or two very simple changes to Apache's configuration file. In fact, you should expect to make a few changes before running Apache. To do this, you'll modify Apache configuration *directives*, the subject of the next chapter. Chances are, the directives you need to learn about and change are those covered in the "Defining the Main Server Environment" section of Chapter 4. If your server won't start, you need to follow the instructions there.

If Apache finds an httpd.conf file that it can read for an acceptable initial configuration, you will see no response, which is good news. To find out if the server is actually running, attempt to connect to it using a Web browser. Your server should display a demo page to let you know things are working. Figure 3.6 shows the demo page from a Red Hat system.

You can also determine if the server is running the slightly more complicated way, and use the Linux process status (or ps) command to look for the process in the Linux process table, as shown below:

```
# ps -ef | grep httpd
root      8764      1  0 13:39 ?        00:00:00 ./httpd
nobody    8765   8764  0 13:39 ?        00:00:00 ./httpd
nobody    8766   8764  0 13:39 ?        00:00:00 ./httpd
nobody    8767   8764  0 13:39 ?        00:00:00 ./httpd
nobody    8768   8764  0 13:39 ?        00:00:00 ./httpd
nobody    8769   8764  0 13:39 ?        00:00:00 ./httpd
```

Figure 3.6 The demonstration Web page installed with the Apache RPM

This list is more interesting than it might appear at first. I used the e argument to ps to display all system processes, the f argument to display the full output format, and then grep to display only those lines containing the string httpd. Note that only one of the httpd processes is owned by root (the user who started Apache); the next few httpd processes in the list are all owned by nobody. This is as it should be. The first process is the main server, which never responds to user requests. It was responsible for creating the five child processes. Note from the third column of the output that all of these have the main server process (denoted by a process ID of 8764) as their parent process. They were all spawned by the main server, which changed their owner to the nobody account. It is these processes that respond to user requests.

Stopping the Apache server is a bit more difficult. When you start Apache, it writes the process ID (or PID) of the main server process into a text file where it can later be used to identify that process and control it using Linux signals. By default, this file is named httpd.pid, and is written in the logs directory under the server root. On my system:

```
# cat /usr/local/apache/logs/httpd.pid
8764
```

You'll note that the number saved in the file is the PID of the main Apache server process we saw in the process status listing earlier. To shut the server down, extract the contents of the `httpd.pid` and pass them to the `kill` command. This is the line that kills Apache:

```
# kill `cat /usr/local/logs/httpd.pid`
```

Using Apachectl

Apache comes with a utility to perform the basic operations of controlling the server. This utility, called `apachectl`, is actually a short shell script that resides in the `bin` directory under `ServerRoot`. It does nothing more than simplify processes you can perform by hand, and for that reason, doesn't require a lot of explanation. All of the functionality provided by `apachectl` is discussed in Chapter 11; for now, I'll show you how to start and stop Apache using this handy utility.

Start the server by invoking `apachectl` with the `start` argument. This is better than simply running `httpd`, because the script first checks to see if Apache is already running, and starts it only if it finds no running `httpd` process.

```
# /usr/local/apache/bin/apachectl start
/usr/local/apache/bin/apachectl start: httpd started
```

Stopping the server is when `apachectl` comes in really handy. Invoked with the `stop` argument, `apachectl` locates the `httpd.pid` file, extracts the PID of the main server, and then uses `kill` to stop the process (and all of its child processes). It is exactly what you did earlier using `ps` and `kill`, but it is much easier. That's what `apachectl` is, really, an easy-to-use wrapper for shell commands.

```
# /usr/local/apache/bin/apachectl stop
/usr/local/apache/bin/apachectl stop: httpd stopped
```

Running Multiple Apache Servers

Many administrators find that they need to run multiple Apache servers on the same physical system. They may want to run a separate server (with its own document space) to provide secure connections using Secure Sockets Layer (see Chapter 15), or run multiple versions of Apache for testing. My Linux server, for example, has Apache production versions 1.3.6, 1.3.9, and 1.3.12 installed, plus the 2.0alpha 2 and 2.0alpha 4 releases. I don't run them all simultaneously (although I could do so, by having each listen for connections on different TCP ports), but I can fire up any one of them at any time.

Apache makes it very easy to install multiple servers on the same box. All you need to do is ensure that each one starts its own unique configuration file. Generally, when you install multiple versions of Apache, you should specify different values for `--prefix` when running `configure`. When installing version 1.3.12, I instructed `configure` to place it in a directory other than the default `/usr/local/apache`:

```
# configure --prefix=/usr/local/apache1_3_12
```

Now, the newly installed 1.3.12 version will have its own configuration file, its own Apache daemon executable (`httpd`), and its own set of DSO modules.

And, if you want to run multiple copies of the same Apache server version, but with alternate configurations, you can use the `-f` argument to `httpd`. This argument lets you choose a configuration file that is read by the Apache daemon at startup and contains all the settings that define the configuration for each particular server.

```
# httpd -1 /usr/local/conf/test.conf
```

Using Defines to Implement Alternate Configurations

Another way to maintain alternate configurations uses a single configuration file. If there are features that you may or may not want to implement, you can place the directives for those features in blocks that, when the configuration file is parsed, will be either read or ignored conditionally. In the configuration file, the `<IfDefine var>` directive is a container for directives that should be run only if *var* has been set. The *var* argument is a type of variable known as a *define*; and on the Linux command line, the `-D` argument to `httpd` sets these variables. A good example of this is provided by the Secure Sockets Layer implementation discussed in Chapter 15. When the module for SSL is installed, all of the directives it adds to the Apache configuration file are placed between `<IfDefine>` directives:

```
<IfDefine SSL>
    Listen 443
</IfDefine>
```

The directives in this container will be read only if the variable SSL is defined. In other words, you want the server to listen for connections on TCP port 443 (the standard port for SSL) only if you defined SSL when you started the daemon. Do this by invoking the Apache daemon, `httpd`, with the `-D` argument, like so:

```
# /usr/local/apache/bin/httpd -D SSL
```

You can do the same to store alternate configurations in a single file, by setting your own defines for the different blocks you want to be active.

Essential Configuration

PART 2

In Sum:

This chapter has presented three methods of installing Apache:

1. From a package prepared for a Linux package manager, such as RPM,
2. From the downloadable binaries available from the Apache Foundation
3. By compiling the binaries yourself from the source files.

Although it's more difficult and time-consuming, compiling from source is the way I prefer to install Apache, because it permits the greatest flexibility in configuration or customization. Complete instructions were given on how to obtain, compile, and install Apache from source code. Many sites will prefer to install ready-made binaries, however, and these offer the quickest and most painless way to install Apache and upgrade it when the time comes. Full instructions on using the Apache Foundation's binary archives and third-party RPM packages were given. In the next chapter, I'll describe the Apache configuration file (httpd.conf) and the most important of the core directives that can be used in that file to customize your Apache server. The core directives are always available in every Apache server, and there is nothing in this chapter that does not apply to your Apache server. It is the most important reading you'll probably do in this book.

4

The Apache Core Directives

We define Apache's behavior and configuration options by using statements called *directives*. Apache directives are rigorously defined in how and where they can be used, and they have a specific syntax, very much like the commands of a programming language. Directives are not commands, though, and using directives is not like programming. Directives are instructions to Apache, telling it how to behave and where to find its resources, but they do not directly control the actions of Apache. Rather, they can be thought of as supplying information to the Apache server engine.

Customizing Apache to meet the needs of your specific Web site means learning the purpose and usage of a number of configuration directives. The most important of these are the core directives. These are the directives that are always compiled into the Apache executable. They are always available and require no special configuration to be used.

Apache directives fall into two groups: those that are always available (the so-called *core directives),* and those supplied by optional add-on *modules*. These configuration directives become available to the administrator only when their modules are added to the server and are meaningless until their modules are enabled. You can do this when compiling Apache, by statically linking the module to the Apache kernel or at runtime, by using the `LoadModule` and `AddModule` directives in `httpd.conf`. The next chapter is devoted to Apache modules and discusses the use of these two directives. Many Apache add-on modules have been adopted by the Apache Software Foundation for inclusion with the Apache distribution, although their use is optional.

Every directive is associated with a specific module; the largest module is the core module, which has special characteristics. This module cannot be unlinked from the Apache kernel and cannot be disabled; the directives it supplies are always available on any Apache server. All of the directives presented in this chapter are from the core Apache module, and all of the most important directives from the core module are covered. The most important other modules and their directives are covered in relevant chapters throughout the book. (For example, mod_proxy and its directives are presented in Chapter 13's discussion of using Apache as a proxy server.) Apache's online documentation includes a comprehensive reference to all the modules and directives; Appendix D shows how to make effective use of this documentation.

The core module provides support for basic server operations, including options and commands that control the operation of other modules. The Apache server with *just* the core module isn't capable of much at all. It will serve documents to requesting clients (identifying all as having the content type defined by the DefaultType directive). While all of the other modules can be considered optional, a useful Apache server will always include at least a few of them. In fact, nearly all of the standard Apache modules are used on most production Apache servers, and more than half are compiled into the server by the default configuration.

In this chapter, we'll see how directives are usually located in a single startup file (httpd.conf). I'll show how the applicability of directives is often confined to a specific scope (by default, directives have a general server scope). Finally, I'll show how directives can be overridden on a directory-by-directory basis (using the .htaccess file).

Using Apache Directives

The emphasis its developers placed on a modular design has proven to be one of Apache's greatest strengths. From the start, Apache was designed with expandability and extensibility in mind. The hooks that were designed into the program allow developers to create modules to extend the functionality of Apache are an important reason for its rapid adoption and huge success. Apache modules add not only new functionality to the server, but also new directives.

In order to get the most out of Apache, you need to be familiar with all the standard modules. You may not need or use all of these modules, but knowing that they exist, and having a basic knowledge of what each does, is very valuable when needs or problems arise in the future.

Read this chapter in conjunction with the book's appendices. This chapter, like all of the others in this book, is a tutorial that explains when a directive should be used, what it does and how you can use it in your server configuration. In addition to this tutorial material,

Appendix A is a tabular list of all directives enabled by the standard set of Apache modules. For each directive the table includes the context(s) in which the directive is permitted, the Overrides statement that applies to it (if any), and the module required to implement the directive. Appendix D is a detailed guide to using the excellent Apache help system, which should be your first stop when you need to know exactly how a directive is used. In configuring Apache, you will need to make frequent reference to these appendices.

The All-Powerful `httpd.conf` File

In keeping with its NCSA httpd origin, Apache originally used three configuration files:

- The main server configuration file, `httpd.conf`
- The resource configuration file, `srm.conf`
- The access permissions configuration file, `access.conf`

The Apache Software Foundation decided to merge these into a single file, and in all current releases of Apache, the only configuration file required is `httpd.conf`. Although there are legitimate reasons to split the Apache configuration into multiple files (particularly when hosting multiple virtual hosts), I find it very convenient to place all my configuration directives into a single file. It greatly simplifies creating backups, and maintaining revision histories. It also makes it easy to describe your server configuration to a colleague—just e-mail them a copy of your `httpd.conf`!

TIP To follow along with the descriptions in this chapter, you might find it useful to open or print the `httpd.conf` on your system to use for reference. On most systems, the file is stored as `/usr/local/apache/conf/httpd`. If you have Apache loaded from a Red Hat Linux distribution CD or a Red Hat Package Manager (RPM) distribution, you'll find the file as `/etc/apache/conf/httpd.conf`. Nearly everything you do to change the Apache configuration requires some modification of this file.

For convenience, the `httpd.conf` file is divided into three sections. Although these divisions are arbitrary, if you try to maintain these groupings, your configuration file will be much easier to read. The three sections of the `httpd.conf` are:

Section 1: The *global environment* section contains directives that control the operation of the Apache server process as a whole. This is where you place directives that control the operation of the Apache server processes, as opposed to directives that control how those processes handle user requests.

Section 2: The *main* or *default server section*, contains directives that define the parameters of the "main" or "default" server, which responds to requests that aren't handled by a virtual host. These directives also provide default values for the settings of all virtual hosts.

Section 3: The *virtual hosts* section contains settings for virtual hosts, which allow Web requests to be sent to different IP addresses or hostnames and have them handled by the same Apache server process. Virtual hosts are the subject of Chapter 6.

Securing Obsolete Configuration Files

Apache looks for the traditional access.conf and srm.conf files each time it loads, even though it runs without these files and won't generate an error if it does not find them. This creates a potential security hole. To eliminate the possibility of someone (perhaps intentionally) writing these files into the location where Apache looks for them, you can disable Apache from performing this search. Apache provides two legacy directives, designed to specify the locations of these once-necessary files, which you can use to indicate /dev/null as the location for both files:

```
AccessConfig /dev/null
ResourceConfig /dev/null
```

Directive Scope and Context

One of the important things to know about any directive is the context in which it operates. The context of a directive determines not only its scope—in other words, its range of applicability—but also where the directive can be placed. There are four contexts in which Apache directives can operate:

The General Server Context: Directives that operate in the general server context apply to the entire server. Some of these directives are only valid in this context, and make no sense in any other. For example, the StartServers directive specifies the number of httpd listener processes that are spawned when Apache is first started, and it makes no sense to include this directive in any other context. Other directives (like ServerName, which is always different for each virtual host) are equally valid in other contexts. When used in the general server context, most of these directives set default values that can be overridden when used in narrower contexts, just as a virtual host will override ServerName to set its own value for this directive.

The Container Context: This group includes directives that are valid when enclosed in one of the three containers: <Directory>, <Files>, or <Location>. These directives are applicable only within the scope defined by the enclosing container. A good example is a Deny directive, which prohibits access to resources. When used within any one of the three containers mentioned, it denies access to the resource or group of resources defined by the enclosing container.

The Virtual Host Context: Although a virtual host is actually defined by the container directive <VirtualHost>, for the purpose of defining directive contexts, it is considered separately because many virtual host directives actually override general server directives or defaults. As discussed in Chapter 6, the virtual host attempts to be a second server in every respect, running on the same machine and, to a client that connects to the virtual host, appearing to be the only server running on the machine.

The .htaccess Context: The directives in an .htaccess file are treated almost identically to directives appearing inside a <Directory> container in httpd.conf. The main difference is that directives appearing inside an .htaccess file can be disabled by using the AllowOverride directive in httpd.conf.

For each directive, Appendix A lists the context in which it can be used and the overrides that enable or disable it. For example, looking at the information for the Action directive, you can see that it is valid in all four contexts but is subject to being overridden, when used in an .htaccess file, by a FileInfo override. That is, if the FileInfo override is not in effect for a directory, an Action directive appearing inside an .htaccess file in that directory is disabled. This is because the Action directive is controlled by the FileInfo override.

The Apache server is smart enough to recognize when a directive is being specified out of scope. You'll get the following error when you boot, for example, if you attempt to use the Listen directive in a <Directory> context:

```
# /usr/local/apache/bin/httpd
Syntax error on line 925 of /usr/local/apache1_3_12/conf/httpd.conf:
Listen not allowed here
httpd could not be started
```

Defining the Main Server Environment

General server directives are those used to configure the server itself and its listening processes. General server directives are not allowed in the other contexts we'll discuss, except for virtual hosts. As you'll see in Chapter 6, general-server directives also provide default values that are inherited by all virtual hosts, unless specifically overridden.

I changed four directives, all of which were modifications of lines found in the default httpd.conf file, to get my server up and running. Once you've installed Apache, you should be able to get the server running by making only these changes, and you probably won't require all four. The default Apache configuration that you installed in Chapter 3 is complete and you can usually start the server using this configuration. However, before doing that, you should understand the purpose of the four directives in this section. These directives, while simple to understand and use, all have a server-wide scope, and affect the way many other directives operate. Because of the importance of these directives, you should take care to ensure that they are set properly.

The ServerName Directive

Apache must always be able to determine a hostname for the server on which it is run. This hostname is used by the server to create *self-referential URLs*—that is, URLs that refer to themselves. Later, we'll see that when more than one virtual host is run on the same system, each will be identified by a unique ServerName directive. For a system that hosts only a single Web server site, the ServerName directive is usually set to the hostname and domain of that server.

When I installed Apache and ran it for the first time, I was presented with the error *httpd: cannot determine local host name*. To correct this, I located the ServerName directive in my httpd.conf file and discovered that the Apache distribution had created the directive, using my fully qualified hostname as the Apache ServerName, but left the directive commented out. The directive was acceptable to me, so I uncommented the line:

```
ServerName jackal.hiwaay.net
```

The ServerRoot Directive

The ServerRoot directive specifies the directory in which the server lives and generally matches the value of the --prefix option that was set during the installation of Apache.

```
ServerRoot /usr/local/apache1_3_12
```

Typically this directory will contain the subdirectories bin/, conf/, and logs/. In lieu of defining the server root directory using the ServerRoot configuration directive, you can also specify the location with the -d option when invoking httpd:

```
/usr/local/apache/bin/httpd -d /etc/httpd
```

While there's nothing wrong with using this method of starting the server, it is usually best reserved for testing alternate configurations and for cases where you will run multiple versions of Apache on the same server simultaneously, each with its own configuration file.

Paths for all other configuration files are taken as relative to this directory. For example, the following directive causes Apache to write error messages into /usr/local/apache/logs/error.log:

```
ErrorLog logs/error.log
```

The ErrorLog directive is covered in detail in Chapter 12.

The `DocumentRoot` Directive

The `DocumentRoot` directive is used to define the top-level directory from which Apache will serve files. The directory defined by `DocumentRoot` contains the files that Apache will serve when it receives requests with the URL /.

It's perfectly acceptable to use the Apache default, which is the directory `htdocs` under the Apache server root, but I usually prefer to change this to the /home filesystem, which is a much larger file system reserved for user home directories.

To change the value of `DocumentRoot` on my system, I commented out the Apache default, and added a new `DocumentRoot` directive of my own:

```
# DocumentRoot "/usr/local/apache/htdocs"
DocumentRoot "/home/httpd/html"
```

Note that a full path to the directory must be used whenever the directory is outside the server root. Otherwise, a relative path can be given. (The double quotes are usually optional, but it's a good idea to always use them. If the string contains spaces, for example, it *must* be enclosed in double quotes.)

When you change the `DocumentRoot`, you must also alter the `<Directory>` container directive that groups all directives that apply to the `DocumentRoot` and subdirectories:

```
# <Directory "/usr/local/apache/htdocs">
<Directory "/home/httpd/html">
```

The `ScriptAlias` Directive

The `ScriptAlias` directive specifies a directory that contains executable scripts; for example, CGI programs that can be invoked from a Web browser. By default, Apache creates a `ScriptAlias` for all URLs requesting a resource in /cgi-bin/.

I also changed the `ScriptAlias` directive for my server. I chose to comment out Apache's default location and add my own, which is colocated with the Web documents on my /home file system. There's nothing wrong with the Apache default location (under the Apache server root directory) for the /cgi-bin directory, but you may want to change the location for ease of maintenance:

```
# ScriptAlias /cgi-bin/ "/usr/local/apache/cgi-bin/"
ScriptAlias /cgi-bin/ "/home/httpd/cgi-bin/"
```

Make sure that only users specifically authorized to create executable scripts can write to the directory you name. I usually assign group ownership of my `cgi-bin` directory to a Web administrator's group:

```
# chown -r nobody.webteam /home/httpd/cgi-bin
# chmod 750 /home/httpd/cgi-bin
```

The name of this group is arbitrary, but I use the command shown above to assign ownership of the cgi-bin directory (and all of its subdirectories and files) to a user named nobody and the group webteam. The default behavior of Apache on Linux is to run under the nobody user account. The group name is arbitrary, but it is to this group that I assign membership for those user accounts that are permitted to create or modify server scripts. The second line ensures that the file owner has full read, write, and execute permission, that members of the webteam group have read and write access, and that all other users have no access to the directory or the files it contains.

More General-Server Directives

There are a number of other general-server directives that you may want to modify before putting your server into operation. These directives are usually acceptable when left at their default values, but changing them rarely carries a significant risk. In all cases, if you feel that you understand the purpose of the directive well enough to add it to your httpd.conf file (or modify it if it's already there) don't be afraid to make such changes. These directives exist to make Apache as customizable as possible; they're for your use.

The ErrorDocument Directive

If Apache encounters an error while processing a user request, it is configured to display a standard error page, which gives the HTTP response code (see Chapter 1) and the URL that caused the problem. Use the ErrorDocument directive to define a custom error response to standard HTTP errors that are more user-friendly and understandable. Using ErrorDocument, you can configure Apache to respond to a particular HTTP error code in either of two ways:

1. By displaying custom error text. For example, the following would display a custom message for HTTP Error Code 403 (Forbidden). Note that the text begins with a double-quote that is not part of the message itself; it is not a quote-enclosed string. Do not end the message with a second quote.

    ```
    ErrorDocument 403 "You are not authorized to view this info!
    ```

2. By issuing a redirect to another URL, which may be external or internal. A fully specified URL that begins with httpd:// is assumed to be an external redirect. Apache will send a redirect to the client to tell it where to request the document, even if the redirect resolves to a resource on the same server. A relative URL is a local redirect, relative to the server's DocumentRoot, and Apache will serve the request directly, without sending a redirect that would require the client to request the document again. Here are examples of each of the possible redirect forms:

    ```
    #HTTP Error 401 (Unauthorized); display subscription page
    ErrorDocument 401 /subscription_info.html
    ```

```
#HTTP Error 404 (Not found); redirect to error script
ErrorDocument 404 /cgi-bin/bad_urls.pl

#HTTP Error 500 (Internal error) Redirect to backup server
ErrorDocument 500 http://jackal2.hiwaay.net
```

NOTE   If you attempt to redirect a request with an ErrorDocument 401 directive
(which means that the client is unauthorized to access the requested document),
the redirect *must* refer to a local document. Apache will not permit an external
redirect for this HTTP error.

The DefaultType Directive

A very rarely used directive in the general server scope, DefaultType can redefine the
default MIME content type for documents requested from the server. If this directive is
not used, all documents not specifically typed elsewhere are assumed to be of MIME type
text/html. Chapter 16 discusses MIME content types.

Apache reads its MIME-type-to-filename-extension mappings from a file named
mime.types, which is found in the Apache configuration directory. This file contains a list
of MIME content types, each optionally followed by one or more filename extensions.
This file is used to determine the MIME content header sent to the client with each
resource sent.

The DefaultType directive is generally used in a directory scope, to redefine the default
type of documents retrieved from a particular directory. In the following example, the
default MIME type for all documents in the /images directory under ServerRoot is
defined to be image/gif. That way, the server doesn't rely on an extension (like .gif) to
determine the resource type. A file with no extension at all, when served from this directory, will be sent to the requesting user with an HTTP header identifying it as MIME type
image/gif.

```
<Directory /images>
    DefaultType image/gif
</Directory>
```

Controlling Server Processes

The following directives are used to control the Linux processes when Apache is run on
that platform. The first directive is used to determine how Linux processes are created to
answer user requests. The remaining three directives all control system settings for the
Apache server processes.

The ServerType Directive

In Chapter 2, I noted that the Linux Apache server usually runs as a pool of listening processes, all of which are under the control of a single main server process that *never* responds to client requests. This standalone mode is by far the most efficient way to run Apache on Linux and the default if no ServerType directive is specified, but it is not the only way that Apache can be run.

The ServerType directive can be used to specify an alternate mode of operation, called *inetd* mode after the Linux process of that same name. When the Apache configuration file contains the directive

```
ServerType inetd
```

there will be no httpd process that binds itself to network sockets and listens for client connections. Instead, the Linux inetd process is configured to listen for client connections on behalf of Apache and spawn httpd processes, as required, to handle arriving connections. This is similar to the way Linux handles services like File Transfer Protocol (FTP).

The Apache inetd mode of operation is not recommended for most Apache installations, although it results in a more efficient use of resources if the server load is very light (a few hundred connections per day), or when the available memory is extremely limited (64MB or less RAM). The Apache server processes spend most of their time in an idle (waiting) state, so not running these processes continuously frees resources (particularly memory) that would otherwise be tied up.

The downside is that, since the system has to create a new listener process for each client connection, there is a delay in processing Web requests. The use of dynamically loadable modules increases the time required for Apache to load and begin responding to user requests. This delay is not usually significant when Apache starts its pool of processes in standalone mode, but in inetd mode, where Apache starts the processes after the request is received, the delay can be noticeable. This is particularly true if a large number of DSO modules have to be loaded and mapped into the Apache kernel's address space. When using Apache in inetd mode, you should avoid using dynamic modules and instead statically link the necessary modules, and eliminate those modules that you aren't using by commenting out or deleting the associated directives in httpd.conf.

NOTE   Some Apache administrators prefer to use inetd and TCP wrappers for all server processes. The Apache Software Foundation questions the security benefits of this practice and does not recommend the use of TCP wrappers with the Apache server.

Setting Up Apache for inetd   Setting up Apache to run in the inetd mode is not quite as simple as running the server in the default standalone mode. Besides adding the ServerType inetd directive to httpd.conf, you must ensure that the Linux system is configured to respond to Web requests and spawn httpd server processes as required. The Linux /etc/services file must contain lines for the TCP ports on which Apache requests will be received. For standard HTTP requests on TCP port 80, the /etc/services file should contain the following line:

```
http 80/tcp
```

If you are running Apache with Secure Sockets Layer (SSL), you should also include a line for the default SSL port:

```
https 443/tcp
```

Additionally, for each of the lines in /etc/services that apply to Apache, you must have a corresponding line in the /etc/inetd.conf file. For the two lines above, you would make sure /etc/inetd.conf contains the following lines:

```
http stream tcp nowait nobody /usr/local/apache/bin/httpd
https stream tcp nowait nobody /usr/local/apache/bin/httpd -DSSL
```

The first argument on each line is the service name and must match an entry in /etc/services. These lines give the inetd server process a full command path and optional arguments to run the Apache server for each defined service. The process will be started with the user ID (UID) nobody, which in Linux is UID -1. The user nobody owns the Apache process, so you should ensure that file and directory permissions permit user nobody to access all resources needed by the server.

Before these changes will be effective, it is necessary to restart Apache or send the HUP (hangup) signal to the running inetd process, as in this example:

```
# ps -ef | grep inetd
root       352      1  0 08:17 ?        00:00:00 inetd
# kill -HUP 352
```

The PidFile Directive

The PidFile directive defines the location and filename of a text file that contains the *process ID* (or PID) of the running Apache server. Processes that need to know the Apache server process ID—for example, the apachectl utility, discussed in Chapter 11—read the PID from this file. It is rarely necessary to change the Apache default PID file, which is stored as httpd.pid in the logs directory under the Apache ServerRoot.

This directive changes the default to place the PidFile in the location that Red Hat Linux uses:

```
PidFile "/var/run/apache.pid"
```

Essential Configuration

PART 2

The User Directive

For Apache servers running in `standalone` mode, this directive defines the Linux user that owns the child processes created to handle user requests. This directive is only meaningful when the Apache server is started as `root`. If the server is started as any other user, it cannot change ownership of child processes.

The default behavior of Apache on Linux systems is to change the ownership of all child processes to UID -1 (which corresponds to user `nobody` in the standard Linux /etc/ `password` file). This is the preferred way to run Apache on Linux systems.

In the following example, I've chosen to run Apace as `www`, a special Web-specific user account that I create on all my Web servers. For ease of administration, Apache resources on my server are usually owned by user `www` and group `wwwteam`.

```
User www
```

The Group Directive

Like the `User` directive, this directive is used to change the ownership of the child processes created to handle user requests. Instead of changing the user ownership of these processes, however, this directive changes the group ownership.

The default behavior of Apache on Linux systems is to change the group ownership of all child process to *group ID* (GID) −1, which corresponds to the `nobody` group in /etc/ `groups`. It often makes more sense to change the group ownership of the Apache server processes than it does to change the user ownership. On Linux servers where I want to give several users read/write access to my Apache configuration files and Web resources, I normally set up a special group with a name like `webteam`:

```
Group webteam
```

I place all the Web developers' accounts in this group and also change the Apache configuration to run server processes owned by this group.

As it must with the `User` directive, a standalone Apache server must be started as `root` to use the group directive. Otherwise, the server can't change the group ownership of any child processes it spawns.

Defining How the Server Listens for Connections

Apache provides three core directives that define the IP addresses and TCP port numbers on which it listens for and accepts client connections. If none of these directives is used, the server listens for connections on TCP port 80 (the HTTP default) on every IP address assigned to the server machine.

The `BindAddress` Directive

This `BindAddress` directive is used to limit the Apache server to listening for client connections on a single IP address. By default, Apache listens for connections on all network interfaces, which is equivalent to including the line `BindAddress *` in `httpd.conf`.

WARNING   Always use a numeric IP address as an argument to the `BindAddress` directive. The directive accepts a fully qualified hostname, but that should be avoided because it forces the server to rely on a successful DNS query to resolve the hostname to an IP address. If the DNS server is unavailable when Apache is started, the DNS query will fail and the Apache server will not start.

This directive is very limited. It can be used only once in an Apache configuration. If multiple directives exist, only the last is used. It cannot specify port values, nor can it be used to specify multiple IP addresses (other than the special case of * or ALL). For these reasons, the `Listen` directive (described shortly) is much more flexible and should usually be used instead.

```
BindAddress 192.168.1.1
```

This example of the `BindAddress` directive (which is always valid only in a server context) causes the Apache server to *bind to,* or listen for, connections on a single network interface (designated by the IP address assigned to that port). By default, Apache listens for connections on all network interfaces on the system. This directive can be used, for example, with an Apache server on an intranet to force it to listen only for connections on the system's local area network address, ignoring connection attempts on any other network adapters that may exist (particularly those accessible from the Internet).

The `Port` Directive

This directive specifies the TCP network port on which Apache should listen for client connections. It does this only if the Apache configuration has no `Listen` directive that specifies a port number for the main server.

The port number can be in the range from 0 to 65535. Port numbers below 1025 are reserved for system services. Each reserved port number is associated with a specific network protocol. The `/etc/services` file lists the reserved ports on your system. The ports in this range are reserved for services that are owned by the system's `root` user. This includes the default port for HTTP servers, port 80. To use port 80, Apache must be started as `root`, although the normal behavior for a standalone server is for this primary server to spawn listener processes that run as nonprivileged users but are still bound to port 80.

Like the `BindAddress` directive, the `Port` directive is limited to a single TCP port for the server and cannot be used to set different port values for different network interfaces. Also, only one `Port` directive is used in `httpd.conf`. If more than one exists, the last one overrides all others. However, while the `BindAddress` directive should be avoided, using the `Port` directive is a good practice. This is because the `Port` directive serves a second purpose: the `Port` value is used with the value of the `ServerName` directive to generate URLs that point back to the system itself. These *self-referential URLs* are often generated automatically by scripts (Chapter 8) or Server-Side Include pages (Chapter 7). While it is acceptable to rely on the default value of the `Port` directive (80), if you wish to create self-referential URLs that use any port other than 80, you *must* specify a `Port` directive. For example:

```
Port 443
```

This directive defines the default port on which Apache listens for connections as TCP port 443, the standard port for Secure Sockets Layer. (SSL is the subject of Chapter 15.) Note that subsequent Listen directives can cause Apache to accept connections on other TCP ports, but whenever the server creates a URL to point back to itself (a "self-referential URL"), the Port directive will force it to include 443 as the designated port for connections.

The `Listen` Directive

The `Listen` directive is used to specify IP addresses or ports on which to accept connections. It incorporates all of the functionality of both the `BindAddress` and `Port` directives but has several important advantages over them. `Listen` should be used instead of `BindAddress` and `Port`. The `Listen` directive has a global server scope and has no meaning inside a container. Apache is smart enough to detect and warn if the `Listen` directive is used in the wrong context. Placing a `Listen` directive inside a virtual host container, for example, generates this error:

```
Syntax error on line 1264 of /usr/local/apache/conf/httpd.conf:
Listen cannot occur within <VirtualHost> section
```

If `Listen` specifies only a port number, the server listens to the specified port on all system network interfaces. If a single IP address and a single port number are given, the server listens only on that port and interface.

Multiple `Listen` directives may be used to specify more than one address and port to listen to. The server will respond to requests from any of the listed addresses and ports.

For example, to make the server accept connections on both port 80 and port 8080, use these directives:

```
Listen 80
Listen 8080
```

To make the server accept connections on two specific interfaces and port numbers, identify the IP address of the interface and the port number separated by a colon, as in this example:

```
Listen 192.168.1.3:80
Listen 192.168.1.5:8080
```

Although Listen is very important in specifying multiple IP addresses for IP-based virtual hosting (discussed in detail in Chapter 6), the Listen directive does *not* tie an IP address to a specific virtual host. Here's an example of the Listen directive used to instruct Apache to accept connections on two interfaces, each of which uses a different TCP port.

```
Listen 192.168.1.1:80
Listen 216.180.25.168:443
```

I use this configuration to accept ordinary HTML requests on Port 80 on my internal network interface; connections on my external interface (from the Internet) are accepted only on TCP Port 443, the default port for Secure Sockets Layer (SSL) connections (as we'll see in Chapter 15).

The Options Directive

The Options directive controls which server features are available in a particular directory. The value can be set to None, in which case none of the extra features are enabled, or one or more of the following:

ExecCGI   Permits execution of CGI scripts.

FollowSymLinks   The server will follow symbolic links (symlinks) in this directory. Following symlinks does not change the pathname used to match against <Directory> sections. This option is ignored if set inside a <Location> section.

Includes   Permits server-side includes (SSI).

IncludesNOEXEC   Server-side includes are permitted, but the #exec and #include commands of SSI scripts are disabled.

Indexes   If a URL that maps to a directory is requested, and there is no
DirectoryIndex (for example, index.html) in that directory, then the server will
return a formatted listing of the directory.

MultiViews   Allows content-negotiated MultiViews. As discussed in Chapter 16,
MultiViews are one means of implementing content negotiation.

All   Includes all options except for MultiViews. This is the default setting.

SymLinksIfOwnerMatch   The server will only follow symbolic links for which
the target file or directory is owned by the same user ID as the link. Like
FollowSymLinks, this option is ignored if set inside a <Location> section.

Normally, if multiple options apply to a directory, the most specific one is used and the
other options are ignored. However, if all the options on the Options directive are preceded by a plus (+) or minus (–) character, then the options are merged. Any options
preceded by a plus are added to the options currently in effect, and any options preceded
by a minus are removed from the options currently in effect.

Since the default setting for the Options directive is All, the configuration file that is
provided with Apache contains the following section, which enables only FollowSymLinks
for every directory on the entire system.

```
<Directory />
    Options FollowSymLinks
</Directory>
```

The following examples should clarify the rules governing the merging of options. In the
first example, only the option Includes will be set for the /web/docs/spec directory:

```
<Directory /web/docs>
    Options Indexes FollowSymLinks
</Directory>
<Directory /web/docs/spec>
     Options Includes
</Directory>
```

In the example below, only the options FollowSymLinks and Includes are set for the /
web/docs/spec directory:

```
<Directory /web/docs>
   Options Indexes FollowSymLinks
</Directory>
<Directory /web/docs/spec>
   Options +Includes -Indexes
</Directory>
```

Using either -IncludesNOEXEC or -Includes disables server-side includes. Also, the use of a plus or minus sign to specify a directive has no effect if no options list is already in effect. Thus it is always a good idea to ensure that at least one Options directive that covers all directories is used in httpd.conf. Options can be added to or removed from this list as required in narrower scopes.

WARNING   Be aware that the default setting for Options is All. For that reason, you should always ensure that this default is overridden for every Web-accessible directory. The default configuration for Apache includes a <Directory> container to do this; do not modify or remove it.

The Container Directives

The scope of an Apache directive is often restricted using special directives called *container directives*. In general, these container directives are easily identified by the enclosing <> brackets. The conditional directives <IfDefine> and <IfModule>, which are not container directives, are an exception. Container directives require a closing directive that has the same name and begins with a slash character (much like HTML tags.)

A container directive encloses other directives and specifies a limited scope of applicability for the directives it encloses. A directive that is not enclosed in a container directive is said to have global scope and applies to the entire Apache server. A global directive is overridden locally by the same directive when it is used inside a container. The following sections examine each type of container directive.

The <VirtualHost> Container

The <VirtualHost> container directive encloses directives that apply only to a specific *virtual host*. As discussed further in Chapter 6, a virtual host is a Web site hosted on your server that is identified by a host name alias. For example, assume your server is www.aulds.com and that it hosts a Web site for a local bait and tackle shop. That shop, however, does not want its customers connecting to www.aulds.com for information; it wants customers to use the Web site www.worms.com. You can solve this problem by creating a virtual host for www.worms.com on the real host www.aulds.com. The format of the <VirtualHost> container directive is:

```
<VirtualHost address>
   directives
</VirtualHost>
```

The directives you enclose in the `<VirtualHost>` container will specify the correct host name and document root for the virtual host. Naturally, the server name should be a value that customers of the Web site expect to see when they connect to the virtual host. Additionally, the file served to the customers needs to provide the expected information. In addition to these obvious directives, almost anything else you need to customize for the virtual host can be set in this container. For example:

```
<VirtualHost 192.168.1.4>
    ServerAdmin webmaster@host1.com
    DocumentRoot /home/httpd/wormsdocs
    ServerName www.worms.com
    ErrorLog logs/worms.log
    TransferLog logs/worms.log
</VirtualHost>
```

The example above defines a single virtual host. In Chapter 6, we'll see that this is one form of virtual host, referred to as *IP-based*. The first line defines the Internet address (IP) for the virtual host. All connections to the Apache server on this IP address are handled by the virtual server for this site, which might be only one of many virtual sites being hosted on the same server. Each directive defines site-specific values for configuration parameters that, outside a `<VirtualHost>` container directive, normally refer to the entire server. The use of each of these in the general server context has already been shown.

The `<Directory>` and `<DirectoryMatch>` Containers

The `<Directory>` container encloses directives that apply to a file system directory and *its subdirectories*. The directory must be expressed by its full pathname or with wildcards. The example below illustrates a `<Directory>` container that sets the `Indexes` and `FollowSymLinks` options for all directories under `/home/httpd/` that begin with `user`:

```
<Directory /home/httpd/user*>
    Options Indexes FollowSymLinks
</Directory>
```

`<Directory>` containers are always evaluated so that the shortest match (widest scope) is applied first, and longer matches (narrower scope) override those that may already be in effect from a wider container. For example, the following container disables all overrides for every directory on the system (/ and all its subdirectories):

```
<Directory />
    AllowOverride None
</Directory>
```

If the `httpd.conf` file includes a second `<Directory>` container that specifies a directory lower in the file system hierarchy, the directives in the container take precedence over those defined for the file system as a whole. The following container enables `FileInfo` overrides for all directories under `/home` (which hosts all user home directories on most Linux systems):

```
<Directory /home/*>
    AllowOverride FileInfo
</Directory>
```

The `<Directory>` container can also be matched against *regular expressions* by using the '~' character to force a regular expression match:

```
<Directory ~ "^/home/user[0-9]{3}">
```

The `<DirectoryMatch>` directive is specifically designed for regular expressions, however, and should normally be used in place of this form. This container directive is exactly like `<Directory>`, except that the directories to which it applies are matched against regular expressions. The following example applies to all request URLs that specify a resource that begins with `/user`, followed by exactly three digits. (The ^ character denotes "beginning of string," and the {3} means to match the previous character; in this case any member of the character set [0–9]).

```
<DirectoryMatch "^/user[0-9]{3}">
    order deny,allow
    deny from all
    allow from .foo.com
</Directory>
```

This container directive would apply to a request URL like the following:

```
http://jackal.hiwaay.net/user321
```

because the `<DirectoryMatch>` container directive looks for directories (relative to `DocumentRoot`) that consist of the word *user* followed by three digits.

Introduction to Regular Expressions

Many Apache configuration directives accept *regular expressions* for matching patterns. Regular expressions are an alternative to wildcard pattern matching and are usually an extension of a directive's wildcard pattern matching capability. Indeed, I have heard regular expressions (or *regexps*) described as "wildcards on steroids."

Introduction to Regular Expressions *(continued)*

A brief sidebar can hardly do justice to the subject, but to pique your interest, here are a few regexp tags and what they mean:

^ and $ Two special and very useful tags that mark the beginning and end of a line. For example, ^# matches the # character whenever it occurs as the first character of a line (very useful for matching comment lines), and #$ would match # occurring as the very last character on a line. These pattern-matching operators are called *anchoring* operators and are said to "anchor the pattern" to either the beginning or the end of a line.

* and ?   The character * matches the preceding character zero or more times, and ? matches the preceding pattern zero or one time. These operators can be confusing, because they work slightly differently from the same characters when used as "wildcards." For example, the expression fo* will match the pattern *foo* or *fooo* (any number of *o* characters), but it also matches *f*, which has zero *o*'s. The expression ca? will match the *c* in *score*, which seems a bit counterintuitive because there's no *a* in the word, but the a? says zero or one *a* character. Matching zero or more occurrences of a pattern is usually important whenever that pattern is optional. You might use one of these operators to find files that begin with a name that is optionally followed by several digits and then an extension. Matching for ^filename\d*.gif will match filename001 .gif and filename2.gif, but also simply filename.gif. The \d matches any digit (0–9), in other words, we are matching zero or more digits.

+   Matches the preceding character one or more times, so ca+ will not match *score*, but will match *scare*.

.   The period character matches any single character except the newline character. In effect, when you use it, you are saying you don't care what character is matched, as long as some character is matched. For example x.y matches *xLy* but not *xy*; the period says the two must be separated by a single character. The expression x.*y says to match an *x* and a *y* separated by zero or more characters.

{n}   This operator (a number between braces) matches the *n* occurrences of the preceding character. For example, so{2} matches *soot*, but not *sot*.

Essential
Configuration

PART 2

Introduction to Regular Expressions *(continued)*

If you're an experienced Linux system administrator, you're already familiar with regular expressions from using grep, sed, and awk. And if you're an experienced Perl user, you probably also have some knowledge of regular expressions. The GNU C++ Regular Expressions library and Windows Scripting Host (WSH) even allow expressions in Microsoft's JavaScript or VBScript programs.

The only way to develop proficiency in using regexps is to study examples and experiment with them. Entire books have been written on the power of regular expressions (well, at least one) for pattern matching and replacement.

Some useful resources on regexps are:

Mastering Regular Expressions, by Jeffrey E.F. Friedl (O'Reilly, 1997)

http://www.perl.com/CPAN-local/doc/manual/html/pod/perlre.html

http://www.delorie.com/gnu/docs/regex/regex_toc.html

http://lib.stat.cmu.edu/scgn/v52/section1_7_0_1.html

The `<Files>` and `<FilesMatch>` Containers

The `<Files>` container encloses directives that apply only to specific files, which should be specified by filename (using wildcards when necessary). The following example allows access to files with the *OurFile* extension only by hosts in a specific domain:

```
<Files *.OurFile>
    order deny,allow
    deny from all
    allow from .thisdomain.com
</Files>
```

Like the `<Directory>` container, `<Files>` can also be matched against *regular expressions* by using the ~ character to force a regular expression match. The following line, for example, matches filenames that end in a period character (escaped with a backslash) immediately followed by the characters *xml*. The $ in regular expressions denotes the end of the string. Thus we are looking for file names with the extension .xml.

```
<Files ~ "\.xml$">
    Directives go here
</Files>
```

The <FilesMatch> directive is specifically designed for regular expressions, however, and should normally be used in place of this form.

<FilesMatch> is exactly like the <Files> directive, except that the specified files are defined by regular expressions. All graphic images might be defined, for example, using:

```
<FilesMatch> "\.(gif|jpe?g|png)$">
    some directives
</FilesMatch>
```

This regular expression matches filenames with the extension *gif* or *jpg* or *jpeg* or *png*. (The *or* is denoted by the vertical bar 'I' character.) Notice the use of the *?* character after the *e*, which indicates zero or one occurrences of the preceding character (*e*). In other words, a match is made to *jp*, followed by zero or one *e*, followed by *g*.

The <Location> and <LocationMatch> Containers

The <Location> container encloses directives that apply to specific URLs. This is similar to <Directory>, because most URLs contain a reference that maps to a specific directory relative to Apache's DocumentRoot. The difference is that <Location> does not access the file system, but considers only the URL of the request. Most directives that are valid in a <Directory> context also work in a <Location> container; directives that do not apply to a URL are simply ignored because they are meaningless in a <Location> context.

The <Location> functionality is especially useful when combined with the SetHandler directive. For example, to enable status requests, but only from browsers at foo.com, you might use the following (note that *status* is *not* a directory; it is a part of the URL, and actually invokes a server-generated status page. There is no /status directory on my system):

```
<Location /status>
    SetHandler server-status
    order deny,allow
    deny from all
    allow from .foo.com
</Location>
```

You can also use extended regular expressions by adding the ~ character, as described for the <Directory> and <Files> container directories; but a special container directive, <LocationMatch>, is specifically designed for this purpose and should be used instead.

<LocationMatch> is exactly like the <Location> container directive, except that the URLs are specified by regular expressions. The following container applies to any URL

that contains the substring */www/user* followed immediately by exactly three digits; for example, */www/user911*:

```
<LocationMatch "/www/user[0-9]{3}">
    order deny,allow
    deny from all
    allow from .foo.com
</Location>
```

The <Limit> and <LimitExcept> Containers

<Limit> encloses directives that apply only to the HTTP methods specified. In the following example, user authentication is required only for requests using the HTTP methods POST, PUT, and DELETE:

```
<Limit POST PUT DELETE>
    require valid-user
</Limit>
```

<LimitExcept> encloses directives that apply to all HTTP methods *except* those specified. The following example shows how authentication can be required for all HTTP methods other than GET:

```
<LimitExcept GET>
    require valid-user
</Limit>
```

Perl Sections

If you are using the mod_perl module, it is possible to include Perl code to automatically configure your server. Sections of the httpd.conf containing valid Perl code and enclosed in special <Perl> container directives are passed to mod_perl's built-in Perl interpreter. The output of these scripts is inserted into the httpd.conf file before it is parsed by the Apache engine. This allows parts of the httpd.conf file to be generated dynamically, possibly from external data sources like a relational database on another machine.

Since this option absolutely requires the use of mod_perl, it is discussed in far more detail with this sophisticated module in Chapter 8.

Apache's Order of Evaluation for Containers

When multiple containers apply to a single incoming request, Apache resolves them in the following order:

1. Apache will first evaluate any <Directory> container (except for those that match regular expressions) and merge any .htaccess files it finds that apply to

the request. <Directory> containers are always evaluated from widest to narrowest scope, and directives found in .htaccess files override those in <Directory> containers that apply to the same directory.

2. Directives found in <DirectoryMatch> containers and <Directory> containers that match regular expressions are evaluated next. Directives that apply to the request override those in effect from <Directory> or .htaccess files (item 1 of this list).

3. After directives that apply to the directory in which the resource resides, Apache applies directives that apply to the file itself. These come from <Files> and <FilesMatch> containers, and they override directives in effect from <Directory> containers. For example, if an .htaccess file contains a directive that denies the requester access to a directory, but a directive in a <Files> container specifically allows access to the file, the request will be granted, because the contents of the <Files> container override those of the <Directory> container.

4. Finally, any directives in <Location> or <LocationMatch> containers are applied. These directives are applied to the request URL and override directives in all other containers. If a directive in a <Location> container directly conflicts with the same directive in *either* a <Directory> or a <Files> container, the directive in the <Location> container will override the others.

Containers with narrower scopes always override those with a wider scope. For example, directives contained in <Directory /home/httpd/html> override those in <Directory /home/httpd> for the resources in its scope. If two containers specify exactly the same scope (for example, both apply to the same directory or file), the one specified last takes precedence.

The following rather contrived example illustrates how the order of evaluation works.

```
<Files index.html>
    allow from 192.168.1.2
</Files>

<Directory /home/httpd/html>
    deny from all
</Directory>
```

In this example, the <Directory> container specifically denies access to the /home/httpd/html directory to all clients. The <Files> directive (which precedes it in the httpd.conf file) permits access to a single file index.html inside that directory, but only to a client connecting from IP address 192.168.1.2. This permits the display of the HTML page by that client, but not any embedded images; these can't be accessed, because the

<Files> directive does not include them in its scope. Note also that the order of the containers within the configuration file is *not* important; it is the order in which the containers are resolved that determines which takes precedence. Any <Files> container directives will always take precedence over <Directory> containers that apply to the same resource(s).

The .htaccess File

Although an Apache server is usually configured completely within the httpd.conf file, editing this file is not always the most efficient configuration method. Most Apache administrators prefer to group directory-specific directives, particularly access-control directives, in special files located within the directories they control. This is the purpose of Apache's .htaccess files. In addition to the convenience of having all the directives that apply to a specific group of files located within the directory that contains those files, .htaccess files offer a couple of other advantages. First, you can grant access to modify .htaccess files on a per-directory basis, allowing trusted users to modify access permissions to files in specific directories without granting those users unrestricted access to the entire Apache configuration. Second, you can modify directives in .htaccess files without having to restart the Apache server (which is the only way to read a modified httpd.conf file).

By default, the Apache server searches for the existence of an .htaccess file in every directory from which it serves resources. If the file is found, it is read and the configuration directives it contains are merged with other directives already in effect for the directory. Unless the administrator has specifically altered the default behavior (using the AllowOverride directive as described below) all directives in the .htaccess file override directives already in effect. For example, suppose httpd.conf contained the following <Directory> section:

```
<Directory /home/httpd/html/Special>
    order deny,allow
    deny from all
</Directory>
```

All access to the directory /home/httpd/html/Special would be denied. This may be exactly what the administrator wants, but it is more likely that the directory exists under the Web server root so that *someone* can get to it with a browser. This can be accomplished by creating an .htaccess file in the Special directory with directives like the following, which overrides the directives already active for the directory:

```
allow from 192.168.1.*
```

Here, we've used a wildcard expression to specify a range of IP addresses (possibly the Web server's local subnet) that can access resources in the Special directory.

The AllowOverrides Directive

By default, whenever Apache receives a request for a resource, it searches for an .htaccess file in the directory where that resource resides, *and in every parent directory of that directory on the file system.* Remember, this search is not limited to DocumentRoot and its subdirectories, but extends all the way up the file system hierarchy to the root directory ("/"). It treats each of these exactly as if it were a <Directory> container for the directory in which it is located. The directives in all .htaccess files found in the requested resource's tree are merged with any other directives already in effect for that directory. Those lower in the file system hierarchy override those higher in the tree; this means you can grant permission to access a directory even if that permission was denied to a higher-level directory (and, consequently, all of its subdirectories). After merging all the relevant .htaccess files with all directives from all applicable <Directory> containers, Apache applies them according to the order of evaluation described earlier.

What I've just described is the default behavior of Apache with regard to .htaccess files. You can modify this behavior through the special directive AllowOverride, which controls how .htaccess files are handled. The AllowOverride directive specifies which directives, when found in an .htaccess file, are allowed to override conflicting directives that are already in effect. AllowOverride is used not to enable or disable directives, but to specify types of directives that can be overridden in .htaccess files.

The following is a list of all permissible arguments to the AllowOverride directive. Each enables or disables a set of directives when these directives are found in .htaccess files. Consult the table in Appendix A for the applicable AllowOverride for each directive for which an override can be specified; the AllowOverride directive does not apply to directives shown in that table with N/A in the Override column.

> All   This enables all .htaccess overrides. Therefore, all directives that are permissible in an .htaccess file, can be used to override settings in the httpd .conf file.

WARNING   The default behavior of Apache is to search for .htaccess files in each directory in the path of a resource as if AllowOverride All had been specified for all directories. This makes the server hard to secure, because anyone who can write a file into any of the directories from which Apache serves files can create a bogus .htaccess file that can be used to subvert system security. It is always best to use AllowOverride to disable .htaccess files in all directories, enabling the use of .htaccess files only for specific purposes and locations, on a case-by-case basis. Disabling the search for .htaccess files also has the added benefit of improving Apache performance (as discussed in Chapter 13).

None   This disables .htaccess overrides. If AllowOverride None is specified for a directory, Apache will not read an .htaccess even if it exists in that directory. If AllowOverride None is specified for the system root ("/") directory, no directory will ever be searched for an .htaccess file.

Authconfig   Allows the use of all user/group authorization directives (Authname, Authuserfiles, Authgroupfile, Require), which are discussed in detail in Chapter 14.

FileInfo   Allows the use of directives controlling document types.

Indexes   Allows the use of directives controlling directory indexing.

Limit   Allow the use of directives that control access based on the browser hostname or network address.

Options   Allow the use of special directives, currently limited to the directives Options and XBitHack.

Setting Up User Home Directories

In nearly every server used to support multiple users, it is useful to provide individual users with their own Web home directories. This is a very common practice among Internet Service Providers that support Web hosting for their users. Providing user home directories is similar to virtual hosting in some respects, but it is much simpler to implement. The functionality is provided by a standard Apache module (mod_userdir) that is compiled into the Apache server by default.

Specifying Username-to-Directory Mappings

If you intend to allow users to publish their own Web pages, the UserDir directive indicates the name of a directory that, if found in the users' home directories, contains Web pages that are accessed with a URL of the form http://serverhostname/~username/. The Apache default is to name this directory public_html. There is absolutely nothing wrong with this default value, but for years, since I first administered a CERN 3.0 server, I have chosen to name this directory WWW. A simple change to the UserDir directive in httpd.conf let me reconfigure this value for all users on the server:

```
UserDir WWW
```

Once I've added this line to Apache's httpd.conf file and restarted the server, each user on my system can now place files in a /WWW subdirectory of their home directory that Apache can serve. Requests to a typical user's Web files look like:

```
http://jackal.hiwaay.net/~caulds/index.html
```

The UserDir directive specifies a filename or pattern that is used to map a request for a user home directory to a special repository for that user's Web files. The UserDir directive can take one of three forms:

A relative path   This is normally the name of a directory that, when found in the user's home directory, becomes the DocumentRoot for that user's Web resources:

```
UserDir public_html
```

This is the simplest way to implement user home directories, and the one I recommend because it gives each user a Web home underneath their system home directories. This form takes advantage of the fact that ~*account* is always Linux shorthand for "user *account*'s home directory". By specifying users' home directories as a relative path, the server actually looks up the user's system home (in the Linux /etc/passwd file) and then looks for the defined Web home directory beneath it).

WARNING   Be careful when using the relative path form of the UserDir directive. It can expose directories that shouldn't be accessible from the Web. For example, when using the form http://servername/~root/, the Linux shortcut for ~root maps to a directory in the file system reserved for system files on most Linux systems. If you had attempted to designate each user's system home directory as their Web home directory (using UserDir /), this request would map to the /root directory. When using the relative directory form to designate user Web home directories, you should lock out any accounts that have home directories on protected file systems (see "Enabling/Disabling Mappings" below). The home directory of the root account (or *superuser*) on Linux systems should be protected. If someone was able to place an executable program in one of root's startup scripts (like .profile or .bashrc), that program would be executed the next time a legitimate user or administrator logged in using the root account.

An absolute path   An absolute pathname is combined with the user name to identify the DocumentRoot for that user's Web resources:

```
UserDir /home/httpd/userstuff
```

This example would give each user their own directory with the same name as their user account underneath /home/httpd/userstuff. This form gives each user a Web home directory that is *outside* their system home directory. Maintaining a special directory for each user, outside their system home directory, is not a good idea if there are a lot of users. They won't be able to maintain their own Web spaces, as they could in their respective home directories, and the entire responsibility will fall on the administrator. Use the absolute form for defining user Web home directories only if you have a small number of users, preferably where each is knowledgeable enough to ensure that their Web home directory is protected from other users on the system.

An absolute path with placeholder   An absolute pathname can contain the * character (called a *placeholder*), which is replaced by the username when determining the DocumentRoot path for that user's Web resources. Like the absolute path described above, this form can map the request to a directory outside the user's system home directory:

```
UserDir    /home/httpd/*/www
```

Apache substitutes the username taken from the request URL of the form http:/ /servername/~username/ to yield the path to each user's Web home directory:

```
/home/httpd/username/www
```

If all users have home directories under the same directory, the placeholder in the absolute path can mimic the relative path form, by specifying:

```
UserDir    /home/*/www
```

The behavior of the lookup is slightly different, though, using this form. In the relative path form, the user's home directory is looked up in /etc/passwd. In the absolute path form, this lookup is not performed, and the user's Web home directory must exist in the specified path. The advantage of using the absolute path in this manner is that it prevents URLs like http://servername/~root from mapping to a location that Web clients should never access.

The disadvantage of using the "absolute path with placeholder" form is that it forces all Web home directories to reside under one directory that you can point to with the absolute path. If you needed to place user Web home directories in other locations (perhaps even on other file systems) you will need to create symbolic links that point the users' defined Web home directories to the actual location of the files. For a small to medium-sized system, this is a task that can be done once for each user and isn't too onerous, but for many users, it's a job you might prefer to avoid.

The use of the UserDir directive is best illustrated by example. Each of the three forms of the directive described above would map a request for

```
http://jackal.hiwaay.net/~caulds/index.html
```

into the following fully qualified path/filenames, respectively:

1. ~caulds/public_html/index.html
2. /home/httpd/userstuff/caulds/index.html
3. /home/httpd/caulds/www/index.html

Redirecting Requests for User Home Directories

Chapter 10 provides a detailed discussion of Apache's tools for redirection, but the topic is worth a quick preview here, in the context of user home directories.

A server cannot *force* a browser to retrieve a resource from an alternate location. It sends a status code showing that the server couldn't respond to the browser's requests, and a Location directive indicating an alternate location. The browser is politely asked to redirect its request to this alternate location. In the case of UserDir, the server issues a redirect request to the client, which will in all likelihood request the resource again from the specified alternate location, and the user is none the wiser. The argument to UserDir can also take the form of a URL, rather than a directory specification, in which case the mapping is sent back to the client as a redirect request. This is most useful when redirecting requests for users' home directories to other servers. The following UserDir directive:

```
UserDir http://server2.hiwaay.com/~*/
```

would cause a request for

```
http://jackal.hiwaay.net/~caulds/docfiles/index.html
```

to generate a URL redirect request that would send the requester to the following resource, which is on a separate server:

```
http://server2.hiwaay.net/~caulds/docfiles/index.html
```

Enabling/Disabling Mappings

Another form of the UserDir directive uses the keywords enabled or disabled in one of three ways:

```
UserDir disabled <usernames>
```

This disables username-to-directory mappings for the space-delimited list of usernames. Example:

```
UserDir disabled root webmaster
```

WARNING If you are running a 1.3 version of Apache, it is strongly recommended that your configuration include a UserDir disabled root declaration.

Using the disabled keyword without username:

```
UserDir disabled
```

turns off all username-to-directory mappings. This form is sually used prior to a UserDir enabled directive that explicitly lists users for which mappings are performed.

```
UserDir enabled <usernames>
```

This enables username-to-directory mappings for the space-delimited list of usernames. It usually follows a UserDir disabled directive that turns off username-to-directory mappings for all users (all are normally enabled). Example:

```
UserDir disabled*
UserDir enabled caulds csewell webteam
```

Using suEXEC with User Directories

Most sites that support user directories also allow users to create and run their own CGI processes. It is easy to see how allowing users to write and run CGI programs that run with the permissions of the Web server could be disastrous. Such a script would have the same access privileges that the Web server itself uses, and this is normally not a good thing. To protect the Web server from errant or malicious user-written CGI scripts, and to protect Web users from one another, user CGI scripts are usually run from a program called a CGI wrapper. A CGI wrapper is used to run a CGI process under different user and group accounts than those that are invoking the process. In other words, while ordinary CGI processes are run under the user and group account of the Apache server (by default that is user nobody and group nobody), using a CGI wrapper, it is possible to invoke CGI processes that run under different user and group ownership.

There are several such CGI wrappers, but one such program, called suEXEC, is a standard part of Apache in all versions after version 1.2 (though not enabled by the default installation). SuEXEC is very easy to install, and even easier to use. There are two ways in which suEXEC is useful to Apache administrators. The most important use for suEXEC is to allow users to run CGI programs from their own directories that run under their user and group accounts, rather than that of the server.

The second way in which suEXEC is used with Apache is with virtual hosts. When used with virtual hosts, suEXEC changes the user and group accounts under which all CGI scripts defined for each virtual host are run. This is used to give virtual host administrators the ability to write and run their own CGI scripts without compromising the security of the primary Web server (or any other virtual host).

Configuring Apache to Use suEXEC

The suEXEC tool is very easy to set up using the APACI installation script. APACI's configure script is provided with a number of options that are used to configure suEXEC. The most important of these is --enable-suexec, which is required to enable suEXEC. All of the other options have default values that you can find by peeking into the makefile in the top Apache source directory. On my system, I chose to use all the available options when running configure. Even when the default values are acceptable, I include them in my build.sh script, borrowing the default values from the makefile and modifying them where I desire. Listing 4.1 shows the complete build.sh script I use to build Apache version 1.3.12 with suEXEC support.

Listing 4.1 A `build.sh` Script for Building Apache 1.3.12 with suEXEC Support

```
CFLAGS="-DUSE_RANDOM_SSI -DUSE_PARSE_FORM" \
./configure \
"--enable-rule=EAPI" \
"--with-layout=Apache" \
"--prefix=/usr/local/apache" \
"--enable-module=most" \
"--enable-module=ssl" \
"--enable-shared=max" \
"--enable-suexec" \
"--suexec-caller=www" \
"--suexec-docroot=/home/httpd/html" \
"--suexec-logfile=/usr/local/apache/logs/suexec_log" \
"--suexec-userdir=public_html" \
"--suexec-uidmin=100" \
"--suexec-gidmin=100" \
"--suexec-safepath=/usr/local/bin:/usr/bin:/bin" \
"$@"
```

To build and install Apache, with suEXEC, I enter three lines in the Apache source directory:

```
# ./build.sh
# make
# make install
```

After building and installing Apache with suEXEC support, you should test it by invoking httpd with the -l argument. If suEXEC is functional, the result will look like this:

```
# ./httpd -l
Compiled-in modules:
  http_core.c
  mod_so.c
suexec: enabled; valid wrapper /usr/local/apache/bin/suexec
```

If Apache is unable to find suEXEC, or if it does not have its user setuid execution bit set, suEXEC will be disabled:

```
# ./httpd -l
Compiled-in modules:
  http_core.c
  mod_so.c
suexec: disabled; invalid wrapper /usr/local/apache1_3_12/bin/suexec
```

Apache will still start, even if suEXEC is unavailable, but suEXEC will be disabled. You have to keep an eye on this; it is unfortunate that, when suEXEC is disabled, no warning is given when Apache is started, and nothing is written into Apache's error log. The error log will only show when suEXEC is enabled. You can check inside Apache's error log (which is in `logs/error.log` under the Apache installation directory, unless you've overridden this default value). If all is OK, the error log will contain the following line, usually immediately after the line indicating that Apache has been started:

```
[notice] suEXEC mechanism enabled (wrapper: /usr/local/apache/bin/suexec)
```

If suEXEC is not enabled when Apache is started, verify that you have the `suexec` wrapper program, owned by `root`, in Apache's `bin` directory:

```
# ls -al /usr/local/apache/bin/suexec
-rws--x--x   1 root     root        10440 Jun 28 09:59 suexec
```

Note the `s` in the user permissions. This indicates that the `setuid` bit is set—in other words, the file, when executed, will run under the user account of the file's owner. For example, the Apache `httpd` process that invokes `suexec` will probably be running under the `nobody` account. The `suexec` process it starts, however, will run under the `root` account, because `root` is the owner of the file `suexec`. Only `root` can invoke the Linux `setuid` and `setgid` system functions to change the ownership of processes it spawns as children (the CGI scripts that run under its control). If `suexec` is not owned by `root`, and does not have its user `setuid` bit set, correct this by entering the following lines while logged in as `root`:

```
# chown root /usr/local/apache/bin/suexec
# chmod u+s /usr/local/apache/bin/suexec
```

If you wish to disable suEXEC, the best way is to simply remove the user `setuid` bit:

```
# chmod u-s /usr/local/apache/bin/suexec
```

This not only disables suEXEC, but it also renders the suEXEC program a bit safer because it will no longer run as `root` (unless directly invoked by `root`).

Using suEXEC

While suEXEC is easy to set up, it's even easier to use. Once it is enabled in your running Apache process, any CGI script that is invoked from a user's Web directory will execute under the user and group permissions of the owner of the Web directory. In other words, if I invoke a script with a URL like `http://jackal.hiwaay.net/~caulds/cgi-bin/somescript.cgi`, that script will run under `caulds`'s user and group account. Note that all CGI scripts that will run under the suEXEC wrapper must be in the user's Web directory (which defaults to `public_html` but can be redefined by the `--suexec-userdir` configuration) or a subdirectory of that directory.

For virtual hosts, the user and group accounts under which CGI scripts are run are defined by the User and Group directives found in the virtual host container:

```
<VirtualHost 192.168.1.1>
    ServerName vhost1.hiwaay.net
    ServerAdmin caulds@hiwaay.net
    DocumentRoot /home/httpd/NamedVH1
    User vh1admin
    Group vh1webteam
</VirtualHost>
```

If a virtual host does not contain a User or Group directive, the values for these are inherited from the primary Web server (usually user nobody and group nobody). Note that all CGI scripts that will run under suEXEC for a virtual host described above must reside beneath the DocumentRoot (they can be in any subdirectory beneath DocumentRoot, but they cannot reside outside it).

Simple Request Redirection

Chapter 10 discusses redirection of HTTP requests in detail, particularly using mod_ rewrite, which permits the use of a series of rules to perform very sophisticated URL rewriting. URL rewriting is a highly flexible way to redirect requests, but it is also quite complicated. For simple redirection, the Alias core directive is very useful. Here's an example of how Alias permits easy access to HTML documents outside the DocumentRoot directory on my server.

Many applications for Linux include documentation in the form of linked HTML pages. These are ordinarily outside the hierarchy of resources that has the Apache DocumentRoot at its top. Apache documentation is no exception. Some provision should be made to allow access to these pages. On my system, the Apache documentation pages are installed in /usr/local/apache/htdocs. I used the Alias directive to alias two directories outside my DocumentRoot to URLs that appear inside the DocumentRoot resource tree. The first of these is the documentation for the MySQL database, which placed its documentation in /usr/doc/MySQL-3.22.29 when installed on my system.

```
# pwd
/usr/doc/MySQL-3.22.29
# ls
PUBLIC   index.html    manual.ps     manual.txt
README   manual.html   manual.texi   manual_toc.html
```

I first granted ownership of this directory to the user and group that Apache processes run under. On Linux systems, these are both user ID -1, which are both named nobody. (Most Unix systems use the same user ID and group ID as Linux. FreeBSD, which does not provide either of these, is the most notable exception.) I changed the ownership of the directory recursively, so that all subdirectories and files would be accessible to the user and group nobody:

```
# chown -R nobody.nobody /usr/doc/MySQL-3.22.29
```

I symbolically linked the top-level HTML file to one that Apache will read when the requested URL names only the directory, and not a particular file (that is, where it matches one of the names specified in DirectoryIndex):

```
# ln -s manual_toc.html index.html
```

Using a symbolic link, rather than copying the file or renaming it, ensures that only one copy of the file exists, but can be accessed by either name. The last step was the insertion of two Alias directives into httpd.conf. Place these in a manner that seems logical to you, probably somewhere in the section of the file labeled 'Main' server configuration, so that you can easily locate the directives at a later date.

```
Alias /MySQL/ "/usr/doc/MySQL-3.22.29/"
Alias /ApacheDocs/ "/usr/local/apache/docs/"
```

Any user can now access these sets of documentation on my server using these URLs:

```
http://jackal.hiwaay.net/MySQL/
http://jackal.hiwaay.net/ApacheDocs/
```

Providing Directory Indexes

I'm ending this chapter with a discussion of a very important set of Apache directories that are not actually part of the core module, but are such a part of the standard distribution that they are used on every Apache server. You might notice that most Web pages are not retrieved by the specific filename. Rather than entering a URL like this:

```
http://jackal.hiwaay.net/dirname/index.html
```

you generally enter a URL like the following:

```
http://jackal.hiwaay.net/dirname
```

This URL actually maps to a directory on the server (a directory named dirname beneath the directory defined in the Apache configuration as DocumentRoot). It is only through a standard Apache module named mod_dir that a specific page is served to clients that send

Essential
Configuration

PART 2

a request URL that maps to a directory. Without mod_dir, the second form, which does not specify a singe resource, would be invalid and would produce an HTTP 404 (Not Found) error.

The mod_dir module serves two important functions. First, whenever a request is received that maps to a directory but does not have a trailing slash (/) as in:

```
http://jackal.hiwaay.net/dirname
```

mod_dir sends a redirection request to the client indicating that the request should be made, instead, to the URL:

```
http://jackal.hiwaay.net/dirname/
```

This requires a second request on the part of the client to correct what is, technically, an error in the original request. Though the time required to make this second request is usually minimal and unnoticed by the user, whenever you express URLs that map to directories rather than files, you should include the trailing slash for correctness and efficiency.

The second function of mod_dir is to look for and serve a file defined as the index file for the directory specified in the request. That page, by default, is named index.html. This can be changed using mod_dir's only directive, DirectoryIndex, as described below. The name of the file comes from the fact that it was originally intended to provide the requestor with an index of the files in the directory. While providing directory indexes is still useful, the file is used far more often to serve a default HTML document, or Web page, for the root URL; this is often called the home page. Remember that this behavior is not a given; mod_dir must be included in the server configuration and enabled for this to work.

The DirectoryIndex Directive

As mentioned, the default value of the file served by mod_dir is index.html. In other words, if the Apache configuration contains no DirectoryIndex directive, it will look for and attempt to serve a file named index.html whenever a request URL resolves to a directory. Although this is a default behavior, the standard Apache configuration will create the following line in the httpd.conf file that it installs:

```
DirectoryIndex index.html
```

The last change I made was to add a second filename to the DirectoryIndex directive. I added an entry for index.htm to cause the Apache server to look for files of this name, which may have been created on a system that follows the Microsoft convention of a three-character filename extension. The files are specified in order of preference from left to right, so if it finds both index.html and index.htm in a directory, it will only serve index.html.

```
# DirectoryIndex index.html
DirectoryIndex index.html index.htm
```

Fancier Directory Indexes

I've described the behavior of Apache when a request is received that maps to a directory on the server. Through mod_dir , Apache serves a file from the directory defined in the DirectoryIndex directive (or index.html if DirectoryIndex is not specified). In cases where no such file exists, Apache uses a second module, mod_autoindex, to prepare an index or listing of the files in the directory.

Figure 4.1 shows the default directory index that mod_autoindex will serve to the requesting client.

Figure 4.1   A plain directory listing

In addition to this plain directory listing, mod_autoindex also allows the administrator full control over every aspect of the directory listing it prepares. This is called *fancy indexing*. You can enable fancy indexing by adding the following directive to httpd.conf:

```
IndexOptions FancyIndexing
```

The default httpd.conf provided with the Apache distribution uses many of the directives that I'll describe in the following sections to set up the default fancy directory for use on your server. Figure 4.2 shows what this standard fancy directory looks like when displaying the results of a directory request.

Figure 4.2   A fancy directory listing

Index Options

IndexOptions can also be used to set a number of other options for configuring directory indexing. Among these are options to specify the size of the icons displayed, to suppress the display of any of the columns besides the filename, and whether or not clicking the column heading sorts the listing by the values in that column. Table 4.1 depicts all possible options that can be used with the IndexOptions directive.

Table 4.1   Index Options

Index Option	Description
FancyIndexing	Enables fancy indexing.
IconsAreLinks	Makes icons part of the clickable anchor for the filename.
IconHeight=pixels	Sets the height (in pixels) of the icons displayed in the listing. Like the HTML tag <IMG HEIGHT=n …>.
IconWidth=pixels	Sets the width (in pixels) of the icons displayed in the listing. Like the HTML tag <IMG WIDTH=n …>.
NameWidth=n	Sets the width (in characters) of the filename column in the listing, truncating characters if the name exceeds this width. Specifying NameWidth=* causes the filename column to be as wide as the longest filename in the listing.
ScanHTMLTitles	Causes the file description to be extracted from the HTML <TITLE> tag, if it exists. The AddDescription directive overrides this setting for individual files.
SuppressColumnSorting	Disables the normal behavior of inserting clickable headers at the top of each column that can be used to sort the listing.
SuppressDescription	Disables the display of the file description.
SuppressHTMLPreamble	Disables automatic HTML formatting of the header file if one is specified for the listing. No <HTML>, <HEAD>, or <BODY> tags precede the header file, and they must be manually placed into the file contents if desired.
SuppressLastModified	Disables the display of the Last Modified column of the listing.
SupressSize	Disables the display of the Size column in the listing.
SupressDescription	Disables the display of the Description column of the listing.
None	Disables fancy indexing.

Options are always inherited from parent directories. This behavior is overridden by specifying options with a + or – prefix to add or subtract the options from the list of

Essential
Configuration

PART 2

options that are already in effect for a directory. Whenever an option is read that does not contain either of these prefixes, the list of options in effect is immediately cleared. Consider this example:

```
IndexOptions +ScanHTMLTitles -IconsAreLinks SuppressSize
```

If this directive appears in an `.htaccess` file for a directory, regardless of the options inherited by that directory from its higher-level directories, the net effect will be the same as this directive:

```
IndexOptions SuppressSize
```

This is because as soon as the `SuppressSize` option was encountered without a + or − prefix, the current list of options was immediately cleared.

Specifying Icons

In addition to `IndexOptions`, `mod_autoindex` provides other directives that act to configure the directory listing. You can, for example, provide a default icon for unrecognized resources. You can change the icon or description displayed for a particular resource, either by its MIME type, filename, or encoding type (GZIP-encoded, for example). You can also specify a default field and display order for sorting; or identify a file whose content will be displayed at the top of the directory.

The `AddIcon` Directive   `AddIcon` specifies the icon to display for a file when fancy indexing is used to display the contents of a directory. The icon is identified by a relative URL to the icon image file. Note that the URL you specify is embedded directly in the formatted document that is sent to the client browser, which then retrieves the image file in a separate HTTP request.

The `name` argument can be a filename extension, a wildcard expression, a complete filename, or one of two special forms. Examples of the use of these forms follow:

```
AddIcon /icons/image.jpg *jpg*
AddIcon (IMG, /icons/image.jpg) .gif .jpg .bmp
```

The second example above illustrates an alternate form for specifying the icon. When parentheses are used to enclose the parameters of the directive, the first parameter is the alternate text to associate with the resource; the icon to be displayed is specified as a relative URL to an image file. The alternate text, `IMG`, will be displayed by browsers that are not capable of rendering images. A disadvantage of using this form is that the alternate text cannot contain spaces or other special characters. The following form is *not* acceptable:

```
AddIcon ("JPG Image", /icons/image.jpg) .jpg
```

There are two special expressions that can be used in place of a filename in the `AddIcon` directive to specify images to use as icons in the directory listing. `^^BLANKICON^^` is used to specify an icon to use for blank lines in the listing, and ^^DIRECTORY^^ is used to specify an icon for directories in the listing:

```
AddIcon /icons/blankicon.jpg  ^^BLANKICON^^
AddIcon /icons/dir.pcx ^^DIRECTORY^^
```

There is one other special case that you should be aware of. The parent of the directory whose index is being displayed is indicated by the ".." filename. You can change the icon associated with the parent directory with a directive like the following:

```
AddIcon /icons/up.gif ..
```

> **NOTE** The Apache Software Foundation recommends using AddIconByType rather than AddIcon whenever possible. Although there appears to be no real difference between these (on a Linux system, the MIME type of a file is identified by its filename extension), it is considered more proper to use the MIME type that Apache uses for the file, rather than directly examining its filename. There are often cases, however, when no MIME type has been associated with a file and you must use AddIcon to set the image for the file.

The AddIconByType Directive   AddIconByType specifies the icon to display in the directory listing for files of certain MIME content types. This directory works like the AddIcon directive just described, but it relies on the determination that Apache has made of the MIME type of the file (as discussed in Chapter 16, Apache usually determines the MIME type of a file based on its filename).

```
AddIconByType /icons/webpage.gif text/html
AddIconByType (TXT, /icons/text.gif) text/*
```

This directive is used almost exactly like AddIcon. When parentheses are used to enclose the parameters of the directive, the first parameter is the alternate text to associate with the resource; the icon to be displayed is specified as a relative URL to an image file. The last parameter, rather than being specified as a filename extension, is a MIME content type (look in conf/mime.types under the Apache home for a list of types that Apache knows about).

The AddIconByEncoding Directive   AddIconByEncoding is used to specify the icon displayed next to files that use a certain MIME encoding. As discussed in Chapter 16, MIME encoding generally refers to file compression schemes and therefore determines what action is required to decode the file for use. Some typical encoding schemes and examples of the use of this directive are:

```
AddIconByEncoding /icons/gzip.gif x-gzip
AddIconByEncoding /icons/tarimage.gif x-gtar
```

Specifying a Default Icon A special directive, `DefaultIcon`, is used to set the icon that is displayed for files with which no icon has been associated with either of the other directives mentioned above. The directive simply identifies an image file by relative URL:

```
DefaultIcon  /icons/unknown.pcx
```

Adding Alternate Text for Images

When an image is displayed in a Web page, the HTML tags used to embed the image in the page provide for an alternate text string that is displayed in browsers that cannot display graphics. This text string is also displayed as pop-up text if the user of a graphical browser right-clicks on the associated image.

There are three directives that are provided by `mod_autoindex` for setting the alternate text associated with a file in the fancy directory listing. Each of these directives is analogous to one of the `AddIcon`... directives shown above and uses the same syntax.

The `AddAlt` Directive The `AddAlt` directive specifies an alternate text string to be display for a file, instead of an icon, in text-only browsers. Like its `AddIcon` counterpart, the directive specifies a filename, partial filename, or wildcard expression to identify files:

```
AddAlt "JPG Image" /icons/image.jpg *jpg*
AddIcon "Image File".gif .jpg .bmp
```

Note that it is possible to use a quoted string with the `AddAlt` directive, which can contain spaces and other special characters. This is not possible when specifying alternate text using the special form of `AddIcon` as shown above.

The `AddAltByType` Directive `AddAltByType` sets the alternate text string to be displayed for a file based on the MIME content type that Apache has identified for the file. This directive works very much like its counterpart, `AddIconByType`.

```
AddAltByType "HTML Document"  text/html
```

The `AddAltByEncoding` Directive `AddAltByEncoding` sets the alternate text string to be displayed for a file, based on the MIME content encoding of the file, as determined by Apache.

```
AddIconByEncoding "GZipped File" x-gzip
```

Specifying File Descriptions

The `AddDescription` directive is used to specify a text string to be displayed in the Description column of the listing for specific files. `AddDescription` is usually used to provide a description for specific files. Files can be identified by a partial or full pathname:

```
AddDescription "My Home Page" index.html
```

Note that this example sets a description to apply to all files named `index.html`. To apply the description to a specific file, use its full and unique pathname:

```
AddDescription "My Home Page" /home/httpd/html/index.html
```

`AddDescription` can also be used with wildcarded filenames to set descriptions for entire classes of files (identified by filename extension in this case):

```
AddDescription "PCX Image" *.pcx
AddDescription "TAR File" *.tgz *.tar.gz
```

When multiple descriptions apply to the same file, the first match found will be the one used in the listing; so always specify the most specific match first:

```
AddDescription "Powered By Apache Logo" poweredby.gif
AddDescription "GIF Image" *.gif
```

In addition to `AddDescription`, there is one other way that `mod_autoindex` can determine values to display in the Description column of a directory listing. If `IndexOptions ScanHTMLTitles` is in effect for a directory, `mod_autoindex` will parse all HTML files in the directory, and extract descriptions for display from the `<TITLE>` elements of the documents. This is handy if the directory contains a relatively small number of HTML documents, or is infrequently accessed. Enabling this option requires that every HTML document in the directory be opened and examined. For a large number of files, this can impose a significant workload, so the option is disabled by default.

Adding a Header and Footer

The `mod_autoindex` module supplies two directives that allow you to insert the contents of a file at the top of the index listing as a page header or at the bottom of the listing as a page footer.

The `HeaderName` directive specifies a filename using a URI relative to the one use to access the directory. The contents of this file are placed into the listing immediately after the opening `<BODY>` tag of the listing. It is usually a good idea to maintain the header file in the same directory it describes, which makes it easy to reference by its filename:

```
HeaderName HEADER.html
```

Files identified by the `HeaderName` directive must be of the major MIME content type text. If the file is identified as type `text/html` (generally by its extension), it is inserted verbatim; otherwise it is enclosed in `<PRE>` and `</PRE>` tags. A CGI script can be used to generate the information for the header (either as HTML or plain text), but you must first associate the CGI script with a MIME main content type (usually text), as follows:

```
AddType text/html .cgi
HeaderName HEADER.cgi
```

The ReadmeName directive works almost identically to HeaderName to specify a file (again relative to the URI used to access the directory being indexed) that is placed in the listing just before the closing </BODY> tag.

Ignoring Files

The IndexIgnore directive specifies a set of filenames that are ignored by mod_autoindex when preparing the index listing of a directory. The filenames can be specified by wildcards:

```
IndexIgnore FOOTER*
```

> **NOTE** The default httpd.conf file provided with Apache contains an IndexIgnore directive that prevents filenames beginning with README or HEADER from being displayed in the index listing by mod_autoindex. This makes these filenames obvious (but not necessary) choices for use as headers and footers for directory listings.

Ordering the Index Listing

The IndexOrderDefault directive is used to change the default order of the index listing generated by mod_autoindex, which is to sort the list in ascending order by filename. This directive takes two arguments. The first must be either Ascending or Descending to indicate the sort direction; the second names a single field as the primary sort key and can be Name, Date, Size, or Description:

```
IndexOrderDefault Descending Size
```

The secondary sort key is always the filename in ascending order.

Example

In order to illustrate typical uses of some of the mod_autoindex directives discussed, I created an .htaccess in the same directory that was illustrated in Figure 4.2. This file contains the following directives, all of which are used by mod_autoindex to customize the index listing for the directory. The result of applying these directives is shown in Figure 4.3.

```
IndexOptions +ScanHTMLTitles
AddIcon /icons/SOUND.GIF .au
AddDescription "1-2-Cha-Cha-Cha" DancingBaby.avi
AddAltByType "This is a JPG Image" image/jpeg
HeaderName HEADER.html
ReadmeName README.txt
```

Figure 4.3   A customized `mod_autoindex` listing

The `IndexOptions` directive is used to enable the extraction of file descriptions from the <TITLE> tags of HTML formatted files (technically, files of MIME content type text/html). In the illustration, you'll see that it did that for the file `indexOLD.html`. If this file had its original name, `index.html`, the index listing would not have been generated; instead, `index.html` would have been sent (by `mod_dir`) to the client.

I've also provided an example of adding an icon using the `AddIcon` directive and a file description using `AddDescription`. The results of these directives can be easily seen in Figure 4.3. The alternate text for JPEG images (added with the `AddAltByType` directive) is not displayed in the figure but would be seen in place of the image icon in text-only browsers. It will also appear in a graphical browser in a pop-up dialog box when the cursor is paused over the associated icon. This gives the page developer a handy way to add help text to a graphics-rich Web page, which can be particularly useful when the icon or image is part of an anchor tag (clickable link) and can invoke an action.

The last two directives I added to the .htaccess file for this directory specify an HTML-formatted file to be included as a page header and a plain text file to be included as a page footer. These both consist of a single line, also visible in Figure 4.3. The header file contains HTML-formatting tags (<H3> ... </H3>) that cause it to be rendered in larger, bolder characters. There is no reason that either the header or footer could not be much longer and contain far more elaborate formatting. Use your imagination.

In Sum

This chapter has covered a lot of ground, because so much of Apache's functionality is incorporated into the configuration directives provided by its core modules. We began with the essential concept of directive *context*, the scope within which particular directives are valid. We then looked at the directives used to configure the basic server environment and how the server listens for connections. These directives are fundamental to Apache's operation, and every administrator needs to be familiar with them.

Later sections of the chapter explored the directives used to create and manage user home directories. These are not only an essential function for any ISP installation of an Apache server, they are also widely used in intranets.

The next chapter moves beyond the core module to the use of third-party modules and the techniques you can use to incorporate them into your Apache server.

5

Apache Modules

I've already discussed the importance of modules to Apache's design philosophy. Without the concept of extension by module, it is unlikely that Apache would have garnered the level of third-party support that directly led to its phenomenal success in the early days of the Web. Apache owes much of that success to the fact that any reasonably proficient programmer can produce add-on modules that tap directly into the server's internal mechanisms. As administrators, we benefit greatly from the availability of these third-party modules.

At one time, it was thought that commercial Web servers, with the support that "commercial" implies, would eventually eclipse the open-source Apache server. It seemed completely logical that when a company began to get serious about the Web, it needed to look for a serious Web engine, a commercial server—not some piece of unsupported free software downloaded from the Internet. But as we've seen, Apache took the top spot from its commercial rivals and has continued to widen that lead, even while most Unix-based applications slowly gave ground to their NT competitors. Apache owes much of its success to a vibrant, innovative, and completely professional community of users and developers that you can be a part of. Apache is as fully supported as any commercial product. Virtually any feature or function you can desire in a Web server is available as an Apache module, usually offered by its author at no cost to all Apache users.

This chapter looks at the types of modules available, how the module mechanism works, how to link modules to Apache as dynamic shared objects (DSOs), and where to find third-party modules. It concludes with a step-by-step example of installing a module.

Types of Apache Modules

Except for the very basic kernel code, virtually all of the capability of an Apache server is implemented in modules. Apache modules can be categorized in three groups:

The core module (httpd_core.c) is the only module that must always be statically linked into the Apache kernel. It is the only module that is absolutely essential to an Apache server. It cannot be removed from the server, and the functions provided by this module are available in *all* Apache servers. The directives furnished by the core module are always available; they are the only directives discussed so far in this book. All of the directives furnished by httpd_core are documented in Appendix A.

The standard modules are provided as part of the Apache distribution and are maintained by the Apache Software Foundation as part of the Apache server itself. Most of the standard modules are compiled by the standard installation scripts (described in Chapter 3) into the Apache code. Unlike the core module, however, any one of the standard modules can be removed at the server administrator's discretion. This might be done for security reasons, but the most common reason for removing a module from Apache is to reduce the amount of memory used by each running instance of the server. (Remember that Apache maintains a pool of server processes to handle user requests. Since each process in the pool requires its own memory space, the amount of space saved by eliminating unused modules can be multiplied by the number of processes in the Apache server pool.)

Third-party modules are modules written, supported, and distributed by sources other than the Apache Group. These modules are not provided as part of the Apache distribution and must be obtained separately.

How Modules Work

Apache modules are able to register callbacks with Apache for the functions they provide. A *callback* is a function that is registered with Apache so that Apache can call the function at various stages of the request processing cycle. Callbacks are generally registered as *handlers* for processing specific events. Callback functions registered with Apache are called at specific times, such as when the module is loaded and initialized, when a new Apache child process is started or shut down, and at various stages of the resource request process. Most of the hooks provided by Apache for modules to register callback functions are part of the HTTP request cycle. There are 11 phases of the request cycle currently defined for which modules can register callback functions, and they occur in the following order:

Post-Read-Request: Actions in this phase take place immediately after the request header has been read. Although any module can register a callback to run at this phase of the cycle, the phase always includes the determination of which virtual host will handle the request. This phase sets up the server to handle the request. Modules that register callbacks for this phase of the request cycle include mod_proxy and mod_setenvif, which get all the information they need from the request URL.

URL Translation: At this stage the URL is translated into a filename. Modules like mod_alias, mod_rewrite or mod_userdir, which provide URL translation services, generally do their main work here.

Header Parsing: This phase is obsolete (superseded by the Post-Read-Request phase); no standard modules register functions to be called during this phase.

Access Control: This phase checks client access to the requested resource, based on the client's network address, returning a response that either allows or denies the user access to the server resource. The only module that acts as a handler for the Access Control phase of the request cycle is mod_access (discussed in Chapter 14).

Authentication: This phase verifies the identity of the user, either accepting or rejecting credentials presented by that user, which are as simple as a username/password pair. Examples of modules that do their work during this phase are mod_auth and mod_auth_dbm.

Authorization: Once the user's identity has been verified, the user's authorization is checked to determine if the user has permission to access the requested resource. Although authenticating (identifying) the user and determining that user's authorization (or level of access) are separate functions, they are usually performed by the same module. The modules listed as examples for the Authentication phase also register callbacks for the Authorization phase.

MIME type checking: Determines the MIME type of the requested resource, which can be used to determine how the resource is handled. A good example is mod_mime.

FixUp: This is a catch-all phase for actions that need to be performed before the request is actually fulfilled. mod_headers is one of the few modules on my system that register a callback for this request phase.

Response or Content: This is the most important phase of the Request cycle; the one in which the requested resource is actually processed. This is where a module is registered to handle documents of a specific MIME type. The mod_cgi module is registered, for example as the default handler for documents identified as CGI scripts.

Logging: After the request has been processed, a module can register functions to log the actions taken. While any module can register a callback to perform actions during this phase (and you can easily write your own) most servers will use only mod_log_config (covered in Chapter 12) to take care of all logging.

Cleanup: Functions registered here are called when an Apache child process shuts down. Actions that would be defined to take place during this phase include the closing of open files and perhaps of database connections. Very few modules actually register a callback for this request phase. In fact, none of the standard modules use it.

Incorporating Perl Scripts with `mod_perl`

Modules already exist for most of the common tasks that Web servers need to perform, and many administrators will never need to write their own. But if you do plan to write your own modules, or even just use modules written by other system administrators, you should know about the `mod_perl` module. As you'll see in Chapter 8, Perl is the scripting language most widely used by system administrators, and `mod_perl` is the tool that makes it available to Apache.

Before there was a `mod_perl`, it was not possible to write an Apache module in anything but C, and for production server applications, I'm not sure I would ever have recommended a scripting language for the task, even if it had been possible to use one. The `mod_perl` module changed that. With its memory-resident Perl interpreter and ability to perform one-time compilation and caching of Perl scripts, it virtually eliminates one of the most valid criticisms leveled at Perl: its lack of speed when compared with binary code compiled from source languages like C.

The `mod_perl` module provides a built-in handler for each of the 11 phases of the Apache request cycle listed above. This makes it extremely easy to invoke a Perl function at any phase. For example, if you want Apache to call a Perl function that will be performed immediately following the receipt of a user request, you can register the function as a callback by placing the following lines in `httpd.conf`:

```
PerlModule Apache::MyModule
PerlPostReadRequestHandler Apache::MyModule::myhandler
```

The first line preloads the module into the `Apache::` namespace. The second line registers the `myhandler` function within that module as a callback during the `PostReadRequest` phase of the request cycle. When a request comes in, Apache will ensure that `myhandler`, which has already been loaded and compiled by `mod_perl`, is called. The function will have access to Apache's internal data structures and functions through the Perl Apache API calls (each of which, in turn, calls a function from the Apache API).

You'll learn more about working with `mod_perl` in Chapter 8. One of the best and most complete sets of online documentation for any Apache module is that available for `mod_perl` at `perl.apache.org/guide/`.

Coming Attraction: `mod_java`

Another scripting option for modules should soon be available—Java. Work began on `mod_java` in 1999 and continues still. The intent of the `mod_java` developers is to create an Apache module that will do for Java developers what `mod_perl` did for Perl coders. When complete, `mod_java` should expose the Apache API through a set of Java classes that will allow Apache extension modules to be written completely in Java (rather than in C or Perl). Watch the progress of the development team at: `http://java.apache.org/`.

Installing Third-Party Modules

There is no rigid specification to which Apache modules from third-party sources must adhere. There is no standard procedure for installing and using Apache modules. There are guidelines, however, that define a "well-behaved" Apache module, and most modules are fairly standard and therefore quite simple to install and configure.

The Two Linking Methods

Apache modules can be installed either within the Apache source tree or outside it. Those installed within the Apache source become, essentially, a part of Apache, even if their inclusion is optional. The standard Apache modules (those that are part of the Apache distribution) fall into this category. A limited number of third-party modules must also be installed in this fashion, particularly if they rely on changes made to the Apache source code. When this method is used, the module source code is usually placed in the `/src/ modules` subdirectory with the rest of the Apache source. Special configuration directives are passed to the APache AutoConf-style Interface (APACI) to compile the module with the rest of Apache, link it with the resulting runtime, and make the necessary changes to `http.conf` to enable the module.

Most third-party modules, though, are better compiled outside the Apache source tree. In other words, they are compiled in a completely separate directory from the Apache source, as dynamic shared object (DSO) modules, and are loaded at runtime by Apache.

Although the module source can be placed inside the Apache source tree and the APACI configuration utility instructed to compile it as a DSO, I strongly recommend against doing this. If you intend to use a module as a DSO, it can be compiled on its own, outside the Apache source tree, using a utility called `apxs`, which is provided with the Apache distribution. One advantage of compiling with `apxs` is that the resulting module, which will have the extension `.so` for *shared object*, is a stand-alone module that can be used with different versions of the server. This allows you to upgrade modules without recompiling Apache, as you must do when a module is compiled within the Apache source tree using

APACI. More importantly, using DSO modules compiled with apxs allows you to upgrade the Apache server without having to rerun the configuration for each module, specifying the new Apache source tree.

There are nearly as many installation procedures as there are modules. Some install inside the Apache tree; most can be compiled separately from Apache. Some simply compile a DSO and leave you to manually edit httpd.conf; some configure httpd.conf for you. Read the INSTALL file carefully before compiling any module, at least to get some idea of how the installation proceeds and what options are available. In general, though, the best way to compile and install Apache modules is to use the utility Apache has provided specifically for this purpose, apxs. Because most third-party modules are best compiled as DSOs using apxs, that is the method I describe in this chapter. The only modules I recommend installing as statically linked modules are those that come with the standard Apache distribution. These are automatically linked to Apache during the server installation unless at least one --enable-shared argument is passed to configure. Chapter 3 describes how standard modules are chosen and identified as statically linked or DSO modules.

Making the Choice

Virtually all Apache modules can be either statically linked or compiled as a DSO to be loaded at runtime, and the choice is usually yours to make. For most Apache sites, the DSO method provides the most flexibility and easiest maintainability, although you pay a small performance cost for it. Administrators should consider statically linking modules only when they rarely alter their Apache configuration.

Table 5.1 summarizes the characteristics of each method of linking a module.

Table 5.1   Static vs. Dynamic Linking

Feature	Statically Linked	Linked as DSO
Installed Using:	APACI	apxs
Module Source Location:	Module source resides in the Apache source tree.	Module source resides outside the Apache source tree.
Impact on Size of Apache Executable:	Increases the size of the Apache runtime executable.	Keeps Apache runtime as small as possible.

Table 5.1   Static vs. Dynamic Linking *(continued)*

Feature	Statically Linked	Linked as DSO
Loading Speed:	Fastest loading.	Increases load time of the module by about 20 percent.
Module Loaded When:	Module always loaded, even if disabled and unused.	Module loaded only when specified in httpd.conf.
Recommended When:	The Apache configuration is simple, requiring few add-on modules and few changes and when fastest possible loading is important.	Server configuration changes frequently or when modules are frequently changed, upgraded, or installed for testing.

Using Dynamically Linked Modules

DSO modules are loaded as part of the Apache server at *runtime*, that is, when the server is started. DSO modules are designed to be dynamically loaded into the running server's address space and are able to access and directly modify internal Apache data structures. Loading a DSO module is approximately 20 percent slower than if the module were statically linked into the server kernel. However, a DSO module, once loaded, is in every respect a part of Apache and there is no performance overhead inherent in running a function in a DSO module rather than as statically linked code.

With two important exceptions, all modules distributed with Apache can be compiled as DSO modules that are loaded at runtime. The first exception is the core module, which must always be statically linked into the Apache kernel. The second module that can never be run as a DSO (for reasons I hope are obvious) is the module that provides the server with the capability of dynamically loading shared objects. No DSO module can be loaded for use by the server without mod_so, and this module must always be statically linked into the Apache kernel when Apache is compiled. When at least one --enable-shared= argument is passed to the Apache configure script (Chapter 3), mod_so automatically links into Apache when it is compiled. You can see the result of this linking by running httpd with the –l switch:

```
# /usr/local/apache/bin/httpd -l
Compiled-in modules:
```

```
http_core.c
mod_so.c
```

This example shows the most basic httpd daemon, which must *always* have the core module linked into it, and optionally, the mod_so module that provides support for DSO modules. All other module support is dynamically linked at runtime to the httpd process. The mod_so module supplies the server with a new directive, LoadModule, that is used in the Apache configuration file to designate a module for dynamic loading. When the server reads a LoadModule directive from the configuration during its initialization, mod_so will load the module and add its name to the list of available Apache modules. The module does not become available, however, until an AddModule directive specifically enables it. The AddModule directive is a core directive and is not specific to DSO modules. All modules, even those that are statically linked into the Apache kernel, must be explicitly enabled with an AddModule directive. Only DSO modules, however, require the LoadModule directive.

A DSO module exposes an external name for itself that does not necessarily have to match the name of the shared object file. For example, if a module calling itself firewall_module is stored in a file mod_firewall.so in the /libexec directory under the Apache ServerRoot, it is enabled for use by the inclusion of the following two lines in the Apache configuration file:

```
LoadModule firewall_module      libexec/mod_firewall.so
AddModule mod_firewall.c
```

The LoadModule directive (supplied by mod_so) links the named module to the httpd process, and then adds the module to the list of active modules. The module is not available, however, until enabled by the AddModule directive, which makes the module's structure, its internal functions, and any directives it supports, available to Apache. As noted above, the LoadModule directive has no meaning for statically linked modules, but an AddModule line is required for all modules before they can be used. This permits the disabling of even a statically linked module by simply commenting out or removing its associated AddModule line in httpd.conf.

These two directives do *not* have to be located together; and in most cases, they are not. Somewhere near the beginning of your httpd.conf file, in the general server configuration, you should find a group of LoadModule directives, followed by a section consisting of AddModule directives. Always remember that when you add a LoadModule directive, you must add a corresponding AddModule directive to enable the loaded module.

If you disable a module by simply commenting out its AddModule directive, you will be loading a module that is never used; and that, of course, is wasteful. Conversely, if you have an AddModule directive without a corresponding LoadModule directive, the module must be statically linked, or you will get a configuration error when you start the server because you will be attempting to enable a module the server knows nothing about. Generally, you should add and delete the LoadModule and AddModule directives in pairs.

The order in which DSO modules are loaded determines the order in which they are called by Apache to handle URLs. As Apache loads each module, it adds the name to a list. DSO modules are *always processed in the reverse* of the order in which they are loaded, so the first modules loaded are the last ones processed. This is a very important thing to remember. In later chapters, you'll encounter some modules that must be processed in the correct order to avoid conflicts. When a module must be processed *before* another, make sure its AddModule line is placed *after* the other module in the httpd.conf file.

The internal list of modules can be erased with the ClearModuleList and then reconstructed with a series of AddModule directives. If you compiled Apache to use DSO modules, you'll find that it does exactly that in the httpd.conf it created, which begins like this:

```
ClearModuleList
AddModule mod_vhost_alias.c
AddModule mod_env.c
AddModule mod_log_config.c
AddModule mod_mime.c
... lines deleted ...
```

You can refer to this section to see the processing order of modules, but change it only with very good reason; altering Apache's default ordering of the AddModule lines can cause undesirable and unpredictable results. There are times, however, when the processing order of modules needs to be changed. You may, for example, want to use multiple modules that provide the same functionality but in a specific order. In Chapter 14, I'll describe how the processing order of authentication modules is often important. There are other cases where some modules fail to function completely if other modules precede them. In Chapter 10, we'll see an example.

If you do venture to change the file, remember the rule of *first loaded, last processed.*

Using apxs

Since the release of Apache version 1.3, Apache has been packaged with a Perl script called apxs (for *AP*ache e*Xten*Sion). This relatively simple utility is used to compile and install third-party modules. One important benefit of using apxs rather than placing the module in the Apache source tree and compiling it with the APACI configure script is that apxs can handle modules consisting of more than one source file; configure cannot.

A few modules have special installation requirements; these modules generally come with detailed instructions (usually in a file named INSTALL) that should be followed carefully. Generally, modules that cannot be installed using the procedures detailed in this section are those that must make modifications to the Apache source. The OpenSSL module (mod_ssl), discussed in Chapter 15, is one such module. As you'll see, during its installation this module makes extensive patches and additions to the Apache source and requires a recompilation of Apache to work.

With those exceptions, however, nearly every Apache module can be compiled with apxs. apxs is the preferred way to compile most third-party modules, and you should become quite familiar with its use.

You can invoke apxs with combinations of the following arguments to control its actions.

-g   Generates a template for module developers; when supplied with a module name (using the -n switch) this option creates a source code directory with that name and installs a makefile and sample module C source code file within it. The sample C program is a complete module that can actually be installed; however, it does nothing but print out a line indicating that it ran. Example:

```
# apxs -g -n mod_MyModule
```

-q   Queries the apxs script for the values of one or more of its defaults. When the apxs script is created during an APACI installation, default values for the following variables are hard-coded into the script: TARGET, CC, CFLAGS, CFLAGS_SHLIB, LD_SHLIB, LDFLAGS_SHLIB, LIBS_SHLIB, PREFIX, SBINDIR, INCLUDEDIR, LIBEXECDIR, SYSCONFDIR. Examples:

```
# /usr/local/apache/bin/apxs -q TARGET
httpd
# /usr/local/apache/bin/apxs -q CFLAGS
-DLINUX=2 -DMOD_SSL=204109 -DUSE_HSREGEX -DEAPI -DUSE_EXPAT -I../lib/
expat-lite
# /usr/local/apache/bin/apxs -q PREFIX
/usr/local/apache
```

TIP The default value for any apxs hard-coded variable can be overridden by specifying a new value with the -S switch, for example:
```
# apxs -S PREFIX="/usr/local/apachetest" -c -n MyModule.so
```

-c   Compiles and links a DSO module, given the name of one or more source files (and, optionally, a list of supporting libraries). Using the -c argument to apxs enables the following options:

-o outputfile   Specifies the name of the resulting module file rather than determining it from the name of the input file.

-D name=value   Specifies compiler directives to be used when compiling the module.

-I `directory` Specifies a directory to add to the list of directories searched by the compiler for include files.

-l `library` Adds a library to the list of libraries to be linked into the module.

-L `directory` Adds a directory to the list of directories to be searched for libraries to be linked into the module.

-Wc, `flags` Passes flags to the compiler. Each flag must be specified as it would appear if it was a command-line argument, and the comma is mandatory:

```
# axps -c -Wc,-O3 MyModule.c
```

-Wl, `flags` Passes flags to the linker. Each flag must be specified as it would appear if it was a command-line argument, and the comma is mandatory:

```
# axps -c -Wl,-t MyModule.c
```

-i Installs a DSO module that has already been created with apxs -c into its correct location, which is determined by the PREFIX variable hard-coded into apxs, if not overridden with a -S switch. Using the -i apxs argument enables two others:

-a modifies the Apache configuration file (httpd.conf) to add LoadModule and AddModule directives to enable the newly installed module.

-A Use this argument to add the lines, but leave them commented out so they don't take effect when Apache is started.

-e Exactly like -i.

-n Works to name a module that is not the same as the DSO file. Example:

```
# apxs -i -a -n mod_MyModule MyModule.so
```

The -c and -i arguments to apxs are usually combined. The following line will compile a DSO from a single source file, install it, and modify the Apache configuration to load it the next time Apache is started:

```
# apxs -c -i -a MyModule.so
```

Where to Find Modules

Third-party Apache modules are available from hundreds of sources; however, I have never used an Apache module that wasn't listed with the Apache Module Registry (modules.apache.org). This site does not attempt to maintain a repository of modules for download. It maintains information about all Apache modules, including a brief description of each one's function, along with information about the author and, most importantly, a link to the site where the latest version of the module is maintained for download. Figure 5.1 shows the search form for this site.

TIP   To request a list of all the modules available on the site, simply enter an empty search string.

Figure 5.1   The Apache Module Registry

Example of Installing a Module

To conclude this chapter, let's work through a complete example of installing, configuring and using a typical module. The module I chose from those available at the Apache Module Registry is Brian Aker's mod_random (Figure 5.2), which performs a very simple task.

Figure 5.2   The Apache Module Registry listing for mod_random

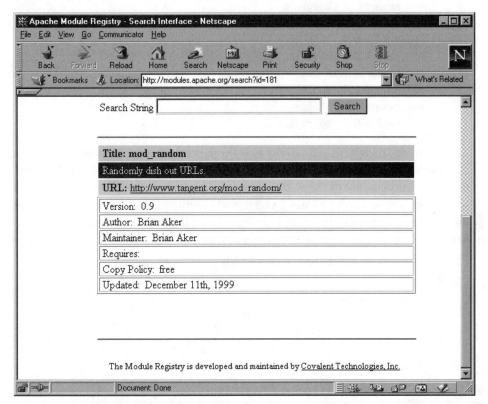

The mod_random module redirects clients to a random URL from a list provided either in Apache configuration directives or in a text file. You could use this module, if you're the serious sort, to implement a simple load-balancing scheme, randomly redirecting clients to different servers. Or, you may (like me) simply use the module for fun.

1. Begin by downloading the module from the author's site (modules.apache.org links to it, but if you need the URL it's http://www.tangent.org/mod_random). Download the latest archive of the module, which was mod_random-0_9_tar.gz when I snagged it. Unpack the archive into a location like /usr/local/src:

```
# pwd
/usr/local/src
# tar xvfz /home/caulds/mod_random-0_9_tar.gz
```

```
mod_random-0.9/
mod_random-0.9/ChangeLog
mod_random-0.9/INSTALL
mod_random-0.9/LICENSE
mod_random-0.9/Makefile
mod_random-0.9/README
mod_random-0.9/TODO
mod_random-0.9/VERSION
mod_random-0.9/mod_random.c
```

As you can see, there's not a lot to the module; the only file you really need is the C source code (mod_random.c). Everything else is simply nonessential support files and documentation. This working core of the module consists of only about 100 lines of easy-to-follow C source code and is worth a glance if you intend to write your own simple module in C. Installing and configuring the module took me about five minutes; if the author has done his part, there's absolutely no reason for anyone to be afraid of a third-party Apache module!

2. Make sure that the directory into which you extracted the files is the working directory:

```
# cd mod_random-0.9
# ls -al
total 14
drwxr-xr-x    2 1001     root     1024 Dec 11 17:48 .
drwxr-xr-x   17 root     root     1024 Mar 15 13:24 ..
-rw-r--r--    1 1001     root       30 Dec 11 17:47 ChangeLog
-rw-r--r--    1 1001     root      779 Dec 11 17:47 INSTALL
-rw-r--r--    1 1001     root     1651 Dec 11 17:47 LICENSE
-rw-r--r--    1 1001     root      820 Dec 11 17:47 Makefile
-rw-r--r--    1 1001     root      738 Dec 11 17:47 README
-rw-r--r--    1 1001     root       72 Dec 11 17:47 TODO
-rw-r--r--    1 1001     root        4 Dec 11 17:47 VERSION
-rw-r--r--    1 1001     root     3342 Dec 11 17:47 mod_random.c
```

3. At this point, you should read the installation instructions (INSTALL) and glance at the contents of the makefile (if one has been provided). The makefile contains instructions for a command-line compilation and installation, and it probably even contains lines for stopping, starting, and restarting the Apache server. These lines are added by the template-generation (-g) argument to apxs, described in the last section. After demonstrating the manual use of apxs to install mod_random, I'll show how the Linux make utility can be used to simplify the already simple procedure.

4. Although you can break this up into a couple of steps, I found it convenient to compile (-c) and install (-i) the module, and configure Apache to use it (-a) all in one command:

```
# /usr/local/apache/bin/apxs -c -i -a -n random mod_random.c
gcc -DLINUX=2 -DMOD_SSL=204109 -DUSE_HSREGEX -DEAPI -DUSE_EXPAT -I../lib/
expat-lite -fpic -DSHARED_MODULE -I/usr/local/apache/include  -c mod_
random.c
gcc -shared -o mod_random.so mod_random.o
cp mod_random.so /usr/local/apache/libexec/mod_random.so
chmod 755 /usr/local/apache/libexec/mod_random.so
[activating module `random' in /usr/local/apache/conf/httpd.conf]
```

5. Make sure that the installation procedure modified httpd.conf to use the new module. I checked using the Linux grep utility to extract mod_random entries from httpd.conf:

```
# grep mod_random /usr/local/apache/conf/httpd.conf
LoadModule random_module      libexec/mod_random.so
AddModule mod_random.c
```

6. Just to be absolutely sure that everything worked, I restarted the server:

```
# /usr/local/apache/bin/apachectl restart
```

7. Then I checked server-info to insure that mod_random is ready to rock (Figure 5.3). This interesting server status page is explored in more detail in Chapter 11.

8. One part of any module configuration is always manual, and that is editing the Apache configuration to make use of the module, usually by specifying the module as a handler, and usually by including directives supplied by the module. Our mod_random is no exception. I added the following section to my httpd.conf file to take full advantage of all the module's features:

```
# Brian Aker's mod_random configuration
#
<Location /randomize>
    SetHandler random
    RandomURL http://www.acme.com/
    RandomURL http://www.apple.com/macosx/inside.html
    RandomURL http://www.asptoday.com/
    RandomURL http://atomz.com/
    RandomFile /usr/local/apache/conf/random.conf
</Location>
```

Figure 5.3   The Server Information page for mod_random

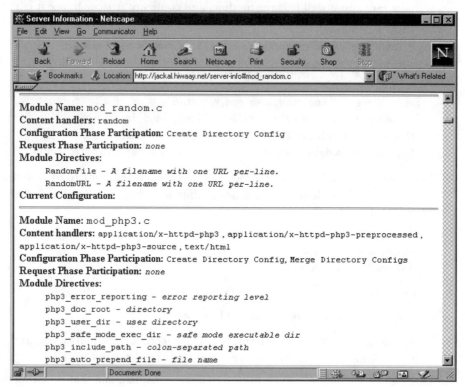

9. I first created a <Location> container, which applies to a partial URL, /randomize. This is not a directory name; it applies to a request URL. All the directives in the <Location> container apply to any arriving requests to a URL that ends in /randomize.

10. Using the RandomURL directive, I manually added a handful of URLs for random selection by the module, and then used the RandomFile directive to point to a file containing a list of URLs (one per line) that are added to mod_random's list of URLs.

11. After creating the necessary <Location> container in httpd.conf, I restarted the server to ensure that it was read, and then pointed a browser at my site, using the following URL:

        http://jackal.hiwaay.net/randomize

12. I was immediately redirected to one of the sites I'd specified for random selection in httpd.conf.

You may or may not eventually have a use for the mod_random module. But the basic procedure demonstrated in this example will be the same for any module you decide to add: download the archived file; extract it into your working directory; compile and install it (after reading the INSTALL file for instructions); check your httpd.conf file to verify that the module has been added; manually edit the configuration file to specify your new module as a handler; and finally test the configuration.

Using the Included Makefile

Most third-party modules, particularly if the author uses the –g template-generating feature of apxs, will include a makefile that can be used with the Linux make utility to do many of the tasks I just described. You can use the included Makefile (if one exists) to perform the steps I described above, but the additional convenience it offers is only slight. If you'll examine the makefile included with mod_random (Listing 5.1), you'll see that it does nothing but invoke the same commands I demonstrated above, using apxs to do the real work.

Listing 5.1   The Makefile Included with mod_random

```
##
## Makefile -- Build file for mod_random Apache module
##
# the used tools
APXS=/usr/local/apache/bin/apxs
APACHECTL=/usr/local/apache/bin/apachectl
# additional defines, includes and libraries
#DEF=-Dmy_define=my_value
#INC=-Imy/include/dir
#LIB=-Lmy/lib/dir -lmylib
# the default target
all: mod_random.so
# compile the shared object file
mod_random.so: mod_random.c
$(APXS) -c $(DEF) $(INC) $(LIB) mod_random.c
# install the shared object file into Apache
install: all
$(APXS) -i -a -n 'random' mod_random.so
# cleanup
clean:
-rm -f mod_random.o mod_random.so
# install and activate shared object by reloading Apache to
```

```
# force a reload of the shared object file
reload: install restart
# the general Apache start/restart/stop
# procedures
start:
$(APACHECTL) start
restart:
$(APACHECTL) restart
stop:
$(APACHECTL) stop
```

The entire process of compiling and installing mod_random, using the supplied makefile, can be summarized as follows:

make	Compiles mod_random.so with apxs.
make install	Uses apxs to copy mod_random.so to Apache and modify server config.
make restart	Restarts Apache using apachectl.

> **NOTE** On the surface, the makefile appears to be the simplest way to install third-party modules, and it often is; but this method depends on the existence of a properly configured makefile. The standard makefile also depends on the values of several environment variables to work properly. If these aren't set on your machine (or if you run multiple Apache configurations), the makefile will not work as expected. This is a good reason to bypass the makefile and invoke the proper apxs commands manually.

In Sum

From the very beginning, the Apache Web server was designed for easy expandability by exposing a set of functions that allowed programmers to write add-in modules easily. Support for dynamic shared objects was added with the release of Apache 1.3. DSO allows modules to be compiled separately from the Apache server and loaded by the server at runtime if desired or omitted by the administrator who wants to reduce the amount of memory required for each loaded copy of Apache.

The modular architecture of Apache is an important factor in the popularity of the server. Because of its fairly uncomplicated programmers' interface for extending the server's capabilities, a large number of modules are available (at no cost) from third-party sources.

6

Virtual Hosting

The term *virtual hosting* refers to maintaining multiple Web sites on a single server machine and differentiating those sites by hostname aliases. This allows companies sharing a single Web server to have their Web sites accessible via their own domain names, as `www.company1.com` and `www.company2.com`, without requiring the user to know any extra path information. With the number of Web sites on the Internet constantly increasing, the ability to host many Web sites on a server efficiently is a critical feature of a first-class Web server engine. Apache provides full support for virtual hosting and is a superb choice of Web engine for hosting large numbers of virtual Web sites (or *virtual hosts*).

This chapter outlines the three basic methods of configuring a single Apache engine to support multiple Web sites: IP-based virtual hosts, name-based virtual hosts, and dynamic virtual hosting. Much of the discussion focuses on the functionality provided by the standard Apache module used for virtual hosting, `mod_virtual`. The `mod_virtual` module supports two types of virtual hosts:

- *IP-based virtual hosts* are identified by the IP address on which client requests are received. Each IP-based virtual host has its own unique IP address and responds to all requests arriving on that IP address.

- *Name-based virtual hosts* take advantage of a feature of HTTP/1.1 designed to eliminate the requirement for dedicating scarce IP addresses to virtual hosts. As mentioned in Chapter 1, HTTP/1.1 requests must have a `Host` header that identifies the name of the server that the client wants to handle the request. For servers not supporting virtual hosts, this is identical to the `ServerName` value set for the primary server. The `Host` header is also used to identify a virtual host to service the request, and virtual hosts identified by the client `Host` header are thus termed *name-based virtual hosts*.

Apache was one of the first servers to support virtual hosts right out of the box. Since version 1.1, Apache has supported both IP-based and name-based virtual hosts. This chapter examines both IP-based and name-based virtual hosts in detail.

The chapter also introduces the concept of *dynamic virtual hosting*, which uses another module, `mod_vhost_aliases`. Dynamic virtual hosts are virtual hosts whose configuration is not fixed, but is determined (using a predefined template) from the request URL. The advantage of dynamic virtual hosts is that literally thousands of these can be supported on a single server with only a few lines of template code, rather than having to write a custom configuration for each.

In general, you will want to use IP-based virtual hosts whenever you must support browsers that aren't HTTP/1.1-compliant (the number of these in use is rapidly dwindling), and when you can afford to dedicate a unique IP address for each virtual host (the number of available IP addresses is also dwindling). Most sites will prefer to use name-based virtual hosts. Remember, though, that with name-based virtual hosting, non-HTTP/1.1 browsers will have no way to specify the virtual hosts they wish to connect to.

Virtual Host Directives

For both IP-based and name-based virtual addressing, the `<VirtualHost>` container directive encloses all directives that apply to a specific virtual host. All directives that are placed in the `<VirtualHost>` container are also applicable in an ordinary single-server context, although their behavior may be altered when they apply to a virtual host. When you examine the examples of virtual host configurations presented in this chapter, remember the following rules:

- Any directive inside a `<VirtualHost>` container applies only to that virtual host.
- All directives in the configuration file that are not part of a `<Virtual Host>` container define the *primary server*. Virtual hosts always inherit the configuration of the primary server, so, in a sense, the primary server configuration defines default values for all virtual hosts. However, directives inside a `<VirtualHost>` container always override the same directive if inherited from the primary server configuration. Keep

virtual host directives to a minimum, overriding or augmenting the inherited primary server directives only where necessary. A `ServerName` directive should be used to override the canonical name of the primary server, and a virtual host will usually have its own `DocumentRoot`. Use care in overriding the primary server directives beyond these two basic directives.

- Before defining virtual hosts, define the network interfaces and ports the primary server will listen to using `BindAddress`, `Port`, and `Listen` (as described in Chapter 4, "The Apache Directive"). These directives are not permissible in a virtual host context.

IP-Based Virtual Hosting

IP-based virtual hosts are defined by the IP address used to access them, and each IP-based virtual host must have a unique IP address. Since no server machine has more than a few physical network interfaces, it is likely that multiple IP-based virtual hosts will share the same network interface, using a technique called *network interface aliasing*. You'll see how to do this on a Linux server later in this section.

Secure Sockets Layer (SSL is the subject of Chapter 15) requires each SSL Web server on the Internet to have a unique IP address associated with its well-known hostname. Most site hosting services and ISPs that provide SSL Web sites for their customers do so by using IP-based virtual hosting, usually by aliasing multiple IP addresses to a small number of actual network interfaces on each server. This has created a demand for IP-based virtual hosts—even though its use was once declining in favor of name-based virtual hosting—and a commensurate increase in demand for IP addresses to support IP-based virtual hosting.

NOTE In September, 2000, one of the world's three registrars of IP addresses, the American Registry for Internet Numbers (ARIN) announced that they would no longer accept IP-based virtual hosting as a justification for new IP number assignments (www.arin.net/announcements/policy_changes.html). The use of IP addresses for IP-based virtual hosting is not restricted or unauthorized, but this policy change could make it difficult for sites trying to obtain a chunk of IP addresses to be used for IP-based virtual hosting.

IP-virtual hosts are quite easy to set up. Use the `<VirtualHost IPaddr>` container directive to enclose a group of directives that apply only to the virtual host specified (and identified by a unique IP address).

Essential Configuration

PART 2

To create two IP-based virtual hosts on my Apache server, I placed the following section in my `httpd.conf` file, making sure that this section followed any global scope directives. In other words, any directives I wanted to apply to the Apache daemon processes or to the primary server and to provide default values for all virtual hosts are placed at the top of the file, and they are the first read when Apache is started. For the following definitions to work, the two IP addresses (192.168.1.4 and 192.168.1.5) must be valid IP addresses for the server, either on separate interfaces or (as in my case) on the same interface using interface aliasing.

```
<VirtualHost 192.168.1.4>
    ServerName vhost1.hiwaay.net
    DocumentRoot /home/httpd/html/vhost1
</VirtualHost>

<VirtualHost 192.168.1.5>
    ServerName vhost2.hiwaay.net
    DocumentRoot /home/httpd/html/vhost2
</VirtualHost>
```

These are quite simple definitions. Appendix A lists all the directives that can be used within a virtual host scope, but here I defined only a `ServerName` for the virtual host and a path to the `DocumentRoot` for each virtual host. Connecting to the first virtual host using the following URL:

```
http://192.168.1.4/
```

causes the server to offer me the documents stored in `/home/httpd/html/vhost1`. Of course, we don't want to require users to enter an IP address. The preferred way to provide access to the virtual host is to add an address record to the network domain name (DNS) server, mapping the IP address to a hostname; this makes it possible, and far more convenient, to connect to the virtual host using this URL:

```
http://vhost1.hiwaay.net/
```

Keep in mind, though, that with IP-based virtual hosts, the hostname is irrelevant (except to human users). Apache uses only the IP address to determine which virtual host will be used to serve a connection. With name-based virtual hosting, as we'll see, the hostname is the determining factor in deciding which virtual host is used to serve a connection. Figure 6.1 illustrates the complete request/resolution process for IP-based virtual hosting. Later in the chapter, you'll compare this to a similar diagram for name-based virtual hosting.

Figure 6.1   IP-based virtual hosting on a server with multiple IP addresses

Using _default_ Virtual Hosts

For IP-based virtual hosting, if no <VirtualHost *IPAddr*> is matched—that is, if the server can be reached on one or more IP addresses for which no virtual host is defined—the primary server is always used to respond to the client's request. (Again, the primary server includes all the directives that are not part of a <VirtualHost> scope.) It is a good idea, when using IP-based virtual hosts, to provide a default server of your own instead of forcing Apache to use the primary server. Virtual hosts defined using _default_ are used for exactly this purpose. When using virtual hosting, it is best to reserve the primary server configuration as a default for directives that apply to *all* virtual hosts. Any _default_ virtual hosts (as I'll illustrate, there can be more than one) answer requests to unrecognized virtual hosts. They can be configured to return an error message to the client browser, for example, or to issue a redirect to one of the legitimate IP-based virtual hosts. A _default_ virtual host provides the flexibility and control needed to handle a variety of misdirected queries.

A special form of the `<VirtualHost>` directive is used to define a default virtual host:

```
<VirtualHost _default_:*>
    DocumentRoot   /home/http/html/defaultvh
</VirtualHost>
```

Here, I've defined a virtual host that will respond to all requests that are sent to any port that is not already assigned to another `<VirtualHost>` on any valid IP address. It is also possible to specify a single port to be used by a `_default_` virtual host, for example:

```
<VirtualHost _default_:443>
    DocumentRoot   /home/httpd/html/securedefault
</VirtualHost>
<VirtualHost _default_:*>
    DocumentRoot   /home/httpd/html/defaultvh
</VirtualHost>
```

This example shows that more than one `_default_` virtual host can be defined. The first `<VirtualHost _default_>` container defines a special default virtual host that is used for unrecognized connections on the Secure Sockets Layer TCP port 443. Connections coming in on that port are served the documents found in `/home/http/html/securedefault`. The second `<VirtualHost _default_>` container handles unrecognized connections on all other ports. It provides those connections access to the documents in `/home/http/html/defaultvh`. Because the specific port 443 is already assigned to another virtual host, the second `<VirtualHost_default_>` directive ignores port 443.

Network Interface Aliasing in Linux

Most modern operating systems have the capability of assigning multiple IP addresses to the same physical network interface, and Linux is no exception. Often referred to as *network interface aliasing*, or sometimes *IP multiplexing*, this is a way to set up multiple IP-based virtual hosts even when you have only a single network interface. It is the method I've used to configure my system to support several IP addresses on its only Ethernet interface. Below, I'll show the commands I used to create separate IP addresses that I later assigned to IP-based virtual hosts. To make this scheme work for virtual hosting, you need to create a separate DNS entry for each virtual host, each with its own IP address.

Assigning multiple IP addresses to your network interface to support additional IP-based virtual hosts has one drawback; like all IP-based virtual hosting, it consumes IP addresses that may be in short supply. However, it makes it very easy to set up virtual hosts that work with older browsers that don't support the HTTP/1.1 `Host` header. Although these browsers are becoming less common (many browsers that don't claim to be fully 1.1-compliant do support `Host`), there are still plenty of them out there. If you can spare an IP address for every virtual host you intend to configure, you may want to use the technique described in this section to give each of your virtual hosts its own IP address. Most organizations, however, will probably opt to use name-based virtual hosts, or because of limited IP address space, use them out of necessity.

To add virtual IP addresses to the network interface on a Linux server, log in as root and use the ifconfig command. In the following example I add two new virtual Ethernet interfaces for the server's one physical Ethernet interface (eth0). These IP addresses do not have to be sequential (as they are here), but they must be on the same network subnet:

```
# /sbin/ifconfig eth0:0    192.168.1.4
# /sbin/ifconfig eth0:1    192.168.1.5
```

To confirm this configuration change, I entered the ifconfig command without arguments. The output is shown in Listing 6.1. As expected, the new virtual interfaces (eth0:0 and eth0:1) appear with the same hardware address (HWaddr 00:60:08:A4:E8:82) as the physical Ethernet interface.

Listing 6.1   The Linux ifconfig command, showing physical and virtual network interfaces

```
# /sbin/ifconfig
eth0        Link encap:Ethernet   HWaddr 00:60:08:A4:E8:82
            inet addr:192.168.1.1  Bcast:192.168.1.255  Mask:255.255.255.0
            UP BROADCAST RUNNING MULTICAST  MTU:1500  Metric:1
            RX packets:463 errors:0 dropped:0 overruns:0 frame:0
            TX packets:497 errors:0 dropped:0 overruns:0 carrier:0
            collisions:0 txqueuelen:100
            Interrupt:11 Base address:0x6100

eth0:0      Link encap:Ethernet   HWaddr 00:60:08:A4:E8:82
            inet addr:192.168.1.4  Bcast:192.168.1.255  Mask:255.255.255.0
            UP BROADCAST RUNNING MULTICAST  MTU:1500  Metric:1
            Interrupt:11 Base address:0x6100

eth0:1      Link encap:Ethernet   HWaddr 00:60:08:A4:E8:82
            inet addr:192.168.1.5  Bcast:192.168.1.255  Mask:255.255.255.0
            UP BROADCAST RUNNING MULTICAST  MTU:1500  Metric:1
            Interrupt:11 Base address:0x6100

lo          Link encap:Local Loopback
            inet addr:127.0.0.1  Mask:255.0.0.0
            UP LOOPBACK RUNNING  MTU:3924  Metric:1
            RX packets:58 errors:0 dropped:0 overruns:0 frame:0
            TX packets:58 errors:0 dropped:0 overruns:0 carrier:0
            collisions:0 txqueuelen:0
```

I created an IP-based virtual host for each new virtual network interface I created on the server, as shown below:

```
<VirtualHost 192.168.1.4>
    ServerName vhost1.hiwaay.net
    DocumentRoot /home/httpd/html/vhost1
</VirtualHost>

<VirtualHost 192.168.1.5>
    ServerName vhost2.hiwaay.net
    DocumentRoot /home/httpd/html/vhost2
</VirtualHost>
```

The Address Resolution Protocol

Linux makes setting up network interface aliasing easy, but how do you advertise the new IP addresses to the rest of the network? For that matter, how do you ensure that Internet packets sent to the new IP addresses are now routed to the correct machine and Ethernet interface? The answer is that both the advertising and the routing are handled automatically by the *Address Resolution Protocol (ARP).*

Your router advertises itself to other routers as a portal or gateway to your network. If you have a properly functioning Internet router, anyone on the Internet can send data to your network through that router. To make a host on your network accessible to the world, you just need to make sure that your router knows how to reach that host by its new IP address.

ARP is a "discovery protocol" used by one host to discover information about another. When you use ifconfig to add an IP address to a Linux interface, you instruct the system to reply to ARP broadcasts for the new IP address with the interface's physical network address. The physical network address of the interface (often called the Media Access Control, or MAC, address) appears in the trace above identified as HWaddr. The manufacturer of the *media access unit (MAU)*, in this case, an Ethernet adapter, works with other manufacturers to ensure that the address is globally unique. Some Ethernet adapters allow this address to be changed, but most have an embedded address that is unalterable.

Adding the IP address 192.168.1.5 to my Ethernet interface (eth0) instructed my Linux server to respond to ARP requests for this IP address with the Ethernet address of that interface. When my router receives an IP packet addressed to 192.168.1.5, it broadcasts an ARP packet to the 192.168.1.0 network. All hosts on that network will receive the broadcast; most ignore it. But my Linux host, now configured to reply to ARP broadcasts for 192.168.1.5, will send an ARP reply to the router instructing it to send all packets addressed to 192.168.1.5 to the Ethernet address of its eth0 interface. A potential for conflict exists if two network devices both respond to the ARP broadcast, claiming to use the same IP address. Most operating systems are designed to prevent such a conflict by detecting the presence of other systems on the network already using their assigned IP address when they boot. (They use ARP to do this, incidentally). The system disables the Ethernet interface with the conflicting address and notifies the administrator of the conflict. In other words, the machine that's already using the IP address gets to keep it, and new machines trying to use the interface politely defer to the incumbent.

Figure 6.2 illustrates how ARP allows other workstations (in this case an NT 4 workstation) to discover the Ethernet address of a Linux workstation that has been configured (as described above) to communicate using three IP addresses on the same Ethernet interface.

Figure 6.2   Address discovery using ARP

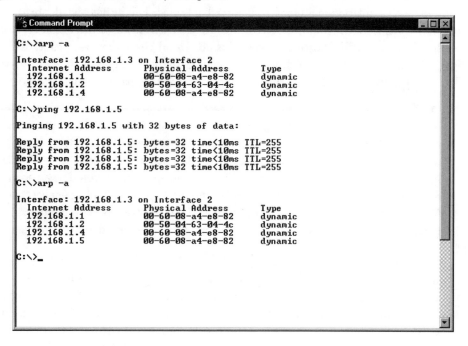

Name-Based Virtual Hosting

Name-based virtual hosting takes advantage of a special request header introduced with HTTP/1.1. As already mentioned, an HTTP/1.1 client browser sends a Host header to identify the hostname of the server that should respond to the request. A standard HTTP/1.0 request usually consists of a single line that identifies the request method, the URI (which is the trailing part of the URL, omitting the protocol and hostname), and the protocol designation:

```
GET / HTTP/1.0
```

The server that receives this request knows only the IP address of the interface on which it was received; it has no way of knowing which DNS name the client used to determine that IP address. To comply with HTTP/1.1, a second header must be present even in a minimal request, to identify the host that should process the request. This is usually the primary Apache server, but it may be any virtual host that has been defined in the Apache configuration. An HTTP/1.1 request would look like this:

```
GET / HTTP/1.1
Host: jackal.hiwaay.net
```

The hostname (and, optionally, the TCP port) that is placed in the Host header by the client browser is determined from the URL of the request itself. In cases where the Web server is using IP-based virtual hosting, or supports no virtual hosts, the Host header is usually ignored. But when name-based virtual hosts are used, the Host header can be very important. The Host header can be used to identify a specific virtual host that has a matching hostname.

> **NOTE** Failure to specify the Host header is an error if the client identifies itself as HTTP/1.1-compliant. A client that does not want to send this header must not specify HTTP/1.1 in its request. Netscape Communicator 4.7 sends the HTTP/1.0 header but also sends the Host field. This is not an error; but it would be an error for Netscape to send the HTTP/1.1 header and omit the Host field. I suspect that Netscape prefers to identify itself as an HTTP/1.0 client because some other behavior of the HTTP/1.1 specification is not fully implemented in Netscape and can't be relied on.

Name-based virtual hosts, which (like IP-based virtual hosts) are handled by the mod_virtual module, make use of a special directive, NameVirtualHost. This directive designates an IP address for name-based virtual hosting. When NameVirtualHost is used, the IP address it specifies becomes available only as a name-based virtual host. It is no longer accessible by non-HTTP/1.1 clients and cannot be used for IP-based virtual hosting.

When Apache encounters the `NameVirtualHost` directive while reading `httpd.conf`, it sets up a virtual host table for the IP address specified. Only a single `NameVirtualHost` address should exist for each IP address, designating that IP address for virtual hosting. Any number of `<VirtualHost>` directives can identify the same IP address, however. As it parses `httpd.conf`, Apache adds virtual hosts to the virtual host table for each IP address whenever it encounters a `<VirtualHost>` directive that specifies the same IP address as one earlier designated for virtual hosting. After parsing `httpd.conf`, Apache has a complete list of all virtual hosts for each IP address specified in `NameVirtualHost` directives.

When it receives a request on any IP address specified by a `NameVirtualHost` directive, Apache searches the associated list of virtual hosts for that IP address. When it finds a virtual host that has a `ServerName` directive matching the `Host` header of the incoming request, Apache responds to the request using the configuration defined in that virtual host's container. This process was illustrated earlier, in Figure 6.1.

In name-based virtual hosting, illustrated in Figure 6.3, the virtual host selected to service a request is always determined from the `Host` header of the request. If no match is found for the virtual host requested by the client, the first virtual host defined for the IP address is served by default. This virtual host is called the *primary virtual host*. Don't confuse this with the primary server, which is defined by the directives outside all virtual host containers. Each request for a name-based virtual host must match an IP address that has been previously designated for virtual hosting with the `NameVirtualHost` directive. Only name-based virtual hosts will be served on an address so designated; the primary server (that is, the configuration defined outside the `VirtualHost` directives) will never serve any client connecting on an IP address designated for virtual hosting.

If Apache receives an HTTP/1.0 request sent to an IP address that you identified for name-based virtual hosting (using a `NameVirtualHost` directive), but the `Host` header is unrecognized (or missing), the primary virtual host always handles the request. The `<VirtualHost _default_>` directive can never be used as a name-based virtual host, because the `<VirtualHost>` directive for name-based virtual hosts must always contain a valid IP address.

With name-based virtual hosting, you should include directives for the main server that apply to *all* virtual hosts rather than trying to use the main server as a repository for directives that apply to the "default" name-based virtual host. The directives for that host should be placed in the virtual host container for the primary virtual host. Remember that the *first* virtual host you define in `httpd.conf` for an IP address previously designated for name-based virtual hosting is the primary virtual host for that address.

On my system (Listing 6.2), I defined two very simple name-based virtual hosts.

Figure 6.3   Name-based virtual hosting on a server with a single IP address

Listing 6.2   Defining two simple name-based hosts

```
NameVirtualHost 192.168.1.1

<VirtualHost 192.168.1.1>
    UseCanonicalName off
    ServerName namedvh1.hiwaay.net
    DocumentRoot /home/httpd/html/
</VirtualHost>
```

```
<VirtualHost 192.168.1.1>
   UseCanonicalName off
   ServerName namedvh2.hiwaay.net
   DocumentRoot /home/httpd/html/NamedVH2
</VirtualHost>
```

The `NameVirtualHost` directive is critical; it identifies the IP address 192.168.1.1 as an interface for name-based virtual hosts. All requests received on this IP address will now be handled by one of the name-based hosts associated with that address. As soon as Apache reads the `NameVirtualHost 192.168.1.1` directive, the primary server can no longer be reached on this IP address. Instead, the server creates a virtual host list for this IP address and adds the names specified by the `ServerName` directive as it processes the virtual host configurations that follow. When this server is loaded, it will have a virtual host list for IP address 192.168.1.1 consisting of the virtual hosts `namedvh1.hiwaay.net` and `namedvh2.hiwaay.net`. As requests arrive, the name specified in `Host` header of each request is compared against this list. When a match is found, the server knows which virtual host will service that request.

Remember that (in contrast to IP-based virtual hosting) any request received on the IP address 192.168.1.1 that does not properly identify one of its name-based virtual hosts will be served by the *first named* virtual host. In Listing 6.2, this is `namedvh1.hiwaay.net`, which becomes sort of a default name-based host for IP address 192.168.1.1. For that reason, I explicitly set its `DocumentRoot` to match that of my primary server. I did this mainly to make the configuration file more readable; it is not necessary to set this value, because virtual hosts inherit the value of this directive, along with that of all other directives, from the primary server.

The second virtual host in Listing 6.2 has a separate `DocumentRoot`, and to HTTP/1.1 browsers that connect to `http://namedvh2.hiwaay.net`, it appears to be completely different from any other Web site on this server; the only hint that it's one virtual host among potentially many others is that it has the same IP address as other Web servers. This is not apparent, however, to users who know the server only by its hostname. When setting up name-based hosts that all apply to the same IP address, you should enter the hostnames as *Canonical Name* or *CNAME* records in the DNS server for the domain. This will place them in the DNS as aliases for the one true hostname that should exist (as an *Address* or *A*) record in the DNS.

There's one more point to note about the example above. The `namedvh2.hiwaay.net` virtual host can only be reached by browsers that send an HTTP/1.1 `Host` request header. It can't be reached at all by browsers that are unable to send this header. If you need to provide access to name-based hosts from browsers that don't support `Host`, read the next section.

Supporting non-HTTP/1.1 Clients

Browsers that do not support HTTP/1.1 are rapidly vanishing from the scene, although the degree to which various browsers support it is the subject of much discussion in the newsgroups. (Some browsers that do not claim to be fully 1.1-compliant actually do support the Host header.) When you're virtually hosting on the Internet, you can't assume what browsers may be out there; and there are special considerations when you're trying to serve pages from name-based virtual hosts to non-HTTP/1.1 browsers. (In a corporate intranet, you as system administrator presumably have some control over the browser software being used.) As mentioned in the last section, any request arriving on an IP address designated for name-based virtual hosts will be served by the first named virtual host if that request does not carry an HTTP Host request header that specifically names one of the virtual hosts assigned to that IP address. Since some HTTP/1.0 browsers will not supply a Host header, you'll have a situation where these legacy browsers are *always* served by the first named virtual host in your list.

Apache provides the ServerPath directive to allow you to serve requests from name-based virtual hosts to clients running non-HTTP/1.1 browsers. This directive is a kludge that you will not want to use unless you must provide support for name-based virtual hosting to HTTP/1.0 browsers.

When the ServerPath directive is used to specify a URL pathname in a <VirtualHost> container, Apache uses that virtual host to serve all requests with URLs that match that pathname. Consider this example:

```
NameVirtualHost 192.168.1.1

    <VirtualHost 192.168.1.1>
        ServerName SomethingBogus.com
        DocumentRoot /home/httpd/
    </VirtualHost>

    <VirtualHost 192.168.1.1>
        ServerName www.innerdomain.com
        ServerPath /securedomain
        DocumentRoot /home/httpd/domain
    </VirtualHost>
```

Here, I've defined a virtual host with the ServerName www.innerdomain.com directive. HTTP/1.1 clients can connect directly to http://www.innerdomain.com. HTTP/1.0 clients will by default reach the SomethingBogus.com virtual host (even though they don't specify it) because it is the first defined, but they can access the innerdomain.com host using a URL that matches the ServerPath, like http://www.innerdomain.com/securedomain. Note, though, that they are selecting the virtual host not with a `Host` header that matches its `ServerName`, but with a URL that matches the `ServerPath`. Actually, it really doesn't matter what hostname a non-HTTP/1.1 client uses as long as it connects on 192.168.1.1 and uses the trailing `/securedomain` in its request URL.

Now, if you publish the URL `http://www.innerdomain.com`, HTTP/1.1 clients will have no trouble reaching the new virtual host; but you need some way to tell non-HTTP/1.1 clients that they need to use another URL, and that's the purpose of the first virtual host. As the first virtual host in the list, it will be the default page served to clients that don't use a `Host` header to designate a name-based virtual host. Choose a `ServerName` for this host that no client will ever connect to directly; this virtual host is a "fall-through" that will only serve requests from clients that don't provide a valid `Host` header. In the `DocumentRoot` directory for this virtual host, you should place a page that redirects non-HTTP/1.1 clients to `http://www.innerdomain.com/securedomain`, similar to this:

```
<HTML>
<TITLE>
Banner Page for non-HTTP/1.1 browser users.
</TITLE>
<BODY>
If you are using an older, non-HTTP/1.1 compatible browser,
please bookmark this page:
<BR>
<A HREF=/securedomain>http://www.innerdomain.com/securedomain
</A>
</BODY>
</HTML>
```

Also, in order to make this work, always make sure you use relative links (e.g., `file.html` or `../icons/image.gif`) in the `www.innerdomain.com` virtual host's pages. For HTTP/1.1 clients, these will be relative to `www.innerdomain.com`; for HTTP/1.0 clients, they will be relative to `www.innerdomain.com/securedomain`.

Dynamic Virtual Hosting

The techniques described above, for IP- and name-based virtual hosting, are sufficient for most applications, but they are limited in the number of virtual hosts that can be set up and administered. The number of Web sites on the Internet has grown so that it is no longer feasible to maintain each site on a single server, or to dedicate an IP address to each. Many sites are now administered by Web hosting services that maintain large "server farms," each server hosting hundreds or even thousands of Web sites. These are usually name-based hosts, each with its own unique Internet hostname and DNS entry. ISPs that provide this service to thousands of customers need a solution for hosting huge numbers of virtual hosts. Even name-based hosting is difficult to set up and maintain for so many virtual sites when an administrator has to set each one up individually, even if only a few lines in the httpd.conf is required for each.

Another technique, called *dynamically configured mass virtual hosting,* is used for very large numbers of Web sites. A standard module provided with the Apache distribution, mod_vhost_aliases, implements dynamically configured hosts by specifying templates for DocumentRoot and ScriptAlias that are used to create the actual paths to these directories after examining the incoming URL.

The entire purpose of mod_vhost_aliases is to create directory paths for DocumentRoot and ScriptAlias based on the request URL. It is a very simple module that is controlled by only four directives, two for name-based and two for IP-based dynamic virtual hosting.

These directives implement name-based dynamic virtual hosting:

VirtualDocumentRoot   Specifies how the module constructs a path to the DocumentRoot for a dynamic virtual host from the request URL.

VirtualScriptAlias   Works like ScriptAlias to construct a path to a directory containing CGI scripts from the request URL.

These implement IP-based dynamic virtual hosting:

VirtualDocumentRootIP   Like VirtualDocumentRoot, but constructs the path to the dynamic virtual host's DocumentRoot from the IP address on which the request was received.

VirtualScriptAliasIP   Like VirtualScriptAlias, but constructs the path to a directory of CGI scripts from the IP address on which the request was received.

Since mod_vhost_aliases constructs paths for dynamic hosts as requests arrive at the server, DocumentRoot and ScriptAlias essentially become variables that change depending on the virtual host the client is trying to reach. Thus they do not have to be explicitly specified for each virtual host in httpd.conf. In fact, no virtual host needs to be specified in httpd.conf; the administrator has only to ensure that a directory exists for each virtual host on the server. If the directory doesn't exist, the requester gets the standard Not Found message (or, if you are being user-friendly, your customized Not Found message).

Each of the directives uses a set of specifiers to extract tokens from the request URL and then embed them into one of two paths, either the path to DocumentRoot or the path to ScriptAlias for the dynamic virtual host. The specifiers that can be used are listed in Table 6.1.

Table 6.1   Specifiers for Dynamic Virtual Host Aliasing

Specifier	Meaning
%%	Translates to a single % character in the path.
%p	The TCP port number of the dynamic virtual host.
%0	The entire server name, as determined by the UseCanonicalName directive (see the following section).
%N	The Nth part of the server name. If the full server name is jackal.hiwaay.net, then %1 resolves to jackal, %2 to hiwaay, and so on.
%N+	The Nth part of the server name, and all parts following. If the full server name is jackal.hiwaay.net, then %2+ resolves to hiwaay.net.
%-N	The Nth part, counting backwards from the end of the string. If the full server name is jackal.hiwaay.net, then %-1 resolves to net, and %-2 resolves to hiwaay.
%-N+	The Nth part, counting backwards, and all parts preceding it. If the full server name is jackal.hiwaay.net, then %-2+ resolves to jackal.hiwaay.

Each of the parts that can be extracted from the server name can be further broken down by specifying a subpart, using the specifier %N.M, where N is the main part, and M is the subpart. If the directive being evaluated refers to a hostname, for example, each part of the URL is separated by the / character; the subparts are the individual characters of each part. A URL beginning with http://caulds.homepages.hiwaay.net would yield the following parts:

```
%1 = caulds
%2 = homepages
%3 = hiwaay
%4 = net
```

Each of these parts can be further broken down into subparts, in this fashion:

```
%1.1 = c
%1.2 = a
%1.3 = u
```

...and so on.

A simple example should illustrate how this works. The mod_vhost_aliases module translates the VirtualDocumentRoot directive specified below into a DocumentRoot path as illustrated in Figure 6.4. The purpose of the UseCanonicalName directive is explained in the next section.

```
UseCanonicalName off
VirtualDocumentRoot /home/httpd/%1/%p
```

This example uses two of the specifiers that create a VirtualDocumentRoot. The first specifier (%1) returns the first portion of the server name. In this case the server name is provided by the client in a Host header of the HTTP request (as described in the discussion of UseCanonicalName). The second specifier (%p) returns the TCP port of the request for the dynamic virtual host—in this case, the Secure Sockets Layer port 443, because this Apache server has been configured to listen for connections on this port. To run CGI scripts from each dynamic virtual host, use a VirtualScriptAlias in exactly the same way to specify a dynamically constructed path to a directory containing these scripts.

Figure 6.4 A simple dynamic virtual host

http://secure.jackal.hiwaay.net:443/login.html

home/httpd/secure/443/login.html
%1   %p

In the next example, an ISP has given its users their own virtual hosts and organized the user home directories into subdirectories based on the first two characters of the user ID. Figure 6.5 shows how the original request URL is mapped to a pathname using parts and subparts.

```
UseCanonicalName off
VirtualDocumentRoot /home/httpd/users/%3.1/%3.2/%2/%1
```

Figure 6.5 Dynamic virtual hosting using subparts[f0605.tif]

http://www.caulds.myisp.com/welcome.html

home/users/c/a/caulds/www/welcome.html
%3.1/%3.2/%2/%1

When using virtual hosts with Apache, you need to give special consideration to the hostname that Apache will use to refer to each virtual host. The next section covers the `UseCanonicalName` directive, which is particularly important for virtual hosting.

The `UseCanonicalName` Directive

An Apache server often has to construct a URL to refer to itself. Such a URL is called a *self-referential URL*. Part of a self-referential URL is the hostname of the server, which should be a hostname that can be resolved by DNS to an IP address for the server. This hostname is often referred to as the *canonical name* for the server.

On my local network, I connect to my Web server using its unqualified name, with a URL like `http://jackal`. This URL would not work for someone on the Internet, so when my server composes a self-referential URL, it always uses a fully qualified hostname and (optionally) the TCP port number. The `UseCanonicalName` directive controls how Apache determines the system's hostname when constructing this self-referential URL. There are three possible ways this directive can be used:

`UseCanonicalName on` Apache constructs a canonical name for the server using information specified in the `ServerName` and `Port` server configuration directives to create a self-referential URL.

`UseCanonicalName off` Apache uses the hostname and port specified in the `Host` directive supplied by HTTP/1.1 clients to construct a self-referential URL for the server. If the client uses HTTP/1.0 and does not supply a `Host` header, Apache constructs a canonical name from the `ServerName` and `Port` directives. The `UseCanonicalName off` form of the directive is usually used with name-based virtual hosts.

`UseCanonicalName DNS` Apache constructs a self-referential URL for the server using the hostname determined from a reverse-DNS lookup performed on the IP address to which the client connected. This option is designed primarily for use with IP-based virtual hosts, though it can be used in a server context. It has no effect in a name-based virtual host context. The `UseCanonicalName DNS` form of the directive should only be used with IP-based virtual hosts.

In addition to controlling how self-referential URLs are constructed, the `UseCanonicalName` directive is also used to set two variables that are accessible by CGI scripts through their "environment," `SERVER_NAME` and `SERVER_PORT`. If you look at a CGI script that displays the environment variables, you can easily see how modifying the `UseCanonicalName` directive affects the value of these two variables. Chapter 8 includes such a script, in the section on CGI programming.

IP-Based Dynamic Virtual Hosts

Dynamic virtual hosts can also be IP-based, although doing so is not common, because each host would require a unique IP address. Since dynamic virtual hosting is typically used in situations where a large number of virtual hosts must be managed on a single server, the IP-based method usually consumes too many precious IP addresses to be feasible. But if you're interested, a simple example illustrates how it works.

Two directives supplied by mod_vhost_aliases, VirtualDocumentRootIP and VirtualScriptAliasIP, support IP-based dynamic virtual hosting. Here's an example of the two directives in use:

```
UseCanonicalName DNS
VirtualDocumentRootIP     /home/httpd/vhost/%4
VirtualScriptAliasIP      /home/httpd/vhost/cgi-bin/%4
```

Notice that the second portion of each directive specifies a pathname constructed from the IP address on which the HTTP request was received. Therefore the %4 in both directives is filled with the fourth part of the request IP address (the fourth number in the traditional dotted quad IP address format). If a request arrives on an interface whose IP address is 127.129.71.225, the paths specified by VirtualDocumentRootIP and VirtualScriptAliasIP directories are translated, respectively, into the following directories:

```
/home/httpd/vhost/225
/home/httpd/vhost/cgi-bin/225
```

These directories need to be created on the server for the server to produce a meaningful response. Since each of the parts of an IP address can take a value from 1 to 254, this scheme permits up to 254 IP-based virtual hosts. The following directives would allow 64516 (254 × 254) virtual hosts, with pathnames like /home/httpd/vhost/116/244/, but would also require an IP address for each. I show this for illustration only; you'd never find something like this being done in the real world.

```
UseCanonicalName DNS
VirtualDocumentRootIP     /home/httpd/vhost/%3/%4
VirtualScriptAliasIP      /home/httpd/vhost/cgi-bin/%3/%4
```

Also note from these examples that no ServerName directive is used to assign each virtual host its name. If the server needs to form a self-referential URL to refer to any of these virtual hosts, the UseCanonicalName DNS directive instructs it to perform a reverse DNS lookup to determine the server name from the IP address. It is *not* necessary for Apache to perform this reverse DNS lookup to serve requests from the virtual host.

Guaranteeing Sufficient File Descriptors

If you're using Apache to provide virtual hosting for a very large number of Web sites, particularly on an older version of Linux, you need to keep in mind the availability of file descriptors.

Whenever Linux opens a disk file or network device for reading or writing, it refers to the open device by a system object known as a *file descriptor* or a *file handle*. The file descriptor is a system resource, and the number of file descriptors each process can have open at any one time is limited by the system. Apache needs one for every open file and another for every open network connection. Web connections are rarely open for very long, as clients connect, retrieve resources, and disconnect. Apache's log files, however, normally stay open for as long as the Apache server is running, in order to minimize the overhead required to open the file, write to it, and close it. This creates a problem when the number of file handles available to the Apache process is limited and a large number of virtual hosts are being supported. Each virtual host has at least two open logs, `error.log` and `access.log`.

File descriptors are usually constrained by three system limits. The first is called the *soft resource limit*. A process cannot use a greater number of file descriptors than this limit, but a user can increase the soft limit using the `ulimit` command up to the *hard resource limit*. A user with root privileges can increase the hard resource limit up to the kernel limit. The kernel limit is an absolute resource limit imposed by the running Linux kernel. Recent versions of the Linux kernel have such a high kernel limit it can be considered unlimited in most environments.

The hard limit and soft limits on the number of file descriptors a process can have open are both set to 1024 in 2.2.*x* kernels. In Linux 2.0 (and older) kernels, these were set to 256. Use the `ulimit` command to determine the hard and soft limits of your Linux kernel, as follows. The number of file descriptors a process can have opened at one time is shown as "open files."

```
[caulds@jackal caulds]$ ulimit -Sa
core file size (blocks)    1000000
data seg size (kbytes)     unlimited
file size (blocks)         unlimited
max memory size (kbytes)   unlimited
stack size (kbytes)        8192
cpu time (seconds)         unlimited
max user processes         256
pipe size (512 bytes)      8
open files                 1024
virtual memory (kbytes)    2105343
```

```
[caulds@jackal caulds]$ ulimit -Ha
core file size (blocks)   unlimited
data seg size (kbytes)    unlimited
file size (blocks)        unlimited
max memory size (kbytes)  unlimited
stack size (kbytes)       unlimited
cpu time (seconds)        unlimited
max user processes        256
pipe size (512 bytes)     8
open files                1024
virtual memory (kbytes)   4194302
```

NOTE I ran the commands as a nonprivileged user. Running them as root produces the same result.

Although it is unlikely that you will ever bump up against Linux's limits on the number of open file descriptors, you should be aware that they exist, especially if you intend to support a large number of virtual hosts, each with its own log files. If you do need to increase the number of file descriptors beyond the system's hard limit, do one of the following things:

- Reduce the number of log files. Simply by having each virtual host write both its error and access logs to the same file, you can reduce the number of required file descriptors by half, though you may not want to do this, because it lumps all logging into a single disk file that fills very rapidly, making it more difficult to locate, isolate, and resolve errors encountered by the server.

- Increase the file descriptor limit to the system's hard limit prior to starting Apache, by using a script like this:

```
#!/bin/sh
ulimit -S -n 1024
/usr/local/apache/bin/apachectl start
```

- On older (pre-2.2.x) kernels, download kernel patches to increase the number of file descriptors supported by the kernel. Look for the Alan Cox kernel patches.

- Increase the 2.2.x kernel limit of 1024 open file descriptors per process to 4096. You can accomplish this using the following instructions:

  A. Add the following lines to the file /etc/security/limits.conf:

  ```
  *       soft    nofile  1024
  *       hard    nofile  4096
  ```

B. Add the following line to /etc/pam.d/login:

```
session required /lib/security/pam_limits.so
```

C. Add the following lines to one of your system startup scripts (probably /etc/rc.d/rc.local):

```
# Increase system-wide file descriptor limit.
echo  8192 > /proc/sys/fs/file-max
echo 24576 > /proc/sys/fs/inode-max
```

D. Finally, always start Apache with a script like the following:

```
#!/bin/sh
ulimit -S -n 4096
/usr/local/apache/bin/apachectl start
```

NOTE   Most situations simply do not call for such a large number of open file descriptors for a single running application or process.

Avoiding DNS Dependence

All of the examples shown so far—including those for name-based virtual hosting—have used only IP addresses in the <VirtualHost> directives. This is not an Apache requirement, but it is the best way to define virtual hosts. While it may seem more intuitive to use the hostname for name-based virtual hosts, that should *never* be done. This example shows why:

```
<VirtualHost vhost1.hiwaay.net>
    ServerAdmin caulds@hiwaay.net
    DocumentRoot /home/httpd/html/vhost1
</VirtualHost>
```

The potential problem is that Apache must know at least one IP address for the virtual host, and we haven't provided it. When Apache starts and reads these lines from its httpd.conf file, it performs a DNS lookup for the IP address of the hostname given in the <VirtualHost> directive. If for some reason DNS is unavailable, the lookup will fail, and Apache will disable this particular virtual host. In versions earlier than 1.2, Apache will then abort.

If we simply swap in the IP address to correct this, we introduce a second problem:

```
<VirtualHost 192.168.1.4>
    ServerAdmin caulds@hiwaay.net
    DocumentRoot /home/httpd/html/vhost1
</VirtualHost>
```

We no longer require Apache to perform a DNS lookup for the value provided by `<VirtualHost>`, but we haven't provided a second important piece of information required for *every* virtual host, the `ServerName`. Apache determines the `ServerName` in this case by performing a reverse-DNS lookup on 198.168.1.4 to find the associated hostname. This reliance on a DNS query when Apache is started means we haven't solved our problem yet. The addition of a `ServerName` directive for the virtual host eliminates the dependence on DNS to start the virtual host. The virtual host specification should read:

```
<VirtualHost 192.168.1.4>
    ServerName vhost1.hiwaay.net
    ServerAdmin caulds@hiwaay.net
    DocumentRoot /home/httpd/html/vhost1
</VirtualHost>
```

Rules for Virtual Hosting

You can avoid many problems when using Apache virtual hosts by adhering to a list of simple rules:

- Always use an IP address in the `<VirtualHost>` directive and in every `Listen` and `BindAddress` directive; *never* use a hostname. Reliance on the DNS to resolve a hostname may prevent Apache from starting. Chapter 4 discusses the `Listen` and `BindAddress` directives.

- Be sure to specify a `ServerName` directive in all virtual hosts; do not rely on reverse DNS lookups to determine the server name for a virtual host.

- IP-based and name-based virtual hosts are independent and must not conflict. However, it is perfectly OK to have both IP- and name-based virtual hosts on the same server; just make sure that the IP addresses specified in each do not conflict.

- Always create a `<VirtualHost _default_:*>` with no pages or with a simple error page. Otherwise, the primary server configuration will be used as the default. Avoid this by providing a default virtual host with some default behavior that you define.

- Ensure that the `NameVirtualHost` directive is used once, and only once, for each IP address on which you intend to host name-based virtual hosts.

> *TIP* When setting up virtual host configurations, it is often helpful to use the `httpd -S` command. This will not start the server, but it will dump out a description of how Apache parsed the configuration file. Careful examination of the IP addresses and server names may help uncover configuration mistakes.

In Sum

Virtual hosting is used to maintain multiple Web sites on a single server machine. The sites are usually identified by unique hostname aliases in the DNS. Virtual hosts can be either IP-based (in which the IP address on which the request was received identifies the virtual host to handle the request) or name-based (in which the client designates the virtual host to handle the request using the HTTP/1.1 `Host` header).

The `mod_vhost_aliases` module provides a way to create dynamic virtual hosts, in which the server knows nothing about the virtual host until a request arrives. All information about a dynamic virtual host is derived from the URL of the request or the IP address on which the request arrived. Dynamic virtual hosts are usually used to support large numbers of virtual hosts on a single server with only minimal configuration changes to the Apache server. Dynamic virtual hosts can also be either IP- or name-based; although IP based dynamic virtual hosts are rarely used because of their requirement that each host have a unique IP address.

Up until this point, I've shown how to set up a working Apache server, but now the focus of the book will change toward determining how that server will respond to requests and how the content it delivers can be customized. In other words, we'll be looking at more than just the Apache engine, which is fairly simple. We'll be looking at requests and responses, and customizing the responses returned by Apache, either by configuration changes, adding additional modules, or by programming. The next chapter discusses one of the simpler, but very efficient, techniques for Web page customization, Server-Side Includes.

Part 3

Advanced Configuration Options

Featuring:

- Configuring Apache to run Server-Side Includes (SSI)
- HotWired's Extended SSI (XSSI)
- Java Server-Side Includes (JSSI)
- The Common Gateway Interface (CGI) and FastCGI
- The mod_perl Perl accelerator
- Using PHP and ASP for Apache
- Java tools for Apache: Apache Jserv, Java Server Pages (JSP), and Resin
- Aliasing and redirection with mod_alias
- URL rewriting with mod_rewrite
- Controlling Apache manually via the command line
- GUI configuration tools

7

Server-Side Includes

Server-Side Includes (SSI) offer the simplest way to add dynamic content to a Web page. When the Web server receives a request for a page that may contain SSI commands, it parses the page looking for those commands. If it finds any, they are processed by the Apache module that implements SSI (usually `mod_include`). The results of this processing—which may be as simple as the document's last-modified date or as complex as the result of running a CGI script—replace the SSI code in the HTML document before it is sent to the requesting user. SSI commands are actually HTML comments (enclosed in `<!--` and `-->` tags) that have special meaning to the SSI processing module. A page that contains SSI commands adheres to the requirements for HTML, and the SSI commands are ignored (as comments) if they happen to reach a client browser without being parsed, processed, and replaced by the server.

Apache has included SSI for a very long time. Although it is implemented as an optional module, this module is compiled into the server by default, and it is available in nearly every Apache server. For simple functions, like automatically including the last date of modification of the enclosing HTML document in the document itself, using SSI is far simpler and more efficient than writing a CGI program to take care of the task. I believe every Apache server should be configured to handle server-parsed documents whenever necessary.

SSI is not powerful enough to replace a programming language for generating complete HTML pages, or for database querying, or any of the fun stuff that requires true programming (although it does allow a page to call CGI scripts that can handle those more complex tasks). SSI can't come close to replacing any of the techniques discussed in Chapters 8 and 9 for Web programming, and SSI shouldn't be considered an alternative to any of them. I prefer to think of SSI as a built-in feature of Apache that can be used to augment these techniques.

The version of SSI included with Apache is XSSI (for eXtended Server-Side Includes). XSSI has been in use for so long that it is generally considered standard SSI. There are extensions to XSSI, the most prominent of which are the HotWired extensions discussed in detail later in this chapter. Another version you may hear of is SSI+, which adds a few tags primarily of interest to Win32 programmers, the most important of which is an ODBC tag used to retrieve data from databases using the Microsoft Open Database Connectivity drivers. At the end of this chapter, Java developers can learn about another option, Java Server-Side Includes (JSSI).

Configuring Apache to Run SSI

SSI documents are an example of a technique called *server-parsed HTML*. Server-parsed documents require two things: a special handler and a way to identify documents that are to be parsed by that handler.

To use SSI on a server, you must make a few changes to the Apache server configuration. First, make sure that the mod_include module is properly installed. You can do this by linking the module to the Apache kernel at compile time, but a better way is to compile the module as a dynamically loadable module (DSO).

1. Check your Apache configuration file. If the two lines shown below are commented out, uncomment them; if they do not exist, add them. Also make sure that the libexec directory holds a copy of mod_include.so:

    ```
    LoadModule includes_module    libexec/mod_include.so
    AddModule mod_include.c
    ```

2. Use an Options directive to enable Includes for the directory (or directories) in which you plan to place your server-parsed pages:

    ```
    Options Includes
    ```

NOTE I first tried to set Options +Includes to say "enable the Includes option" but, much to my surprise, this did *not* work! The + operator *adds* options to an Options list that already exists. Since I had no Options list already set for my DocumentRoot directory, the statement had no effect. It was necessary for me to remove the + for the Options directive to take effect.

3. Specify a MIME content type for files with the `.shtml` extension:

   ```
   AddType text/html .shtml
   ```

4. Add an Apache handler for `.shtml` files:

   ```
   AddHandler server-parsed .shtml
   ```

NOTE   The choice of `.shtml` as the extension for SSI files is conventional but not strictly necessary. You just need to specify the same extension in both the AddType and AddHandler statements, and save all HTML files containing SSI commands with that extension.

5. Check the Apache configuration file syntax:

   ```
   # /usr/local/apache/bin/apachectl configtest
   Syntax OK
   ```

6. And then restart the server:

   ```
   # /usr/local/apache/bin/apachectl restart
   /usr/local/apache/bin/apachectl restart: httpd restarted
   ```

SSI Tags

Part of the beauty of SSI is that it is implemented through such a simple mechanism, embedded HTML tags that have special meaning only to the SSI parser. SSI commands are legitimate HTML comments that appear between HTML comment tags <!– and --> and would be ignored by the client browser if they weren't parsed and removed by the Web server. SSI commands have the following general syntax:

```
<!--#command attribute=value attribute=value ... -->
```

Most SSI commands require at least one `attribute=value` pair. Only a few SSI commands (such as `printenv`) can be used without an `attribute=value` pair. To prevent confusion in interpreting the SSI line, it is a good practice to enclose the `value` in double quotes, even if that value is a nonstring data type like an integer. The comment terminator (`-->`) at the end of the line should be offset with white space. (This is not always required, but I had problems running SSI when I failed to separate the final SSI token from the comment terminator.)

SSI commands are parsed in-place and do not need to be placed at the beginning of the line; you can use an SSI command to replace a single word in the middle of a sentence. In Listing 7.1 and its output (Figure 7.1) you'll see how SSI commands can be used to insert values right in the middle of a line of text.

The <config> Tag

The config tag specifies how certain elements of SSI are formatted or displayed. The tag has three defined attributes in standard SSI:

errmsg   The value of errmsg is displayed in the client browser if an error is returned while parsing the SSI document (see Figure 7.1, which displays an error at the bottom for any line that could not be parsed). The custom error message we create for this example is unable to tell us anything about the nature of the error (indicating the almost nonexistent error-handling capability of SSI), and is only marginally better than the default SSI error message, which is *[an error occurred while processing this directive]*. The error in Figure 7.1 occurred because I specified a full pathname as the value of the include file attribute. This must always be expressed as a path relative to the directory in which the SSI page resides.

sizefmt   Determines how the SSI parser displays file sizes returned by the fsize tag. The value of sizefmt can be set to either bytes or abbrev (which displays the file size in either KB or MB, whichever is most appropriate for the size of the file). The sizefmt attribute affects only the use of the fsize tag and has no meaning otherwise. You'll see a demonstration later in this chapter, when we discuss fsize.

timefmt   Allows great flexibility in formatting the strings used to display date and time information. This option will be familiar to anyone who has ever worked with the Linux date utility. SSI calls the Linux strftime() routine to yield % values from Table 7.1.

Table 7.1   Format strings used with the <config> SSI tag

String	Meaning
%%	Escapes a % character
%a	Day of the week abbreviated (Wed)
%A	Full name of day of the week (Wednesday)
%w	Number of day of the week (0–6; Sunday is 0)
%b	Month abbreviated (Oct)
%B	Full name of month (October)
%d	The day of the month (01–31)
%e	The day of the month (1–31)
%H	24 hour of the day (00–23)

Table 7.1   Format strings used with the <config> SSI tag *(continued)*

String	Meaning
%I	12 hour of day (01–12)
%j	Day in the year (001–366)
%M	Minute (00–59)
%p	A.M. or P.M.
%S	Second (00–59)
%y	Last two digits of the year (00–99)
%Y	The four-digit year
%Z	The time zone (CST)

Listing 7.1 is an example of a Web page, formatted in HyperText Markup Language (HTML), that uses most of the time format tags from Table 7.1. Figure 7.1 shows how that page will look when viewed in a Web browser. HTML, as you may remember from Chapter 2, is a standard method of formatting documents for display, or *rendering*. By definition, a Web browser must be able to interpret some version of HTML. Most modern browsers support HTML 4, which includes nearly every element or tag one might conceivably require (version 4 is described at www.w3.org/TR/html4/). HTML is a work in progress, and variants of it have been spawned (with names like Extended HTML or Dynamic HTML) but all Web-browser software supports basic HTML.

Listing 7.1   A Test Document for the SSI config Tag

```
<HTML>
<HEAD>
<TITLE>SSI "config" Element Test Page</TITLE>
</HEAD>
<BODY>
<center>
<H1>SSI "config" Element Test Page</H1>
</center>
<!--#config errmsg="mod_include unable to parse your code!" -->
<!--#config timefmt="%A" -->
Today is <!--#echo var="DATE_LOCAL"-->.
```

```
<!--#config timefmt="%B %d, %Y" -->
The date is:  <!--#echo var="DATE_LOCAL"-->
<!--#include file="footer.html"-->
<!--#include file="/home/httpd/html/footer.html"-->
</BODY>
</HTML>
```

Figure 7.1 The SSI config test document displayed in a browser

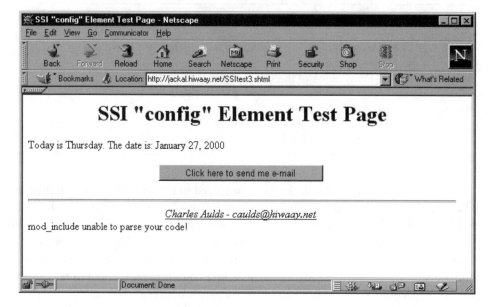

Some familiarity with HTML will be necessary to understand the SSI examples in this chapter, but the important tags, and the only ones that will be explained in detail, are the SSI tags. These can be identified in this example as those enclosed in slightly modified brackets, <!--# -->. The first SSI tag in Listing 7.1, <!--#config, changes the default error message to be displayed when the SSI parser encounters a problem. One of the two include file tags, which attempt to bring HTML formatted documents into this one as a page footer, is incorrect and will cause this error message to be displayed. The other footer is correct, so you can see the result in Figure 7.1. Note that HTML tags in that footer are properly rendered (as a button and as an embedded hyperlink).

This example also serves to illustrate the use of the config timefmt SSI tag to display the current system time and date. Compare the SSI tags against the output, glancing back at Table 7.1, and you can pretty easily see how these work.

As you can see, at least one statement in the HTML could not be parsed. But which one? Where did the links to my e-mail come from? And why are there two separate references to a `footer.html` file? Not surprisingly, the answers to all those questions are related. The e-mail links are part of my standard page footer, displayed by calling my `footer.html` file. One of the `#include` statements is correct and displays the footer page, but the other has incorrect syntax and displays the error message. You'll see exactly what the error is when we look at the `#include` tag later in the chapter.

The <echo> Tag

The `echo` tag prints the values of SSI variables and requires at least one attribute, the name of the variable to be printed. If the variable identified in the attribute is not set, it is displayed as (`none`), and no error occurs. In addition to the variables available in the standard Common Gateway Interface (CGI) environment (the full list of these variables is included in the discussion of CGI in Chapter 8), SSI also sets the following SSI-specific variables:

`DATE_GMT`   The current system date in Greenwich Mean Time.

`DATE_LOCAL`   The current system date in local time.

`DOCUMENT_NAME`   The filename of the SSI document requested by the user.

`DOCUMENT_URI`   The URL path of the SSI document requested by the user.

`LAST_MODIFIED`   The last modification date of the SSI document requested by the user. (When displayed by `echo`, will be formatted according to `"config timefmt"`.)

Listing 7.2 illustrates how the `echo` tag is used to display the values of all four of the SSI-specific variables shown above, along with several selected variables from the CGI environment. Figure 7.2 shows the results in a browser. The two time variables (`DATA_LOCAL` and `DATE_GMT`) are displayed using the SSI default format, but could be tailored by preceding them with a `"config timefmt"` tag, as described in the last section.

Listing 7.2   A Test Document for the SSI echo Tag

```
<HTML>
<HEAD>
<TITLE>SSI Variable Include Test Page</TITLE>
</HEAD>
<BODY>
<center>
<H1>SSI Variable Include Test Page</H1>
</center>
<FONT SIZE=+1>
<ul>
Special mod_include Includes:
<ul>
```

```
DATE_LOCAL:<!--#echo var="DATE_LOCAL"--> <br>
DATE_GMT:<!--#echo var="DATE_GMT"--> <br>
DOCUMENT_NAME:<!--#echo var="DOCUMENT_NAME"--> <br>
DOCUMENT_URI:<!--#echo var="DOCUMENT_URI"--> <br>
LAST_MODIFIED:<!--#echo var="LAST_MODIFIED"--> <br>
<p>
</ul>
Includes from the CGI Environment:
<ul>
SERVER_NAME:<!--#echo var="SERVER_NAME"--> <br>
SERVER_SOFTWARE:<!--#echo var="SERVER_SOFTWARE"--> <br>
HTTP_USER_AGENT:<!--#echo var="HTTP_USER_AGENT"--> <br>
</ul>
</FONT>
<!--#include file="footer.html"-->
</BODY>
</HTML>
```

Figure 7.2 The SSI echo test document displayed in a browser

The <exec> Tag

The exec tag executes an external command and displays the command's standard output (stdout). The command can be either a Linux shell command in this format:

```
<!--#exec cmd="shell-command arg1 arg2 ..." -->
```

for example:

```
<!--#exec cmd="/usr/bin/parser.sh rfc2626.html" -->
```

or a CGI script:

```
<!--#exec cgi="/cgi-bin/mycgi.cgi" -->
```

If the script returns a Location: HTML header instead of output, this header is translated into an HTML anchor (an embedded hyperlink). Listing 7.3 is an example of the exec tag at work. The CGI script that it calls consists of only three lines; while it could do many other things, it simply returns a Location: string (SSI is smart enough to translate this into an anchor tag or hyperlink):

```
#!/usr/bin/perl -Tw
# This is anchor.cgi
use CGI;
print "Location: http://www.apache.org\n\n";
```

Figure 7.3 shows how a browser renders the results.

Listing 7.3   A Test Document for the SSI exec Tag

```
<HTML>
<HEAD>
<TITLE>SSI "exec Tag with Location:" Test Page</TITLE>
</HEAD>
<BODY>
<center>
<H1>SSI "exec Tag with Location:" Test Page</H1>
</center>
<br>
Clickable hyperlink:  <!--#exec cgi="/cgi-bin/anchor.cgi" -->
<p>
<!--#include file="footer.html"-->
</BODY>
</HTML>
```

Advanced
Configuration Options

PART 3

Figure 7.3 The SSI exec tag used as anchor

If an `IncludesNOEXEC` option is in effect for the directory containing the SSI file being parsed, the `exec` tag will be ignored. The directive `Options IncludesNOEXEC` should be in the `.htaccess` file in the directory or in the `httpd.conf` file.

> **WARNING** For security reasons, you should avoid the use of the `<exec cgi>` SSI tag, which will execute a file anywhere in the file system. This violates an accepted Apache standard practice, that CGI scripts reside only in special protected directories and have specific filename extensions. Instead, use `<include virtual>`, which can execute only standard CGI scripts that are accessible only through a URL that is acceptable to Apache. This allows Apache to apply the security measures applied to ordinary CGI scripts.

The `<fsize>` Tag

The `fsize` tag inserts the size of a given file into a server-parsed HTML file. It has two forms, each of which is a different way of locating the file whose size is to be displayed:

 `file`   Identifies a filename and path relative to the directory containing the SSI document being parsed.

virtual   The virtual variable is set to the filename or path relative to Apache's DocumentRoot. Use this when you want to specify a file using a partial URL.

The fsize and flastmod tags are examples of what I like best about SSI: They both have very simple syntax and offer a very efficient way of doing what they do. Moreover, neither tries to do too many things, but each of them comes in very handy when you need it. The next section illustrates them both in the same example (Listing 7.4) because they are used in exactly the same manner. Figure 7.4 then shows how both tags are rendered by a browser.

> **TIP** Use the config tag as described above to format the file size printed by the fsize tag.

The <flastmod> Tag

The flastmod tag inserts the date of last modification of a specified file into the SSI document being parsed at the location of the flastmod tag. Like fsize, the file is specified in one of the following two ways:

file   Identifies a filename and path relative to the directory containing the SSI document being parsed.

virtual   The virtual variable is set to the filename or path relative to Apache's DocumentRoot. Use this when you want to specify a file using a partial URL.

> **TIP** The format of the date printed by the flastmod tag is controlled using the config tag as described earlier.

Listing 7.4 is an example of a document that makes use of both the SSI fsize and flastmod tags. By referring to Figure 7.4, you can easily determine the use of each of these tags. Note that the first fsize tag uses the file keyword to indicate that the referenced file is relative to the directory in which the SSI document resides (in this case they must be in the same directory). The second fsize tag makes use of the virtual keyword to indicate that the file is relative to the Apache DocumentRoot (the file must be in the docs subdirectory of that directory).

Listing 7.4   A Test Document for the SSI fsize and flastmod Tags

```
<HTML>
<HEAD>
<TITLE> SSI fsize and flastmod Test Page</TITLE>
</HEAD>
```

Advanced Configuration Options

PART 3

```
<BODY>
<center>
<H1>SSI Test Page</H1>
<H3>Testing fsize and flastmod</H3>
</center>
<!--#config sizefmt="bytes" -->
<!--#config timefmt="%I:%M %P on %B %d, %Y" -->
<p>Size of this file (bytes): <!--#fsize file="SSItest6.shtml" -->
<br>Last modification of this file:
<!--#flastmod file="SSItest6.shtml" -->
<p>Size of mod_fastcgi.html (bytes):
<!--#fsize virtual=filemod_fastcgi.html" -->
<br>Size of mod_fastcgi.html (KB):
<!--#fsize virtual="/docs/mod_fastcgi.html" -->
<!--#include file="footer.html"-->
</BODY>
</HTML>
```

Figure 7.4 The SSI fsize and flastmod test document displayed in a browser

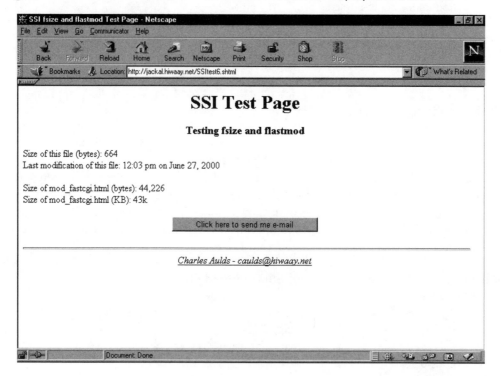

The `<include>` Tag

The `include` tag runs an external file, captures its output, and places that output in the document being parsed. There are two possible formats for the tag:

include file   The `include file` SSI tag is used in the examples throughout this chapter to include an HTML file as a page footer. This is the simplest possible use of the tag. When it's used in this fashion, the included file must be specified by a path relative to the directory of the calling document. (A fully qualified pathname will *not* work; that's why the second `include` statement back in Listing 7.1 triggered the error message you saw in Figure 7.1.) Any access restrictions upon the directory in which the called file resides remain in effect for its inclusion in the calling document.

include virtual   The preferred way to use the `include` tag is to specify `include virtual`, which identifies the included resource by a relative URL, not by filename or path. (This is preferred because the design of the Web is to ensure that all resources are referenced by URI, making their location as independent of system path as possible.) When used in this fashion, `mod_include` constructs a URL from the `include virtual` command, and embeds the results of this URL (what would be returned if the URL was called directly by the client) into the calling document. If the resource indicated by the URL itself includes SSI commands, these are resolved, which allows include files to be nested.

Regardless of the calling method, the included resource can also be a CGI script, and `include virtual` is the preferred way to embed CGI-generated output in server-parsed documents (always use this method rather than `exec cgi`, which the SSI developers do not recommend). Incidentally, if you need to pass information to a CGI script from an SSI document, you *must* use `include virtual`; it isn't possible using `exec cgi`.

Also, attempting to set environment variables (such as QUERY_STRING) from within an SSI page in order to pass data to a CGI script won't work. This sets a variable accessible only to `mod_include` and doesn't alter the environment variable with the same name. Instead, pass variables to CGI scripts by appending `?variable=value` to the query string of the calling URL, as shown in Listing 7.5. This script demonstrates how a CGI script is called, passed a variable and value, and the results embedded in an HTML document passed to the browser. Figure 7.5 shows the resulting document displayed in a browser.

Advanced Configuration Options

PART 3

Listing 7.5 A Test Document for the SSI `include` Tag

```
<HTML>
<HEAD>
<TITLE>include virtual Test Page</TITLE>
</HEAD>
<BODY>
<center>
<H1>Test of include virtual SSI Tag</H1>
</center>
<!--#include virtual="/cgi-bin/test1.cgi?testvar=Testing+for+Carl" -->
<!--#include file="footer.html"-->
</BODY>
</HTML>
```

Listing 7.6 The CGI Script Used with the SSI `include` Tag Test Document

```
#!/usr/bin/perl -Tw
#This is test1.cgi
#
#queries a table for a value

use strict;
use CGI qw(:standard);
use CGI::Carp;

my $output=new CGI;

my $TEST=param('testvar') if (param('testvar') );

print $output->header;
print h3("Variable passed to and returned from CGI script:");
print h4("$TEST");
print $output->end_html;
```

Figure 7.5   The SSI include test document displayed in a browser

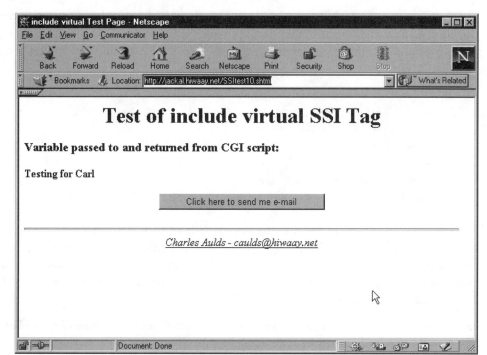

The <printenv> Tag

Of all the SSI tags, printenv is probably the easiest to use. It has no attributes and simply performs a single function; it returns all the system environment variables in one unformatted list. Since the list is not HTML formatted, it is usually a good idea to enclose the printenv tags in standard HTML <pre> or <code> tags that normally enclose unformatted text in an HTML page:

```
<pre>
<!--#printenv -->
</pre>
```

The <set> Tag

The set tag sets the value of a variable, creating the variable if it doesn't already exist. It takes two attributes: the name of a variable to be set, and a value attribute that is assigned to this variable. Both the var and value attributes need to be specified separately:

```
<!--#set var="FOO" value="someval" -->
```

Flow Control

The so-called *flow control* elements of SSI implement only the most basic execution control element, an if/else operator; they don't provide the functions of execution branching or nesting found in a real programming language. Here's the basic implementation of the if tag in SSI:

```
<!--#if expr="test_condition" -->
    HTML-formatted text
<!--#elif expr="test_condition" -->
    HTML-formatted text
<!--#else -->
    even more HTML-formatted text
<!--#endif -->
```

Note that expr is a keyword and must be present. The if expr element works like the if statement in a true programming language. The test condition is evaluated and, if the result is true, the text between it and the next elif, else, or endif tag is included in the output stream, and subsequent endif tests are ignored. If the result is false, the next elif is evaluated in the same way.

SSI test conditions are almost always simple string comparisons, and return True or False based on the result of one of the following possible operations:

Syntax	Value
string	True if *string* is not empty; False otherwise
string1 = *string2*	True if *string1* is equal to *string2*
string1 != *string2*	True if *string1* is not equal to *string2*
string1 < *string2*	True if *string1* is alphabetically less than *string2*
string1 <= *string2*	True if *string1* is alphabetically less than or equal to *string2*
string1 > *string2*	True if *string1* is alphabetically greater than *string2*
string1 >= *string2*	True if *string1* is alphabetically greater than or equal to *string2*
Condition1 && *condition2*	True if both conditions are True (the AND operator)
Condition1 || *condition2*	True if either condition is True (the OR operator)

An alternate form is to compare a string against a regular expression. If *string2* in any of the operations above is expressed as */string2/*, a regular expression comparison is made against string1:

```
<!-if expr=string1=/string2/ -->
```

Generally, you will be looking only for the existence of a match (using the = operator) when working with regular expressions:

```
<!-if expr=$DOCUMENT_URI=/^cgi-bin/ -->
```

However, you can also test for an expression that is not matched by negating the results of the match using the != operator:

```
<!-if expr=$DOCUMENT_URI!=/^cgi-bin/ -->
```

Use parentheses for clarity when expressing SSI tags with several comparisons:

```
<!--#if expr="($a = test1) && ($b = test2)" -->
```

The following example evaluates to True if the request URI begins with either /cgi-bin/ or /cgi-vep/, False otherwise:

```
<!--#if expr="($DOCUMENT_URI=/^\/cgi-bin/) || ($DOCUMENT_URI=/^\/cgi-vep/)" -->
```

Listing 7.7 illustrates a very practical use of the if/else tag in SSI. If the IP address of the connecting host, which is stored in the environment variable REMOTE_ADDR, matches the regular expression in the first if expr expression, it indicates that the client is on the Apache server's subnet, and the user is presented with some information that external users will *never* see. If the REMOTE_ADDR does not match in this expression, the user is not on the local subnet, and the text in the else clause is sent to the requester. This contains a line to simply tell remote users that some aspects of the page are invisible to them. In real life, you'd probably keep them from knowing even that, instead presenting them with a document intended for their eyes. Figure 7.6 shows how the results of Listing 7.7 are displayed in a browser.

Listing 7.7   An SSI Flow-Control Test Document

```
<HEAD>
<TITLE>SSI File Include Test Page</TITLE>
</HEAD>
<BODY>
<center>
<H1>SSI File Include Test Page</H1>
<!--#if expr="$REMOTE_ADDR = /^192.168.1./" -->
```

Advanced
Configuration Options

PART 3

```
        <H3>You connected from the local network!</H3>
<!--#else -->
        <H3>Remote users cannot see some aspects of this page!</H3>
<!--#endif -->
<center>
<FORM METHOD = "POST" ACTION = "mailto:caulds@hiwaay.net">
<INPUT TYPE = "SUBMIT" VALUE="Click here to send me e-mail"></FORM>
</center>
<HR>
<ADDRESS>
<center>
<A HREF="mailto:caulds@hiwaay.net">Charles Aulds - caulds@hiwaay.net</A>
<BR>
</ADDRESS>
</center>
</BODY>
</HTML>
```

Figure 7.6   The SSI Flow-Control test document displayed in a browser

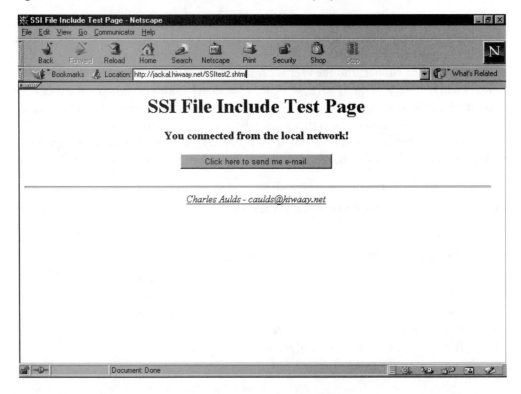

The XBitHack Directive

Although mod_include extends the Apache server to enable the parsing of a number of different tags, the module adds only one directive to Apache, and it's kind of a strange one. The XBitHack directive is very aptly named. It is a genuine hack, an alternative to the "proper" way of doing things. It uses the access permission attributes of a file in a completely different way than they are intended. For that reason, I don't actually recommend its use, but if you can identify a need, it works as advertised.

XBitHack allows the system administrator to identify ordinary HTML documents as candidates for server-side parsing. Whenever the XBitHack directive is applied to a directory from httpd.conf or from an .htaccess file, all documents in that directory that are identifiable as MIME-type text/html can be handled by mod_include, based on the Linux permissions set for the files.

The XBitHack directive can take three values; the behavior of each is described below:

XBitHack Off   Disables all treatment of text/html files as server-parsed documents.

XBitHack On   Tests every text/html document within the scope of the directive to see if it should be handled as server-parsed by mod_include. If the user-execute bit is set, the document is parsed as a SSI document. If an XBitHack On directive applied to the directory in the following example, index.html would not be identified as server-parsed until the chmod statement was issued to set the execute bit for the user:

```
# ls -al index.html
-rw-r--r--   1 www       www            3844 Jan 28 14:58 index.html
# chmod u+x index.html
# ls -al index.html
-rwxr--r--   1 www       www            3844 Jan 28 14:58 index.html
```

XBitHack Full   Works just like XBitHack On except that, in addition to testing the user-execute bit, it also tests to see if the group-execute bit is set. If it is, then the Last-Modified date set in the response header is the last modified time of the file. If the group-execute bit is not set, no Last-Modified header is sent to the requester. This XBitHack feature is used when you want proxies to cache server-parsed documents; normally, you would *not* want to do this if the document contains data (from a CGI include, for example) that changes upon every invocation. Here's an example of setting the group-execute bit:

```
# ls -al index.html
-rw-r--r--   1 www       www            3916 Mar 10 08:25 index.html
# chmod g+x index.html
# ls -al index.html
-rw-r-xr--   1 www       www            3916 Mar 10 08:25 index.html
```

HotWired's Extended SSI (XSSI)

HotWired makes available an extended version of the Apache SSL module (`mod_include`) that contains some really nifty, easy-to-use features. Unlike most third-party Apache modules, HotWired's module replaces the standard Apache `mod_include`, and it supports all the standard SSI functions. It also does the following:

- Adds a new directive, `parse_form`, which parses the input GET string from the client browser and sets variables from that string for use by SSI.

- Adds a new directive, `random`, which generates a random number and assigns it to a variable for use by SSI.

- Extends the SSI `echo` directive to make it easier to include HTML escape characters in SSI `echo` statements, and also to provide a default value to `echo` for variables that have not been set.

NOTE   The XBitHack directive, discussed in the last section, is fully implemented in the HotWired Extended XSSI. Do *not*, however, expect it to be available when using any other SSI implementation (like Apache JSSI).

Installing HotWired's Extensions

The simplicity of the HotWired SSI Extensions is part of its attraction—it consists of a single C file that compiles into a module that replaces the standard `mod_include` packaged with Apache. Download the extensions from HotWired's WebMonkey site at:

```
http://www.hotwired.com/webmonkey/99/10/index0a.html
```

A disclaimer on HotWired's Web site states that the module has not been thoroughly tested when compiled as a DSO module, but that is the way I compiled and tested it, and I had no problems. I was unable to use HotWired's instructions for compiling the module from within the Apache source directory, disabling the standard `mod_include` and enabling the HotWired version. Instead, I recommend compiling the module outside the Apache source directory, as a DSO, and replacing the `mod_include.so` that came with Apache. I used the following command line to compile the module, install it into Apache's `libexec`, and add the `LoadModule` and `AddModule` lines to Apache's `httpd.conf`. The `LoadModule` and `AddModule` lines will already exist if you are using the standard Apache `mod_include`; they will be created, otherwise:

```
/usr/local/apache/bin/apxs -i -a mod_include.so
```

Another way to do this is simply to replace the standard Apache `mod_include.c` found in the `src/modules/standard` directory in the Apache source tree with the HotWired version and recompile Apache. I actually used both methods. I replaced the standard `mod_ include.c` in Apache, but rather than recompiling the entire server, I chose to make `mod_ include.so` with `apxs` and simply restarted the server. The next time I compile Apache, I'll be compiling the HotWired version of `mod_include`.

The HotWired `parse_form` Tag

The `parse_form` tag is used to extract information from the `QUERY_STRING` variable and place it into named variables for use by XSSI. The data items in variable/value pairs usually originate as entries in a Web form and arrive at the server (using the HTTP GET Method) appended to the URL, as shown in the `Location:` field of Figure 7.7. Generally, such a URL is generated from a Web form designed to use the GET method. The HTML to generate such a form might include lines like the following (note that this is just part of a complete HTML document):

```
<input type="text" name="var1" id="var1" value="Test variable">, etc...


<FORM METHOD="GET"
    ACTION="http://jackal.hiwaay.net/SSItest5.shtml">
    <LABEL>Enter var1: </LABEL>
    <INPUT type="text" name="var1" id="var1"><BR>
    <LABEL>Enter var2: </LABEL>
    <INPUT type="text" name="var2" id="var2"><BR>
    <INPUT TYPE="submit" VALUE="Submit">
</FORM>
```

Listing 7.8 illustrates how the `parse_form` tag is used to create two SSI variables (`form_ var1` and `form_var2`) from information entered by a user in a Web form, and made available to the SSI page through the variable `QUERY_STRING`. The purpose of the `parse_form` tag is to easily convert user input into variables that can be used by other SSI code. These variables might be used, for example, in an `<include virtual>` SSI tag to specify an external document for inclusion in the HTML sent to the browser:

Listing 7.8   A Test Document for the HotWired `parse_form` Tag

```
<!--#parse_form -->
<HTML>
<HEAD>
<TITLE>HotWired's XSSI Test Page</TITLE>
</HEAD>
<BODY>
<center>
```

```
<H1>HotWired's XSSI Test Page</H1>
<H3>Testing parse_form</H3>
</center>
<p>form_var1: <!--#echo var="form_var1" escape="html" -->
<p>form_var2: <!--#echo var="form_var2" escape="html" -->
<!--#include file="footer.html"-->
</BODY>
</HTML>
```

Figure 7.7 The HotWired parse_form test page displayed in a browser

---

NOTE In order for the parse_form tag to be enabled, it is necessary to add
–DUSE_PARSE_FORM to CFLAGS before compiling Apache. This can be done by setting the CFLAGS environment variable or by modifying CFLAGS (or EXTRA_CFLAGS)
in the Apache configuration file.

The HotWired Extended echo Tag

The HotWired XSSI extension adds two attributes to the standard SSI echo tag. The first is a default string, which is printed whenever the echo tag is used with a variable that has not been set. The second attribute is escape, which can currently take only one value, html. The escape attribute performs the following substitutions:

&lt for the character < ("less than")

&gt for the character > ("greater than")

&amp for the character & (ampersand)

&quot for the character " (quotation)

This allows variables containing those HTML characters to be displayed in a Web browser. Without the escape attribute, these characters cannot be displayed because they have special significance in the HTML syntax.

The example in Listing 7.9 illustrates the use of both the default and escape attributes to HotWired's XSSI echo tag. Note that the first time we echo FOO, the variable has not been set, and the default attribute is used by echo. Then, using SSI's set var= tag, we set the value to <p>. The second time it is echoed, the value is interpreted by the browser as a page tag. The third time we echo the value of FOO, using escape=html, the <> characters are replaced with &lt and &gt before value of FOO is sent to the browser. Figure 7.8 shows the result of HotWired XSSI parsing the echo test document.

Listing 7.9   A Test Document for the HotWired echo Tag

```
<HTML>
<HEAD>
<TITLE>HotWired's XSSI Test Page</TITLE>
</HEAD>
<BODY>
<center>
<H1>HotWired's XSSI Test Page</H1>
</center>
<p>First: <!--#echo var="FOO" default="<b>Not Set</b>" -->
<!--#set var="FOO" value="<p>" -->
<p>Second: <!--#echo var="FOO" -->
<p>Third: <!--#echo var="FOO" escape="html" -->
<!--#include file="footer.html"-->
</BODY>
</HTML>
```

Figure 7.8 The HotWired echo test page displayed in a browser

The HotWired random Tag

The random tag is used to set a variable to a randomly generated integer, which can be bounded. The XSSI script in Listing 7.10 shows one way this can be used. The random tag is used in the example to set value of rnd to a random value between 1 and 10. The value of rnd is then used to select one of ten different footers to include at the bottom of the XSSI-parsed file. Figure 7.9 shows how the results are displayed in a Web browser. Not terribly impressive, I guess, but handy if you can think of a really neat way to use the capability. The classic example is that of randomly generated banner advertisements. You could also use this to display a random help tip.

Listing 7.10 A Test Document for the HotWired random Tag

```
<HTML>
<HEAD>
<TITLE>HotWired's XSSI Test Page</TITLE>
</HEAD>
<BODY>
<center>
```

```
<H1>HotWired's XSSI Test Page</H1>
</center>
<!--#random var="rnd" low="1" high="10" -->
<center>
rnd = <!--#echo var="rnd" -->
<!--#include file="footer$rnd.html" -->
</BODY>
</HTML>
```

Figure 7.9   The HotWired random tag test page displayed in a browser

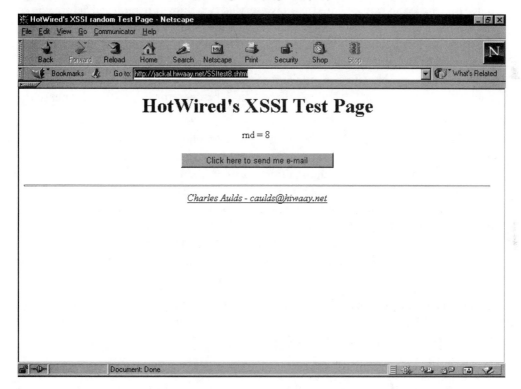

NOTE   To enable the random tag, you need to add –DUSE_RANDOM_SSI to CFLAGS before compiling Apache. This can be done by setting the CFLAGS environment variable or by modifying CFLAGS (or EXTRA_CFLAGS) in the Apache configuration file.

Java Server-Side Includes (JSSI)

Chapter 9 covers two of the most important tools for using Java with Apache: JServ and Java Server Pages (JSP). In addition, the Java Apache Project (`http://java.apache.org`) makes available an Apache add-on called Apache Java Server-Side Includes (JSSI). JSSI permits an SSI page to execute Java servlet code and then place the output of the server in the page sent to the requester. Apache JSSI is fairly simple and straightforward to install, since it is implemented as a single Java servlet class (based on the 2.0 JavaSoft Servlet API) that is used to parse an HTML file interpreting any JSSI (or standard SSI) tags it finds there.

Since Apache JSSI is implemented as a Java servlet, two things are required before you can use it. First, you must have a fully functioning Java runtime environment, which requires the installation of a Java Development Kit or JDK. You must also install the Java Servlet Development Kit (JSDK), which supports the 2.0 Servlet API. Chapter 9 discusses in detail how you set these up to run Java servlets under Apache. If you need either of these components, read Chapter 9 and install them both before returning to this chapter to read about JSSI.

Once installed, Apache JSSI is used as an Apache handler to process files that are identified in the Apache configuration as Apache JSSI files. By default, Apache JSSI files are given the `.jhtml` extension, although this is arbitrary and can be changed. Unlike most Apache handlers, JSSI does not have a special module and does not add any configuration directives. Instead, it looks for information to process within the body of the `.jhtml` file, particularly the <SERVLET> tag. This tag indicates that the module should process the enclosed strings as Java servlets and replace the <SERVLET> tag with their output. All the action takes place on the server; this makes JSSI simpler than using the Java <APPLET> tag, which specifies a Java applet to run within the client browser.

Another nice feature of Apache JSSI is that it supports most traditional SSI elements, so you don't have to give up SSI functionality by letting Apache JSSI parse your server-side includes. Apache JSSI supports the following SSI directives:

- config
- echo
- fsize
- flastmod
- include

You will not, however, be able to use the HotWired XSSI extensions (as discussed immediately above) or XBitHack with Apache JSSI. Those are available only in `.shtml` files processed with the HotWired `mod_include` module.

WARNING   Unlike Apache mod_include, Apache JSSI does not implement the IncludesNOEXEC feature, nor does it support an exec tag. The only way to run external programs from Apache JSSI is through the <SERVLET> tag.

Although JSSI is a nice add-on if you are already running Java servlets, it does not justify the complexity involved in installing servlet capability in Apache. SSI is simply not the best use of Java. Java Server Pages are the ticket, now and for the future. If you run JSP, then Apache JSSI is a simple installation and well worth the time spent to install it. If you don't already have servlet capability, look for a better reason than Apache JSSI to install it.

Installing Apache JSSI

Compared to the time needed to add Java servlet capability to an Apache server, the installation of Apache JSSI is surprisingly simple and straightforward.

1. Download the latest version of Apache JSSI from java.apache.org and unpack it in /usr/local/src directory:

   ```
   # pwd
   /usr/local
   # ls /home/caulds/ApacheJSSI*
   /home/caulds/ApacheJSSI-1_1_2_tar.gz
   # tar xvzf /home/caulds/ApacheJSSI-1_1_2_tar.gz
   ApacheJSSI-1.1.2/
   ApacheJSSI-1.1.2/CHANGES
   ApacheJSSI-1.1.2/docs/

   ... many deleted lines ...
   ```

2. Change to the src/java subdirectory under the newly created ApacheJSSI source directory and type **make** to create the ApacheJSSI.jar Java archive (*jar*) file:

   ```
   # cd ApacheJSSI-1.1.2/src/java
   # make

   ... many deleted lines ...

   # ls -al ApacheJSSI.jar*
   -rw-r--r--    1 root     root        70135 Mar  9 12:21 ApacheJSSI.jar
   -rw-r--r--    1 root     root        68859 Mar  9 12:01 ApacheJSSI.jar.ORIG
   ```

3. The newly created ApacheJSSI.jar file appears first, and the file that came with the Apache JSSI distribution is shown with the .ORIG extension appended. A .jar

file can reside anywhere on your system, as long as the Java servlet runner can locate it. I place mine in the lib subdirectory of my Java Servlet Development Kit (JSDK):

```
# cp ApacheJSSI.jar /usr/local/JSDK2.0/lib
```

Wherever you choose to place the `ApacheJSSI.jar` file, you will point to it, explicitly, from one of your Apache JServ configuration files. For now, just locate it in a place that makes sense to you.

> **NOTE** If you are unable to make the `ApacheJSSI.jar` file, don't worry; the Apache JSSI archive contains an `ApacheJSSI.jar` file that you can probably use with your Apache setup without running make. When I first ran make, the file I created was identical to the one provided with Apache JSSI. When I did it a second time, the file differed in size (it was about 2% larger) but worked perfectly. I think the difference is that I had changed JDK or JSDK versions. Keep in mind that you aren't compiling a system binary; you are compiling Java pseudocode, which should compile and run the same on different system architectures. The Java *Virtual Machine (VM)* interprets this pseudocode at runtime into machine-specific binary code, which does differ drastically between machines.

4. The next steps are small changes to the Apache JServ configuration files to permit Apache JServ to locate and run the Apache JSSI servlet. The first change is to the main Apache JServ configuration file, which is actually called from the main Apache `httpd.conf` by an `Include` line like this one taken from my system:

```
Include /usr/local/apache/conf/jserv/jserv.conf
```

5. In `jserv.conf`, ensure that the `ApJServAction` line for the Apache JSSI servlet is uncommented; this line works like `AddHandler` in `httpd.conf` to define a servlet as the proper handler for files with the `.jhtml` extension (again, that's an arbitrary choice of extension, but as good as any other). Note that a different servlet is specified to run JSP (`.jsp`) pages; the other `ApJServAction` lines in my configuration aren't used and are commented out:

```
# excerpted from: /usr/local/apache/conf/jserv/jserv.conf
# Executes a servlet passing filename with proper extension in
PATH_TRANSLATED

# property of servlet request.
# Syntax: ApJServAction [extension] [servlet-uri]
# Defaults: NONE
# Notes: This is used for external tools.
```

```
ApJServAction .jsp /servlets/org.gjt.jsp.JSPServlet
#ApJServAction .gsp /servlets/com.bitmechanic.gsp.GspServlet
ApJServAction .jhtml /servlets/org.apache.servlet.ssi.SSI
#ApJServAction .xml /servlets/org.apache.cocoon.Cocoon
```

6. Point to the Apache JSSI classes (the `ApacheJSSI.jar` file) in one of your Apache JServ *servlet zones*. You may have a number of different servlet zones, each probably corresponding to a different application, but you should always have a *root servlet zone* defined, which is the default zone, and defined by the file `zone.properties`. It is this file that I edited to add a class repository for Apache JSSI (note that a repository can be a directory like `/usr/local/apache/servlets` which contains individual class files, or it can point to an archive of classes in a `.jar` file):

```
# excerpted from: /usr/local/apache/conf/jserv/zone.properties:
# List of Repositories
######################
# The list of servlet repositories controlled by this servlet zone
# Syntax: repositories=[repository],[repository]...
# Default: NONE
# Note: The classes you want to be reloaded upon modification should be
# put here.
repositories=/usr/local/apache/servlets
repositories=/usr/local/JSDK2.0/lib/ApacheJSSI.jar
```

7. Apache JSSI only sets the following variables for use by SSI: DATE_GMT, DOCUMENT_NAME, and LAST_MODIFIED. To enable Apache JSSI to work with the entire set of standard SSI tags, it is necessary to pass the Apache JSSI servlet an initial argument.

8. The exact method of doing this varies between different implementations of the Java servlet engine. For Apache JServ, I added a single line to my `zone.properties` file, at the very end, in a section reserved for passing initialization arguments to Java servlets (the file contains simple syntax examples and instructions):

```
# Aliased Servlet Init Parameters
servlet.org.apache.servlet.ssi.SSI.initArgs=SSISiteRoot=/home/httpd/html
```

9. This line simply tells the servlet engine where to find the Java classes that implement Java Server-Side Includes.

You're now ready to install the following simple test application and crank her up.

Sample JSSI Application

My very minimal sample Apache JSSI application consists of two parts, unlike the plain SSI pages earlier this chapter. The first (Listing 7.11) is the Apache JSSI page (which must be named with a .jhtml extension.) The second part (Listing 7.12) is the Java servlet that the JSSI page will call, and which will run inside the Java servlet engine:

Listing 7.11   A JSSI Test Document

```
<HTML>
<HEAD>
<TITLE>Java Server-Side Include (JSSI) Test Page</TITLE>
</HEAD>
<BODY>
<center>
<H1>Java Server-Side Include (JSSI) Test Page</H1>
</center>
<h3>Traditional SSI Includes:</h3>
<ul><b>
DATE_LOCAL:  <!--#echo var="DATE_LOCAL"--> <br>
DATE_GMT:  <!--#echo var="DATE_GMT"--> <br>
DOCUMENT_NAME:  <!--#echo var="DOCUMENT_NAME"--> <br>
DOCUMENT_URI:  <!--#echo var="DOCUMENT_URI"--> <br>
LAST_MODIFIED:  <!--#echo var="LAST_MODIFIED"--> <br>
</b>
<SERVLET CODE="HelloWorld.class">
Your Web server has not been configured to support servlet tags!
</SERVLET>
<!--#include file="footer.html" -->
```

Note that I included some regular SSI so that you can see that the SSI tags work with Apache JSSI. Three of the SSI variables used are available; two are simply not set by Apache JSSI. The include tag works pretty much as you would expect. The real tag of interest is <SERVLET>, which runs the servlet shown in Listing 7.12, displaying the output formatted by the servlet to the client browser. Figure 7.10 shows how the output will look in the user's browser.

Listing 7.12   A Java Servlet Called from a JSSI Document

```java
import java.io.*;
import javax.servlet.*;
import javax.servlet.http.*;

/**
 * This is a simple example of an HTTP Servlet.  It responds to
 * the GET and HEAD methods of the HTTP protocol.
 */
public class HelloWorld extends HttpServlet
{
  /**
   * Handle the GET and HEAD methods by building a simple web
   * page. HEAD is just like GET, except that the server returns
   * only the headers (including content length) not the body we
   * write.
   */
  public void doGet (HttpServletRequest request,
                     HttpServletResponse response)
    throws ServletException, IOException
    {
        PrintWriter out;
        String title = "Example JSSI Servlet";

        // set content type and other response header fields first
        response.setContentType("text/html");

        // then write the data of the response
        out = response.getWriter();

        out.println(title);
        out.println("<H1>" + title + "</H1>");
        out.println("<H2> Congratulations, if you are reading this, <br>"
            + "Java Server-Side Include (JSSI) 1.1.2 is working!<br>");
    out.close();
    }
}
```

Figure 7.10   The result of the Apache JSSI example displayed in a browser

What's going on in this example? When you request a file with the .jhtml extension, the Apache JServ module (mod_jserv.so) loads and runs the proper servlet to handle the file. We could define any servlet to handle .jhtml files, but we defined org.apache.servlet .ssi.SSI, which resides in a Java archive named ApacheJSSI.jar. The servlet is loaded and run in a Java virtual machine created by Apache JServ, and it runs the servlet classes, passing them the .jhtml file. The file is parsed, the standard SSI tags resolved, and any Java classes defined in <SERVLET> tags are run and the output pasted back into the .jhtml file, which is sent on to the requesting browser after being parsed. Notice the doGet method, which is automatically called whenever the servlet is invoked by an HTTP request using the GET method. This is provided, in accordance with the specification for Java servlets, by the HttpServlet class from which our HelloWorld class is derived (illustrating class inheritance).

For the little it accomplishes, that's a pretty expensive piece of code. Apache JSSI is far more overhead than I required for my trivial application. Nevertheless, you can see that a very powerful servlet could be used here, perhaps with a remote database query or something equally complex.

In Sum

Server-Side Includes or SSI (often called server-parsed HTML) provides one of the simplest ways to produce dynamic Web pages without true programming. SSI is implemented through special SSI tags, but otherwise the instructions consist of standard HTML text. SSI is usually used to provide features like displaying the current time, the date and time of the last file modification, or including standard text from other documents. Although SSI is rarely an alternative to a real programming language, it can be used for tasks like querying or updating a database, sending an e-mail message, or using conditional statements to determine whether certain actions are taken or whether or not specific text is displayed.

In the next chapter, we begin a journey through the most popular programming techniques used by Web site designers today. As an Apache administrator, you require a working familiarity with each, and in particular, knowledge of how they interface with Apache. The next two chapters will tell you what you need to know to install and use the programming methodologies that power the majority of the dynamic Web sites on the Internet.

8

Scripting/Programming with CGI and Perl

In the early days of the Web, programming usually meant enhancing a Web site by adding simple user interactivity, or providing access to some basic services on the server side. Essentially, programming for the Web in those days meant interpreting input from the user and generating specific content for that user dynamically ("on-the-fly"). A simple Web program might take user input and use it to control a search engine or a database query.

Web programming has evolved from those very simple programs that added user interactivity and automation to Web pages. Today, Web-based applications are often full-fledged production systems, complete electronic storefronts, or front ends to complex, powerful databases. Such applications are often implemented using the three-tier business computing model, where the application or Web server usually makes up the middle tier, and the Web browser is often used as the bottom tier or user interface. The top tier of this model usually consists of large database server systems and has no direct interaction with the end user (or bottom tier).

Changes in the requirements for Web programming are a direct result of the changing role of the Internet Web server. The Web is no longer simply a delivery medium for static Web pages. Chances are, if you are writing programs for the Web today, they are likely to be an integral part of someone's Internet business strategy. Your ability to program an application, even a very simple application, is probably critical to the success of your Web project.

Although larger Web sites generally have both a Webmaster and a content provider, often with sharply divided responsibilities, at many sites the two roles have been increasingly merged. I don't know any sharp Apache administrator who isn't keenly interested in programming techniques for the Web. Like the topic of security (discussed in Chapters 14 and 15 of this book), programming is one of those formerly peripheral topics that have become an integral part of the Apache administrator's required knowledge base.

This is the first of two chapters on scripting/programming for the Apache server. There are a number of good programming methodologies for the Web; no single language is clearly superior to all the rest, and each has its adherents and, in many cases, religious zealots. There will always be someone who will try to tell you that there's only one way to program a Web-based application, and if you aren't using that technology, you're behind the times. Don't believe it. Your choice of programming language or methodology shouldn't be based on what is most popular at the moment, but rather should fit your particular need, as well as the skills you already possess. When selecting a programming methodology, you must look at what your competencies are, and what you enjoy most; all the programming tools discussed for Web programming in this chapter and the next are quite adequate for developing commercial-quality Web applications.

In this chapter we'll cover what is still the most widespread approach—using the Common Gateway Interface (CGI) or its newer variant, FastCGI, and the Perl scripting language. Chapter 9 will look at some of the newer tools and techniques available, including PHP, Apache JServ, ASP, JSP, and Resin. Each of these tools can be used to successfully create real-world Web-based applications. They can all be used on the same server, and a single Web application might make use of more than one tool.

The goal of these chapters is not to teach you "how to program" in the languages covered; entire books have been written on those topics. The focus instead is on how the tool is used with Apache. A simple programming example for each tool will serve to show the basics of how it is used. The examples I provide are simple, but not trivial. Each demonstrates how to extract data from a database using a simple Structured Query Language (SQL) query. In essence, each is a full three-tier application, providing a simple user-input form along with a mid-tier server program that takes the user input and uses it to query the third tier, a database engine, that might be on a completely separate server.

For additional information on all of the programming methodologies mentioned in this chapter and the next one, be sure to see the "Programming Resources" section of Appendix B. The best of these provide numerous examples of working code. Since I believe studying program examples is undoubtedly the best way to learn programming techniques, I have provided working examples in each topic discussed in the next two chapters.

The Common Gateway Interface (CGI)

The Common Gateway Interface (CGI) is a very simple mechanism that permits a Web server to invoke any program, capture the output of that program, wrap it in the most basic HTTP headers, and return it to the Web browser. That's only a slight oversimplification; in fact, CGI *is* very simple. And since CGI is provided through one of the standard Apache modules (`mod_cgi`), it is available on every Apache server. I think of CGI as a given, a feature I can count on finding on any Web server. Among the Apache programming interfaces, it's the equivalent of the `vi` text editor—ubiquitous and capable enough for the most essential applications.

CGI was first implemented in the NCSA `httpd` Web server and quickly adopted as the de facto programming interface for the Web. Today every major Web server supports CGI. The current working specification for CGI (version 1.1) dates back to 1995. Although the 1.1 specification is still a draft IETF standard, there is already a 1.2 version of the CGI specification in the works. Progress on version 1.2 has been slow, and there doesn't appear to be a big demand for any of the changes under consideration for the new version. For most purposes, CGI can be considered a fairly static mechanism. Learning CGI means that you won't soon have to learn a new programming methodology or see your Web-based application suddenly become obsolete.

Any program that can be executed from the command line on the server can be used with CGI. This includes compiled programs written in C or C++, or even COBOL or Fortran. Scripting languages like Perl, Tcl, or shell scripting languages are the most popular ways to write CGI programs. Scripts are usually much quicker to write than compiled programs. Since the client browser provides the user interface for Web applications, the scripts contain only the basic code required for data I/O and are smaller and easier to maintain. Minor code changes to scripts don't require compilation and linking, which speeds up and simplifies code design, testing, and maintenance.

As a general-purpose programming interface, CGI offers some advantages over proprietary Web programming interfaces like Netscape's NSAPI, Microsoft's ISAPI, and even the Apache programming interface. Although these interfaces offer the programmer substantially better performance and easier access to the inner workings of the Web server, CGI is far more widely used for several reasons. The first is that CGI is independent of both server architecture and programming language, allowing the programmer great freedom to choose the language best suited for a particular programming task. I regularly use a combination of C, Tcl, Perl, and even shell scripts for CGI programming tasks.

CGI also offers complete process isolation. A CGI program runs in its own process address space, independently of the Web server, and it communicates only input and output with the server. Running CGI programs outside the program space of Apache not only protects the server from errant CGI processes (even the most serious errors in a CGI program cannot affect the Web server), it also provides protection against deliberate attempts to compromise the security or stability of the server.

Last, but certainly not least, CGI offers the tremendous advantage of being a simple interface to learn and use. For most programming tasks, CGI offers more than enough functionality and adequate performance, without imposing heavy demands on the programmer.

Scripting languages are so popular for CGI Web programming tasks that many texts simply refer to CGI programs as *CGI scripts*. In fact, the Perl language owes much of its popularity to its early adoption by Web site administrators for CGI applications. In the past few years it has seen wide acceptance as a general-purpose scripting language, especially where cross-platform compatibility is a strong concern. Many programmers consider Perl to be the de facto standard for writing CGI scripts. Actually, nearly any language can be used to write CGI programs, including compiled languages like C. But Perl is the most popular, and it's the one I've chosen to best illustrate the use of CGI. Just remember that CGI is not limited to scripting languages, and Perl is not limited to Web programming.

The CGI examples provided in this section are all written in scripting languages, but there is no reason that a compiled language like C could be used in exactly the same way.

How CGI Works

Programs that run under CGI require no special hooks into the Web server and use no CGI-specific API calls. Communication between Apache and the CGI program does not use special protocols. It is kept as simple and as generic as possible, using two mechanisms that all programs can access: the process *environment*, and the standard input and output pipes.

The System Environment

In Linux, when a program is invoked, it is passed a set of data called the process *environment*. This is a list of *name=value* pairs. Typically, one process that is invoked by another inherits a copy of that process's environment (it is said to *inherit* the environment of its *parent* process). This provides one way for a process to pass data to a process it creates. By tailoring its own environment before starting a process, the parent process can control the environment of the process it invokes.

When Apache receives a request for a resource that it recognizes as a CGI script or program, it spawns the process by making calls to the Linux operating system. The process is completely independent of Apache, with one important exception: Its standard output pipe remains connected to the Apache server process, so that Apache receives all output from the program that is directed to standard output (or *stdout*). If the CGI program is a Linux shell script, like the example below, the echo statement is used to send text to stdout. (Later in this chapter, in the section "A Script to Return the Environment," we'll add a little formatting to this script to generate the output shown in Figure 8.1.)

```
#!/bin/sh
echo "Content-type: text/plain"
echo
echo "Environment variables defined:"
echo
env
```

Apache does not communicate directly with the CGI process it spawns. Instead, as the parent of the process, it has some degree of control over the environment in which the process runs. In order to pass data to the process it creates, Apache places its data in environment variables that can be read by the process. In our simple CGI process, the shell command env reads the environment and reports it to its standard output file handle (stdout). Apache receives this output through the pipe it maintains to the script's stdout handle and sends it to the requesting user.

To test this script, create a new file in a directory defined by a ScriptAlias directive in httpd.conf, and place in the file the statements shown above. (Chapter 4 shows how to use ScriptAlias.) You must also ensure that the file has an extension associated in httpd.conf with an Apache handler as described in the next section. In the default httpd.conf file provided with the Apache distribution, you will find the following line:

```
#AddHandler cgi-script .cgi
```

Removing the leading # character that marks this line as a comment causes Apache to treat all files with a name ending in the .cgi extension as CGI scripts, and they will be executed using the CGI mechanism. Under Linux, it is not necessary to identify each type of script by a different extension, and I use the .cgi extension to identify all CGI scripts on my systems, without regard to the actual content of the file. The first line of all scripts should contain the full pathname of the script processor, preceded by the hash-bang (#!) characters, as in our example:

```
#!/bin/sh
```

Identifying CGI Resources

The important thing to remember is that the CGI resource (whether identified by its file-name or extension, or its location in Apache's document space) must be associated with a *handler* provided by the mod_cgi module if it is to be executed as a CGI script. There are several ways that resources can be identified to Apache as candidates for treatment as CGI files. Each method is discussed separately in these sections.

The Concept of the "Handler"

Apache uses the concept of a *handler* to determine how it should process scripts and other dynamic resources before handing the results to the requester. Each Apache handler is usually associated with a particular module that performs the handler's work. By defining a handler to process a particular resource or collection of resources, we actually specify a module that receives and processes the resource before it is passed on to the requester.

The default Apache distribution comes with a number of built-in handlers, including one for CGI programs. The CGI handler is cgi-script, which is provided by the standard module, mod_cgi. Configuring a script or program to be treated as a CGI resource is as simple as defining cgi-script as its handler. In the next sections, I'll show four ways to do this.

> **NOTE**   Every resource served by Apache that is not associated with a specific handler is processed by a handler named (not surprisingly) *default-handler*, provided by the core module.

Defining Directories

The most common way to define resources for execution as CGI programs is to designate one or more directories as containers for CGI programs. Security is enhanced when CGI programs reside in a limited number of specified CGI directories. Access to these directories should be strictly controlled, and careful attention paid to the ownership and permissions of files that are stored there.

Two slightly different directives provide a means of identifying a directory as a container for CGI scripts: ScriptAlias (introduced in Chapter 4) and ScriptAliasMatch. Both directives work like a simple Alias directive to map a request to a directory that may not exist under DocumentRoot, and they designate a directory as a container for CGI scripts. ScriptAlias is simpler, so we'll look at it first.

The following line, found in the standard Apache distribution, defines a directory to contain CGI scripts:

```
ScriptAlias /cgi-bin/ "/usr/local/apache/cgi-bin/"
```

When a request comes in with a URL like `http://jackal.hiwaay.net/cgi-bin/example.cgi`, Apache looks for a file named `example.cgi` in the `/usr/local/apache/cgi-bin` directory and (if it finds the file) executes the file as a CGI script. In the sample request URL, `cgi-bin` appears to be a subdirectory of `DocumentRoot`; however, the directory's actual name and location are arbitrary and it could be anywhere on the file system.

Pay very close attention to the permission settings for directories identified as containers for CGI scripts. Apache itself does not apply any kind of security checking to directories identified using `ScriptAlias`. It is up to the Apache administrator to ensure that only designated users can write to or execute files in those directories. If users need to be able to maintain their own Apache-executable scripts but not those of other users, consider using multiple `ScriptAlias` directives to identify several CGI directories and grant separate access permissions to different Linux groups. Also make sure that the account under which Apache runs has execute permission for the files in each directory. Always remember that the only security provided for CGI scripts is that of the Linux operating system, and Apache does not concern itself with protecting those resources.

Finally, make sure that the `user` execute bit is set (avoid setting the `group` or `other` execute bits). On all Apache servers that I've administered, I've created a `www` group account that includes the user accounts of all the members of the Web team. A directory listing of one of my CGI directories is shown below. You can see that the CGI scripts are all owned by the `nobody` user (that is, the Apache `httpd` process running as `nobody`), although members of the `www` group have full read-write privileges, and all other users are strictly disallowed.

```
# ls -al
total 31
drwxr-x---  2 nobody   www     1024 Apr 20 16:39 .
drwxr-x---  7 www      www     1024 Mar 25 13:20 ..
-rwxrw----  1 nobody   www      743 Feb 25 15:10 CGIForm.cgi
-rwxrw----  1 nobody   www      685 Feb 25 16:40 CGIForm2.cgi
-rwxrw----  1 nobody   www     2308 Feb  9 16:20 CGITest1.cgi
-rwxrw----  1 nobody   www      738 Feb 29 16:04 JavaForm.cgi
-rwxrw----  1 nobody   www      987 Feb  9 11:34 MySQLTest1.cgi
-rwxrw----  1 nobody   www      987 Feb  9 17:06 MySQLTest2.cgi
-rwxrw----  1 nobody   www      736 Mar  1 15:06 PHPForm.cgi
-rwxrw----  1 nobody   www    15100 Feb  9 09:11 cgi-lib.pl
-rwxrw----  1 nobody   www      349 Feb  9 11:24 environ.cgi
-rwxrw----  1 nobody   www      443 Feb 26 13:57 environ.fcgi
```

Advanced
Configuration Options

PART 3

```
-rwxrw----   1 nobody   www    762 Jan 27 11:43 simplesend.cgi
-rwxrw----   1 nobody   www    844 Feb 10 14:28 zipcodes.cgi
-rwxrw----   1 nobody   www   1051 Mar  1 10:05 zipcodes.fcgi
```

Defining Request URLs

The ScriptAliasMatch directive works just like ScriptAlias but uses a regular-expression match instead of a relative URL to match the request. In the following example, ScriptAliasMatch is used to produce the same behavior as the ScriptAlias example shown earlier:

```
ScriptAliasMatch ^/cgi-bin(.*) /usr/local/apache/cgi-bin$1
```

Here, any request URL that begins with /cgi-bin (followed by any other characters) will be mapped to the file system using the fixed path /usr/local/apache/cgi-bin with the content of the first back-reference to the regular expression match appended. The back-reference $1 is filled with the contents of that part of the request URL that matched the portion of the regular expression contained in parentheses. In this case, it should always match a slash followed by a valid filename containing the CGI script.

In general, use ScriptAliasMatch only when you find it impossible to phrase your URL match as a plain string comparison. I have never found it necessary to use ScriptAliasMatch, and I consider regular expressions unduly complicated for this purpose.

Defining Files

Although the simplest and most commonly used means of identifying files as CGI scripts is to place them into directories reserved for scripts, you can also identify individual files as CGI scripts. To do this, use the AddHandler directive, which maps an Apache handler to files that end with certain filename extensions. The following line, for example, defines the standard cgi-script handler to be used for processing all files ending with the extensions .pl or .cgi. Typically CGI scripts will be given the .cgi extension, but since CGI scripts can be written in more than one language, you may prefer to retain the .pl extension to more easily identify scripts written in Perl.

```
AddHandler cgi-script .cgi .pl
```

The AddHandler directive is valid only in a directory scope, either within a <Directory> container in http.conf or as part of an .htaccess file. It cannot be used as a global directive, and therefore can't be used to define all files with a certain extension as CGI scripts, regardless of where they occur.

Defining Methods

Although you are unlikely to ever need it, the `Script` directive, provided by the `mod_actions` module, invokes a CGI script whenever the requesting client uses a specified HTTP request method. The request method must be `GET`, `POST`, or `DELETE`.

The following `Script` directive calls a CGI script to handle all user `DELETE` requests:

```
Script DELETE /cgi-bin/deleteit.cgi
```

Defining Media Types

An alternative to writing a module to add a handler to Apache is to use the `Action` directive to define an external program (or script) as a resource handler. The `mod_actions` module provides one last method of defining CGI scripts. The `Action` directive provided by this module invokes a CGI script whenever a resource of a particular MIME type is requested. You could use this, for example, to invoke a CGI script to process all HTML pages served. This might be a script written to search for and replace offensive words in every Web page before passing it on to particularly sensitive viewers:

```
Action text/html   /home/httpd/cgi-bin/ParseMe.cgi
```

This example defines a particular CGI script as the handler for all HTML files. When any HTML file is requested, the file will first be passed through the script `ParseMe.cgi` which does a string search for dirty language and replaces it with more acceptable text.

Controlling the Environment

I've already mentioned that a CGI script receives data from Apache only through the system environment it inherits from the server when it is started. This section lists all the environment variables that are made available to a CGI script, although some of them will not always be set. In most cases, all the information the script needs is contained in this set of variables.

The following environment variables are not request-specific and are set for all requests:

SERVER_SOFTWARE	The name and version of the information server software answering the request (and running the gateway). Format: name/version.
SERVER_NAME	The server's hostname, DNS alias, or IP address, as it would appear in self-referencing URLs.
GATEWAY_INTERFACE	The revision of the CGI specification to which this server complies. Format: CGI/revision.

The following environment variables are specific to the request being fulfilled by the gateway program:

SERVER_PROTOCOL	The name and revision of the information protocol this request came in with. Format: protocol/revision, as HTTP/1.1.
SERVER_PORT	The port number to which the request was sent.
REQUEST_METHOD	The method with which the request was made. For HTTP, this is GET, HEAD, POST, etc.
PATH_INFO	The extra path information, as given by the client. In other words, scripts can be accessed by their virtual pathname, followed by extra information at the end of this path. The extra information is sent as PATH_INFO. The server should decode this information if it comes from a URL before it is passed to the CGI script.
PATH_TRANSLATED	The server provides a translated version of PATH_INFO, which takes the path and does any virtual-to-physical mapping to it.
SCRIPT_NAME	A virtual path to the script being executed, used for self-referencing URLs.
QUERY_STRING	The information that follows the question mark in the URL that referenced this script. This query information should not be decoded in any fashion. This variable should always be set when there is query information, regardless of command-line decoding.
REMOTE_HOST	The hostname making the request. If the server does not have this information, it should set REMOTE_ADDR and leave this unset.
REMOTE_ADDR	The IP address of the remote host making the request.
AUTH_TYPE	If the server supports user authentication, and the script is protected, this is the protocol-specific authentication method used to validate the user.
REMOTE_USER	Set only if the CGI script is subject to authentication. If the server supports user authentication, and the script is protected, this is the username they have authenticated as.
REMOTE_IDENT	If the HTTP server supports RFC 931 identification, then this variable will be set to the remote username retrieved from the server. Usage of this variable should be limited to logging only, and it should be set only if IdentityCheck is on.

CONTENT_TYPE	For queries with attached information, such as HTTP POST and PUT, this is the content type of the data.
CONTENT_LENGTH	The length of the content as given by the client.

The following variables are not defined by the CGI specification but are added by Apache for your convenience:

DOCUMENT_PATH_INFO	Any additional path information that was passed to a document.
DOCUMENT_ROOT	The pathname specified in Apache's DocumentRoot directive.
PATH	Corresponds to the shell environment variable PATH that was set when Apache was started.
REMOTE_PORT	The TCP port used on the client-side of the HTTP connection.
SERVER_ADDR	The IP address on which the server received the connection.
SCRIPT_FILENAME	The absolute path to the CGI script.
SERVER_ADMIN	The e-mail address provided in Apache's ServerAdmin directive.

The following variables are not defined by the CGI specification but are added by the mod_rewrite module, if it is used:

SCRIPT_URI	The absolute URL, including the protocol, hostname, port, and request.
SCRIPT_URL	The URL path to the script that was called.
REQUEST_URI	The URL path received from the client that led to the script that was called.

In addition to the headers shown above, header lines from the client request are also placed into the environment. These are named with the prefix HTTP_ followed by the header name. Any - characters in the header name are changed to _ characters. The server may choose to exclude any headers it has already processed and placed in the environment, such as Authorization or Content-type.

As a good example of how this works, consider the User-Agent request header. A CGI script will find the value of this header, extracted from the user request, in the environment variable HTTP_USER_AGENT.

Modifying the CGI Environment

Two modules, both compiled into the default configuration of the Apache server, provide a mechanism for the server to set variables in its environment that are inherited by CGI scripts. Setting environment variables is one way of passing arbitrary data to scripts. Later, I'll illustrate how an environment variable can be set to indicate to CGI scripts that the requester has been identified as a Web indexing robot. In practice, I've found this technique to be of limited use, mainly because most information available to the server about an incoming request is already available to the CGI script through existing environment variables. All HTTP headers in the request, for example, are passed to every CGI script.

You should read this section well enough to know what the directives do, and realize that they are easily available for your use through two standard Apache modules. When a real need arises that can be best fulfilled by one of these directives, you should have it in your toolkit.

The mod_env Module

The first of the modules that can be used to set environment variables to be passed to CGI scripts is mod_env, which contains three very simple directives:

The SetEnv Directive   Sets the value of an environment variable to be passed to CGI scripts, creating the variable if it doesn't already exist:

```
SetEnv PATH /usr/local/bin
```

This changes the value of the PATH variable passed to CGI scripts to include only a single path. All programs called by the CGI script must reside in this path (or be called by their full pathname).

The UnsetEnv Directive   Removes one or more environment variables from the environment before it is passed to CGI scripts:

```
UnsetEnv PATH
```

You might remove the PATH variable from the CGI environment to avoid the possibility of a malicious hacker planting a Trojan horse somewhere in the PATH where it would be executed instead of a legitimate program the script was trying to call. In general, however, the PATH that is passed to CGI scripts (inherited from the Apache httpd process that called the script) should contain only protected directories that nonprivileged users cannot write to. Many site administrators prefer to remove the PATH and reference all external scripts or utility programs by their full pathname. This is certainly safe, but it is much better to protect the directories that are included in the PATH variable passed to CGI scripts.

The PassEnv Directive   Specifies one or more environment variables from the server's environment to be passed to CGI scripts:

```
PassEnv USER
```

The PassEnv directive cannot be used to create a new ENV variable; it can only designate a variable in the httpd process's environment that is to be included in the environment that CGI scripts inherit. In this case, we are passing the value of USER, which indicates the Linux user ID under which the Apache httpd process is running (by default, this is UID -1, corresponding to user nobody). You might wish to have a script abort with an error message if this value is not what the script expects.

The mod_setenvif Module

This module provides four additional directives that set environment variables based on the results of conditions that are specified in the directives themselves: SetEnvIf, SetEnvIfNoCase, BrowserMatch, and BrowserMatchNoCase. For efficiency and clarity, however, it is usually better to rely on the CGI script itself to perform these conditional tests on request header information and perform the necessary actions. Replace the BrowserMatch directive, for example, with lines in your CGI program that test the User-Agent header of the request to identify the browser used to send the request, and take action accordingly.

The SetEnvIf Directive   Defines one or more environment variables based on an attribute that is associated only with the current request being processed. In most cases this attribute is one of the HTTP request headers (such as Remote_Addr, User_Agent, Referer). If not, the attribute is tested to see if it is the name of an environment variable set (by other SetEnv or SetEnvIf directives) earlier in the processing cycle for the current request (or in a wider scope, such as the server scope).

The syntax of the SetEnvIf directive is

```
SetEnvIf attribute regex envvar[=value] [...]
```

If the attribute matches *regex*, then *envvar* is set to a value defined in *=value* (if it exists) or set to 1 otherwise. If the attribute does not match *regex*, no action is performed.

The SetEnvIfNoCase Directive   The SetEnvIfNoCase directive performs its regular expression match without regard to the case of the characters but is otherwise identical to the SetEnvIf directive.

The BrowserMatch Directive   The BrowserMatch directive defines environment variables based solely on the User-Agent HTTP request header field. The first argument is a regular expression that is matched against this field. If there is a match, the rest of the arguments set environment variables and (optionally) define values to assign to them.

In this directive the variable names can be defined in three ways:

varname   Sets varname to 1.

!varname   Unsets or removes the variable if it exists.

varname=value   Sets the variable to the specified *value*.

If a User-Agent string matches more than one entry, they will be merged. Entries are processed in the order in which they appear, and later entries can override earlier ones. Example:

```
BrowserMatch ^Robot IS_ROBOT
```

CGI scripts can be written so that the presence of the environment variable IS_ROBOT, indicating that the script's output will go to a Web-indexing robot, can be tailored for indexing engines. Web indexing robots generally ignore and don't download embedded graphics or banner ads; therefore, the page returned to robots should be text-rich and packed with key words and phrases for the indexing engine.

> **NOTE**   Keep in mind that the BrowserMatch and BrowserMatchNoCase directives are special cases of the SetEnvIf and SetEnvIfNoCase directives, and they offer no additional functionality.

The BrowserMatchNoCase Directive   The BrowserMatchNoCase directive performs its regular-expression match regardless of the case of the characters but is otherwise identical to the BrowserMatch directive.

Securing Your CGI Scripts

CGI is often criticized as an insecure way to run programs on a Web server. Though security holes have been discovered in a number of commonly used CGI scripts, these are not the result of inherent security weaknesses in CGI. Problems in these ready-made scripts that can be downloaded from the Internet are usually the result of inattention to the potential for misuse, and most have been modified to improve their security. When using scripts that you didn't write, make sure you have the latest available version and that the author has tried to address security concerns with CGI.

CGI has been used for dynamic Web programming for a very long time (since 1993) and for that reason, most of the vulnerabilities inherent in the use of CGI have been widely publicized. These problems are not show-stoppers, as long as you pay proper attention to detail, particularly when preparing user input to be passed to another program via the shell—for example, passing the user's address to a mail agent like sendmail. The next sections of this chapter describe how to write a safe CGI script. Remember that Unix was once criticized as inherently more insecure than Microsoft Windows NT, largely because the Unix vulnerabilities had received so much exposure. Now that NT is more widely used in a server role, it is also suffering (perhaps unfairly) from the perception that its network security model is weak. When it comes to security, neither Linux nor NT has an indisputable advantage over the other; both platforms contain vulnerabilities that can be exploited by a malicious attacker. I believe that the Linux community is more open about security risks, though, and it acts more quickly to solve those that are discovered.

A properly written CGI script is no more insecure than any other Web program. A few simple guidelines can be very helpful in writing secure CGI scripts.

General Tips for Safe CGI Use

There are some general rules for safe CGI use. These rules do not absolutely guarantee secure CGI scripts, but adherence to them will protect you from the most serious, and most exploited, security vulnerabilities in CGI.

Never run your Apache server as `root`. The main Apache daemon, which does *not* respond to client connections, should be owned by `root`, but the child `httpd` processes it creates should be owned by a user account with limited privileges. This is covered in detail in Chapter 14.

Avoid passing user input of any kind to the shell for processing. Perl scripts pass data to the shell for processing in several ways. Perl spawns a new shell process to execute commands enclosed in backtick characters (`` ` ``) or included as arguments to `system()` or `exec()` function calls. This should be avoided. The following examples illustrate how user data might end up being interpreted by a shell process:

```
system("/usr/lib/sendmail -t $foo_address < $input_file");
```

or

```
$result=`/usr/lib/sendmail -t $foo_address < $input_file`;
```

In both of these lines, the shell is passed user input as an argument to the `sendmail` process. In both examples, the shell that processes the line can be tricked into executing part of `$input_file` as a separate process. If a malicious person were able to trick your system into running a line like this:

```
rm *
```

you could be in trouble. That is the main reason why the Apache processes that respond to user requests should never run as `root`. The code below shows a better way to pass data to a process. Note that, while the shell is used to run `sendmail`, the user input is passed to the `sendmail` process through a pipe, and the shell never sees the contents of the variable `$stuff`:

```
open(MAIL, "|/usr/lib/sendmail -t");
print MAIL "To: $recipient\n";
print MAIL $stuff;
```

PART 3

Advanced Configuration Options

In all CGI scripts, explicitly set the value of the PATH environment variables, rather than simply accepting the value inherited from the Apache process. I recommend setting this value to a single directory in which you place scripts or other executable programs you trust. I've already shown one way to do this using the SetEnv and UnSetEnv directives. You can also do the same thing from within CGI scripts if, for example, you don't have access privileges that allow you to modify the httpd.conf to modify the environment for all CGI scripts. The following line, when included in a Perl CGI script, clears all environment variables and resets the value of PATH to a "safe" directory:

```
delete @ENV{qw(IFS CDPATH ENV BASH_ENV)};
$ENV{"PATH"} = "/usr/local/websafe";
```

Alternatively, set PATH to a null value and call all external programs from your CGI script using their fully pathname. Basically, before doing a system call, clear the PATH by issuing a statement like the following:

```
$ENV{"PATH"} = "";
```

Always use Perl taint checking. See the following section.

If you are using the CGI support modules, always use the latest version. For example, for Perl, be sure to download current versions of either cgi-lib.pl or CGI.pm.

Using Perl Taint Checking

Perl has an optional mode of operation called *taint checking*. It is designed to prevent security problems with scripts that are run with special privileges on behalf of unknown or unprivileged users. This is exactly what happens when you use CGI; you are allowing outside users to run programs on your Web server, with the privilege level assigned to the Web server.

In Perl 5, you can enable taint checking by invoking Perl with the -T command-line argument. In a CGI script, the first line of the script should look like this (the -w argument enables the output of warning messages):

```
#!/usr/bin/perl -T -w
```

Taint checking derives its name from the fact that Perl considers any data that your script receives from an outside source, such as unmodified or unexamined user input from a Web form, to be *tainted*. Perl will not allow tainted variables to be used in any command that requires your script to fork a subshell. In other words, if taint checking is enabled and you attempt to fork a shell and pass it data that Perl regards as tainted, Perl aborts your script, reporting an error similar to the following:

```
Insecure dependency in `` while running with -T switch at temp.pl line 4,
<stdin> chunk 1.
```

A Web programmer often needs to use external programs, passing data that was received as input from an unknown user. One of the most common examples of this is using a mail transport agent (on Linux, this is most likely the ubiquitous `sendmail` utility) to e-mail data using input received from a client. The following line is the most commonly cited example of an absolute CGI scripting no-no:

```
system("/usr/sbin/sendmail -t $useraddr < $file_requested");
```

This takes a user-entered address and filename and mails the requested file to the user. What's wrong with this? By inserting a ; character into the `$file_requested`, you can easily trick the shell into believing it is being passed one command, separated from a second distinct command by this special shell *metacharacter*. The shell will often be quite happy to run the second command, which might try to do something nasty on behalf of your attacker.

If Perl is so careful not to use tainted input from the client, how is it possible to pass any input safely? There are basically two ways.

The first way is to avoid passing data directly to the shell. This works because most hackers are trying to exploit the shell itself and trick it into running unauthorized commands on their behalf. You can avoid the use of the shell by opening a system *pipe* to the program intended to accept the input. Replace the `system` command above with the following lines:

```
open(PIPE, "| /usr/sbin/sendmail -t");
print PIPE "To: $useraddr\n";
open (INFILE, "$file_requested);
while (<INFILE>) {
    print PIPE $_;
}
```

In this example, the shell never sees the user's input, which is piped directly to the `sendmail` executable. This means that attempts to exploit the shell are thwarted.

The second way is to "untaint" the data. To do this, use a regular expression pattern match to extract data from the tainted variable using () groups and back-references to create new variables. Perl will always consider new variables created from data extracted from a tainted variable in this manner to be untainted. Of course, Perl has no way of knowing whether the new variables have been examined carefully to ensure that they present no security risk when passed to the shell, but it gives the programmer the benefit of the doubt. Perl assumes that any programmer who has applied a regular expression match to tainted variables has also taken enough care to remove dangerous metacharacters from the variable. It is the programmer's responsibility to make sure this assumption is a correct one.

For the e-mail example above, you could untaint the $file_requested variable using the
following section of Perl code:

```
if ($file_requested =~ /(\w{1}[\w-\.]*)\@([\w-\.]+)/) {
  $file_requested = "$1\@$2";
} else {
    war ("DATA SENT BY $ENV{'REMOTE_ADDR'}IS NOT A VALID E-MAIL ADDRESS:
        $file-requested: $!");
    $file_requested = ""; # successful match did not occur
}
```

In this example, the variable is matched to ensure that it conforms to the proper format
for an e-mail address. The regular expression in the first line takes a little work to interpret. First, remember the regular expression rules that { } braces enclose a number specifying how many times the previous character must be repeated to make a match, that []
brackets enclose sets of alternative characters to be matched, and that \w refers to a word
character (defined as characters in the set [a-zA-Z0-9]). The first line can thus be read as
"if the content of $file_requested matches any string containing at least one word char-
acter, followed by any number of word characters, dashes, or periods, followed by the lit-
eral character @ followed by at least one pattern consisting of word characters, dashes or
periods, then perform the following block." The parentheses are used to enclose sections
of the regular expression that are later substituted into $n back-references, where n cor-
responds to the number of the parenthetical match. In the next line, the first set of parentheses (which matches that portion of the variable to the left of the @ character) is later
substituted into $1; the second set of parenthesEs (matching the portion of the variable to
the right of the @ character) is substituted for $2. The result then replaces the old value
of $file_requested, which, having been processed by a regular expression, is now
marked as untainted for future use by Perl.

The else clause of the if statement handles those situations where the regular expression
fails to match $file_requested, which means that the variable does *not* have the
expected format of an e-mail message. In this case, the script will print a warning, which
will be written to Apache's error log, along with the IP address of the remote host that
submitted the tainted data and a copy of that data. This information might be helpful in
locating a hacker trying to exploit a CGI weakness on the server. Immediately after logging the failure to match, the Perl script empties the $file_requested variable, essen-
tially discarding the user's input.

Avoid the temptation to untaint your Perl variables without doing any real checking. This
would have been easy to do in the previous example with two lines of code:

```
$file_requested =~ /(.*)/;
$file_requested = $1;
```

This fragment matches anything the user enters and simply overwrites the variable with its existing contents, but Perl assumes that a check for malicious input has been performed and untaints the variable. Absolutely nothing has actually been done, however. The programmer who does this should probably just turn off taint checking rather than resort to this kind of deception. It is likely to lull other programmers into a false assumption that since the script is taint-checked, it must be safe.

Debugging CGI Scripts

The mod_cgi module provides a special logging capability designed specifically to aid the debugging of CGI scripts. Rather than intermingle your CGI errors with Apache's error log, you can choose to capture the output and error messages generated by CGI scripts in a special file.

The ScriptLog directive identifies a file for logging CGI output. This directive serves the purpose of enabling CGI script logging and specifying a file (either by absolute path or a path relative to ServerRoot) for the log. Here's the directive for an absolute path:

```
ScriptLog /var/log/cgilog
```

And here's what it looks like for a path relative to ServerRoot:

```
ScriptLog logs/cgilog
```

The Apache httpd process owner should have write access to the log you specify. Note that the ScriptLog is valid only in a server context, in other words, you cannot place the directive within a container directive. In particular, you cannot specify different log files for different virtual hosts.

> **NOTE** Script logging is a debugging feature to be used when writing CGI scripts and is not meant to be activated on production servers. It is not optimized for speed or efficiency.

Since the output of *all* CGI scripts will be logged (not just error messages), your logfile will tend to grow rapidly. The ScriptLogLength directive is useful for limiting the size of the logfile. The maximum byte size set with this directive limits the size to which the log file will grow (the default value of ScriptLogLength is 1MB). The following line would set the maximum log file size to half a megabyte:

```
ScriptLogLength 524288
```

Remember that when the value of ScriptLogLength is reached, no further logging occurs; logging is simply disabled.

Advanced Configuration Options

PART 3

One other directive is used to control CGI logging. `ScriptLogBuffer` can be used to limit the size of entries written to the CGI log. This can be especially useful in limiting the growth of the log when the entire contents of PUT or POST requests (in which the client browser sends data to the server) are being logged. Since the contents of these two HTTP request methods are unlimited, they can quickly fill a log file. The default value of this directive is 1KB (1024 bytes). The following line will limit entries written to the CGI log to one-fourth that size:

```
ScriptLogBuffer 256
```

Using CGI.pm

Lincoln Stein's `CGI.pm` is a very large Perl module that uses Perl 5 objects to perform simple Web-related tasks, such as the HTML tagging required by many HTML elements (headers, forms, tables, etc.). The module also manages the CGI interface to the Web server by providing a mechanism for capturing user input into a Perl *hash* or two-dimensional array. This hash contains environment variables and their values as easy-to-access data pairs. For example, in Perl, you can access (or *dereference*) the value of the environment variable QUERY_STRING using $ENV{QUERY_STRING}.

The module also provides some of the more advanced features of CGI scripting, including support for file uploads, cookies, cascading style sheets, server PUSH, and frames. The `CGI.pm` Perl module is designed to be used with standard CGI or Apache `mod_perl` (discussed in a later section) and simplifies the use of these Web programming techniques, but does not replace either. The module is far too extensive to cover in detail here, but my CGI examples throughout this chapter make use of it, and illustrate some of the basic `CGI.pm` methods (or functions, for those not yet thinking in object terms). Speaking of object-orientation, though, `CGI.pm` makes internal methods (or functions) accessible either as Perl 5 objects or as traditional functions. With `CGI.pm`, you can choose to use either form, or both, if you wish. `CGI.pm` even emulates the `ReadParse` function from `cgi-lib.pl` (a Perl/CGI library that many Web programmers cut their teeth on). This means "legacy" Perl/CGI scripts don't have to be rewritten to use `CGI.pm`.

You can obtain `CGI.pm` from the Comprehensive Perl Archive Network (or CPAN) search site at

```
http://search.cpan.org/
```

or directly from its author at

```
http://www.genome.wi.mit.edu/ftp/pub/software/WWW/cgi_docs.html
```

or

```
ftp://ftp-genome.wi.mit.edu/pub/software/WWW/
```

A Script to Return the Environment

In Linux, every process is started by the operating system kernel and inherits an address space referred to as the *process environment*. Prior to starting every process, Linux tailors this environment by creating variables that the process will inherit, and setting the values of these variables to contain information that the process can later read. It is through the environment that information is traditionally passed to CGI scripts. When Apache starts a CGI process, it sets a number of environment variables that the CGI process can read to determine things like the request headers that were sent to Apache by the client and the request URL (which, in the case of a GET request, can contain data from a form).

Listing 8.1 depicts a Perl script that returns a neatly formatted listing of all environment variables set for the CGI script prior to its execution.

Listing 8.1   The `Environ.cgi` Script

```
#!/usr/bin/perl
#Environ.cgi - Show environment variables set by the server
#
print "Content-type: text/html\n\n";
print "<HTML><HEAD><TITLE>Environment Variables</TITLE></HEAD><BODY>";
print "<H2>Environment Variables:</H2>";
print "<HR>\n";
foreach $evar( keys (%ENV)){
        print "<B>$evar:</B> $ENV{$evar}<BR>";
}
print "</BODY></HTML>\n";
```

The first line of the script designates Perl as the script interpreter; in other words, this is a Perl script (the `.cgi` extension says nothing about the contents of the file, but it ensures that Apache spawns the file using CGI). The output of the script (the `print` statements) is redirected to the requester's browser in the form of an HTTP response. Note that the first response is the `Content-type` HTML header, which causes the browser to render the rest of the output as HTML-formatted text. This header is followed by two consecutive newline characters (/n/n), an HTTP convention used to separate HTTP headers from the HTTP content or payload. Figure 8.1 shows the page as rendered by a Web browser.

If you know a little Perl, you'll realize that the script accesses a hash (or indexed two-dimensional array) named `%ENV`, iterating through the hash, displaying each hash entry key and value. The `%ENV` hash contains the environment inherited by all Perl scripts; access to the environment, therefore, requires no special function in Perl—it is provided without charge by the Perl interpreter.

Figure 8.1 Environ.cgi in a Browser

This script is extremely handy to have in your CGI directory. Take a moment now to install it and execute it from a Web browser. This will allow you to use it to view the environment provided through CGI, and that environment will change as you add certain modules or use different request methods. I can access this file on my server using

```
http://jackal.hiwaay.net/cgi-bin/Environ.cgi
```

As an experiment, you can pass a variable to any CGI script using a request URL such as:

```
http://jackal.hiwaay.net/cgi-bin/Environ.cgi?somevar=somevalue
```

When you try that on your server, you should see the additional data you passed in the environment variable QUERY_STRING: somevalue=somevar. That's how information is passed to CGI scripts when the GET request method is used. More often, however, data is sent to the Web server with the POST request method. When POST is used, Apache uses the script's standard input handle (*stdin*) to send the data to the script in a data stream.

A CGI script that handles POST requests is a bit more difficult to write, but utilities like the Perl CGI.pm (discussed earlier) module make this much easier. Remember, CGI.pm is *not* required for using Perl with CGI and Apache; it is a convenience, but one well worth taking the time to learn.

A Simple Database Query Example

To demonstrate the use of the various Web programming techniques described in this chapter, I created a simple relational database. It consists of a single table that contains slightly more than 47,000 five-digit US postal delivery codes (the so-called "Zip codes") with the associated U.S. city and state for each. I chose this data because it is public domain information, and I was able to download the 47,000-line file in comma-separated value format.

Although any database that supports SQL queries could be used, I chose the very powerful, yet completely free, MySQL relational database management program.

MySQL, a Simple Relational Database for Linux

Many of the Web programming examples in this book make a simple query of a relational database management system using the structured query language (SQL). With slight modification, these examples will work with virtually any RDBMS you can run on Linux.

I chose to use an open-source freely obtained database system called MySQL. MySQL is available from http://mysql.com.

You can download the very latest development releases or the latest stable production release, as well as binary distributions, or contributed RPMs, from http://mysql.com/. I have downloaded the source code for MySQL and found it easy to compile and install, but since I wanted only a running SQL engine and had no interest in customizing the code, I have since taken to installing MySQL from RPMs. You can get these from the mysql.com site, but I prefer to use the old standby, RPMFind.net.

MySQL's version numbers change pretty rapidly; the version I installed may be behind the current release by the time you read this. It's a database server and performs a pretty mundane role, when you get right down to it. I don't worry too much about having the latest version; I'm happy as long as I've got a stable SQL engine that is always available.

MySQL, a Simple Relational Database for Linux *(continued)*

You'll need to get several pieces for a whole system. For the 3.22.29 version I last installed, for example, I downloaded the following four RPMs:

`MySQL-3.22.29-1.rpm`	The database engine itself. The most essential piece.
`MySQL-client-3.22.29-1.rpm`	The standard MySQL clients. You'll need these to perform chores like creating databases and setting up security from the Linux command line.
`MySQL-devel-3.22.29-1.rpm`	The development header files and libraries necessary to develop MySQL client applications. Though not strictly necessary, if you ever attempt to compile another application to use MySQL (like a Perl DBD driver), the linker will need these header files and libraries.
`MySQL-shared-3.22.29-1.rpm`	Shared libraries (*.so*); required by certain languages and applications to dynamically load and use MySQL.

Installation of MySQL is as simple as applying each of these RPMs:

```
rpm -i MySQL-3_22_29-1_i386.rpm
rpm -i MySQL-client-3_22_29-1_i386.rpm
rpm -i MySQL-devel-3_22_29-1_i386.rpm
rpm -i MySQL-shared-3_22_29-1_i386.rpm
```

I took one more step, however, to make the excellent documentation that is provided easily available from my server through a Web browser. Adding the following line to my `httpd.conf` allows me to read the MySQL docs using the URL `http://jackal.hiwaay.net/MySQL`.

```
Alias /MySQL "/usr/doc/MySQL-3.22.29"
```

The documentation provided with MySQL is the same superlative documentation available online at `mysql.com/documentation`. The local documentation is quicker to read and better formatted for printing, but the online documentation is indexed for searching. I use them both.

In MySQL, the `mysqladmin` program is used to create new databases.

```
# mysqladmin -p create zipcodes
Enter password:
Database "zipcodes" created.
```

The -p argument in the command line above (and in subsequent examples) causes MySQL to prompt for the user's password. In this case, the MySQL user's identity is that of the invoking user (and I was logged in as `root` when I invoked these commands). MySQL is started and the database is opened like this:

```
# mysql -p zipcodes
Enter password:
Welcome to the MySQL monitor. Commands end with ; or \g.
Your MySQL connection id is 105 to server version: 3.22.29

Type 'help' for help.
```

I created a single table in the database. Named `zips`, it consists of three fields: a 25-character string for the city name, a two-character string for the state abbreviation, and a five-character string for the postal Zip code, which is the primary index into the table and, therefore, cannot be empty (NOT NULL).

```
mysql> create table zips (city char(25), state char(2),
    -> zip char(5) NOT NULL, primary key (zip) );

Query OK, 0 rows affected (0.00 sec)
```

The 46,796 rows of the database were retrieved from a text file using the following MySQL command line:

```
mysql> LOAD DATA LOCAL INFILE "zips.txt" INTO TABLE zips
    -> FIELDS TERMINATED BY ', ' ENCLOSED BY '"';
Query OK, 46796 rows affected (2.66 sec)
Records: 46796 Deleted: 0 Skipped: 0 Warnings: 0
```

This specifies the field delimiter as a comma followed by a space character and tells MySQL that the string fields in the original file are enclosed in quotes. Even on my old Pentium 200 MMX server, this database was loaded (and indexed) in less than three seconds (impressive).

For each Web programming language and technique in this chapter and the next one, I'll present an example that accepts a five-digit Zip code entered by a user in a Web form, looks up the associated city and state from the database, and returns the result to the user. This will demonstrate not only how to program an application to accept data from a Web client, but also how to interface the application to a common database system, make a query of a database, and return the results to the requester. Although it is quite simple, the application demonstrates the basics of Web programming, particularly for database access, one of the most common tasks that must be performed by Web servers on behalf of the end user.

The input form will be the same for each Web programming example that accesses the Zipcodes MySQL database, a very simple HTML form that takes a single input, the U.S. Postal Service Code to be looked up in a database. The Web form used to get user input is shown in Figure 8.2.

Figure 8.2 The Zipcodes database query form

The HTML for the form is also quite simple, as you can see in Listing 8.2.

Listing 8.2   HTML Code to Produce the Zipcodes Query Form

```
<!DOCTYPE HTML PUBLIC "-//IETF//DTD HTML//EN">
<HTML><HEAD><TITLE>Zip Code Database Query Form</TITLE>
</HEAD><BODY><H1>Zip Code MySQL Database Query Form</H1>
<FORM METHOD="POST" ACTION="http://Jackal.hiwaay.net/cgi-bin/zipcodes.cgi"
ENCTYPE="application/x-www-form-urlencoded">
<EM>Enter a 5-digit Zip Code:</EM><BR><INPUT TYPE="text" NAME="zip"
SIZE=6><P><INPUT TYPE="reset" VALUE="Clear"><INPUT TYPE="submit"
NAME=".submit" VALUE="Submit Search"></FORM><HR>
<HR>
<ADDRESS>Charles Aulds</ADDRESS><BR>
<A HREF="/">Home Page</A>
</BODY></HTML>
```

I didn't actually write the HTML you see above; I used CGI.pm module to do much of the work for me. Along with the features noted earlier, this module provides the ability to create most of the features of an HTML document. CGI.pm can do this using either "traditional" or object-oriented programming mechanisms. The first method uses standard Perl function calls. For those programmers who aren't completely comfortable with programming through objects, this may seem the simplest and most intuitive way to use CGI.pm. The function-oriented CGI script in Listing 8.3 generated the HTML for the simple input form shown in Listing 8.2.

Listing 8.3   Using CGI.pm to Generate the HTML for a Web Form

```
#!/usr/bin/perl -Tw
use CGI;
use CGI::Carp;

use CGI qw/:standard/;

print header;
print >start_html("Zip Code Database Query Form");
print "<H1>Zip Code MySQL Database Query Form</H1>\n";
&print_prompt($query);
&print_tail;
print end_html;
sub print_prompt {
my($query) = @_;
print startform(-method=>"POST",-action=>"http://Jackal.hiwaay.net/cgi-bin/
zipcodes.cgi ");
```

Advanced Configuration Options

PART 3

```perl
print "<EM>Enter a 5-digit Zip Code:</EM><BR>";
print textfield(-name=>'zip', -size=>6);
print "<P>",reset('Clear');
print submit(-value=>'Submit Search');
print endform;
print "<HR>\n";
}
sub print_tail {
print <<END;
<ADDRESS>Charles Aulds</ADDRESS><BR>
<A HREF="/">Home Page</A>
END
}
```

To use CGI.pm in object-oriented style, you create a CGI object and then make use of methods and properties that it exposes. This is the form I recommend, for two reasons: First, it is the modern programming paradigm; second, nearly all good examples you'll find for using CGI.pm, including those in the CGI.pm documentation, use this style. Listing 8.4 is the same script, but written to use the CGI object methods rather than functions.

Listing 8.4   Using CGI.pm in Object-Oriented Fashion

```perl
#!/usr/bin/perl -Tw
use CGI;
use CGI::Carp;

$query = new CGI;

print $query->header;
print $query->start_html("Zip Code Database Query Form");
print "<H1>Zip Code MySQL Database Query Form</H1>\n";
&print_prompt($query);
&print_tail;
print $query->end_html;
sub print_prompt {
my($query) = @_;
print $query->startform(-method=>"POST",-action=>"http://Jackal.hiwaay.net/
cgi-bin/zipcodes.cgi ");
print "<EM>Enter a 5-digit Zip Code:</EM><BR>";
print $query->textfield(-name=>'zip', -size=>6);
```

```
print "<P>",$query->reset('Clear');
print $query->submit(-value=>'Submit Search');
print $query->endform;
print "<HR>\n";
}
sub print_tail {
print <<END;
<ADDRESS>Charles Aulds</ADDRESS><BR>
<A HREF="/">Home Page</A>
END
}
```

Notice several things about both examples above. First, the CGI scripts are designed only to return an HTML page to the client browser; they contain no code for data manipulation, either I/O or computation. It might seem far easier to write the HTML and save it on the server as `filename.html`. In this case, it probably is … but when you are required to generate your HTML dynamically or on-the-fly, `CGI.pm` will repay the effort you take to learn the module. Use `perldoc CGI` to generate the excellent documentation for the module, full of good examples.

Also note that many functions (or methods) have defaults. In the case of the `header` function (or method) above, I used the default, which sends the following HTML header to the client:

```
Content-Type: text/html
```

You can override the default to specify your own content type using either of these forms, which are equivalent:

```
print header('mimetype/subtype')
```

or

```
print $query->header('mimetype/subtype');
```

The third point to note is how easily an HTML form can be created with `CGI.pm`. With `CGI.pm`, it isn't necessary to know the HTML tags used by the browser to render the HTML page. Comparing the CGI scripts above with the generated HTML, you can easily see how the script generated the form. `CGI.pm` is best learned in exactly that fashion, comparing a script with its output. Later in this chapter, I'll demonstrate how `CGI.pm` is used to receive user-generated input.

Finally, note that, even if you are using `CGI.pm`, you can use `print` statements to output anything else from your script. For some of the simpler lines, I did just that, using `print` to output tagged HTML.

CGI::Carp

Carp is a module that was developed to increase the usefulness of the standard warnings and error messages returned when things go wrong in a Perl script. When you include the Carp module in a Perl script by placing the line

```
use Carp;
```

somewhere near the beginning of the file, standard error messages are displayed with the name of the module in which the error occurred. This is handy whenever you are running Perl scripts that, in turn, call other scripts.

Errors returned from CGI scripts (normally written to the script's standard output) are automatically diverted into the Apache log. The problem is that the errors written there are not time-stamped and, even worse, sometimes don't identify the CGI script in which the error occurred. For example, I deliberately broke a CGI script by calling a nonexistent function, and then ran the script from a Web browser, which wrote the following line into Apaches error.log file:

```
Died at /home/httpd/cgi-bin/CGIForm.cgi line 12.
```

This isn't bad; it tells me the script name and even the line number where the error occurred. When I added the line

```
use CGI::Carp;
```

to the beginning of the script, however, the same error caused the following lines to be written. They give a time and date stamp, as well as identifying the script where the error or warning occurred, and listing the calling subroutine(s) when these apply:

```
[Fri Feb 25 14:37:55 2000] CGIForm.cgi: Died at /home/httpd/cgi-bin/
CGIForm.cgi line 12.
[Fri Feb 25 14:37:56 2000] CGIForm.cgi: main::print_me() called at /
home/httpd/cgi-bin/CGIForm.cgi line 8.
```

CGI::Carp can tremendously speed your troubleshooting of Perl/CGI scripts, particularly when you have large scripts with many subroutines.

Listing 8.5 shows the actual CGI script that performs the database lookup, taking one parameter, a postal (Zip) code entered by the user in the Web form. This script also loads CGI.pm, which makes it very easy to receive user form input. CGI.pm provides a Perl function (or method) called param. This function can be called with the name of a field in a Web form to retrieve the value entered by the user in that field. In this example, the value entered by the user in the zip field is obtained by calling param('zip').

Listing 8.5   The zipcodes.cgi Script for a Database Query

```perl
#!/usr/bin/perl -w
# queries a MySQL table for a value and returns it in
# an HTML-formatted document
#
use strict;
use DBI;
use CGI qw(:standard);
use CGI::Carp;
#
# Create a new CGI object
my $output=new CGI;
#
# What did the user enter in the query form?
my $zipentered=param('zip') if (param('zip') );
my($server, $sock, $db);
#
# Connect to mysql database and return a database handle ($dbh)
my $dbh=DBI->connect("DBI:mysql:zipcodes:jackal.hiwaay.net","root","mypass");
#
# Prepare a SQL query; return a statement handle ($sth)
my $sth=$dbh->prepare("Select * from zips where zip=$zipentered");
#
# Execute prepared statement to return
$sth->execute;
my @row;
print $output->header;
print $output->start_html("Zip Code");
print h1("ZipCODE");
#
# Return rows into a Perl array
while (@row=$sth->fetchrow_array() ) {
print "The US Postal Service Zip Code <font size=+1><b>$row[2]</b></font> is
for: <font size=+2><b>$row[0], $row[1]</b></font>\n";
}
print "<p>\n";
print "<h3>GATEWAY_INTERFACE=$ENV{GATEWAY_INTERFACE}</h3>";
print $output->end_html;
```

```
#
# Call the disconnect() method on the database handle
# to close the connection to the MySQL database
$dbh->disconnect;
```

The database query is performed using the `DBI.pm` module (see the accompanying discussion). Although DBI has a number of functions, the most basic use of the module is to create a connection, compose and send a query, and close the connection. The comments in Listing 8.5 serve to explain what each line is doing. Using this example, you should be able to quickly write your own CGI script to connect to and query a relational database on your own server. You may not choose to use MySQL as I did, but by changing one line of this script (the line that calls the `DBI->connect` method) you can make this same script work with nearly all major relational database servers.

DBI.pm

Certainly one of the most useful of all Perl modules is the DBI module (`DBI.pm`). DBI stands for "DataBase Independent," and the DBI module provides a standard set of programming functions for querying a wide variety of databases. While a full discussion of the DBI module is beyond the scope of this chapter, I have used DBI to illustrate database querying from standard CGI scripts.

You install the DBI module once. Then you install a DataBase Dependent (or DBD) module for each database that you intend to access. As with most Perl modules, the latest versions of the DBD modules are available from the Comprehensive Perl Archive Network (`search.cpan.net`). Better yet, using the `CPAN.pm` module, download and install them in one easy step. To install the latest `DBI.pm` module and the MySQL DBD module, I entered two commands after loading `CPAN.pm` (as described in Chapter 1):

```
# cpan
cpan> install DBI
cpan>install DBD::mysql
```

One very interesting module that I use quite frequently is `DBD::CSV`, which allows you to create a flat text file consisting of rows of comma-separated values and work with it as you would a true relational database. Each line of the file is a separate data record or row, and the values on the line, separated by commas, are separate data fields. Using `DBD::CSV` allows you to develop database applications without having access to a true relational database. When you have things the way you want them, you simply modify your application to use a true database-dependent driver (by loading a new DBD module).

FastCGI

CGI was the first general-purpose standard mechanism for Web programming, and for a long time it remained the most used application programmer's interface to the Web server. But it has always been hampered by a performance bottleneck: Every time a CGI application is called, the Web server spawns a new subsystem or subshell to run the process. The request loads imposed on many modern servers are so large that faster mechanisms have been developed, which now largely overshadow CGI. Among the first of these was FastCGI, a standard, which allows a slightly modified CGI script to load once and remain memory-resident to respond to subsequent requests.

FastCGI consists of two components. The first is an Apache module, mod_fastcgi.so, that modifies or extends the Web server so that it can properly identify and execute programs designed to run under FastCGI. The second component is a set of functions that are linked to your FastCGI programs. For compiled languages, these are provided as a shared library; for Perl, these functions are added using the FCGI.pm Perl module.

To make the functions exported from these libraries available to your program, you include a C header file or, in scripting languages like Tcl or Perl, place a line at the beginning of the script to include code necessary to enable FastCGI support in the script. FastCGI libraries are available for C, Perl, Java, Tcl, and Python. In this section I'll demonstrate how to make the necessary modifications to the Apache server and how to modify the CGIForm.cgi Perl script to allow it to run as a FastCGI script.

How FastCGI Works

FastCGI is based on a very simple concept. Whenever a FastCGI program is loaded into memory, it remains there until it is purged as part of the cleanup process when the Web server shuts down. In other words, programs identified as FastCGI scripts are run in *persistent processes*. The overhead associated with initializing a new system process and loading the CGI script into the process's memory space becomes negligible, as these tasks are performed only once, the first time the program is requested by a client. In order for this to work, it is necessary to edit standard CGI programs to include an infinite loop. A FastCGI program actually sits idle most of the time, waiting for a signal from the mod_fastcgi module to wake up and process a request. When it receives this signal, the script processes a new iteration of the loop, which handles all of the normal functions of a CGI script. That is, it reads new information from the environment or standard input handle, processes it, and writes some kind of output to its standard output handle. Note that, with FastCGI, the process's environment may change many times during the lifetime of the process, once for each new request to be processed. This is part of the magic of FastCGI.

Advanced Configuration Options

PART 3

Installing and Compiling mod_fastcgi

To get started, download the latest version of mod_fastcgi from www.fastcgi.com. The module is a cinch to compile and use as a DSO.

1. Download the latest version of the module (2.2.4 when I wrote this) and then extract it into your /usr/local/src directory with this command:

   ```
   # tar xvfz /home/caulds/mod_fastcgi_2_2_4_tar.gz
   ```

2. Moving to the new source directory created, you can use a single command line to invoke the apxs utility to compile and install the module:

   ```
   # cd mod_fastcgi_2.2.4
   # /usr/local/apache/bin/apxs -i -a -o mod_fastcgi.so -c *.c
   ```

3. Then verify that the following lines have been added to httpd.conf:

   ```
   LoadModule fastcgi_module      libexec/mod_fastcgi.so
   AddModule mod_fastcgi.c
   ```

4. The last step is to restart the server, and you're in business.

Modifying CGI Scripts to Use FastCGI

FastCGI was designed to make conversions of existing CGI files as simple as possible. To illustrate, consider Listing 8.6, a simple modification of the Environ.pl script shown in Listing 8.1. The first thing you have to do is acquire a copy of the FCGI.pm module for Perl. If you are already using the CPAN.pm module (see the earlier sidebar) to maintain your installed Perl modules, this is as easy as issuing the command install FCGI in CPAN.pm's interactive mode. Including the line use FCGI; at the beginning of a Perl script ensures that it will work with CGI (you would link your object code to the FCGI library to accomplish the same thing with a compiled language like C).

Now, create a loop that executes once each time a call to FCGI::accept returns with a value that is not negative. When this call returns with a value less than zero, the loop terminates and the program ends. Everything within the loop should look like regular CGI stuff. Incidentally, using the ab benchmark utility that comes with Apache, I evaluated the speed of this script in responding to 10,000 requests, and measured it to be 328% faster than the plain CGI script. That's a very significant increase.

Listing 8.6   The Environ.fcgi FastCGI Script

```
#!/usr/bin/perl -Tw
#Environ.cgi - Show environment variables set by the server
use FCGI; # Imports the library; this line required
```

```perl
while (FCGI::accept >= 0) {
  print "Content-type: text/html\n\n";
  print "<HTML><HEAD><TITLE>Environment
    Variables</TITLE></HEAD><BODY>";
  print "<H2>Environment Variables:</H2>";
  print "<HR>\n";
  foreach $evar( keys (%ENV)){
    print "<B>$evar:</B> $ENV{$evar}<BR>";
  }
  print "</BODY></HTML>\n";
}
```

You might note a new environment variable that appears when you call this script from a browser:

```
FCGI_APACHE_ROLE= RESPONDER
```

This indicates that FastCGI is operating in one of three different application *roles* it can assume. The *Responder* role provides the functionality of ordinary CGI, which cannot operate in the other two roles that FastCGI can assume. The first of these alternate roles is the *Filter* role, in which a FastCGI script is used to process a file before it is returned to the client. The other role is the *Authorizer* role, in which a FastCGI application is used to make decisions about whether or not to grant a user's request. In this role, FastCGI acts as an authorization module, like those described in Chapter 14. Both of these roles are too complex for discussion here, and neither is used often. If you're interested in exploring either of them further, your first stop to learn more should be www.fastcgi.com.

Note that other Perl modules can still be used in same fashion as ordinary CGI scripts. Listing 8.7 illustrates this. It's a FastCGI rewrite of the zipcodes MySQL query script, rewritten to take advantage of the efficiency of FastCGI.

Listing 8.7 The zipcodes.fcgi FastCGI Script

```perl
#!/usr/bin/perl -Tw
use CGI;
use CGI::Carp;
use FCGI; # Imports the library; required line
$query = new CGI;
# Response loop
while (FCGI::accept >= 0) {
  print $query->header;
```

```
print $query->start_html("Zip Code Database Query Form");
print "<H1>Zip Code MySQL Database Query Form</H1>\n";
&print_prompt($query);
&print_tail;
print $query->end_html;
sub print_prompt {
my($query) = @_;
print $query->startform(-method=>"POST",- action=>"http://Jackal.hiwaay.net/
cgi-bin/zipcodes.cgi ");
print "<EM>Enter a 5-digit Zip Code:</EM><BR>";
print $query->textfield(-name=>'zip', -size=>6);
print "<P>",$query->reset('Clear');
print $query->submit(-value=>'Submit Search');
print $query->endform;
print "<HR>\n";
}
sub print_tail {
print <<END;
<ADDRESS>Charles Aulds</ADDRESS><BR>
<A HREF="/">Home Page</A>
END
}
} # End FCGI loop
```

Listing 8.8 shows a simple FastCGI script written in C.

Listing 8.8   A Simple C Script in FastCGI

```
#include <fcgi_stdio.h>

void main(void)
{
   int I = 0;
   while(FCGI_Accept() >= 0) {
      printf("Content-type: text/html\r\n\r\n");
      printf("<H1>Hello World!</H1>");
      printf("<p>You've requested this FastCGI page
         %d times.\n", i++);
   }
}
```

Notice the #include statement that is necessary to use FastCGI. The program goes into a loop that is processed once every time a call to FCGI_Accept() returns with a result greater than zero. I set an integer counter outside the loop, which is incremented during the processing of the loop. Can you see how a different value of the counter is returned for each request for this FastCGI program?

The mod_perl Perl Accelerator

Traditional Perl, as an interpreted language, has always had a reputation of being relatively slow, and this reputation is at least partially deserved. Perl certainly isn't a speed demon, but the runtime performance of Perl scripts is far less important in most situations than the fact that the Perl interpreter has to be loaded each time a script is invoked. On a Web server that may be running thousands of Perl scripts through the CGI interface every hour, launching a separate Perl interpreter in a new Linux shell process for each request can result in a substantial performance impact on the server.

My favorite Apache module, mod_perl, eliminates virtually all the overhead associated with Perl/CGI and puts Perl in the same league with the very fastest server-side Web programming techniques. Add to this a tremendous wealth of modules that mod_perl enables, and mod_perl becomes a virtual gold mine for Web program authors and Apache administrators.

mod_perl starts by linking the Perl runtime library into the Apache server, thereby giving each running copy of Apache its own Perl interpreter. This is accomplished in two ways; first, the Perl function libraries can be statically linked to the Apache httpd process (which requires recompiling Apache from the source code). Alternatively, the Perl libraries can be linked into the mod_perl DSO module that is loaded in Apache's address space at runtime. If the DSO option is chosen, you have a choice of obtaining the DSO as an RPM, or compiling it yourself. All of these methods of installing mod_perl are discussed in the next few sections. This completely eliminates the need to start a new instance of the Perl interpreter in its own Linux process each time a Perl CGI script is called, which significantly improves the response time and total runtime of scripts. Consequently, this increase in server throughput results in a dramatic increase in the number of client requests that can be serviced in a given time.

The really cool thing is that mod_perl runs nearly all Perl scripts without modification. The only thing you have to do is specify mod_perl as the Apache handler for the scripts, instead of the default mod_cgi. On my server, I set up mod_cgi to handle requests to /cgi-bin and mod_perl to handle all requests to /perl.

**Advanced
Configuration Options**

PART 3

The advantages of using mod_perl don't stop there, however. An integral part of mod_perl is Apache::Registry, which is probably the most valuable Perl module for use with Apache. Used together, these modules increase the execution speed of Perl scripts dramatically. The Apache::Registry module creates its own namespace and compiles Perl scripts that are called through mod_perl into that namespace. It associates each script with a time-stamp. The next time that script is used, if the source files aren't newer than the compiled bytecodes in the Apache::Registry namespace, the module is not recompiled. Some Perl code that is called frequently (like CGI.pm) is only compiled once, the first time it is used!

Two other important features that mod_perl adds to Apache are of special interest to hard-core programmers. The first is a set of functions that give Perl scripters access to the Apache internal functions and data structures. This permits Apache modules to be written completely in Perl, rather than in C, and a large number of such modules exist. (I'll describe a few shortly.) The second programming feature is a set of easy-to-use handler directives for all the phases of the Apache request processing cycle. These permit the specification of Perl modules to handle virtually any task, without explicitly adding the module to the Apache configuration.

Installing mod_perl

Installing mod_perl is a bit more complex than installing most Apache modules, mainly because it consists of so many components. As described, the actual mod_perl Apache module (compiled from C source) is only one part of the puzzle. In addition, the Perl interpreter library needs to be linked either to the Apache kernel or directly to the mod_perl module (if it's compiled as a DSO). A number of supporting Perl scripts are also included with mod_perl and provide essential pieces of its functionality. There are two easy ways to acquire all the parts and install them simply. The first is to obtain mod_perl as an RPM, which I recommend only if you are using a copy of Apache that has been installed using an RPM, most likely as a part of a standard Linux distribution.

If you are using Apache source that you compiled or installed from a binary distribution, you should consider using the CPAN.pm module to acquire and install the latest source distribution of mod_perl, and all the required support files. If you use this method, however, I recommend that you decide between statically linking mod_perl to Apache and compiling it as a DSO module. In either case, you should reconfigure, recompile, and reinstall the module directly from the source code downloaded and extracted to your hard disk by CPAN.pm. Instructions for both methods are given.

Traditionally, mod_perl has experienced problems when built as a DSO module on some platforms. The documentation for the module warns that it may not work, and says that for some platforms it *will not* work. However, I have compiled mod_perl as a DSO (libperl.so) and it has worked fine for me under Linux, running every CGI script I have without problems, even during intense activity driven by the ApacheBench benchmarking utility. And since mod_perl is provided as a DSO with the Red Hat Linux distribution, the module probably doesn't deserve its reputation for presenting problems when run as a DSO (at least not on Linux). I recommend that you compile mod_perl as a DSO and reserve static linking as a means of solving any problems that occur. I'm willing to bet you will have no problems using the module as a DSO.

Using the RPM

The easiest way to install mod_perl is using the prepackaged RPM. I use RPMs whenever I can, particularly when I need to update a system library (for example, the GNU C library or *glibc*) that belongs in a well-established location or standard location (like /lib). As an Apache extension, the mod_perl RPM will place its files in the locations where it expects to find the Apache binaries. For most RPMs, these will be the Red Hat default locations. The paths do not match the Apache defaults. Sure, you can manually put things in their "proper" locations, but this is more trouble than it is worth, negating the benefits of the RPM.

If you have a Red Hat Linux system, or you installed Apache from a downloaded RPM, chances are you already have mod_perl installed. You can tell if you have the module installed by running rpm -qa | grep mod_perl. If you simply want to reinstall or upgrade the module, I recommend you download and install the mod_perl RPM. If you've installed Apache from a binary distribution for your platform, or compiled it from the source, however, don't use the RPM method described here. Instead, use the CPAN install method to retrieve the source as a Perl or bundled distribution.

The only place you really need to look for Linux RPMs is Rpmfind.Net (http://rpmfind.net). This site hosts a database and repository of thousands of RPMs, built on systems around the world. Figure 8.3 shows the mod_perl 1.22 RPM that I downloaded for installation on my server. This RPM contains mod_perl built as a loadable module (DSO) that installs as /usr/lib/apache/libperl.so. If you are installing mod_perl for the first time, you will need to configure Apache manually to load and use the module as described below.

Installing the RPM is as easy as downloading the package and entering the following command line:

```
# rpm -i mod_perl-1.22-2.i386.rpm
```

Figure 8.3   mod_perl RPMs on the rpmfind.net site

Using CPAN.pm to Retrieve the Source

It's important to understand that mod_perl (like so many Perl modules) was not developed in a stand-alone fashion, but borrows much of its functionality from other Perl modules. That is how object orientation is implemented in Perl. Rather than defining standard interfaces for shared objects (like Microsoft's OLE and COM), Perl does things far more simply; it permits one Perl program to load another into its own *namespace*. This allows the calling program to reference variables and functions in the program it loaded, as long as they were declared as public. Simple, but very effective, and it takes a lot of the pain out of "code reuse."

Most of mod_perl is the Perl module itself, which is library object code that must be compiled into a module that Apache can use (either by statically linking it to the Apache kernel or as a dynamically loadable module). Other parts of mod_perl, however, make use of the following Perl modules:

```
MIME::Base64 - Used in authentication headers
Digest::MD5 - Needed to do Digest authentication
URI 0.10 - There are URIs everywhere
```

```
Net::FTP 2.00 - If you want ftp://-support
HTML::HeadParser - To get the correct $res->base
LWP - The reason why you need the modules above
Devel::Symdump - Symbol table browsing with Apache::Status
Data::Dumper - Used by Apache::PerlSections->dump
CGI - CGI.pm
Tie::IxHash - For order in <Perl> sections
Apache - Perl interface to Apache server API
Apache::DBI - Wrapper around DBI->connect to transparently maintain persistent
connections
Apache::DB - Run the interactive Perl debugger under mod_perl
Apache::Stage - Management of document staging directories
Apache::Sandwich - Layered document maker
Apache::Request - Effective methods for dealing with client request data
```

You should have the latest versions of all these modules installed on your machine (as well as an up-to-date version of Perl, at least 5.004, although 5.005 is much better). Don't despair if there seems to be far too many pieces of the puzzle; it's easy to snag them all with CPAN.pm, where you can download mod_perl and all those other pieces as a single bundle and install them all at one time.

You can install the mod_perl bundle from CPAN using the following command line:

```
# perl -MCPAN -e 'install mod_perl'
```

I do *not* recommend this method of using the CPAN.pm module, however, particularly since many of the installation scripts (makefiles) require some user input. Always invoke CPAN.pm in the interactive mode (as described in the sidebar earlier in the chapter) and use the install command, as shown below. The components of the mod_perl package that are already installed on your machine are flagged as "up to date" and will be skipped during the installation.

```
# cpan
cpan shell -- CPAN exploration and modules installation (v1.54)
ReadLine support enabled

cpan> install mod_perl
```

A lot of stuff happens at this point (the trace was over 1500 lines long). Don't let it scare you; it's mostly information that you can safely ignore, but some parts of the install will require user input. For example, in installing the libnet portion, you will be asked for some information about your network, including the names of mail servers, your domain name, and that sort of thing. Do your best to answer these, but don't fret if you can't answer a question; the module will work without all that information; accept the default response for any question you can't answer and things will be just fine. Everything is built relative to your Apache source code, so when you're asked to supply that, make sure you enter the correct path to the src directory under the Apache source directory:

```
Please tell me where I can find your apache src
[] /usr/local/src/apache_1.3.9/src
Configure mod_perl with /usr/local/src/apache_1.3.9/src ? [y]
Shall I build httpd in /usr/local/src/apache_1.3.9/src for you? [y]
```

During the installation procedure (which takes quite some time), the CPAN.pm module downloads mod_perl and all of the support modules listed above, and it runs Makefile scripts for each to compile and install them. When the process is completely, I usually reenter the install line as a test. If all went well, instead of 1500 lines of output, you should see this:

```
cpan> install mod_perl
mod_perl is up to date.
```

Installing as a Static Module

If you intend to link the module to Apache statically, you will need the Apache source and the mod_perl source code. If you installed mod_perl using the CPAN.pm module, you will find the source package in a directory reserved for these, arranged by the authors' ID as found on the CPAN archive site. When I installed mod_perl, the GZIP archive was downloaded into

```
/root/.cpan/sources/authors/id/DOUGM/mod_perl-1.24.tar.gz
```

Unless specifically reconfigured, the CPAN.pm module creates a source and a build directory under a .cpan directory beneath the current user's home directory. I always use the root account when I use CPAN to download and install Perl packages, so all my source archives and builds fall under /root/.cpan, and I've found no reason to change this. It seems like a good location, well protected, and I don't recommend that you change these default locations.

In addition to the sources directory, you should find a build directory, which the CPAN.pm module uses to build Perl packages. It does this by extracting the files from the source archive and running the provided Makefile.PL to configure the application (which may query you for information it needs) and then running make and then makefile. This is the same procedure that you would use if installing the package by hand. Most modules will not require you to go into the build directory and run the install by hand, but because of the number of configuration options for mod_perl, that is exactly what you should do after running CPAN.pm.

You should find a directory under build that matches the name of the Perl package you installed using CPAN.pm. In my case, the directory for mod_perl version 1.24 was /root/ .cpan/build/mod_perl-1.24. In this directory, enter the following to configure mod_ perl, adding several configuration options:

```
# perl Makefile.PL \
> APACHE_SRC=/usr/local/src/apache_1.3.9/src \
> USE_APACI=1 \
> PREP_HTTPD=1 \
> DO_HTTPD=1 \
> EVERYTHING=1
```

Note that this is a single command line; the backslash at the end of the first five lines concatenates the following line. The most important option here is PREP_HTTP, which causes the source files to be moved into the Apache source tree (defined by APACHE_SRC) but not built. After you enter the above command line, the configuration will proceed, printing many lines of information. The EVERYTHING variable instructs the configuration to include all features of mod_perl, even those considered experimental. This will enable, for example, features like support for Server-Side Include parsing. Using EVERYTHING=1 is the equivalent of specifying all of the following:

```
# ALL_HOOKS=1 \
> PERL_SSI=1 \
> PERL_SECTIONS=1 \
> PERL_STACKED_HANDLERS=1 \
> PERL_METHOD_HANDLERS=1 \
> PERL_TABLE_API=1
```

You can now compile and install Apache by typing the following command *while still in the mod_perl source directory*:

```
# make
# make install
```

This is the way mod_perl is documented, and it works perfectly well, but if you compile the module from this location you will need to remember that subsequent Apache builds need to be run from the mod_perl directory, instead of from the Apache source tree. This is awkward, but there is a better way. If you prefer to rebuild Apache from the Apache source tree as described in Chapter 3, use the following instructions.

After running the `perl Makefile.PL` just shown, you'll find a new directory, `src/modules/perl`, inside the Apache source directory. It contains everything APACI needs to compile this module into the Apache server. However, to compile Apache and include the `mod_perl` module, you will need to modify the `LIBS` and `CFLAGS` variables and add an `--activate-module` option when running the Apache `configure` utility. The following script (run from within the top-level directory of the Apache source tree) is the one I use to configure, compile, and install basic Apache with `mod_perl` support:

```
#!/bin/sh
LIBS=`perl -MExtUtils::Embed -e ldopts` \
CFLAGS=`perl -MExtUtils::Embed -e ccopts` \
./configure \
"--activate-module=src/modules/perl/libperl.a" \
"$@"
make
make install
```

Installing `mod_perl` as a DSO

Again, in order to compile `mod_perl` as a DSO module, locate yourself in the CPAN build directory, which will probably be `/root/.cpan/build/mod_perl-1.24` if you run CPAN as `root`. The following command line uses the Apache `apxs` utility to compile the module:

```
# perl Makefile.PL \
> APACHE_SRC=/usr/local/src/apache_1.3.9/src \
> USE_APXS=1 \
> WITH_APXS=/usr/local/apache/bin/apxs \
> EVERYTHING=1
```

It's a single command line, spanning several lines concatenated using the trailing \ character on the first four lines. Now run `make` to compile the DSO. When it completes the task, you should find the DSO, compiled as `libperl.so`, residing in the `apaci` directory. The size of this file (nearly a megabyte on my machine) seems excessive, but remember that it has the entire Perl interpreter linked into it, which largely accounts for the size.

```
# ls -al apaci/libperl.so
-rwxr-xr-x   1 root     root        947311 Apr  8 15:24 apaci/libperl.so
```

You can reduce the size of the file somewhat by stripping unnecessary debugging symbols (using the Linux `strip` command):

```
# strip apaci/libperl.so
# ls -al apaci/libperl.so
-rwxr-xr-x   1 root     root        872676 Apr  8 15:30 apaci/libperl.so
```

A reduction of only eight percent seems modest, but worth the little time it took. The last step is to run make install to install the module:

```
# make install
[root@jackal mod_perl-1.24]# make install
(cd ./apaci && make)
make[1]: Entering directory `/root/.cpan/build/mod_perl-1.24/apaci'

   lines deleted

make[1]: Entering directory `/root/.cpan/build/mod_perl-1.24/apaci'
/usr/local/apache/bin/apxs -i -a -n perl libperl.so
cp libperl.so /usr/local/apache/libexec/libperl.so
chmod 755 /usr/local/apache/libexec/libperl.so
[activating module `perl' in /usr/local/apache/conf/httpd.conf]
make[1]: Leaving directory `/root/.cpan/build/mod_perl-1.24/apaci'
Appending installation info to /usr/lib/perl5/i586-linux/5.00405/perllocal.pod
```

This last step uses apxs to install the module into Apache's libexec directory, and even modifies the Apache httpd.conf file to use it, by adding the following two lines to that file:

```
LoadModule perl_module        libexec/libperl.so
AddModule mod_perl
```

Advanced Configuration Options

PART 3

BEGIN and END Blocks: A Word of Caution

If you are running Perl scripts that contain BEGIN and END blocks, under mod_perl these may not behave as you intend. Because scripts are compiled and cached for later reuse by Apache::Registry, these blocks will not be executed each time the script is called (as usually intended). Instead, the BEGIN block will be executed once by Apache::Registry when it is loaded. The END block receives special treatment by mod_perl. For scripts loaded at runtime by Apache::Registry, the END block is called when the script finishes running; this occurs for all invocations of the script, even if it has been compiled and cached. In scripts loaded at server startup (using PerlModule or PerlRequire), the END block is executed only once, when the main server is shut down.

The behavior of BEGIN and END blocks under mod_perl does not render them unusable, but you should probably avoid their use in scripts intended to be cached by Apache::Registry. The BEGIN block particularly is to be avoided.

Running Perl Scripts with `mod_perl`

In general, `mod_perl` functions as a drop-in replacement for CGI (for Perl scripts only, of course). Using `mod_perl` requires no modification to ordinary CGI Perl scripts, but it runs them far faster than they run under standard CGI. This section describes how to set up `mod_perl` to run Perl scripts and then discusses a few modules that build on the capabilities `mod_perl` adds to Apache. While the most common use of `mod_perl` is to accelerate Perl/CGI, these extension modules are becoming quite popular for the development of extensive Web-based applications, and they put `mod_perl` squarely in the same field as competitors like PHP or Java Servlets (both discussed in Chapter 9).

Passing Data to `mod_perl` Scripts

Since `mod_perl` emulates the CGI interface so that traditional CGI scripts can run unaltered, the best way to pass data to `mod_perl` scripts is through the system environment it inherits. Two directives can be used in `httpd.conf` to pass information to `mod_perl` scripts. These are analogous to the `SetEnv` and `PassEnv` directives already discussed, but they must be used in place of those directives to modify the special environment that `mod_perl` sets up for scripts that run under its control. The `PerlSetEnv` directive creates a new environment variable and sets its value for a Perl script to retrieve from the `%ENV` hash:

```
PerlSetEnv logfile /var/logs/Mylog.txt
```

The second directive, `PerlPassEnv`, takes the name of an existing variable from the main server's environment (usually the environment of the user who started Apache, typically `root`). This environment variable will be included in the environment set up for the CGI script:

```
PerlPassEnv USER
```

If you are not passing data to your `mod_perl` scripts through the environment, you can instruct `mod_perl` not to set up an environment to be inherited by CGI scripts. The speed gain and memory savings are usually not substantial enough to warrant disabling this feature, but it can be done for an extra performance boost:

```
PerlSetupEnv Off
```

Another directive is `PerlSetVar`, provided by `mod_perl` to pass arbitrary data pairs to `mod_perl` scripts without using the environment. This directive is a tool primarily used by module programmers and generally not used by Web scripters. Retrieving this information requires a call to a special `mod_perl` method, `dir_config()`, which in turn requires a modification of standard CGI scripts. The directive looks like this:

```
PerlSetVar MyVar some_arbitrary_data
```

Supplying Perl with Command-Line Switches

The first line of a traditional Perl/CGI script specifies a path to a script interpreter (typically/usr/lib/perl) and generally looks something like #!/usr/lib/perl. Using mod_perl, however, this line is ignored because Apache::Registry knows about (and uses) only a single script interpreter, the one that is linked into mod_perl during its installation. Since this line will be ignored when processing scripts with mod_perl, instructions to the interpreter that are normally passed as arguments on this line are also ignored.

The two most important of these to CGI programmers are the -T switch to enable taint checking and the -w switch, which instructs Perl to print warnings. mod_perl provides two directives that pass these switches to the Perl interpreter. I find it very useful to include both directives in my httpd.conf file.

```
PerlTaintCheck On
PerlWarn On
```

Using mod_perl with SSI

If Apache's mod_include module has been compiled with the proper switches (SSI = 1 or EVERYTHING = 1, as discussed earlier in the chapter), it can support Perl callbacks as SSI tags. The syntax for an SSI line that uses this special tag is

```
<--#perl sub=subkey -->
```

The *subkey* can be a call to an external Perl script or package name (which calls the handler method of the package by default), or it can specify an anonymous function expressed as sub{}:

```
<--perl sub="SomePackage" arg="first" arg="second" -->
<--perl sub="sub {for (0..4) { print \"some line\n\" }}" -->
```

Apache Modules Packaged with mod_perl

For the administrator who merely wants to write dynamic or interactive Web content or access a database from Web forms, the real benefit of mod_perl comes not from its API but from a number of existing modules written to work with Apache and mod_perl. Some of these come packaged with mod_perl to extend its functionality, but there are others that perform a wide variety of different functions. Examples include modules to authenticate clients using a wide variety of databases and authentication schemes, modules that implement server-side HTML parsing using the ASP and SSI specifications, and modules that maintain shared, persistent, connections to back-end databases for the quickest possible access to data stores.

All Apache modules, including older versions, are archived and available at:

```
www.perl.org/CPAN-local/modules/by-module/Apache/
```

Advanced
Configuration Options

PART 3

To find only the most recent version of each, go to the CPAN search site and search for modules matching the string *Apache*. As a shortcut, you can use the following URL:

```
search.cpan.org/search?mode=module&query=Apache
```

The Apache::Registry Module   Of all the support modules that mod_perl relies on, Apache::Registry is without question the most important. The module is so important that mod_perl can't be installed or used without it. The two work hand in hand, and many of the functions we think of as part of mod_perl are actually performed by the Apache::Registry Perl module. The module performs two tasks that greatly extend mod_perl. First, it provides a full emulation of the CGI environment, allowing CGI scripts to be run under mod_perl without modification. Remember, mod_perl only provides a Perl programmer's interface to Apache and embeds a Perl interpreter into the Apache kernel. It is these functions of mod_perl that Apache::Registry uses to provide CGI emulation to Apache and its Perl interpreter. Although it is a separate Perl module, Apache::Registry is inseperable from mod_perl, and each depends on the other.

The second essential Apache::Registry function is called *script caching*. Perl CGI scripts are automatically loaded into a special namespace managed by Apache::Registry and maintained there, rather than being unloaded from memory after they are used. This means that a CGI program is loaded and compiled only the first time it is called, and subsequent calls to the same program are run in the cached code. This greatly increases the throughput of the Perl engine, as I'll show in a later section on benchmarking mod_perl.

Although Apache::Registry provides the functions of CGI emulation and script caching, these are usually attributed to mod_perl, and for that reason I won't refer again to Apache::Registry. Whenever I refer to mod_perl, I'm speaking of mod_perl with Apache::Registry and other support modules of lesser importance. Without these, mod_perl doesn't do much for the typical Apache administrator but is merely a programmer's interface.

Configuring Apache to Use Apache::Registry   To use mod_perl to run CGI scripts, you need to declare Apache::Registry as the handler for those scripts. On my server, I used the following <Location> section to specify Apache::Registry as the handler for request URLs ending in /perl:

```
<Location /perl>
    SetHandler perl-script
    PerlHandler Apache::Registry
    PerlSendHeader On
    Options +ExecCGI
</Location>
```

The PerlSendHeader On line causes mod_perl to generate common HTTP headers just as mod_cgi does when processing standard CGI. By default, mod_perl sends no headers. It is a good idea to always enable the PerlSendHeader directive, especially when using unmodified standard CGI scripts with mod_perl.

I used the following Alias directive to assign a directory outside Apache's DocumentRoot to the /perl request URL:

```
Alias /perl/ /home/httpd/perl/
```

The directory so defined does not have to be located under the Apache DocumentRoot, and in my case, it is not. I used the following Linux command lines to create the new directory, copy the environ.cgi script to it, and then change the ownership of the directory and its contents to the nobody account and the group ownership to www. On your system, ensure that the file is owned by the same user account under which the Apache httpd processes run, and that the group ownership is set to a group that includes your Web administrators.

```
# mkdir /home/httpd/perl
# cp /home/httpd/cgi-bin/environ.cgi /home/httpd/perl
# chown -R nobody.www /home/httpd
```

After installing mod_perl, I called http://jackal.hiwaay.net/perl/environ.pl, and the changes made to the server are highlighted below:

```
Content-type: text/html
SERVER_SOFTWARE: Apache/1.3.9 (Unix) ApacheJServ/1.1 PHP/3.0.15 Resin/1.1 mod_
fastcgi/2.2.2 mod_perl/1.24 AuthMySQL/2.20
DOCUMENT_ROOT = /home/httpd/html
GATEWAY_INTERFACE = CGI-Perl/1.1
UNIQUE_ID = OFF8fn8AAAEAAAhZDWw
REMOTE_ADDR = 192.168.1.2
SERVER_PROTOCOL = HTTP/1.0
SERVER_SIGNATURE =
Apache/1.3.9 Server at Jackal.hiwaay.net Port 80

REQUEST_METHOD = GET
QUERY_STRING =
HTTP_USER_AGENT = Mozilla/4.7 [en] (WinNT; I)
PATH = /bin:/usr/bin:/usr/ucb:/usr/bsd:/usr/local/bin
HTTP_CONNECTION = Keep-Alive
HTTP_ACCEPT = image/gif, image/x-xbitmap, image/jpeg, image/pjpeg, image/png,
*/*
```

```
REMOTE_PORT = 2102
SERVER_ADDR = 192.168.1.1
HTTP_ACCEPT_LANGUAGE = en
MOD_PERL = mod_perl/1.24
SCRIPT_NAME = /perl/environ.cgi
SCRIPT_FILENAME = /home/httpd/perl/environ.cgi
HTTP_ACCEPT_ENCODING = gzip
SERVER_NAME = Jackal.hiwaay.net
REQUEST_URI = /perl/environ.cgi
HTTP_ACCEPT_CHARSET = iso-8859-1,*,utf-8
SERVER_PORT = 80
HTTP_HOST = Jackal
SERVER_ADMIN = root@jackal.hiwaay.net
```

A Few Other Important Apache Modules   Two other Apache modules for Perl, `Apache::ASP` and `Apache::DBI`, are worth mentioning but are too ambitious to cover in detail here. Both allow you to add extensive functionality to Apache. Because each of them relies on the mechanisms of `mod_perl`, they also offer efficiency and speed. They are available, and documented, from the `perl.apache.org` and `search.cpan.org` sites.

`Apache::ASP`   This Perl module provides Active Server Pages (ASP), a popular Microsoft-developed technology that originated with the Microsoft IIS server. The Microsoft Win32 version of ASP for IIS allows the embedding of Perl, VBScript, and JScript code in HTML documents. Using `Apache::ASP`, programmers already proficient in ASP on IIS servers can leverage this knowledge by programming ASP pages in Perl. Although VBScript and JScript cannot be used with `Apache::ASP`, there is an effort underway to bring these to non-Microsoft platforms in a product called OpenASP (see "ASP for Apache" in Chapter 9).

`Apache::DBI`   This module (which should not be confused with the standard `DBI.pm` module) enables the caching of database handles in the same way that Perl code is cached and reused by Perl scripts. The section "Persistent Database Connections" later in this chapter discusses `Apache::DBI` in detail.

Embedded Perl Solutions

A very popular technique used by Perl Web programmers today is embedding Perl in HTML code, in very much the same way that Active Server Pages are used. The two most popular embedded Perl techniques, however, are designed specifically for Perl, riding on top of the `mod_perl` Apache module for efficiency. I will briefly describe these two embedded Perl systems. Both are complete development systems in their own right, and can be used to develop complete Web-based applications.

HTML::EmbPerl   Although mod_perl and mod_include work together to allow embedded Perl in server-parsed HTML pages, this module provides another way to embed Perl in HTML documents. EmbPerl provides its own tags and commands for processing conditional statements and loops, evaluating Perl code, and building HTML structures such as tables or drop-down lists. Essentially, EmbPerl defines a new specification for server-parsed embedded HTML content. The module, although well documented (see http://perl.apache.org/embperl/), does require learning a new, nonstandard, method of using server-side includes. The module offers far more functions than are available in standard SSI provided through mod_include, and it is a rich set of development tools for programmers who prefer the embedded code approach to developing dynamic Web pages. EmbPerl enjoys active and strong support from its author as well as a large user community, an asset whose value is hard to quantify, but it is unquestionably one of the major reasons to use EmbPerl.

HTML::Mason   The newer HTML::Mason Perl module appears, on the surface, to work remarkably like its cousin, EmbPerl, but there are some critical differences between the two. While EmbPerl tends to take a grass-roots approach, starting with HTML and enhancing it, Mason takes a top-down view of things. Before the HTML or Perl code ever comes into play, Mason starts with a master plan, in which Web pages are composed of the output of *components*. These components are usually mixtures of HTML, embedded Perl, and special Mason commands. The emphasis is on site design and page structure, rather than on simply embedding Perl functions in HTML documents. This approach encourages code and design component reuse. Mason is full of functions to facilitate the reuse of code, either by simple inclusion in a document, or through filters (which modify the output of a component) and templates (which work somewhat like style sheets to apply a format to an entire directory of pages).

HTML::Mason is not strictly an Apache add-on. It will work in stand-alone mode or CGI mode, but the developers highly recommend that it be used with Apache supporting the mod_perl module. HTML::Mason is well documented at the author's Web site, which also hosts a small library of user-written components that can be downloaded and used or examined to learn the use of the product.

Improving the Performance of mod_perl

The techniques covered in this section are not required for using mod_perl, but they offer ways to significantly increase its performance. Mod_perl relies on a memory-resident Perl interpreter for part of the magic that allows it to increase the speed of Perl/CGI scripts; it uses caching to achieve the rest. You'll see two ways of using mod_perl's caching engine more efficiently, and then the results of a few benchmark tests I ran to verify that mod_perl does, indeed, deliver on its promise of greatly increasing your Perl script performance.

Persistent Database Connections

Although our database query example was made more efficient using mod_perl because the DBI and DBD::mysql modules are cached and reused, most of the processing overhead associated with these modules occurs in establishing database connections. This is particularly true if the connections are to a remote database server, which is quite often the case on today's networks. Far greater efficiency can be realized through the use of persistent database connections, in which the database connection is opened once by Apache and shared among all clients.

The Apache::DBI module provides automatic connection caching and sharing. If this module is used instead of the regular DBI.pm module, it monitors all DBI (Database Independent module) requests issued through mod_perl. As Apache::Registry does for scripts, Apache::DBI caches database connections. For each running httpd process, only the first DBI->connect actually results in a new database connection. After that, whenever a script calls DBI->connect, it is given a cached database handle, rather than a new handle resulting from a fresh connection. When the script uses the disconnect call to close the handle, Apache::DBI handles this request by returning the handle to its cache rather than actually closing the database connection. The use of shared persistent database connections results in a significant improvement in the speed of Perl DBI database operations.

To use Apache::DBI, install it using CPAN.pm:

```
# cpan
cpan shell -- CPAN exploration and modules installation (v1.54)
ReadLine support enabled

cpan> install Apache::DBI
```

Then remove all use DBI lines from scripts that should use cached database handles. This will prevent calls to DBI functions from being handled by the standard DBI module. All such calls will instead be handled automatically by Apache::DBI module.

You should *never* attempt to open a database connection during Apache's startup sequence (for example, from a mod_perl startup script). This may seem like a logical way to open database connections for later use, but the database handles created this way are shared among the httpd child server processes, rather than being opened one-per-httpd-process. This can create conflicts between httpd processes trying to use the same database handle simultaneously.

Preloading Modules

Remember that the main Apache httpd process creates child httpd processes to handle all user requests, and these child processes inherit the namespace of the main process. Each child process inherits its own copy of the Perl modules loaded by the main server to support mod_perl. As requests for CGI scripts are fulfilled, each process will also load its own copy of Apache::Registry and maintain its own cache of compiled Perl scripts. These child httpd processes are usually killed after answering a fixed number of requests (configured using the MaxRequestsPerChild directive). This can mitigate problems associated with potential memory leaks, but it also destroys each httpd process's Apache::Registry cache and requires that each be built again from scratch. This can happen thousands of times during the lifetime of the main server process.

To prevent cached Perl code from being destroyed along with the child process that loaded it, mod_perl provides two configuration directives that enable Perl scripts to be preloaded into the namespace of the main server and inherited by all the child processes it creates.

The first of these is PerlRequire, which specifies a single Perl script to load when Apache starts up:

```
PerlRequire startup.pl
```

Generally, this script contains use statements that load other Perl code. This directive is used to preload external modules that are common to a number of Perl scripts:

```
# contents of startup.pl
use Apache::Registry;
use CGI;
use CGI::Carp;
use Apache::DBI;
```

The script specified must exist in one of the directories specified in the @INC array (described in the next section).

The second directive that can be used for this purpose is PerlModule, which can specify a single module to preload when Apache starts. The startup.pl script shown can also be rewritten entirely in httpd.conf with these four directives:

```
PerlModule Apache::Registry
PerlModule CGI
PerlModule CGI::Carp
PerlModule Apache::DBI
```

Advanced Configuration Options

PART 3

The advantage of using `PerlModule` is that an external startup script is not required. A limitation of `PerlModule`, however, is that no more than 10 modules can be preloaded using `PerlModule` directives. For most sites, this limitation is not significant, but if you need to preload more than 10 modules, you will need to use a startup script.

Including External Code

Whenever a Perl script contains a `use` or `require` statement to pull in external code, it searches a path defined in the `@INC` array. This array is created for each Perl script from information compiled into the Perl interpreter. Under mod_perl, two additional directories are added to this array, both under the directory where Apache is installed. You can view this array on your system by running `perl -V`, which lists all compiled-in values. Scripts running under mod_perl on my server search this array for external code:

```
@INC =
/usr/lib/perl5/5.00503/i386-linux
/usr/lib/perl5/5.00503
/usr/lib/perl5/site_perl/5.005/i386-linux
/usr/lib/perl5/site_perl/5.005
.
/usr/local/apache/
/usr/local/apache/lib/perl
```

The last two directories will appear only if mod_perl is used. The last directory specified in this array provides a convenient location for storing Perl scripts that are intended for use only with mod_perl. Although Perl fills `@INC` from values compiled into Perl when you run a program, you can add directories to this array with the `use lib` statement, which is best placed in a startup script to ensure that all processes inherit the modified `@INC` array. To add the directory /usr/local/perlstuff to the @INC array, add a line like the following somewhere at the beginning of your startup script:

```
use lib /usr/local/perlstuff
```

Unlike ordinary scripts, code loaded through `use` and `require` modules is not automatically reloaded if it is changed. For this reason, you should use these statements only to call code that will not change, particularly if you are loading it into the main server namespace, which will not be refreshed as child processes expire and are killed.

Handling Server Restarts

The default behavior of mod_perl is to retain all cached Perl code when the server is restarted using `apachectl restart` (as opposed to being stopped and then started). Use the `PerlFreshRestart` directive to ensure that the cached code resulting from

PerlRequire and PerlModule directives in httpd.conf is refreshed when Apache is restarted:

```
PerlFreshRestart on
```

Benchmarking mod_perl

To find out just how much faster mod_perl runs than a traditional Perl script invoked through the CGI interface, I used the excellent ApacheBench benchmarking tool that comes packaged with Apache (you'll find it as ab in the bin directory where Apache is installed).

Listing 8.9 shows a very simple CGI script that does nothing but return the system environment.

Listing 8.9   A Test Script Used with ApacheBench

```perl
#!/usr/bin/perl
#ReportWho.cgi - Show environment variables set by the server

print "Content-type: text/html\n\n";
print "<HTML><HEAD><TITLE>Environment Variables</TITLE></HEAD><BODY>";
print "<H2>Environment Variables:</H2>";
print "<HR>\n";
foreach $evar( keys (%ENV)){
        print "<B>$evar:</B> $ENV{$evar}<BR>";
}
print "</BODY></HTML>\n";
```

I used ab to execute this script as ordinary CGI with the following command line:

```
# ab -n 10000 -c 20 192.168.1.1:80/cgi-bin/environ.cgi
```

Here, -n represents the number of requests to make, and -c indicates the number of concurrent connections to my server that would be opened by ab.

I collected statistics on 10,000 requests to /cgi-bin/environ.cgi, and then I executed the following command line to collect the same statistics on /perl/environ.cgi. These requests are handled by mod_perl and Apache::Registry.

```
# ab -n 10000 -c 20 192.168.1.1:80/perl/environ.cgi
```

Advanced Configuration Options

PART 3

The results of my benchmark test (Tables 8.1 and 8.2) show the number of requests that can be answered is 350% that of unmodified Apache.

Table 8.1 Perl/CGI versus mod_perl Benchmark Results

	Apache 1.3.9/CGI	Apache 1.39/mod_perl 1.21
Server Hostname	192.168.1.1	192.168.1.1
Server Port	80	80
Document Path	/cgi-bin/environ.cgi	/perl/environ.cgi
Concurrency Level	20	20
Elapsed Time	348.735 seconds	97.294 seconds
Complete requests	10000	10000
Failed requests	0	0
Total transferred	12530000 bytes	11067762 bytes
HTML transferred	10510000 bytes	10817587 bytes
Requests per second	28.68	102.78
Transfer rate	35.93 Kbps received	113.76 Kbps received

Table 8.2 Perl/CGI versus mod_perl Benchmark Results—Connection Times (ms)

	Apache 1.3.9/CGI			Apache 1.39/mod_perl		
	Min	Avg	Max	Min	Avg	Max
Connect	0	0	192	0	58	231
Processing	31	696	1963	86	134	1160
Total	31	696	2155	86	92	1391

If the additional efficiency that could be obtained through persistent database connection sharing were introduced, these numbers would be even more impressive. That's why I ran the second set of tests shown in Tables 8.3 and 8.4.

The results in these tables show an even more remarkable improvement in speed using mod_perl. This example queries the zipcodes MySQL database 1000 times, using this command line:

```
# ab -n 1000 -c 20 192.168.1.1:80/cgi-bin/zipcodes.cgi?zip="35016"
```

I then ran the same test through mod_perl, using this command:

```
# ab -n 1000 -c 20 192.168.1.1:80/perl/zipcodes.cgi?zip="35016"
```

This test really gave mod_perl a chance to shine. It not only takes advantage of the embedded Perl interpreter, which eliminates the shell process creation overhead associated with CGI, but also allows Apache::Registry to open a database connection and pass the database handle to processes that ordinarily would have to open and close their own connections. With absolutely no attempt to optimize mod_perl, I saw an increase of nearly 1400% in the number of connections served per second. I'm no benchmarking expert, and these results are from something less than a controlled scientific experiment, but they were enough to convince me that mod_perl runs circles around conventional CGI.

Table 8.3 Benchmarking Results Using Database Connection Sharing

	Apache 1.3.9/CGI	Apache 1.39/mod_perl 1.21
Server Hostname	192.168.1.1	192.168.1.1
Server Port	80	80
Document Path	/cgi-bin/zipcodes .cgi?zip="35801"	/perl/zipcodes .cgi?zip="35801"
Concurrency Level	20	20
Elapsed Time	962.537 seconds	63.691 seconds
Complete Requests	1000	1000
Failed Requests	0	0

Table 8.3 Benchmarking Results Using Database Connection Sharing *(continued)*

	Apache 1.3.9/CGI	Apache 1.39/mod_perl 1.21
Total Transferred	566000 bytes	690000 bytes
HTML Transferred	333000 bytes	457000 bytes
Requests per Second	1.04	15.70
Transfer Rate	0.59Kbps received	10.83Kbps received

Table 8.4 Benchmarking Results Using Database Connection Sharing—Connection Times (ms)

	Apache 1.3.9/CGI			Apache 1.39/mod_perl		
	Min	**Avg**	**Max**	**Min**	**Avg**	**Max**
Connect	0	0	35	0	25	1810
Processing	12328	19099	39583	110	962	31039
Total	12328	19099	39618	110	962	32849

Checking the Status of mod_perl

mod_perl also comes with a nice built-in handler for checking the status of the module. In order to use the status handler, make sure you have a section like the following in your Apache httpd.conf to define the Apache::Status module as a handler for a special request URL:

```
<Location /perl-status>
    SetHandler perl-script
    PerlHandler Apache::Status
</Location>
```

Figure 8.4 shows this status page, which was invoked on my server using the URL http://jackal.hiwaay.net/perl-status.

Figure 8.4   Displaying the status of mod_perl

The first part of the display shows the embedded Perl version, along with the server string that identifies many of the capabilities of the server, as well as the date when the server was started. The lower part of the display is a menu of links to more detailed information about specific areas. Particularly check out the Loaded Modules page, shown in Figure 8.5. This page lists all of the Perl modules that have been compiled and are held in cache by Apache::Registry. When Apache is first started, this page shows the 21 modules loaded into cache and available to be run by the embedded Perl interpreter.

These are the modules preloaded by mod_perl and required to implement and support it. After running a single script (the Perl/CGI zipcode query), I checked this page again, and discovered that the following scripts had been loaded, compiled, and cached:

```
Apache::Registry
CGI
CGI::Carp
CGI::Util
DBI
DBD::mysql
```

Figure 8.5 The Loaded Modules status page

These are the modules that were called for use in my query program, except for Apache::Registry, which is loaded at the same time as the first CGI request. (Remember that in httpd.conf, we specified Apache::Registry as the handler for scripts called with the URL /perl/*.)

The modules CGI.pm and DBI.pm have been loaded, as well as the database-dependent module for MySQL. These have actually been loaded for only one httpd daemon. If that daemon receives another request for a Perl/CGI script that needs these module, they do not have to be loaded or compiled, and there is no need to spawn a Perl process to run them because there is one already running (mod_perl's embedded Perl interpreter). This gives Perl scripts blinding speed under mod_perl.

Use the mod_perl status pages to ensure that the module is properly installed and is caching your scripts as they are executed. Particularly, ensure that the most frequently accessed scripts are preloaded when Apache starts. By viewing the status pages immediately after starting Apache, you can see which scripts are preloaded, compiled, and cached for arriving requests.

Programming With mod_perl

In addition to acting as an accelerator for Perl scripts run from Apache through CGI, mod_perl also provides two other features for programming Apache. The first allows Apache modules to be completely written in Perl (freeing Apache module developers from having to use C). The second feature, far less useful, allows the Apache httpd.conf file to include Perl code so that Apache directives can be dynamically created when Apache is loaded.

Using Perl Handlers

Besides linking the Perl interpreter to the Apache kernel, mod_perl has another important feature. It allows us to write Apache modules in Perl. We do this by using special mod_perl directives in httpd.conf to specify Perl programs as callbacks during stages of the Apache request processing cycle and by providing the module programmer with a rich set of Perl functions that correspond to functions in the Apache API. (These were formerly accessible only to programs written in C.)

The following configuration directives are defined by mod_perl, each corresponding to a different phase in the Apache request processing cycle:

```
PerlHandler - Perl Content Generation handler
PerlTransHandler - Perl Translation handler
PerlAuthenHandler - Perl Authentication handler
PerlAuthzHandler - Perl Authorization handler
PerlAccessHandler - Perl Access handler
PerlTypeHandler - Perl Type check handler
PerlFixupHandler - Perl Fixup handler
PerlLogHandler - Perl Log handler
PerlCleanupHandler - Perl Cleanup handler
PerlInitHandler - Perl Init handler
PerlHeaderParserHandler - Perl Header Parser handler
PerlChildInitHandler - Perl Child init handler
PerlChildExitHandler - Perl Child exit handler
PerlPostReadRequestHandler - Perl Post Read Request handler
PerlDispatchHandler - Perl Dispatch handler
PerlRestartHandler - Perl Restart handler
```

A caution may be in order here, that you are entering real programmers' territory—but actually all of these handlers are very easy to use. They allow you to specify Perl code to

Advanced
Configuration Options

PART 3

perform functions at various stages during the handling of an HTTP request without having to use the specialized functions of the Apache API (although those are still available). The most important of these directives is `PerlHandler`, which defines a Perl module that is called by Apache during the Content Generation phase immediately after a document is retrieved from disk. The module defined by `PerlHandler` can do whatever it wants with that document (for example, it is this handler that is used to parse an SSI document). Previously, I showed how to use this directive to define `Apache::Registry` as the handler for scripts identified (by the /perl/ in their URL) to be run under `mod_perl`.

Listing 8.10 illustrates a very simple Perl logging program to write request information to a MySQL database. The $r in this example is an object that represents the HTTP request headers and is extracted from another object that is passed to the script by `mod_perl`, which contains everything Apache knows about the HTTP request being processed.

Listing 8.10 A Logging Program for `mod_perl`

```perl
package Apache::LogMySQL;

# Pull httpd.h constants into this namespace
use Apache::Constants qw(:common);

use strict;

# uncomment if Apache::DBI not used
# use DBI ();

use Apache::Util qw(ht_time);

sub handler {
    my $orig = shift;
    my $r = $orig->last;
    my $date    = ht_time($orig->request_time, '%Y-%m-%d %H:%M:%S', 0);
    my $host    = $r->get_remote_host;
    my $method  = $r->method;
    my $url     = $orig->uri;
    my $user    = $r->connection->user;
    my $referer = $r->header_in('Referer');
    my $browser = $r->header_in('User-agent');
    my $status  = $orig->status;
    my $bytes   = $r->bytes_sent;
```

```
    my $dbh =
        DBI->connect("DBI:mysql:mydblog:jackal.hiwaay.net","root","password")
            || die $DBI::errstr;

    my $sth = $dbh->prepare("INSERT INTO accesslog VALUES(?,?,?,?,?,?,?,?,?)")
                | die $dbh->errstr;

    $sth->execute($date,$host,$method,$url,$user,
                    $browser,$referer,$status,$bytes) || die $dbh->errstr;
    return OK;
}


1;
__END__
```

If this file is saved as LogMySQL.pm under the Apache package directory (/usr/lib/
perl5/site_perl/5.005/Apache on my system), it can be specified as a handler for the
logging phase of Apache's HTTP request cycle with the single directive:

```
PerlLogHandler Apache::LogMySQL
```

Each time a request is handled, at the Log Handler phase, this program is called. Note
that it creates its own namespace (Apache::LogMySQL). There's not a lot to know about
this application, except that $r refers to the Apache request object, and all the informa-
tion required for the log is retrieved from that object. A special function, ht_time() in the
Apache::Util module is used to format the request timestamp that is logged. Also note
the commented Use DBI() line; that line is required only if Use Apache::DBI was not
specified in a startup.pl script so that database connections will be shared. In this
example, since Apache::DBI is used, each time this handler script calls DBI->connect, it
is handed a database handle for a database connection already opened (by Apache::DBI)
to use. This handle is returned when the script finishes, and it is used over and over.

This example is a bare skeleton of what is required to set up a Perl handler. Although it
is a real example, it is minimal. You should evaluate DBI logging modules already written
(Apache::DBILogConfig or Apache::DBILogger) before you write your own, although
you may want to do it just for fun. Look for Apache logging modules at http://
search.cpan.org/.

Using mod_perl to Modify httpd.conf

Another enhancement to Apache added by mod_perl is the ability to include Perl code
within <Perl> sections in httpd.conf. These are interpreted when the server is started
and used to dynamically generate configuration directives. I haven't found this feature

very useful, and it tends to overcomplicate the server configuration. Furthermore, although using Perl code in your `httpd.conf` file may simplify and shorten that text file, the configuration that is eventually loaded by Apache and stored in memory is identical to the configuration that would be constructed using conventional configuration directives. There are no efficiency benefits to the use of Perl sections.

There are cases, however, when this feature might simplify the configuration process. You might consider using <Perl> sections when configuration directives can be generated programmatically (for example, by retrieving their values from a relational database). Another use is when a loop can be used to configure a number of sections (as, for example, when a list of virtual hosts is used to construct a number of <VirtualHost> sections).

To enable this capability, when installing mod_perl using the APACI or apxs methods described in this chapter, you need to specify PERL_SECTIONS=1:

```
perl Makefile.PL PERL_SECTIONS=1
```

To use <Perl> sections, you need only create variables with the same names as valid configuration directives and assign values to these, either as scalars or as Perl lists, which are interpreted later as space-delimited strings. In other words, if you wanted to create a Port directive and assign it the value 80, you could use the following <Perl> section:

```
<Perl>
    $Port=80;
</Perl>
```

When Apache is started and this configuration file is parsed, these variables are converted to regular configuration directives that are then treated as though they were read directly from `httpd.conf`. A couple of examples will illustrate how this works. Here, a Perl section is used to configure some general server directives:

```
<Perl>
@PerlModule = qw(Apache::Include Apache::DBI CGI);
$User="wwwroot";
$Group="wwwgroup";
$ServerAdmin="caulds@hiwaay.net";
__END__   # All text following this token ignored by preprocessor
</Perl>
```

The following example illustrates how hashes are used to store the contents of container directives. Nested containers are stored as nested Perl hashes.

```
<Perl>
$Directory{"/secure/"} = {
```

```
      @AllowOverride = (FileInfo AuthConfig Limit);
      AuthUserFile => "/usr/local/adminpwds";
      AuthGroupFile => "/usr/local/groups";
      AuthType => "Basic";
      Limit => {
         METHODS => "GET POST",
         Require => "group Webteam";
      }
   }
   __END__
</Perl>
```

Of course, the Perl sections in these examples offer no benefit over the use of ordinary configuration directives. The real benefit would be in cases where Perl code dynamically creates (potentially hundreds of) virtual hosts. Suppose, for example, that we had a text file that consisted of virtual host definitions, one per line, stored as `sites.conf`. This is a very simple example that does virtually no sanity checking, but it could be used to generate a number of IP-based virtual hosts. Whenever virtual hosts in the list need to be added, deleted, or modified, the change is made to `sites.conf`, and `httpd.conf` doesn't need to be changed.

```
<Perl>
open SITECONF, "< /usr/local/apache/conf/sites.conf" or die "$!";
while (<SITECONF>) {
   chomp;
   next if /^s*#/ || /^s*$/; # Skip comments & blank lines
   my @fields = split(/:/,$_,-1);
   die "Bad sites.conf file format" unless scalar(@fields)==6;
   my ($sitename, $sadmin, $ip, $http_dir, $errlog, $tfrlog)= @fields;
   $VirtualHost{$ip} = {
      ServerName => $sitename,
      ServerAdmin => $sadmin,
      DocumentRoot => "/home/httpd/".$http_dir,
      ErrorLog => "logs/".$errlog,
      TransferLog => "logs/".$tfrlog
   };
}
close SITECONF;
__END__
</Perl>
```

If you choose to use Perl sections to configure virtual hosts dynamically, remember that you can run `httpd -S` to display the virtual host configuration.

In Sum

The earliest method of interfacing external programs to the Apache Web server is the Common Gateway Interface, once the de facto standard for programming Web applications. CGI remains a viable technique for Apache programming.

The biggest drawback of traditional CGI (poor performance) has been largely eliminated, first by the use of FastCGI (implemented in the Apache module `mod_fastcgi`) and more recently by `mod_perl`. Both of these Apache add-ons eliminate the overhead of starting a new Perl interpreter process each time a CGI script is called. The `mod_perl` module goes a step farther and uses a caching mechanism to ensure that scripts, once compiled into Perl pseudo-code, are available for subsequent invocation without requiring recompilation.

This chapter has shown how to modify Apache to use these programming techniques, and it has illustrated the use of each with a simple, yet useful, application that queries a relational database using user-entered data as a search key. The next chapter examines programming techniques that are somewhat newer than CGI, each of which has garnered a lot of attention and a large number of devotees in the past few years.

9

Other Apache Scripting/Programming Tools

No aspect of Apache administration has changed as much as the need to support a variety of programming languages and tools. Where only a few short years ago, a Web server with built-in support for CGI scripting was sufficient, today as an Apache administrator you may be expected to understand and support a number of other programming methodologies.

This chapter will introduce you to the most widely used Web program development systems used on Apache servers today. The emphasis of the chapter is on installing the systems discussed and verifying their workability. As an administrator, you may not be called on to program using these tools, but I hope this chapter helps you understand how they work and enables you to install basic Apache support for each.

PHP

If you've been involved in Web site development in the last couple of years, you probably know about PHP (originally called Personal Home Page Tools). Developed in 1994 as a simple HTML-embedded (server-parsed) tool for creating dynamic content in Web pages, PHP has steadily grown into a powerful Web development tool. It is also becoming one of the most popular. In fact, it is by far the most widely used Apache module. The April 2000 survey from SecuritySpace.com (`www.securityspace.com`) shows that three times as many Internet sites use PHP as `mod_perl`. PHP is based on years of effort from a large number of contributors and is distributed under an open source license from `www.php.net`. PHP is not a toy, and it is far more than an enhanced server-side includes.

PHP built a reputation as a powerful scripting language that was simple enough to appeal to site designers who weren't necessarily professional programmers. In this regard, it has succeeded admirably. For many Web designers, embedding code in HTML pages is natural and intuitive (even though most programmers find that approach messy and inelegant). I was surprised at how quickly I could create interesting and useful applications with PHP. There is almost nothing that can be done with CGI that cannot be done with PHP.

PHP greatly enables server-parsed scripting, and it has a place in any Web programmer's toolkit. Intermixing code with HTML is great for simple requirements, but when the amount of code significantly exceeds the HMTL, the pages become difficult to read. Particularly for pages that rely on the inclusion of external documents or scripts, the benefits of server-parsed HTML can be debated.

PHP has always been great for rapid development of dynamic Web pages, but with the release of PHP 4.0 in May 2000, PHP has acquired a sorely needed performance boost and features that are required of any top-shelf Web application development environment.

PHP Documentation

One of the really nice features of PHP is the documentation provided by the developers. Not only is the documentation thorough and helpful, but there's a lot of it. You can download the entire manual as a huge two-part PDF file (for printing and binding), or you can download the HTML version of the manual and put it on your own server. The PHP manual is also available as an RTF file or a DOC file for the PalmPilot (for the PHP enthusiast on the go). There are even translations of the manual into French and Japanese.

The PHP HTML online manual is the real star of the show, though. There are hundreds of functions in the PHP language, and this well organized and easy to search online manual is truly an essential resource. Bookmark it at a `php.net` mirror site near you (Figure 9.1), particularly if you are outside the United States. You'll see that I read the manual from the US mirror site (`us.php.net`), which may not be your best choice.

One of the really interesting and valuable features of the online HTML documentation is the user notes section at the bottom of each page. Viewers can submit notes on the page and read notes submitted by previous visitors. The comments are often informative and interesting and are a tremendous enhancement to the developer-supplied documentation. This is a feature I would like to see in the online documentation of other sites.

Figure 9.1   Bookmarking the PHP HTML documentation

PHP 4.0

PHP 4.0 was released in May 2000, and it is the features added to that version that make PHP highly appealing. It is to the credit of the PHP development team that this new release is intended to eliminate the most significant weaknesses in PHP 3.0 rather than simply stuffing in as many new eye-catching features as possible. The new release makes real progress in dealing with most of the drawbacks of using PHP on a real-world server, particularly its poor speed and lack of object orientation. If you are considering PHP, you should definitely plan to download this latest version.

Virtually all changes to PHP in version 4.0 are internal and don't affect the way PHP is used. There should be no difference in the way PHP 4.0 and PHP 3.0 are installed, and all scripts that run in 3.0 should work without modification in 4.0.

The most significant change in PHP 4.0 is a compete rewrite of the PHP scripting engine, incorporating a language parser called the Zend Engine, from Zend Technologies Ltd. (www.zend.com). This odd partnership between the open-source PHP development team and a commercial firm has far-reaching impact. Zend Technologies will also offer a freely available tool called the Zend Optimizer, which examines PHP code and performs optimizations that are claimed to double the running speed of most PHP applications. And, finally, there are plans to release the Zend Compiler. The compiler will function much like a Java pseudocode compiler to compile PHP into code that is not only faster at runtime, but also unreadable (for those developers who want to distribute their product, but not in source format). The compiler is the one component that won't be free.

Database Support in PHP

One of the reasons often given for PHP's wide acceptance by Web developers is its strong support for databases. The latest version of PHP supports all of the following database engines (although a special configuration directive is required for each to compile this support into the resulting module):

Adabas D

dBase

DBMaker

Empress

filePro

IBM DB2

Informix

InterBase

LDAP

Linux/Unix DBM

Microsoft SQL Server

mSQL

MySQL

Oracle

PostgresSQL

Solid Embedded Engine

Sybase

Velocis

Installing PHP as a Red Hat Package

The easiest way to install PHP is with a prepackaged RPM, but I only recommend this when you have not compiled the Apache source code yourself (usually because you installed Apache as an RPM, or it was installed as part of your Linux distribution). If you're looking for the easiest possible installation of PHP, grab the RPM; it's very complete and probably meets all of the requirements of most sites. If you did compile Apache yourself, you'll want to install PHP as a DSO, as described in the next section.

The site to search first for downloadable copies of the RPM is the Rpmfind.Net repository (`http://rpmfind.net/`). Look for an RPM with a name beginning with *php*. By the time you read this, PHP4 should be available as RPMs.

Before installing PHP from an RPM, first determine if PHP is already installed on your system (you can do this with the command `rpm -qa | grep PHP`). I had trouble installing PHP the first time from an RPM and encountered errors about conflicting files. I recommend that you uninstall any previous version of PHP (using `rpm -e`) before installing a new version of the RPM.

Installing the RPM was as easy as entering this line:

```
# rpm -i php-3.0.16-2.i386.rpm
```

The RPM will install all the files in their "proper" locations. Note that the RPM installs PHP as a DSO module. Although the RPM will install a number of files, including documentation, the only file you really need is the DSO module, `libphp3.so`. To use the module, it is necessary to manually modify the Apache configuration files to add or uncomment the following lines (note that these will be slightly different if you are installing the PHP4 RPM):

```
LoadModule php3_module          libexec/libphp3.so
AddModule mod_php3.c


AddType application/x-httpd-php3 .php3
AddType application/x-httpd-php3-source .phps
```

To see what these configuration statements do, skip ahead to the section "Configuring Apache to Run PHP."

Installing PHP from Source Code

By far the best way to install PHP is from up-to-date source code, as a DSO module. If you'll pardon a lame pun, you should go straight to the source for your PHP source code (`www.php.net`). The Downloads section of that site contains source code for the latest production release versions, as well as for older versions no longer supported (at least as far back as PHP/FI version 1.99, dated May 1996).

I extracted my source files (as I normally do) into the /usr/local/src directory on my Linux server:

```
# cd /usr/local/src
# tar xvzf /home/caulds/downloads/ /home/caulds/
php-4.0.1pl2/
php-4.0.1pl2/build/
php-4.0.1pl2/build/build.mk
php-4.0.1pl2/build/build2.mk
php-4.0.1pl2/build/buildcheck.sh
php-4.0.1pl2/build/dynlib.mk
php-4.0.1pl2/build/fastgen.sh
php-4.0.1pl2/build/library.mk
php-4.0.1pl2/build/ltlib.mk
php-4.0.1pl2/build/mkdep.perl
php-4.0.1pl2/build/program.mk
... many lines deleted ...
```

Move into the PHP source directory:

```
# cd /php-4.0.1pl2
```

On my system, I created a file (build.sh) that contains all the options I used to configure the source for compilation. There are a huge number of configuration options for PHP; too many to list here. To obtain a list of all valid options, run the configure script with just the --help argument. The subset below is minimal, but completely sufficient for everything I do with PHP.

```
# cat build.sh
./configure --with-apxs=/usr/local/apache/bin/apxs \
--enable-debug=no \
--enable-safe-mode \
--with-mysql=/usr \
--with-exec-dir=/usr/bin \
--with-regex=system \
--with-xml
```

In most cases, the default values provided with PHP are well thought out and completely adequate. The only options I used that were essential were –apxs, which enables the use of `apxs` to compile and install PHP as a DSO module, and `--with-mysql`, which will compile support for the MySQL relational database into the resulting module. (You must have MySQL installed on the same server for this to work.)

You may need to enable support for other databases or multiple databases. Without a database behind it, PHP is only half the development system.

All available options to `configure` are well described in the PHP documentation, but the odds are you will never need to know about or use more than a few. Keep things simple. It's probably *not* worth your time to read the many pages of documentation that cover all the options. If you ever need an additional feature of PHP, you'll be able to easily determine which `configure` options are used to enable that feature.

The procedure used to build and install PHP is like most others described in this book: run the `configure` script (either by invoking it as a shell script like the `build.sh` file I created, or manually from the command line). PHP is an extensive system, and the configuration will run for some time, displaying hundreds of lines describing what it does. Following the configuration, run `make` and then `make install` to complete the process.

```
# ./build.sh
# make
# make install
```

The `make install` step places the compiled DSO into a location from which it can be loaded by Apache and then modifies `httpd.conf` to use the module. This should work properly for you, although my prerelease copy of PHP4.0 failed to make the correct entries in `httpd.conf`.

Configuring Apache to Run PHP

As noted in the previous two sections, installing PHP from an RPM requires you to modify your Apache configuration file manually, but compiling source code and running `make install` should add the necessary statements automatically. Either way, you need to ensure that your `httpd.conf` includes the proper lines.

```
LoadModule php4_module        libexec/libphp4.so

AddModule mod_php4.c

AddType application/x-httpd-php .php .php4
```

By now, you should recognize the `LoadModule` and `AddModule` lines as the directives required to load the PHP module and make it available to Apache. The first `AddType` directive specifies files ending in .php or .php4 to be of type x-httpd-php, for which the server knows that PHP is the proper handler. In other words, when a file with one of these extensions is read from disk, Apache gives it to PHP to be parsed before sending it to the requester.

Optional PHP Configuration Directives

Beyond the minimal configuration we've just looked at, Apache offers many configuration options that can be used with PHP. These can be placed not only in locations where normal Apache configuration directives are allowed (anywhere in httpd.conf or in .htaccess files), but also in a special file named php.ini file. This file is read only once, when Apache starts up, and it offers no advantages over placing the PHP directives directly in httpd.conf. It does, however, offer a convenient location to keep these directives separate from the basic Apache configuration. The path to the php.ini file (if used) is compiled into Apache by specifying

```
--with-config-file-path=PATH
```

when the configure script is run. An alternative is to specify this path in an environment variable, PHPRC.

PHP configuration options are all fairly advanced, and they all have default values that rarely need to be overridden. Chapter 3 of the PHP Manual discusses these directives, and is worth a quick review, but most administrators will never need to modify the default values provided by the PHP developers.

Another very useful technique, particularly for those learning PHP, is to use the AddType directive to define a filename extension to be associated with a new MIME content type that PHP adds:

```
AddType application/x-httpd-php-source .phps
```

This takes advantage of an ingenious feature for debugging HTML pages with embedded PHP commands. When a file ending in .phps is loaded, it is displayed in a Web browser with the PHP code (instead of being executed) highlighted in color to separate it from the surrounding HTML. To use this feature, you can take regular PHP source files, with the extension .php or .php4, and copy them to a file with the extension .phps. When requested from Apache with this filename, the page rendered in the browser will not execute PHP commands embedded in the documents, but will display them using colors to make them stand out. For simple HTML applications, seeing this source code is very instructional; for large applications where there's a lot of PHP in a page, it can be a tremendous debugging aid.

Configuration Changes from PHP 3 to PHP 4

Apache administrators upgrading from PHP 3 to PHP 4 need to be aware that the format of PHP directives used in the Apache configuration file (httpd.conf) has changed. In version 3.0, there were a large number of PHP directives that could be placed in httpd.conf. In 4.0, only four directives can be placed there, each of which includes the old PHP directive as an argument. The four possible PHP directives in PHP 4.0 are these:

```
php_value directive value
php_flag directive On | Off
php_admin_value directive value
php_admin_flag directive value
```

For example, these PHP3 directives:

```
include_path=/usr/local/phplib
display_errors On
```

would need to be expressed in PHP4 as:

```
php_admin_value include_path /usr/local/phplib
php_admin_flag display_errors On
```

The php_value directive is used with PHP directives that are set to a (non-Boolean) value, while php_flag is used with directives that can only be set to On or Off. The php_admin_* variants of both can be used only in server-wide configuration files (they are not permitted in .htaccess files or in a <Directory> container). The php_admin_* form is the only permitted way to specify certain PHP configuration directives in PHP 4.0. Restricting certain directives to server-wide use is only permitted when specified with the php_admin_* form; these directives can never be overridden in a narrower context (this is primarily to prohibit them from being overridden in an .htaccess file).

Users of PHP 3.0 transitioning to PHP 4.0 can take advantage of two shell scripts provided with PHP 4.0 that automatically convert PHP 3.0 configuration directives to the new PHP 4.0 format (these scripts are included with the PHP distribution):

apconf-conv.sh   The name of an Apache configuration file can be passed to this script as an argument:

```
apconf-conv.sh /usr/local/apache/conf/httpd.conf
```

aphtaccess-conf.sh   The name of an .htaccess file is passed to this script as an argument. It's best used with a Linux find command to perform this action for all .htaccess files:

```
find / -name .htaccess -exec /path/aphtaccess-conv.sh {} \;
```

Some PHP Examples

To test your PHP installation to make sure that everything is working, create a simple file like the one shown in Listing 9.1. Make sure the script is accessible from the Web (in Apache's DocumentRoot, for example) and has a .php extension (or .php3 if you are using PHP 3.0). Accessing this page from a browser, you should see something like Figure 9.2.

Listing 9.1   The Simplest PHP Example

```
<!-- HelloWorld.php -->
<html>
<body>
<? echo "Hello World -- PHP works!" ?>
</body>
</html>
```

Figure 9.2   The simplest PHP example viewed in a browser

The HelloWorld example is the simplest of all PHP scripts, useful for no more than testing the server. The script in Listing 9.2 is equally simple but does far more. This PHP script calls a built-in PHP function called phpinfo() and displays the output of that function. Figure 9.3

shows the resulting screen, which contains a wealth of information about PHP. Note that the exact configuration command used to build PHP is displayed. That's useful, isn't it? Take the time to review the information presented by this script. It's a good idea to save this script somewhere under a more descriptive name for future use, but make it something obscure, or better yet, restrict access to it (as described in Chapter 14) because it contains information that is better kept from public view.

Listing 9.2   PHPinfo.php

```
<!- PHPinfo.php -->
<html>
<body>
<?php
  phpinfo();
?>
</body>
</html>
```

Figure 9.3   The results of running PHPinfo.php

Note one other thing from Listing 9.2. The leading PHP tag is <?php, rather than the shorter <? form expressed in Listing 9.1. Either form can be used, but the short form is in conflict with the Extended Markup Language (XML) specification. If you are not using XML on your server it's safe to use the short form, but its use is discouraged and is best avoided completely. In fact, one of the newer PHP configuration options is --disable-short-tags, which disables support for this tag. Always use <?php and you should never have a problem.

Using Alternative Tags

Besides the <? and <?php tags, there are two other ways to escape PHP from the surrounding HTML, both probably best left alone by Linux Apache programmers. The first is a generic tag for specifying embedded scripts in an HTML document:

```
<script language="php">
   echo "PHP commands go here …";
</script>
```

The second form is familiar to anyone who has experience using Microsoft Active Server Pages.

```
<%
   echo "Parse this as PHP …";
%>
```

This last form must be explicitly enabled by including the following configuration directive in Apache's httpd.conf, an .htaccess file, or by a line in the php.ini file:

```
asp_tags on
```

Listing 9.3 is an example of PHP that's a bit more complicated, but quite easy to understand. This example simply tests to see if the user's browser is Microsoft Internet Explorer and displays one line if it is, or reports the browser identification string in its reply if it is not IE. This is useful to the server administrator who wants to customize source documents depending on the browser that the client is using.

Listing 9.3 BrowserTest.php

```
<!-- BrowserTest.php -->
<HTML>
<HEAD>
<TITLE></TITLE>
</HEAD>
```

```
<BODY>
<H1>Browser Test PHP Script</H1>
<?php
  if(strstr($HTTP_USER_AGENT, "MSIE")) {
?>
You are using <b>Internet Explorer</b>
<?php
} else {
  echo "Your browser identified as: <b>$HTTP_USER_AGENT</b><p>";
}
?>
</BODY>
```

One of the things that makes PHP so easy to use is that it automatically makes a large number of variables available as standard variables. (The phpinfo() function we used earlier displays all these variables and their values.) In this example, I've used another PHP function, strstr(), to compare the environment variable $HTTP_USER_AGENT against the string "MSIE". If the string matches, the lines within the if clause (surrounded by the first set of {} braces) are processed. What may not seem completely intuitive, however, is that the line we want displayed in the browser is *not* part of the PHP. It is preceded by the ?> closing tag so that it is not processed as PHP but is rendered as HMTL-formatted text.

The else clause should be easy enough to understand. It is processed if the user's browser is not identified as Internet Explorer (that is, if the $HTTP_USER_AGENT variable does not contain the "MSIE" string). Note, however, that the line to be displayed is contained within <?php … ?> tags. The echo function has to be used to output the information, which contains HTML tags and one variable value that is first interpreted.

Study this example until you understand it thoroughly. It contains the most essential elements of PHP (flow-control, use of functions, variable testing). Test it on your machine, and modify it to do other things, or perform tests of other variables.

The last example I'll give introduces PHP's strongest feature: support for databases. Listing 9.4 is the HTML form introduced in Chapter 8 to grab user input in order to query the Zipcodes database. Note this time, however, that the form does not call a CGI script, but calls a PHP file in the <FORM> tag (Listing 9.5) which happens to reside in my DocumentRoot. This means that with PHP, there is a tendency to mix static HTML documents and program code. There is nothing inherently wrong with this; in fact, PHP is intended to facilitate this mixture of coding and display formatting. This tends to fly in the face of traditional CGI programming practice, which would dictate that all programming code be placed in reserved, protected directories separate from static Web pages. I'll admit, it made me a bit uncomfortable at first, particularly when I realized how powerful PHP is. PHP is not CGI, however, and the PHP parser has been designed to avoid the well-known security vulnerabilities. PHP pages cannot really be made more secure by changing their location on the server (except perhaps from users who have local access to the server). Just try to avoid a false belief that PHP files in a special directory are automatically safer to publish on the Web.

Listing 9.4   PHPForm.html

```
<!-- PHPForm.html -->
<HTML><HEAD><TITLE>Zip Code Database Query Form</TITLE>
</HEAD><BODY><H1>Zip Code MySQL Database Query Form</H1>
<FORM METHOD="POST" ACTION="http://Jackal.hiwaay.net/zipcodes.php3"
ENCTYPE="application/x-www-form-urlencoded">
<EM>Enter a 5-digit Zip Code:</EM><BR><INPUT TYPE="text" NAME="zip"
SIZE=6><P><
INPUT TYPE="reset" VALUE="Clear"><INPUT TYPE="submit" NAME=".submit"
VALUE="Submit Search"></FORM><HR>
<ADDRESS>Charles Aulds</ADDRESS><BR>
<A HREF="/">Home Page</A>
</BODY></HTML>
```

Listing 9.5   zipcodes.php

```
<!-- zipcodes.php -->
<HTML>
<HEAD>
<TITLE>Zip Code</TITLE>
<H1>ZipCODE</H1>
</HEAD>
<BODY>
<?php
  $db=mysql_connect("localhost", "dbuser", "mypasswd");
  mysql_select_db("zipcodes", $db);
  $result = mysql_query("SELECT * FROM zips WHERE zip = '$zip'");
  if($myrow = mysql_fetch_array($result)) {
    do {
      printf("The US Postal Zip Code <font size=+1><b> $myrow[zip] </b>
        </font> is for:  <font size=+2><b> $myrow[city] , $myrow[state]");
```

```
        } while ($myrow = mysql_fetch_array($result));
    }
?>
</body>
</html>
```

This example uses four PHP directives that are specific to MySQL (`mysql_connect`, `mysql_select_db`, `mysql_query`, and `mysql_fetch_array`). Using a different relational database, you would replace these with equivalent functions that are specific to that database. This is a bit more awkward than using Perl with the database-independent (DBI) programming interface that does not require program code to be altered when the database on the back-end changes. However, using functions specific to, and optimized for, a single database leads to greater efficiency and processing speed. PHP does support at least one database-independent programmer's interface, Open Database Connectivity (ODBC), which is able to query any ODBC-compliant database. Usually this is a database on a Windows NT or Windows 2000 server that exposes the database interfaces through a data set name (or *DSN*).

PHP includes an alternate function for most PHP-supported databases (in the case of MySQL, the function is `mysql_pconnect`) that opens a persistent database connection (that is it doesn't close when the PHP script ends). Instead (just as in mod_perl), subsequent connect calls to the same database that use the username and password are simply passed a handle to the open database connection.

Note that `zipcodes.php` contains passwords to the MySQL database. It's a good practice to place this information in a separate file that is stored somewhere other than `DocumentRoot`. For example, you could use the PHP `include` statement to insert this information when `zipcodes.php` is loaded, by placing this line after the `<?php` tag:

```
include "/usr/local/apache/conf/dbinfo.php";
```

The contents of the file specified in the `include` statement should look like this:

```
<?php
    $username="dbuser";
    $password="mypasswd";
?>
```

The PHP tags instruct Apache to parse the contents of this file as PHP when it loads the file. The values of the variables are set and later used in the `mysql_connect` function. If you do something like this, make certain that the filename has an extension that will cause the file to be parsed by PHP. If you name the script to be included with a special extension (like `.inc`), for example, make certain that Apache is configured to process `.inc` files with PHP.

ASP for Apache

Active Server Pages (ASP) or *Active Scripting* was a Microsoft invention and for many years has been a favorite Web application development environment for Microsoft Internet Information Server (IIS) for Windows. In 1998 a group called the ActiveScripting Organization (www.activescripting.org) began an effort to write an open-source ASP engine for Apache. The product they began developing, called OpenASP for Apache, was designed to bring popular IIS programming languages like Microsoft's VBScript and JScript, as well as ActiveState's PerlScript, to the Apache Web platform under an open-source license. The intent was to make Apache more desirable and accessible to IIS developers already familiar with the scripting languages of that platform and thus to bring Microsoft's Active Scripting host to Apache running on popular Unix systems like Solaris and Linux as well as Apache/Win32 for NT.

Currently, the only version of OpenASP for Apache is a first beta release for the Win32 version of Apache. The ActiveScripting Organization has not yet released a Unix version, although they still promise one. It may be that the demand for ASP on Apache, especially for Unix-like operating systems, turned out to be less than estimated, particularly in view of the high performance benchmarks set by IIS on NT.

Currently, the only open-source ASP for Apache on Linux is the Apache::ASP Perl module (see Chapter 8), which is not too shabby and allows ASP programming (only in PerlScript, of course) on Apache systems. Experienced ASP programmers might want to take a look at Apache::ASP. Again, remember, that you will only be able to code ASP in Perl using this module.

Most programmers who are adept at using ASP, however, are transitioning from a Microsoft IIS environment, and most of them will have learned to code in VBScript or perhaps JScript. Currently, there are two commercial products available that permit the use of ASP for Apache on Linux and allow coding in these two Microsoft-specific languages. InstantASP is a product from Halcyon Software that enables ASP on any Java servlet-enabled Web server. The other commercial ASP product on Linux is from a company called Chili!Soft (www.chilisoft.com). Chili!Soft ASP for Linux is a platform-independent version of ASP that strives to be functionally equivalent to Microsoft ASP. The target market for the product consists of firms that are trying to leverage the skills of programmers already proficient with ASP on Microsoft IIS. One feature of Chili!Soft ASP for Linux is particularly interesting. The product contains ports of the Microsoft Active Data Objects (ADO) that allow use of these Microsoft-specific objects to access non-Microsoft-hosted databases. The product also supports access to objects from the Common Object Request Broker Architecture (CORBA) world, although most shops already using that heavily Unix-oriented technology are unlikely to move to a Microsoft technology like ASP.

One last ASP solution deserves mention, particularly for use by sites that are trying to transition completely away from ASP or IIS to PHP4 on Apache. An application called asp2php, written by Michael Kohn (http://asp2php.naken.cc) converts ASP pages written in VBScript into PHP. While the FAQ for the utility admits that it won't convert everything, the program's author offers to assist in converting any VBScript the program won't handle (you don't get that kind of support everyday, even for commercial products). And they have a really nice logo and T-shirt.

Apache JServ

Sun Microsystems (http://java.sun.com) introduced the Java programming language in 1995. At that time, the software that was changing the face of computing wasn't coming from the traditional big players like Sun. Java didn't even have the status of a "killer" user application; it was just a developer's tool. I can't think of less likely beginnings for something that has been successful as Java. Nonetheless, Java put Microsoft into a frenzy of concerned activity, and there is no better indicator of a product's potential than Microsoft's knee-jerk reaction.

While it is true that Java has fallen far short of the predictions made by most of its staunchest proponents (it certainly hasn't made the Windows PC obsolete), it has managed to secure an unshakable position as a programming environment for Internet-based applications. Initially, Java was used solely to produce *applets*, programs that were downloaded to the client browser and run on the client's computer in a special Java Virtual Machine (JVM), also called a Java Runtime Environment (JRE), which is provided in most modern browser software. This model has largely given way to enterprise application development that leverages brokered objects, transaction processing, and strong database connectivity. The cornerstone of Web-based applications developed in Java is now usually a Web server capable of running *servlets*, which are nothing more than Java programs that run on the server. Sun maintains strong control over the future development of Java by releasing the base Java development tools (like the Java Development Kit or JDK), programmer's interface specifications to which Java products adhere, and Java classes that implement many of the APIs.

Apache JServ is a set of programs that enable Java servlets to run under Apache and has been the de facto standard for running Java servlets on Apache Web servers for several years now. Although Apache JServ is still the servlet engine that continues to be used on most production servers, there are no plans to upgrade it to support the newest versions of the Java Servlet API Specification 2.2. Many sites still require support for the older Java Servlet Specification 2.0. If you will be required to install Apache JServ, the following section should prove useful in negotiating the sometimes tricky steps involved. If, however, your site is able to move to the newest Java Servlet Specification, I strongly urge you to consider a product called Resin from Caucho Technologies. The final sections of this chapter discuss Resin in some detail; it is far easier to set up than Apache JServ, performs better, and as an added bonus, supports Java Servlet Pages (JSP) out of the box (Apache JServ requires an additional add-on to support JSP).

NOTE To get the most out of this discussion of JServ, you need a working familiarity with the Java programming language. This chapter is not a tutorial on Java programming, and in order to present practical examples of the Apache JServ interface, I've had to use many Java techniques and features that may be unfamiliar to newcomers.

The current version implements Sun's Java Servlet API Specifications 2.0. To install and use Apache JServ, you need three essential components: a working Apache server, some version of the Sun JDK (see the sidebar), and the Java Servlet Development Kit version 2.0 (JSDK2.0). Apache JServ will *not* work with classes that implement the Servlet API version 2.1 (packaged with the JavaServer Web Development Kit 1.0.1) or those that implement Servlet API version 2.2 (packaged with a new reference implementation called Tomcat from Jakarta, discussed in the section "Java Server Pages (JSP)" later in this chapter).

If all this seems confusing, keep in mind that what Apache JServ does is simple. It enables the use of Java servlets, Java programs that run on your server rather than in the client's browser. The capability to run servlets is required for using other technologies that are written as Java servlets. The two most important of these are Java Server Pages (discussed later in this chapter) and Java Server-Side Includes (discussed in Chapter 7).

JDK for Linux

All the Java Servlet or JSP applications are provided as Java classes and require a Java runtime, or *virtual machine (VM)* to run them. The original sources for these Java runtime utilities are the Java Development Kits (JDKs) from Sun Microsystems. Although Sun tries to maintain a strong involvement in the development of Java (and thus some control over it), it is no longer the only source for the JDK. Most of the other options are ports of the JDK released by Sun for its Solaris operating system.

For Linux systems, the most widely used ports of the JDK are those released by Blackdown.com (www.blackdown.com). These are precompiled and ready to go, if you have the supporting utilities. (You can also get the JDK for Linux from Sun Microsystems, www.sun.com.) I downloaded the latest version of the Blackdown JDK, which, as of this writing, was JDK1.2.2, Release Candidate 4:

```
jdk-1.2.2-RC4-linux-i386-glibc-2.1.2.tar.bz2:
```

JDK for Linux *(continued)*

This is a "bzipped tarball" and requires a very small, easily installed, utility called bzip, which can be downloaded from `http://sourceware.cygnus.com/bzip2/index.html`. Download the `bzip` executable file, place it wherever you want, rename it to make it easier to call, make sure it is marked as executable, and invoke it directly. The version I downloaded was `bzip2-095d-x86-linux20`.

After downloading this file, I used the following commands to make it more usable:

```
# cp bzip2-095d-x86-linux20 /usr/sbin/bzip
# chmod 755 /usr/sbin/bzip
```

Once you have `bzip` installed and have downloaded the JDK, installation is a cinch. The JDK from Blackdown consists of precompiled binaries, already optimized for Linux. You only have to extract them into a location of your own choosing. I recommend `/usr/local`:

```
# cd /usr/local
# tar xvfI /downloads/jdk-1.2.2-RC4-linux-i386-glibc-
2.1.2.tar.bz2
```

Incidentally, if you find that you need to upgrade your C runtime library, `glibc`, to a newer version to support this package, your best bet is to download the required upgrades as Red Hat Package Manager (RPM) files. From Rpmfind.net (`http://rpmfind.net`), download the following RPMs and install them using the –i (install) command line switch:

```
rpm -i glibc-2_1_2-11_i386.rpm.
```

While it may seem logical to upgrade your existing `libc` to the latest version, it is better to install the newer GNU `libc` alongside the existing one. For Linux, three major `libc` versions are available (`libc-4`, `libc-5`, and `libc-6`) and you can have any combination of these three installed to support applications with dependencies on each of them.

```
rpm -U glibc-devel-2_1_2-11_i386.rpm
```

Apache JServ consists of two separate parts (Figure 9.4). The first part, called the Apache-side component, is an Apache module written in C (`mod_jserv`). The second part, or Java-side component, is Java code that implements the Java servlet API in a Java Virtual Machine (JVM). The two components communicate using a special protocol called the Apache JServ Protocol (AJP).

Figure 9.4   Apache JServ Architecture

The Apache-side component is responsible only for the exchange of information between Apache and the Java-side component. In the automatic mode of operation, mod_jserv starts the JVM in which the Java-side component runs. Like most Apache modules, mod_jserv can be statically linked to the Apache executable file (httpd) or compiled as a DSO and dynamically linked to the server at runtime.

The Java-side component is written in Java and runs inside a JVM. The Java-side component implements the Java servlet API and does most of the work of running servlets. It has no direct contact with the client, communicating only with mod_jserv using the AJP protocol.

Although the automatic mode of operation is the simplest and recommended mode, the JVM and Java engine can be started separately and allowed to run outside the control of Apache and mod_jserv, but responding to AJP connections. This so-called *manual mode* of operation can be used to run the Java servlet engine on a separate computer from the Apache server, or to allow multiple Java servlet engines to be running in separate JVMs, each listening for AJP connections on its own port. Later in this section, I'll show how to configure multiple Java servlet engines running in separate JVMs.

Installing Apache JServ

Before installing Apache JServ, make sure you have a working JDK. On my machine the following lines show that I have the JDK 1.2.2 installed and entered in my PATH environment variable. Although I have several other versions of the JDK on the system, this would be the one used when the Java executable is called without a qualifying path. To use other JDKs, you need to reference them explicitly. See the sidebar above on installing the JDK.

```
# echo $PATH
/usr/bin:/bin:/sbin:/usr/bin:/usr/sbin:/usr/local/bin:/usr/local/sbin:/usr/
bin/X
11:/usr/X11R6/bin:/root/bin:/usr/local/jdk1.2.2/bin:.
# java -version
java version "1.2.2"
Classic VM (build Linux_JDK_1.2.2_RC4, native threads, sunwjit)
```

You should find the second required component, the JSDK 2.0 in the Downloads archive section at http://java.sun.com/products/servlet/download.html. The file you are looking for is named jsdk20-solaris2-sparc.tar.Z. Don't let the name fool you; nothing in the package is compiled as a Solaris on SPARC binary. The Java classes will work on your Linux system. Again, do *not* attempt to use the 2.1 or 2.2 version of the JSDK with Apache JServ. (The 2.2 version is currently packaged only with the Tomcat reference implementation, and it is unlikely that you will download this JSDK by mistake.) Unpack the JSDK someplace convenient, like /usr/local:

```
# cd /usr/local
# tar tvfz /home/caulds/jsdk20-solaris2-sparc_tar.gz
# ls -al | grep JSDK
drwxr-xr-x   7 nobody    nobody          1024 Apr 21  1998 JSDK2.0
# chown -R root.root JSDK2.0
```

Download Apache JServ. You should be able to find the most current version at http://java.apache.org/jserv/dist/. The latest stable release was 1.1 when I downloaded it. Again, extract the file into a good location to build it (like /usr/local/src):

```
# cd /usr/local/src
# tar xvfz /home/caulds/ ApacheJServ-1.1.tar.gz
# cd ApacheJServ-1.1
# ls
INSTALL       Makefile.in    acinclude.m4   configure      example
LICENSE       README         aclocal.m4     configure.in   index.html
Makefile.am   README.build   conf           docs           src
```

As I do with many other Apache modules that use a configuration script, I built a shell file to hold my command line. The script I call build.sh contains all the configure options on separate lines, but concatenated so that they are passed to the shell and executed as a single line. It looks something like this:

```
# cat build.sh
#!/bin/sh
./configure \
--prefix=/usr/local/jserv \
--with-apxs=/usr/local/apache/bin/apxs \
--with-jdk-home=/usr/local/jdk117 \
--with-JSDK=/usr/local/JSDK2.0/lib/jsdk.jar \
--enable-EAPI \
--disable-debugging
```

You can enter `configure --help` to list all the options, but for the most part, those shown above are the ones you need. You can see that I'm creating a DSO module with `apxs`, and I'm specifying the locations for the JDK home directory and the JSDK Java archive, `jsdk.jar`, which should already be installed. The last options enable the Apache Extended API and disable debugging (which means that the Java compiler will not write debugging information into `.class` files it creates). The following lines build the module (`mod_jserv.so`), install it, and modify Apache's `httpd.conf` to load it:

```
# sh ./build.sh
# make
# make install
```

As a result of this installation, another file is installed inside the Apache `libexec` directory. Named `ApacheJServ.jar`, it consists of the classes necessary to implement the Java-side component of Apache JServ:

```
# ls -al /usr/local/apache/libexec | grep -i jserv
drwxr-x---   2 root      root           1024 Jan 29 08:22 .
-rw-r--r--   1 root      root          87882 Jan 29 08:22 ApacheJServ.jar
-rwxr-xr-x   1 root      root         234780 Jan 29 08:22 mod_jserv.so
```

Take a look at some of the freebies you get with Apache JServ. Copies of all the configuration files required to set up Apache JServ with a single servlet zone (called the *root* zone) are automatically written into the `jserv` directory under the Apache `conf` directory. The ones without the `.default` extensions are the working copies you should modify.

```
# ls -al /usr/local/apache/conf/jserv
total 56
drwxr-xr-x   2 root      root           1024 Jan 29 08:42 .
```

```
drwxr-xr-x   8 root      root           1024 Jan 29 08:42 ..
-rw-r--r--   1 root      root           6422 Apr 19 16:07 jserv.conf
-rw-r--r--   1 root      root           6422 Apr 19 16:07 jserv.conf.default
-rw-r--r--   1 root      root          13191 Apr 19 16:07 jserv.properties
-rw-r--r--   1 root      root          13191 Apr 19 16:07 jserv.properties.default
-rw-r--r--   1 root      root           5940 Apr 19 16:07 zone.properties
-rw-r--r--   1 root      root           5940 Apr 19 16:07 zone.properties.default
```

Some sample servlets are also installed, so you can test Apache JServ to see if it's working:

```
# ls -al  /usr/local/apache/servlets
total 14
drwxr-xr-x   2 root      root           1024 Jan 29 08:42 .
drwxr-xr-x  13 root      root           1024 Jan 29 08:42 ..
-rw-r--r--   1 root      root           1132 Jan 29 08:42 Hello.class
-rw-r--r--   1 root      root           1301 Jan 29 08:42 Hello.java
-rw-r--r--   1 root      root           2119 Jan 29 08:42 IsItWorking.class
-rw-r--r--   1 root      root           4542 Jan 29 08:42 IsItWorking.java
```

And, under the directory you specified in the --prefix option when you ran configure, you'll find a full set of HTML documentation files:

```
# ls -al  /usr/local/jserv/docs
total 214
drwxr-xr-x   7 root      root           1024 Jan 29 08:42 .
drwxr-xr-x   3 root      root           1024 Jan 29 08:42 ..
-rw-r--r--   1 root      root           1131 Jan 29 08:42 FAQ.html
-rw-r--r--   1 root      root          10117 Jan 29 08:42 STATUS.txt
drwxr-xr-x   3 root      root           1024 Jan 29 08:42 api
-rw-r--r--   1 root      root           2632 Jan 29 08:42 bugs.html
-rw-r--r--   1 root      root          59771 Jan 29 08:42 changes.html
-rw-r--r--   1 root      root           2123 Jan 29 08:42 contributing.html
-rw-r--r--   1 root      root           9816 Jan 29 08:42 contributors.html
-rw-r--r--   1 root      root           5060 Jan 29 08:42 features.html
drwxr-xr-x   2 root      root           1024 Jan 29 08:42 future
-rw-r--r--   1 root      root           4561 Jan 29 08:42 glossary.html
-rw-r--r--   1 root      root          44979 Jan 29 08:42 howto.load-balancing.html
drwxr-xr-x   2 root      root           1024 Jan 29 08:42 images
-rw-r--r--   1 root      root           7791 Jan 29 08:42 index.html
drwxr-xr-x   2 root      root           1024 Jan 29 08:42 install
```

**Advanced
Configuration Options**

PART 3

```
-rw-r--r--   1 root      root          3732 Jan 29 08:42 license.html
-rw-r--r--   1 root      root          8056 Jan 29 08:42 modules.html
-rw-r--r--   1 root      root          8208 Jan 29 08:42 operation.html
drwxr-xr-x   2 root      root          1024 Jan 29 08:42 protocol
-rw-r--r--   1 root      root          3324 Jan 29 08:42 security.html
-rw-r--r--   1 root      root          5257 Jan 29 08:42 sendbug.html
-rw-r--r--   1 root      root          1067 Jan 29 08:42 support.html
-rw-r--r--   1 root      root          5590 Jan 29 08:42 upgrade.html
-rw-r--r--   1 root      root          8460 Jan 29 08:42 y2k.html
-rw-r--r--   1 root      root          7476 Jan 29 08:42 zones.html
```

One way to make these documentation files easily accessible is to include the following directive in your `httpd.conf` file and restart Apache:

```
Alias /JServDocs "/usr/local/jserv/docs"
```

A request to `http://<servname>/JservDocs` should now give access to excellent documentation, not only on Apache JServ but on the Java classes that make it work (Figure 9.5).

Figure 9.5   Apache JServ documentation

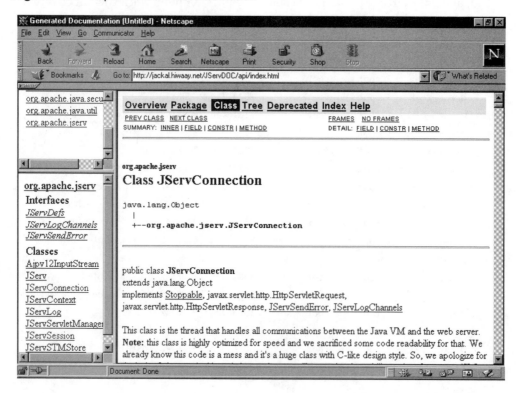

The final step is to ensure that everything's working. Restart Apache and connect to one of the following URLs:

```
http://<servername>/servlets/Hello
http://<servername>/servlets/IsItWorking
```

The results should indicate that Apache JServ is working (Figure 9.6)

Figure 9.6   Apache JServ is working!

Viewing the Apache JServ Status Page

Apache JServ includes a special handler, `jserv-status`, that allows the `mod_jserv` module to be queried via a Web browser for a wide variety of useful information. As part of the Apache JServ installation, the following `<Location>` container is included in the default `jserv.conf` file:

```
<Location /status/jserv>
    SetHandler jserv-status
    order deny,allow
```

```
        deny from all
        allow from localhost
    </Location>
```

This permits a browser on the server system to access the Apache JServ status information with the URL http://localhost/status.jserv (you can add other host systems to the allow from directive to enable remote status monitoring). This will invoke a status page for the server from which you can determine information about the Linux, Apache, and Apache JServ software versions and the Apache JServ configuration.

Additional status information is enabled by including the following line in jserv .properties:

```
    security.selfservlet=true
```

If this option is used, make sure that only valid hosts are allowed to access the status page.

Figure 9.7 is an example of the very complete, very useful information that is available through the status handler.

Figure 9.7   The Apache JServ status handler

Configuring Apache JServ

Each component of Apache JServ has its own configuration file, generally located in the Apache conf/jserv directory. In Apache JServ, all possible directives are included in each of three files (though many are commented out) which are written into the Apache Root/conf/jserv directory by the Apache JServ installation. These files are intended to be self-documenting, so I will only discuss the directives that the Apache administrator is most likely to change. Most of the directives can remain as they are installed and can be thought of as setting default values. You should print out and review the following three files:

jserv.conf   The configuration file for the mod_jserv Apache module.

jserv.properties   The configuration file for the Java servlet engine (the Java-side of Apache JServ).

zone.properties   The configuration file for the root servlet zone (other zones may be created, as described shortly, but the root servlet zone is required and is properly configured during the Apache JServ installation).

The next three sections discuss these files and their Apache JServ components.

Configuring the mod_jserv Module

The Apache component of Apache JServ (the Apache module mod_jserv) is usually configured through a file named jserv.conf, which is referenced by an include statement in Apache's httpd.conf file:

```
Include /usr/local/apache/conf/jserv/jserv.conf
```

The directives in this file are all valid in the Apache httpd.conf file, and it is not necessary to place them in a separate file, although that is the recommended standard practice. Keeping the Apache JServ configuration file separate from the Apache configuration makes them much easier to find and edit, and access permissions can be different from those that apply to the Apache httpd.conf file. Just remember that the directives included in jserv.conf apply to the Apache server (and mod_jserv Apache module), and are equally valid inside the Apache httpd.conf. Listing 9.6 depicts the jserv.conf file created on my server by the Apache JServ installation (after removing all comments).

Listing 9.6   The jserv.conf file as Installed by Default

```
LoadModule jserv_module
/usr/local/apache/libexec/mod_jserv.so
<IfModule mod_jserv.c>
  ApJServManual off
  ApJServProperties /usr/local/apache/conf/jserv/jserv.properties
  ApJServLogFile /usr/local/apache/logs/mod_jserv.log
```

```
ApJServLogLevel notice
ApJServDefaultProtocol ajpv12
ApJServDefaultPort 8007
ApJServSecretKey DISABLED
ApJServMount /servlets /root
ApJServMount /servlet /root
ApJServMountCopy on
<Location /jserv/>
  SetHandler jserv-status
  order deny,allow
  deny from all
  allow from localhost
</Location>
</IfModule>
```

LoadModule is the first directive in the file, a very nonstandard location for that directive. The rest of the directives in the file are enclosed in an IfModule directive that renders them ineffective if mod_jserv is not installed or has been temporarily disabled.

ApJServManual enables or disables Apache JServ manual mode. The default setting for this directive is off, meaning that Apache JServ operates in automatic mode and Apache automatically starts the Java portion of Apache JServ. This is the most convenient way to run Apache JServ, and when using a single JVM it is the best way. The main reason to change this setting is to run multiple JVMs, each of which must be manually started (as described later).

ApJServProperties names a path to a file containing configuration directives that apply to the Java side of Apache JServ.

```
ApJServProperties /usr/local/apache/conf/jserv/jserv.properties
```

This file is described in the next section.

The ApjServMount directive names a servlet zone and a URL that Apache uses to identify client requests that are served from this zone. This URL is called the servlet's *mount point*. In the default example, the root servlet zone is named, and the URL /servlets is its mount point. Client requests to this URL are intercepted and served from the root zone. The root zone should not be removed (although you may choose to modify the URL of the servlet mount point), but additional servlet zones can be added, as described in the section "Servlet Zones" later in the chapter.

The remaining directives you'll find in the provided jserv.conf file specify various default values that are better left unchanged. These are well documented in the file, however, and you should review the directives and their associated comments.

Configuring the Apache JServ Engine

The Java-side component of Apache JServ is configured in the file `jserv.properties`, which was pointed to by the `ApJServProperties` directive in `jserv.conf`. Remember that the Java side of Apache JServ is a set of Java classes. The lines in `jserv.properties` are not *directives*, as we are used to seeing in Apache configuration files, but rather *properties* that are set to various values to control the operation of the Java-side component. The properties in the `jserv.properties` file are configured to define a Java runtime engine (or JVM) to start, a set of classes to load, and other parameters that are used by the classes.

The `wrapper.bin` property is set to the name of the desired JVM to run. It must point to an executable file, usually named `java`. This can be any JVM supported by Apache JServ. Apache JServ was defined on my server to run the JVM provided with JDK 1.1.7:

```
wrapper.bin=/usr/local/jdk117/bin/java
```

The `wrapper.classpath` property is used to define a string to add to the CLASSPATH environment variable that is passed to the JVM. The CLASSPATH is used by the JVM to locate Java classes when they are used by Java servlets. The values placed in `wrapper.classpath` can be either a directory that contains Java classes (in `.class` files) or it can identify a Java archive (a single Java archive, or `.jar` file). If you have multiple entries to add, specify them with multiple `wrapper.classpath` property lines. The first two lines below are required to run Apache JServ, and they identify the classes that implement the Java-side component of Apache JServ and also the Java Servlet Development Kit classes that implement servlets. The third line adds a directory that contains classes to implement a JDBC driver for the MySQL database. In our Apache JServ application example, we'll use these classes to query our Zipcodes database with a Java servlet.

```
wrapper.classpath=/usr/local/apache/libexec/ApacheJServ.jar
wrapper.classpath=/usr/local/JSDK2.0/lib/jsdk.jar
wrapper.classpath=/usr/local/mm.mysql.jdbc-1.2c
```

Two other properties are set to define the required root servlet zone. The first property (*zone*) is used to store the name of the zone. The second, *zone*`.properties`, which derives its name from the value of *zone*, stores the name of a properties file for that zone. Later, I'll show how these properties can be used to add a servlet zone. A running Apache JServ engine, however, requires only the `root` zone:

```
zones=root
root.properties=/usr/local/apache/conf/jserv/zone.properties
```

The remaining properties in the `jserv.properties` file set values that are generally adequate for most servers. Read about these, and tweak them, only when optimizing the performance of an already working Apache JServ engine.

Configuring Servlet Zones

The last configuration files that Apache JServ uses are the properties file for each zone specified. A minimal Apache JServ implementation requires only a single servlet zone (the root zone). After a standard Apache JServ installation, the root zone has its properties stored in the file zone.properties.

This file sets only one property that is essential and worth discussing here; the remaining properties change the behavior of Apache JServ and are mainly used for optimization. The repositories property is set to the value of a directory that will contain Java classes specific to this zone. This directory is generally specific to a Java application or project and is made accessible to a developer or group of developers for that project.

The installation default value for the root servlet zone is:

```
repositories=/usr/local/apache/servlets
```

Java classes placed in this directory are available to clients making requests to the URL /servlets. If Java source files are placed in this directory, they are automatically compiled to .class files when accessed. The "Automatic Class Reloading" section below discusses how classes are automatically reloaded when they are changed.

Logging

Logging is automatically set up during the Apache JServ installation, and most administrators don't need to change it, so this section is just a short introduction to the Apache JServ logging features you'll get. There are two files into which Apache JServ will write logging information. On the Apache side, mod.jserv will write into a log file defined in jserv.conf with a line like this:

```
log.file=/usr/local/apache/logs/mod_jserv.log
```

Generally, you'll find this line already in the file after installation. It is recommended that a full path be used here (rather than something like ./logs/mod_jserv.log) if it isn't already specified as a full path.

> **NOTE** Setting this value to DISABLED does not disable logging by mod_jserv; instead, the messages are redirected into Apache's error log.

The only change you might want to make to jserv.conf is to the logging level. By default, this is set to notice by the following directive:

```
ApJServLogLevel notice
```

This directive can take one of the following eight values, each defining a lower level of verbosity. The emerg level, for example, logs only the most critical errors and represents the lowest possible level of logging:

```
debug
info
notice
warn
error
crit
alert
emerg
```

While testing my server, I set the value to debug, so that I got all kinds of notices, but later downgraded my level of debugging to warn.

On the Java side, logging is enabled through the jserv.properties file, through a group of properties:

```
log=true
log.file=/usr/local/apache/logs/jserv.log
log.timestamp=true
log.dateFormat=[dd/MM/yyyy HH:mm:ss:SSS zz]
log.queue.maxage = 5000
log.queue.maxsize = 1000
log.channel.servletException=true
log.channel.jservException=true
log.channel.warning=true
log.channel.servletLog=true
log.channel.critical=true
```

These are the default settings after installation on my server, and I have not seen fit to change them. The first property can be set to false to disable logging, and the second property defines the log file. The level of logging (defined by the different log channels) seems adequate. This log file can be very useful when debugging Java servlets.

A common problem (and one I encountered while setting up Apache JServ) is that the Java-side component may not be able to write to its log file. You must ensure that the user account under which the Apache httpd processes run (nobody, in my case) can write to this file. The following lines set user and group ownership of all Apache log files to the nobody user and group, and then change the file access permissions to grant read/write access to the file owners, read access to the nobody group, and no access at all to other users:

```
# chown nobody.nobody /usr/local/apache/logs/*
# chmod "640" /usr/local/apache/logs
# ls -al /usr/local/apache/logs/*
total 25681
drw-r--r--   2 nobody    nobody        1024 Apr 19 16:37 .
drwxr-xr-x  13 nobody    nobody        1024 Apr 18 18:02 ..
-rw-r-----   1 nobody    nobody     7906272 Apr 19 16:10 access_log
-rw-r-----   1 nobody    nobody      919250 Apr 19 16:37 error_log
-rw-r-----   1 nobody    nobody           6 Apr 19 16:37 httpd.pid
-rw-r-----   1 nobody    nobody         500 Apr 19 16:10 jserv.log
-rw-r-----   1 nobody    nobody       18692 Apr 19 16:37 mod_jserv.log
-rw-r-----   1 nobody    nobody    17335811 Apr 11 09:05 mod_rewrite.log
-rw-r-----   1 nobody    nobody        2084 Apr 11 15:53 ssl_engine_log
-rw-r-----   1 nobody    nobody           0 Apr 11 11:00 ssl_request_log
```

Servlet Zones

The concept of servlet zones is central to Apache JServ. All servlets (whether as .class files or .jar archives) are associated with servlet zones and are said to run within their respective zones. A servlet's zone is a container for the servlet and allows the administrator to configure zones independently, usually for security reasons (often individual developers or project teams are given their own servlet zone), but also to distribute servlet engines among more than one server.

In order to define a new server zone, you need to modify all three Apache JServ configuration files. I'll demonstrate the steps required to add a new servlet zone named auldszone to my Apache server. Servlets that are intended to reside in this zone must be requested with a URL of the form http://jackal.hiwaay.net/myservlets/.

In jserv.conf, it is necessary to specify a mount point for the new zone. This mount point is used to map a request URL to a named zone. The default configuration defines a mount point that maps URLs requesting /servlets to the /root zone. I added this line:

```
ApJServMount /myservlets /auldszone
```

This accomplishes a URL-to-servlet zone mapping in Apache, but the zone does not exist until specified in jserv.properties (the properties file for the Java-side component). To do that, I added the following two lines to that file:

```
zones=root, auldszone
auldszone.properties= /usr/local/apache/conf/jserv/auldszone.properties
```

Now the zone has been added to Apache JServ's list of known servlet zones and, a properties file has been defined to describe that zone. This file (`auldszone.properties`) still needs to be created. The only line that absolutely must exist in that file sets the repository (or repositories) for classes that are run within the zone:

```
repositories=/home/httpd/MyServlets, /home/caulds/servletstuff
```

Note that the directories specified as servlet zone repositories need to exist, and they need to be accessible to the Apache JServ component (which will normally run under the same user account as the Apache server processes, typically the nobody account). Servlets are added to a servlet zone by placing the compiled class files into one of the directories defined as repositories in the properties file for that zone. Naturally, these, too, must be readable by the servlet engine (Java-side process).

Multiple JVMs

By far the easiest way to run Apache JServ is as I have described, by leaving `ApJServManual` set to on, which causes `mod_apache` to start the Java-side servlet engine automatically in a JVM on the same server. The servlet engine (and its JVM) can also be started manually. There are usually two reasons for doing this. The first is when the JVM is to be run on one or more separate machines, often in order to implement load balancing for efficiency on multiple high-volume servers. The special load-balancing features in Apache JServ are complex and beyond the scope of this book, but an excellent discussion of Apache JServ load balancing is given in `http://java.apache.org/jserv/howto.load-balancing.html`.

The other reason is usually to increase security by running a separate servlet engine for each zone, each in its own JVM so that they don't share instantiations of the same classes. I'll describe running two instances of the Java-side servlet engine, each in a separate JVM, one on the local server, one on a remote host. Both are defined to listen on different TCP ports, though this would not be necessary if they were on separate servers.

The first thing that must be done is to ensure that Apache JServ is run in manual mode. Do this by setting the `ApJServManual` directory to `jserv.conf`:

```
ApJServManual off
```

In the same file, define separate multiple mount points for each servlet engine (in other words, define different engines and servlet zones to handle requests using different URLs):

```
ApJServMount /myservlets ajpv11://localhost:9000/localzone
ApJServMount /hisservlets ajpv12://rascal.hiwaay.net:9001/remotezone
```

NOTE   Note that servlet mount points and zones can be specified within `<virtual host>` containers, as another way of separating servlet engines and giving each virtual host its own servlet engine.

The Java-side component of Apache JServ consists of nothing but Java code and can run on any machine that can run a JVM. In this example, requests for /myservlets connect to TCP port 9000 on the local host (which should have a servlet engine process bound to it and listening) and use the AJP version 1.1 protocol to communicate to the servlet engine. Requests for /hisservlets are directed to the *remotezone* servlet zone on rascal.hiwaay.net, which must have a servlet engine running on TCP port 9001. AJP version 1.2 is used to communicate with this engine.

These two alternate forms of the ApJServMount directive specify not simply a named zone on the same server, but either a local or a remote zone. They do this by specifying a communication protocol (usually some version of AJP), the hostname, TCP port number for the connection, and optionally a named servlet zone on that host. The remote servlet zone does not have to be specified but can be taken from the request URL.

Omitting the remotezone name in the second line in the example above would require that request URLs specify the servlet zone before the requested servlet. If the remotezone name was not specified in this line, servlets in that zone could still be requested with a URL like this:

```
http://thishost/hisservlets/remotezone/HelloWorld
```

By contrast, this request would *not* work:

```
http://thishost/hisservlets/HelloWorld
```

The next step is to create an Apache JServ engine properties file (jserv.properties) on each machine where a servlet engine is to be manually started. On the local host, jserv.properties should contain at least the following lines:

```
port=9000
zones=localzone
localzone.properties=/usr/local/apache/conf/jserv/localzone.properties
```

And on rascal.hiwaay.net, there should be a jserv.properties file containing the following lines:

```
port=9001
zones=remotezone
remotezone.properties=/usr/local/apache/conf/jserv/remotezone.properties
```

Each zone.properties files should contain at least a repositories line:

```
# localzone.properties (on the localhost)
repositories=/usr/local/apache/servlets
```

```
# remotezone.properties (on rascal.hiwaay.net)
repositories=/usr/local/servlets
```

Each JVM is started on its host machine using command lines like the following. I start mine from `/etc/rd.d/rc.local`:

```
/usr/local/jdk117/bin/java -classpath            \
   /usr/local/apache/libexec/ApacheJServ.jar: \
   /usr/local/JSDK2.0/lib/                       \
   org.apache.jserv.JServ                        \
   /usr/local/apache/conf/jserv/localzone.properties


/usr/local/jdk1.2.2/bin/java -classpath          \
   /usr/local/apache/libexec/ApacheJServ.jar: \
   /usr/local/JSDK2.0/lib/jsdk.jar               \
   org.apache.jserv.JServ                        \
   /usr/local/apache/conf/jserv/remotezone.properties
```

Automatic Class Reloading

Each servlet zone is given its own class reloader that loads classes from the repositories defined for the zone, along with supporting classes in the $CLASSPATH environment variable or specified with a -classpath argument when the servlet engine is started in its JVM. The class reloader also monitors the classes in each class repository for changes. If a change is detected in any class, all classes that have been loaded from that repository are automatically reloaded if the autoreload.classes property is set to true in the zone properties file:

```
autoreload.classes=true
```

While automatic class reloading is a very useful feature on development servers where servlets are frequently changed, there are drawbacks to its use that administrators of production servers should consider. Before the execution of a servlet in a zone where automatic class reloading has been enabled, the class reloader must check every class in every repository specified for that zone. This happens every time a servlet is loaded from that zone, which significantly slows the server engine.

The servlet loader works on an all-or-nothing basis. If it finds that any class in a zone has changed, it reloads all the classes in all the repositories for that zone. This is not generally a problem if the zone contains only a few classes, but if the zone consists of several large repositories, reloading all the classes can take some time.

Advanced Configuration Options

PART 3

Another problem occurs if session tracking is in effect (that is, if the state is maintained between servlet executions): reloading classes destroys client state information if the state data is maintained in memory. This problem can be eliminated by maintaining session data in disk files or databases (which also allows state data to persist across Apache restarts and even server reboots).

Administrators of production servers should consider disabling automatic class reloading or moving large classes to the system class path (a directory defined in $CLASSPATH or the -classpath argument to the servlet engine). No classes in the system class path are affected by class reloading.

A Database Query Using Apache JServ

Again, I'll use my Zipcodes database to illustrate a very simple Java servlet running in an Apache JServ engine. Listing 9.7 is the servlet I wrote to accept Web form input and query the MySQL database.

Listing 9.7   A Java Servlet to Query the Zipcodes Database

```
// /usr/local/apache/servlets/ZipCodes.java
import java.io.*;
import java.sql.*;
import javax.servlet.*;
import javax.servlet.http.*;

public class ZipCodes extends HttpServlet
{
    public void service (HttpServletRequest request, HttpServletResponse
response)
       throws ServletException, IOException
  {
       super.service(request, response);
  }

    public void doGet (HttpServletRequest request,
      HttpServletResponse response)
      throws ServletException, IOException
  {
        // compose a SQL query string using the user input zip
      String query = "select * from zips where zip=\"" +
        request.getParameter("zip") +"\"";
```

```
try {
  // Load the MySQL JDBC driver
  Class.forName("org.gjt.mm.mysql.Driver").newInstance();
}
catch (Exception Err) {
    System.err.println("Unable to load JDBC driver.");
    Err.printStackTrace();
}
try {
    // make a connection to the zipcodes MySQL database
    // on localhost, using root account and password
    Connection Conn = DriverManager.getConnection
      ("jdbc:mysql://localhost/
      zipcodes?user=root&password=notmypasswd");
    try {
        // create a statement object which will send
        // the SQL query
        Statement Stmt = Conn.createStatement();
        // send the query, store the results in a
        // ResultSet object
        ResultSet RS = Stmt.executeQuery (query);

        String title = "Example Database Servlet";

        // set content type and other response header
        // fields first
        response.setContentType("text/html");

        // then write the data of the response
        PrintWriter out = response.getWriter();

        out.println("<HTML><HEAD><TITLE>");
        out.println(title);
        out.println("</TITLE></HEAD><BODY bgcolor=\"#FFFFFF\">");
        out.println("<H1>" + title + "</H1>");
        out.println("<H2>US ZipCode Lookup<br></h2>");

        while (RS.next()) {
```

```
                    out.println("The US Postal Service Zip Code <font size=+1><b>"
                    + RS.getString(3) + "</b></font> is for <font size=+2><b>" +
                    RS.getString(1) + ", " + RS.getString(2) + "</b></font><br>");
                }
                out.println("</BODY></HTML>");
                out.close();
                RS.close();
                Stmt.close();
                Conn.close();
            }
            catch (SQLException Err) {
                System.out.println("SQLException: " +
                    Err.getMessage() );
                System.out.println("SQLState:    " +
                    Err.getSQLState() );
                System.out.println("VendorError:  " +
                    Err.getErrorCode() );
            }
        }
        catch (SQLException Err) {
            System.out.println("SQLException: " +
                Err.getMessage() );
            System.out.println("SQLState:    " +
                Err.getSQLState() );
            System.out.println("VendorError:  " +
                Err.getErrorCode() );
        }
    } //doGet()
} //Class
```

Using the Apache JServ installation defaults, I installed the servlet into /usr/local/
apache/servlets, which is defined as the repository for the root servlet zone and
mapped to the /servlets request URL.

Because Java can be daunting to a beginner, I tried to keep this example as simple as possible. To be honest, there's more code here than I would have liked in such a simple
example. The try, throw, and catch error-trapping commands are necessary; removing
them causes errors, as the Java objects appear to expect error handling. I'm sure they dramatically increase the reliability of my code, but this enforces a lot of discipline on the
programmer (you can be the judge of whether that's good or bad).

The `import` statements make support classes available. Generally you import classes whenever you intend to use methods from those classes. The `javax.servlet.*` and `javax.servlet.http.*` classes are necessary to run Java servlets and are provided as part of the Java Servlet Development Kit (the JSDK). The `java.sql.*` classes implement the database calls through JDBC as explained in "Installing JDBC."

I defined a new `ZipCodes` class that is derived from (or *extends*) the `HttpServlet` class. By declaring it so, I essentially created a new class that inherited all the methods and properties of a servlet. My class, therefore, implements the standard methods of the Java servlet API. The `service` method is called by the servlet engine when a new user request needs to be handled. If that request is an HTTP GET request, the standard method `doGet` is called. Any servlet you write should implement at least one of the following methods: `doGet`, `doPost`, `doPut` or `doDelete`, each of which corresponds to a type of HTTP request.

The `doGet` method is passed two objects by the servlet engine: the `request` object and the `response` object. These correspond, respectively, to the HTTP client request being processed and the response to that client. Every servlet operates on these two objects. To summarize briefly, the input from the user is retrieved by calling the `getParameter` method of the `request` object, passing it the name of the field in the Web form. This value is used to construct a SQL query, which is passed through a set of methods and objects supplied in classes provided as part of the JDBC driver for MySQL (`org.gjt.mm.mysql.Driver`). These methods and objects are standard in the Java Database Connectivity (JDBC) database-independent programmer's interface, and will work with little or no modification for other databases. You will, of course, need to supply the proper JDBC driver classes for each database you use. See the sidebar "Installing JDBC" for instructions on downloading and installing the JDBC drivers for MySQL.

Advanced Configuration Options

PART 3

Installing JDBC

Java Database Connectivity (JDBC) is a programmer's interface for relational database management systems (RDBMS). It provides a consistent set of methods for programming database applications in Java that do not change when the database on the back end changes. A complete change from Sybase to Oracle, for example, requires only new JDBC drivers to allow most Java database programs to work unaltered. This fits nicely into the trademarked paradigm of Java programming, which has always been to create "Write Once, Run Anywhere" programs. If you're familiar with database programming for Perl, recognize that JDBC functions a lot like the Perl DBI (database independent API) module.

Installing JDBC *(continued)*

The definitive site for information related to JDBC is maintained by Sun Micro-systems at:

```
http://java.sun.com/products/jdbc/
```

In order to write the simple Java examples in this chapter that query the MySQL data-base on my Linux server, I had to download a JDBC driver for MySQL. You download a different JDBC driver for each RDBMS that you want to manipulate with Java. The Sun site maintains a database of JDBC drivers for different database engines. For my use with MySQL, I downloaded the latest release version of Mark Matthew's highly respected MM MySQL driver directly from his site at `www.worldserver.com/ mm.mysql`.

One of the really nice things about JDBC (as with most Java add-ons) is that it is avail-able as a collection of Java classes. In other words, the only thing you have to do to install JDBC is ensure that your Java engine knows where to locate these classes. The JDBC classes come prepackaged as a Java archive (or `.jar` file), and I recommend using the archive as is. Although you can easily recompile the archive yourself from the `.java` files containing the source by using the makefile included with the MM MySQL driver, compiling the source yourself won't necessarily lead to optimizations for your hardware.

I extracted MM MySQL to my `/usr/local` directory, and the *only* thing I had to do to make it work was to include the JDBC classes in my system's CLASSPATH environ-ment variable. You can do this by editing the CLASSPATH variable in `/etc/profile`). My CLASSPATH looks like this:

```
CLASSPATH=/usr/local/apache/libexec/ApacheJServ.jar:/usr/local/
JSDK2.0/lib/jsdk.jar:/usr/local/mm.mysql.jdbc-1.2c:
```

Java Server Pages (JSP)

Java Server Pages (JSP) is a set of Java servlet classes that enables Java code to be embedded inside HTML documents. These documents are parsed by the JSP classes, and the embedded Java code is compiled and executed before the document is returned to the requester. Even though JSP is itself implemented as a Java servlet and requires some implementation of the Java servlet API, it is according to some sources the logical and inevitable successor to Java servlets. For simply automating Web pages, that may be true, but large Web-based applications will probably keep Java servlets in use for a very long time to come.

Formerly, installing Java Server Pages meant installing one of two sets of JSP classes on top of Apache JServ. These were the GNU Server Page (GSP), available from www.bitmechanic.com, and GNU JavaServer Pages (GNUJSP), which can be obtained from www.klomp.org/gnujsp. These Apache JServ add-ons were never widely accepted, and both tended to lag the latest versions of the JSP specification (1.1) and the latest specifications for the Java Servlets API (2.2).

In 1998, Sun Microsystems and the Apache Software Foundation formed the Jakarta Project (http://jakarta.apache.org) to complete a combined official reference implementation of the Java Server Pages version 1.1 specification running as a servlet that adhered to the latest Java Servlet API version 2.2 specification. This product, dubbed Tomcat, was designed to make obsolete Apache JServ and JSP implementations based on the older JSP 1.0 and Java Servlet 2.0 specification. Tomcat actually replaces the Java-Server Web Development Kit (JSWDK), which formerly included the reference implementation of the JSP and Java Servlet specifications.

The first releases of Tomcat intended for production use became available in 2000.

By the time of Tomcat's release, however, another product based on JSP 1.1 and Java Servlet API 2.2 was already widely accepted by Java/Apache aficionados, quite stable, and turning in very respectable benchmark test results. That product is Resin from Caucho.com, a discussion of which concludes this chapter.

At this point in the game, if you intend to develop new projects with Java Server Pages, you should bypass GSP and GNUJSP running on top of Apache JServ. Instead, install either the Jakarta Project's Tomcat or try the excellent Resin product.

A Simple Java Server Pages Example

Listing 9.8 is a very simple Java Server Pages application that returns HelloWorld in HTML formatting, does a simple mathematical calculation, and sets a variable for later reference. It isn't meant to be useful, but merely illustrates the simplest use of JSP. Figure 9.8 shows the results in a browser.

Listing 9.8   A Very Simple JSP Example

```
<%
// Create a string variable named title and assign
// it a value
//
String title = "Hello, world!";
%>
```

```
<!DOCTYPE HTML PUBLIC "-//W3C//DTD HTML 4.0 Transitional//EN">

<head>
<meta http-equiv="Content-Type" content="text/html; charset=ISO-8859-1">

<!-- The expression tags interpolate script variables into the HTML -->

<title><%= title %></title>
</head>

<body bgcolor=white>
<h1><%= title %></h1>

<!-- JSP can be used to perform mathematical
     computations -->
<h2>2 + 2 = <%= 2 + 2 %></H2>

</body>
```

Figure 9.8   The simple JSP page in a browser

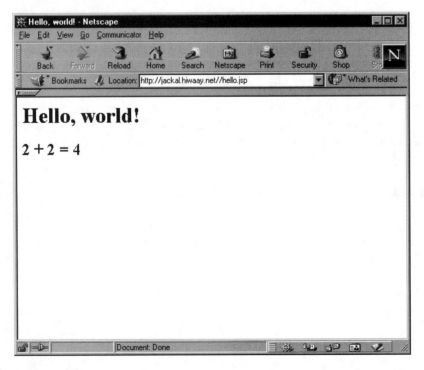

The Database Example in Java Server Pages

Coding my database query application in JSP was easier in some ways than writing it as a Java servlet. For one thing, it wasn't necessary to use the exception handling that was required in the servlet apps (the try and catch blocks). Apparently, JSP takes care of that automatically, though I couldn't find that stated in the documentation. All I know is that my application was a lot shorter in JSP. Listing 9.9 is as simple as I could make it. This JSP page, when called from a Web form and passed a postal code, performs a lookup in the MySQL database. There is no output at all from the Java code embedded in the page; it was far simpler to use HTML to format the output, inserting the values of variables where needed, using a <%=   %> JSP tag.

Listing 9.9   A JSP ZipCode database query example

```
<title>JSP Example Using MySQL Query</title>
</head>

<H1><center>Simple JSP Example Using MySQL Query</H1>
<body bgcolor='white'>

<%
// Use the request object to get user input
String zip=request.getParameter("zip");
%>

<h1>Zip entered was: <%= zip %> </h1>

<%
// It's really a cinch to use JDBC with JS
Class.forName("org.gjt.mm.mysql.Driver").newInstance();
Connection Conn = DriverManager.getConnection(
   "jdbc:mysql://localhost/zipcodes?user=root&password=
   notmypassword");
String query = "select * from zips where zip=\"" +
   request.getParameter("zip") + "\"";
Statement Stmt = Conn.createStatement();
ResultSet RS = Stmt.executeQuery (query);
%>

<h1><%= zip %> is the zip code for
<%= RS.getString(1) %>, <%= RS.getString(2) %>!
```

Advanced Configuration Options

PART 3

While this is much easier than writing a complete servlet for a simple application, when things get more complex, JSP can become more mangling than mingling of HTML and Java code. In complex applications, some portion of the Java code is usually separated from the HTML and imported as a Java bean. JSP supports a special `<jsp:useBean` tag to create an object that instantiates an external class. The properties and methods of the object are then called from the code fragments embedded in the Java server page.

An excellent guide to the advanced use of JSP can be found on Sun's Java technology site at `http://java.sun.com/products/jsp/docs.html`.

Resin

Make no mistake about it, installing Apache support for Java Servlets or Java Server Pages can be a very confusing, often frustrating task. If you find the number of options (from different sources) too confusing, you may want to simply install a product called Resin. Like the newer Tomcat product, Resin is a single solution that implements both servlets and JSP with one installation. It is freely available under an open-source license from Caucho Technology (`www.caucho.com`). While it may not have the large number of collaborating developers that some other Java applications do, Resin seems to be very well supported and quite stable. It is billed as "the fastest servlet and JSP engine available," and independent benchmark tests seem to support the claim.

Resin remains quite up-to-date with the ever-changing Java specifications from Sun Microsystems. The version I installed, while still a beta release (Resin 1.1b6) was quite current, supporting the Java Server Pages 1.1 specification and the Java Servlet 2.2 specification; these are the very latest releases of these specs that are suitable for production software. This was right on par with the Tomcat "reference implementation" from Sun and the Apache Software Foundation.

Resin on Apache (like Apache JServ) consists of two separate parts: an Apache module (written in C) and a Servlet runner (written in Java, of course). Figure 9.9 depicts this configuration. A user request identified in Resin's configuration as a candidate for processing by the Servlet runner is sent to that engine, through a standard TCP socket connection. The Servlet runner (or *srun*) is a separate program, which runs Java servlets (including the servlet that parses Java Server Pages) in a standard Java Virtual Machine (VM) or runtime environment. Notice the similarity to the Apache JServ architecture shown earlier, in Figure 9.4.

Figure 9.9   The architecture of Resin on Apache

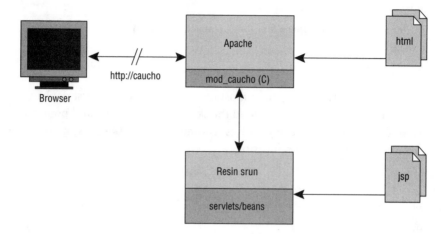

Installing Resin

While Resin is designed primarily for improving the performance of Java applications, it is also extremely simple to install, configure, understand, and upgrade.

The first step is, of course, to download the latest version from www.caucho.com. I downloaded the 1.1 beta 6 release as resin-1_1_b6_tar.gz and extracted the contents into /usr/local:

```
# pwd
# tar xvfz /downloads/resin-1_1_b6_tar.gz
# cd /usr/local/resin1.1
```

NOTE   While Resin is available under an open-source license for free downloading and use, the authors of the product reserve a copyright on their work and encourage all "funded projects" to purchase a license for the product. While a license is not required to use Resin, the developers believe that anyone making money using Resin should be fair in giving something back to ensure the future development and quality of the product. The current license requires a one-time fee of $500 per production server. My opinion? It's worth it.

The package was a cinch to install with three commands, each issued in /usr/local/resin1.1:

```
# pwd
# ./configure --with-apache=/usr/local/apache
# make
# make install
```

Alternatively, you can issue a command like the following, substituting the full path to your apxs script, if necessary:

```
# ./configure -with-apxs=/usr/local/apache/bin/apxs
# make
# make install
```

The Resin install is smart enough, in most cases, to make the necessary changes to your Apache server's httpd.conf file to load the mod_caucho module and point to the resin.conf configuration file in your Resin home directory. On my system, the following lines were added in the proper locations:

```
LoadModule caucho_module       libexec/mod_caucho.so


AddModule mod_caucho.c
```

And at the end of the file, Resin added:

```
<IfModule mod_caucho.c>
    CauchoConfigFile /usr/local/resin1.1/resin.conf
    <Location /caucho-status>
       SetHandler caucho-status
    </Location>
</IfModule>
```

This section tells mod_caucho where to look for its configuration info, and also adds a special handler for the Resin status page (Figure 9.10). It is recommended that the <Location /caucho-status> section be removed on production servers, but for testing, it can be quite useful.

Before starting the servlet runner, it is necessary to modify the file resin.conf in the Resin home directory. For a simple JSP and Java Servlet, I used the following:

```
<caucho.com>
  <http-server srun-port=6802 srun-host=localhost
     app-dir='/home/httpd/html'>
     <servlet-mapping url-pattern='/servlets/*'
         servlet-name='invoker'/>
     <servlet-mapping url-pattern='*.jsp'
         servlet-name='com.caucho.jsp.JspServlet'/>
     <servlet-mapping url-pattern='*.xtp'
         servlet-name='com.caucho.jsp.XtpServlet'/>
  </http-server>
</caucho.com>
```

Figure 9.10   The Resin status page

This file specifies that mod_caucho.so will contact the servlet runner using TCP port 6802 on the local system (localhost). Three servlet mappings will be used. The first mapping is for Java servlets identified by their class names. The default configuration file included with Resin looks for servlet classes in RESIN_HOME/doc/WEB-INF/classes. This behavior is defined by the Java Servlet 2.2 specification but can be modified with the <classpath> directive. The following lines could be added immediately following the <httpd-server> directive:

```
<classpath id='/home/httpd/html/classes'
    source='/home/caulds/servletsources'>
<classpath>
```

These lines redefine the location where Resin will look for supporting Java classes and servlet classes. The optional source keyword defines a directory where the Java source files for classes reside. If you supply source, Resin will automatically compile the classes for you whenever they change (or from the source if the class file doesn't already exist).

I modified my Resin configuration file to use my Apache `DocumentRoot` as the `app-dir`, and retained `/servlets/*` as the URL mapping. What this means is that if a request comes in for a resource:

```
/servlets/someclass
```

The Resin servlet runner will attempt to run:

```
/home/httpd/html/WEB-INF/classes/someclass.class
```

Unlike Apache JServ, which is configured with "servlet zones," Resin uses either virtual hosts or Web-apps to separate workspaces. Each workspace is identified by a different relative path to the `app-dir`, and each workspace contains a directory `WEB-INF` that, in turn, contains subdirectories such as `classes`. Although Caucho developers are still debating the usefulness of a hard-coded dependence on the `WEB-INF` directory, it is necessary to provide this directory in your main `app-dir` or `web-app` directories.

My second mapping defines `com.caucho.jsp.JspServlet` as the servlet that the servlet runner should use to preprocess or parse all files designated as Java Server Pages (by the `.jsp` extension). The last servlet mapping defines `com.caucho.jsp.XtpServlet` as the servlet to use for processing Extended Markup Language (XML) templates and can be omitted if you aren't using these. If you attempt to load a Java Server Page at this point, you will probably encounter the error shown in Figure 9.11, indicating that the Resin servlet runner has not been started. Unlike Apache JServ, the servlet runner is not started automatically, and must be invoked manually (usually while logged on as `root`) or from Linux system startup scripts for automatic start at system boot.

The servlet runner is located in the `bin` directory under the Resin Home and is a shell script named `srun.sh`. The actual work, however, is performed by a Perl script in the same directory, `wrapper.pl`. On my system, it was necessary to make two small modifications to this script. First, I manually set the `$RESIN_HOME` variable to point to my installed location for Resin (this may not be necessary for you). Second, I manually pointed to the version of the Java Development Kit I wanted to use (since I had two installed on my system). The third change you may want to make is to modify the `$CLASSPATH` variable rather than allowing the script to read the `CLASSPATH` from the system environment, depending on whether you have the value properly set in your system or shell profile. Although I set the variable here, it is not necessary to do so if you are relying on the system's `CLASSPATH` environment variable. Listing 9.10 depicts the first lines of `srun.sh` on my server.

Figure 9.11   The error message displayed when SRUN.SH has not been started

Listing 9.10   A partial listing of SRUN.SH

```
#! /usr/bin/perl
# This is /usr/local/resin1.0/bin/wrapper.pl
#! /usr/bin/perl
#
# The following variables are usually automatically set or set from the
# command line.  They can be set here if necessary.
#
# location of the Resin directories, usually scripts can find it
#
$RESIN_HOME="/usr/local/resin1.1";
#
# location of JAVA_HOME, usually scripts can find it
#
$JAVA_HOME="/usr/local/jdk1.2.2";
#
```

```
# location of java executable, usually scripts can find it
#
$JAVA_EXE="";
#
# additional args to pass to java
#
$JAVA_ARGS="";
#
$CLASSPATH="usr/local/resin1.1/lib/resin.jar:/usr/local/resin1.1/lib/
jsdk22.jar:/usr/local/resin1.1/lib/jdk12.jar:/usr/local/mm.mysql.jdbc-1.2c";
```

When all these changes have been made, you should be able to start the servlet runner manually using the following commands (though you will probably want to configure Linux to do this automatically when the system is started):

```
# pwd
/usr/local/resin1.1/bin
# bin/srun.sh start
start srun
```

Alternatively, you can use the -verbose argument to display the most important user-selectable settings that apply to the servlet runner:

```
# pwd
/usr/local/resin1.1/bin
# srun.sh -verbose start
JAVA_HOME:      /usr/local/jdk1.2.2
RESIN_HOME:     /usr/local/resin1.1
CLASSPATH:
        /usr/local/resin1.1/lib/resin.jar
        /usr/local/resin1.1/lib/jsdk.jar
        /usr/local/resin1.1/lib/jsdk12.jar
        /usr/local/resin1.1/classes
        /usr/local/resin1.1/lib/resin.jar
        /usr/local/jdk1.2.2/lib/tools.jar
        /usr/local/jdk1.2.2/jre/lib/rt.jar
        /usr/local/resin1.1/lib/jsdk22.jar
java:        /usr/local/jdk1.2.2/bin/java
args:
class:       com.caucho.server.http.RunnerServer
start srun
```

In Sum

Most comparisons of Web-server programming methodologies give performance considerations special emphasis, citing benchmark tests that prove one technique is unquestionably better than another. These benchmarks usually measure the ability of a Web server to generate and serve HTML pages to large numbers of concurrently connected clients. Raw performance can be a significant consideration when choosing a programming technique for a heavily-trafficked site, particularly if that Web server is furnishing data through a very large pipe (and this means more than a single T1 circuit, which has a bandwidth slightly larger than 1.5Mbps).

The truth is, though, most Web sites receive no more than a few thousand hits in a single day. Other considerations can be far more significant than raw performance in choosing a Web programming tool.

When choosing a Web programming tool or technique, don't make your decision based on a set of numbers in a table of benchmark scores. Instead, leverage capabilities and talents that you already have in-house.

Always remember, too, that Web programming languages are not mutually exclusive; you don't have to choose one technique to the exclusion of all others.

Advanced
Configuration Options

PART 3

10

Aliasing and Redirection

Nearly every Apache administrator needs to know how to implement the *aliasing* and *redirection* of client requests. Apache simplifies the process of locating resources by assuming that the request URL always represents a path to a resource relative to the server's DocumentRoot. This assumption provides for extremely fast resource retrieval, but it is not always correct. Often the requested resource is stored in a nonstandard location; it may be under DocumentRoot but not in a location that can be deduced from the URL, or it may be in a completely different location on the system.

Aliasing is the process of mapping a client's request URL into a nonstandard location and automatically retrieving the resource from this location.

Redirection is the process of responding to a request with a new location URL and a request to redirect the request to the new URL. A redirection response also includes an HTTP response code indicating the reason for the redirection. An entire class of HTTP status codes is dedicated to request redirection. As you'll see later in the chapter, however, only seven codes are currently used.

Aliasing and redirection are related tasks with a fundamental difference: aliasing is performed solely at the server; redirection requires the client browser to issue a second request for the desired resource at a new location. Aliasing is completely transparent to the requesting user. When a URL is aliased, the requester receives the requested document as usual but does not know that its location on the server was identified by means of an alias.

In redirection, however, the client (that is, the browser) receives a new URL, which will be reflected in its Location: field. The user can then bookmark this new URL for future use, and it is usually cached by the browser or any proxy server acting on the client's behalf.

The most common redirection is almost certainly that which occurs when a request for a directory does not include a trailing slash. In Chapter 4, I discussed how mod_dir automatically issues a redirect for such requests, which are technically incorrect. For example, on my server, if I use the URL http://jackal.hiwaay.net/Docs, where Docs is a subdirectory of my document root, I don't immediately receive a listing of that directory (or a default index page). Instead, the server sends the following redirect response:

```
HTTP/1.1 301 Moved Permanently
Date: Mon, 17 Jul 2000 17:29:45 GMT
Server: Apache/1.3.12 (Unix) mod_perl/1.24 PHP/4.0.1pl2
Location: http://jackal.hiwaay.net/Docs/
Content-Type: text/html; charset=iso-8859-1
```

Upon receiving this response, my browser automatically reissues the request to the URL specified in the Location: header, http://jackal.hiwaay.net/Docs/. The second request is automatic and performed without my knowledge. The time required to re-request the resource is minimal, but it is unnecessary. Whenever possible, ensure that hyperlinks embedded in documents you serve contain properly formatted URLs for directories (which always include the trailing slash character).

The Apache distribution provides two modules to handle URL aliasing and redirection, mod_alias and mod_rewrite. Although mod_alias is probably the more important and more generally useful of the two modules, more than half of the chapter discusses mod_rewrite. The amount of space I devote to mod_rewrite is a measure of its complexity, size, and flexibility, not necessarily its usefulness. In fact, for the sake of efficiency, you should use mod_alias whenever possible, and use mod_rewrite only when you need the extra flexibility it offers.

The mod_alias Module

The mod_alias module handles the basic functions of both request redirection and URL aliasing. For most installations, this module (which is compiled into the basic server by default) has more than enough flexibility and power to handle all of the administrator's needs. You should strive to understand all of the directives provided by mod_alias and use them whenever they are sufficient to meet the requirement at hand. Reserve the more powerful (but complex) mod_rewrite for those situations that mod_alias can't handle.

Aliasing with mod_alias

The mod_alias module is probably used most often for aliasing URLs, and nearly every Apache server includes at least one directive from the module in its configuration. mod_alias provides the following directives for the purpose of aliasing URLs:

```
Alias
AliasMatch
ScriptAlias
ScriptAliasMatch
```

The Alias Directive

The Alias directive allows a nonstandard mapping of a URL to a destination filename. In other words, using Alias, you can store documents in locations that aren't under the server's defined DocumentRoot. The directive specifies a full pathname to a directory or file for a single URL.

An excellent example is an alias to a directory containing icons or images. Here is one I use on my machine:

```
Alias /icons "/usr/local/apache/icons"
```

I also use an Alias directive to make my Apache documentation accessible to a browser, even though I'm storing those files outside my defined DocumentRoot:

```
Alias /ApacheDocs "/usr/local/apache/htdocs"
```

Note that if you include a trailing slash on the URL, the server will require a trailing slash in requests. If I had used trailing slashes in the above, for example, a request for //jackal.hiwaay.net/ApacheDocs would fail; the server would only respond to http://jackal.hiwaay.net/ApacheDocs/.

The AliasMatch Directive

The AliasMatch directive is functionally equivalent to Alias but extends it to use standard regular expressions (including back-references) to match against the request URL. For example, I might use this directive to express both of the examples given for the Alias directive as:

```
AliasMatch ^/icons/(.*) "/usr/local/apache/icons/$1"
AliasMatch ^/ApacheDocs(.*) "/usr/local/apache/htdocs$1"
```

The ScriptAlias Directive

The ScriptAlias directive works like the Alias directive to handle nonstandard URL mapping, with one important additional feature. It also identifies the target directory as

Advanced Configuration Options

PART 3

containing CGI scripts (it sets the MIME-type of all files in the identified directory to `application/x-httpd-cgi`).

Here's an example:

```
ScriptAlias /cgi-bin/ "/usr/local/apache/cgi-bin/"
```

With this directive in effect, a request to `//jackal.hiwaay.net/cgi-bin/test.txt` would attempt to run the file `/usr/local/apache/cgi-bin/test.txt` as a CGI script. But if that file is (as its extension indicates) simply a text file, it is unlikely that it can be run as a shell script (though it is possible, depending on the contents of the file). If the shell is unable to parse and run the contents of this file as a script, the result will be a "Premature end of script" error in the Apache error log, and Apache will send an HTTP error code 500 (Internal Server Error) to the requester, along with a default error page indicating that the server administrator should be contacted.

The `ScriptAliasMatch` Directive

The `ScriptAliasMatch` directive is almost equivalent to `ScriptAlias` but permits the use of a standard regular expression for the URL match. The example given for `ScriptAlias` can be rewritten with `ScriptAliasMatch` like this:

```
ScriptAlias ^/cgi-bin/(.*) "/usr/local/apache/cgi-bin/$1"
```

Redirection with `mod_alias`

`mod_alias` also provides basic redirection, which should be used whenever a simple one-to-one match can be defined between the request URL and a destination to which you want to redirect the requester. The `mod_alias` module supplies the following directives for the purpose of redirecting requests:

```
Redirect
RedirectMatch
RedirectTemp
RedirectPermanent
```

The `Redirect` Directive

`Redirect` is the simplest Apache directive for redirection. It has the following syntax:

```
Redirect [status] oldURLprefix newURLprefix
```

The directive performs a match against a URL prefix (in other words, it looks to see if the request begins with the specified prefix). If the request begins with this prefix, it is mapped into a new URL that begins with a new prefix; this prefix is returned to the client with a redirect message indicating that the location of the resource has changed and that it can now be reached at the new URL. It is the client's responsibility to fetch the resource with a second request using the new URL. Web browsers generally do this without notice to the user, and almost invisibly. The Redirect directive can be given an optional status, which specifies the HTTP response code sent to the client. (Table 10.1 lists the HTTP response codes for request redirection.) If no status is given, the HTTP response code sent is 302. The status code can be any valid numeric code or one of these four values, which return the HTTP status codes shown:

permanent   Status code 301: Moved Permanently

temp   Status code 302: Found

seeother   Status code 303: See Other (indicates that the resource has been replaced rather than simply relocated).

gone   Status code 410: Gone (indicates that the resource no longer exists; used without the newURL)

If a numeric status code between 300 and 399 is given, the newURL field must be given; otherwise this field must be omitted.

Table 10.1   HTTP Request Redirection Codes

Status Code	Meaning	Explanation
300	Multiple Choices	Used when there are multiple variations of the requested resource. The server provides alternate URLs for the variations available and requests that the client select one and send a separate request for it.
301	Moved Permanently	The requested resource has been permanently assigned a new URL. The client is asked to redirect the request to this URL and is informed that it should use the new URL for all future requests.
302	Found	The requested resource is temporarily unavailable at the request URL the client used, but that address is still valid and the client should continue to use it. The client is asked to redirect the current request but keep the old URL on file (or in cache).
303	See Other	Works like status code 307 to redirect the request temporarily. The difference between status codes 307 and 303 is subtle; code 303 should *not* be interpreted as an "alternate location for the requested resource." It is used when the usual and accepted response to the initial request is a redirection to an alternate URL (usually generated programmatically).

Table 10.1 HTTP Request Redirection Codes *(continued)*

Status Code	Meaning	Explanation
304	Not Modified	Used when the client has issued a conditional request (for example, using the `If-Modified-Since:` header) and the requested document has not been modified. In such a case, the server responds with status code 304 to inform the client to use the document he already has. Technically, the server is not responding with a redirect request.
305	Use Proxy	This code informs the client that the original request URL was good, but the resource must be obtained through a proxy server. The `Location:` field of the HTTP response message contains the URL of the proxy server (rather than an alternate URL for the resource).
306	(Unused)	HTTP status code 306 is obsolete and should not be used with the current version of the protocol.
307	Temporary Redirect	Works just like status code 302. The requested resource is temporarily unavailable at the request URL the client used, but that address is still valid and the client should continue to use it. The client is asked to redirect the current request, but keep the old URL on file (or in cache). Status code 307 is usually used with newer browsers that behave according to the HTTP/1.1 specification. Older browsers, which understand only status code 302, often violated the specification, which states that the client browser is not allowed to change the method of a redirected request.

For example, with the following directive in effect:

```
Redirect permanent /download  http://dlserver.hiwaay.com/archives/
```

a request for `http://jackal.hiwaay.net/download/test.zip` will be redirected to `http://dlserver.hiwaay.com/archives/test.zip`. The request URL is tested only to see if it begins with the specified prefix; whatever follows that prefix is written onto the end of the new URL prefix.

NOTE Redirect directives always take precedence over Alias or ScriptAlias directives, regardless of their relative ordering in the configuration file.

Matching Regular Expressions: RedirectMatch

The RedirectMatch directive is functionally equivalent to Redirect but allows the use of standard regular expressions in matching the request URL prefix.

```
RedirectMatch (.*)\.gif$ http://2ndserver.hiwaay.com$1.jpg
```

In this example, the request URI (that portion of the URL that follows the hostname) is compared to see if it ends with the characters .gif. The $ character matches the end of the string. The backslash is necessary to *escape* the following character, a period. In other words, it tells the regular-expression engine to interpret the period literally; that is the character we are looking for here. The previous period, within the parentheses, is regular-expression shorthand meaning "any single character." The portion of the expression within parentheses is read as "any character (.) repeated any number of times (*)". This portion of the URI is used to fill in the back-reference $1 in the new URL portion of the directive. This directive would redirect a request for

```
http://jackal.hiwaay.net/images/uparrow.gif
```

to

```
http://2ndserver.hiwaay.com/images/uparrow.jpg
```

Redirecting to a Temporary Location: RedirectTemp

When you've had to move material on your site temporarily, use RedirectTemp, which has the following syntax:

```
RedirectTemp oldURLprefix newURLprefix
```

It sends a Redirect to the client with HTTP status code 302 (Found) and is exactly equivalent to Redirect temp.

```
RedirectTemp /mystuff /home/caulds/
```

This directive performs a very simple redirect, redirecting all requests using URLs ending in /mystuff to /home/caulds. There is no advantage to using RedirectTemp over Redirect (which has the default behavior of sending status code 302) to indicate a temporary redirect. Use RedirectTemp only to make your purpose obvious in the configuration file.

Advanced Configuration Options

PART 3

Redirecting Permanently: `RedirectPermanent`

When material on your site has moved permanently, use `RedirectPermanent`, which has this syntax:

```
RedirectPermanent oldURLprefix newURLprefix
```

This directive sends a `Redirect` to the client with HTTP status code 301 (Permanently Moved) and is exactly equivalent to `Redirect permanent`. For example, the following two directives have identical effects:

```
RedirectPermanent /mystuff /home/caulds/
Redirect permanent /mystuff /home/caulds/
```

The `mod_rewrite` Module

The `Alias` directive is often quite adequate for simple URL rewriting and request redirection. For more complicated URL redirection, particularly when URL rewriting is conditional, is based on information contained outside the URL, or involves database or file lookups, there's a far more powerful module called `mod_rewrite`.

Its author, Ralf S. Engelschall, describes `mod_rewrite` as a "rule-based rewriting engine." The purpose of the module can be stated quite simply; it is responsible for rewriting incoming URLs using a set of rules and then redirecting the requester to the newly rewritten URL. The power of `mod_rewrite` lies in the tremendous flexibility that its rules can give Apache administrators in redirecting requests, and it has numerous uses on most Apache servers, although `mod_alias` is usually sufficient for most request redirection needs.

The module is complex, so I'll begin by describing how it is intended to function. Armed with this understanding of what's going on in the module (and a familiarity with basic regular expressions), you'll be able to study the examples that follow. I will start with the essential `mod_rewrite` directives and the simplest possible uses for `mod_rewrite`, and then talk about the optional directives and show examples that use the functionality these directives add. It is important to realize, though, that `mod_rewrite` is so complex and so flexible that it would be impossible to list all the different ways in which it can be used. The examples in this chapter illustrate only a fraction of the potential power of this module; the real limitation is your imagination.

Try to learn `mod_rewrite` in pieces. If you understand what's happening in each example I introduce, by the end of this section, you'll know `mod_rewrite` well enough to decide whether you have a need for it. Even more important than understanding how to set up URL rewriting rules with `mod_rewrite` is understanding what the module is capable of. Someday you'll encounter a problem or requirement for which `mod_rewrite` will be the perfect solution.

How mod_rewrite Works

As described in Chapter 5, most Apache modules can register internal functions as *callbacks* with the Apache server, so that the server calls these functions at one or more phases of the document request cycle. Mod_rewrite registers two callbacks: one in the *URL Translation* phase (in which the URL is translated to the name of a file on the server) and the other in the *Fixup* phase, which handles any final processing that may be required before the request is fulfilled.

When an HTTP resource request arrives at the server, the first phase of the request cycle (called the *Post-Read-Request* phase) is generally used to configure the server to handle the request. It is here, for example, that Apache decides which virtual host will handle the request. The very next phase is *URL Translation*, and it is here that mod_rewrite does its work.

The mod_rewrite module can also be used on a per-directory basis, rather than applying rewriting rules to all incoming URLs, usually by adding mod_rewrite directives to .htaccess files. However, Apache processes .htaccess files well after the request URL has already been translated into a filename (that's how Apache was able to locate and read the proper .htaccess file). In order to perform a second URL translation, mod_rewrite performs a bit of magic. The module registers a callback with the server for the Fixup phase of the request cycle, which normally performs only perfunctory duties after all the real work of processing a request has been completed. During this late cycle phase, mod_rewrite applies any per-directory rewriting rules. By this time, however, the URL has already been reduced to a single filename, so mod_rewrite reconstructs a URL and resubmits it to the server for processing, and the request processing cycle begins all over again. The process is a lot more involved than that of straight per-server rewriting, and heavy use of per-directory rewriting can cause a significant decrease in server efficiency in processing requests. There's no general rule of thumb regarding per-directory rewrites, but they should be used only when necessary and their impact always kept in mind. Attempt to reduce the number of URLs that are processed using per-directory rewriting.

Setting Up mod_rewrite

Mod_rewrite is a standard module provided with the Apache distribution, so you should have it available without having to download and install it, as you would a third-party module. To ensure that you can use the module, make sure your httpd.conf file includes the following lines (for a DSO module that has been statically linked to the Apache kernel, only the second line is needed to enable it):

```
LoadModule rewrite_module    libexec/mod_rewrite.so
AddModule mod_rewrite.c
```

If you've implemented virtual hosting (as described in Chapter 6), however, you may have more work to do before mod_rewrite is ready to use. The first time I tried to use mod_rewrite, I spent hours trying to figure out why it wouldn't work.

I restarted Apache with the original plain-vanilla httpd.conf and mod_rewrite worked, writing its actions into the log file I'd defined. Obviously, some change I'd made to httpd.conf had broken mod_rewrite. I suspected a module I'd added was somehow refusing to let mod_rewrite do its job, and I began to take lines out of my httpd.conf file, one by one, hoping to find the conflicting module or directive. It wasn't until I began to remove my <VirtualHost> configurations that I realized what was going on. When setting up the virtual hosts, I had taken great pains to ensure that my main Apache server never handled requests. As you saw in Chapter 6, it's generally a good practice to configure one of your virtual hosts as a default for requests that resolve to no other virtual host, in order to prevent your main server from providing request responses. I had done exactly that, and my mod_rewrite ruleset (being applied to the main server) was never given anything to do by Apache.

The problem is that mod_rewrite directives, unlike most configuration directives, are not inherited from the primary server configuration by virtual hosts. To use rewriting rules in virtual host contexts, you must either redefine URL rewriting rules for each virtual host or use the RewriteOptions directive to enable the inheritance of rewriting rules by virtual hosts (see the discussion on this mod_rewrite directive later in the chapter).

Note that if you intend to use both mod_alias and mod_rewrite, you must load mod_alias first, which means (as you may remember from Chapter 5) that it is processed after mod_rewrite. The reason you must do this is that mod_alias translates URLs to filenames. If mod_rewrite is processed after mod_alias, the URL it expects will have already been translated to a filename that it can't process. You may be wondering why mod_rewrite (which also functions as a URL-to-filename translator) doesn't break mod_alias. Ordinarily, it will, but it includes a special *passthrough* flag that causes mod_rewrite to change Apache's internal representation of the request from a filename to a URL when it has completed its work. This flag is discussed later with the RewriteRule directive.

Rulesets

The URL rewriting engine of mod_rewrite works on *rulesets* that consist of rewriting rules and their optional conditions. A rewriting rule looks very much like the Redirect directives we saw in the earlier discussion of mod_alias; it consists of a pattern that is matched (using a regular expression match) against the request URL and a substitution that is applied if the URL matches the pattern.

For example, what you already know about mod_alias redirection applies to a simple rewriting rule like the following:

```
RewriteRule /mystuff /home/caulds/
```

Examining a simple rewriting rule like this one, you're probably wondering what advantage mod_rewrite provides over mod_alias. Indeed, for simple request redirection, there are no significant advantages, and that is why I recommend using the simpler mod_alias whenever possible. The advantages of using mod_rewrite only become important when multiple rules must be applied, often based on conditional tests, and that is the purpose of rulesets.

A simple mod_rewrite ruleset might have a single rewriting rule preceded by a conditional test:

```
RewriteCond %{REMOTE_ADDR} ^192\.168\.1\..*
RewriteRule .* /localpages/ [R]
```

The details of how this simple (yet quite useful) example works will become apparent as you read the descriptions of the two mod_rewrite directives it uses. The purpose of this ruleset is to redirect all requests submitted to my server from local clients (anyone on the subnet 192.168.1.*) to a different set of Web pages. The optional flag [R] that ends the RewriteRule directive stands for Redirect and indicates that the rule performs the URL substitution and returns the results to the requester as a redirect.

Per-server rulesets are read from httpd.conf once when the server is started; per-directory rulesets are read from .htaccess files at runtime as the server follows the path to a directory corresponding to the request URL.

Although the order of the rules in a mod_rewrite ruleset is very important, their processing is not completely sequential. The rewriting engine starts at the beginning of the defined ruleset and works its way through the rules until it reaches the end. If the URL does not match the pattern specified in a rule, processing of that rule ends, and the rewriting engine proceeds to the next rule in the set. When it finds a rule with a pattern that matches the URL, mod_rewrite does not immediately process that rule, but first evaluates any rewriting conditions that apply to the rule. Like a rewriting rule, a condition contains a pattern that is matched against the URL, using regular expression matching with some enhancements added by mod_rewrite. The pattern resolves as either True or False, and based on this result, the substitution part of the corresponding rewriting rule is either applied or ignored.

After applying a rewriting rule, the rewriting engine continues processing additional rules in the ruleset—unless that rule has the l flag appended (which indicates it is the last rule to be processed). It's generally a good idea to use the l flag to step out of the processing loop (much like a using the last command in a Perl loop or the break command in C). There are times, however, when you do wish to apply a rule and continue processing the ruleset. In complex mod_rewrite rulesets, often two or more rules must be applied to completely rewrite the URL.

The Essential Rewriting Directives

Only two of the mod_rewrite directives are required for the module to work. The first of these, RewriteEngine, enables the rewriting engine. The second, RewriteRule, is the only directive that must be present in all rewriting rulesets. I'll discuss these directives before presenting a very simple but useful example of a ruleset that contains only a single rewriting rule.

Turning the Rewrite Engine On or Off: RewriteEngine

The RewriteEngine directive is very simple, but it is essential to mod_rewrite. It enables or disables the URL rewriting engine:

```
RewriteEngine on | off
```

By default, the engine is off and the module does absolutely nothing. To use mod_rewrite, you must have at least one RewriteEngine on directive, either in httpd.conf or in an .htaccess file.

By default, mod_rewrite rewriting configurations are not inherited (see the section on RewriteOptions later in this chapter for how to alter this behavior). This means that virtual hosts do not inherit the rewriting configuration from the primary server as they do most other general server configuration directives, and so you normally need a RewriteEngine directive in each virtual host to use mod_rewrite in that context.

Defining the Ruleset: RewriteRule

It should come as no surprise that the RewriteRule directive is the most important part of mod_rewrite. Without a RewriteRule directive, no other mod_rewrite directive has any effect. Each RewriteRule directive expresses a single matching rule of the form:

```
RewriteRule Pattern Substitution
```

Each rule consists of patterns against which the original URL is matched and actions to be taken if the match is successful. In most cases, the action is a simple replacement of the original URL with a new one that can contain fragments from the original, data taken from Apache or the system environment, or the results of lookups from static text files or even databases.

The Pattern is a regular expression that is matched to the current URL when the rule is applied. This current URL might not be the original request URL, which may have been altered by preceding `RewriteRule` directives or an `Alias` directive. `mod_rewrite` expands the regular expression matching in the following important ways:

- The regular expression can be negated by preceding it with the logical NOT character (`!`).

- `RewriteRule` back-references can be used in the regular expression. These are back-references of the form `$N`, where `N` can be an integer value 0 through 9 and is filled with the contents of the `N`th set of parentheses in the `Pattern` portion of the rule. For example, in the following `RewriteRule`, the portion of the URL that matches the expression within the first set of parentheses replaces `$1` in the substitution, and the portion matching the second set replaces `$2`:

  ```
  RewriteRule ^/~(.*)/(.*) /home/$1/$2
  ```

- `RewriteCond` back-references can be used in the regular expression. These are back-references of the form `%N`, where `N` can be an integer value 0 through 9 and is filled with the contents of the `N`th parentheses in the last matched `RewriteCond` directive. Later in the chapter, when conditional rewriting (using the `RewriteCond` directive) is discussed, we'll see examples of `RewriteRule` directives that use back references to use a value obtained from a previous `RewriteCond` directive.

- Environment variables: The special format `%{variable}` is filled with the value of `variable` from Apache's environment. This is particularly useful when previous `RewriteRule` directives have been used to set arbitrary environment variables. As we'll see in later examples, environment variables play a more important role in conditional rewriting. Occasionally, though, you may wish to use the value of an environment variable for rewriting a URL using a `RewriteRule` directive.

- Mapping-function calls: These are calls to mappings previously defined with `RewriteMap` and take the form `${mapname:key|default}`.

All the rewriting rules are applied to the substitution (in the order of definition in the configuration file). The URL is completely replaced by the substitution and the rewriting process goes on until there are no more rules, unless a `RewriteRule` in the set is explicitly terminated by an `[L]` flag.

If the substitution consists of the single character - (minus), no substitution is performed and the URL is passed unaltered to the next `RewriteRule`. This is useful when you want to make multiple matches (using the `[C]` flag to chain server `RewriteRule` directives) before you rewrite the URL. Another use for this is to have a `RewriteRule` that does not rewrite the URL but instead has a flag that indicates a certain response to send the user (like the `[F]` flag, which returns a response with an HTTP 403 (Forbidden) status).

One more note: You can even create URLs in the substitution string containing a query string part. Just use a question mark inside the substitution string to indicate that the following stuff should be reinjected into the `QUERY_STRING`. When you want to erase an existing query string, end the substitution string with just the question mark. Use the [QSA] flag to force the query string to be appended to QUERY_STRING. The following directive extracts a filename from the request URL and then rewrites the URL to pass this filename to a CGI script (parser.cgi), which will preprocess the file before it is served to the requester:

```
RewriteRule ^(/.*)$  /cgi-bin/parser.cgi?file=$1
```

If the rewritten URL is expressed as a relative URL, it goes back to the server engine for processing. However, if the rule precedes the rewritten URL with http:// (which makes the new URL a URI), the rewritten URL is returned to the client as an external redirect even if the [R] flag is not used.

> **NOTE** When you prefix a substitution field with the prefix http://thishost [:thisport] (in other words, if you point to the local server by server name and port), mod_rewrite automatically strips this prefix. This auto-reduction on implicit external redirect URLs is a useful and important feature when you use a RewriteMap to generate the hostname part. The result of this, though, is that an unconditional external redirect to your own server will not work with the prefix http://thishost. To achieve such a self-redirect, you must use the [R] flag (see below) to force an external redirect.

Additionally you can set special flags for Substitution by appending [flags] as the third argument to the RewriteRule directive. Flags is a comma-separated list of the following flags:

R|redirect [=code]   Treats the rewritten URL as a redirect. The default HTTP status code of 302 (Found) is placed on the response. You can define another response code in the range 300–400 by appending =code to the [R] flag, where code can be the number or one of the following symbolic names: temp (default), permanent, or seeother.

F|forbidden   The client is immediately sent an HTTP response with status 403 (Forbidden).

G|gone   The client is immediately sent an HTTP response with status 410 (Gone).

P|proxy   Forces the rewritten URL to be processed internally by the proxy module, mod_proxy, which must be present for this to work. (Chapter 13 discusses mod_proxy.) This flag also causes mod_rewrite processing to cease at once and implies an [L] flag.

L|last   Indicates that mod_rewrite processing should cease with this ruleset. Note that this flag is only effective if the Pattern matches the URL. If the match fails, rewriting processing proceeds immediately with the next RewriteRule directive in the current ruleset.

N|next   Starts the rewriting process over, with the first RewriteRule directive in the current ruleset. The rewriting process begins with the rewritten URL from the last RewriteRule directive.

C|chain   Chains the current rule with the next rule. If any rule in a set of chained rules fails to match, all following rules in the chain are ignored.

T|type=MIME-type   Forces the target file of the rewritten URL to be of a specified MIME-type. This is often used to simulate the ScriptAlias directive, which forces all files inside a target directory to have the MIME-type application/x-httpd-cgi.

NS|nosubreq   Causes the current rule to be skipped if the current request is an internal subrequest. Subrequests from CGI scripts often cause problems, so it is often desirable to use this flag when rewritten URLs target CGI scripts that make requests of the server.

NC|nocase   Forces the Pattern match against the URL to be case-insensitive.

QSA|qsappend   If the URL being rewritten is a query string, and the rewritten URL is also a query string (that is, begins with a question mark) this flag forces the rewriting engine to append the rewritten query string part to the existing URL instead of replacing it. Use this when you simply want to add more data to the query string via a rewriting rule.

S|skip=num   Forces the rewriting engine to skip the next num rules if the Pattern matches the URL in the current rule.

E|env=var:value   Sets an environment variable if the Pattern matches the URL in the current rule. The value can contain both RewriteRule and RewriteCond back-references ($N and %N, respectively). This flag is used in a similar way to the SetEnvIf directive. It is often used to set access control conditions. You can use the flag more than once in a single RewriteRule directive to set more than one environment variable.

PT|passthrough   Forces the rewriting engine to set the URI field of the internal request_rec structure to the value of the filename field. Since mod_rewrite translates URLs to filenames, the rewritten URL is known internally to the server as a filename. This flag does not change the output of a RewriteRule directive but internally designates it as a URI, so that it can, in turn, be processed by other URI-to-filename translators, such as the Alias, ScriptAlias, and Redirect directives from mod_alias. Failure to use this flag will prevent these directives from being able to process mod_rewrite output.

A Simple Redirection Example

Here's what may be the simplest (and possibly most useful) example of how a RewriteRule might be used. This example illustrates all of the critical elements that must be understood to use the RewriteRule directive, so be sure you understand how it works before reading further in this chapter. It begins with an example of a URL rewriting rule that I actually use on my server. This example is quite simple and could just as easily be implemented using the Redirect directive in mod_alias. The purpose of the following rewriting rule is to rewrite requests for a non-existent file environ.html to a CGI script that generates the HTML output. I did this primarily to disguise the fact that a CGI script is actually being used.

```
# mod_rewrite stuff
#
RewriteEngine on
RewriteRule    ^/environ\.html$  /environ.cgi [L, R]
```

Placed in the general server configuration section of my httpd.conf, this ruleset first turns the rewriting engine on (you only need to do this once in the general server context). The RewriteRule then matches against any URL that requests environ.html from my server and rewrites the URL to /environ.cgi. The [L] flag says "let this be the last rule." If this rule is processed (that is, if the match to environ.html is successful), the rewriting engine stops processing this ruleset and ignores any RewriteRule directives following this one.

TIP One of the best ways to understand how mod_rewrite works is to practice with it. Try entering a simple rule like the one in this example in your Apache httpd.conf and restart the server. Modify the filenames used in the example, to substitute one HTML file for another, for instance. The remaining examples in this chapter will be much easier to understand if you practice with them; so I've tried to keep them simple enough that they can be implemented, with only minor changes, by the administrator of any working Apache server with mod_rewrite enabled.

Changing the rule above to include the [R], as in the following line, changes the RewriteRule to a forced redirect:

```
RewriteRule    ^/environ\.html$  /environ.cgi [L,R]
```

The effect is that the browser will now redirect its request to /environ.cgi, and that URL will display in the Location: field of the browser where, before, the user only saw environ.html. Note that the request must now be submitted twice (by the client browser) before it is fulfilled.

In addition to the forced or explicit redirect I just demonstrated, redirection can also occur implicitly, and that's what will happen if the RewriteRule is modified to this:

```
RewriteRule    ^/environ\.html$  http://192.168.1.1/environ.cgi [L]
```

Note that the [R] is missing, but the inclusion of http:// will always cause an implicit external redirect unless the server name in the rewritten URL matches the ServerName defined for the local server. That's why my rewriting rule used the IP address of the server. Had I used its hostname, the redirect would have been handled as an internal redirect. The use of http:// in the rewritten URL is the best way to handle redirects to other servers.

There's something else that can be learned from this example. When I use a relative URL to rewrite the request URL to /environ.cgi, this URL will be processed as relative to DocumentHome. For this to work, I had to enable CGI processing in that directory on my server, something I do *not* recommend for production Apache servers. In fact, I generally prefer to keep my /cgi-bin directory completely separate from the entire DocumentRoot. If you need to rewrite the URL to /cgi-bin/environ.cgi (which is mapped by a ScriptAlias directive to another part of the file system) you must use the pass-through [PT] flag so that mod-alias will be able to process the rewritten URL.:

```
RewriteRule    ^/environ\.html$  /cgi-bin/environ.cgi [L,PT]
```

The result of using the pass-through flag is that the rewritten request, which is normally identified by the server as a path and filename, is now marked internally as a URL for subsequent processing by modules with registered handlers for URL translation (like mod_alias). It will then be processed by any other URL translation modules in the server configuration. Thus, /cgi-bin/environ.cgi is no longer a relative path and filename but is now a URL, and mod_alias translates that URL into a path, using a ScriptAlias directive, like the one I have defined for my server:

```
ScriptAlias /cgi-bin/ "/home/httpd/cgi-bin/"
```

Conditional Rewriting: The RewriteCond Directive

RewriteRule directives can be preceded with one or more RewriteCond directives, each of which defines a single rule condition that evaluates to True or False to determine whether the rule will be applied. Before any RewriteRule is applied, the rewriting engine evaluates all preceding conditions. The RewriteRule is applied only if all the RewriteCond directives immediately preceding it evaluate to True. Unless multiple RewriteCond conditions are joined using an [OR] flag and evaluated as a single rule, a RewriteRule will be ignored if any condition preceding it fails. RewriteCond has the following syntax:

```
RewriteCond MatchString Pattern
```

The MatchString Argument

The MatchString is a plain-text string, which can also contain the following constructs that are expanded before comparing the string to the Pattern:

RewriteRule back-references These are back-references of the form $N, where N can be an integer value 0 through 9 and is filled with the contents of the Nth set of parentheses in the pattern portion of the following RewriteRule.

RewriteCond back-references These are back-references of the form %N, where N can be an integer value 0 through 9 and is filled with the contents of the Nth set of parentheses in the last matched RewriteCond directive.

Server variables These are variables of the form %{VARIABLE_NAME} where VARIABLE_NAME is one of the following:

HTTP headers: HTTP_USER_AGENT, HTTP_REFERER, HTTP_COOKIE, HTTP_FORWARDED, HTTP_HOST, HTTP_PROXY_CONNECTION, HTTP_ACCEPT

Connection and request: REMOTE_ADDR, REMOTE_HOST, REMOTE_USER, REMOTE_IDENT, REQUEST_METHOD, SCRIPT_FILENAME, PATH_INFO, QUERY_STRING, AUTH_TYPE

Server internals: DOCUMENT_ROOT, SERVER_ADMIN, SERVER_NAME, SERVER_ADDR, SERVER_PORT, SERVER_PROTOCOL, SERVER_SOFTWARE

System values: TIME_YEAR, TIME_MON, TIME_DAY, TIME_HOUR, TIME_MIN, TIME_SEC, TIME_WDAY, TIME

Special variables: API_VERSION, SCRIPT_URI, SCRIPT_URL, REQUEST_URI, REQUEST_FILENAME, IS_SUBREQ

Environment variables The special format %{ENV:variable} is filled with the value of variable from Apache's environment. This is particularly useful when previous RewriteRule directives have been used to set arbitrary environment variables.

HTTP headers The special format %{HTTP:header} is filled with the value of header from the HTTP request being evaluated.

Look-aheads The special format %{LA-U:variable} is filled with the value of variable that will normally be set later in the request cycle based on the URL. For example, if you wanted to condition your rewriting on the value of REMOTE_USER in a per-server context (that is, using directives in httpd.conf), you must use a look-ahead, because mod_rewrite does its work before the authorization phases set the variable. When the rewriting occurs in a per-directory context (from an .htaccess file), it occurs in the Fixup phase of the cycle and after the authorization phases. Another form of the look-ahead uses the format %{LA-F:variable}, which is filled with the value of *variable* based on the filename, rather than URL. This form is rarely needed.

The Pattern Argument

The Pattern in a RewriteCond directive is a regular expression that is compared to the directive's MatchString. If it matches, the entire RewriteCond directive evaluates to True. If it fails to match, the directive evaluates to False. This regular expression has been extended by mod_rewrite in the following ways:

- You can prefix the Pattern with a ! character to specify a non-matching pattern.
- Instead of a regular expression match, you can use one of the following comparisons to match the MatchString and Pattern. Each comparison evaluates to True or False.

  <Pattern   Treats the Pattern as a plain string and compares it lexically (using alphanumeric and other characters) to MatchString. Evaluates to True if MatchString is lexically less than Pattern.

  >Pattern   Treats the Pattern as a plain string and compares it lexically to MatchString. True if MatchString is lexically greater than Pattern.

  =Pattern   Treats the Pattern as a plain string and compares it lexically to MatchString. Evaluates to True if MatchString is lexically equal to Pattern. If the Pattern is just " " (two quotation marks), this compares MatchString to the null string. Use this to determine if a particular variable is set.

  -d   Treats MatchString as a pathname and tests whether it exists and is a directory.

  -f   Treats MatchString as a pathname and tests whether it exists and is a regular file.

  -s   Treats MatchString as a pathname and tests whether it exists and is a file with size greater than zero.

  -l   Treats MatchString as a pathname and tests whether it exists and is a symbolic link.

  -F   Treats MatchString as a pathname and tests whether it exists and is accessible via all of the server's currently configured access controls for that path. This uses an internal subrequest to make the determination, so there is a performance degradation with heavy use of this option.

  -U   Treats MatchString as a URL and tests whether it is accessible via all the currently configured access controls for that path. This option uses an internal subrequest to determine the check, so there is a performance degradation with heavy use.

- Additionally, you can set special flags for `Pattern` by appending `[flags]` as the third argument to the `RewriteCond` directive. The flags can be either or both of the following (separated by a comma):

    `ornext|OR`   Combines the current condition and the next condition with a logical OR instead of the implied AND. In other words, if either statement is true, together they both evaluate as True.

    `nocase|NC`   Disregards character case in comparing the `MatchString` and `Pattern`.

An Example of Conditional Rewriting

To rewrite the default page of a site according to the `User-Agent:` header of the request, you can use ruleset shown in Listing 10.1:

Listing 10.1   Ruleset for Conditional Rewriting Based on Client Browser Type

```
# Match strings beginning with Mozilla, followed by
# anything
RewriteCond  %{HTTP_USER_AGENT}  ^Mozilla.*
# Match strings that do NOT contain the string MSIE
RewriteCond  %{HTTP_USER_AGENT}  !^.*MSIE.*
# Rewrite the URL to /nscape.index.html
RewriteRule  ^/$              /nscape.index.html  [R,L]

# Above rule not applied, match URLs containing MSIE
# anywhere in the string
RewriteCond  %{HTTP_USER_AGENT}  ^.*MSIE.*
# Rewrite the URL to /ie.index.html
RewriteRule  ^/$              /ie.index.html  [R,L]

# Neither rule above applied, match URLs beginning with
# Lynx, followed by anything
RewriteCond  %{HTTP_USER_AGENT}  ^Lynx.*
# Rewrite the URL to /text.index.html
RewriteRule  ^/$              /text.index.html  [R,L]

# None of the previous rules applied, rewrite the URL
# to the default /index.html
RewriteRule  ^/$              /index.html  [R,L]
```

A site visitor who uses the browser Netscape Navigator (which identifies itself as *Mozilla* but does not contain the *MSIE* string) will be served the `nscape.index.html` page, which is optimized for the Netscape browser. Anyone using Microsoft Internet Explorer (which also identifies itself as *Mozilla*, strangely enough, but contains *MSIE*) will get `ie.index.html`. A visitor using Lynx, a text-only browser, will reach a text-only page, `text.index.html`. And finally, if none of the other conditions are met, the user will see the regular `index.html`. Maybe this is similar to what certain Web sites seem to do so that they appear broken when used with a competitor's browser?

The `[R,L]` flag that ends each `RewriteRule` directive indicates that a redirect response with the rewritten URL should be returned to the requesting client and that this should be the last `RewriteRule` processed in the current ruleset. By default, the response sent to the client will carry a status code of 302 (Found).

An Example of Automatic Page Creation

Listing 10.2 depicts an interesting example of how a static Web page can be automatically created if it does not already exist. The `!-s` flag at the end of the `RewriteCond` directive tells `mod_rewrite` to interpret the match string as a path and filename to be tested to see if the file exists and has a size greater than 0 bytes. The `RewriteCond` directive tests to see if the requested file exists. If it does, no rewriting occurs and the document is served from the disk file. If the file does not exist (or is zero-length), the request is redirected to the CGI script shown in Listing 10.3. This script creates the requested file and then sends the lines written to this file as a response to the client. Subsequent requests for the file will not result in a redirection to this script, but will be served from the disk file.

What practical use does this have? Suppose there is a page on the server that needs to be updated on a regular basis; for example, it may contain a daily bulletin that is generated from other text files on the server. As administrator, you can schedule a process (using the Linux `cron` utility) to delete the file automatically at a specified time, perhaps midnight. The first request for this file after it has been deleted will cause the CGI script to run and generate a new file.

Listing 10.2   Ruleset to Create a Page Automatically When Needed

```
# Test REQUEST_FILENAME to ascertain if it exists. The
# ! operator means that this condition evaluates to TRUE
# if the file does not exist, or if it has a length of 0
# bytes
RewriteCond /home/httpd/html%{REQUEST_FILENAME}  !-s
#
# Rewrite the URL to redirect the request to the
# dynindex.cgi CGI script.
RewriteRule dynindex\.html$ /cgi-bin/dynindex.cgi [L]
```

Advanced
Configuration Options

PART 3

Listing 10.3   Perl Script That Uses the Page-Creation Ruleset

```perl
#!/usr/bin/perl
#
open(OUTFILE, "> /home/httpd/html/dynindex.html");
#open(OUTFILE, "> /tmp/dynindex.html");
print OUTFILE <<END;
<TITLE>Charles Aulds's Home Page</TITLE>
</HEAD>
<body background="IMAGES/ftbckgrd.jpg">
<center>
<h1>This is my home page ...</h1>
<p>
<FORM METHOD = "POST" ACTION = "mailto:caulds\@hiwaay.net">
<INPUT TYPE = "SUBMIT" VALUE="Click here to send me e-mail"></FORM>
</center>
<HR>
<p>
</BODY>
</HTML>
END
close OUTFILE;
system("/bin/chown www.www/home/httpd/html/dynindex.html;/bin/chmod 755 /home/
httpd/html/dynindex.html");
print<<END;
Content-type: text/html\n\n
<TITLE>Charles Aulds's Home Page</TITLE>
</HEAD>
<body background="IMAGES/ftbckgrd.jpg">
<center>
<h1>This is my home page ...</h1>
<p>
<FORM METHOD = "POST" ACTION = "mailto:caulds\@hiwway.net">
<INPUT TYPE = "SUBMIT" VALUE="Click here to send me e-mail"></FORM>
</center>
<HR>
<p>
</BODY>
</HTML>
END
```

An Example of Reusing Conditions

Listing 10.4 illustrates how the result of one or more mod_rewrite directives can be reused (by setting the value of an environment variable that is referenced in later conditions). This example first uses the SetEnv directive to set the value of an environment variable trustedhost to *no*. Then it uses three RewriteCond directives to test the network address of the requesting client to see if the request came from one of three subnets. The RewriteCond directives are joined by [OR] flags to create one test that will result in a True condition if any one of the directives finds a match. The first RewriteRule directive will be evaluated only if any one of the three conditions is met. The rewriting rule is simple; it makes no actual substitution (denoted by the - character) but uses the [E] flag to set the trustedhost environment variable to *yes*, which indicates the request came from one of the trusted subnets.

The rest of the ruleset consists of two additional rewriting rules, only one of which will be applied to each request, depending on the value of the trustedhost variable. The flowchart in Figure 10.1 illustrates the logic.

Listing 10.4   Reusing the Result of a RewriteCond Directive

```
# Create a new environment variable and set its
# value to "no".  The SetEnv directive requires
# mod_env
SetEnv trustedhost=no

# Test the request URL against two IP addresses
# and one hostname
RewriteCond %{REMOTE_ADDR} ^192\.168\.1\.* [OR]
RewriteCond %{REMOTE_ADDR} ^216\.78\.169\.* [OR]
RewriteCond %{REMOTE_HOST} ^rascal\.hiwaay\.net$
# At least one of the conditions above evaluated
# to true; special RewriteRule does no rewrite
# but [E] flag resets trustedhost to yes
RewriteRule .* - [E=trustedhost=yes]

# trustedhost=no then TRUE, otherwise FALSE
RewriteCond %{ENV:trustedhost} ^no$
# not a trusted host, rewrite URL to standard
# index.html, send redirect to client
RwriteRule .* /index\.html [R]
```

```
# trustedhost=no then TRUE, otherwise FALSE
RewriteCond %{ENV:trustedhost} ^yes$
# is a trusted host, rewrite request to special
# /trusted directory, send redirect to client
RewriteRule (.*) /trusted/$1 [R]
```

Figure 10.1   Flowchart for Reusing a RewriteCond Directive

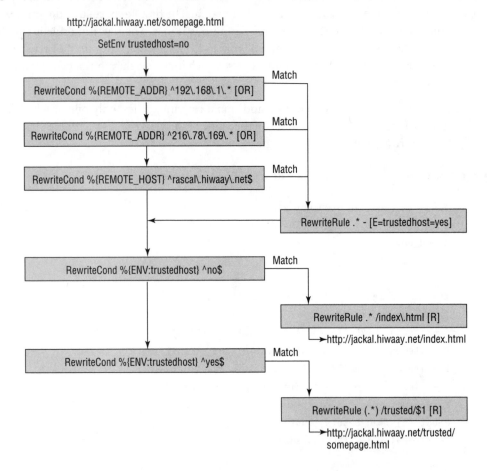

Special Considerations for Per-Directory Rewriting

Anyone planning to use mod_rewrite in a per-directory rather than a per-server context needs to be aware of a few special considerations. First, mod_rewrite uses a somewhat unusual mechanism for security. Whenever RewriteRule directives are included in a per-directory context, the FollowSymLinks option must be enabled for the intended directory.

If this option is not enabled for a directory in which an .htaccess file containing mod_rewrite rules resides, the server will log the following error:

```
[Thu Mar 30 09:58:14 2000] [error] [client 192.168.1.3] Options FollowSymLinks
or SymLinksIfOwnerMatch is off which implies that RewriteRule directive is
forbidden: /home/httpd/html
```

In addition, the client request for a resource subject to URL rewriting is rejected with an HTTP request response code of 403 (Forbidden).

To prevent this, make sure that any .htaccess file or <Directory> container that includes mod_rewrite URL rules also contains the following lines:

```
RewriteEngine On
Options FollowSymLinks
```

Another important consideration is the different behavior of mod_rewrite in per-directory and per-server contexts. In a per-directory context, mod_rewrite strips the per-directory prefix, which is added back after substitution occurs. For that reason, a per-server RewriteRule that contains the pattern ^/docs/.*$ will not match in a per-directory context. Since the directory prefix is stripped from the URL by mod_rewrite in a per-directory context, this pattern would be reduced to ^.*$ in a RewriteRule applied in a per-directory context to the /docs directory (probably in an .htaccess file inside that directory). In other words, whenever you include rewriting directives in an .htaccess file, make sure your MatchString does not include the directory path.

The RewriteOptions Directive

mod_rewrite settings are not inherited by default; this behavior must be explicitly enabled in every context where such inheritance is desired. For this purpose you can use the RewriteOptions directive. Although it was designed as a general-purpose directive to set special options for the mod_rewrite module, there is only one option that can currently be set, inherit; so there is only one form of the directive:

```
RewriteOptions inherit
```

This causes the current configuration to inherit the mod_rewrite settings of its parent. There are two completely different ways it is used, depending on the context:

Virtual host   If the RewriteOptions inherit directive is set in a virtual host context, the mod_rewrite settings are inherited from the primary server. This includes rewriting conditions, rules, and maps. (We'll look at rewriting maps and the RewriteMap directive later in the chapter.)

Directory   In a directory context (for example, when the RewriteOptions inherit directive is contained in an .htaccess file), the mod_rewrite settings are inherited from the parent directory's .htaccess file, if it exists.

Logging Rewriting Actions

When using mod_rewrite, it is always a good idea to enable logging for the module, especially when debugging your rewriting rules. The logging provided by the module is very complete and very useful. It can also be educational, if you take the time to follow the progress of the rewriting engine through the rulesets. I recommend that you enable logging for all servers using the module, even if you enable it only at a low level of verbosity on production servers. To use logging, you need to identify the file where the log will be maintained, and you need to set the level of information that will be logged. The mod_rewrite module provides a separate directive for each task.

Specifying the Log File Location: RewriteLog

The RewriteLog directive specifies the name of a file into which the server logs the rewriting actions it performs. Here's an example:

```
RewriteLog "/usr/local/apache/logs/mod_rewrite.log"
```

Unless the name begins with a slash (/), it is assumed to be relative to the ServerRoot. The directive should occur only once per server configuration.

To disable rewrite logging, do *not* set the filename to /dev/null (although this may seem intuitive). Although no log appears to be written, this does not actually disable logging—it simply redirects logging output to the system null file handle (the so-called *bit bucket*, which essentially destroys the information). The logging activities are still performed and consume processor resources. To disable logging, either remove the RewriteLog directive or use RewriteLogLevel 0.

Setting the Logging Level: RewriteLogLevel

The RewriteLogLevel directive sets the verbosity level of the rewriting log file. The default level of 0 means no logging, while 9 or more means that practically all actions are logged. Example:

```
RewriteLogLevel 2
```

A RewriteLogLevel of 2 produces a log that very nicely shows the various stages of the rewriting process and can be useful in examining the effect of each RewriteCond and RewriteRule directive. Values greater than 2 will slow down your Apache server significantly and should be used only during debugging.

Listing 10.5 shows a Level 2 rewrite log for a single request handled by a RewriteRule in my httpd.conf file (that is, in a per-server context). The actual rule is the one used in my first mod_rewrite example:

```
RewriteRule    ^/environ\.html$         /environ.cgi [L]
```

In the sample log, you'll see that almost every step of the rewriting process is logged even at this minimal level of verbosity. mod_rewrite logging can be very useful in understanding both the process of URL rewriting and the behavior of the module in processing your rewriting rules. When developing rewriting rules, always examine the log so that you understand what's going on.

Listing 10.5   A Sample from a RewriteLog

```
192.168.1.3 - - [04/Apr/2000:09:33:31 -0500] [jackal.hiwaay.net/
sid#80bcb1c][rid

#84cb144/initial] (2) init rewrite engine with requested uri /environ.html

192.168.1.3 - - [04/Apr/2000:09:33:31 -0500] [jackal.hiwaay.net/
sid#80bcb1c][rid

#84cb144/initial] (2) rewrite /environ.html -> /environ.cgi

192.168.1.3 - - [04/Apr/2000:09:33:31 -0500] [jackal.hiwaay.net/
sid#80bcb1c][rid

#84cb144/initial] (2) local path result: /environ.cgi

192.168.1.3 - - [04/Apr/2000:09:33:31 -0500] [jackal.hiwaay.net/
sid#80bcb1c][rid

#84cb144/initial] (2) prefixed with document_root to /home/httpd/html/
environ.cgi

192.168.1.3 - - [04/Apr/2000:09:33:31 -0500] [jackal.hiwaay.net/
sid#80bcb1c][rid

#84cb144/initial] (1) go-ahead with /home/httpd/html/environ.cgi [OK]

192.168.1.3 - - [04/Apr/2000:09:33:31 -0500] [jackal.hiwaay.net/
sid#80bcb1c][rid

#84cb144/initial] (1) [per-dir /home/httpd/html/] pass through /home/httpd/html/
environ.cgi
```

Setting a Base URL: The RewriteBase Directive

The RewriteBase directive explicitly sets the base URL for per-directory rewriting. The directive is applied only on a per-directory basis, possibly in a <Directory> container, but usually in an .htaccess file. It is necessary whenever the request URL does not match the local file system, usually because an Alias directive has been used to redirect requests to locations outside Apache's DocumentRoot.

Why is it necessary to use RewriteBase? Whenever a rewriting rule modifies a location on a per-directory basis, the actual rewriting occurs late in the request cycle, after almost all other actions have already happened. I've said that mod_alias should process the URL only after mod_rewrite has had its turn, but in a per-directory context, the rewriting rules are applied at a very late stage in the request processing cycle, after both per-server mod_rewrite rules and mod_alias have had their turns.

To make per-directory rewriting work, the URL resulting from these late-cycle rewrites is resubmitted to the server (internally), and a new request cycle begins. The URL is said to be "reinjected" into the server engine. The rewriting rule, when applied in a per-directory context, strips off RewriteBase (which, by default, is the local directory prefix), applies the rule to the remainder of the URL, and then prepends the RewriteBase. In a case where the incoming URL does not map to the local file system, you want to change the RewriteBase so that it matches the incoming URL prefix, not the local directory prefix.

For example, assume the Ruleset shown in Listing 10.6 is an .htaccess file in the /usr/local/docs directory and an Alias directive in httpd.conf has mapped this directory to the URL /docs.

Listing 10.6   A Ruleset Using the RewriteBase Directive

```
#   /usr/local/docs/.htaccess - a per-dir config file
#   The following Alias directive in the server config
#   maps this directory to /docs:
#
#          Alias /docs/ "/usr/local/docs/"
#
RewriteEngine On
#
#
RewriteBase    /docs
#
RewriteRule    ^FAQ\.html$  faqlist.html
```

Here, a request to /docs/FAQ.html is mapped (by the Alias directive) to /usr/local/docs/FAQ.html. The .htaccess file is read, and the RewriteRule strips the local directory prefix from the URL and then maps the remainder (FAQ.html) to faqlist.html. Before reinjecting the request to the server engine, mod_rewrite first prepends the value of RewriteBase, so that the reinjected URL is processed as /docs/faqlist.html. If the RewriteBase directive is removed from the .htaccess file, mod_rewrite would, instead, prepend the local directory prefix (which is the RewriteBase default) and submit the URL /usr/local/docs/faqlist.html for processing. The server would reject this request as invalid.

Mapped Rewriting: The RewriteMap Directive

The RewriteMap directive names a rewriting map for later use in a RewriteRule, and specifies the rewriting map source that can be used to look up information based on a key search and later inserted into the RewriteRule substitution string. It has the following syntax:

```
RewriteMap MapName MapType:MapSource
```

A rewriting map is essentially a lookup table. It consists of any number of variable/value pairs and is analogous to a Perl *hash* (or *associative array*) or a *dictionary object* in VBScript or JavaScript. The closest analogy in C would be a two-dimensional array in which the name of the variable is used as a lookup for its value.

When one of the following constructs is placed inside the substitution string of a `RewriteRule`, it will be filled by the result of the `RewriteMap` lookup if the key is found in the map; otherwise the construct is replaced by the `DefaultValue` (if specified) or with an empty string.

```
${ MapName : LookupKey }
${ MapName : LookupKey | DefaultValue }
```

The `RewriteMap` directive can occur more than once. For each mapping function, use one `RewriteMap` directive to declare its rewriting mapfile. While you cannot *declare* a map in a per-directory context, you can *use* this map in per-directory context.

The following combinations for `MapType` and `MapSource` can be used:

Standard Plain Text (`MapType txt`)

Randomized Plain Text (`MapType rnd`)

Hash file (`MapType dbm`)

External Function (`MapType prg`)

Internal Function (`MapType int`)

> **NOTE** For plain-text and DBM format files, the looked-up keys are cached in-core until the modification time of the mapfile changes or the server is restarted. This way, you can have map functions in rules that are used for every request. This is no problem, because the external lookup only happens once!

Standard Plain Text

The standard rewriting map is one in which the `MapSource` is a plain-text file that contains key/value pairs, one per line (blank lines are ignored, as well as parts of any line beginning with the character #).

For example, you might create the following text file as `/usr/local/apache/conf/userlist.txt` to serve as a rewriting map of usernames to home directories:

```
##
##  map.txt -- rewriting map
##
```

```
caulds  /           # Charles Aulds
csewell /carlstuff/ # Carl Sewell
larry   /larry/     # Larry H
```

The following `RewriteMap` directive would enable this file as a plain-text rewriting map that can be referred to in subsequent `RewriteRule` directives by the name `userlist`:

```
RewriteMap userlist txt:/usr/local/apache/conf/userlist.txt
```

A `RewriteRule` to access this map might look like:

```
RewriteRule  ^.*\/userdir\/(.*)$  ${userlist:$1}
```

The pattern in this rule matches URLs that end in /userdir, followed by some string that will always be a username. The contents of the parentheses enclosing that username fill the $1 token in the substitution, so that the username (for example, `caulds`) becomes the key in a lookup of the previously defined rewriting map named `userdir`. The value (a relative path to that user's Web home directory, which is in this example `DocumentRoot`) is used verbatim in constructing the rewritten URL. For this example to work, each user's Web home directory must be relative to the server `DocumentRoot`.

The example of access multiplexing presented later in this chapter gives another complete (and potentially useful) demonstration of a simple plain-text rewriting map.

Randomized Plain Text

This map type is a variation on the plain-text rewriting map just described. It looks up its value in exactly the same manner, but it performs some additional processing after the lookup. If the value retrieved contains one or more | characters, it is assumed to contain more than one alternative value, and the value substituted in the `Substitution` field of a `RewriteRule` that references this map is chosen at random from this list.

This may sound like a frivolous feature, but it was designed for load balancing in a reverse-proxy situation where the looked-up values are server names. Later in this chapter, the section "An Example of Randomly Generated URLs" illustrates one possible use of this feature.

Hash File

The hash file rewriting map is used exactly like a plain-text map lookup, except that the text file is first compiled into a Linux binary DBM format. DBM is implemented in Linux as a library of routines that manage datafiles containing key/value pairs and provide optimized lookups of data based on string keys. This greatly speeds the lookup process, but in most situations, a plain-text lookup will be nearly as fast as using a DBM retrieval and easier to maintain. A DBM hash file should be used only when your rewriting map grows in size until it is several hundred lines long and you are tuning for the most speed possible.

You can create a DBM hash file from a plain-text file with any DBM tool or with the script shown in Listing 10.7.

It isn't necessary to understand how the script works to use it. Use a text file to create the file on your system (naming it anything you desire, but the name txt2dbm is used in this example). Make sure the script is executable (by running chmod 755 scriptname) and then feed it the names of the text file you want converted to a DBM file with a command line like this:

```
# txt2dbm somefile.txt somefile.dbm
```

Listing 10.7 A Script to Convert a Text Map to a DBM File

```perl
#!/path/to/bin/perl
##
##  txt2dbm -- convert txt map to dbm format
##  Usage: txt2dbm textfile dbmfile

($txtmap, $dbmmap) = @ARGV;
open(TXT, "<$txtmap");
dbmopen(%DB, $dbmmap, 0644);
while (<TXT>) {
    next if (m|^\s*#.*| or m|^\s*$|);
    $DB{$1} = $2 if (m|^\s*(\S+)\s+(\S+)$|);
}
dbmclose(%DB);
close(TXT)
```

Internal Functions

There are four internal Apache functions that can be called using a rewriting map:

toupper   Converts the key to all uppercase characters.

tolower   Converts the key to all lowercase characters.

escape   Escapes special characters in the key, translating them to hex-encodings. This properly formats the key for use as a URL.

unescape   Converts escaped characters in the key (a URL with hex-encodings) back to special characters.

The first two functions are not terribly useful, but the last two can be very useful if you ever have to work with URLs containing special characters that must be hex-encoded for processing. The following RewriteRule takes a URL that may have been processed by previous RewriteRule directives and escapes it. The [R] flag then redirects the request:

```
RewriteRule  ^(.*)  ${escape:$1} [R]
```

URL escaping is often required when a URL might include characters that have special meaning. A URL that contains a ? character for example, needs to be escaped so that the character isn't interpreted by the server as indicating parameters passed to a script. Note from this example that no RewriteMap directive is required to use these internal functions, since they already exist as built-in rewriting maps.

An External Rewriting Program

The map source can also be a user-written program. The program can be written in any language that can accept input on its *standard input* (stdin) file handle, manipulate it, and return a value on its *standard output* (stdout) file handle. Since the program will perform little more than a simple mapping of the input key into its corresponding output value, interpreted shell scripts (and particularly Perl) work well for this purpose.

This program (which must have its Linux execute bit set) is started once, when the Apache server starts up. It is designed to enter a continuous loop in which it waits indefinitely for input on its standard input. When it receives a key value from mod_rewrite, it performs some lookup and returns the associated value (always followed by a newline character) for inclusion in a RewriteRule substitution string. If the program finds no associated value for the key it is given, it should return either an empty string or the four-letter string NULL. The program should be kept as simple and as resilient as possible. If your program hangs, the Apache server will hang at the point that it processes the RewriteRule that sends data to the external program. The following example illustrates the use of an external rewriting program to authenticate users against a MySQL database.

An Example of Access Control Using mod-rewrite

Using an external program to do rewrite mapping offers only one clear advantage over a standard text mapping; it allows you to use any database you choose to hold the information. Listing 10.8 shows a very simple Perl external rewriting program. It illustrates one very important rule that must be remembered about external rewriting programs: You must *never* use buffered I/O. In Perl, you can specify unbuffered (or *raw*) I/O by setting the special variable $| to 1.

Listing 10.8 An External mod_rewrite Program

```perl
#!/usr/bin/perl
# /usr/local/bin/host_deny.pl
#
use strict;
```

```
use DBI      # Use DBI for database
$| = 1;      # use raw I/O
my $value;   # create variable to hold lookup result
#
# Create database handle
my $dbh=DBI->connect("DBI:mysql:hostsdb:jackal.hiwaay.net","root","password");
while (<STDIN>) {
    $value=$dbh->prepare("Select value from denytable where key=$_");
    if $value {
        print "$value\n";
    }
    else {
        print "NULL\n";
    }
}
```

This program can be used with rewriting rules like the following:

```
RewriteMap prg hosts-deny:/usr/local/bin/hosts_deny.pl
RewriteCond ${hosts-deny:%{REMOTE_ADDR}|NOT_FOUND} !=NOT_FOUND
RewriteRule ^/.* - [F]
```

The RewriteMap directive defines the program in Listing 10.8 as a rewriting map named hosts-deny. Using the value of the HTTP header REMOTE_ADDR, the RewriteCond directive submits the remote host IP address to the external program, which attempts to find it in the MySQL database named hostsdb. If no match is found for the IP address in table denytable, the RewriteCond directive sets the value of the lookup to NOT_FOUND.

The RewriteRule shown in this example demonstrates a use for the special - (minus sign) form of a RewriteRule, which performs no rewrite at all. The [F] flag at the end of the rule indicates that the current URL is forbidden, and the request is answered with an HTTP response code of 403 (Forbidden). This rule will not be applied, though, unless the RewriteCond evaluates to True; in other words, the remote host's IP address is found in the MySQL table of denied hosts. If the host is not found in the table, the rule is not applied and the client's request is honored.

The RewriteLock Directive

The RewriteLock directive sets the filename for a synchronization lock file, which mod_rewrite needs to communicate with external RewriteMap programs. A lock file is used to prevent multiple attempts to access the same datafile, as might happen if multiple instances of mod_rewrite (running as part of different httpd processes) attempt to open the same file. If a RewriteLock directive is present, mod_rewrite will create this lock file whenever it accesses an external program and remove it when it is done. For simple programs that do not alter data, locking is generally not required, but if you are attempting to use a program that writes data to disk or makes modifications to a database, it is a very good idea to use this directive. This will ensure that your program does not conflict with other instances of the program that may have been spawned from other Apache processes running on the same machine. A conflict can occur when two httpd processes receive requests that cause them to run the same external program simultaneously.

Note that a lock is only required for external rewriting map programs and is *not* required for other types of rewriting maps. The lock file must always be set to a local path (never to a file on an NFS-mounted device).

For example, the following directives demonstrate the use of a lock file to prevent simultaneous attempts to access a single Perl mapping script (hosts_deny.pl):

```
RewriteLock /var/lock/rewrite_lock
RewriteMap prg hosts-deny:/usr/local/bin/hosts_deny.pl
```

An Example of Access Multiplexing

Rewriting maps can be used to redirect requests based on information in the request header. For example, mod_rewrite can be used by a very large international organization to attempt to redirect download requests to a server that's geographically nearer the requester. (In practice, this rarely works well because of the large number of sites in top-level domains, such as .com, that give no clue as to where in the world they are located. Most organizations that host mirror sites around the world just let the user choose one near them, which usually works pretty well. But I'm not trying to solve a problem with the Internet domain naming system here; my intention is to demonstrate the technique of reading information from a request header and processing it through a rewriting map.)

In this example, a RewriteRule examines the REMOTE_HOST header of the request, which identifies the Internet hostname of the requester's system, and attempts to choose a download site more suitable for the requester's location.

Start by creating a text file with a one-to-one mapping of top-level domains to URLs for mirror systems set up in those domains. Assume the file is stored as /usr/local/apache/conf/multi.txt, and looks like:

```
com     http://dlsite.com/download     # com domain
net     http://bigsite.net/download    # net domain
edu     http://bigsite.edu/download    # edu domain
org     http://bigsite.org/download    # org domain
```

```
au        http://bigsite.au/download    # australia
de        http://bigsite.de/download    # deutschland
uk        http://bigsite.uk/download    # united kingdom
... possibly many others ...
```

The following rewriting rules do the work:

```
# define a plain text rewriting map called multiplexer
# that points to the multi.txt file
RewriteMap multiplexer txt:/usr/local/apache/conf/multi.txt
#
# Convert the request URL to one of the form:
# remotehost::<request> and chain to the next rule
RewriteRule ^/download/(.*) ${REMOTE_HOST}::$1 [C]
#
# Look up the new URL prefix in the multiplexer
# rewriting map (or apply default dlsite.com)
# and append the request
RewriteRule ^.+\.[a-zA-Z]+)::(.*)$
    ${multiplexer::$1|dlsite.com/download/}$2 [R,L]
```

The RewriteMap directive specifies the multi.txt text file as a rewriting map called multiplexer. The first RewriteRule matches all URLs of the form /download/somefile and translates the URL to one of the form requester.domain.tld::somefile. The [C] is used to chain the next rule to this one. In other words, the two RewriteRule directives function as a pair; either *both* work, or *neither* works and the URL passes through the ruleset unaltered.

The last rule has been passed the rewritten URL requester.domain.tld::somefile from which it strips the top-level-domain (tld) and uses it as a back-reference ($1) to look up a corresponding URL in the multiplexer rewriting map. If no match is found, it uses the default value dlsite.com/download/. To this URL is appended somefile, which by back-reference fills $2.

The flags [R,L] indicate that the URL is returned to the requester as a redirection, and no further rewriting rules are processed.

An Example of Randomly Generated URLs

Here's a very simple example that redirects requests (at random) to one of the URLs defined in a simple text file that looks like the following:

```
URL freshmeat.net|www.acme.com/|www.asptoday.com/
```

Advanced Configuration Options

PART 3

Note that the file actually consists of a single line that begins with the index value or key of URL. The rest of the line is a list of all the URLs to be randomized, separated by the | character.

Listing 10.9 shows how a request for the URL outside.html is redirected to one of the URLs in the text file that is specified as a randomized plain-text rewriting map called servers.

Listing 10.9   Randomly Generating URLs

```
# Defines a randomized plain text rewriting map
# named servers.rnd
RewriteMap servers rnd:/usr/local/apache/conf/servers.rnd
#
# All requests to outside.html are rewritten to one of
# the servers chosen at random from the servers map
# note: the key into the file is URL
RewriteRule outside\.html$ http://${servers:URL} [R,L]  .
```

User Home Directories with mod_rewrite

One of the many potential uses for the mod_rewrite module is to provide access to user Web directories by rewriting request URLs. The RewriteCond directive must contain a set of parentheses for a back-reference to file %1, as follows:

```
RewriteCond %{HTTP_HOST} ^www\..+\.jackal\.hiwaay\.net$
RewriteRule ^(.+) /home/%1$1
```

Here's what happens. When a URL comes in of the form http://www.username.jackal .hiwaay.net, the rewriting condition evaluates to True, and the username (for example, caulds) fills the %1 back-reference. (Remember that %1 is filled with contents matched within the first set of parentheses in the last RewriteCond directive.) The RewriteRule is then used to translate the URL, taking the username from the back-reference filled by RewriteCond, and adding it, plus the request path, to /home (which fills the $1 back-reference). Thus a URL like:

```
http://www.caulds.jackal.hiwaay.net/someresource.html
```

is the equivalent of:

```
http://jackal.hiwaay.net/home/caulds/someresource.html
```

Note a couple of things about this example, however. First, you'll need to provide each user with a DNS entry for their virtual Web site, as their username is part of the hostname used to access the site. Also note that, unlike a true virtual host, this method does not allow you to apply custom directives to your new virtual hosts (like a custom log file or server admin e-mail address). The advantage of this method is that it will support any number of user directories very efficiently with just two lines added to `httpd.conf`.

Again, this example is just to show you what kinds of things can be done. I'm sure there are a number of ways you can improve this skeletal example. You might use `RewriteMap` to define paths for each user; if these paths are not under the same directory on your system, this might be one way to avoid having too many users on a single file system. Use your imagination.

In Sum

Two modules (`mod_alias` and `mod_rewrite`) provide the functions of URL aliasing and URL redirection to the Apache server. Aliasing is the process of mapping a URL to a non-standard location on the system, and occurs completely at the server. Redirection is the process of mapping a URL to a different URL and furnishing this URL to the requester, with a request to redirect the request to the new URL.

While `mod_alias` is far less complex and less extensive than `mod_rewrite`, it is generally more useful, almost essential on most servers, and should be used in all situations that do not required the additional functionality and flexibility of `mod_rewrite`.

The `mod_rewrite` module offers the additional functionality of conditional rewriting, multiple rules for a single operation, and access to environment variables for use in rewriting URLs. In addition, it can use previously defined rewriting maps to store rewriting information that is queried based on information provided in the request URL.

So far, this book has moved progressively into advanced topics for Apache server administrators such as programming, and URL rewriting; topics centered on configuring Apache to make it do what you want it to. The remainder of the book is concerned with administering an already configured server. The next chapter covers the most basic administrative task of all, stopping and starting the server. There are, however, a surprising variety of ways to do this, as you'll see.

11

Controlling Apache

It's conventional to think of configuring a Web server and managing it as two separate activities: you configure the server to do what you need, and then you start it running; everything after that is "management" (until you encounter something that requires you to "reconfigure"). Microsoft IIS, for example, provides a management interface called the Microsoft Management Console that allows administrators to perform tasks like creating log files, creating new virtual hosts, or setting Web client access permissions. In Apache, that model is a less useful way of describing the administrative process. Virtually all instructions to the server take the form of directives within the `httpd.conf` file. Even if you are using a GUI tool, what you essentially do to make any change in the server's operation is modify `httpd.conf` and restart Apache.

This chapter serves as a transition. Earlier parts of the book focused on Apache's directive command language and the production- or user-oriented services you can set up Apache to provide, such as virtual hosting and aliasing/redirection. Later chapters will focus on maintenance issues such as performance and security. Your administrative activity will still be configuration—that is, you will still be modifying `httpd.conf`—but the goal will be to optimize the server's operation internally. Here, we'll take a close look at a relatively narrow topic: the different ways you can instruct the server to do routine operations like starting and stopping. In other words, the subject of this chapter is how to issue configuration commands for day-to-day administration. That may seem pretty basic, but the fact that there are several ways to accomplish these routine administrative tasks often confuses new Apache administrators.

Apache can be controlled in several ways: by invoking the httpd command with various arguments, by using a Perl script provided with Apache called apachectl, by sending various Linux signals to the running Apache daemon process, and through several GUI administration tools. This chapter discusses all of these options, in order to help you evaluate which one best meets your needs.

Controlling Apache Manually

Before too long, we may have really useful GUI administrative tools for Linux; certainly there is tremendous potential in that approach. It's really nice to have all the configuration settings available from a consistent interface, and GUI tools are generally easier to learn and to remember than the command line. The tools available today, however, are a long way from achieving their potential. Until I can administer my entire server from within a single graphical utility, I will continue to work from the command line. The Linux command line is the only interface that is at all consistent between all Linux versions and vendor distributions. Even if you would prefer to use a GUI tool, you should learn the basic command-line tools for administering Apache. The main reason for this is that most Apache configuration changes are made the same way: edit httpd.conf, and then restart the server. In many respects, a graphical interface that forces you to search through a settings tree for one of a hundred different property dialogs can get in the way.

httpd Command-Line Arguments

One way to control Apache is to invoke the httpd utility and provide it one of several command-line arguments. Invoking httpd with no arguments simply starts the server *daemon*, or master process, which then starts child processes to listen for and respond to requests. The httpd daemon process should run continuously as long as the server is up. In fact, the server is properly shut down when the daemon is sent a signal telling it to shut down (the Linux -TERM signal). Before actually stopping, the daemon sends signals, in turn, to each of the child processes that it has started or *spawned*, telling them to clean up and cease their activities. To see what the httpd utility can do, enter the command with the –h option:

```
# httpd -h
Usage: httpd [-D name] [-d directory] [-f file]
             [-C "directive"] [-c "directive"]
             [-v] [-V] [-h] [-1] [-L] [-S] [-t] [-T]
Options:
-D name          : define a name for use in <IfDefine name> directives
-d directory     : specify an alternate initial ServerRoot
-f file          : specify an alternate ServerConfigFile
```

```
-C "directive"    : process directive before reading config files
-c "directive"    : process directive after  reading config files
-v                : show version number
-V                : show compile settings
-h                : list available command line options (this page)
-l                : list compiled-in modules
-L                : list available configuration directives
-S                : show parsed settings (currently only vhost settings)
-t                : run syntax check for config files (with docroot check)
-T                : run syntax check for config files (without docroot check)
```

Here's a closer look at the Apache httpd arguments:

-d directory   Specifies the initial ServerRoot directory to use instead of the compiled-in default value. Example:

```
# /usr/local/apache/bin/httpd -d /home/alternateWeb
```

-D name   Sets a value for use with the <IfDefine> directive. In the following example, a variable DSS is set to indicate that httpd should be started with Secure Socket Layer enabled:

```
# /usr/local/apache/bin/httpd -DSSL
```

-f filename   Specifies the server configuration file to use instead of the compiled-in default value. Example:

```
# /usr/local/apache/bin/httpd -f /usr/local/apache/conf/test.conf
```

-C "directive"   Processes the specified directive before reading the configuration file(s). Example:

```
# /usr/local/apache/bin/httpd -C "ScriptAlias /usr/tmp"
```

-c "directive"   Processes the specified directive after reading the configuration files(s). Example:

```
# /usr/local/apache/bin/httpd -c "DocumentHome /home/altwebhome"
```

-v   Displays the Apache version number. Example:

```
# ./httpd -v
Server version: Apache/1.3.12 (Unix)
Server built:   May 11 2000 17:46:09
```

-V   Displays compilation settings. Example:

```
# ./httpd -V
Server version: Apache/1.3.12 (Unix)
Server built:   May 11 2000 17:46:09
```

```
Server's Module Magic Number: 19990320:7
Server compiled with....
 -D EAPI
 -D HAVE_MMAP
 -D HAVE_SHMGET
 -D USE_SHMGET_SCOREBOARD
 -D USE_MMAP_FILES
 -D USE_FCNTL_SERIALIZED_ACCEPT
 -D HTTPD_ROOT="/usr/local/apache"
 -D SUEXEC_BIN="/usr/local/apache/bin/suexec"
 -D DEFAULT_PIDLOG="logs/httpd.pid"
 -D DEFAULT_SCOREBOARD="logs/httpd.scoreboard"
 -D DEFAULT_LOCKFILE="logs/httpd.lock"
 -D DEFAULT_XFERLOG="logs/access_log"
 -D DEFAULT_ERRORLOG="logs/error_log"
 -D TYPES_CONFIG_FILE="conf/mime.types"
 -D SERVER_CONFIG_FILE="conf/httpd.conf"
 -D ACCESS_CONFIG_FILE="conf/access.conf"
 -D RESOURCE_CONFIG_FILE="conf/srm.conf"
```

-l Lists modules compiled into the Apache executable. Example:

```
# ./httpd -l
Compiled-in modules:
  http_core.c
  mod_so.c
  mod_include.c
  mod_define.c
  mod_auth_mysql.c
```

-L Lists available configuration directives. Example:

```
# ./httpd -L
<Directory (http_core.c)
        Container for directives affecting resources located in
        the specified directories
        Allowed in *.conf only outside <Directory>, <Files> or
        <Location>
</Directory> (http_core.c)
        Marks end of <Directory>
        Allowed in *.conf only inside <Directory>, <Files> or
        <Location>

Many lines deleted
```

```
Auth_MySQL_Encryption_Types (mod_auth_mysql.c)
        Encryption types to use
        Allowed in *.conf only inside <Directory>, <Files>
        or <Location> and in .htaccess
        when AllowOverride includes AuthConfig
Auth_MySQL_Non_Persistent (mod_auth_mysql.c)
        Use non-persistent MySQL links
        Allowed in *.conf only inside <Directory>, <Files> or
        <Location> and in .htaccess
        when AllowOverride includes AuthConfig
```

-S   Shows parsed settings (currently only for virtual hosts). Example:

```
# ./httpd -S
VirtualHost configuration:
192.168.1.1:80          is a NameVirtualHost
default server namedvh1.hiwaay.net (/usr/local/apache/conf/httpd.conf:988)
port 80 namevhost namedvh1.hiwaay.net (/usr/local/apache/conf/
httpd.conf:988)
port 80 namevhost namedvh2.hiwaay.net (/usr/local/apache/conf/
httpd.conf:994)
192.168.1.5:80          vhost2.hiwaay.net (/usr/local/apache/conf/
httpd.conf:981)
192.168.1.4:80          vhost1.hiwaay.net (/usr/local/apache/conf/
httpd.conf:975)
```

-t   Runs a syntax test on configuration files without starting the server. This command checks to see if all DocumentRoot entries (for the main server and all virtual hosts) exist and are directories. Example:

```
# ./httpd -t
Syntax error on line 378 of /usr/local/apache/conf/httpd.conf:
DocumentRoot must be a directory
```

-T   Runs a syntax check on configuration files (without the DocumentRoot check) but does not start the server. Example:

```
# ./httpd -T
httpd: cannot determine local host name.
Use the ServerName directive to set it manually.
```

-X   The Apache server runs as an ordinary single process. In other words, it does not fork any child processes and does not detach from the terminal and run in the background. This is used for debugging purposes and has no usefulness in a production environment.

Controlling Apache with Linux Signals

As a true Unix daemon, the Linux Apache server provides the administrator no way to communicate directly with the running server. The Apache daemon responds only to signals from the Linux operating system. Rather than communicate directly with the Apache daemon, the Apache administrator uses Linux programs to send signals from the operating system to the Apache daemon process (which must be identified by its Linux process ID or PID). This can be done using either the Linux command line or a script. Utilities have been written to make this process more straightforward, including the apachectl shell script supplied with Apache (covered later in this script), but beneath these utilities, a fixed set of Linux control signals is used to control the running server. The Linux signals that Apache responds to are –TERM, -HUP, and –USR1; and the Linux kill command is used to transmit them. In this section, I'll discuss the use of each of these signals. In order to use this technique, however, you need to understand the role of the process ID.

> **NOTE**   All kernel signals, along with their numeric values and mnemonic equivalents, are stored in a rather unusual spot on Linux systems. You'll find them in the file /usr/include/bits/signum.h, or get a list by entering the command kill -1.

The Process ID

The process ID of the root Apache server (also known as the Apache daemon) is saved in a file named httpd.pid, which the default Apache configuration stores in /usr/local/ apache/logs. The full path to this file can be changed with the PidFile directive. If installed from Red Hat's Linux distribution RPM, the file is /var/run/httpd.pid.

> **NOTE**   A process ID (PID) is a number that uniquely identifies a running Linux process. Process IDs are also used to maintain parent/child relationships between processes; the parent of every running process is maintained as an attribute of that process.

If this file doesn't exist for some reason, or if it doesn't contain the proper process ID for the Apache daemon process, you can determine the proper PID using the process status or ps command:

```
# ps –ef | grep httpd
root      1090     1  0 17:21 ?    00:00:00 /usr/local/apache/bin/httpd
nobody    1092  1090  0 17:21 ?    00:00:00 /usr/local/apache/bin/httpd
nobody    1093  1090  0 17:21 ?    00:00:00 /usr/local/apache/bin/httpd
```

```
nobody  1094  1090  0 17:21 ?      00:00:00 /usr/local/apache/bin/httpd
nobody  1095  1090  0 17:21 ?      00:00:00 /usr/local/apache/bin/httpd
nobody  1096  1090  0 17:21 ?      00:00:00 /usr/local/apache/bin/httpd
root    1299  1010  0 18:35 pts/0   00:00:00 grep httpd
```

The first process shown (owned by root, and with the lowest PID of the httpd processes, indicated in the second column of the listing) is the Apache daemon process. This is the PID you'll use to stop and start the server. The third column of the listing shows the PID of the parent process for each process. Note that all of the httpd processes (except the main httpd process) display the PID of the root process in this column. This parent/child relationship (maintained by Linux) is what enables you to control all of the httpd processes in the process group through the main httpd process. (The last process in the list, incidentally, should be ignored. It is the grep process used to extract the httpd processes from the full list of Linux processes.)

The kill Command and the Apache Signals

The kill command, when issued from the Linux command line and used with the process ID of the root Apache server, sends a control signal to the Apache daemon. Apache recognizes these control signals:

-TERM   This signal is used to instruct any running process to shut down in an orderly manner (closing open files and device handles and, in general, doing its housekeeping work before ending). When sent to the parent process or primary server, it causes Apache to kill off all its children and then kill itself (sounds gruesome, but that's the correct terminology for what happens). Example:

```
# kill -TERM <pid>
```

where <pid> is the process ID of the Apache daemon. Another way to express this is:

```
# kill -TERM 'cat /usr/local/apache/logs/httpd.pid'
```

This is especially useful if you are writing scripts to control Apache. The portion of the above command line between the single quote marks is evaluated by the shell, and returns the contents of the httpd.pid file, which is then passed as the final argument to the kill command.

-HUP   Restarts the server immediately. When the daemon process receives this signal, it kills all of its children processes (the httpd listener processes) but does not itself die. The daemon closes all open logs, rereads the httpd.conf file (reinitializing itself), reopens its logs, and spawns new child processes to handle client requests. This is the signal you should use after making changes to the Apache configuration. Here's an example:

```
# kill -HUP 'cat /usr/local/apache/logs/httpd.pid'
```

-USR1   Graceful restart. The daemon process signals all of its child processes to exit as soon as they've fulfilled their current requests. Processes that are not actively responding to a client request die at once. The daemon process closes all open logs, rereads the `httpd.conf` file (reinitializing itself), reopens its logs, and spawns new child processes to replace those that are dying at its request. Gracefully restarting Apache is kind to any clients that may be connected (by not forcing them to wait for an abruptly closed connection to time-out). Here's an example:

```
# kill -USR1 'cat /usr/local/apache/logs/httpd.pid'
```

While the Linux `kill` program is used to stop or kill running processes, that name is a bit misleading because the fundamental purpose of the program is to send kernel signals to running processes. It just so happens that several of the signals that can be sent using the `kill` program result in the termination of the process.

The signal names shown above are actually mnemonic equivalents for signal numbers, which can also be used. The following lines, for example, are equivalent, and send the KILL signal (which means unblockable, absolute death to any process) to the process with the PID of 931:

```
# kill -9 931
```

or

```
# kill -KILL 931
```

The default signal value (if the `kill` command is invoked with just a process ID) is to send the -TERM (15) signal to the designated process. When signal 9 (the KILL signal) is issued, Apache never actually receives the signal. Instead, Linux immediately terminates the running process, giving it no prior warning. Killing a process in this manner is a bit heavy-handed, as it gives the process no opportunity to close in an orderly fashion, after having closed any files or database connections it has open. Issuing the -KILL signal should be a last-resort method of shutting down Apache, used only in cases where the process refuses to shut down after receiving an -HUP signal.

The apachectl Utility

The Apache server is provided with a Perl utility named `apachectl` that handles many of the tasks already described. We first looked briefly at `apachectl` in Chapter 3 as a tool for starting Apache after installation. It is a very useful tool, but remember that it is merely a shell script that performs the tasks of invoking `httpd` or sending Linux signals to the Apache daemon process. It can simplify those tasks, but if you intend to control Apache programmatically (through your own shell scripts or programs), don't use `apachectl`, although you may want to borrow from the script or even rewrite it. `apachectl` is an interactive utility; that is, it's not meant to be scripted.

You'll find `apachectl` in the `/src/support` directory under the Apache source home. Apache's installation process will copy this file into the `/bin` directory under the Apache home directory (the default location is `/usr/local/apache/bin/apachectl`).

You can invoke `apachectl` with any one of the following arguments (these arguments are not meant to be used in combination):

`start`   Starts Apache. This is the same as entering `httpd` without arguments. Nothing special about this option, and yet it is the one you will use most often. Example:

```
# /usr/local/apache/bin/apachectl start
/usr/local/apache/bin/apachectl start: httpd started
```

`startssl`   Starts Apache in SSL mode. This is the same as entering `httpd -DSSL`. Example:

```
# /usr/local/apache/bin/apachectl startssl
/usr/local/apache/bin/apachectl startssl: httpd started
```

`stop`   Stops Apache. This is the same as entering `kill -TERM <httpd PID>`. This option is quite handy because it eliminates the need to look up the PID of the Apache daemon process. Example:

```
# /usr/local/apache/bin/apachectl stop
/usr/local/apache/bin/apachectl stop: httpd stopped
```

`restart`   Restarts Apache if it is already running. This is identical to `kill -HUP <httpd PID>`. Again, useful because the `httpd` PID does not have to be determined. Example:

```
# /usr/local/apache/bin/apachectl restart
/usr/local/apache/bin/apachectl restart: httpd restarted
```

`status`   Dumps a short status screen. Using it requires the character browser `lynx` along with the `mod_status` module. It's not very useful; it is far better to use a Web browser to access the server status screen, but there may be times when you need the status information and, for some reason, have only the command-line interface at your disposal (perhaps because you're using a `telnet` connection). Be sure to pipe the output to `more` because it will scroll off the screen.

`fullstatus`   Dumps a complete status screen. It also requires the character browser `lynx`, along with `mod_status`. Its display looks like the regular status screen, but with more information. Later in the chapter, I'll show how to access this same information using a graphical Web browser. You'll almost certainly prefer that method, as the information is much easier to read, but be aware that the text status screens are available if you ever find yourself without Web access to the server—for example, if you are dialed in on a standard serial modem connection.

graceful Performs a graceful Apache restart. Causes Apache to wait for all open requests to be serviced. This is identical to kill -USR1 <http PID>. Example:

```
# /usr/local/apache/bin/apachectl graceful
/usr/local/apache/bin/apachectl graceful: httpd gracefully restarted
```

configtest Performs a syntax test on Apache configuration files. I rely heavily on this option for discovering problems that prevent Apache from starting, particularly with virtual hosts. It's a good idea to run this before restarting Apache after making extensive edits to httpd.conf. Example:

```
# /usr/local/apache/bin/apachectl configtest
Syntax error on line 641 of /usr/local/apache/conf/httpd.conf:
ScriptAlias not allowed here
```

help Prints a screen describing apachectl usage.

Starting Apache Automatically

The techniques you've just seen for starting and stopping Apache are useful whenever manual intervention is needed. Most of the time, of course, you can simply let Apache start automatically, launching it along with Linux. Apache has two modes of automatic operation: standalone and inetd, both of which are discussed in earlier chapters.

The standalone mode is the default and is described in Chapter 2. As discussed there, it operates as a process swarm, in which a single daemon process (usually an httpd process owned by root) starts a number of child httpd processes that run under a nonprivileged system account and respond to client requests. The daemon process is responsible for keeping an eye on all its child processes, starting new ones whenever necessary to meet increases in server load and periodically killing excess processes. This mode of operation maintains a pool of processes that are waiting to respond to client HTTP requests and is generally very efficient because it eliminates the overhead associated with creating new processes.

The inetd mode, discussed in Chapter 4, uses the Linux inetd module to listen for client connections on behalf of Apache and spawn httpd processes, as required, to handle arriving connections. This mode is recommended only for installations with extremely light server load or limited memory.

GUI Configuration Tools

When I began to write this chapter, I had no experience with any of the Apache/Linux configuration tools that use a graphical user interface (GUI), but I had high hopes of finding one that would simplify routine administration chores and save time. It simply didn't happen. I tried them all and found something to like about all of them, and someday I'll do virtually all of my Linux administration with utilities that use a graphical interface. But the tool I'll use will be a single configuration utility that will provide a consistent interface to managing all of the system software services and applications, hardware configurations, network settings, and user accounts. For that reason, I tend to shy away from Apache-only configuration utilities. I would use any of the tools discussed below if it meant I had to know nothing about the `httpd.conf` file and how to configure it. But for now, you cannot be a strong Apache administrator unless you learn to use its configuration directives.

Another problem with many of the tools here is their dependencies. Nothing hurts a good Linux utility like dependence on supporting software that may or may not be on the system you're administering. If a utility requires that I be at an X-Window console to use it, I'm not interested. The utilities that show the most promise are those that offer the simplest interfaces; either a character-based interface that can be used via a `telnet` session or, better yet, HTML support for browser management.

Admittedly, the tools with the nicest interfaces are those that require specialized support from the system. It comes at a price, though. Not only do these often present difficulties in managing the system across the network, but X Window and function libraries built on it (like Tk) impose serious performance demands on even the most powerful server. On a real-world Web server with many connecting clients, if you devote half your CPU cycles to the X sessions running on the console, you definitely won't need to spend time worrying about increasing the speed of your Web programs. While I'm at it, I might mention that running CPU-intensive screensavers on your system console is a very bad idea if you are hosting services supporting other users.

The conclusion I drew from practicing with each of the GUI configuration utilities I discuss is that the best compromise between a pure command-line tool and a full GUI interface is a browser-based tool. Offering complete portability across platforms, and acceptable performance across a network, browser tools are ideal for this purpose, even if they are always just a little less than what you *really* want.

Comanche

Comanche (a freely available product supported by Covalent Technologies, `www.covalent .net/projects/comanche`) is an ambitious attempt to develop a cross-platform GUI administrative interface for Apache. Not only is Comanche (the name derives from COnfiguration MANager for ApaCHE) intended to run on all platforms that support Apache (Unix flavors, Linux, and NT), it is also designed to be extended modularly and to provide multi-language support. Figure 11.1 gives some idea of the interface Comanche provides in an X-Window session.

Figure 11.1   Using Comanche in an X-Window environment

The source package for Comanche for Unix requires functions from the Tcl and Tk libraries (as well as the wish Tk interpreter), which is usually not a problem since these are installed by most standard Linux distributions. The standard package also contains a single (enormous) binary that includes all the parts needed to run it. Needless to say, it also requires X Window and does not function without it (from the command line or from a Web browser).

Comanche has always given me the impression that it's a tool under development and not ready for real-world use. While development of Comanche continues, I'll use other methods to administer my Apache, but I'll check back with the Comanche developers from time to time to see how things are coming along.

TkApache and Mohawk

The Web site for TkApache (`http://eunuchs.org/linux/TkApache/`) describes it as "a configuration tool written primarily to be extremely easy to grasp and also to provide a really cool interface." How cool? I can't say, because I couldn't get the product to run. It requires a version of the `Perl::Tk` module (800.011) that is no longer available on the CPAN site. (The current version of `Perl::Tk` is 800.022.) The documentation I saw, however, suggests that it is too large and complex a tool for the simple task it was developed to perform.

The same developers have announced a new configuration tool, called Mohawk, as "the next-generation TkApache." It's not available for download yet, and the developers invite collaborators. Mohawk, intended to replace TkApache, is written completely in C, using the GTK+/GNOME graphical libraries, for performance that far exceeds Perl using Tk. In addition to providing the Apache administrator with a GUI utility to change configuration parameters, Mohawk is also intended to be used as a performance monitoring tool, providing real-time statistics as well as graphs to show historical trends. Mohawk will even include an e-mail and pager alert system to notify the administrator of abnormal conditions on the server.

Webmin

Of all the GUI configuration and administration tools for Linux, Webmin (`www.webmin.com/webmin/`) is my hands-down favorite (Figure 11.2). Originally developed by an independent group, the Webmin project received a tremendous shot in the arm when it was acquired by Caldera, and now enjoys full support from that company. Webmin is packaged as the standard administration tool with Caldera OpenLinux eServer bundle, but can be freely downloaded and used with any other Linux.

Webmin is a modular product, and Apache is one of many servers administered through Webmin using an add-on module. You can easily add further modules (downloadable as single files with the `.wbm` extension), to upgrade an existing Webmin. If you're adventurous, add-on modules can be written for Webmin. This is actually a pretty neat feature, because the BSD license under which Webmin has been released permits anyone to modify and distribute the product and new modules for either commercial or noncommercial reasons. That's a pretty broad license.

Figure 11.2   The Webmin Apache administration module

Another strong feature of Webmin is its support for SSL connections. Using the OpenSSL library (we'll install it for SSL support in Chapter 15) and the Apache Net::SSLeay module (easily retrieved and installed using the Apache CPAN module), Webmin communicates with your browser over an SSL connection.

While its Apache administration module could be a bit stronger, Webmin is a good sound tool, well documented, efficient, secure, and extendable. As a general-purpose utility for Linux administrators, it holds great promise. Web-based administration tools aren't the easiest and most enjoyable to use, but they sure are liberating—using a Web browser and Webmin, you can handle most Linux admin chores. You won't be able to completely administer an Apache server with just this GUI product (or any other), but it's another one that shows great promise.

Linuxconf

Linuxconf is a general-purpose administration tool for Linux, downloadable from www.solucorp.qc.ca/linuxconf. Some version of Linuxconf has always been distributed with the most popular Linux distribution (Red Hat), and it has always been closely associated with that distribution, but Linuxconf can be used with any Linux distribution.

By far the nicest feature of Linuxconf is that it provides full support for three different user interfaces. Use them interchangeably; they all modify the same files and have the same functionality (although the HTML version has some limitations for security reasons). In fact, they are all run from the same executable file (/bin/linuxconf):

Character The character interface to Linuxconf appears when you invoke Linuxconf from the command line while operating in a character shell (like you would from a telnet or ssh session). Figure 11.3 depicts Linuxconf operating in character mode. Although everything is in character mode, very good use is made of the *ncurses* library, which allows a carefully written character application to support features like scrolling windows, and here we see a tree structure with nodes that can be expanded. Standard DEC VT100 terminal emulation on a telnet client is all that is required to make this work.

Figure 11.3 The Linuxconf character interface

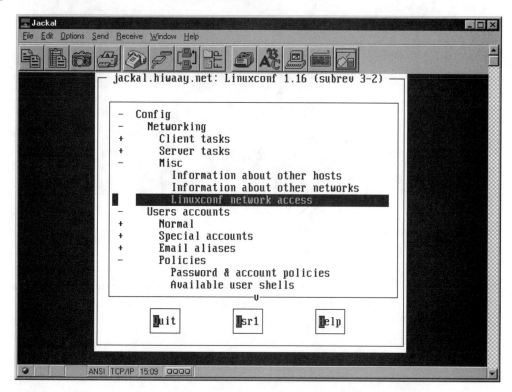

Graphical   Figure 11.4 shows Linuxconf in a graphical environment (in this case the Gnome desktop). You invoke the same executable for graphical Linuxconf as you do for the character-based interface. Linuxconf is intelligent enough to recognize when it has been invoked from the command line in a windowed shell and will run itself in graphical mode.

Figure 11.4   The Linuxconf graphical (Gnome) interface

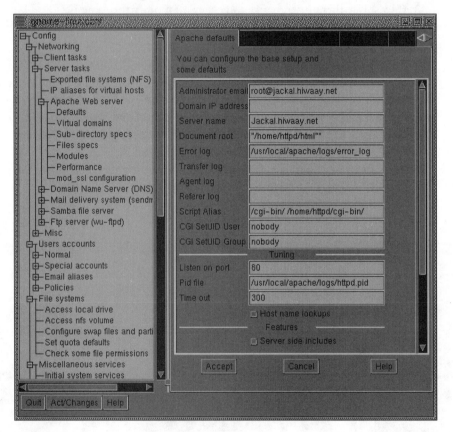

Web   The Web or HTML version of Linuxconf is what I like best about it. It's not the fanciest way to go, but it sure is convenient (Figure 11.5). Note that I access Linuxconf by connecting to TCP port 98 on my Apache server. Linuxconf is set up so that the very same executable that is used for the character and graphical interfaces is spawned (with a special switch) to handle the request.

Figure 11.5   The Linuxconf HTML interface

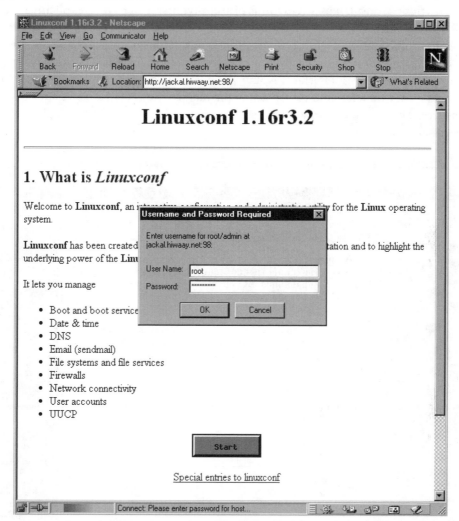

Linuxconf is written in C. It requires no special libraries and no special configuration to operate. You won't, of course, be able to use the graphic version unless you are running some graphical Linux shell. I have found that the HTML version is quite adequate for the tasks I needed it to perform.

A drawback of using Linuxconf with a Web browser is that it doesn't (yet) support SSL connections. Instead, it uses two forms of security; first, you have to explicitly list every IP address from which you are willing to accept connections to the Linuxconf management socket (port 98). Figure 11.6 shows how this is done using the character interface. Figure 11.7 illustrates how easily you can view and modify basic Apache server parameters using the HTML interface. Notice the line of links at the top of the page, which makes it easy to determine your place in the hierarchy of HTML pages and to ascend the tree. There is no tree view of all pages in the HTML interface, although it is rarely necessary.

Figure 11.6   Configuring Linuxconf for HTML clients from the character interface

Figure 11.7   Basic server parameters in the Linuxconf HTML interface

Apache's Built-In Web Monitors

This chapter has been devoted to the tools available for stopping and starting the server, but it hasn't said anything so far about how you determine the need to intervene and take those steps. Here's a quick look at the two Apache modules, mod_status and mod_info, that provide the capability to serve status and information pages. For monitoring Apache and getting a formatted listing of its configuration, the status pages provided by mod_status are the best things going.

When `mod_status` is compiled into Apache (or linked as a DSO module), it installs a new handler, `server-status`. This handler must be specified as a handler for requests to the URL /server-status by including a `<Location>` section like the following in `httpd.conf`:

```
<Location /server-status>
    SetHandler server-status
    Order deny,allow
    Deny from all
    Allow from 192.168.1.*
</Location>
```

You'll find such a section in the default `httpd.conf` after installation, but it will be commented out. Uncomment the lines, and be sure to specify your network subnet number (or a list of individual IP addresses) for those hosts that are allowed to access the status screen (shown in Figure 11.8). This status page is accessible from a browser on any computer attached to the subnet 192.168.1.*. An attempt from any other site will be rejected.

Figure 11.8   The basic status screen displayed by `mod_status`

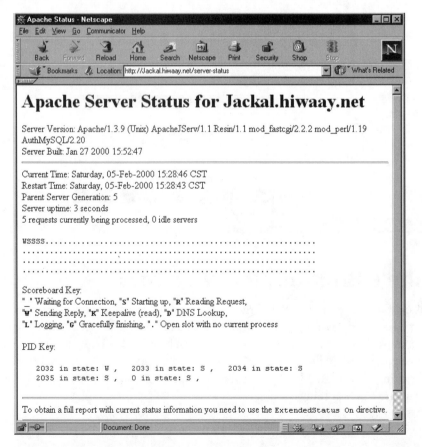

You can display additional status information, including information on requests answered by each child `httpd` process, by enabling `mod_status`'s only directive, `ExtendedStatus`. Set the value of this directive to On to enable extended status information (shown in Figure 11.9).

        ExtendedStatus On

This directive is also provided for you in the default `httpd.conf` file, but it is commented out.

Figure 11.9   You can display greater detail by using the ExtendedStatus On directive.

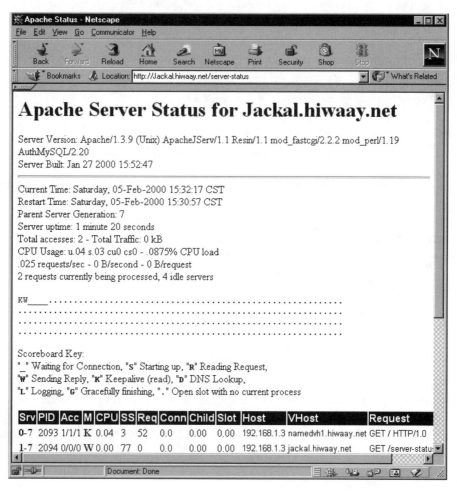

There are several options you can specify when retrieving `mod_status` pages. One of the most useful is `refresh`. Appending `?refresh=` N to the URL used to retrieve the status page will cause your browser to update the page every *N* seconds, as in:

```
http://jackal.hiwaay.net/server-status?refresh=5
```

Not specifying the number of seconds causes the page to refresh every second:

```
http://jackal.hiwaay.net/server-status?refresh
```

By default, the page that is returned uses HTML tables. To view a page with a browser that does not support tables (very rare these days), you can specify the `notable` option:

```
http://jackal.hiwaay.net/server-status?notable
```

Finally, the `auto` option returns a page of raw data, intended for parsing by a script or program:

```
http://jackal.hiwaay.net/server-status?auto
```

These options can be also used in combination:

```
http://jackal.hiwaay.net/server-status?notable?refresh=5
```

The module `mod_info` (installed in the standard Apache configuration) provides additional server configuration information, as shown in Figure 11.10. This information is available through another `<Location>` directive, again provided in the default `httpd .conf` file but commented out.

```
<Location /server-info>
    SetHandler server-info
    Order deny,allow
    Deny from all
    Allow from 192.168.1.1
    Allow from 192.168.1.3
</Location>
```

The information provided by `mod_info` is static; it will not change between invocations unless the configuration files are edited. The information is read from the Apache configuration files and may not necessarily reflect the contents of those files when the server was started.

Figure 11.10 The Apache server-info page

Nonetheless, the information provided by mod_info can be very useful. It shows not only the default settings for the Apache daemon, but which modules are enabled, with a little about what each of those modules does. Scrolling further in the page (which should be quite long), you can see in Figure 11.11 that for each module, mod_info shows any handlers provided by the module, which phases of the HTTP request cycle are handled by the module, and any directives provided by the module.

Figure 11.11 Module information displayed by mod_info

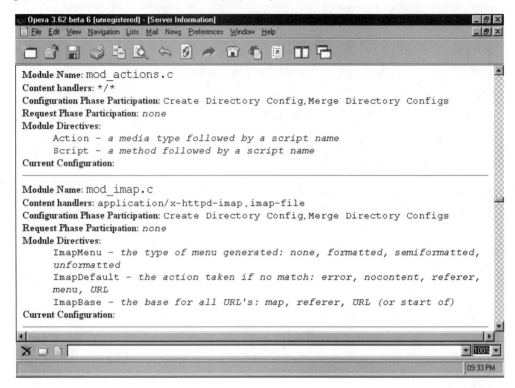

In Sum

This chapter has focused on the various ways of controlling Apache—starting and stopping the server, and performing other routine administrative tasks. The variety of methods available often seems daunting to new Apache administrators.

We first looked at the tools for starting and stopping Apache manually: the command-line arguments you can use with httpd, the Linux signals transmitted to Apache via the kill command, and the Perl utility apachectl. The chapter then surveyed the graphical utilities currently available for Apache administration. I found something to like about each of them, but abandoned them all to go back to using the traditional and "standard" means of administering Apache. In the hands of an experienced Linux administrator, Apache's configuration text files offer a flexibility that is unmatched by any graphical utility currently available. The last section showed how to use the mod_info and mod_status monitoring tools, so you'll be aware of conditions that might require you to stop and restart the server manually.

The next chapter, which begins Part IV: "Maintaining a Healthy Server," continues the topic of monitoring by exploring Apache's logging tools.

Part 4

Maintaining a Healthy Server

Featuring:

- Error and access logging

- Tracking user sessions

- Using log analyzers

- Controlling listener processes

- Using Apache as a proxy server

- Accelerating Apache with kHTTPd

- Apache's basic security tools

- Implementing Secure Sockets Layer in Apache

- Using metainformation for content negotiation

12

Apache Logging

The previous chapter showed how you can display the current status and configuration of an Apache server. This information, while important, cannot inform the administrator of a working server about unusual conditions, problems, or client usage. Those kinds of information are written (or *logged*) continuously to files that provide a historical record of the activity of the server and any unusual conditions it encounters. There are two main types of log files that are important to the Apache administrator. Request logs (also called *transfer logs*) record the network activity of the server, and they include all log files that record information about client requests and information that can be gathered about the clients making the requests. The most important request log is the access log, which contains a single line entry for each HTTP request the server receives. The second type of log provided by Apache is the error log, in which the server records errors, warnings, and unusual conditions it encounters while running.

Apache has a very complete, highly configurable, logging capability. Error logging, intimately associated with the inner workings of the Apache server engine, is provided by the core module. The standard request logging, provided by the mod_log_config module, is designed to capture information about all client requests and also to store errors generated by the server or other processes (like CGI scripts) that it spawns. Additional modules designed to track an individual user's chain of requests (a *session*) provide information that you can later use to determine user preferences or predict user behavior. This chapter covers both the standard logging capabilities and the use of add-on modules to support session logging. The chapter includes a look at two third-party log analyzers I've used, Analog and Webalizer, and a brief look at one log analyzer that is available commercially, Enterprise Reporting Server by WebTrends.

Error Logging

Two basic logs are a part of every standard Apache installation: an error log and a request log. Most of the chapter is devoted to request logging, simply because that is a more complex topic and Apache's capabilities for it are more extensive. Error logging is pretty straightforward.

On a properly functioning server, error logs should be fairly small, and they can be examined directly by the administrator to determine problems that need to be corrected. The majority of these will be malformed HTTP requests, usually requiring modification of Web pages that contain "broken" links. Though less frequent, errors are also written by the server if it encounters problems performing its function. These usually require the attention of the administrator; particularly those that are written immediately after the server is started. Typical log entries indicate problems in loading modules, implementing configuration directives, or setting up virtual hosts.

Apache's error logging is provided by the core module (mod_core) and is an error log that Apache uses to contain error messages that it generates, or that one of its modules generates, or that Apache captures from a process it spawns (like a CGI script). You don't need to do anything to enable the Apache error log. By default, Apache will write its errors into logs/error_log under the directory defined as ServerRoot. The ErrorLog directive, however, allows you to control the location of the error log (or even turn it off). This directive takes several forms, each of which is illustrated below by example. This line uses ErrorLog to redefine the log location by giving the full path to a new log file:

```
ErrorLog /var/logs/apache/error_log
```

This line redefines the name of the error log but doesn't specify a full path to the file:

```
ErrorLog logs/newname_log
```

If the file pathname does not begin with a slash (/), it is assumed to be relative to the directory defined as ServerRoot.

The following directive uses the special keyword syslog to indicate that logging should be performed by the system logging daemon (or syslogd):

```
ErrorLog syslog
```

The syslogd utility is a part of every Linux system and provides not only system kernel logging, but also a means for applications to use it for logging, via a set of syslog *facilities* that are defined in /etc/syslog.conf. By default, Apache will use the facility designated as local7 in /etc/syslog.conf. If you look in that file, you'll find a line like the following:

```
local7.*              /var/log/boot.log
```

If you use the `ErrorLog syslog` directive without specifying a syslog facility, your Apache errors will be logged with all the other stuff in the system boot log (`/var/log/boot.log`). If you use `syslogd` for Apache error logging, you should set up a special facility for Apache logging. Do this by creating a new line in `/etc/syslog.conf` like the following:

```
local5.*                /var/log/apache/httpd_error.log
```

Here, I'm using one of the predefined facilities `syslogd` provides for application use (`local0-local7`). For this change to take effect, you need to send the -HUP signal to the running `syslogd` process. Use the `ps` command to determine its process ID (302 in the following example) and the `kill` command to send the -HUP signal to the process:

```
# ps -aux | grep syslogd
root     302  0.0  0.8  1156  528 ?       S   07:34   0:16 syslogd -m 0
root     580  0.0  0.7  1168  456 pts/1   S   16:24   0:00 grep syslogd
# kill -HUP 302
```

Once you've configured `syslogd` to use the new `httpd` facility, you must use the following directive in your Apache `httpd.conf` file to ensure that Apache pipes its log output to the syslog daemon.

```
ErrorLog syslog:local5
```

The last form of the `ErrorLog` directive opens a system pipe to a program or script that processes errors written to the log. The process starts when Apache is invoked, and the pipe stays open until Apache is shut down. System pipes are an efficient mechanism for interprocess communication, and this can actually be a pretty efficient way to handle logging information, particularly if you want it parsed in stream:

```
ErrorLog |/usr/local/apache/bin/logfilter.pl
```

In this case, `logfilter.pl` is a Perl script that is designed to accept error-logging information from Apache. Such a filter could be used to check each error message as it is written to the log. A script could easily be written in Perl to notify the Administrator immediately when specific messages are written to the log. Notification could be via e-mail, pager, console message, or a combination of all three.

> **WARNING** If error logging is defined by `ErrorLog` as a pipe to a program, that program will run under the user who started `httpd`. This is normally `root`, so precautions should be taken to ensure that the program is secure (that is, an ordinary user cannot write to it).

The `LogLevel` directive is used to specify which of eight verbosity levels Apache is to use in logging errors. Table 12.1 lists these levels, which correspond to the same error levels used by the Linux system log. To set the `LogLevel` to `error` (no lower level of verbosity is recommended), use this directive:

```
LogLevel error
```

Error logging is automatically enabled for all levels in Table 2.1 above the one specified. That is, if you have used `LogLevel` to set the error logging level to `warn`, Apache will also write all errors that are defined for levels `emerg`, `alert`, `crit`, and `error`. The `LogLevel` directive is an Apache core directive; always available, and applicable to all modules that use logging. The default value is the same as specifying `LogLevel` error, which on production servers is generally verbose enough to diagnose most errors. I recommend setting the verbosity level at least one step higher (`warn`) and I usually use `LogLevel info` on my servers. Many of the additional log entries are useful and informative, but not so numerous that they fill the log file too quickly. `LogLevel debug` is usually useful only to programmers, particularly when they have written modules specifically to write debugging messages, and should never be enabled on a production server. Never reduce the logging verbosity level below `LogLevel crit` (in other words, never use the `emerg` or `alert` levels); this will cause you to miss important warning and error conditions that can warn of problems either present or impending.

Table 12.1   Error Logging Levels

Level	Description	Example
emerg	Emergency conditions that render the system unusable	"No active child processes: shutting down."
alert	Conditions that require immediate action	"Child 1234 returned a Fatal error...Apache is exiting!"
crit	Critical conditions	"Parent: Path to Apache process too long."
error	Error conditions	"master_main: create child process failed. Exiting."
warn	Warning conditions	"child process 1234 did not exit, sending another SIGHUP."
notice	Advisory conditions that do not indicate abnormal activity	"httpd: SIGUSR1 received. Doing graceful restart."

Table 12.1   Error Logging Levels *(continued)*

Level	Description	Example
info	Informational only.	"Shutdown event signaled. Shutting the server down."
debug	Messages displayed only when running in debug mode	"loaded module mod_vhost.c."

Request Logging

In addition to logging errors, the standard Apache configuration also allows administrators to log all access to the server. Access logging is also known as *request logging*.

The most basic request logging capability is provided in Apache by the standard module mod_log_config, which is either compiled into the server or compiled as a DSO and loaded at runtime. This standard module does the work that was formerly performed by three modules, mod_log_common, mod_log_agent, and mod_log_referer. Those modules were used for logging all user accesses, the user-agent (browser) used, and any referring URLs, respectively. They were made obsolete by mod_log_config and should not be used in Apache with a version number higher than 1.3. Check your httpd.conf file to see if they are enabled. If they are, ensure that mod_log_config is either compiled into Apache or loaded at runtime as a DSO, and remove the other modules.

The mod_log_config module provides a number of directives to enable standard logging using what is called the *Common Log Format (CLF)*, which is discussed in the next section. The simplest of these access-logging directives is TransferLog, which can be used to enable access logging into a file it defines:

```
TransferLog /usr/local/apache/logs/access_log
```

When enabled with TransferLog, Apache logging uses the format defined by the most recent LogFormat directive or, if no format has been defined, it uses the CLF, described in the next section. Like the ErrorLog directive, TransferLog can also pipe its output to a filter program that receives the logging information via its standard input.

The TransferLog directive is provided in mod_log_config for backward compatibility with the original, but now obsolete, Apache logging module, mod_log_common. That module was very basic, supporting only CLF logging to a single file. The mod_log_config module is capable of defining multiple logs, each with its own custom log format. The standard Apache configuration no longer includes the mod_log_common module. It has been replaced by mod_log_config, which replaces TransferLog with the LogFormat and CustomLog directives. These are used, as described below, to implement all logging, even traditional CLF logging. While you can still use `TransferLog`, I recommend that you learn and begin using the newer directives instead.

Unlike error logging, which is written to a default location even if no `ErrorLog` directive is specified, access is not logged unless either a `TransferLog` or `CustomLog` directive is used to specify a location for an access log.

WARNING As with error logging, if access logging is defined by `TransferLog` as a pipe to a program, that program will run under the user who started `httpd`. This is normally root, so the same precautions should be taken to ensure that the program is secure.

The Common Log Format

Most Apache servers use the common log format (or some close variant of that format) for access logging. The common log format was loosely defined way back in the beginning by the World Wide Web Consortium (W3C) and is documented at `www.w3.org/Daemon/User/Config/Logging.html`. The format is not complex or rigidly defined, but it has become the default format for logging in most Unix-based Web servers, and it has always been the default access log format for Apache.

Each request received by the server makes up one line of the access log, and each line in CLF is defined as follows:

```
remotehost identd authuser [date] "request URL" status bytes
```

The fields mean the following:

remotehost The IP address of the client that sent the request or the client's fully qualified hostname if hostname lookup is enabled. (Performing hostname lookups for each request can significantly slow an Apache server; see the discussion of `logresolve` later in the chapter.)

identd If the `identd` protocol is used to verify a client's identity, this is the identity information resulting from an `identd` response from the client. `identd` is a user identification protocol (defined by RFC 1413) in which a machine is queried for the identity of the user who owns a process that initiated a TCP/IP connection. The protocol is not widely implemented and imposes a burden on the server, which must wait for `identd` responses from each client, most of which probably do not even support `identd`. Consequently, `identd` checking is disabled by default, and this field is normally filled by a hyphen character as a placeholder.

authuser If the request was for a protected document and requires user ID and password information, the user ID furnished by the client fills this field. If no credentials were required to access the requested resource, this field normally contains a hyphen in the log.

`date`   A date-and-time stamp for the request, filled in by the server and enclosed in brackets [].

`"request URL"`   The URL received from the client, enclosed in quotes, and omitting the leading `http://servername` portion.

`status`   The three-digit status code returned to the client.

`bytes`   The number of bytes returned in the body of the response to the client (does not include any of the response headers).

Each field of the CLF line is delimited (set apart from surrounding text) by the space character. The two fields that commonly contain spaces are enclosed in special delimiter characters: braces ([]) enclose the request date, and quotes ("") enclose the request URL. Any CLF log analyzer or filter program needs to be able to deal with these characters.

Here are three lines I pulled from my `access.log` to give you an idea of what CLF format looks like when written to the Apache log.

```
192.168.1.2 - - [20/May/2000:13:33:27 -0500] "GET / HTTP/1.1" 200 3918
192.168.1.2 - - [20/May/2000:13:37:41 -0500] "GET / HTTP/1.1" 304 -
192.168.1.2 - caulds [20/May/2000:13:38:41 -0500] "GET /AuthTest/secret.html
HTTP/1.1" 200 221
```

The first line shows a request for my home page (the URL is simply /), which was answered with an OK response (code 200) and a 3918-byte response body (my `index.html` page). The second line is for the same resource, but it's a bit more interesting. The browser I used this time was HTTP/1.1 compliant and sent with its request a special header, `If-Modified-Since`, with the timestamp of the resource it has previously requested and cached. Since the resource hasn't changed since last requested, the server doesn't send a new copy of the resource, it simply provides a 304 (Not Modified) header in response. Neat, huh? For large files (like images) this can greatly reduce the response time for the client and ease the burden on your server.

The last line shows a request for a resource in a protected area. I was required to furnish a username and password to retrieve the resource, and my username was logged in the third field.

That's common log format, and it is (as the name implies) the most commonly used Web log format. Although several other "standard" log formats have been developed, none of them has seen such widespread use, and most sites that don't use CLF use a custom log format that is usually a slightly modified version of CLF.

Maintaining a
Healthy Server

PART 4

One attempt to standardize a modified CLF log is the Extended Common Logfile Format, also known as the combined log format. First introduced in NCSA httpd 1.4, this is the standard CLF with two additional fields, referer and agent, which appear at the end of the line enclosed in quotation marks. While there is no official standard for this format, it is the most commonly used alternative to CLF and is supported by most Web servers and logfile analyzers. The referer field logs the value of the Referer HTTP header (if it exists). The presence of this field in a request indicates that the request was generated by clicking a link in a page from another site, and the content of this header indicates the URL of this page. The content of the agent field indicates the browser type used by the client that sent the request. The Extended Common Logfile Format is specified by the W3C organization as Working Draft WD-logfile-960323 (www.w3.org/TR/WD-logfile.html).

Defining What to Log: Using LogFormat

The most important directive provided by mod_log_config is LogFormat. This directive allows a great deal of customizability in defining the format of each line written to the access log (which is defined in a CustomLog directive as discussed in the next section). The LogFormat directive consists of two parts, a format string and a nickname used to refer to the defined format. In the default httpd.conf, you will find the following line, which defines the common log format with the tokens enclosed in quotes, and assigns the format to the nickname common.

```
LogFormat "%h %l %u %t \"%r\" %>s %b" common
```

The default value of LogFormat is the CLF, but without a nickname. Any CustomLog directive that does not reference a named format uses the CLF. A % character always precedes the tokens in the format specification. The flexibility of LogFormat lies in the wide variety of log parameters that can be specified using these tokens, including all HTTP request headers and the contents of any environment variable. The possible tokens are:

%a   The remote host IP address.

%A   The local host IP address.

%B   The number of bytes sent, excluding HTTP headers.

%b   The number of bytes sent, excluding HTTP headers. Sends a dash (-) character rather than a zero when no characters are sent, to comply with the CLF specification.

%{ENV VAR}e   The contents of the environment variable specified by ENV VAR.

%f   The filename of the logfile.

%h   The Remote hostname (requires the HostnameLookups directive to enable reverse hostname lookups). If HostnameLookups has not been enabled, or if a reverse hostname lookup cannot resolve a client IP address to the hostname, the IP address of the requestor is logged.

%H   The request protocol and version (for example, HTTP/1.1).

%{header_line}i   The contents of one or more header_line entries, each specified within braces, taken from the request sent to the server.

%l   The remote logname (from identd, if IdentityCheck is enabled) supplied by the client machine, if it is running identd.

%m   The request method (typically GET).

%{note}n   The contents of one or more note entries specified within braces, taken from another module.

%{header_line}o   The contents of one or more header_line entries, specified within braces, taken from the reply to the client.

%p   The canonical TCP port of the server serving the request (set by the Port configuration directive).

%P   The process ID of the child httpd process that serviced the request.

%q   The query string (prefixed with a ? if a query string exists; otherwise an empty string).

%r   The first line of the request.

%s   Status. For requests that were redirected internally, this is the status of the original request. Using %>s returns the status of the last request.

%t   The time, in CLF time format (standard English format).

%{format}t   The time, in the form specified by the format template within the braces, which must follow the Linux strftime rules).

%T   The time taken to serve the request, in seconds.

%u   The remote user. (Unauthorized). A 401 response could mean that the user ID supplied by the user (and logged) was bogus; or the user ID could be OK but the password missing or incorrect. It may be unreliable if the return status (%s) is 401.

%U   The URL path requested.

%v   The canonical ServerName of the server serving the request.

%V   The server name according to the UseCanonicalName setting.

Custom Logging Options

The default httpd.conf file provided with Apache contains the following line, which defines the Extended Common Log Format discussed earlier, which Apache refers to by the nickname combined:

```
LogFormat "%h %l %u %t \"%r\" %>s %b \"%{Referer}i\" \"%{User-Agent}i\"" combined
```

Maintaining a
Healthy Server

PART 4

The format remains unused, however, until a `CustomLog` directive names the `combined` format.

In addition, it is possible to insert any number of HTTP response codes behind the % character to apply the token conditionally. The following token, for example, will log referring URLs only in cases where the response is 404(Not Found); in other words, it will log Web pages that contain a link to a resource that's not on the current site.

```
LogFormat "%h %l %u %t \"%r\" %s %b %404{Referer}i"
```

You can also use the ! (negation) character to precede the list of HTTP response codes, so that the format specification will be used only when the response code is not in the list:

```
LogFormat "%h %l %u %t \"%r\" %s %b %!200,304,302{Referer}i"
```

In this case, the referring URL is appended to the log line only if the response code is not 200 (OK), 302 (Found), or 304 (Not Modified). Note that the negation refers to the entire list of codes, not just to the single code it precedes.

Here are two sample `LogFormat` directives, with examples of lines that will be written to the logs using these formats:

```
LogFormat "%h %l %u %t \"%r\" %>s %b" common
192.168.1.2 - - [23/Mar/2000:12:44:20 -0600] "GET / HTTP/1.0" 304 -

LogFormat "%h %l %u %t \"%r\" %>s %b %{User-agent}i" common
192.168.1.2 - - [23/Mar/2000:12:44:48 -0600] "GET / HTTP/1.0" 304 - Mozilla/
4.7[en] (WinNT; I)
```

In both cases, the first field shown (corresponding to the %h specifier) is the IP address of the requestor. The second two fields, shown here as dashes, are filled in only if the request was for a resource that requires authentication of the requestor (as described in Chapter 14). The second field, rarely used, corresponding to the %l specifier, is the remote user's login name, as determined by `identd` authentication. The third field, also represented by a hyphen in these examples, is filled in with the requesting user's name, if authentication is enabled and a username and password are supplied with the request.

Creating the Log File: Using `CustomLog`

Whether you specify a custom access logging format with the `LogFormat` directive or decide to use the default CLF, you need to use the `CustomLog` directive to instruct Apache to use the format. This directive actually creates and enables a logfile. It specifies the location and name of the logfile and, optionally, the name of a previously defined log format to use for that logfile. If no named format is specified, `CustomLog` uses either the last `LogFormat` directive that did not assign a name or CLF, if no previous `LogFormat` has been specified.

The default Apache configuration file configures CLF logging into the access.log file using this pair of directives:

```
LogFormat "%h %l %u %t \"%r\" %>s %b" common
CustomLog /usr/local/apache/logs/access_log common
```

An alternate way, perhaps simpler, is to define a LogFormat without a name and follow it with a CustomLog directive, also without a name:

```
LogFormat "%h %l %u %t \"%r\" %>s %b"
CustomLog /usr/local/apache/logs/access_log
```

Actually, since the default value of LogFormat is the CLF, that directive is redundant even in the simplified example above.

The standard Apache file also defines three other formats:

```
LogFormat "%h %l %u %t \"%r\" %>s %b \"%{Referer}i\" \"%{User-Agent}i\"" combined
LogFormat "%{Referer}i -> %U" referer
LogFormat "%{User-agent}i" agent
```

CustomLog directives that use these formats are also included in the httpd.conf file but commented out.

```
#CustomLog /usr/local/apache1_3_12/logs/access_log common
#CustomLog/usr/local/apache1_3_12/logs/referer_log referer
#CustomLog /usr/local/apache1_3_12/logs/agent_log agent
```

The last two define logs that are separate from, and written in addition to, the regular access_log file. The combined log format, intended to replace the CLF log, should be uncommented only if you comment out the common log format. Otherwise, you will have two CustomLog directives defining the same file. This is permissible, but you will have two lines, with slightly different formats, written to that file for every server request.

Conditional Logging

The CustomLog directive has a special conditional format that determines whether a particular request is logged based on the existence or absence of a particular environment variable. This is usually used in conjunction with a SetEnvIf directive, as the following example illustrates:

```
SetEnvIf Request_URI \.gif$ image
SetEnvIf Request_URI \.jpg$ image
SetEnvIf Request_URI \.png$ image
CustomLog logs/images_log common env=image
CustomLog logs/access_log common env=!image
```

Maintaining a Healthy Server

PART 4

Here we simply want to log requests for images separately from other access. The SetEnvIf directives define an environment variable, image, for request URLs that indicate a request for images. Log entries will be written to one of two logs based on whether this variable is set (env=image) or not set (env=!image).

Here's an example where we log all requests from a particular network into a special directory for later review, possibly because we suspect malicious behavior originating from there. Note that, in this case, those requests will be written twice, once to the intruder_log, and once to the normal access_log:

```
CustomLog logs/access_log common
SetEnvIf Remote_Addr ^208\.229\.24 intruder
CustomLog logs/intruder_log common env=intruder
```

Logging for Virtual Hosts

If you're implementing virtual hosts on your server, as described in Chapter 6, it is often useful to log those hosts separately. To do that, you can create separate logging directives within each <VirtualHost> container so that all requests handled by that virtual host are written to a log separate from the primary server and all other virtual hosts. Otherwise, if a <VirtualHost> section contains no TransferLog or CustomLog directives, the logs defined for the main server are inherited and used by that virtual host.

Each log file opened by Apache consumes a new system file handle, a resource for which there are hard limits imposed by the Apache kernel. Although in recent versions of Apache these limits are usually so large they aren't a concern, Apache could run out of file handles if you use a large number of virtual hosts, and each opens two logs (an access log and an error log). An alternative to using separate log files for each virtual host is to log the server name with each log entry in the main server log. The %v format specification is used to log the name of the server that handles each request. For example, the following directives accomplish this by making a slight modification to the common log format. Note that I renamed the format revised to distinguish it as a custom format:

```
LogFormat "%h %l %u %t \"%r\" %>s %b Serving Host: %v" revised
CustomLog /usr/local/apache/logs/access_log revised
```

A request for http://namedvh2.hiwaay.net/ is now logged as:

```
192.168.1.2 - - [23/Mar/2000:15:35:55 -0600] "GET /oracle-b.gif HTTP/1.0" 404
281 Serving Host: namedvh2.hiwaay.net
```

Logfile Security

There are two reasons that adequate measures must be taken to ensure that nonprivileged users cannot access Apache logfiles. First, the data in the Apache logs should be considered sensitive, and could reveal information about your server configuration that could aid hackers in infiltrating your system. Second, since the root user can write to Apache logs, you must ensure that no one else also has write access. A malicious hacker who has write access to these files could create a symbolic link from an Apache log to a critical system file; the next time Apache tries to open the logfile for writing, the symbolic link will open that file instead and the system file will be corrupted.

While in the Apache `logs` directory, under `ServerRoot`, issue the following commands to correctly set the ownership and permissions of that directory and the files it contains:

```
# pwd
/usr/local/apache/logs
# chown 0.www . *
# chmod 750 .
# chmod 650 *
# ls -al
total 799
drwxr-x---   2 root     www         1024 Jul 29 14:43 .
drwxr-x---  12 root     www         1024 Jul 29 12:24 ..
-rw-r-----   1 root     www      1107233 Jul 29 15:41 access_log
-rw-r-----   1 root     www        31705 Jul 29 12:55 error_log
-rw-r-----   1 root     www            5 Jul 29 12:55 httpd.pid
```

The first command, `pwd`, was issued to ensure that we are in the proper directory; the `chown` command sets both the user and group ownership of the directory, and all of its files, to `root`. The results of the `chmod` command (the first of which sets permissions on the `logs` directory and the second for its files) are shown in the `ls` listing produced by the last command, essentially granting read and write access to the `root` user, read-only access to members of the `www` group, and no access at all to all other users. Incidentally, permissions on the `bin` and `conf` directories under the Apache `ServerRoot` should be set with the same ownership and access permissions shown here for the `logs` directory.

Tracking User Sessions

User tracking, or the logging of a user-specific piece of information for each Web request, permits a later analysis of the logs to compile information on user habits or preferences: Which of our pages did a particular user access? What link was followed to reach our page (derived from the `Referer` header)? How long did the user stay at our site? This analysis is usually designed to reveal the behavior of the typical user. When combined with demographic data (hopefully volunteered by the user), user tracking data maintained in log files can be used to determine buying habits and Web viewing habits of different population groups. The proliferation of Web-based commerce has made session

Maintaining a
Healthy Server

PART 4

logging more important than in the past, as companies use their Web access logs to develop Web usage profiles of their clientele.

The standard logging of error messages and HTTP requests in Apache that we've discussed so far, however, cannot provide this information about individual user sessions. While it might seem that the IP address would uniquely identify each connecting user in the logs, in practice, this doesn't work. Business users are increasingly hidden behind firewalls and HTTP proxy servers that effectively mask their IP addresses, so that they appear to be using the IP address of the proxy server. Also, most ISPs dynamically assign IP addresses to their users, which is not helpful in identifying particular users.

To meet this need, Apache provides two modules, mod_usertrack and mod_session, that attempt to track users by assigning a unique piece of information to a connecting user and including this information with the log entry of each HTTP request received from that user. Both of these modules that implement user tracking will be discussed.

Cookies

When Netscape introduced *cookies*, they were quickly and widely adopted as an efficient way to track user information. Cookies are pieces of information generated by the Web server and stored by the client browser. When the same browser makes subsequent requests to the server that issued the cookie, it attaches the cookie to the request. This enables the Web server to identify the user and perhaps load a customized page or return to a stored state in a transaction session.

Cookies are very simple to use. To set a cookie on a client's workstation, the server sends a Set-Cookie header with its HTTP response. That header looks like the following and passes five fields (only one of which is mandatory) in no specific order:

```
Set-Cookie: name=value; expires=date;path=path; domain=domain_name; secure
```

Unless the user's browser is incapable of storing cookie data (highly unlikely these days) or the user has specifically disabled the browser from accepting and storing cookies, the cookie data is written somewhere on the client's hard disk by the browser. The following data fields are passed to the browser in a cookie:

name   The name of the cookie. This is the only required attribute of a cookie. This field can be set by the CookieName directive in mod_usertrack but defaults to Apache.

expires   A date string that specifies a time and date after which the cookie is considered expired and is no longer used or stored on the client's machine. The CookieExpires directive in mod_usertrack sets this field. If this optional field is not specified, the cookie is expired when the current session ends (usually when the browser is closed).

path   The URLs on the server for which the cookie is valid. If this optional field is not specified, it is assumed to be the same path as returned in the header that contains the cookie.

domain   Used as a key to look up the cookie in the stored cookies file, this is usually set to the server host or domain name. If this optional field is not specified, it is assumed to be the host name of the server that generated the cookie.

secure   This is a keyword that, if present, will mark the cookie to be transmitted only over an encrypted communication channel (essentially meaning SSL). If not included, the cookie will be sent as regular, unencrypted traffic.

Netscape cookies were first implemented in Apache by a now-obsolete module called mod_cookies. That module has since been replaced with one called mod_usertrack, which implements user tracking (primarily using the standard Apache log) with cookies.

One of the nice things about cookies is that they are so simple to use, and mod_usertrack is a simple module. It is enabled in the default Apache configuration, and its facilities should be available in the standard Apache server. All you need to do to use cookies for user tracking is enable this feature with the CookieTracking directive:

```
CookieTracking on
```

When thus enabled, mod_usertrack will start generating and sending cookies for all new user requests for resources within the scope of the directive. The CookieTracking directive can be used to enable user tracking in virtual hosts, directory contexts, and .htaccess files, but it is not permitted in <Files> containers. This means that we can't elect to disable the use of cookies for tracking requests of a specific file type (like .GIF files), although we can disable cookies for a specific directory that might be reserved to contain files of type GIF:

```
CookieTracking on

<Directory /images>
  CookieTracking off
</Directory>
```

The CookieName directive is used to set the name of generated cookies for tracking purposes. If the directive is not used, the name of all cookies issued by mod_usertrack is Apache. The CookieExpires directive is expressed as a duration for which the cookie is valid, and it takes a single argument that can be expressed either as number of seconds or as a time period expressed in combinations of years, months, weeks, hours, minutes, and seconds. The following example illustrates the use of all three mod_usertrack directives:

```
CookieTracking on
CookieName MyApacheCookie
CookieExpires "2 days 1 hour"
```

Placing these directives in my `httpd.conf` file caused the response header I received for a simple HTTP query to look like the following:

```
HTTP/1.1 200 OK
Date: Tue, 23 May 2000 13:38:35 GMT
Server: Apache/1.3.12 (Unix)
Set-Cookie: MyApacheCookie= 192.168.1.2.1173959089422918; path=/; expires=Thu,
25-May-00 14:38:35 GMT
Last-Modified: Sat, 20 May 2000 18:33:25 GMT
ETag: "34062-f4e-3926da75"
Accept-Ranges: bytes
Content-Length: 3918
Connection: close
Content-Type: text/html
```

The `Set-Cookie` line includes the new name of my server-issued cookies and a value that is unique to this server/browser session. Note that it sends an expiration time relative to the server clock time, rather than sending the cookie's duration of validity and letting the browser compute the expiration time.

The Netscape browser records the issued cookie as follows:

```
jackal.hiwaay.net       FALSE   /       FALSE   959265865       MyApacheCookie
192.168.1.2.1173959089422918
```

Note that the expiration date appears to have been converted into a large integer (959265865), which is the number of seconds since a relative time base (usually referred to as the *epoch*, discussed later in the chapter).

Session Tracking

Many people are leery of accepting cookies because they fear that it jeopardizes their privacy or the security of their computers. For that reason, the use of cookies has lost much of its effectiveness as more people disable the acceptance of cookies in their Web browsers (all major browsers permit the user to do that). Many Webmasters are supplementing the use of cookies with a second method of tracking users that, while not as efficient, is supported by every browser.

HTTP is a *connectionless* protocol, meaning that persistent connections aren't maintained between server and browser between transactions (or client requests). Maintaining state information between connections in a user session (for example, when a user is working through a Web shopping application) is critical to many Web-based applications. The user's shopping cart may be stored on the server. The shopping application is able to look at the session ID or cookie for new requests in order to associate the new connection with an existing session. From the user's point of view, it is not apparent that the connection to the e-commerce server is intermittent rather than continuous. Properly implemented, session tracking gives the user the impression of an unbroken connection between the browser and the server.

Session tracking (as opposed to simple user tracking) is usually a programming mechanism for storing persistent user data that can be recovered for a particular user session (based on a cookie or session ID provided by the user). Using these mechanisms, a client can be restored to a previous session even after a server reboot. The programming techniques used to implement sessions that emulate continuous connections differ depending on the programming tools used. Sessions are implemented in Perl, for example, using the Apache::Session module; in Java, using the HttpSession object of the servlet classes; and in PHP through a number of built-in functions for session control.

A detailed discussion of HTTP session programming is beyond the scope of this book, but there is a general-purpose module designed for session tracking that you should be aware of. The module mod_session is not part of the standard Apache distribution, but a link to the most recent version is maintained in the Apache Module Registry (http://modules.apache.org).

Using mod_session

The mod_session module (which is a single C source file that includes all of its documentation in the form of comment lines) is quite easily compiled and installed as a DSO using apxs:

```
# /usr/local/apache/bin/apxs -c -i -A mod_session.c
```

This module provides the same cookie tracking features as mod_usertrack, although it has completely different configuration directives and more of them. It differs from mod_usertrack in that it can add session keys to URLs returned to individual users, but will do this only for browsers that will not accept cookies.

Like the mod_usertrack module, mod_session has a directive for setting the cookie name:

```
SessionCookieName   MyApacheCookie
```

In addition, you must also set a name for the session ID, which is appended to URLs furnished by the client:

```
SessionUrlSidName sid
```

This SessionUrlSidName will generate URLs of the form:

```
http://servername.dom/resource?sid=xxxxx
```

Maintaining a Healthy Server

PART 4

Session tracking using URL modification is much more work than using cookies, because each new user connecting to the server is first sent to an entry point for the Web-based application. From there, the browser is redirected to a new URL that has the session key attached, as shown in the last example line. Once the browser has a session key, you must make sure that hyperlinks in the page it reaches are dynamically generated to contain this session key. This is normally done by post-processing (or filtering) all HTML documents requested by the client so that any embedded hyperlinks are modified to contain the client's session key. The module includes such a filter, which is specified using the module's `SessionFilter` directive:

```
SessionFilter /cgi-bin/filter
```

Session key and cookie expiration times are set as follows. Note that the argument to both directives can only be expressed in seconds:

```
#Expire time set to 4 hours
SessionCookieExpire 14400
SessionUrlExpire 14400
```

The following directives apply only when cookies are used; they set values that the browser stores with each cookie:

```
SessionCookieDomain /thisdomain.com
SessionCookiePath /valid_url/
```

The `SessionValidEntry` directive is used to specify entry points that a client can access without a session key or cookie. A new session key will be generated for requests made to this area:

```
SessionValidEntry / /index.html /cgi-bin/newuser.cgi
```

All areas not included in the `SessionValidEntry` line must have a session key to be accessed, or the request will be automatically redirected to a location defined by the `SessionTop` variable:

```
SessionTop http://jackal.hiwaay.net/index.html
```

Some resources on your server should be exempted from session control. You don't want a session key generated for icons and images, for example, because that will prevent them from being properly cached by proxy servers. By default, `mod_session` automatically exempts files of type `image` from session control. To exempt other media types and handlers, use the `SessionExemptTypes` directive (which accepts regular-expression arguments):

```
SessionExemptTypes image/.* audio/.* cgi-script
```

You can also exempt resources from session control by location (expressed by URL or URL regular expression):

```
SessionExemptLocations  /images/.*    /sounds/.*
```

You can disable session control by setting an environment variable, `nosessioncontrol`, using either the `SetEnvIf` or `BrowserMatch` directive. This is used to disable session control for robots that might visit, for example:

```
BrowserMatchNoCase     infoseek/.*      nosessioncontrol
BrowserMatchNoCase     .*spider.*       nosessioncontrol
BrowserMatchNoCase     .*spyder.*       nosessioncontrol
BrowserMatchNoCase     .*bot.*          nosessioncontrol
BrowserMatchNoCase     .*harvest.*      nosessioncontrol
BrowserMatchNoCase     .*crawler.*      nosessioncontrol
BrowserMatchNoCase     .*yahoo.*        nosessioncontrol
```

Creating the Session Log

Once you've got `mod_session` working, how do you make use of it by logging user sessions? The session key of every request made to your server is recorded by `mod_session` as an internal Apache data structure called a *note*, which is referenced like a system environment variable. This note (SESSION_KEY) is logged using the `LogFormat` command as discussed earlier in the chapter. To append the session key to a CLF log entry, use:

```
LogFormat "%h %l %u %t \"%r\" %>s %b %{SESSION_KEY}n" common
CustomLog /usr/local/apache/logs/access_log common
```

You could also leave your CLF-formatted access log intact and create a second log specifically for session logging, using commands like these:

```
LogFormat "%{SESSION_KEY}n %t \"%r\" " session
CustomLog /usr/local/apache/logs/session_log session
```

You can also log the session key type (either URL or cookie) using the SESSION_KEY_TYPE note:

```
LogFormat "%{SESSION_KEY}n %{SESSION_KEY_TYPE)n %t \"%r\" " session
CustomLog /usr/local/apache/logs/session_log session
```

The `mod_session` module is more difficult to set up than `mod_usertrack` and it should be used only in situations where cookie tracking is insufficient, and something more robust is needed.

Maintaining a
Healthy Server

PART 4

Follow2

A shareware program called Follow2 (available from `www.mnot.net/follows2/`) can be used to track user sessions without cookies or session keys. This program, which is *not* open source or public domain, requires only that your access log be in combined log format. I have not used this program and merely call it to the reader's attention.

Analyzing Logs

On any server with a significant amount of client traffic, Apache access logs rapidly grow until they become so large that you'll need a good program to analyze the data they contain. Simple Perl scripts are one good way to extract specific information from Apache's access logs, for those who have the time and inclination to write them. Most site administrators, however, are better served by one of the many good log analyzers available for download on the Internet.

What makes a good log analyzer? The most important criterion is efficiency or speed in processing the log file. I have used analyzers that produced useful statistics or charts but ran so slowly that it took literally hours to get the results. A good analyzer should also be configurable for a wide variety of log formats. Ideally, you should be able to configure your analyzer to read any format you can express using the `LogFormat` directive described earlier in the chapter. The other criterion of major importance for a log analyzer is that the information it returns is useful and presented in a fashion that makes it easy to understand. Basically, you want to know which of your pages are most popular, where the majority of your clients are from, which of your pages generated errors, and what other sites on the Internet are referring people to your own (referers).

Of the many analyzers available, here are two I'm familiar with.

Analog

I have for years relied only on one log analyzer, Dr. Stephen Turner's Analog (`www`
`.analog.cx`), or its predecessor, `getstats` (written by Kevin Hughes). These two have long held the distinction of being the most popular Web access log analyzers available, and for good reason. Analog meets all the important criteria for a log analyzer: it is fast, extensively configurable, and produces a fully-customizable output that includes practically everything that can possibly be extracted from the access log.

Analog is an easy program to compile and install. Download the latest source archive (a file named `analog-4_1_tar.gz` when I wrote this) and create a directory to hold it.

Unlike most programs, Analog isn't packaged to install into a working directory from a separate source directory. Unpack the distribution archive into the parent directory of Analog's intended home and then go to that directory:

```
# pwd
/usr/local
# tar xvzf /home/caulds/analog-4_1_tar.gz
# cd /usr/local/analog-4.1
```

Analog has a configuration file, analog.cfg, into which you can set a large number of values to control it. Each of these values (C program variables) is also initialized in several include files (header files with a .h extension). Prior to compiling the program, you can modify these header files to change the compiled program's default values, but I don't recommend this. Instead, make all your configuration edits to analog.cfg. There are a huge number of configuration values, most of which will never concern you. They are well documented both in the included HTML files and on the Analog Web site and its mirrors.

Compiling Analog is as simple as typing:

```
# make
```

The installation is complete when the program is compiled. You'll find a single executable file (named analog) in the directory where you installed the program. Invoke that executable to generate a report:

```
# ls -al /usr/local/analog-4.1/analog
-rwxr-xr-x   1 root       root      213584 May 24 18:20
    /usr/local/analog-4.1/analog
```

I won't attempt to show even a small percentage of the many configuration variables that can be used in Analog. Instead, I'll explain the configuration values you will probably want to consider changing from their defaults, and I'll show you the values I used for each.

In the file analog.cfg, I changed or added the following seven values before running Analog the first time:

HOSTNAME   This is simply the name that will appear at the top of the Analog report; it does not have to be a hostname. Enclose it in quotes if the value contains spaces:

```
HOSTNAME "My Apache Server"
```

HOSTURL   The name entered in the configuration file as HOSTNAME is a hyperlink on the display report. When the link is clicked, this is the URL to which the browser is redirected:

```
HOSTURL "http://jackal.hiwaay.net"
```

ANALOGDIR   The directory where Analog will look for its support files and configuration when loaded:

```
ANALOGDIR "/usr/local/analog-4.1/"
```

LOGFILE   The location of your Apache access file:

```
LOGFILE "/usr/local/apache/logs/access_log"
```

OUTFILE   By default, this is set to stdin (the Linux standard output file handle). You may want to change this to the name of file, as I did, or you may want to run Analog from a script that automatically redirects the output to a specially generated filename (that might, for instance, contain a datestamp):

```
OUTFILE "/home/httpd/html/analog.html"
```

IMAGEDIR   The directory in which Analog will look for the support images it displays. (Note that the value of IMAGEDIR is used to form URLs to reference the images, and should be expressed as a URI that can be reached on your server.) I placed the images that came with Analog in my Apache image file and set this variable to that directory:

```
IMAGEDIR "icons/"
```

LOGFORMAT   The same as the LogFormat directive used in Apache to create your log. In fact, the Analog documentation for the use of this configuration variable refers to the Apache docs.

```
LOGFORMAT "%h %l %u %t \"%r\" %>s %b \"%{Referer}i\" \"%{User-Agent}i\""
```

Properly configured, Analog will know where to find the Apache logs and where you write them. The default value is to send the output to the Linux stdout handle, which means your screen. You'll need to redirect the output into an HTML file that you can retrieve using a Web browser:

```
# /usrlocal/analog-4.1/analog > /home/httpd/html/May24Log.html
```

With the configuration changes I made to analog.cfg, all I had to do to generate a report for my Apache logs was enter this command:

```
# /usr/local/analog-4.1
```

The results were instantly available on my server and are shown in Figure 12.1.

Figure 12.1 A report generated by Analog 4.1

Another strong feature of Analog is its multilanguage support. As of this writing, Analog can provide output in any of 31 different languages (with more promised) using a variable called LANGUAGE. Refer to the documentation for a list of the supported languages. The default is:

```
LANGUAGE ENGLISH
```

Analog also supports another way of adding language support, from a special language file that you can download, either from the Analog site or from another user:

```
LANGFILE lang/hindi.lng
```

Analog offers plain text as an optional alternative to HTML-formatted output, which is nice for reports that are later cut and pasted into other documents, or for e-mail that doesn't support HTML formatted message bodies. Use the following configuration line to produce plain text output:

```
OUTPUT ASCII
```

Listing 12.1 is a sample of the plain text output from Analog, showing only a few of the 13 output reports it can generate.

Listing 12.1   Plain text output from Analog

```
Web Server Statistics for My Apache Server
==============================================
Program started at Thu-25-May-2000 08:20.
Analysed requests from Fri-19-May-2000 09:54 to Wed-24-May-2000 20:04 (5.4
days).
------------------------------------------------------------------------------
General Summary
---------------
Successful requests: 1,320
Average successful requests per day: 243
Successful requests for pages: 598
Average successful requests for pages per day: 110
Failed requests: 74
Redirected requests: 9
Distinct files requested: 42
Distinct hosts served: 6
Data transferred: 4.329 Mbytes
Average data transferred per day: 817.397 kbytes
------------------------------------------------------------------------------
Directory Report
----------------
Listing directories with at least 0.01% of the traffic, sorted by the amount
of traffic.
reqs: %bytes: directory
----: ------: ---------
579: 57.10%: [root directory]
48: 20.40%: /webalizer/
510: 12.54%: /cgi-bin/
117: 6.19%: /~caulds/
44: 1.76%: /IMAGES/
1: 1.28%: /MySQL/
6: 0.52%: / http/
2: 0.17%: [no directory]
```

```
12: 0.03%: /icons/
1: : [not listed: 1 directory]
------------------------------------------------------------------------
Request Report
--------------
Listing files with at least 20 requests, sorted by the number of requests.
reqs: %bytes: last time: file
----: ------: ---------------: ----
560: 47.46%: 24/May/00 20:02: /
510: 12.54%: 23/May/00 20:21: /cgi-bin/environ.cgi
43: 1.64%: 24/May/00 20:02: /~caulds/IMAGES/emailed.gif
43: 1.71%: 24/May/00 20:02: /IMAGES/ftbckgrd.jpg
164: 36.64%: 24/May/00 20:03: [not listed: 38 files]
------------------------------------------------------------------------
This analysis was produced by analog 4.1.
Running time: Less than 1 second.
```

The best way to find out what Analog can do is to compile a copy and run it on your server logs. Even if you're running another log analyzer, it is quite likely that some features of Analog will be useful in augmenting the other analyzer.

Webalizer

The only other Web log analyzer I have used regularly is Brad Barrett's Webalizer (www .mrunix.net/webalizer/), mostly for its excellent use of graphics. While Analog excels at in-depth statistics about your Web server's activity, Webalizer does an excellent job of providing high-level summaries of the data, presented in bar-charts, pie charts, and tables that highlight trends and time period comparisons (Figure 12.2). Webalizer compiles hourly, daily, monthly and yearly summaries in both tabular and a variety of graphic formats.

Webalizer is a good tool to use in conjunction with other log analyzers. One of its limitations is that it doesn't support fully customized logs. Currently it only supports CLF, combined, and two less-used formats, squid and wu-ftp logs. In the next release, it is expected to include support for native IIS and W3C extended logs.

> **NOTE** The W3C format (www.w3.org/TR/WD-logfile) is an extensible format in which the format specification is included within the log itself (something like XML).

Figure 12.2 Webalizer can provide graphical summaries of Web access statistics.

Webalizer makes use of the GD libraries to render its graphics. Quite honestly, I didn't think I had them on my Linux system, having never linked to or used them before. However, these were part of my Red Hat installation, and I was able to compile and install Webalizer with the following simple commands:

```
# ./configure
# make
# make install
```

Webalizer installs its executable (by default) into /usr/local/bin/webalizer. It also creates a sample configuration file, /etc/webalizer.conf.sample. This file should be renamed webalizer.conf, and modified as necessary. I made two modifications to it, pointing Webalizer to the proper Apache access log, and also specifying a location for Webalizer's output files. Webalizer will write HTML files and supporting GIF images (all of which will automatically be assigned a name that includes the current date) into this output directory:

```
LogFile       /usr/local/apache/logs/access_log
OutputDir     /home/httpd/html/webalizer
```

Webalizer allows incremental processing, so you can process small pieces of a log rather than trying to accumulate weeks or months of data into one huge log. With incremental logging, you can rotate your logs, for example, on a weekly basis and process each weekly log separately, combining the results. Monthly summaries, too, are saved, eliminating the need to have previous log files available for generating long-term historical charts.

Webalizer is very fast and quite easy to use. While it might not answer all of everyone's log analysis needs, it is one program I highly recommend to all Apache administrators, even those already happily using another log analyzer.

Advanced Log Analyzers

In today's new electronic commerce world, Web site traffic analysis is often far more sophisticated than the methods I've described in this chapter. Newer tools for analyzing Web access patterns usually work pretty much the same as the standard logging methods I've described, analyzing standard log files. In addition, however, most attempt to draw conclusions from that data about client usage patterns. The high-end variety often correlate log data in some way with demographic data supplied by the site's customers and stored in databases. This type of customer profiling is usually aimed at determining not just what visitors to your site access while there, but how they got there in the first place, and the paths they followed once they arrived.

Most of these commercial log analyzers are able to work with a large number of log formats, although the Extended Common Log Format is the format most often used on Apache servers. These advanced analyzers should be considered separate products in their own rights, and not as Apache add-ons. For that reason, I will only mention one, as an example of the best of breed. Although the number of commercial Web site tracking tools is constantly increasing, and the field is in constant fluctuation, the current stand-out favorite for Apache on Linux Web servers is Enterprise Reporting Server by WebTrends (www.webtrends.com).

The value of these commercial Web site log analyzers lies in the efficiency with which they can summarize extremely large log files (WebTrends claims to be able to analyze daily log files of over 160 million requests), and the quality of the summary reports they generate from standard log data. WebTrends will output its reports in both Microsoft Word and HTML for viewing, and also in Microsoft Excel format for analysis.

An even newer approach to Web customer profiling is behavioral analysis. This involves embedding metadata within HTML-formatted documents. When the document is retrieved, this special code is "fired" to record information about the retrieving client, often temporary data that is accumulated from the user during the current session and will not be written to log files for later retrieval. Again, WebTrends stands as a current best-of-breed example of such a product with its high-end CommerceTrends engine.

Rotating Apache Logs

On heavily trafficked Apache servers, logfiles often grow quite large (and quite rapidly). Most sites use some scheme to *rotate* logfiles. In other words, at specific time intervals (usually daily, and usually during a period of low traffic volume) they quit writing to the current log, close it, rename it, and begin logging to a fresh, empty logfile. At first glance, it might seem impossible (or at least a *very* bad) idea to close and rename a file that Apache is actively using for its logfile. The Apache developers have made this easy, however, and you can change the active log without having to shut down the server completely. It's actually quite simple and completely safe, though there is a small trick involved.

Apache knows the logfile by its initial *inode*, rather than its filename. The inode is a numerical entry into a table that shows how disk clusters are allocated to files. When you rename a file, the file itself remains unchanged on the hard disk. Since Apache is writing to the file by inode, changing its name has no effect; and when the logfile is renamed, Apache continues to write to the file by its new name. This allows you to issue a command like the following to change the name of the Apache request logfile on the fly:

```
# mv /usr/local/apache/logs/access_log /usr/local/apache/logs/access.0730
```

You can do this through a script (usually scheduled to run automatically under Linux's cron utility). After renaming the file, the Apache server is restarted by sending it the -USR signal. This signal causes Apache to perform a graceful restart, ensuring that all current connections are closed only after their requests are fulfilled and there will be no interruption of service. The restart will cause Apache to read its configuration file, and it will create a new logfile using the name specified in the TransferLog of the configuration file and begin writing its logging information there. Use either the Linux kill command or the apachectl utility to perform a graceful restart (as described in Chapter 11):

```
# kill -USR1 'cat /usr/local/apache/logs/httpd.pid'
# /usr/local/apache/bin/apachectl graceful
```

Although this process is quite simple and easy to script, it is essentially a manual process and Apache provides an alternative method. In Apache's bin directory you will also find another utility called `rotatelogs`. This utility is designed to be used with the log-to-pipe functionality described earlier in this chapter. The utility must be used with a `TransferLog` directive that indicates that logging should be piped to this utility, as in this example:

```
TransferLog "|rotatelogs /usr/local/apache/logs/access_log 86400"
ErrorLog "|rotatelogs /usr/local/apache/logs/error_log 86400"
```

In this example, `rotatelogs` will automatically rotate your logs, appending the system time to the filename specified, so that a filename like `error_log.0964828800` is created. The number at the end is the number of seconds that has elapsed since a fixed point in time called the *epoch*; every second, that large integer is incremented by one. Without doing the math, I will accept the Linux designers' word that the epoch is 00:00:00 on January 1, 1970, Coordinated Universal Time, or UTC.

The numeric argument to `rotatelogs` is the number of seconds between each log rotation. In the example, `rotatelogs` will rotate `access_log` to `access_log.nnnn` every 86400 seconds (24 hours), and open up a new `access_log` file.

One disadvantage of `rotatelogs` is that it does not permit a lot of control over the names assigned to the rotated logfiles. Also, the extension that it assigns to rotated files can be inconvenient for people. Your log analyzers won't care about the long numeric extension (they will use only the internal dates in preparing their summary statistics), but it will make it difficult for human administrators to find the log entries for a particular day, for example. For that reason, you may wish to consider an open-source alternative to `rotatelogs` called `cronolog` (available from `www.ford-mason.co.uk/resources/cronolog`). This program works quite similarly to Apache's `rotatelogs`, except that it determines the frequency of log rotation and directory paths to the rotated logs according to a template that uses the same format specifiers as the Linux `date` command. For example, if you wanted to rotate your logs on a daily basis, you would use a template like the following:

```
TransferLog "|bin/cronolog /usr/local/apache/logs/%Y/%m/%d/access.log
ErrorLog "|/bin/cronolog /usr/local/apache/logs/%Y/%m/%d/errors.log
```

This template would maintain logfiles in separate directories for each year, month, and day, as follows:

```
/usr/local/apache/logs/2000/07/27/access.log
/usr/local/apache/logs/2000/07/27/errors.log
```

Maintaining a
Healthy Server

PART 4

Using `logresolve`

Although Apache logging can be configured to look up and log hostnames for every request, this is never desirable on heavily loaded servers. Reverse DNS lookups (in which the DNS is queried to find the hostname corresponding to an IP address) require time and put Apache processes into a wait state while the results are being fetched. Eliminating the requirement for the hostname lookup eliminates these expensive wait states. You should enable `HostnameLookups` only on a lightly used server.

If you desire hostnames instead of IP addresses in your log analyses, you can use an Apache utility named `logresolve` to perform the reverse-DNS lookups on entire log files prior to analysis. You'll find this utility in the `bin` subdirectory under the Apache installation directory (usually `/usr/local/apache`).

Do not use `logresolve` with an open logfile; but after having rotated your logfile (as described in the previous section), you can run `logresolve` on the file to convert IP addresses into hostnames (assuming the IP address can be resolved into a hostname). The utility is very simple, reading from its standard input handle and writing to its standard output handle. You use I/O redirection to specify the input and output, as follows:

```
logresolve < access.log > access.log.resolved
```

The `logresolve` utility can take two optional arguments. Provide the `-s` argument to have `logresolve` write statistics it gathers to a separate file as in:

```
logresolve -s logstats.txt < access.log > access.log.resolved
```

The `-c` option instructs `logresolve` to use double-reverse DNS lookups. This is a check for bogus (*spoofed*) hostnames by checking that a hostname associated with an IP actually maps to that IP address. After resolving an IP address to a hostname (with a reverse DNS lookup), `logresolve` will then do a DNS lookup for the IP address of that hostname (it may receive several). Before `logresolve` will accept a hostname it has determined from a reverse DNS lookup, one of the IP addresses it receives when supplying this hostname in an address lookup query must match the original IP address. I do not recommend using this feature, for two reasons: it will greatly increase the time required to process a log, and the benefits are minimal. When used with `logresolve`, double-reverse DNS lookup does nothing to enhance the security of your site, and the bogus entries it catches are far more likely to be the result of misconfigured DNS servers than the result of deliberate attempts to spoof a hostname.

In Sum

Logging is an essential function of any Web server. This chapter discussed how Apache provides logging, both as part of the core module for error logging and through the `mod_log_config` module for request logging. It showed how to configure an Apache server for logging, how to specify the location for log files, how to determine the severity of errors that will be logged, and how to customize request logs.

Although request logs are often examined in detail, usually to determine the action logged for a specific request, these logs are so extensive that they are viewed in summary to determine client patterns, trends and preferences. Scripting languages like Perl or Python are very useful for summarizing Apache request logs. For most administrators, however, a far more convenient solution is to use one of the many log analyzers written for just this purpose. Some of the best are freely available as open source. I offered two as examples of the best of these: one that produces graphical, or presentation-oriented, output; the other produces tabular, textual data. I have found both quite useful. There is also a new breed of log analyzer, tailored to electronic commerce solutions, and generally targeted at creating a profile of customer preferences usually correlated with demographic data from another data source.

The next chapter continues the discussion of administering a working server; it discusses a number of ways to increase the performance of an Apache server, particularly the use of proxying and caching.

Maintaining a
Healthy Server

PART 4

13

Proxying and Performance Tuning

Once you have a working Apache Web server, you will want to tune the server to optimize its performance. This would mean minimizing the delay experienced by users in retrieving resources from your server and maximizing the number of requests you can adequately respond to in a given time.

Well, if you're the type who likes to tweak software, the bad news is that there's not a lot you can do to improve the performance of Apache. The good news is that it usually isn't necessary; Apache is already well tuned for the highest performance, and most of the development work being done on Apache now (for the 2.0 release) is geared more toward higher performance than feature enhancement.

In this chapter, I'll first discuss the few performance directives you have at your disposal as an administrator and then one of the most important tools you can use to minimize document retrieval times on a local area network, Web caching using Apache as a proxy server.

Performance Directives

One way to optimize Apache's performance is by increasing the number of process threads available to handle requests. Recall from Chapter 2 that Apache's default *standalone* mode of operation starts the main Apache process at boot time. The main Apache process starts the process pool (or *swarm*), which consists of up to 256 Apache server processes that handle incoming requests. Apache's pool of waiting processes is under the control of the main Apache server process (which does not, itself, respond to client requests). The number of processes in the pool is not static; it changes as requirements dictate. The server administrator sets three parameters in `httpd.conf` to control the number of processes started when Apache is invoked. The following general server directives (which have server-wide scope) are used for that purpose:

`MinSpareServers`   Specifies the minimum number of spare servers (idle servers waiting for incoming connections) that reside in the process pool. The main Apache process ensures that at least this many idle servers are always available to handle client requests. The default value of five spare servers is usually changed only on servers with very heavy or light loads. With a heavily loaded server, you'll increase this value to ensure more standby servers so that clients never experience a delay while a new process is created. On very lightly loaded servers you may choose to reduce the number of servers waiting idle but consuming system memory.

`MaxSpareServers`   Specifies the maximum number of spare servers in the process pool. If the number of idle servers exceeds this number, the main Apache server kills excess servers until there are fewer idle Apache processes than specified in this directive. The default value of 10 is usually changed only on very heavily or very lightly loaded servers.

`StartServers`   Specifies the number of spare server processes that are created when Apache is started. The default value of 5 rarely needs to be changed, although it may be increased on heavily loaded servers to ensure an adequate pool of Apache processes to handle a large number of client connections. I usually set this value on my servers to match `MinSpareServers`.

Here's an example. My personal Apache/Linux server, which is used mainly for testing and to host resources that are shared with colleagues, is very lightly used. The number of connections is measured in hundreds per day. Listing 13.1 is an `httpd.conf` file that starts 10 listener processes when Apache starts (twice the Apache default), always keeps 10 in reserve, and ensures that the number of active listener processes is always 10 or greater.

Listing 13.1   Allocating Listener Processes

```
#MinSpareServers 5  Apache default
MinSpareServers 10

#MaxSpareServer 10  Apache default
MaxSpareServers 20
```

```
#
# Number of servers to start initially --- should be
# a reasonable ballpark figure.
#StartServers 5      Apache default
StartServers 10
```

A benchmarking utility like ApacheBench (demonstrated in Chapter 8) or the excellent WebStone utility (open-source software available from MindCraft, www.mindcraft.com/webstone) can be used to determine when these values need to be increased. If you can run these benchmarking tools on a nonproduction server, you should do so with a large variety of test URLs, varying the number of server processes and concurrent client processes. Strive to get a baseline estimate of the number of requests your server is capable of processing; look for the breakpoint where increasing the number of server processes no longer results in a performance increase. WebStone can be configured to automatically increment the number of concurrent client processes at each of several iterations of a benchmark test. The results can then be used to predict performance decreases that will occur as request loads increase.

There is no hard-and-fast rule for determining the optimum number of httpd processes, but in general, you should increase the number of running listener processes whenever measured connection times start to increase (indicating that client connections are being queued to be handled by the next available listener process). Collecting benchmark data regularly is the best way to discern trends in server usage and keep an eye on server response. You will need to experiment with different values of the Apache performance directives to optimize them for your server, but most sites will probably find that the Apache defaults are perfectly adequate.

Controlling Client Connections

In addition to the directives available for controlling server processes, Apache also provides a set of directives you can use to control the number and size of client connections.

MaxClients   This directive sets a limit to the number of httpd listener processes that can run simultaneously (one per connected client). The default is 256, which is the maximum that can be set without modifying the value of HARD_SERVER_LIMIT in *Apache_source*/include/httpd.h and recompiling the server. This parameter rarely needs to be increased. If you do increase the value, make sure your system can handle the load (it needs a fast CPU and fast disk I/O, but especially, lots of system RAM). This limit is a fail-safe value to keep your server from crashing under extreme load, and the value you set should exceed the number of clients you are actually serving by about 25 percent. If your server load is so heavy that you find 256 processes insufficient, consider adding another physical server on your network. You may wish, however, to limit the total number of Apache server processes that can run if you have a system with limited resources (particularly if you have only 32 or 64MB of RAM). There is no hard-and-fast way to determine, however, the maximum number of processes your system can support. You might need to experiment a little. If your system is crashing because of an excessive number of Apache processes, however, you should immediately reduce the maximum number specified in this directive.

ListenBacklog   Apache does not immediately refuse new client connections once the maximum number of httpd processes has reached MaxClients. Instead, it holds them in a queue to be handled by the httpd processes that complete the servicing of a request and are free to accept a new one. This queue can grow up to the number of requests specified in ListenBacklog. When the queue reaches this limit, all arriving connections are rejected with a 503 (Service Unavailable) HTTP response code. By default, this value is set to 511, and it rarely needs to be changed. If your number of backlogged connections consistently grows to this size, you should try to reduce the backlog rather than increasing the allowable number of backlogged connections.

Timeout   Apache uses a single value to determine when to time out and close a connection when waiting for a response from a client. When any of the following three wait intervals exceeds the value set by the Timeout directive, the client connection is closed:

- The time it takes to receive a GET request from a client after that client connects.
- The time between receipt of individual TCP packets on a POST or PUT HTTP request, in which the server is accepting a stream of data from the client.
- The time Apache will wait for acknowledgments (ACKs) to individual TCP packets it sends.

The default value for Timeout is 300 seconds, or 5 minutes. That's an extraordinarily long time to wait for any one of the three responses for which this timeout is valid. For most servers, this value can safely be reduced to something like 60, with this directive:

```
Timeout 60
```

Clients on very slow links may be disconnected prematurely, but a value of a full minute is not unreasonably small in today's Internet.

SendBufferSize   This value (expressed in kilobytes) will set the size of the TCP output buffer size. The default value of this buffer is set in the Linux kernel, but you can override it, particularly if you need to queue data for high-latency links (where the time required to receive an acknowledgment to a sent packet is in the range of 100ms or more).

KeepAlive   This simple directive can be set to either On or Off to enable or disable HTTP/1.1 persistent connections. HTTP/1.1-compliant browsers use persistent connections to submit multiple requests over a single TCP connection to a Web server. Enabling this feature usually offers a tremendous speed advantage over traditional connectionless HTTP, in which the client has to establish a new connection to the server for each request. A Web page that has a number of inline images can request all of these over the same TCP connection, rather than opening a new request for each.

The default value of KeepAlive is On, which means Apache will allow persistent connections requested by browsers that support them (as nearly all up-to-date browsers now do). It should never be necessary to disable this feature, except for browsers that do not properly support persistent connections but request them anyway. The default Apache configuration identifies two such browsers and disables persistent connections for them by setting the nokeepalive environment variable using a BrowserMatch directive. You can also set this environment variable to disable persistent connections selectively, but you are safe in leaving the directive set to KeepAlive on.

KeepAliveTimeout   Specifies the length of time Apache will wait for a subsequent request after receiving a client request with an HTTP Keep-Alive header requesting a persistent connection. The default value is 15 seconds, which you will find defined in your default Apache configuration by this directive:

```
KeepAliveTimeout 15
```

If no subsequent request is received in this length of time, Apache completes the processing of the current request for that client and closes the connection.

MaxKeepAliveRequests   Limits the number of requests allowed per persistent connection. By default the value is set to 100, which should be a sufficient value for all sites:

```
MaxKeepAliveRequests 100
```

If the number is set to 0, unlimited requests will be accepted over a single request. This is something you should never do, however. It opens your Apache server to a form of denial-of-service attack in which a malicious client opens, but doesn't close, a large number of persistent HTTP connections.

LimitRequestBody   Sets a limit, in bytes, to the size of an HTTP request body. You can set the value to any number from 0 (the default, which means "unlimited") up to 2,147,483,647 bytes (2GB). Use this directive to set a limit on the size of data sent by a client in a POST or PUT HTTP request. This directive is valid in a directory context. To set the value to 10KB for CGI scripts that receive client uploads, use this:

```
<Location /cgi-bin/*>
LimitRequestBody 10240
</Location>
```

NOTE   In Linux 2.4, which should be available shortly after this book is published, the 2GB limit for an HTTP request body will be eliminated.

LimitRequestFields   Allows the Apache administrator to limit the number of HTTP headers that can appear in a single client request. The default value is 100, which well exceeds the typical number of headers in a request (rarely over 20). This directive is rarely needed, but many administrators choose to set a lower limit than the default value to provide some measure of protection against malformed requests using a directive like this:

```
LimitRequestFields 40
```

LimitRequestFieldSize   Limits the size (in bytes) of all HTTP request headers. Here again, the value rarely needs to be changed from its compiled-in default of 8190 bytes. If you wish to reduce or increase this limit, however, you can do so with a directive like this:

```
LimitRequestFieldSize 1000
```

To increase the value beyond 8190 bytes, it is necessary to modify the value of DEFAULT_LIMIT_REQUEST_FIELDSIZE in *Apache_source*/include/httpd.h, and recompile the Apache kernel.

LimitRequestLine   Limits the allowable size (in bytes) of all HTTP request lines. The request line consists of the HTTP method, the URI, and optionally the protocol version. This value rarely needs to be changed from its compiled-in default of 8190 bytes. To decrease it, use a directive like this:

```
LimitRequestLine 500
```

To increase the value beyond 8190 bytes, you'll need to modify the value of DEFAULT_LIMIT_REQUEST_LINE in *Apache_source*/include/httpd.h and recompile the Apache kernel.

Listing 13.2 is a portion of an httpd.conf file for controlling the number and size of client connections.

Listing 13.2   Controlling Client Connections

```
MaxClients 512
ListenBacklog 1000
Timeout 45
SendBufferSize
KeepAlive on
KeepAliveTimeout 30
MaxKeepAliveRequests 50
LimitRequestBody 10000
LimitRequestFields 40
LimitRequestFieldSize
LimitRequestLine 1000
```

First, the MaxClients 512 directive increases the maximum number of simultaneous httpd processes from the default of 256. Next, the ListenBacklog 1000 directive increases the number of TCP connections that will be waiting for an available httpd process from its default of 511, again to prevent connections from being rejected on our heavily loaded server.

We also decrease the length of time that our server will wait for a response from each client before closing the connection from the default of 300 seconds (5 minutes) to 45 seconds.

The SendBufferSize directive is usually changed only when the Apache server will be communicating over high-latency links (like intercontinental transmission lines), and it isn't changed in this example.

The KeepAlive on directive enables HTTP/1.1 persistent connections, and the KeepAliveTimeout 30 directive doubles the default value of 15 seconds for the maximum time that Apache will wait for a second request from a client with an open persistent connection. MaxKeepAliveRequests 50 sets a limit on the number of requests that will be permitted from a client on a single persistent connection, reduced by half from its default value of 100.

On this server we are not accepting uploads from clients (in the form of PUT requests), so the LimitRequestBody 10000 directive limits the byte size of HTTP requests. The LimitRequestsFields 40 directive then greatly reduces the number of headers that can be received in a single HTTP request; the default setting of 8190 is far too many for a legitimate request. Again, we do this to reduce the potential for abuse of the server. With the LimitRequestFieldSize directive, we accept the (quite sane) default limit of 8190 bytes on the size of a single HTTP request header. Finally, the LimitRequestLine 1000 directive reduces the default limit of 8190 characters on the length of a single request line. The default is probably larger than will ever be necessary, but not unreasonably so; this line is included mainly for the purpose of illustration.

Using Apache as a Proxy Server

So far in this chapter you've seen how to tune Apache's performance by adjusting the values of various parameters related to server processes and client connections; and you've seen that the benefits of that approach are limited, because Apache's default values for these parameters are already well optimized for performance.

Thanks to its mod_proxy module, Apache can also be used as a proxy server, a strategy that can provide significant performance benefits on intranet or LAN installations and enhance security on all Apache servers. The remainder of this chapter examines the different approaches to proxying and the tools that Apache's mod_proxy module provides.

How Proxies Work

The most common form of proxy server is a *forwarding proxy server,* illustrated in Figure 13.1. Notice that the server designated as the proxy server sits outside the requesting network's firewall and responds to requests from internal hosts for resources on the Internet. The proxy server forwards these requests to the remote Internet host, often because (for security reasons) the originator of the request does not have direct access to the Internet. The request is not literally forwarded; the proxy server reissues it with a new IP header. The remote server responds directly to the proxy server and is unaware that the request originated on another system. When the proxy server receives the response, it replaces the IP header with a new header, which has the address of the internal host that originated the proxy request.

Most proxy servers are capable of performing this task for a variety of application protocols. The protocols that are most often proxied are HTTP (Web connections), Secure HTTP (HTTPS), and the File Transfer Protocol (FTP). While the original purpose of using proxy servers was to provide Internet access through a network firewall, that role has changed significantly. Today, as more Web servers are used in intranets, the importance of a proxy server is increasingly with *caching* HTTP requests. A proxy server configured for HTTP caching saves a copy of each Web object (pages, images, files) that it retrieves on behalf of clients. These saved copies of Web objects are written to disk storage on the proxy server. If a subsequent request for a cached Web object is received (and the object's expiration time has not passed), the proxy server sends the cached object, rather than making a new request of the remote host from which it was originally obtained. From the requester's point of view, this greatly speeds the retrieval of the resource.

Figure 13.1   A forwarding proxy server

HTTP caching results in two forms of performance improvement for intranets. First, whenever a Web object is served from cache, rather than by making an HTTP request of a remote host, there is a significant reduction in the *latency* of the request. In other words, the requester gets the object much faster when it comes from cached data. This has the effect of making the network appear much faster than it actually is. The second improvement that is realized from HTTP caching is reduced bandwidth usage. Every request that can be served from cached data means less traffic on the Internet connection. Of course, both benefits depend on the assumption that in a given network, a high percentage of Web traffic will go to a relatively small number of sites whose content does not expire too frequently.

Most Web browser software is capable of caching copies of retrieved documents. For resources that rarely change and are frequently reused (like inline image and icons), retrieval from cache storage rather than from the remote server can significantly reduce the amount of time required to load a Web page. A browser-based cache is often referred to as a *private cache*. When the cache resides on a proxy server that is capable of serving locally stored copies of documents to a number of client browsers, it is called a *shared cache*. On my local network, I set up `mod_proxy` on my Apache server and configured all my browsers to retrieve HTTP and FTP documents through it. Since I have only a few client workstations, I did not expect shared caching to significantly affect the way my browsers performed. I was very surprised, particularly when requesting documents with a large number of embedded images, to discover that mod_proxy caching on my Apache server is significantly faster than the browser cache on my client workstations. While this seems implausible, and I can't guarantee you'll have the same experience, I do recommend mod_proxy for shared Web caching even on a small local LAN with a shared Internet connection. It seems to work nearly as well on a small scale as it does on a large one.

Reverse Proxying

As illustrated in Figure 13.2, proxy servers can also be configured to work in the opposite direction. A *reverse proxy* server sits outside the serving network's firewall and is configured to respond to requests from HTTP clients on the Internet for resources that reside on internal Web servers. The proxy server in this scheme takes these external requests and forwards them to the correct internal server. The reverse proxy server here primarily plays a security role, providing access to internal data providers that are not directly accessible from the outside world. Caching of these resources is generally a secondary concern when a reverse proxy is used.

Figure 13.2 A reverse proxy server

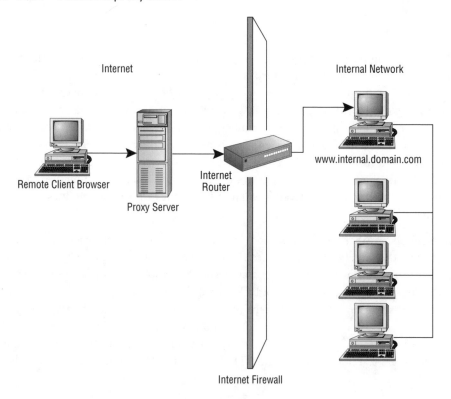

In the following sections I'll show how to set up mod_proxy as a forward and reverse proxy. Keep in mind that a single proxy server can simultaneously serve in both roles. You do not have to select one role to the exclusion of the other.

The mod_proxy Module

Apache's tool for implementing a proxy/cache is the mod_proxy module. It implements proxying capability for HTTP/0.9, HTTP/1.0, and FTP. Using the CONNECT protocol, which supports TCP port 443 for SSL, and TCP port 563 for Snews by default, the module can also be configured to connect to other proxy modules for these and other protocols.

Setting Up a Forward Proxy

To use mod_proxy as a forward proxy, you just need to ensure that the module is either statically linked into the Apache kernel or compiled as a DSO module and dynamically loaded at runtime.

> **TIP** You can verify the availability of this or any other module by running httpd -l, or via the URL /server-info, if you have that enabled capability as described in Chapter 11.

If you used the --enable-shared=most switch when running the Apache configure script, you'll find that the module is compiled as libproxy.so (not mod_proxy.so). Ensure that your httpd.conf file contains the directives necessary to load and enable the module

```
LoadModule proxy_module        libexec/libproxy.so
AddModule mod_proxy.c
```

A properly installed mod_proxy will add a number of directives to your httpd.conf file, in a section clearly labeled *Proxy server directives*. Like all optional directives, they are initially commented out, so you'll need to uncomment them. While you will probably not need to change any of these directives to use Apache as a proxy server, this chapter describes all of them, and you should understand what each one does. The most important directive you'll need to enable in httpd.conf is this:

```
ProxyRequests on
```

Once this forward proxying is enabled, the Apache server will respond to requests for resources on the server by sending them directly, as usual. But it will proxy requests for all other resources by attempting to retrieve the resource from the server named in the URL, and returning the results to the requesting client. In networks where a firewall blocks internal hosts from direct access to the Internet, this is the only way that these hosts can retrieve Web resources from the Internet.

While it is perfectly okay to let your main Apache server proxy requests for documents that it cannot serve directly from its own local stores, I usually prefer to set up a virtual host, listening on a TCP port other than the main server's default of port 80, to handle proxy requests. My Apache httpd.conf file contains this <VirtualHost> container:

```
<VirtualHost 192.168.1.1:8080>
  ServerName jackal.hiwaay.net
  ProxyRequests on
</VirtualHost>
```

This container ensures that only requests received on TCP port 8080 are proxied. It's only a convention, but that is the TCP port proxy servers commonly use, and you'll often see that port used in documentation on configuring proxy clients. Note that my httpd.conf must also contain a Listen 8080 directive (outside the virtual host container) to ensure that Apache accepts connections on that port.

The ProxyRequests directive is used to halt proxy services as follows (this is the default setting for the directive):

```
ProxyRequests off
```

I doubt you'll ever have an occasion to specify this directive.

Mirroring Remote Sites

One common use of a proxy server is to mirror remote Web sites, making them appear to be local. The ProxyPass directive is used to map remote Web URLs to a URL that would ordinarily point to a resource on the local server.

For example, the following directive can be used to make documentation from the Linux Documentation Project's main site appear to be local to my server (and once a resource has been retrieved by the proxy, and held in cache, it will be served as a local resource):

```
ProxyPass /LinuxDocs/ http://www.linuxdoc.org/
```

Here, whenever my proxy server receives a request from a client trying to connect to http://jackal.hiwaay.net/LinuxDocs/, the request is automatically and invisibly referred to linuxdoc.org.

Setting Up a Reverse Proxy

You can also use mod_proxy to configure your Apache server as a reverse proxy, which gives remote clients access to resources on your internal servers without exposing those servers to direct connections from the outside. Indeed, in most situations where a proxy server is used in this manner, an Internet firewall renders servers totally invisible and completely inaccessible from the outside world.

As with forward proxying, the first step to setting up a reverse proxy server is to ensure that mod_proxy is either compiled into Apache or loaded as a DSO module. And just as you do for a forward proxy server, enable proxy services with this directive:

```
ProxyRequests On
```

Some special considerations are necessary to ensure reverse proxy operation, however. First, the goal is to provide outside clients with transparent access to resources on your internal servers, without connecting to those servers directly. These remote clients will see only one server, your proxy server, and will connect only to that system. This server only appears to serve all the resources the client requests. To perform this feat of magic, some means is necessary to map each requested URL received from remote clients by the proxy server to a URL on an internal server. This is provided by the ProxyPass directive, and you will need one to map each request into a URL that can be used to request the resource from an internal server. Here's an example that maps requests to /CPAN on the proxy server to a server named archive.fubar.com, and all imbedded images are retrieved from a second server, rascal.fubar.com:

```
ProxyPass /CPAN/ http://archive.fubar.com/CPAN/
ProxyPass /images/ httpd://rascal.fubar.com/images/
```

The second configuration that's necessary for reverse proxy use is to include a ProxyPassReverse directive. Because the internal server that eventually answers a request from a remote host will place its own hostname in the Location header of redirect requests sent to the client, the Apache reverse proxy server needs to replace this hostname with its own; that's what the ProxyPassReverse directive does. This ensures that redirected requests from an internal Web server are adjusted so that the proxy server receives them.

To make things really convenient, the ProxyPassReverse directive takes exactly the same arguments as the ProxyPass directive, and you can easily create a matching ProxyPassReverse directive for each ProxyPass directive.

```
ProxyPassReverse /CPAN/ http://archive.fubar.com/CPAN/
ProxyPassReverse /images/ httpd://rascal.fubar.com/images/
```

Configuring a Browser for Your Proxy

Once you have an Apache server configured with mod_proxy to act as a (forward) proxy server for HTTP (and FTP) requests, you only need to configure your client browsers to make requests of this server, rather than trying to connect to the desired resource directly.

When a browser is configured to use a proxy server, it will connect to that server, and make a request for that server to act as a proxy in retrieving the desired resource from the remote server. Every browser has its own procedure for configuring it to use one or more proxy servers. The procedure I describe is for Netscape Communicator/Navigator and serves only to illustrate the basic steps required.

In Communicator, select Preferences from the Edit menu and, in the Preferences window, expand the Advanced node in the command tree, and click Proxies. The window will now look like Figure 13.3.

Figure 13.3 Begin configuring a Netscape Communicator/Navigator browser by opening the Preferences window.

Make sure Manual Proxy Configuration is enabled and click the View button. In the dialog box that appears (Figure 13.4), enter the IP address (or hostname) of your proxy server for each protocol you intend to proxy (the Security option means SSL). In Figure 13.4, I've configured my browser to connect to TCP port 8080 on my Apache server for HTTP and FTP requests. That TCP port number is commonly used by proxy servers, but it is arbitrary. In fact, I usually configure my Apache server to proxy requests received on the standard HTTP port (80). The module will proxy only those requests that it cannot satisfy directly (in other words, only remote resources).

Figure 13.4   Manual proxy configuration in Netscape

Now that Netscape is configured to use a proxy to retrieve resources, when you request a document with a URL like this:

```
http://www.apache.org
```

the browser will connect to TCP port 8080 on the proxy server, and issue a request that looks like this:

```
proxy://www.apache.org
```

This tells the server to fulfill the request by proxy.

If you have many client browsers behind a firewall that need to be set up to use a proxy server, consider distributing these instructions to your users. Setting up Web browsers to use a proxy server is a straightforward process that administrators shouldn't be burdened with performing for every client workstation.

Controlling Resource Expiration

A crucial element of caching is the concept of document or resource expiration. Web users don't just want their requests served immediately; they want to be sure they have retrieved the most current version of the resource. A proxy server that implements a cache needs some way to determine whether it can safely return the copy of a given resource it has already cached or needs to retrieve a newer one. That is the role of the

Maintaining a Healthy Server

PART 4

HTTP `Expires` header, the most important tool for controlling caching server behavior. This is the basic header sent by a server with each HTTP response to control how that document should be treated by all caching mechanisms (not only proxy server shared caches, but browser-based private caches as well). This header declares a date and time, expressed in Greenwich Mean Time (GMT), after which the document can no longer be considered valid and should not be served from cache without first *validating* the document with the server from which it was originally retrieved.

To validate a document, the proxy server checks with the origin server to see if the document has changed in any respect since it was last retrieved and stored to cache. The proxy server does not retrieve a new copy of the document unless the origin server indicates that the modification time of the original document is later than the timestamp on the copy in cache. If the document has been modified since it was cached, a new copy is requested, and the old cached copy is deleted.

The `mod_expires` module gives the Apache administrator control over the `Expires` header, and you should make certain this module is enabled on your Apache server. It is probably a part of your standard Apache build, especially if you ran Apache's configure script with the `–enable-shared=most` option. The module is simple to use, supplying only three directives for controlling `Expires` headers: `ExpiresActive`, `ExpiresDefault`, and `ExpiresByType`.

NOTE In the HTTP/1.1 protocol, the functionality of the `Expires` header has been superseded by the Cache-Control header (which is discussed in "HTTP/1.1 Support for Caching" later in this chapter). However, this directive has not been fully incorporated in all Web caching engines (proxy servers and browsers). Apache's mod_proxy, for example, is not even aware of the Cache-Control header. Until the use of this directive becomes more widespread, the `Expires` directive remains the predominant mechanism for controlling Web resource caching. Apache administrators can use both headers to increase the odds that caching proxies will properly handle expiration dates associated with resources.

Enabling the `Expires` Header

The `ExpiresActive` directive, which can take only the values on and off, enables the generation of `Expires` headers for the documents in its scope (for example, if you place this directive in an `.htaccess` file, `Expires` header generation is enabled only for the directory that contains that file).

```
ExpiresActive on
```

Setting a Default Expires Value

The ExpiresDefault directive specifies a time offset for generating the default value of the Expires header for all documents affected by the directive. You can apply the ExpiresDefault directive in several different <Directory> containers or .htaccess files to specify different values for different scopes. The time value that will be generated for a document can be relative either to the last modification time of the file or to the time of the client's last access to it. The time intervals can be expressed in two different formats. One is more economical but more cryptic, and the other is a little more verbose but more easily understood. In the first format, the time is always expressed in seconds and prefixed with an A if it's relative to the last access or with an M if relative to modification. In this example, we set the default expiration to one week (604,800 seconds) after the browser's last access:

```
ExpiresActive on
ExpiresDefault A604800
```

In the easier-to-use alternate form, we express the time in terms of years, months, weeks, days, hours, minutes and seconds, relative to either access or last modification times. Rewriting the example in this syntax gives us the following equivalent set of directives:

```
ExpiresActive on
ExpiresDefault access plus 1 week
```

After enabling the Expires header with the previous directives, I got the following headers placed on the response from my server:

```
HTTP/1.1 200 OK
Date: Tue, 30 May 2000 16:20:00 GMT
Server: Apache/1.3.12 (Unix)
Cache-Control: max-age=604800
Expires: Tue, 06 Jun 2000 16:20:00 GMT
Last-Modified: Wed, 24 May 2000 13:45:21 GMT
ETag: "34062-f66-392bdcf1"
Accept-Ranges: bytes
Content-Length: 3942
Connection: close
Content-Type: text/html
```

Note that the time given in the Expires header is exactly one week after the date of access. Notice also that mod_expires has created a Cache-Control header, stating that under no circumstances should this document be served from any cache when it has been there for more than 604,800 seconds (one week). All HTTP/1.1-compliant browsers and proxy servers are required to honor this directive from the server. While mod_expires appears to be somewhat compliant with HTTP/1.1, I looked at the source code and found that it supports only the max-age directive (one of 19 directives that HTTP/1.1 defines for the Cache-Control header). Generating this header is a nice "extra" from mod_expires, but you will not be able to make further use of the Cache-Control header with this module (or with mod_proxy, which has no support yet for the Cache-Control header). Until HTTP/1.1 becomes more widely used, the Expires header is the tool you will manipulate and use to control the caching of documents served from Apache.

Expires Headers for a Specific MIME Type

The ExpiresByType directive specifies the value of the Expires header for a specific MIME type (e.g. text/html). Again, the time value that will be generated can be relative either to the last modification time of the disk file or to the time of the client's access. Here's an example in which the Expires: header generated for documents of type text/html will be relative to the last modification time of the document, but relative to the client's access time for inline images:

```
ExpiresActive on
ExpiresByType text/html M604800
ExpiresByType image/gif A2592000
```

Rewriting the example in the alternate (but equivalent) syntax yields:

```
ExpiresActive on
ExpiresByType text/html modification plus 1 week
ExpiresByType image/gif access plus 1 month
```

This distinction based on type would make sense for sites in which graphic images are part of the site's design or decoration (such as a corporate logo) and presumably change much less frequently than the site's text. Of course, for art that's closely related to the site's text content, you would not do this.

Controlling the Proxy Engine

The mod_proxy module contains a number of directives that basically fit into either of two categories: those that control the module's proxy engine in receiving resources on the behalf of clients, and those that control the caching of resources already retrieved and stored by the proxy engine. This section discusses the first group; I've already shown two of these, ProxyPass and ProxyPassReverse. The next section, "Controlling the Proxy Cache," covers this second category of directives.

Increasing Throughput of Proxied Requests

Although mod_proxy rarely requires performance tuning, there is one directive that is specifically designed to increase request throughput. The ProxyReceiveBufferSize allows the administrator to set a buffer size for HTTP and FTP requests. The directive takes one argument, the desired buffer size in bytes, which must be greater than 512:

```
ProxyReceiveBufferSize 4096
```

In Linux, I prefer to explicitly set the buffer size to 0, which indicates that the system's default buffer size is used. The Linux default buffer size of 64KB is already set to the maximum value that the operating system will allow.

Setting a Default Proxy Domain

In an intranet, you may want users to be able to omit your domain name from the URL when requesting resources from internal servers. To do this, you can use the ProxyDomain directive to specify a default domain to which the Apache proxy server belongs. This works just like the default domain name defined for the Linux server itself. If a request that omits the host's domain name is received to be proxied, the proxy server appends the domain defined by ProxyDomain before attempting to fulfill the request.

To illustrate, if the following ProxyDomain directive was in effect:

```
ProxyDomain intranet.corporate.com
```

the proxy server would attempt to proxy a request for:

```
http://somehost/docs/index.html
```

by retrieving a resource from:

```
http://somehost.intranet.corporate.com/docs/index.html
```

Forwarding Proxy Requests

Often, it is desirable to configure a proxy server to redirect a part of its workload to other proxy servers. This is one way to distribute the tasks of resource retrieval and caching among several proxy servers. Use the ProxyRemote directive to define proxies to which the server will send certain requests instead of trying to retrieve the resource directly. Here's an example of how this might be used:

```
ProxyRemote http://www.thissite.org/
    http://proxy.corporate.com
```

Here, whenever my local Apache server, acting as a proxy, receives a request destined for www.thissite.org, it will automatically refer the request to a corporate proxy server. The corporate proxy not only caches responses from Internet Web sites, it is also the only way to retrieve Web resources through the corporate firewall, so it accomplishes two goals: enhanced security for the corporate intranet and more efficient Web retrieval.

Because mod_proxy can only communicate using HTTP, this directive will not support any other protocol for communication with the remote server. You can, however, refer requests received with other protocols, if you specify only HTTP in the remote URL, as in:

```
ProxyRemote ftp http://ftpproxy.mydomain.com:8080
```

Here, any attempt to proxy an FTP request is referred to an FTP proxy server (which can't be Apache running mod_proxy, of course, and is probably a dedicated proxy server). Note that HTTP is used to communicate with this remote proxy server. The original FTP request is encapsulated in HTTP for this request, which is probably not the most efficient technique. In these cases, it is usually better if the client browsers are configured with separate proxies for the HTTP and FTP protocols.

The special character * means "all requests," as in the following example, where all requests to this server are sent through a remote proxy:

```
ProxyRemote * http://proxy.mydomain.com
```

The NoProxy directive, which has a misleading name, is used to turn off ProxyRemote behavior for specific hostnames, domains, subnets and individual IP addresses. For example:

```
ProxyRemote * http://proxy.mydomain.com
NoProxy 192.168.1 www.corporate.com
```

In this case, we've used ProxyRemote to specify that all requests received should be forwarded to a remote proxy. Then the NoProxy directive is used to identify all sites on the local subnet and one specific Web site as exclusions from this rule. The proxy server handles requests received for these sites directly, all others being forwarding to the remote proxy to be served.

Blocking Proxy Requests

It is sometimes necessary to block certain remote sites from being accessed by a proxy server or, alternatively, to block certain clients from using the proxy server. The ProxyBlock directive accomplishes the first task. Provided with a list of words, hostnames, or domain names, this directive blocks all proxy requests for URLs containing these keywords and site names:

```
ProxyBlock sexsirens.com gambling
```

In the above example, our proxy would refuse to honor requests for anything from the site sexsirens.com (a fictitious domain, at least when I wrote this), or any URL that contains the string *gambling*. This is not really the best way to block a large number of sites, but it can come in handy if your proxy server is your LAN's only HTTP access to the Internet, and you need to block access to a few sites.

Interestingly, if a hostname is specified that can be resolved to an IP address when Apache starts, this IP address is cached, so that users can't bypass your ProxyBlock by using the blocked site's IP address instead of its hostname.

While ProxyBlock is useful in blocking specific remote sites from your proxy clients, it cannot be used to prevent specific clients from using the proxy server. To do that, you can instead take advantage of the fact that when a proxy client is configured to request HTTP resources through a proxy server, the URL it submits begins with the word proxy://, rather than with http://. Therefore, you can use a <Directory> section like the following to prohibit or allow use of the proxy by specific clients:

```
<Directory proxy:*>
  Order deny,allow
  Deny from all
  Allow from 192.168.1
</Directory>
```

In this case, I am permitting use of my proxy server only from hosts connected to my local subnet (198.168.1).

Controlling the Proxy Cache

The second category of mod_proxy directives controls the caching of resources that have already been retrieved and stored by the proxy engine.

CacheRoot   Sets the name of the directory to contain cached files. This directive is mandatory for caching, but if it does not exist, Apache won't generate an error; it simply won't do any caching. The value on my server is:

```
CacheRoot /usr/local/apache/proxy
```

CacheSize   Sets the maximum size of the cache (expressed in kilobytes). The cache can exceed this value but will be cut back to this size during a regular cleanup phase (the frequency of which you set with the CacheGcInterval directive). The default value of this parameter is a ridiculously small 5KB. On my server, I set my cache size to 40MB:

```
CacheSize 40960
```

CacheGcInterval   Sets the interval (in hours) between cache size checks and garbage collection. During the garbage collection phase, the cache is purged of its oldest entries until it occupies less disk space than specified in the CacheSize directive. Beware: if you do not specify this directive, the garbage collection task will never run, and your cache will grow indefinitely. My server is set to perform this cleanup every 90 minutes:

```
CacheGcInterval 1.5
```

`CacheDefaultExpire`   If a resource is retrieved that does not have an expiry time, this value (in hours) is used. The default value is a very short one hour. On my server, I increased this to 48 hours:

```
CacheDefaultExpire 48
```

`CacheMaxExpire`   Sets a maximum time for which cached resources are served without being validated by the origin server. This directive specifies the absolute maximum time that a cached document will be considered valid. This restriction applies even if the origin server specified a later expiry date for the resource or if `CacheDefaultExpire` is set to an even larger time interval. The default is 24 hours, which I extended on my server to three days (or 72 hours):

```
CacheMaxExpire 72
```

`CacheLastModifiedFactor`   Specifies a factor used to estimate an expiry date for a document that was delivered without one. The following formula is used to estimate the expiry period, which is always relative to the time of the last modification of the document:

expiry-period = time since last modification × *factor*

If the factor were set to 0.1 (the default value, and the one I use on my server) this essentially resolves to an expiry period equal to one-tenth the time elapsed since the document was last modified. In other words, if a received document was last modified 10 days ago, compute an expiry date based on one-tenth this time interval (or one day from the date of receipt).

`CacheDirLevels`   Sets the number of subdirectory levels that can be used to store the cache. For extremely large caches, a larger number of directories can be used to speed searching the cache. It is rarely necessary to change this directive, however, from its default value of 3.

`CacheDirLength`   Sets the number of characters in proxy cache subdirectory names. This leads to subdirectories of the cache (taken from letters in the URL used to retrieve resources) that look like:

```
/usr/local/apache/proxy/A/n/w
```

I have never found it necessary to change this from its default value of 1.

`CacheForceCompletion`   Sets a percentage value that is used to determine if a document being retrieved to cache should be completely downloaded and cached if the HTTP transfer is aborted. For example, if this value is set to 90 (the default) and the user aborts the retrieval while the document is still only 80 percent transferred, the portion already received will be discarded and the document will not be cached. But if the transfer is 91 percent complete when aborted, the document will be completely retrieved and cached. I set the value of this directive to 75 percent on my server:

```
CacheForceCompletion 75
```

NoCache   Specifies a list of keywords, hostnames, and/or domains from which documents retrieved are never saved in cache. You might use this, for example, to ensure that documents retrieved from certain Web sites are always retrieved fresh and never cached, such as a page for currency exchange rates that your financial analysts consult many times a day:

```
NoCache xchange.corporate.net
```

Proxying other Protocols

The CONNECT method is not really defined by the HTTP specification but is reserved in that specification as an alternate method to be implemented by proxy servers. It is an HTTP request method (like GET or PUT) that allows connections via other protocols to be tunneled for security through a proxy server to a remote server. The AllowConnect directive specifies a list of port numbers through which clients using the proxy CONNECT method can connect to your Apache server. A CONNECT request is issued by a client that wishes to connect to a remote server via some protocol other than HTTP or FTP. CONNECT requests are commonly issued by SSL browsers, which connect to the proxy server using a URL that begins with https:// in order to connect using HTTP proxy tunneling to some remote server—for example, when the user of an e-commerce site clicks a link that initiates a secure transaction. The proxy server establishes the connection to the remote server, and it maintains this connection (using the client's desired CONNECT protocol), throughout the entire session. All traffic received by the proxy server from the remote is tunneled to the client, which also maintains a connection to the proxy server for the entire session.

Two of the most common protocols tunneled in this fashion are provided in the default configuration: TCP port 443, which is SSL; and TCP port 563, which is Snews. To override this default and specify telnet (TCP port 23) as an additional CONNECT protocol instead of Snews, use the directive as follows:

```
AllowConnect 443 23
```

A web browser that is configured to use a proxy server for protocols other than HTTP or FTP (for example, the Telnet protocol) will connect to that proxy server and issue a

CONNECT request. For example, a client can establish an ordinary HTTP connection to the proxy server and issue a CONNECT command that looks like the following:

```
CONNECT remotehost.com:23 HTTP/1.0
```

The proxy server will establish a connection to remotehost.com on its TCP port 23 (a telnet daemon or server will accept the connection) and this connection will be tunneled to the requesting client using HTTP.

HTTP/1.1 Support for Caching

The HTTP/1.1 protocol significantly extends support for proxy caching through the addition of two new headers (HTTP/1.1 is documented in RFC 2616). Of these, the only new header that is implemented in Apache mod_proxy (which is still considered an HTTP/1.0 compliant proxy server) is the Via header, discussed in the next section. Most of the enhanced support for caching in HTTP/1.1, however, is in the new Cache-Control header, which is not implemented in the current version of mod_proxy. This new HTTP response header is actually a container for 19 directives to caching servers in the response chain (which may be proxy servers or even a caching Web browser). According to the HTTP/1.1 specification, these directives must be obeyed by all caching mechanisms that call themselves HTTP/1.1-compliant, and they must be passed through to all caching mechanisms further downstream (closer to the requesting client).

The directives that can be specified in the Cache-Control header fall into four categories, all defining in different ways what can be cached. There are directives that determine which HTTP responses can be cached, directives that specify what types of resources can be cached, directives to control the expiration of resources (which do the work of HTTP/1.0's Expires header), and directives that control revalidation and reloading of cached resources. A typical Cache-Control header, using two of the directives defined in RFC 2616, might be this:

```
Cache-Control: max-age=3600
```

This header instructs all proxy servers that cache copies of this document to consider the cached copy *stale* after 6 hours (3600 seconds). After that, whenever the server receives a new request for a resource the proxy server must check the server for a fresh copy of the document, and if it finds one, download it to replace the one in cache. Another common use of the Cache-Control header is shown below:

```
Cache-Control: must-revalidate
```

This header instructs cache servers to always connect to the server and check for a fresh copy of the cached documents before serving it to the requesting client. The proxy server still saves time by not downloading the document from the server if validation determines that the cached copy is still fresh.

Since mod_proxy, in its current state, does not support the HTTP/1.1 Cache-Control header, I will simply mention several of the most interesting of the directives it implements. These will, eventually, become the directives used to control HTTP caching server behavior.

public   Marks the HTTP response message as cacheable, even if it normally would not be. For instance, normal cache server behavior is to never cache responses that require username/password authentication. This directive marks those responses as cacheable.

private   Indicates that the response message is intended for a single user (hence, the name of the directive) and must never be cached by a shared cache (one used by more than one user), though it can be cached by a browser.

no-cache   Forces cache engines (both proxy server and browser) to always validate the request with the origin server before releasing a cached copy. Note that the requester may still receive a cached copy of the requested resource, but that copy will have been validated by the origin server (to ensure either proper authentication or freshness of the cached date).

max-age=[n]   Specifies the maximum amount of time (in seconds) that an object will be considered fresh.

s-maxage=[n]   Like max-age, but only applies to shared (proxy server) caches, not to browser caches.

max-stale   This directive can be placed in a Cache-Control header by a client browser, and it indicates to cache engines that the client is willing to accept responses that have exceeded their expiration times. An origin server can override this directive with the must-revalidate directive.

must-revalidate   Tells cache engines that they must validate all subsequent requests for this requested object with the origin server. This is to prevent a caching server from being configured to ignore the server's instructions on expiration intervals. This directive relies on all HTTP/1.1-compliant caching servers adhering to the rule that they must obey all Cache-Control directives.

proxy-revalidate   Like must-revalidate, but applies only to proxy caches (not browser caches).

Using HTTP/1.1 Caching with Apache

I've mentioned eight of the directives that can be used with the HTTP/1.1 Cache-Control header. These are the most useful, and should serve to give you some idea of the usefulness

Maintaining a
Healthy Server

PART 4

of this method of caching control when it does become widely available. Until mod_proxy (or a replacement module) fully implements HTTP/1.1 caching control, you can still manually add the header to your Apache responses, using the Header directive. This directive is provided by a standard module, mod_header, which is compiled into Apache by default. The Header directive is the only directive supplied by mod-header, and it implements the only function of the module, which is to allow the Apache administrator to customize the HTTP response headers by adding an arbitrary header or removing standard headers.

The Header directive is valid in nearly every possible context, so it can apply to a specific directory, to all files of a specific MIME type, or to specific files by name. The following directive, for example, appends the specified Client-Control header to all response messages to which the directive applies:

```
Header append "Client-Control: max-age=3600, must-revalidate"
```

The Via Header

Although mod_proxy is described as implementing an HTTP/1.0-compliant caching proxy server, it does include support for one new header from the HTTP/1.1 specification. The Via HTTP header is used to track the flow of a response through a chain of proxy servers and gateways, providing a record of all parties in the request chain. Its purpose is to identify the flow of a request, avoiding possible loops, and to identify the supported protocol of all proxies in the chain. According to the HTTP/1.1 specification, all HTTP/1.1-compliant proxy servers must attach a Via header that indicates the server's identity (and optionally a comment indicating that server's software revision levels).

I'm sure you've seen e-mail messages in which the message headers indicate all the mail servers that have handled the message (using the Simple Mail Transport Protocol Received header). The HTTP Via header is designed to work similarly to that, providing some record of all the servers that have had a hand in delivering an HTTP resource.

Apache's mod_proxy support for the Via header is minimal, with one directive, ProxyVia, taking one of the following four values:

off   The default setting for ProxyVia, this indicates that no Via header will be added to any HTTP response handled by mod_proxy. Since mod_proxy doesn't aspire to be an HTTP/1.1 proxy, it does not have to adhere to that specifications requirement that all proxy servers append a Via header.

on   Adds a Via header that identifies the current server to every request handled by mod_proxy.

full   Generates a Via header that includes an optional comment field displaying the Apache server version.

`block`   Removes all `Via` headers from requests passed through `mod_proxy`. Actually, this is something of a no-no, as it violates a requirement of the HTTP/1.1 specification that these headers be passed through all proxy servers unaltered. It's not illegal yet, but it is probably bad behavior. Don't use `ProxyVia block`.

Squid: A Proxy Server for Linux

Apache, with the `mod_proxy` module, is quite adequate for most site administrators. Its caching engine is quite efficient and robust. In spite of its ability to tunnel other protocols, `mod_proxy` is primarily an HTTP proxy server. Sites that find it necessary to proxy other protocols should consider the use of a dedicated proxy server specifically designed to handle simultaneous requests from multiple clients and high loads. Although many commercial proxy servers are available, there is an open-source alternative that has an excellent reputation among its users on Linux platforms.

If a full-featured, dedicated proxy server is what you need, be sure to evaluate Squid, an open-source solution, freely available from `www.squid-cache.org`. Squid proxies not only HTTP but FTP, WAIS, Gopher, and SSL.

kHTTPd: An Apache Accelerator

A recent development in serving Web pages from Linux is an open-source project called kHTTPd (`www.fenrus.demon.nl`). kHTTPd is designed to serve static Web resources (including embedded image files) as fast as physically possible from a Linux server, and it runs from within the Linux kernel as a device driver. kHTTPd is designed solely to respond to requests for static resources, and that is just about all it does. kHTTPd has an extremely limited (almost nonexistent) feature set and does not support any of the Apache features discussed in this book (virtual hosts, customizable logging, user authentication, programming, and so on). Support for HTTP/1.1 persistent connections (in which the Web server responds to more than a single HTTP request through a single TCP connection) is currently available as a test patch for kHTTPd and should be included in the base release as soon as it is thoroughly tested.

kHTTPd is not designed to be used as an alternative to a full-featured, highly configurable Web server like Apache. Instead, kHTTPd runs in addition to, and augments, a regular Web server, passing that server any request that it cannot fulfill. Apache is unaware of kHTTPd and receives the TCP connection (from kHTTPd) without knowing that the connection has first been handled by kHTTPd just as it is unaware of any other device driver that handled a network datagram previously. Apache receives only requests that kHTTPd cannot process, as new incoming connections, requiring absolutely no configuration changes in Apache.

For most sites, kHTTPd greatly reduces the load on an Apache server by directly handling requests for static Web pages and images, alleviating the need for Apache to handle these requests. kHTTPd can be thought of as an accelerator for an Apache server, not as a separate Web server.

Traditionally, kHTTPd has been provided as a set of C source files that compile into a single Linux module (khttpd.o) and a set of patches to a few Linux kernel source files to make it work. To install kHTTPd, it was necessary to patch the Apache kernel source and build a new Apache kernel; not a terribly difficult process, if you're already familiar with it, but finding and applying the proper kHTTPd patches made it more difficult than it should have been.

As of version 2.3.14, the kHTTPd patches are part of the Linux kernel source. That version, and all future versions of Linux, will have kHTTPd in the kernel, though probably labeled *experimental*. If you are compiling the Linux kernel, you will need to answer two questions in the affirmative during the configuration portion of the kernel compilation.

In order to be prompted to install modules labeled as experimental, answer yes (or "y") to the following prompt:

```
Prompt for development and/or incomplete code/drivers (CONFIG_EXPERIMENTAL)
[N/y/?] y
```

The following prompt, which asks if you want to include support for *kernel httpd acceleration*, must be answered "y" to build kHTTPd support into the kernel executable. Answering "m" will build kHTTPd as a dynamically loadable kernel module (to be loaded with a utility like modprobe or insmod before use).

```
Kernel httpd acceleration (experimental) [N/m/y/?] y
```

Hopefully, by the time kHTTPd becomes a production-ready application, there will be an easy interface to configure it. Currently, however, the only way to do this is to send strings to the pseudo-filesystem /proc. Listing 13.3 shows a script that can be used to start kHTTPd. Note that each line simply echoes a string of characters to an entry in the /proc filesystem.

In this example, kHTTPd has been compiled as a kernel module and properly installed in a directory under /lib/modules that matches the current running kernel. The first line in Listing 13.3 ensures that the khttpd module is loaded into the kernel's memory and is ready to run. Subsequent lines set kHTTPd parameters, and the last line kicks the kHTTPd server into gear.

The clientport parameter is set to indicate the port on which kHTTPd will listen and serve requests for static pages. The serverport parameter identifies the port on which your Apache server will listen for requests to be passed to it by kHTTPd, presumably all requests for dynamically generated pages (either from scripts or server-parsed files like SSI or ASP pages). The documentroot parameter corresponds directly to Apache's DocumentRoot directive. The dynamic parameter is used to specify strings that, if found in a URL, identify a request for a dynamically generated resource, which are immediately passed to the Apache Web server. By default, any request that contains the string cgi-bin is automatically passed to Apache. In this example, I've added three more strings to indicate dynamic resources, each of which will occur as a filename extension for files to be parsed as PHP or SSI.

Listing 13.3   A kHTTPd Startup Script

```
modprobe khttpd
echo 8080 > /proc/sys/net/khttpd/clientport
echo 80 > /proc/sys/net/khttpd/serverport
echo /home/httpd/html > /proc/sys/net/khttpd/documentroot
echo php > /proc/sys/net/khttpd/dynamic
echo php3 > /proc/sys/net/khttpd/dynamic
echo shtml > /proc/sys/net/khttpd/dynamic
echo 1 > /proc/sys/net/khttpd/start
```

Listing 13.4 shows a typical script (or sequence of Linux commands) that might be used to shut down kHTTPd. The first line stops the server; the second prepares it for unloading, and the last line actually removes the module from the memory space of the running Linux kernel.

Listing 13.4   A kHTTPd Shutdown Script

```
echo 1 > /proc/sys/net/khttpd/stop
echo 1 > /proc/sys/net/khttpd/unload
rmmod khttpd
```

Controlling Web Robots (Spiders)

To find information on the World Wide Web, nearly everyone, at one time or another, has used one of the major Internet search engines and will recognize names like Yahoo!, Excite, AltaVista, or Google. Each of these builds its indexed databases of Web sites using *robots.* Also known as *Web crawlers* or *spiders*, these are programs designed to traverse the Internet, parsing Web pages for embedded hyperlinks that are followed to discover new sites, storing what they find in huge databases that the public can then search by topic or keyword.

Most public Web sites welcome and try to attract the attention of the major search engines that serve as indexes for the Internet. In fact, there have been books written on how to attract visitors to Web sites, and inclusion by these search engines in their indexes of Web sites is a important part of publicizing a Web site. There are times, however, when it is desirable to limit the activities of these robots. The most important reason for controlling robots is to prevent the wide publication of Web sites that are not intended for the general public, although they may be generally accessible. Another reason, less important today than in earlier years, is that Web robots can reduce the performance of a Web site by crawling it too rapidly, degrading the response time for real users.

In 1994, the major Web robot developers of the time agreed on a scheme that Web site administrators could use to identify their preferences to visiting Web robots. This scheme is informally known as the robot exclusion standard. Adherence is completely voluntary, but it has always been the accepted way to limit the activities of Internet Web robots. When I first heard about this standard, I was skeptical—it would only control well-behaved robots, not the ones I wanted to keep off my site. The truth is, though, that most search engines that crawl the Web are well behaved and will abide by the conditions you specify.

Using the robot exclusion standard is very simple. It specifies the URL /robots.txt as the location where search engines will look for your instructions about what to exclude. First of all, your Web site must be able to respond to a request for a resource at that URL. The simplest way to do this is to create a file named robots.txt under your server's DocumentRoot, although (using techniques like URL rewriting) you could also serve this file from other locations or even scripts. Well-behaved Web robots will ask for this file before taking any other action, and they will comply with the instructions you place in it.

The syntax to use in the robots.txt file is fairly simple. The file should contain one or more sections (separated by blank lines) that apply to different Web robots or groups of robots. Each section begins with one or more User-Agent: lines. These identify robots that should comply with the rules in that section. Remember that the robots themselves read robots.txt, and if one finds the section that applies to itself, it is responsible for reading the rules of that section and abiding by them. One and only one default section can exist, which contains rules that apply to all robots not matching one of the other sections. The default section begins with the line:

```
User-agent: *
```

Each section then contains a `Disallow:` rule, which identifies portions of the site that are not to be crawled and indexed by any of the robots identified in the section's `User-Agent:` lines. These portions are identified by partial URL. To specify that no robot should access any portion of your Web site, for example, you could have a `robots.txt` file that contains only the following two lines:

```
User-agent: *
Disallow: /
```

This asks all robots not to request any URL beginning with a / character, which will, of course, include all possible request URLs.

Listing 13.5 is a `robots.txt` file that first requests all robots to refrain from requesting resources using URLs that begin with the string `/private/`. The next section removes this restriction for a single robot, InfoSeek. One spider, NastySpider, is asked not to index any resource on the site.

Listing 13.5   A Sample `robots.txt` File

```
#robots.txt
User-agent: *
Disallow: /private/

User-agent: InfoSeek
Disallow:

User-agent: NastySpider
Disallow: /
```

Unfortunately, now that robot technology is being used in all sorts of end-user products, the `robots.txt` file is becoming less useful. Many spiders that crawl the Web today don't use the file, which formerly would have been considered extremely antisocial behavior. Still, it is a good idea to create the file if you want to control the behavior of robots that are indexing your public Web site, even if your file only includes a single default rule section.

Besides following the rules in all `robots.txt` files it encounters, a socially responsible robot should be registered with the Web Robots Database, at `http://info.webcrawler` `.com/mak/projects/robots/active`. The same site also provides a FAQ (`/robots/faq` `.html`) that describes the complete syntax and is very useful in determining `User-agent:` strings to use in your `robots.txt` file for various robots.

In Sum

The default configuration provided with Apache is highly optimized for performance on Linux servers. As a result, there is very little that the administrator needs to do to tweak more performance out of the server. There are several server performance directives that the administrator should understand and be able to modify. These were discussed in this chapter, with examples of their use.

Generally, however, when additional performance is required from an Apache server, it is obtained through the use of a module designed to improve the performance of the Apache engine. In Chapter 8, I mentioned mod_perl and mod_fastcgi, both of which are common methods of squeezing extra performance out of Apache running scripts through the CGI interface. In this chapter, I mentioned two more mechanisms, mod_proxy and kHTTPd, both of which are designed to optimize the performance of Apache when serving static HTML pages.

The chapter closed with a discussion of the robot exclusion standard, which is used to prevent server performance degradation caused by Web spiders attempting to index all the resources on the site. This is primarily of importance to the administrators of sites that have a very large number of Web pages publicly accessible through the Internet.

The next two chapters discuss securing an Apache server. Chapter 14 covers basic user authentication; Chapter 15 discusses one of the most widely used Apache modules, mod_ssl, which provides Secure Sockets Layer, the underpinning of most secure Web e-commerce sites on the Internet today.

14

Basic Security for Your Web Server

Security is an essential topic for administrators of both Internet-connected and internal (intranet) servers. Web servers are particularly attractive targets, it seems, for purveyors of mayhem on the Internet or (even more seriously) those who have the goal of compromising system security and stealing information such as credit card numbers. Security is a very broad topic, about which many books have been written. This chapter and the next focus on the security precautions you can easily take to protect Apache.

Most organizations that maintain Web servers usually divide them into two groups, separated by a firewall router. Internal Web servers (inside the firewall) are those intended for access only by the organization's internal hosts, and external servers are those outside the firewall, exposed to access from the Internet. The most certain way to protect a Web server completely from unwanted access is to ensure that it can't be accessed from the Internet. This is perfectly fine for intranet Web servers, but it defeats the very purpose of most Web servers, which are public information systems or Internet commerce servers (supporting marketing, sales, ordering/shipping, product support, and customer relations).

The best thing we can do to protect a Web server from malicious intrusion is to protect private resources using some mechanism that forces users to enter a set of credentials to identify themselves. In this chapter I discuss those security measures that you can take to protect a Web server by ensuring that you know who is connecting to the server (*authentication*) and establishing rules that govern what these users are permitted to access (*authorization*).

Chapter 15 covers Secure Sockets Layer (or SSL), which goes a bit further than basic authentication and creates an encrypted connection with Web browsers to permit the secure exchange of sensitive information (the most common example being credit card numbers). By providing users with a sense of confidence and trust in the privacy and security of Web servers, SSL has been a vital component in making electronic commerce a reality.

Apache's Basic Security Tools

The modules that are responsible for controlling access to Apache resources are implemented fairly simply. Regardless of the complexity of an access control module, its task is to make a judgement about a single HTTP request and return one of two values to Apache: OK if the request should be honored; FORBIDDEN if the request should be denied.

Modules that are responsible for safeguarding protected resources in Apache are applied during three phases of the request processing cycle:

Access Control   During this standard phase of the Apache request processing cycle, a module can deny access to the requested resource based on information provided by the HTTP request or encapsulating IP packet. The only module discussed in this chapter that operates in this request phase is mod_access, which is responsible for allowing or denying client access based on the network address from which the request originates.

Authentication   Any module that is called during the verification phase must verify the identity of the requester, based on credentials presented by the user. These credentials can be as elaborate as a digital certificate, perhaps signed by a trusted third-party certificate authority. By far the most common user credential is a simple username/password pair provided by the user through a standard dialogue box provided by a Web browser, or perhaps furnished from cached data.

Authorization   When a module is called during the authorization phase, the user's identity is assumed to be already known, and the module checks access control information (such as access control lists) to determine if the user has permission to access the requested resources. Again, the response of the module must be either OK or FORBIDDEN.

Most modules that restrict access based on user identification provide handlers for both of the latter two phases, first identifying the user (authentication) and then determining if that user, once identified, will be permitted access to the requested resource (authorization). Most of this chapter is devoted to these modules, but first I'll discuss mod_access, a module that functions during the access control phase of the request cycle to restrict access to clients based on the IP address from which the request originates.

Restrictions Based on Client Origin

The very simplest means of restricting access is provided by the standard mod_access module, which operates at the access control stage of the Apache request cycle (very early in the cycle, before almost anything else has been done). At this phase, Apache knows nothing about the user request; indeed, it has not even examined any of the HTTP headers. During the access control phase, mod_access is used to determine if the request will be honored, based solely on the requesting client's hostname or IP address.

Although it is quite simple, the functionality this module provides is very useful. The directives supplied by the module operate in a directory context (either in a <Directory> container or an .htaccess file). Access restrictions imposed by these directives apply to all resources in the applicable directory and cannot be used to restrict access to specific files.

In most cases, mod_access is used to deny access to clients connecting from locations (IP addresses) that are either specifically prohibited or absent from a list of addresses that are specifically approved. Two basic directives are used to specify hosts that are either permitted or prohibited access to resources in a directory:

allow   Specifies hosts that can access resources in the associated directory.

deny   Specifies hosts that are denied access to resources in the associated directory.

Hosts can be specified in these directives using any of the following forms:

- The special all keyword, meaning all hosts:

    ```
    deny from all
    ```

- Partial or full IP addresses:

    ```
    allow from 192.168.1.1 192.168.1.2
    ```

- Partial domain names:

    ```
    deny from .some.domain.com
    ```

- A network-number/subnet-mask pair. All of the following are equivalent:

    ```
    allow from 192.168.1
    allow from 192.168.1.0/255.255.255.0
    allow from 192.168.1.0/24
    ```

Another directive, order, determines the order in which the allow and deny directives are applied. The order directive can take one of three possible forms:

order deny,allow   Applies all deny directives before the allow directives. This is generally used to prohibit most hosts from accessing a directory but specifically allow access from a select few. This works much like tight firewall (least permissive) rules; generally access is first denied to all and then opened for a limited number of users. Typically this order is used with a `Deny All` directive, which will be applied before all `Allow` directives.

`order allow,deny`   Applies all `allow` directives before the `deny` directives. This is generally used to allow most accesses, but specifically designating a few hosts or Internet subnets as prohibited. Typically this order is used with an `Allow All` directive, which will be applied before all `Deny` directives.

`mutual-failure`   Allows access to any hosts that appear on the `allow` list but not on the deny list.

NOTE   Make sure that you enter these directives exactly as shown. The `order` directive takes only a single argument. A common mistake administrators make is adding a space character within the argument. That is, the directive `order  deny,allow` will generate an Apache error; it needs to be entered as `order  deny,allow`.

To better understand the use of the `order` directive, consider an example. Suppose the following directives appeared in a `<Directory>` container or an `.htaccess` file:

```
order deny,allow    # this is the default value
allow 192.168.1
deny from all
```

They would deny all access to the relevant directory except from the 192.168.1 subnet, because the `order` directive causes the `deny from all` directive to be applied first, even though it follows the `deny` directive in the configuration. Now suppose the `order` directive were changed to this:

```
order allow,deny
```

This time, the `allow` directive, being applied first, would grant access to the 192.168.1 subnet, but that access would be immediately overridden by the `deny from all` directive that is applied last. The order of the directives in the configuration file is irrelevant, so pay close attention the `order` directive, which defaults to `order deny,allow` if not specified.

An alternate form of the `allow` and `deny` directives can be used to control access to a directory based on the existence of an environment variable:

```
allow from env=<env var>
deny from env=<env var>
```

These directives determine whether to allow or deny a request based on the existence of an environment variable. Usually this variable is *set* or created by a preceding `BrowserMatch` or SetEnvIf directive that has performed some test on one or more of the HTTP request headers. Here's an example:

```
BrowserMatch MSIE ie_user
<Directory /Explorer>
    order deny,allow
    deny from all
    allow from env=ie_user
</Directory>
```

Here, if the requester is using the Microsoft Internet Explorer browser (determined by the User-Agent HTTP request header of the request), an environment variable ie_user is set and later used to allow access to the /Explorer directory. Users of other browser types will receive a 403-Forbidden response. Consider another example, where SetEnvIf is used to set a variable based on an arbitrarily chosen header:

```
SetEnvIf Referer "someremotehost\.com"    deny_this
<Directory /audio>
    order allow,deny
    allow from all
    deny from env=deny_this
</Directory>
```

In this example, requests for audio files are denied if those requests are the result of a link in a page on a host that is known to provide links to audio files on our server, effectively stealing our bandwidth. All other requests for the same files are honored.

Restrictions Based on User Identification

You've seen that it's easy to configure access restrictions based on the origin of the request (that is, the IP address), a technique that's useful when you want to grant only a few hosts or network subnets access to certain resources (like server status pages). This approach, however, is not very flexible. For one thing, you are basing access on the network address of the client, something that you do not always control and that is subject to change. In most cases, this is fine if you want to restrict access only to subnets or hosts under your control, but a good general access control method involves both the identification of a user (authentication) and some means of controlling what resources that user can access (authorization).

The HTTP protocol describes two types of authentication that should be supported by all Web servers and clients (browsers). The first of these, which is by far the most commonly used, is basic HTTP authentication, which involves the unencrypted exchange of user authentication information, consisting of a username and password combination. The

HTTP standard also describes a second form of user authentication, called digest authentication, that works similarly but uses a mechanism to encrypt user credentials before transmission, essentially eliminating the threat of passwords being intercepted in transit. You'll learn about digest authentication later in the chapter.

Apache's standard method for basic HTTP authentication stores user credentials in text files, and I'll discuss that method first. The use of text files for storing user information imposes performance penalties that become significant when those text files grow large (roughly 1000 users or more). Most sites that use basic HTTP authentication use some type of database to store user information. Two common methods are discussed: DBM is a common key/value database method that is included in all Linux distributions; I'll also discuss authentication against a relational database. My example uses MySQL, a common Linux relational database, but the configuration described will be almost identical for any authentication module that uses another relational database, and modules are available for virtually every database system in use on Linux.

Basic HTTP Authentication

RFC 2617, "HTTP Authentication: Basic and Digest Access Authentication" defines the requirements of basic and digest authentication that are implemented in all HTTP-compliant Web servers and browsers. When the server receives a request for a resource that has been identified as protected using basic authentication, it returns a 401 (Unauthorized) response. The response also includes an HTTP WWW-Authenticate header, which contains a *challenge* to the user and identifies the authentication *realm*. The authentication realm is defined in the HTTP protocol standard as a "protection space." This means, essentially, that it is a set of resources that are logically related but may not be in the same directory. All resources in a realm are usually protected with the same authentication scheme and authorization datasource. This means that a user who has been validated for a specific realm should not have to enter a new username and password for other resources in the same realm during the same browser session. After the first authentication, subsequent requests for resources in the same realm result in credentials being supplied from the browser cache.

If no credentials are held in cache for an authentication realm, the browser will attempt to get this information from the user by presenting a dialog box like that shown in Figure 14.1. The username and password are forwarded to the server in the Authorization header in a new request.

If the browser has cached user credentials for the identified realm, it will automatically (and transparently to the user) repeat the initial HTTP request that returned a 401 error, adding an Authorization header containing the cached credentials without requesting them again from the user.

Figure 14.1   The Netscape browser's username/password dialog box

When the server receives a resource request with an Authorization header, it will first attempt to verify the validity of the information provided and then, if the user is identified, check to see if the user has been granted access to the resource. If the username is not valid, if the password can't be matched, or if the user is denied access to the resource, the server returns a second 401 (Unauthorized) response. The browser will interpret this second response as an authorization failure and will usually generate a dialog box like that shown in Figure 14.2.

Figure 14.2   The Netscape browser's "Authorization Failed" dialog box

Clicking OK to retry the request will bring up the authentication dialog (Figure 14.1) a second time; clicking Cancel should bring up a page like that shown in Figure 14.3.

Incidentally, this is a standard error page for HTTP response code 401 that can be over-ridden using the ErrorDocument directive:

```
ErrorDocument 401 /401.html
```

You can place this directive in httpd.conf to designate a new error page for response code 401 wherever authorization errors occur. You can also use this directive in narrower contexts (in an .htaccess file, for example, to designate a special page that applies only to a specific directory). My revised version of the 401 error page (named 401.html and stored in my DocumentRoot) is shown in Figure 14.4.

Figure 14.3 The Netscape browser's authorization error message

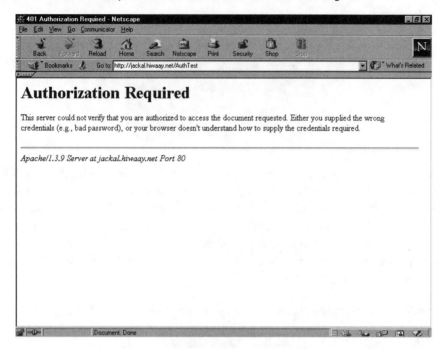

Figure 14.4 A customized error page displayed using the ErrorDocument directive

---

TIP To simplify creating a customized error page, start by deliberately generating the standard error page. Then use your browser's View Source option and copy the HTML source code for the page to a document you can edit.

Apache Modules for Authentication and Authorization

By now, you should understand that authentication (who is the user?) and authorization (what is the user allowed to access?) are separate functions. In fact, the Apache request-processing cycle includes separate phases for each of these functions. Most Apache authorization modules (and there are many), however, perform both authentication and authorization by providing callback functions for both phases of request processing. In general, when you apply an authorization module (to authenticate a user against a text file, database, or authentication server) that module both identifies the user with an acceptable degree of accuracy and also determines whether the user's request should be honored, based on an access rights list of some kind.

Just like the simpler mod_access described in the last section, the more sophisticated modules that restrict access based on a user's identity and an access rights list also return a simple OK or FORBIDDEN response. In addition, however, most can also be set to be *authoritative*; in other words, the access they grant or deny cannot be superseded by a lower-level module. Multiple authentication modules can be specified in httpd.conf, for example:

```
AddModule mod_auth.c
AddModule mod_auth_anon.c
AddModule mod_auth_dbm.c
```

The task of authenticating user requests can be passed from one module to the next, based on the *reverse* of the sequence in which the AddModule statements are added to the Apache module list. That is, the priority order of the modules is determined by the order of the AddModule statements. The modules will have an order of priority in *reverse* of their order of appearance in the Apache configuration file. In the example above, mod_auth_dbm will have the highest priority, mod_auth_anon will be next in priority, and mod_auth will have the lowest priority.

If any of these modules is specified as authoritative (the default behavior for most modules), authentication will not be passed to lower-priority modules, and acceptance or rejection of user connections by that module will be absolute. In order to allow authentication to be passed to lower-level modules, it is usually necessary to specify nonauthoritative behavior explicitly, as in:

```
AuthDBMAuthoritative off
```

Authentication by mod_auth is performed against a text file that is created by htpasswd, a utility that is packaged as a standard "accessory" with Apache. You should find this script in the /bin directory under the Apache installation directory. This utility is used to create a user file that contains usernames and associated passwords. While the file is an ordinary text file, it does not store passwords as readable text. Instead, it will encrypt the password for each user using one of several schemes. The default encryption scheme uses the standard Unix crypt function to encrypt the password.

You can enter htpasswd, with no command-line arguments, to get a listing of all the options for the function. Usually, though, you will create a new user file with htpasswd, using a line like this:

```
htpasswd -c /usr/local/apache/auth/userfile caulds
```

The -c argument is used here to create a new file (userfile in the auth directory under the Apache home). The htpasswd always requires a username argument. In this case, the new file will be created with one user, caulds, and htpasswd will prompt for that user's password and then prompt again for confirmation. The password is encrypted (using the Unix crypt system function by default) and the contents of the file will look like this:

```
caulds:cnVPtfAz2xw6o
```

Additional users are added to this file by simply omitting the creation (-c) argument:

```
htpasswd  /usr/local/apache/auth/userfile csewell
```

Adding the -b switch instructs Apache to read the password from the command line, with no prompts, and is useful for batching user account creation:

```
htpasswd -b /usr/local/apache/auth/userfile csewell fubar
```

The other arguments, -m, -s, and -p, are used to specify alternate forms of password encryption: respectively, MD5, SHA, and plain text (no encryption). Regardless of the encryption chosen, mod_auth will usually be able to authenticate users, although some configurations do not allow plain text passwords (which aren't a good idea, anyway). Here's a user file that contains one example of each encryption type (crypt, MD5, SHA, and plain text). I used this file without problems, proving that it is safe to mix and match encryption types:

```
caulds:Xsfs6UqwWLZJY
csewell:$apr1$44SVx...$YMk.PPHr7HvBHf3hCIAdMO
linda:{SHA}lituavWnx6/8ZLKNZVc4F2rbpSU=
donkey:mypasswd
```

To enable authorization for an HTTP authentication realm (in practice, usually a directory), you create an .htaccess file in the directory to be protected. This file must contain, as a minimum, the following lines:

```
AuthName        "mod_auth Test Realm"
AuthType Basic
AuthUserFile /usr/local/apache/auth/userfile
require user caulds csewell linda donkey
```

The first line defines the authorization realm, and the second specifies the authorization type (currently only Basic and Digest are supported). The next line specifies that a user file is created using htpasswd, and finally a require user line specifies a list of users who are permitted access. Note that even if the user provides a username and password that are valid in the AuthUserFile, if that valid account is not specified in the require user line, the request is rejected. In that case, the user passed the test of authentication, but failed the authorization test. Remember, most authentication modules perform both functions.

You can avoid specifying all valid users by creating a group file that contains a list of groups and members of each of those groups. This file is a plain text file and is generally created and edited with your favorite text editor. An example of such a file would be:

```
admins: caulds csewell
friends: linda csewell
associates: donkey
```

Here, I've broken my user file into three groups: admins, friends, and associates. Note that a user can be a member of more than one group.

The group file is specified in .htaccess as follows:

```
AuthName        "mod_auth Test Realm"
AuthType Basic
AuthUserFile  /usr/local/apache/auth/userfile
AuthGroupFile /usr/local/apache/auth/groupfile
require group admins friends
```

In this example, authorization is being granted to members of the admins and friends groups. One of my users (donkey) is not a member of either group and will be denied access to the resources in this directory.

Group files are used to provide authorization information. That is why the AuthUserFile line is still required. That line identifies a file used to verify users; the require group line is used to determine whether the user is authorized to access the protected resources, not to verify the validity of the credentials that user presents.

All user authentication schemes use similar configuration directives. Each will provide:

- An `AuthName` directive identifying an authentication realm.
- An `AuthType` directive specifying either basic or digest authentication.
- A directive indicating the source file or database for the user/password information pairs. Each module will have a different form of this directive, as in these examples:

  ```
  AuthUserFile /usr/local/apache/auth/userfile
  AuthDBMUserFile /usr/local/apache/auth/password.dbm
  ```

- A directive indicating a file to contain group names and members. Again, different modules will express different forms of this directive. This directive is optional and used only when access is being granted to groups rather than individual users.
- A directive indicating which users or groups are granted access; typically, this is the `require` directive.
- A directive to indicate whether the module is authoritative in its decision to accept or reject a user's request. If the module is not authoritative, any existing lower-level authentication modules are then used to process the request, any one of which may be able to authenticate the user. This directive is optional, and the default value is On, but it is a good idea to explicitly specify whether or not each module is authoritative.

I mentioned earlier that the HTTP standard provides for two types of user authentication. Basic user authentication, just described, is by far the most common of these. The next section discusses the other method, called message digest authentication.

Message Digest Authentication

Regardless of the authentication method used on the server, basic authentication uses the procedure already described, in which the server returns a 401 (Not Authorized) response and the client sends user credentials in plain text. HTTP also provides a second authentication type, called digest access authentication. Like basic authentication, this scheme proceeds as a challenge-response dialog. The difference is that the password is never sent across the wire; it is used only by the browser to compute a checksum that must match the same checksum created on the server in order for user authentication to succeed. Various checksum schemes can be used but, by default, digest authentication uses Message Digest 5 (MD5).

Although digest authentication is more secure than basic authentication, it is limited in significant ways. For one thing, the only part of the communication between browser and server that is protected is the password. All other communication is completely in the clear. Also, digest authentication is not consistently implemented in most browser software. If your site requires greater security than that offered by the basic authentication schemes described here, you should consider using SSL, as described in the next chapter, rather than using digest authentication.

If you do attempt to use MD5 authentication, be aware that not all browsers support it fully.

Implementing Digest Authentication in Apache

Digest authentication is provided by two standard Apache modules, mod_digest and the newer mod_auth_digest. Both are included in the standard Apache distribution, but neither is compiled into the server in the default configuration.

Once you've made these modules available, use the htdigest file command to create a user database for MD5 authentication:

```
# htdigest -c /usr/local/apache/auth/password.md5 "Simple Authentication Test"
caulds[
Adding password for caulds in realm Digest Authentication Realm.
New password:
Re-type new password:
```

This produces the following file:

```
# cat /usr/local/apache/auth/password.md5
caulds:Digest Authentication Realm:49afdef1311ec591ed02559e2a19ef45
```

Notice that the authentication realm is stored with each user's information. Since the same username cannot be stored twice in the same file, it is usually necessary to have separate files for each authentication realm. Group files are in the same format as ordinary mod_auth group files; in fact, the same group files can be used and specified by the AuthDigestGroupFile directive. The following example of a Location directive specifies a location (URL) to protect with digest authentication:

```
<Location /MD5Protected/>
   AuthName "Digest Authentication"
   AuthType Digest
   AuthDigestFile /usr/local/apache/auth/password.md5
   AuthDigestGroupFile /usr/local/apache/auth/groups
   AuthDigestDomain /MD5Protected/ /private/
   Require group WebAdmins
</Location>
```

In this example, notice first that the AuthDigestDomain directive lists URLs that are part of this authentication realm. The directive should always be specified and should contain at least the root URL. Also note that there is no directive to specify whether digest authentication is authoritative. When digest authentication is used, it is always authoritative, and other authentication schemes cannot be used to grant access to an MD5-protected realm.

Database Authentication (Berkeley DB)

Basic authentication is perfectly adequate for many systems, particularly if no more than about 1000 users must be authenticated. The level of confidence that can be placed in the identity of users authenticated by mod_auth is as good as other schemes that use the basic HTTP authentication. However, a significant drawback of mod_auth is that it does use unindexed text files to store user and group information. To match user-provided credentials against these text files, the file must be opened and a string comparison made of each username against each line of the text file until a match is made or the end of file is reached.

When the number of users for whom credentials are maintained on the server grows to 1000 or greater, it's time to move to some type of database to store the information. There are many options, and modules are available to provide basic HTTP authentication against all major commercial relational databases as well as some lightweight, but highly efficient, open-source alternatives (like my favorite, the MySQL database). Table 14.1 lists most available database authentication modules; check modules.apache.org if your database isn't listed.

Table 14.1   Some Database Authentication Modules

Module	Database Used With
mod_auth_db	Berkeley DB
mod_auth_dbm	Unix DBM
mod_auth_mysql	MySQL
mod_auth_ora7	Oracle Version 7
mod_auth_ora8	Oracle Version 8
mod_auth_pgsql	PostgreSQL
mod_auth_tds	Microsoft SQL Server and Sybase
mod_auth_solid	Solid

Using the DBM Database for Authentication

All distributions of Linux (like virtually all Unix systems) come with at least one variation of a database system called DBM, usually implemented as a system object code library that can be linked into other programs. Not only are these databases built-in system functions, they also use highly optimized indexing schemes for super-fast lookups. There are two major databases used, either Berkeley DB (sometimes called BSD DB) or one of several schemes called DBM that go by names like NDBM, SDBM, and Gnu DBM (GDBM). Since all use a common set of functions, changing from one package to another usually doesn't require rewriting applications but can be accomplished by recompiling with a new header file and linking to the new database library. In the case of an interpreted language like Perl, changing database packages usually means simply reading the new module into the script's namespace. The functions that are called within the Perl program remain the same. The major difference between the different DB and DBM variants is the file format, which is incompatible between them. That means, simply, that if you create a file for DB or one of the DBM libraries, you can read that file only with applications designed to read files of the same type.

All DB and DBM implementations are designed to provide quick retrieval of data based on a key value, and all systems are implemented as key/value pairs, in much the same way that Perl uses hashes. In fact, a common way to use DB or DBM with Perl is to *tie* the DB/DBM database to a standard Perl hash and then manipulate the hash, without regard to the underlying database or file system. Perl simply thinks it's working with an in-memory hash. I mention Perl because a Perl script is provided with Apache to create and maintain a DB or DBM database which contains user authentication information. In fact, you should read the Perl documentation for more information on the different system databases supported by Perl. Enter the following to see that formatted page:

```
# perldoc AnyDBM_File
```

User authentication against DBM databases is provided by a standard module called mod_auth_dbm. This module is problematic on Linux systems, where DBM support is provided by the Gnu DBM library, which provides an imperfect emulation of DBM schemes like NDBM. On Linux, the use of mod_auth_dbm should be avoided. Instead, you should use mod_auth_db, which authenticates users against a database stored in Berkeley DB format.

Enabling mod_auth_db   The mod_auth_dbm module, which is part of the default Apache configuration, compiles just fine in versions of the Red Hat distributions prior to version 7.0, but under Red Hat 7.0, you will see the following error if you attempt to use this module:

```
mod_auth_dbm.c:79:22: db1/ndbm.h: No such file or directory
```

Apache on Linux users should disable this module, and enable, instead, the Berkeley DB Authentication module (mod_auth_db) which is cleanly supported by all Linux distributions.

This is done by including both of the following options in the `configure` script when preparing Apache for compilation:

```
--enable-module=auth_db
--disable-module=auth_db_dbm
```

In version 7.0, however, Red Hat inexplicably failed to provide a symbol header file (`/usr/include/db.h`) for Berkeley DB, although the DB library is installed. Trying to compile Apache with mod_auth_db support under Red Hat 7.0 will yield this error:

```
Error: None of Berkeley-DB 1.x, 2.x or 3.x libraries found.
       Either disable mod_auth_db or provide us with the paths
       to the Berkeley-DB include and library files.
       (Hint: INCLUDES, LDFLAGS, LIBS)
```

If you encounter this problem, you need to load the development RPM that matches the DB utility RPM used by your Linux distribution. Red Hat 7.0 loads the Berkeley DB support from this RPM:

```
db3-3.1.14-6.i386.rpm
```

The matching development RPM has the closely matching name:

```
db3-devel-3.1.14-6.i386.rpm
```

Specifically, you are looking for a single file that this RPM installs:

```
/usr/include/db.h
```

You may be safe in simply moving this file from another Linux system, but the better course is to acquire the RPM (from a site like `rpmfind.net`) and install it like this:

```
# rpm -i db3-devel-3.1.14-6.i386.rpm
```

Managing a Berkeley DB User Database   In order to create a Berkeley DB user file, you use a special script named `/usr/bin/dbmmanage`. This Perl script is similar to the `htpasswd` script described for mod_auth authentication in the last section. The file it creates is a set of username/password pairs. The main difference is that this file will be in DB format, not viewable or editable with a text editor, but far more efficient for looking up a specific user's information.

If you open the `dbmmanage` script with a text editor, you'll find the following line:

```
BEGIN { @AnyDBM_File::ISA = qw(DB_File NDBM_File GDBM_File)}
```

This line expresses the script author's preferences for Berkeley DB, because the string `DB_File` (actually the name of a Perl module) appears first in the `@ISA` array. When `dbmmanage` is invoked with this line, it will use the Berkeley DB libraries if they are available; failing that, the script will choose NDBM. If the NDBM libraries do not exist, the script uses GDBM. You *must* change the order of entries in this line if you intend to use mod_auth_dbm. For Berkeley DB, no change is required (and that suits us just fine).

Invoking dbmmanage with no argument lists all the available command line options. Each of these will be explained by example:

```
# dbmmanage
usage: /usr/bin/dbmmanage filename
[add|adduser|check|delete|import|update|view][username]
```

Use the adduser command to add a new user to the database or to create a new database:

```
# dbmmanage /usr/local/apache/auth/dbmpasswds adduser caulds
New password:
Re-type new password:
User caulds added with password encrypted to .1iWwtF3v4Qkw
```

Note that the user's password isn't displayed when typed, so that a person looking over your shoulder has to read your fingers instead. No dbmmanage command will ever display a user readable password. The view command can be used to display the database entry for a specific user:

```
# dbmmanage /usr/local/apache/auth/dbmpasswds view caulds
caulds:.1iWwtF3v4Qkw
```

The dbmmanage script encrypts passwords using the standard Linux crypt system function. The crypt function is based on the Data Encryption Standard (DES). It would be pretty easy to modify dbmmanage (which is a short, simple Perl script) to use other methods of encryption, but I'm not sure mod_auth_dbm could handle these. Unless you have very good reasons for using another encryption scheme, crypt is good enough and should be used. If a hacker has unrestricted access to your DB database, given enough time and the right cracking tools, that person will break any standard encryption method.

The import command is used to import data from a username/password list. The most common use of this command is importing a standard mod_auth authorization file. (Note that the passwords in this file are already encrypted; import does not permit the encryption of plain text passwords being imported.) I converted my AuthUserFile with this command line:

```
# dbmmanage /usr/local/apache/auth/dbpasswds import < userfile
User caulds added with password encrypted to I7G7qC9E9DgPc
User csewell added with password encrypted to FoebWZ210Tef.
User linda added with password encrypted to cj70MmHuU6xsk
User larry added with password encrypted to NFrrBvMvm0O56
```

The entire contents of the database can be viewed with the view command omitting without expressing a user name:

```
# dbmmanage /usr/local/apache/auth/dbpasswds view
caulds:I7G7qC9E9DgPc
linda:cj70MmHuU6xsk
larry:NFrrBvMvmOO56
csewell:FoebWZ210Tef.
```

The add command adds one user whose username and encrypted password are both passed on the command line (some method of encrypting the password has to be used first, perhaps the password was copied from a user file on another Linux system):

```
# dbmmanage /usr/local/apache/auth/dbpasswds add AdminGuy I7G7qC9E9DgPc
User Administrator added with password encrypted to I7G7qC9E9DgPc
```

Use the update command to change a user's password in the database:

```
# dbmmanage /usr/local/apache/auth/dbpasswds update larry
New password:
Re-type new password:
User larry updated with password encrypted to 1tLbQexG8jRXc
```

The check command checks the password in the database for a user. It will tell you if the password you are attempting to use, when encrypted, matches the one in the database:

```
# dbmmanage /usr/local/apache/auth/dbpasswds check linda
Enter password:
password ok
```

Finally, the delete command removes the database entry for a single user:

```
# dbmmanage /usr/local/apache/auth/dbpasswds delete linda
`linda' deleted
```

Configuring Apache for DB Authentication   If you've compiled mod_auth_db support into your server, at least one of the following lines will be in your httpd.conf file:

```
#   grep dbm /usr/local/apache/conf/httpd.conf
LoadModule db_auth_module     libexec/mod_auth_db.so
AddModule mod_auth_db.c
```

The LoadModule line is required only if you've compiled mod_auth_db as a DSO; the AddModule line must be there to enable use of the module.

DB authorization is easy to set up, and it works very much like standard mod_auth authorization. The following .htaccess file protects resources on my server by authenticating users against a DBM database:

```
AuthName        "DB Authentication Realm"
AuthType        basic
AuthDBUserFile /usr/local/apache/auth/dbpasswds
require valid-user
AuthDBAuthoritative Off
```

The AuthName directive, which is required, names a new authentication realm. Remember that users, once authenticated against the realm, are automatically granted access to other areas that specify the same realm. AuthType is, again, basic, which is really the only value you will ever use for this directive. The AuthDBUserFile points to a DB database of usernames and password, as described in the next section. The require directive, again, grants access to any user presenting credentials that can be validated against this DB database. Finally, the AuthDBAuthoritative Off directive specifies that the acceptance or rejection of a user by this module is not authoritative and the user credentials should be passed to any lower-level authentication module in the Apache module list. (Remember, these would be specified in AddModule directives appearing before AddModule mod_auth_dbm in the Apache configuration file.)

A group file can also be used; again, this is a list of groups and members and is identical in format to the group file used for mod_auth authorization in the last section. In fact, you can use the same file:

```
AuthName        "DB Authentication Realm"
AuthType        basic
AuthDBUserFile   /usr/local/apache/auth/dbpasswds
AuthDBGroupFile  /usr/local/apache/auth/groups.dbm
require group WebAdmins
AuthDBAuthoritative On
```

Using the MySQL Database for Authentication

Table 14.1 listed Apache modules for authenticating users against some of the most common database management systems, both flat and relational. This section describes the installation and use of mod_auth_mysql to create a user database in the MySQL database and authenticate Apache users against that database.

The mod_auth_mysql module allows you to authenticate users against a MySQL database (running on either the same server or another). For heavily loaded servers, it is considered far more efficient than flat-file-based searches, and probably more secure. The user passwords are stored in DES-encrypted form in the MySQL database. Really nice.

As in all authentication schemes, mod_auth_mysql is responsible for accepting credentials presented by a user (usually by entering username and password information into a dialog presented by a Web browser) and then comparing this information against a collection of username/password pairs in a data repository of some kind (in this case, a MySQL database and table). The module returns a status of OK or FORBIDDEN to state whether the user will be granted access to the requested resource.

> **NOTE**   There are two versions of mod_auth_mysql, from different third-party sources, but I've been able to use only one of them, Vivek Khera's mod_auth_mysql, available from ftp://ftp.kciLink.com/pub/.

Vivek Khera's mod_auth_mysql module, designed to be used as a DSO, is provided as a single C source file, intended to be compiled and installed with the apxs utility. It is a quick, painless install, and it goes like this:

```
# gunzip mod_auth_mysql.c.gz
# apxs -c -i -a -L/usr/local/lib/mysql -lmysqlclient \
> -lm mod_auth_mysql.c
gcc -DLINUX=2 -DMOD_SSL=204109 -DUSE_HSREGEX -DEAPI -DUSE_EXPAT -I../lib/
expat-lite -fpic -DSHARED_MODULE -I/usr/local/apache/include  -c mod_auth_
mysql.c
gcc -shared -o mod_auth_mysql.so mod_auth_mysql.o -L/usr/local/lib/mysql -
lmysqlclient -lm
cp mod_auth_mysql.so /usr/local/apache/libexec/mod_auth_mysql.so
chmod 755 /usr/local/apache/libexec/mod_auth_mysql.so
 [activating module `mysql_auth' in /usr/local/apache/conf/httpd.conf]
```

That's all there was to it. I downloaded the file mod_auth_mysql.c.gz, ran gunzip to decompress it, and then used apxs to compile the DSO, including the -i (install) and -a (activate) switches and providing the other switches as described in the 12-line file mod_auth_mysql.build, which you should also download with the module.

I had MySQL authorization working only minutes after discovering this module.

Using a relational database for authenticating users is really no more difficult than using a flat file. You only have to create the database and fill it with user data; the module itself knows how to look up user information. The following instructions apply to MySQL, but you will follow very similar steps in creating a database for another relational database application like Oracle or PostgreSQL.

Although there are directives that allow you to change the name of the database and tables that mod_auth_mysql expects to contain user data, there is no real reason to change these. Save yourself some trouble, and create a database named http_auth that contains a single table named mysql_auth. Create the database as follows (entering the password of a MySQL user who has been granted database creation rights):

```
# mysqladmin -p create http_auth
Enter password:
Database "http_auth" created.
```

Now, invoke the mysql process and connect to the newly created database:

```
# mysql -p http_auth
Enter password:
Welcome to the MySQL monitor.  Commands end with ; or \g.
Your MySQL connection id is 10 to server version: 3.22.29
```

Use the following commands to create a single table, named mysql_auth that contains the three columns shown, with the column "username" designated as the primary index key:

```
Type 'help' for help.
mysql> create table mysql_auth (
    -> username char(25) NOT NULL,
    -> passwd char(25),
    -> groups char(25),
    -> primary key (username)
    -> );
Query OK, 0 rows affected (0.00 sec)
```

By default, mod_auth_mysql looks in the user database for passwords encrypted with the Data Encryption Standard (DES). The easiest way to fill the database, especially if it is very large, is to create a text file, each line of which is a single user's database record. The record should contain three fields, separated by tab characters, each of which corresponds to one of the three database fields (username, passwd, and groups). The following very simple example will be used to add two users, one of whom is a member only of the webteam group and the other a member of groups Admin and webteam:

```
caulds  ojWrh3YkcsRoo   Admin,webteam
csewell zv2cdTYCoc4Bw   webteam
```

One way to create the encrypted passwords, which actually makes a call to the Unix crypt() function (which is based on DES), is to use the ENCRYPT function in MySQL. It's a bit awkward, but you can use cut-and-paste to place the results in your tab-delimited flat file.

Maintaining a Healthy Server

PART 4

Load MySQL and use a line like the following to obtain each of the encrypted passwords:

```
mysql> select ENCRYPT("mypasswd");
+----------------------+
| ENCRYPT("password") |
+----------------------+
| ojWrh3YkcsRoo        |
+----------------------+
1 row in set (0.01 sec)
```

From within MySQL, I used the following line to load my MySQL database from the tab-delimited text file I named mod_auth_mysql_userfile:

```
mysql> LOAD DATA LOCAL INFILE "mod_auth_mysql_userfile" INTO TABLE mysql_auth;
Query OK, 1 row affected (0.00 sec)
Records: 1  Deleted: 0  Skipped: 0  Warnings: 0

Connection id: 14   (Can be used with mysqladmin kill)

mysql> select * from mysql_auth;
+----------+---------------+--------+
| username | passwd        | groups |
+----------+---------------+--------+
| caulds   | GeZtKIGBlQJSk | Admin  |
+----------+---------------+--------+
1 row in set (0.00 sec)
```

Once the database is created, the .htaccess file shown in Listing 14.1 can be used to grant access to a directory only to those users with an entry in the database. Most of the directives in this listing are the same as those used in basic authentication. Three directives are specific to the mod_auth_mysql module: Auth_MySQL_Info is used to specify the information needed to connect to the database (hostname, user ID, and password), Auth_MySQL_General_DB identifies the name of the MySQL database that contains the list of authorized users, and the AuthMySQL On directive enables mod_auth_mysql to perform client authentication and authorization.

Listing 14.1   An .htaccess File That Uses mod_auth_mysql

```
# The following lines are required to make a connection to
# the MySQL database, identifying the database by name,
# the server name (localhost), userid and password required
```

```
# to access the table.
Auth_MySQL_Info localhost root password
Auth_MySQL_General_DB http_auth

# Enable the mod_auth_mysql module
Auth_MYSQL on

# Make MySQL authentication authoritative. In other words,
# if this module accepts or denies access to a user, that
# decision is final; no other auth module can override
Auth_MySQL_Authoritative on

# The following directives are identical to those
# used for Basic authorization

AuthName        "MySQL Authorization Test="
AuthType Basic
#
# standard "require" to specify authorized users
require user caulds csewell
#
# or use groups to control access
# require group Admin
```

In addition to modules that provide true user authentication, there is one module you should be aware of, although it isn't widely used. The next section discusses mod_auth_anon, which provides "anonymous" Web access in the same fashion that many FTP servers provide anonymous or guest accounts.

"Anonymous" Authentication: the mod_auth_anon Module

The mod_auth_anon module (part of the standard Apache distribution, though not compiled into the default configuration) provides an interesting form of authentication. This module allows "anonymous" user access to specified areas in the same way that anonymous access is provided on many FTP servers. The user who enters one or more "magic" usernames is allowed access without having to provide a password. A long-standing convention with anonymous FTP servers is to request that users enter their complete e-mail addresses for logging purposes, though this is usually not required. To use this module, make sure that the following lines are in your httpd.conf file:

```
LoadModule anon_auth_module    libexec/mod_auth_anon.so
AddModule mod_auth_anon.c
```

Maintaining a
Healthy Server

PART 4

The .htaccess file in Listing 14.2 provides examples of all possible mod_auth_anon directives. The comments in the listing provide all the information you need to make this simple module work.

Listing 14.2   An .htaccess File That Uses mod_auth_anon

```
# .htaccess file for anonymous HTTP access
# The AuthType directive is required
AuthType basic
#
# Provides the prompt in user's login dialog box
AuthName "Use 'anonymous' & Email address for guest entry"
#
# Specify logins 'anonymous' and 'guest' for anonymous
# access; this directive required
Anonymous anonymous guest
#
# Do not permit blank username field, set to on to
# allow null usernames
#
Anonymous_NoUserId off
#
# User must specify an e-mail address as a password; set
# to off to allow null passwords.
Anonymous_MustGiveEmail on
#
# Set to on to check for at least one '@' character and
# one '.' character in password provided; does NOT guarantee
# that the e-mail address is valid
Anonymous_VerifyEmail on
#
# When set to on, this directive causes the user e-mail
# address (password) to be written in error.log
Anonymous_LogEmail on
#
# Set to On to disable fall-through to other authorization
# methods.  Access is by use of anonymous usernames only
Anonymous_Authoritative On
```

```
#
# Mandatory, even though no user file is used or specified
require valid-user
```

Authentication Servers

In addition to modules that authenticate users against databases, there are a large number of third-party Apache modules to provide authentication against directory services and specialized authentication servers. For a complete and up-to-date list of these, enter **authentication** as the search term at modules.apache.org. Table 14.2 lists modules for the most widely used user authentication schemes.

Table 14.2   Authentication Server Apache Modules

Module	Authentication Scheme
mod_auth_kerb	Kerberos
mod_auth_ldap	LDAP
mod_auth_nds	NDS (Novell)
mod_auth_notes	Lotus Notes
mod_auth_nt_lm	NT domain controller
mod_auth_radius	RADIUS server
mod_auth_samba	Samba
mod_auth_smb	SMB (LAN Manager)
mod_auth_sys	Authentication against system files
mod_auth_tacacs	TACACS+
mod_auth_yp	NIS (Yellow Pages)
mod_securid	SecurID token authentication

In most cases, these authentication modules work just like authentication modules for database authentication. The actual querying of the authentication server takes place behind the scenes. From the client standpoint, there is no difference; users are presented with the standard dialog for their browser and prompted for a username and password, exactly as in any other scheme.

The Remote Authentication Dial-In User Server (RADIUS) is one the most common authentication servers in use today, providing authentication of dial-in users for most large Internet Service Providers (ISPs). To provide Web services for client users only, ISPs might choose to authenticate Web client access against their existing RADIUS database. The mod_auth_radius module makes this a fairly straightforward task. While the details aren't important, the process is as simple as compiling mod_auth_radius as a DSO module (using the apxs utility, as described in Chapter 5), configuring Apache to load the module, and ensuring that the module can locate and communicate with a RADIUS server by adding a line like the following to the httpd.conf file:

```
AddRadiusAuth radius01.hiwaay.net:1645 tanstaafl
```

The line shown above identifies the hostname of the RADIUS authentication server (and connection port number), and a shared secret used to establish encrypted communication with this server. Listing 14.3 shows a simple .htaccess file that can be created in a directory to grant access to that directory only to valid RADIUS account holders.

Listing 14.3   An .htaccess File That Uses mod_auth_radius

```
# Use basic password authentication.
AuthType Basic
#
AuthName "RADIUS authentication for jackal.hiwaay.net"
#
# Use mod_auth_radius for authentication
AuthRadiusAuthoritative on
#
# mod_auth_radius grants access to all valid RADIUS users
#
require valid-user
```

In Sum

Securing an Apache Web server is probably one of the most important topics covered in this book, especially to administrators of Internet-accessible servers (as most are today).

This chapter and the next both discuss mechanisms that are used with Apache to provide three types of security:

- Access control based solely on the details of the incoming request packet, which essentially means controlling access based on the network address of the originator. A single module, mod_access, provides this functionality in Apache.

- User authentication is any mechanism used to verify the identity of the user. This chapter has discussed authentication modules that match unencrypted usernames and passwords against stored data on the server; the next chapter discusses the use of digital *certificates* to facilitate a public key exchange that permits encryption of all data (including user passwords) between a Web server and client browser.

- Authorization is the determination of what resources a user is permitted to access. Although the functions of user authentication and authorization are completely separate, most Apache modules for controlling access to server resources perform both roles.

Because of the additional security required to implement real business applications on the public Internet, the simple user authentication and authorization discussed in this chapter are rapidly being replaced by Secure Sockets Layer, which encrypts the data passing between server and client browser. Apache is easily modified to support SSL. Because of the importance of this technology, the next chapter is devoted to SSL.

15

Secure Sockets Layer

The last chapter discussed common methods used by all Web servers to authenticate users. In Apache, these are implemented as modules that perform both user authentication and access authorization. There are two weaknesses of this traditional Web security model. First, the data transmitted between Web server and client browser is not secure from eavesdropping, and there is a possibility (if slight) that someone with malicious intent and the ability to snoop on the network packets passing between the two can read sensitive information (the prime targets are passwords). The second weakness of conventional security is that, while the Web server has a reasonable degree of assurance about the client user (through the use of a login user ID and password), the client has no way of determining if the Web server is the correct one. Thieves have been known to spoof servers on the Internet, attempting to appear, in every respect, like the legitimate host and capture information that the unwitting user thinks he is sending to a completely different server. These so-called "man in the middle" schemes, while rare and requiring a good deal of knowledge and planning to execute, are likely to become more common as the stakes in the Internet commerce game increase (with the proliferation of such things as Internet banking).

In the mid-nineties, Netscape Communications developed a scheme to close both of the security vulnerabilities in the Web security model. The Secure Sockets Layer (SSL) protocol seeks to provide a private channel of communication between Web server and browser and assure clients that the Web server to which they are connected is the proper one (using digitally signed certificates of authenticity).

SSL is based on cryptography, specifically on what is referred to as public key cryptography (an asymmetric encryption scheme in which the key used to encode data is different from, but mathematically related to, the key used to decrypt the same data). The next section is a very basic primer on cryptography. Cryptography is math, but you don't need to be a mathematician to understand how it is used. You should read the following section as an introduction to the use of digitally signed certificates, the basis of SSL.

Symmetric and Asymmetric Encryption Schemes

There are two major types of encryption schemes, symmetric and asymmetric. In symmetric key encryptions, a single key is used to encrypt and decrypt a message or a communication stream. Symmetric key encryption schemes have the advantage of being very fast and are normally used when large amounts of data must be encrypted before being sent and rapidly decrypted on the opposite end (like data passing between sites in a communication session). The disadvantage of symmetric key systems is that both participants must know the single key used.

Asymmetric encryption is so called because two keys are used. An encryption key is used to encode a message or transmission, and a completely different decryption key is used to decode it. How is it possible to encode a message with one key and decode it with another key? For this to work, the two keys are generated at the same time, and they are related to one another mathematically. Although there are several accepted ways to generate asymmetric encryption keys, they all work pretty much the same. A block of data that is encrypted with one of the two keys in the pair can be decrypted only by the other key in the pair, and vice versa.

While the mathematical operations used to compute two such keys are quite complex, the use of asymmetric key schemes is actually pretty easy to understand. It's based on the concept of a *public key encryption system*, in which one of the two keys in the key pair is considered the *public key*, and the other, the *private key*. The public key (as its name implies) is usually distributed in some fashion (by download from a Web or FTP site, for example). The owner of the key pair keeps the private key a closely guarded secret. The simplest exchange of information using a public key encryption system works like this: A user wishing to send confidential information to the owner of a public key encrypts that information with the other user's public key (remember, the public key is not a secret). Now only the holder of the private key matching the public key used to encrypt that information can decrypt and view it. Unless that private key has been compromised, only the intended recipient of the message can view it.

Public key encryption systems are not commonly used for encrypting data, however, they are more often used to authenticate individuals, and it is in authentication that public key encryption plays a strong role in SSL, as I'll show. Authentication using public key encryption works like this. If you encrypt a block of data (any data) with your private key, only the matching public key can be used to decrypt that data. If the public key correctly decrypts the data, it is known with a high degree of certainty that the private key holder encrypted the data. In other words, the recipient of the data is assured of the identity of the sender; the sender's identity has been authenticated.

The mathematical operations (or algorithms) used to implement public key encryption are complex, comparatively slow, and CPU-intensive (*expensive* might be a better term). For that reason, in practice, public key encryption is used to securely pass a symmetric encryption key between the SSL server and client. This symmetric key is then used to encrypt and decrypt the data being transmitted between the two. Symmetric key schemes are far more efficient, remember.

That brings us to SSL. Secure Sockets Layer uses both symmetric and asymmetric encryption. When an SSL connection is established between a Web server and a browser, the communication session between the two is encrypted and decrypted using an efficient symmetric key algorithm, agreed on by the two sides, and using a single shared key. The real genius in SSL is a secure method of exchanging this symmetric *session key*. That's where public key encryption plays a part. For SSL to work, all SSL servers hold digital authentication *certificates* to identify themselves.

The certificates used by SSL are basically digital packages that contain the public half of a key pair belonging to an SSL Web server. The certificate is used as a trusted means of putting this public key in your hands. Once you have the public key of an SSL Web site, you can encrypt a message to that site that can be decrypted only by the holder of the unique private half of the key pair. This allows you to transmit the aforementioned session key, which is used to set up a secure tunnel through the Internet for communication between you and the SSL site.

These SSL certificates are issued by organizations known as *certificate authorities* (CAs). These CAs are organizations that are trusted to certify that the certificate owner is exactly what it claims to be. Web browsers come prepackaged with a long list of CAs from which they'll accept certificates of authenticity. You might be surprised at how many CAs your browser trusts. If you doubt this, take a look. In Netscape Navigator 4.7, there are over 50 certificate signers listed as trusted! Uncover this information in Netscape by selecting Communicator ➤ Tools ➤ Security Info. Figure 15.1 shows part of the list.

Figure 15.1 Netscape trusted certificate signers

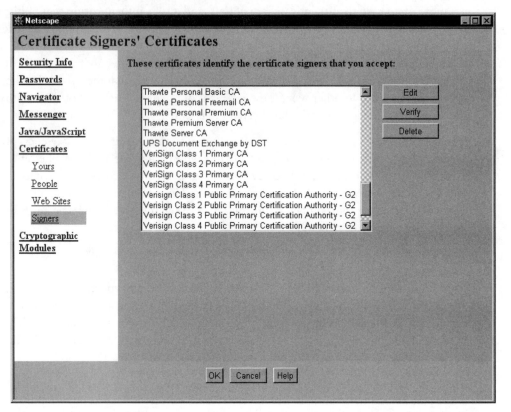

Several formats have been proposed for digital certificates to fulfill this purpose. Only one of these is in widespread use. Originally proposed in 1988 as part of the X.500 directory services by the organization now known as the International Telecommunication Union (ITU), the X.509 certificate specification was adopted for use with SSL. The X.509 standard is now a joint international standard of the ITU and the International Organization for Standardization (ISO), and it is the only type of digital certificate you will probably ever need to be concerned about, especially for SSL.

Besides the certificate holder's public key, an X.509 certificate also contains information such as the expiration date of the certificate, details about the certificate's issuing authority and the certificate holder (Figure 15.2 shows the certificate for my Web site). The most important element of the certificate, though, is the wrapper or envelope that you don't see. The wrapper that encloses the certificate information contains the signature of the certificate's issuing authority. This signature indicates that the contents of the certificate have been verified and can be trusted (as long as you trust the issuing certificate authority).

Figure 15.2   Viewing the Contents of an X.509 Certificate

The SSL certificate authentication scheme works like this:

1. A site that wishes to use SSL presents a *certificate request* to a certificate authority. This request contains the site's public key, along with other information about the company.

2. The certificate authority, after verifying that the certificate request is valid and came from the source it claims to represent, creates a certificate that it then encrypts with its private key. The certificate is returned to the site that requested it.

3. Now, whenever an SSL-capable client connects to the site's SSL Web server, this certificate is sent to the client.

4. The client, which trusts the CA that issued the certificate, validates the certificate with the trusted CA's public key, which ensures that the certificate was signed by that CA with its closely guarded private key. A certificate is considered valid for the server that presents it if it meets three criteria:

   - A CA trusted by the browser must issue the certificates.

   - The certificate must not be expired (its expiration date and time must be later than the current system date and time).

   - The certificate must be for the server that the browser believes it is connected to, in other words, the certificate offered by the server *must* match the URL used to make the request.

5. Having validated the certificate, the client now opens it and extracts the Web server's public key.

6. The client then generates a symmetric session key and encrypts that key with the Web site's public key. Remember, *only* the site holding the correct private key can decrypt the session key, so when it is properly decrypted, only the browser that generated the key and that Web site know it.

7. For the rest of the SSL session, the client and the server use this shared symmetric key to encrypt all traffic. The slower public key encryption scheme is used only to authenticate the server to the browser and to ensure a safe transmission of the session key between the two.

This whole process is actually more complex than I've described. Although you don't need to understand all the details in order to set up SSL for an Apache server and use it, it is important to understand enough of what's going on to follow the many setup steps required.

A Matter of Trust

Recent developments in the field of encryption technology tend to gloss over the fact that all such security is built on systems of trust. This is particularly true where the encryption software is sold as a complete solution or product add-on to companies that have very little knowledge of the underlying mathematics; and it's ironic in a business world where suspicion of one's competitors and even business partners is often the rule.

Most authentication and data encryption schemes rely on the use of public key encryption. This is true even of SSL, which uses certificates that have been signed with the private key of a known and trusted certificate authority. The public keys of these CAs are public knowledge, incorporated into browser software, and the ability to open and read a certificate with one of these public keys ensures that the CA did, indeed, sign the certificate using one of its highly secret, closely guarded, private keys.

Originally, the plan for public key distribution was to have public keys registered with trusted "escrow" holders, third parties trusted by both partners in a public key exchange. In other words, we would all go to these escrow servers to get public keys that we would trust because we trust the escrow holder. The early designs for these systems would require that every time I need to validate a certificate from a certificate authority, I'd retrieve the public key of that CA from an escrow server.

A Matter of Trust *(continued)*

The problem was that no one wanted to trust any of the entities that offered their services as pubic key escrow holders. The United States government drew the loudest protestations when the National Security Agency proposed that it be the key escrow holder for everyone who wanted to engage in Internet commerce (this was back when the US government thought it owned the Internet, because it built the initial infrastructure). The resistance was especially strong after it was revealed, upon orders of a US Federal court judge, that anyone's private key could be delivered to law enforcement bodies. Private corporations didn't receive too much support either, primarily because of their profit motivations.

When I started learning about SSL and certificate authorities, I was very curious to know how they planned to implement it without the use of an escrow server, or trusted third party, for every transaction. Certificate authorities do not hold private keys in escrow; instead, they enclose the public-key half of the pair in a so-called digital certificate that is signed with the CA's private key. Since the public keys of the CAs are available to everyone who has a browser, these certificates can be opened by virtually anyone and the contents examined. If a particular CA's public key successfully opens a certificate, that is considered absolute proof that the CA's private key was used to create/encrypt the certificate. This is how a certificate is known to be trustworthy and valid. The public key it contains for the Web server it represents is considered absolutely reliable. The world's certificate authorities, while they don't possess the private keys of the companies they certify, are like escrow servers in one important sense: everyone has to trust them explicitly for this whole scheme to work.

There is absolutely no reason that large corporations can't act as their own certification authorities, and many do, setting up complex hierarchies of certificate servers that ensure the privacy of their internal communications and data transfer and even, in some cases, with trading partners. The US automobile industry set up one of the most elaborate and successful systems. Largely because the technologies underlying public key authentication and encryption are not well understood, and because of the difficulty of setting up hierarchies of trusted certificate servers, companies like VeriSign and Thawte have assumed the role of trusted authorities, and they do it for money. The two companies recently merged to form a single group that, as of April 2000, furnished fully 90 percent of all certificates in use on the Internet (according to the April 2000 survey of Internet SSL servers from SecuritySpace.com). Who monitors the activities and motivations of these certificate authorities to ensure that they always act in the best interest of the global Internet community? No one, actually, but we trust them anyway—perhaps because they've never betrayed that trust.

Maintaining a
Healthy Server

PART 4

> ### A Matter of Trust *(continued)*
>
> Perhaps this is a fundamental flaw in the system of universal trust that makes Internet commerce possible. Perhaps this is simply another example of commerce and industry failing to understand the implications of a technology that marketers have said we must implement. Or perhaps I'm just being paranoid.

Implementing SSL in Apache

Part of the confusion about SSL is that it is implemented for Apache in two completely separate packages, both of which appear to be actively supported. The first of these is Apache-SSL, available from `www.apache-ssl.org`. The other is Ralf S. Engelschall's `mod_ssl` module, which was originally based on Apache-SSL code but evolved away from it until the two no longer share a large common code base. `mod_ssl` did not replace or make obsolete Apache-SSL, and both can be used and perform basically the same functions. This is largely because both are based on a package called OpenSSL (`www.openssl.org`).

> ### SSLeay: What Is It?
>
> If you have any experience at all with SSL, you will have heard about SSLeay. SSLeay was the first open-source implementation of a number of encryption methods and protocols already publicized as part of Netscape's Secure Sockets Layer. Like OpenSSL, SSLeay is a set of function libraries that program developers can use to create SSL-enabled products. There have been no new releases of SSLeay since the release of version 0.9.0b in 1998, and OpenSSL appears to have taken up where SSLeay left off. This is not to say that SSLeay is not a complete work or that OpenSSL is necessarily better; it just means that some applications are based on SSLeay and require it, while other SSL implementations require the OpenSSL libraries. Some applications even provide support for both (an example is the Perl module `Crypt::SSLeay`). In most cases, OpenSSL can be considered a replacement for SSLeay, and when installing an SSL library, you should always install OpenSSL. If you encounter documentation that refers to SSLeay, mentally substitute the word OpenSSL.

You will need to download and install OpenSSL to use either Apache-SSL or `mod_ssl`. OpenSSL is described as a "toolkit" that implements SSL and a large number of cryptography schemes. It consists of two libraries. The OpenSSL SSL/TLS library (`libssl.a`) contains functions that implement the Secure Sockets Layer and Transport Layer Security protocols, and the Crypto library (`libcrypto.a`) contains a huge number of functions that implement a wide array of cryptographic algorithms. Make no mistake about it; OpenSSL is a massive application and a very impressive piece of work, especially considering its ease of installation, complete reliability, and price (essentially free).

OpenSSL contains a number of different mathematical libraries to perform the nitty-gritty functions of encryption required to implement SSL, and it allows you to use these implementations of complex algorithms without having to understand them. Later, when you install `mod_ssl`, you will generate a public key pair for your server. `Mod_ssl` will use the OpenSSL libraries to do this, and you will be offered a choice of two public key encryption schemes. The most widely used digital public key encryption system for SSL is the RSA public key cryptosystem. The mathematical algorithm for RSA was protected by a US patent issued to RSA Security (`www.rsasecurity.com`), until the expiration of that patent on September 20, 2000. Although OpenSSL provides the Digital Signature Algorithm (DSA) as an alternative to RSA to comply with this patent, there is no longer any reason to use DSA instead of RSA encryption; nor is there any need to buy a commercial OpenSSL package simply to acquire the RSA license. The examples in this chapter illustrate the use of RSA encryption.

So, here are the pieces you'll need to install SSL on Apache:

1. The source code for OpenSSL. Even if your system already has OpenSSL installed (it installs as part of Red Hat 7.0), the application source code will be required in order to install SSL.

2. The source code for either Apache-SSL or `mod_ssl`. I installed `mod_ssl`, because it is very well documented, easier to configure, and better supported by its author and by the Internet public. The procedure I recommend below applies only to `mod_ssl`.

Installing OpenSSL

The purpose of installing the OpenSSL package is to create the following system libraries that are used to implement, respectively, cryptographic functions and SSL functions:

- `libcrypto.a`
- `libssl.a`

In addition, you'll get an extensive command-line utility (`/sbin/openssl`) that is used to access these functions for manipulating keys, certificates, etc.

1. If your system does not have OpenSSL installed, download the latest version of OpenSSL from `www.openssl.org` and uncompress it into a convenient location like `/usr/local/src`. If your Linux distribution installed a version of OpenSSL, you should look for a version of the source code that matches the installed version. Red Hat 7.0 installs OpenSSL version 0.9.5a; you can find the RPM with matching

source code on the second Red Hat CD in the SRPMS (Source RPMs) tree as openssl-0.9.5a-14.src.rpm.

```
# cd /usr/local/src
# tar xzf /downloads/openssl-0_9_5a_tar.gz
# cd openssl-0.9.5a
```

2. Run the `config` utility, using the following command line:

```
# ./config
```

3. The following commands complete the process. They will take quite some time, and generate *lots* of output:

```
# make
# make test
# make install
```

The `make install` command will create the libraries `libcrypto.a` and `libssl.a` under a special directory, `/usr/local/ssl/lib`. It will also create the `openssl` utility in `/usr/local/ssl/bin`.

4. To see if things are working, try entering a couple of `openssl` commands. For example, the `version` command reports the `openssl` version—not much of a test, but at least it will show you that the command-line tool and libraries are in place:

```
# /usr/local/ssl/bin/openssl version
OpenSSL 0.9.5a 1 Apr 2000
```

Installing `mod_ssl`

When downloading `mod_ssl` from www.modssl.org, be sure to get a version of the program that is written for your version of Apache. As of October 2000, the latest version of `mod_ssl` is 2.6.6-1.3.12, which is for use with Apache 1.3.12 only. If you are still using 1.3.9, the latest version is 2.4.9-1.3.9.

1. Download the `mod_ssl` source file and uncompress it into a convenient location like /usr/local/src:

```
# cd /usr/local/src
# tar xvzf /downloads/ mod_ssl-2.6.6-1.3.12.tar.gz
```

2. You should use the APACI install as follows. From within the source directory, run the `configure` utility and specify all the options that you might normally use to configure Apache, plus the `--with-ssl` option, which should point to your OpenSSL directory:

```
# ./configure \
> --prefix=/usr/local/apache \
```

```
> --enable-module=most \
> --enable-shared=max \
> --with-apache=../apache_1.3.12 \
> --with-ssl=../openssl-0.9.5a \
```

This will actually configure Apache to build itself with the SSL extensions.

3. When the configuration completes, providing there are no errors to resolve, change to the Apache source directory and make Apache:

```
# cd /usr/local/src/apache_1.3.12
# make
```

Apache will make itself, with a host of new options for SSL.

4. When it's done, the next step, prior to running Apache's make install, is to run a new make option, make certificate. This step is necessary to create a server SSL certificate, and for test purposes, mod_ssl will sign this certificate using a dummy certificate authority called the Snake Oil CA. Later you will want to replace this signed certificate with either a self-signed certificate (in which you act as your own CA in authenticating your own certificate) or with a certificate signed by one of the well-known certificate authorities.

5. After running a make certificate command, complete the installation of mod_ssl by running:

```
# make install
```

Listing 15.1 traces each step of make certificate. It is very interactive in gathering information to build a server certificate. If you mess up during the process, you can always make a new certificate.

Listing 15.1   Running the make certificate Process

```
# make certificate
make[1]: Entering directory `/usr/local/src/apache_1.3.12/src'
SSL Certificate Generation Utility (mkcert.sh)
Copyright (c) 1998-1999 Ralf S. Engelschall, All Rights Reserved.


Generating test certificate signed by Snake Oil CA [TEST]
WARNING: Do not use this for real-life/production systems
_____


STEP 0: Decide the signature algorithm used for certificate
The generated X.509 CA certificate can contain either
```

RSA or DSA based ingredients. Select the one you want to use.

Signature Algorithm ((R)SA or (D)SA) [R]:R

STEP 1: Generating RSA private key (1024 bit) [server.key]

794906 semi-random bytes loaded

Generating RSA private key, 1024 bit long modulus

...............................+++++

...........+++++

e is 65537 (0x10001)

STEP 2: Generating X.509 certificate signing request [server.csr]

Using configuration from .mkcert.cfg

You are about to be asked to enter information that will be incorporated
   into your certificate request.

What you are about to enter is what is called a Distinguished Name or a DN.

There are quite a few fields but you can leave some blank

For some fields there will be a default value,

If you enter '.', the field will be left blank.

-----

1. Country Name   (2 letter code) [XY]:**US**
2. State or Province Name   (full name)   [Snake Desert]:**Alabama**
3. Locality Name   (eg, city)   [Snake Town]:**Huntsville**
4. Organization Name   (eg, company)   [Snake Oil, Ltd]:**Sybex**
5. Organizational Unit Name   (eg, section)   [Webserver Team]:**Author**
6. Common Name   (eg, FQDN)
   [www.snakeoil.dom]:**jackal.hiwaay.net**
7. Email Address   (eg, name@FQDN)
   [www@snakeoil.dom]:**caulds@hiwaay.net**
8. Certificate Validity   (days)   [365]:

STEP 3: Generating X.509 certificate signed by Snake Oil CA [server.crt]

Certificate Version (1 or 3) [3]:**3**

Signature ok

subject=/C=US/ST=Alabama/L=Huntsville/O=Sybex/OU=Author/
   Email=caulds@hiwaay.net

Getting CA Private Key

Verify: matching certificate & key modulus

read RSA private key

```
Verify: matching certificate signature
../conf/ssl.crt/server.crt: OK
```

```
STEP 4: Enrypting RSA private key with a pass phrase for security [server.key]
The contents of the server.key file (the generated private key) has to be
    kept secret. So we strongly recommend you to encrypt the server.key file
    with a Triple-DES cipher and a Pass Phrase.
Encrypt the private key now? [Y/n]: y
read RSA private key
writing RSA private key
Enter PEM pass phrase: <not shown>
Verifying password - Enter PEM pass phrase: <not shown>
Fine, you're using an encrypted RSA private key.
```

```
RESULT: Server Certification Files
```

```
WARNING: Do not use this for real-life/production systems
```

```
make[1]: Leaving directory `/usr/local/src/apache_1.3.9/src'
```

> **NOTE** Don't encrypt your server key if you intend to start Apache automatically during system bootup. Encrypting the server key means that someone will have to enter a password phrase when Apache is started. This is a good security measure, as the server key is unusable without the pass phrase, but having to start Apache manually can be very inconvenient. If you choose not to encrypt the server private key, take extra precautions to protect the key. That key is the identity of your server; don't let someone steal it! Make sure that the file can be read only by root by running a command line like this: # **chmod 400 server.key**

You'll find that the new server certificate and other SSL files are written into the conf directory under the Apache source home. The SSL directories all have names that begin with ssl. These are the most important:

- ssl.csr   Contains *certificate signing request* files. These are the files that are sent to certificate authorities, which will use them to generate certificates that are returned to you. The mod_ssl installation creates ssl.csr/server.csr. This certificate signing request is unique to your server and organization and is ready to be signed.

- `ssl.crt`   Contains X.509 certificates. The default certificate created by the mod_ssl installation is `ssl.crt/server.crt`.

- `ssl.key`   Contains the private key halves of an RSA public key encryption pair. The server private key is stored here as `ssl.key/server.key`. You need to take great care in protecting these keys. These will be copied from the Apache source directory to the Apache configuration directory. Remember to protect both locations. My server key (encrypted) looks like this:

```
# cat ssl.key/server.key
-----BEGIN RSA PRIVATE KEY-----
Proc-Type: 4,ENCRYPTED
DEK-Info: DES-EDE3-CBC,EE3509ECF1D9E04E

O8m+/dXypT31/2M9jUYV/Sx8MijQLfmekUm+VtK6aZ+zxCrV7P8vL9LFxzy+MYDY
zy/7uVPXvKK4Y3c83vQ9yUYTR5b9u7U/Zzf8eaQShk7ijuGYegjty/SeK/z5tAhA
ts81Z9Sh7bD3vztGBCwGLvbQeaiQHOiwImI6eBHcfa4WcrhW7ryyJViUh75J43mK
0AQqy2E/RCbZytPuAgLDShpLP8+Zp3n616xRWQhKkCZiV3LQhBXU93U2TlH0ayxT
qa5g8wQnsx3oZIAIQkoGhvSaxJgwrfmglZoYa9ADOQDt9qh0ac2p1ulUPbwMcnjQ
e/T/2rH0h8dkQmloCuPA2dedrLFsHS7EIu28VYpMMAqLWzgkvRShyg0a5u1eva6F
3+z71wc1jfZPRCk+x8pj3wfoMjtWFdj073upd6bUSGsi/QI15/QE0xqZzFDj3PeZ
gogmqZUtE3SW46K1TAclKD7HfoOujqRUVEy/MTD0dOFlycics7DclDJWCkma/lfe
00C0t439gWk3EA8TmJWWGXjPmWOMiI1GgPAiuS+44q+EZWn5R4L3wjCmwbvzIjZO
KFyzicQO2g3Zs4Lo/2dz/Xd+5zXPbjYwO3y1DQmEI3FUE79CEtKzm/xrYGsLGGyb
hzIhlJzOE5Qu1nPFW1cz9tx89zF1eLa5ntDOyQIeC1/ewFta5bKncKOtLIIgG8ei
qWaRnezb7DCa8GsZQDfH1ZzV46SYEyMIXEnqOddD/gvBWSxTvCdV+yLu4fu8i4Hy
LP3x0YWvTgQ9uE5F/traJR2RIamoChfPXA0GhB/4xbUUyCvQdQEQHw==
-----END RSA PRIVATE KEY-----
```

Using the SSL Server

You'll find that the installation procedure makes some extensive modifications to your server's `httpd.conf.default` configuration file. Fortunately, it does a good job of this. Make sure that all the SSL lines are copied to the server's working configuration (usually `httpd.conf`), and you should be able to start the server in SSL mode by using the following command line:

```
# /usr/local/apache/bin/httpd -DSSL
```

or its equivalent:

```
# /usr/local/apache/bin/apachectl startssl
```

Either way, if you encrypted your server key, you will be prompted for your pass phrase. The server cannot be started in SSL mode unless the key can be decrypted and read, which requires the manual entry of a secret pass phrase.

The commands to load and enable the SSL module are wrapped in <IfDefine SSL> commands. I discovered that the installation routines for adding new modules to the server configuration often write lines in these two containers, where they don't belong. Remember that, if you have trouble getting a module to work. The only lines that belong in these containers are those for the mod_ssl module:

```
<IfDefine SSL>
LoadModule ssl_module          libexec/libssl.so
</IfDefine>
<IfDefine SSL>
AddModule mod_ssl.c
</IfDefine>
```

The installation will also create a new virtual host to respond to connections on the default SSL TCP port 443:

```
<VirtualHost _default_:443>
#  General setup for the virtual host
#DocumentRoot "/usr/local/apache/htdocs"
DocumentRoot "/home/httpd/SSLHome"
ServerName jackal.hiwaay.net
ServerAdmin root@jackal.hiwaay.net
ErrorLog /usr/local/apache/logs/error_log
TransferLog /usr/local/apache/logs/access_log
ScriptAlias /cgi-bin/ "/home/httpd/SSLcgi-bin/"
#    SSL Engine Switch:
#    Enable/Disable SSL for this virtual host.
SSLEngine on
-- other lines deleted --
</VirtualHost>
```

I've deleted most of the lines that mod_ssl places in the virtual host container. These control default settings for mod_ssl that are better left alone. Each of these directives is thoroughly documented in comment statements that precede it in the file.

You can change the locations where mod_ssl will look for its certificate and key files, for example (using the SSLCertificateFile and SSLCertificateKeyFile directives, respectively), but the default values are as good as any other, and most administrators will decide to use them. The important thing to realize is that SSL is implemented in Apache as a virtual host that can have its own DocumentRoot and ServerAdmin settings, among

Maintaining a
Healthy Server

PART 4

others. For all purposes, you should consider the SSL server a separate server of its own, granting access only to resources that require the protection of SSL. For a corporate intranet server, you may even want to disable connections on Port 80 (the standard HTTP port) and use only SSL.

Start the server in SSL mode, and attempt to connect to it using a URL beginning with `https`, rather than `http`:

> `https://jackal.hiwaay.net`

This will initiate a connection to the default SSL TCP port 443. If an alternate TCP port was chosen, you can use a command like the following instead (this one assumes that SSL is configured to accept connections on port 8001):

> `http://jackal.hiwaay.net:8001`

As a test, try connecting to the SSL-protected site. The first time you connect, your browser should present a dialog box like Figure 15.3.

Figure 15.3 Netscape's New Site Certificate dialog box

Click the Next button for each dialog box that is presented to accept the test certificate that is signed by the dummy Snake Oil CA. You may want to accept it for the current session only (Figure 15.4), rather than storing the certificate permanently. In the next step, we'll sign our own certificate rather than use the test certificate.

Figure 15.4   Accept the Certificate for a Single Session

I copied my environ.cgi script to the directory defined by a ScriptAlias as a CGI directory for my SSL server. Running the script, I saw a lot of new information that was added by the SSL module, as shown in Listing 15.2. Note the large number of environment variables that have been added by SSL. The information provided by these variables is available to your CGI scripts, and indicate exactly the type of encryption used as well as providing details about the X.509 certificate used to authenticate the connection. For the most part, this is information you will not need to pass to back end scripts; it's actually more interesting to review than it is useful.

Listing 15.2   Running the environ.cgi Script

```
SSL_SESSION_ID =
    8FDD7AD978C891A290AF79E7B422407102DBB7B0D0635B2866E32C6BD4AAC027

SSL_SERVER_I_DN = /C=XY/ST=Snake Desert/L=Snake Town/O=Snake Oil, Ltd/
    OU=Certificate Authority/CN=Snake Oil CA/Email=ca@snakeoil.dom

SERVER_SOFTWARE = Apache/1.3.12 (Unix) mod_ssl/2.6.4 OpenSSL/0.9.5a GATEWAY_
    INTERFACE = CGI/1.1

DOCUMENT_ROOT = /home/httpd/html

SSL_SERVER_I_DN_C = XY

SSL_PROTOCOL = SSLv3

SSL_CIPHER_ALGKEYSIZE = 128

SSL_SERVER_I_DN_OU = Certificate Authority

REMOTE_ADDR = 192.168.1.2
```

```
SSL_SERVER_I_DN_ST = Snake Desert
REQUEST_METHOD = GET
SSL_SERVER_A_SIG = md5WithRSAEncryption
SSL_VERSION_LIBRARY = OpenSSL/0.9.4
SSL_SERVER_S_DN = /C=US/ST=Alabama/L=Huntsville/O=Sybex/OU=Author/
    CN=jackal.hiwaay.net/Email=caulds@hiwaay.net
QUERY_STRING =
SSL_SERVER_I_DN_L = Snake Town
SSL_SERVER_S_DN_C = US
SSL_CIPHER_EXPORT = true
SSL_SERVER_S_DN_OU = Author
SSL_SERVER_I_DN_O = Snake Oil, Ltd
HTTP_ACCEPT = image/gif, image/x-xbitmap, image/jpeg, image/pjpeg, image/png, */*
SSL_SERVER_A_KEY = rsaEncryption
REMOTE_PORT = 1158
SSL_SERVER_S_DN_ST = Alabama
SERVER_ADDR = 192.168.1.1
HTTP_ACCEPT_LANGUAGE = en
HTTPS = on
HTTP_ACCEPT_ENCODING = gzip
SCRIPT_FILENAME = /home/httpd/cgi-bin/environ.pl
SSL_SERVER_S_DN_L = Huntsville
SERVER_NAME = jackal.hiwaay.net
SSL_SERVER_S_DN_O = Sybex
SSL_SERVER_M_VERSION = 3
SERVER_PORT = 443
SSL_CIPHER_USEKEYSIZE = 40
SERVER_ADMIN = root@jackal.hiwaay.net
UNIQUE_ID = OHS3Tn8AAAEAABmkEkI
SSL_CLIENT_VERIFY = NONE
SSL_VERSION_INTERFACE = mod_ssl/2.4.9
SERVER_PROTOCOL = HTTP/1.0
SERVER_SIGNATURE =
Apache/1.3.9 Server at jackal.hiwaay.net Port 443
SSL_SERVER_I_DN_Email = ca@snakeoil.dom
SSL_SERVER_V_START = Jan 5 21:05:41 2000 GMT
HTTP_USER_AGENT = Mozilla/4.7 [en] (WinNT; I)
SSL_CIPHER = EXP-RC4-MD5
PATH = /usr/bin:/bin:/sbin:/usr/bin:/usr/sbin:/usr/local/bin:/usr/local/sbin:/
    usr/bin/X11:/usr/X11R6/bin:/root/bin
```

```
HTTP_CONNECTION = Keep-Alive
SSL_SERVER_I_DN_CN = Snake Oil CA
SSL_SERVER_S_DN_Email = caulds@hiwaay.net
SSL_SERVER_V_END = Jan 4 21:05:41 2001 GMT
SSL_SERVER_M_SERIAL = 05
SCRIPT_NAME = /cgi-bin/environ.pl
REQUEST_URI = /cgi-bin/environ.pl
HTTP_ACCEPT_CHARSET = iso-8859-1,*,utf-8
SSL_SERVER_S_DN_CN = jackal.hiwaay.net
HTTP_HOST = Jackal
```

Locate the server certificate on your server; more than likely it resides in the /usr/local/
apache/conf/ssl.crt directory as a file named server.crt. Use the openssl utility to
view the contents of the server certificate.

This X.509 certificate is stored in a format called PEM (Privacy Enhanced Mail), but can
be viewed with the following command line:

```
# openssl x509 -in server.crt -noout -text | more
```

The PEM-formatted certificate looks like this:

```
-----BEGIN CERTIFICATE-----
MIIC7jCCAlegAwIBAgIBATANBgkqhkiG9w0BAQQFADCBqTELMAkGA1UEBhMCWFkx
FTATBgNVBAgTDFNuYWtlIER1c2VydDETMBEGA1UEBxMKU25ha2UgVG93bjEXMBUG
A1UEChMOU25ha2UgT21sLCBMdGQxHjAcBgNVBAsTFUN1cnRpZm1jYXRlIEF1dGhv
cml0eTEVMBMGA1UEAxMMU25ha2UgT21sIENBMR4wHAYJKoZIhvcNAQkBFg9jYUBz
bmFrZW9pbC5kb20wHhcNOTgxMDIxMDg1ODM2WhcNOTkxMDIxMDg1ODM2WjCBpzEL
MAkGA1UEBhMCWFkxFTATBgNVBAgTDFNuYWtlIER1c2VydDETMBEGA1UEBxMKU25h
a2UgVG93bjEXMBUGA1UEChMOU25ha2UgT21sLCBMdGQxFzAVBgNVBAsTD1d1YnN1
cnZlciBUZWFtMRkwFwYDVQQDExB3d3cuc25ha2VvaWwuZG9tMR8wHQYJKoZIhvcN
AQkBFhB3d3dAc25ha2VvaWwuZG9tMIGfMA0GCSqGSIb3DQEBAQUAA4GNADCBiQKB
gQDH9Ge/s2zcH+da+rPTx/DPRp3xGjHZ4GG6pCmvADIEtBtKBFAcZ64n+Dy7Np8b
vKR+yy5DGQiijsH1D/j8HlGE+q4TZ8OFk7BNBFazHxFbYI4OKMiCxdKzdif1yfaa
lWoANF1Az1SdbxeGVHoTOK+gT5w3UxwZKv2DLbCTzLZyPwIDAQABoyYwJDAPBgNV
HRMECDAGAQH/AgEAMBEGCWCGSAGG+EIBAQQEAwIAQDANBgkqhkiG9w0BAQQFAAOB
gQAZUIHAL4DO9oE6Lv2k56Gp38OBDuILvwLg1v1KL8mQR+KFjghCrtpqaztZqcDt
2q2QoyulCgSzHbEGmiOEsdkPfg6mpOpenssIFePYNI+/8u9HT4LuKMJX15hxBam7
dUHzICxBVC1lnHyYGjDuAMhe3961YAn8bCld1/L4NMGBCQ==
-----END CERTIFICATE-----
```

Maintaining a
Healthy Server

PART 4

When you receive a certificate from a commercial certificate authority, incidentally, it will be in PEM format. The format is encoded so that people cannot read it, but don't make the mistake of thinking it is encrypted. It is not, and can be easily converted into its human-readable form, which is shown in Listing 15.3.

Listing 15.3   A Test Certificate in Readable Form

```
# openssl x509 -noout -text -in server.crt
Certificate:
    Data:
        Version: 3 (0x2)
        Serial Number: 5 (0x5)
        Signature Algorithm: md5WithRSAEncryption
        Issuer: C=XY, ST=Snake Desert, L=Snake Town, O=Snake Oil, Ltd,
            OU=Certificate Authority, CN=Snake Oil CA/Email=ca@snakeoil.dom
        Validity
            Not Before: Jan  5 21:05:41 2000 GMT
            Not After : Jan  4 21:05:41 2001 GMT
        Subject: C=US, ST=Alabama, L=Huntsville, O=Sybex, OU=Author,
            CN=jackal.hiwaay.net/Email=caulds@hiwaay.net
        Subject Public Key Info:
            Public Key Algorithm: rsaEncryption
            RSA Public Key: (1024 bit)
                Modulus (1024 bit):
                    00:bb:80:16:1c:31:25:40:68:58:d3:85:c5:6d:a9:
                    54:34:9f:b5:ea:23:89:d9:00:50:e0:2c:01:ed:d1:
                    f7:32:9d:f4:59:03:44:ee:18:4c:b9:2b:2a:ba:d9:
                    52:cb:9f:74:e8:6e:ba:83:88:66:8a:05:1a:05:5f:
                    51:23:8d:d4:d2:65:94:52:7f:de:cc:09:47:21:a5:
                    ab:4d:6e:b2:5c:8d:af:36:0f:f7:b4:be:be:16:23:
                    f5:2e:a6:28:9a:df:b3:e6:d9:14:d7:f1:05:a8:04:
                    85:cb:44:7b:0f:6a:a5:66:af:77:b1:ba:8c:b9:35:
                    85:ae:e2:d8:f5:bb:18:bd:2b
                Exponent: 65537 (0x10001)
        X509v3 extensions:
            X509v3 Subject Alternative Name:
                email:caulds@hiwaay.net
            Netscape Comment:
                mod_ssl generated test server certificate
```

```
        Netscape Cert Type:
            SSL Server
    Signature Algorithm: md5WithRSAEncryption
        3b:39:a6:ac:2d:fe:91:fb:f0:cb:1e:2f:9b:a6:58:fc:56:4f:
        da:7f:f1:b6:e1:79:de:90:c5:3c:20:3f:67:d7:34:11:f0:9e:
        ee:13:39:dc:23:06:29:5b:89:94:3a:06:f8:34:23:3a:d5:db:
        1c:7c:87:26:31:ed:df:e7:54:67:74:78:cd:5c:38:36:04:ed:
        2d:75:93:51:f8:46:8d:74:6f:81:09:9e:46:82:53:2b:36:72:
        0a:c4:6b:e4:5f:7d:27:da:03:a0:5b:d2:04:f8:c9:e3:03:8e:
        f5:ee:20:57:b9:0d:db:60:59:03:e4:7f:f5:fd:ca:32:44:41:
        db:be
```

You'll note that the certificate contains a lot of information. The essential elements of all X.509 digital certificates are these:

- The certificate owner's common name (usually the hostname of the Web server)
- Additional information like an e-mail address for a contact at the site
- The site's public key (the matching private key is on the server, closely guarded, but must be accessible by the SSL code)
- The expiration date of the public key
- The identity of the CA that issued the certificate
- A unique serial number for the certificate
- The digital signature of the issuing CA

Signing Your Own Certificate

The final step I'll demonstrate is creating a self-signed certificate. This is often all that is required, if all of your clients (for example) are willing to accept a certificate signed by your server acting as its own certificate authority. In a corporate intranet, for example, this might be feasible. On the World Wide Web, however, you will probably send your server.csr (certificate signing request) to a third-party certificate authority for signing.

To create a self-signed certificate, use the following command line:

```
# openssl req -x509 -key ./ssl.key/server.key \
> -in ./ssl.csr/server.csr -out ./ssl.crt/server.crt
```

Here, openssl creates an X.509 certificate from the server's certificate signing request (server.csr) and signs it with the server's private RSA key (server.key). The result is a signed certificate, output as a file named server.crt.

After creating your self-signed certificate, install it in the location defined by the `SSLCertificateFile` directive in `httpd.conf`, overwriting the test certificate there, the location is probably:

```
usr/local/apache/conf/ssl.crt/server.crt
```

After restarting Apache in SSL mode, I reconnected to my server and ran `environ.cgi` a second time to make sure that my server was using the new certificate. This time, in the output, note the change in the following environment variable:

```
SSL_SERVER_I_DN: /C=US/ST=Alabama/L=Huntsville/O=Sybex/OU=Author/
    CN=jackal.hiwaay.net/Email=caulds@hiwaay.net
```

This is the *distinguished name* of the issuing certificate authority, in this case derived from my server's private RSA key.

Client Certificates

So far, I've talked only about server certification, where a client receives a digital certificate from an SSL server, and if a trusted CA has signed the certificate, the server is also trusted and an SSL connection established. SSL also permits *client* certification, where the server maintains its own list of trusted CAs and will establish SSL connections only with clients who can furnish a certificate signed by one of those CAs. By default, `mod_ssl` accepts certificates signed with its own private key, so you can set up SSL to accept only certificates signed by itself. This can be useful for corporate intranets, for example, to gain some measure of control over who connects to the server. Currently, this is the most common use for client certification, but in the future, it is conceivable that many commercial Web sites might require client authentication using digital certification, perhaps in lieu of credit card numbers and other forms of identification that are more open to fraudulent use.

Though there appears to be little impetus toward the goal of more rigid client authentication, I'll describe how the scheme would work in SSL. The server would maintain a list of acceptable well-known certificate authorities, and only certificates signed by any one of these CAs are accepted. There are two ways that such certificates can be maintained. First, each individual certificate can be placed in the location identified by the `SSLCACertificatePath` directive in `httpd.conf`. This is the directory that, by default, contains the server certificate (it is usually `/usr/local/apache/conf/ssl.crt`), meaning that the server accepts a certificate signed by itself. You can obtain individual server certificates, place them in this directory, and within that directory run `make update` to create a hash for the files:

```
# pwd
/usr/local/apache/conf/ssl.crt
# make update
```

```
ca-bundle.crt    ... Skipped
server.crt       ... 8393c41e.0
snakeoil-ca-dsa.crt ... 0cf14d7d.0
snakeoil-ca-rsa.crt ... e52d41d0.0
snakeoil-dsa.crt ... 5d8360e1.0
snakeoil-rsa.crt ... 82ab5372.0
verisign.crt     ... e52d41d0.1
```

For a small number of certificates, or if you intend to sign all client certificates yourself, this is not a terribly inconvenient way to deal with certificates. (Of course, those dummy snakeoil certificates are for testing purposes and should be deleted from your active certificate directory.)

A second way to do this is to concatenate all your server certificates into a single file named ca-bundle.crt. Take a look at the one that came provided with mod_ssl; it includes a very large number of well-known certificate authorities. Bear in mind, though, that these are certificates that all have an expiration date, and eventually you'll need an updated list of certificates. These can be obtained from a variety of sites by downloading them across the Internet. There is no need to create hash values for this file. To use the list, simply include a reference to it in httpd.conf with the SSLCACertificateFile directive, like this:

```
SSLCACertificateFile conf/ssl.crt/ca.crt
```

Certificate Revocation Lists

In a corporate intranet, client certificates need to be revoked when employees leave. So when using client certification, it is usually necessary to maintain *certificate revocation lists* (CRLs). A CRL is a group of certificates that have been revoked before their scheduled expiration dates. A CRL is a group of certificates, just like those maintained in your browser's list of acceptable CA issued certificates, and there are two ways to maintain CRLs.

First, CRLs are usually obtained from the issuing CAs, and once you've downloaded a CRL file, you can place current certificates into the directory defined in httpd.conf with the SSLCARevocationPath directive:

```
SSLCARevocationPath /usr/local/apache/conf/ssl.crl/
```

Copy the CRL files here and then run make update to ensure that a hash is created for each.

Alternatively, most CAs issue their revocation lists as single files containing concatenated certificates. These are much easier to use. You need to acquire current CRLs for the CAs you support, concatenate them into one large file, and then point to this file in `http.conf` using the `SSLCARevocationFile` directive:

```
SSLCARevocationFile /usr/local/apache/conf/ssl.crl/ca-bundle-client.crl
```

You can use this method in place of or in addition to maintaining individual CRL files.

Getting Certificates from a Commercial CA

I've demonstrated how to set up `mod_ssl` with the dummy test certificate signed by the bogus Snake Oil CA, and also how to sign your certificates with your own server's private key. Most SSL Web sites, however (particularly those engaging in e-commerce over the Internet), will want to take advantage of a certificate issued by one of the well-known certificate authorities. There are a number of these, but, as I mentioned in the sidebar earlier in the chapter ("A Matter of Trust"), the VeriSign/Thawte merger resulted in approximately 90 percent of all digital certificates traversing the Web being issued by this one CA.

Use a CA whose certificates are recognized by all common browser software. Although new certificate authorities can be added to the list of those recognized by the client's browser (refer back to Figure 15.1), this is an imposition on the certificate user. Private companies that sign their own certificates as described above and configure all their internal browsers to accept those certificates are, in effect, acting as a *private* CA, a term you may hear. That approach requires the certificate issuer to have some measure of control over all the client browsers in order to configure them to accept the certificates so issued. For Internet commerce, that just isn't possible. To make things easy for the client (especially for nontechnical users) to use SSL with your server, you will probably go with one of the big certificate authorities.

While the procedure for obtaining a digital certificate varies between issuing CAs, the procedure is basically as follows:

1. You submit a certificate signing request (CSR). This is often as simple as pasting a PEM-formatted (i.e. unencrypted) CSR into a Web form on the CA's site. On my server, I used the contents of the file `/usr/local/apache/conf/ssl.csr/server.csr`. See Figure 15.5.

2. Much of the information required by the CA is read from the CSR. You will be asked to verify it, possibly explain or correct any inconsistencies, and provide some additional information they will use to identify your organization.

3. You will need to submit some documentation of your organization's identity. VeriSign requires, for example, your Dun & Bradstreet number to more accurately identify your organization (Figure 15.6). This assumes Dun & Bradstreet (a major provider of credit information for business-to-business commerce) has already performed some verification of your information, which was not the case in my test application. Higher levels (or *classes*) of authentication are also available, though not widely used. These involve much more stringent procedures for identifying yourself to the CA.

4. Once you've completed all the required information in the certificate application and arranged to pay for the digital certificate, the certificate will be mailed to you. It will arrive in clear text (not encrypted) but encoded in PEM format along with instructions for using it. For Apache with mod_ssl, all you have to do is paste the certificate text into the proper CRT file. (For the default Apache configuration, this will be /usr/local/apache/conf/ssl.crt/server.crt.)

Figure 15.5 Entering your site's CSR

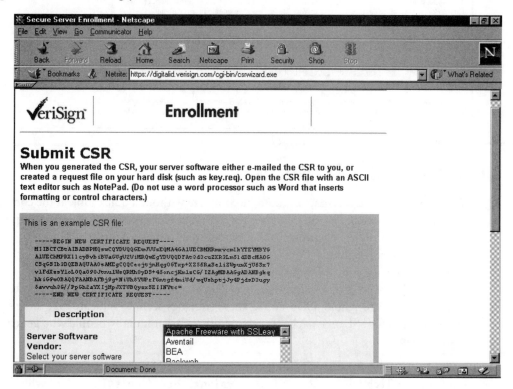

Figure 15.6 Documentation of identity

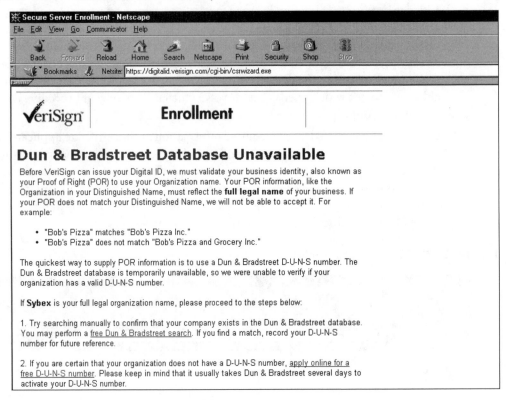

Commercial SSL Servers

No discussion of SSL on Apache would be complete without a quick look at the commercial versions of Apache, already patched for SSL, that eliminate all of the effort required to compile and install the various packages required to make it work. The most widely used of these is Stronghold from C2Net (www.c2.net). The April 2000 surveys of SSL from SecuritySpace.com showed that while Stronghold servers make up less than 1 percent of all Web servers on the Internet, over 30 percent of all SSL-traffic on the Internet is generated by Stronghold SSL servers. These statistics seem to indicate that there's a strong demand for SSL on Apache servers, but there are not many people who get enthusiastic about setting it up.

Two other popular Apache-SSL implementations are Red Hat's Secure Web Server (SWS) and Covalent Technology's Raven (www.covalent.net/raven/ssl), both of which use Apache.

I don't personally recommend using a commercial Apache SSL server unless you find the procedures discussed in this chapter too time-consuming. All three of those I mentioned are based on mod_ssl and OpenSSL and offer no features you can't put together for free (not counting your investment in perspiration and time). Prior to the expiration of the patent restricting the commercial use of RSA Data Security's encryption algorithms, the included license was a major benefit to most sites that chose commercial SSL applications. This benefit is no longer relevant.

You might consider commercial vendor support a major benefit of these commercial mod_ssl offerings. It might be; the fact is, though, all the software is open source and is best supported by the open-source community. When you run into problems, chances are you'll turn to a stranger on the Internet for help, and the one thing that might prevent you from getting that help is some obscure difference between the commercial version you are using and the "real" open-source version. So although I don't advise you *not* to choose a commercial Apache+SSL product, I do advise you to consider the open source alternative first. After all, this is Linux we're talking about, right?

In Sum

The Secure Sockets Layer (SSL) protocol enables a greater degree of security than the standard user authentication methods described in the preceding chapter. SSL uses a public key encryption certification scheme to securely pass information between SSL Web servers and SSL client browsers. The SSL server provides a *certificate* to the SSL browser that is examined for authenticity. The browser, already configured with the public keys of a number of *certificate authorities* (CAs), is able to decode this certificate, authenticating the Web server and extracting its public key. This public key is used to encrypt a *session key* that only the legitimate Web server can decode. This session key is used to establish an encrypted data tunnel with the server. During the entire SSL session, all information passing between Web server and client browser is encrypted to protect against eavesdropping. The benefits of certificate authentication of SSL servers (by widely trusted certificate authorities) and secure data communications have made SSL the de facto standard for today's electronic commerce applications; and it has been deemed secure enough for applications that range from on-line credit card sales to electronic banking.

Adding SSL to Apache is not terribly complicated, but it is quite a bit more involved than adding a standard Apache module. The SSL implementation described in this chapter (mod_ssl) requires installation of an open-source library of the encryption functions used by SSL, patching the Apache source, and recompiling the server. Finally, the server must be provided with a digital certificate to authenticate itself to the client browser. For

Maintaining a
Healthy Server

PART 4

Internet servers, this certificate is obtained from one of the accepted certificate authorities. For intranets, the server can use a self-generated certificate or one generated by a corporate certificate authority. For this to work, however, the client browsers must be configured to recognize the authority of the certificate signer. In this chapter, I demonstrate both methods.

The next and final chapter of this book discusses HTTP/1.1 content negotiation, something that most site administrators really don't need to know a lot about. If you are running a server that has multilingual content and serves a variety of different pages to clients with different needs, however, you will want to know how Apache can be configured to support this feature.

16

Metainformation and Content Negotiation

In most cases, the resources a Web server delivers to a client are documents formatted in HyperText Markup Language. This is, essentially, a default resource type, but the HTTP protocol is capable of delivering virtually any type of information. We have all used Web browsers to retrieve many different types of data, including embedded images, streaming multimedia, binary data files, Java applets ... there is no limit to the variety of data types that can be delivered by a Web server.

In order to do its job and deliver the optimum content acceptable to each client, Apache needs to know as much as possible about each resource that it serves. Information about other information, often called *metainformation*, not only tells the server how to process the data, it also instructs the client browser on how to handle the data, determining which application to pass the data to if the browser is incapable of dealing with it directly. There are four items of metainformation that the server and the browser need for any resource:

- The content type
- The language used for text
- The character set used for text
- The encoding, usually a compression scheme

> **NOTE** You may also hear the term metainformation used to describe informa-
> tion within HTML-formatted documents in the form of META tags embedded
> inside the document. The HTML META tag is reserved for use with information
> types that do not correspond to standard HTTP headers, and may describe the
> document's authors, revision history, and that sort of thing. Apache is not con-
> cerned with this type of metainformation, so it is not discussed in this chapter.

The subject of this chapter is this metainformation—how Apache determines it for the
files it serves, and the three ways in which it is used. Each of the uses for metainformation
is discussed in a separate section of the chapter:

- To instruct the browser how to handle the document. Special HTTP headers that
  precede data sent from Apache convey information to the receiving browser.
  Information that Apache can send the browser includes the type of the resource,
  its language, and the character set required to display it.

- To determine an appropriate Apache handler for the document before it is delivered to the requesting client browser. A content handler is usually an Apache
  module that performs certain functions with Web-delivered data before it is sent
  to the client. The most common example is that of server-parsed HTML, in which
  an Apache module scans the document looking for "tags" that it replaces with
  program-generated text before forwarding the document to the client. Chapter 7
  introduces server-side includes, which do just that.

- To negotiate a suitable version of a document with an HTTP/1.1-compliant
  browser. When multiple versions of a document exist, Apache uses content negotiation to send a version of the document that best meets the preferences
  expressed by the client.

We'll examine several directives that are supplied by this module. The first, `AddType`,
maps a MIME content type to one or more file extensions. The module provides similar
directives to map the other three types of metainformation to additional filename extensions: `AddLanguage`, `AddCharset`, and `AddEncoding`. You'll see that two other Apache
modules can also play a role: `mod_mime_magic` implements the traditional Unix technique
of determining a file's type by looking at its first few bytes for a "magic number," and
`mod_negotiation` implements the process of content negotiation.

First, we'll look at the four types of metainformation Apache works with.

Passing Metainformation to the Apache Server

Before Apache can use the metainformation about a file in any of the ways outlined above, the file's creator first needs to inform Apache about the four basic characteristics. As you'll see, the most common method is via the filename extension. For the content type, a second method, using Unix "magic numbers," is also available but less efficient.

The MIME Content Type

Without a doubt, the most critical piece of metainformation that Apache needs to know about a file is its content type, usually referred to as the MIME type of the file. Originally, MIME (which stands for *Multipurpose Internet Mail Extensions*) was introduced as a standard method of encoding nontext files for attachment to Internet electronic mail messages. MIME is documented in RFC 1521 and RFC 1522 ("Multipurpose Internet Mail Extensions, Parts 1 and 2"). This specification describes a method for encoding a binary file as standard ASCII text characters for transmission (called MIME Base-64 encoding), and also a standard means for the sender to describe the encoded attachment.

The adoption of MIME as a standard for encoding e-mail attachments is what permits the exchange of binary (or nontext) files between e-mail applications from different vendors. Today, virtually all e-mail attachments that cross the Internet use MIME encoding, preceded by MIME *headers*, which include information about the attachment (or each of the attachments, if multiple attachments are used). Typical MIME headers for an e-mail message look like this:

```
Content-Type: image/gif; name="cancun.gif"
Content-Transfer-Encoding: base64
```

Here you see the two main parts of MIME: the type description in the `Content-Type` header, and the identification of the standard MIME Base-64 encoding format in the `Content-Transfer-Encoding` header. These headers will instruct the e-mail application that receives the message how to decode the attachment and then how to interpret the results. Even if the decoded file did not carry the `.gif` extension, the `Content-Type` header instructs the receiving application how to interpret the file, in some cases by invoking a separate application that knows how to handle files of that type.

The best method of telling Apache the content type of a document is by associating the document's filename extension with one of the standard MIME types. The list of all MIME types that Apache knows about and supports is stored in the default location `conf/mime-types`, under the Apache directory. This file contains a list of MIME types and subtypes, along with the filename extensions that Apache associates with each. For example, here is the entry in this file for JPEG-encoded images:

```
image/jpeg                    jpeg jpg jpe
```

When Apache receives a request for a file that has the extension jpg, jpeg, or jpe, this line in the mime-types file instructs it to use a Content-Type HTTP header to identify the file as MIME type image, subtype jpeg.

You can edit this file directly to add new content types, which may or may not be officially recognized by the Internet Assigned Numbers Authority (IANA). In the early days of the Web, when new multimedia applications and "plug-ins" were constantly being introduced, I had to edit this file several times a year to accommodate new applications. Adding new MIME types isn't required nearly so often today. In fact, direct editing of the mime-types file is no longer even recommended. To add a new type (or a new filename extension) to the list of types that Apache recognizes, use the AddType directive instead. This directive has basically the same format as a line in mime-types. To illustrate, suppose we want Apache to recognize files with the extension .giff as GIF images. You would use the following AddType directive in httpd.conf:

```
AddType image/gif       gif giff
```

The AddType directive overrides (or replaces) the same MIME type in the mime-types file, so when you are trying to replace an existing mapping, make sure you specify all filename extensions you want to map, not just the new ones you want to add.

If you also wanted to add support for an application you've written that writes files ending in the extension .myapp, you could add the following line:

```
AddType application/myapp .myapp
```

Incidentally, you can change the location of the mime-types file using the TypesConfig directory, specifying a new relative or absolute path to the file:

```
TypesConfig /usr/local/apache1_3_12/conf/mime-types
```

Using Magic MIME Types

Reading a filename extension is an efficient means of determining the MIME type of the file's contents. With this method it isn't necessary to open the file or read metainformation about the file from some other source. It is essentially the same method used by most PC operating systems, which maintain an *association* between the extension of a file's name and the application required to read it. Traditionally, however, Unix systems haven't used this mechanism. Linux (and most versions of Unix) come with a utility named `file` that is used to guess the nature of a file by opening it and reading the first few bytes, in this way:

```
# file *.EXE *.gif *.gz
PLAYER.EXE:                    MS-DOS executable (EXE)
sound1.gif:                    GIF image data, version 89a
apache_1_3_12.gz:              gzip compressed data
```

The `file` utility takes a peek into a file and attempts to determine the file type from the bytecodes it finds there. Programmers often include a few bytes (commonly called *magic numbers*) somewhere near the beginning of a datafile that uniquely identify that file to be of a specific type.

Here are a couple of examples to illustrate how the contents of a file can be used to identify the MIME type of it contents. I'm using a standard Linux utility, od (octal dump), to view the contents of a GIF file, piping the output to the head command so that only the first four lines are displayed.

```
# od -a leftarrow.gif | head -4
0000000   G   I   F   8   9   a dc4 nul syn nul   B nul nul del del del
0000020 del   3   3   L del del   L   L   L  em  em  em   f nul nul   3
0000040   3   3 nul nul nul   !   ~   N   T   h   i   s  sp   a   r   t
0000060  sp   i   s  sp   i   n  sp   t   h   e  sp   p   u   b   l   i
```

As defined in the Graphics Interchange Format specification, the first three characters of any GIF file are G, I, and F. In a moment, I'll show how we can use this fact to identify a GIF file by these magic characters. First, though, let's look at a JPEG representation of the same image:

```
# od -h leftarrow.jpg | head -4
0000000 d8ff e0ff 1000 464a 4649 0100 0001 0100
0000020 0100 0000 dbff 4300 0800 0606 0607 0805
0000040 0707 0907 0809 0c0a 0d14 0b0c 0c0b 1219
0000060 0f13 1d14 1f1a 1d1e 1c1a 201c 2e24 2027
```

In this case, it isn't as obvious, but all JPEG files can be identified by the first 16 bits of the file. On an Intel machine (which is often referred to as "little-endian" because the bytes at lower addresses have lower significance) these 16 bits are shown as the two hex bytes d8 and ff. The same file stored on a "big-endian" machine (such as a machine built around one of the Motorola family of chips) might be stored with the bytes that make up this 16-bit value reversed. For that reason, when looking for byte values in a file, you must specify the order. In this case, to identify a JPEG image, we would look for the file to begin with 0xd8ff in little-endian order, or 0xffd8 in big-endian order.

The standard Apache module mod_mime_magic can determine a file's type by opening the file and searching for magic numbers it recognizes. The module supplies a single directive, MimeMagicFile, which specifies the location of a text file that maps recognized magic numbers and other data patterns to associated MIME types. Note that there is no default value provided for this directive. As a result, mod_mime_magic is only activated when httpd.conf contains a line like the following:

```
MimeMagicFile conf/magic
```

The active lines in this file contain four mandatory fields and an optional (rarely used) fifth field, in this format:

```
byte_offset data_type_to_match match_data MIME_type [MIME_encoding]
```

The fields are as follows:

byte_offset   The byte number to begin checking from; > indicates continuation from the preceding line

data_type_to_match   The type of data to match, whether a string or some type of integer

match_data   The specific contents to match, such as the string "GIF"

MIME_type   The MIME type Apache should assign to the file

MIME_encoding   The MIME encoding Apache should assign to the file (optional)

To determine the content type of a file, mod_mime_magic compares the file against each line of the magic file. If a successful match is found, the associated MIME type is returned (along with the optional encoding if specified).

As an example, consider this line from the standard magic file that comes with the module:

```
0        string        GIF             image/gif
```

Here, mod_mime_magic is being instructed to begin matching with the first byte of the file (offset 0) and look for a string matching the pattern "GIF". If that's found, the MIME type returned for the file is image/gif. That's simple enough to understand. To identify a file containing a graphic image in JPEG format, this line is used:

```
0        beshort       0xffd8          image/jpeg
```

Here, the magic number we are looking for is a two-octet or 16-bit (short) integer value, but we aren't sure exactly how these two bytes will be stored—in other words, our match needs to be independent of the machine we run it on, so we have specified big-endian notation for the match. That way, regardless of whether the file contains the bytes stored big-end first or little-end first, the two octets are converted to big-endian notation before matching against 0xffd8. In big-endian format, where the most significant byte is expressed first, this will always equal 0xffd8, regardless of the actual ordering of the octets.

The following data types are defined for the `magic` file:

Data Type	Explanation	Example
Byte	Single byte	64
Short	machine-order 16-bit integer	0xffd8
Long	machine-order 32-bit integer	0x4e54524b
String	text string	HTML
Leshort	little-endian 16-bit integer	0xffd8
Beshort	big-endian 16-bit integer	0xd8ff
Lelong	little-endian 32-bit integer	0x4e54524b
Belong	big-endian 32-bit integer	0x4b52544e

Provided with `mod_mime_magic` is an example file that includes most standard file formats. It is unlikely that you will need to edit this file to add other formats. You will need specific knowledge of file formats, though, if you intend to describe them so that `mod_mime_magic` can identify them. If you wrote the file format, that shouldn't be too big an order to fill. The example file provided with the module serves as an excellent example for creating your own magic file entries. The documentation for the module is not terribly instructive, and the source code not especially easy to follow. The best way to learn to write patterns for your magic file is to study the examples already there to determine what patterns they are looking for in existing file formats.

In the magic file that comes with the module, you'll see some lines preceded with the greater-than (>) character. This identifies the line as a continuation of the preceding line. Think of this line as a conditional line; it will only be used if the preceding line matched. The example for a compiled Java file demonstrates how this works:

```
0        short        0xcafe
>2       short        0xbabe        application/java
```

Here, the second line will be used to test the file only if the first 16-bit short value equals 0xcafe. (Since the Java file is compiled to a specific machine, the byte order is not significant here, because it will always be the same for files compiled to run on this machine's specific architecture, and no other notation needs to be considered.) We need to do this because identifying a compiled Java file requires matching the first two octets, ignoring the second two, but requiring a match of the third pair of octets. Kind of tricky. If the first 16 bits of the file (offset 0) match 0xcafe, then (and only then) compare the third 16 bits (offset 2), and if they match 0xbabe, consider this a file containing content of type application/java.

Additional levels of indentation can be used to further nest conditional statements, but you will probably never need to do this.

mod_mime_magic is almost never used as the primary means of identifying a file's content type, mainly because it is inefficient to open the file and compare its contents against stored data, looking for comparison clues. It is far more efficient to use a mechanism like the filename extension (or file location) for this purpose.

MIME Language

There are no international boundaries to the Internet, and an increasing number of Web sites are offering their Web pages in more than one language. Later in the chapter, I'll show how the new HTTP/1.1 standard supports content negotiation, a methodology that can be used to provide content according to the requester's language preference.

In addition to content type, the language used in a Web-based document can be identified. Again, a filename extension is usually used to inform Apache of what language to associate with a resource. mod_mime supplies the AddLanguage directive to make the association between content languages and filename extensions. An AddLanguage directive should be used for each language type supported, although a single AddLanguage directive can associate a single language with multiple filename extensions.

The default httpd.conf provides a number of these directives for the most widely used languages of the world, and these serve as good examples of the use of the AddLanguage directive:

```
AddLanguage en .en
AddLanguage fr .fr
AddLanguage de .de
AddLanguage da .da
AddLanguage el .el
AddLanguage it .it
```

The two-letter language extensions are usually used in addition to any other extensions used to identify the content type of the same file, a valid filename for an HTML document in Italian might be

```
index.html.it
```

The two-letter language tags used are those defined by the International Standards Organization in ISO 639, "Names of Languages." If you need a reference to these, refer to this site:

```
www.unicode.org/unicode/onlinedat/languages.html
```

MIME Character Set

In addition to different languages, documents can also use different character sets. Client browsers also need to support these character sets, and Apache needs to pass along the information about them.

The `AddCharset` directive maps a character set to one or more filename extensions. The following lines were included in my default `httpd.conf` file, although I make use of neither (the first includes several character sets used for rendering Japanese text; the second supplies glyphs needed for some Central European languages):

```
AddCharset ISO-2022-JP .jis
AddCharset ISO-8859-2 .iso-pl
```

The character encoding specified provides a mapping between each character in the set and the numeric representation of that character. In order to use an alternate character set, you first create documents using that character set, which usually requires a special (non-English) version of your software application. You would assign the file you create an extension that relates it to the character set used, and then, using `AddCharset`, ensure that Apache is able to determine the character set for purposes of informing client browsers and in content negotiation as discussed later in this chapter.

The character set names are registered with the IANA and can be found at:

```
www.isi.edu/in-notes/iana/assignments/character-sets
```

Note that the IANA does not act as a standards body, and the various encoding schemes registered with the IANA conform to a number of different specifications, published by a wide number of different standards organizations.

MIME Encoding

In addition to a MIME content type, language, and character set, a Web-delivered document can also have an encoding. Fortunately, this one's easy to deal with. As far as Apache is concerned, the encoding of a file is generally a compression scheme.

The `AddEncoding` directive maps an encoding type to one or more filename extensions. The default `httpd.conf` file comes preconfigured for two:

```
AddEncoding x-compress Z
AddEncoding x-gzip gz zip
```

You may want to add directives for the more common compression schemes, such as this:

```
AddEncoding mac-binhex40 hqx
```

Maintaining a
Healthy Server

PART 4

Some browsers have been written that allow on-the-fly decompression of data compressed with one of these schemes. Most browsers, however, use information about the compression scheme to spawn an external application to decompress the data.

MIME encoding is not used in content negotiation, and it is important only in informing the client browser how data is compressed so that it can properly deal with the data.

How Apache Uses Metainformation

Once Apache has learned a document's content type, language, character set, and encoding, how does it carry out the essential tasks of conveying the metainformation to the browser, assigning a handler for any server-side processing the content type may require, and performing content negotiation with HTTP/1.1 browsers? That's what we'll explore in the rest of this chapter.

Instructing the Browser

HTTP has always been a binary transfer protocol. In other words, no special encoding of data is required to deliver it to the recipient. However, all HTTP transmissions begin with a set of headers that describe the data to follow. One of the most important of these is borrowed directly from MIME, the Content-Type header, which is a mandatory header on all HTTP responses from a Web server and is the last header in the sequence. A typical HTTP response header, this one for an image to be used as an embedded icon in a Web page, looks like this:

```
HTTP/1.1 200 OK
Date: Sat, 03 Jun 2000 20:33:15 GMT
Server: Apache/1.3.12 (Unix)
Last-Modified: Thu, 22 Feb 1996 11:46:09 GMT
ETag: "fc0a5-112-312c5781"
Accept-Ranges: bytes
Content-Length: 274
Connection: close
Content-Type: image/gif
```

The Content-Type header always identifies a content media type, which can be anything the browser recognizes as a valid media type. In nearly every case, however, the header will contain one of the many commonly recognized Internet media types. The IANA maintains a list of Internet media types, which constitutes the de facto standard for the Content-Type MIME (and HTTP) header. You can find this list at

www.isi.edu/in-notes/iana/assignments/media-types/media-types

Just as Apache comes preconfigured to recognize most common MIME types, most browsers also recognize many common document types. Figure 16.1 shows the Netscape configuration for documents received of type image/gif. Notice that Netscape is defined as the handler for documents of this type. In other words, Netscape uses its internal image viewer to display GIF images. A user who preferred a different image viewer could configure Netscape to invoke that application to display GIF images. Use the Edit button to edit the configuration for known types.

Figure 16.1   The Netscape browser's default configuration for the GIF_Image MIME type

Generally, the only MIME types you will serve from Apache are the standard types that most browsers already recognize and support. If it's necessary to define new MIME types in Apache, however, you will also need to configure the browser to recognize those types. In that case, you can use the Add button in the Preferences window to add new MIME types to Netscape. For example, if you have configured Apache to serve files with the extension .myapp, adding a Content-Type header identifying these as type application/myapp, you must also configure your browser to handle these. Figure 16.2 shows how Netscape is configured to add support for files of this type.

Figure 16.2   Adding a MIME type (Netscape)

Since every browser has to be individually configured to support nonstandard MIME types, you would normally only do this in an environment where you have some control over the client browser, such as a corporate intranet. In a manufacturing facility, I have had to configure client browsers to automatically recognize CAD/CAM formats and invoke the appropriate application to view these. This gave line workers the ability to use a standard Web browser to view manufacturing specifications and engineering drawings on the shop floor, without having a CAD/CAM workstation.

The content media type of a Web-delivered document is by far the most important piece of information furnished to the client browser. However, when relevant, Apache also furnishes other information about the document, also in the Content-Type header. The possible options that can be set are the language, character set, and encoding. Oddly enough, the character set is specified with the media type in the Content-Type header:

```
Content-Type: text/html; charset=windows-1251
```

The language encoding and compression (if used) are specified with two HTTP headers used specifically for that purpose:

```
Content-Language: it
Content-Encoding: gzip
```

Setting a Handler

The second purpose for identifying a file's content type is so that Apache can invoke a content handler for that type of file. Most documents (such as HTML-formatted documents and image files) pass through a handler called `default-handler`, which is implemented in the Apache core. Apache's `default-handler` performs the task of serving every document to the browser, and every resource served will pass through this handler. Files that need server-side processing, however, such as server-parsed HTML (for example, server-side includes, discussed in Chapter 7), Java Server Pages, and CGI scripts, also require special handlers. The handler is normally supplied by a loaded module and supplies one or more names by which the handler is called. One way to see all available content handlers for the currently running Apache server is to invoke the Server Info screen, as described in Chapter 11.

To specify a handler for a file, it is usually best to directly associate a filename extension with a handler by name instead of associating a filename extension with a MIME type (using the `AddType` directive) and relying on a handler being defined for that MIME type. `mod_mime` supplies the `AddHandler` directive that is used to create this association. Two handlers that you will probably find in your default `httpd.conf` are:

```
AddHandler cgi-script .cgi
AddHandler server-parsed .shtml
```

These identify the handlers named `cgi-script` and `server-parsed` as handlers for files with names ending with the extensions `.cgi` and `.shtml`, respectively. The two handlers are supplied by the modules `mod_cgi` and `mod_include.c`, and they will not be recognized until the modules have been enabled with an `AddModule` directive in `httpd.conf`. The directives to enable these modules are included in the default `httpd.conf` file provided with the Apache distribution. You might note that, in addition to the handler names used above, both modules still support an alternate handler name in the MIME type/subtype format:

```
application/x-httpd-cgi
text/x-server-parsed-html , text/x-server-parsed-html3
```

If you'll check the `magic` file, however, you'll see no mention of these MIME types, nor are they defined by the IANA as registered Internet MIME types. The use of such nonstandard MIME types for defining server-based content handlers is not recommended. Instead, rely on the `AddHandler` and `SetHandler` directives to perform this task.

The `SetHandler` directive is used to associate a named handler with a specific directory or request URI.

```
<Location /status/jserv>
  SetHandler jserv-status
  order deny,allow
  deny from all
  allow from localhost, 192.168.1.2, 192.168.1.3
</Location>
```

In this example, the SetHandler directive is applied to the URL identified in the <Location> container directive. Note that this SetHandler directive is applied to all request URLs that begin with /status/jserv, which may not map to a specific directory (and probably doesn't). All requests the server receives that begin with this pattern, however, are passed to the jserv-status handler for processing.

Content Negotiation

So far in this chapter we've discussed the four elements of metainformation that Apache can maintain about any resource: MIME content type, language, character set, and the encoding (compression scheme), if any. We've also looked at two of the ways Apache can use that information: simply passing the information to the browser via headers, and selecting a handler for any server-side processing that needs to be done. Now it's time to examine the most complex and powerful use of metainformation: *content negotiation*.

Content negotiation is a process that occurs between Apache (or other servers) and HTTP/1.1-compliant browsers when the server has multiple variants of a given resource available for serving. It is the process by which the server attempts to match the needs of the client user as closely as possible.

What is a variant of a resource? A *resource*, as the term is used in Internet documentation (and as I've used it throughout this book), is any entity that can be identified by a URL. It may be a single file or a directory. A given resource may exist in more than one *representation*, or version, varying by the categories of metainformation discussed at the beginning of this chapter. Each of these versions is known as a *variant*.

Three elements are necessary for the server to begin the negotiation process when it receives a request for a resource:

Identifying Variant Types   The server first needs to identify the content type and other metainformation variables for all resources, using the methods discussed earlier.

Determining the Client Preference   The server also needs to know what content types, etc., the client browser can accept.

Determining the Available Variants   The server finally needs to know what variants it has available for a requested resource.

Client Preference

Probably the most important part of the content-negotiation process is the client's preference. In most cases, the client's stated document preference is honored, if the server has a matching version of the requested document. Why serve the client English text, if the client's browser has stated a preference for Italian and the server has an Italian version ready for delivery? Content negotiation is a process that attempts to find a suitable compromise between server and client document preferences, but usually the only relevant preference is that of the client. I'll discuss first how client preferences are communicated to Apache.

HTTP/1.1 defines four headers that clients can use in their request to a Web server: `Accept`, `Accept-Language`, `Accept-Charset`, and `Accept-Encoding`.

The Accept Header The `Accept` header lists the MIME content types that the client is willing to accept. These types are the same as those that Apache uses in its `mime-types` file. Here's an example:

```
Accept: text/html, text/plain
```

This client is expressing a willingness to accept either an HTML-formatted document or one that is in plain ASCII text. The browser has not expressed a preference, however, and the server is completely at liberty to serve either. In such a case, the server will use its own preference settings to determine which variant (among those that are stored on it) it will serve, and we'll cover this later in the chapter.

The browser can also send `Accept` headers that contain an optional quality value for each media type. This quality factor (expressed as a q value) can take a value of 0.000 (completely unacceptable) to 1.000 (the highest preference). Here, the media types that are acceptable to the client are given quality values:

```
Accept: text/html, application/pdf;q=0.8, text/plain;q=0.4
```

Since the default quality value is 1.0, HTML-formatted text is requested with the strongest preference value, and a PDF document is acceptable with a slightly lower preference, but the user will accept plain text if that's all the server has to offer.

The `Accept` header can also contain wildcard characters for the media types. If the client browser sent the following `Accept` header, it would be expressing a willingness to accept any document that has a text MIME type, regardless of the subtype:

```
Accept: text/html, text/*
```

The PDF version would *not* be acceptable in this case.

Many browsers send a wildcard (*.*) with each request, as a way of saying "if you don't have the explicit types I asked for, send whatever you have":

```
Accept: image/gif, image/jpeg, *.*
```

Since no quality values are assigned to any of the preferences expressed in this example, you might assume that all have an equal preference (the default quality value of 1.0). But Apache doesn't assign default preference to wildcards. Instead, it assigns a quality value of 0.01 to `*.*` and 0.02 to a wildcard subtype, like our example of `text/*`.

The `Accept-Language` Header   The `Accept-Language` header identifies all languages that the client will accept, with an optional quality value (defaults to 1.0 if not specified).

```
Accept-Language: en;q=0.8, de;q=0.4, it;q=0.2
```

Here, the client has expressed a preference for English but is willing to accept German or Italian (a very multilingual reader here), with successively lower degrees of enthusiasm.

Figure 16.3 shows how language preferences are configured in a client browser (in this case, Netscape Navigator). This information will be conveyed to the server in an `Accept-Language` HTTP header.

Figure 16.3   Client browser language preference

The Accept-Charset Header   Accept-Charset identifies all character sets the client is willing to accept. Again, quality values can be used; if they are not used, ISO-8859-1 (the Latin-1 set for West European languages, the standard U.S. encoding) is deemed to be acceptable to every client. Note, too, that if the media type of a document on the server is text/html, and no other character set is associated with the document (either by a file-name extension or type-map file), the document is assumed to be in ISO-8859-1.

```
Accept-Charset: ISO-2022-JP;q=1.0, ISO-8859-2;0.5
```

The line above expresses a preference for a Japanese character set, with a lesser preference for ISO-8859-2 (Latin-2, which covers most Central European languages). If neither of these is available, the server will send the document in ISO-8859-1, which is always deemed acceptable to any client.

The Accept-Encoding Header   The Accept-Encoding header identifies all encodings the client will accept. Quality values can be assigned by the client. Unencoded versions of files are always preferred and will be served, if they exist.

```
Accept-Encoding: gzip;q=0.8, zip;q=0.5
```

Determining Source Variants

The final requirement for content negotiation is the determination of what variants of each document are available to be served by Apache. When Apache receives a request for a resource, it uses one of two different methods—Multiviews or a type map—to build a list of all servable variants of that document. The number of variants potentially includes all combinations of the four ways in which a document can be classified.

Multiviews   Multiviews is an Apache option that can be set on a per-directory basis. Multiviews is enabled by including the following line in the directory's .htaccess file:

```
Options +Multiviews
```

Multiviews works by using filename extensions to create a list of all source variants for a given resource. When a request is received for a resource—for example, /somedoc—and Multiviews is enabled for the directory indicated, mod_negotiation looks for all resources in the directory that match the name, using the filename extensions to build a list of variants for that document. It may find the following files in the directory, for example:

```
somedoc.html
somedoc.html.en
somedoc.html.de
somedoc.pdf.en
somedoc.pdf.de
```

Maintaining a
Healthy Server

PART 4

This would indicate to mod_negotiation that five variants of the same resource exist: English language versions of the file formatted in HTML and PDF, and German versions formatted in both HTML and PDF. What about the file that has no two-letter language code extension? That file can be interpreted in two ways by mod_negotiation. Usually it is interpreted as having no language attribute, and will be served only if the client expresses no language preference, but you can modify this behavior using the DefaultLanguage directive. When this directive is used in a per-directory context (in either a <Directory> container or an .htaccess file), it specifies a language to be assigned to all files in that directory that do not have a language attribute assigned:

```
DefaultLanguage en
```

The DefaultLanguage directive can only specify a single language.

When Multiviews is used to create a list of variants for a resource, the LanguagePriority directive can also be used to set a precedence for language selection that is used whenever a client does not express a language preference:

```
LanguagePriority en de
```

If the above directive were in effect, and a client requests /somedoc.html, then the English version, formatted as HTML, would always be served. The German version will only be served to clients that specifically express a preference for it, by sending a header like the following:

```
Accept-Language: de;q=1.0, en;q=0.6; fr;q=0.2
```

The Type-Map File   An alternative to Multiviews is the use of a type-map file, a document used to itemize a list of document variants that Apache can serve. This file contains a section for each document that can be served from the directory containing the type-map file and uses a set of headers to define the available variants for each document.

Type-map is actually the name of an Apache handler, supplied by mod_negotiation, and the use of type maps is enabled by using the AddHandler directive to associate this handler with a filename extension. By convention, .var (for *variant*) is usually appended to the name of the type-map file:

```
AddHandler type-map .var
```

Since type-map is defined as a handler for documents saved as files ending in .var, type maps are invoked when the client requests a resource that ends with .var. Of course, you've never actually submitted a request like http://jackal.hiwaay.net/somedoc.var, though that would be a valid way to call a type map. Most servers use some form of URL rewriting (discussed in Chapter 10) to redirect a request to a type map. Using mod_rewrite, for instance, you could redirect all requests for files ending with `.html` in the `DocumentRoot` directory to an associated type-map file using these directives:

```
<Location />
RewriteRule ^(.*)\.html$ $1.var [NS]
</Location>
```

The advantage of using type maps instead of Multiviews is that they allow you to set a server precedence for variants of a document. For each variant of a document, type maps can instruct `mod_negotiation` to use a *quality source factor* (or `qs` value). Remember that the quality value included in a client's `Accept` request header is distinctly different from the quality source factors assigned to resources on the Apache server. Content negotiation is basically a process in which the server objectively arrives at a compromise between the client's expressed preference and the server's. The server uses a fixed algorithm to perform this arbitration, as described in the next section. Fortunately, it is rarely necessary to understand this process, although you might find it helpful to know how it is done. Generally, your work is complete when you assign quality source factors `qs` to create a precedence for different variants of the same document.

The contents of a type-map file are a set of records, one for each variant of the document (each of which is stored under a different filename, of course). The attributes of each variant are expressed on a separate line within each variant record, and each must begin with one of the following headers:

URL   The URI of the file that contains the variant (even though the header is URL, the resource is identified by a URI). This URI is always relative to the type-map file, a URI that consists of only a filename is assumed to be in the same directory as the type-map file. Note that variants defined by the type-map file do not have to be in the same directory as that type-map file, and a single type-map file can contain variants from any number of directories.

Content-Type   The MIME content media type of the variant, and optionally, the quality source factor, or `qs`. The `qs` level has the same meaning as that expressed by the client in `Accept` headers. The `qs` factor for a variant must be expressed only in the `Content-Type` header for that variant and cannot be placed after any other header.

Content-Language   The language in which the variant was written, using one of the two-character codes defined in ISO 639.

Content-Encoding   If the file is compressed or otherwise encoded, rather than simply raw data, this describes the encoding used, typically `x-gzip` or `x-compress`.

Content-Length   The byte size of the file.

Description   A human-readable description of the variant. If Apache cannot find an appropriate variant to return, it will return an error message that lists all available variants, with these descriptions. The client can then request one of these directly.

Consider a sample .var file:

```
URI:  somedoc.html.en
Content-Type: text/html; qs=1.0
Content-Language: en
Description: "English Language Version"


URI: somedoc.html.de
Content-type: text/html; qs=0.8
Content-Language: de
Description: "Deutsche Sprachversion"
```

This is a very simple example, in which our server maintains separate English and German versions of the same HTML-formatted document. The English version is preferred.

Like the client-preference q value, the qs factor can take values of 0.000 to 1.000. A value of 1.000 is assigned to any variant in the file for which a qs factor is not expressed. A variant with a value of 0.000 will never be served. The quality source factor expressed in the type map is combined with the quality value expressed by the client browser to negotiate the variant actually sent to the client. In this case, if the client sent a header such as:

```
Accept-Language: de; q=1.0, en; q=0.6; fr; q=0.2
```

mod_negotiation will multiply the quality source factors for the server and the quality value provided by the browser to derive a joint factor:

en: $1.0 \times 0.6 = 0.6$

de: $0.8 \times 1.0 = 0.8$

In this case, even though English is preferred on the server side, the German version wins out and is the one that will be returned to the client. And although the client expressed a willingness to accept French, there is no matching variant on the server, so this doesn't enter into the content negotiation process.

The Apache Negotiation Process

Whenever there are multiple variants of the same document, trying to determine which is the optimum variant to send to the client can be very confusing. Fortunately, we don't get involved in that process; mod_negotiation takes care of it for us. There may be times, however, especially when using type maps, that we want to influence mod_negotiation's selection process. For that reason, I'll describe the content negotiation process the module follows whenever a request is received for a document that has multiple variants to select and return a single variant to the client (or an error if the request can't be resolved to a single variant).

1. Build a list of all available variants of the requested file, either from a type map or using Multiviews. If a type map is used, prioritize these according to quality (qs) values in the type map, assigning default values where no qs value is specified. If a type map is used, all variants have equal priority.

2. Extract the Accept headers from the client request, and build a list of the variants the client can accept. Prioritize these according to quality values, if provided; otherwise assign default values. Compare this list against the list of available variants compiled in step 1, eliminating any server variants the client hasn't specified as acceptable. When this step is complete, you should have a list of all variants available on the server that are acceptable to the client. From this list, one will be chosen as optimum, and served to the client.

3. If no variant on the server is acceptable to the client, a 406 (No acceptable representation) HTTP error is returned to the client. The error message will also contain a list of all available variants, using the Description header from the type map (if available), allowing the client to resubmit a request for one of these variants.

4. For each variant in our list, multiply the quality factor from the client Accept header with the server's qs factor (which is taken from the type map, if used, or always 1.0 for Multiview). If one variant has a higher score than the rest, it is chosen and sent to the client. If the high score is tied between two or more variants, eliminate all other variants and continue.

5. The list has now been reduced to variants that have matching scores. Of these, consider only the client's language quality value, as specified in the Accept-Language header. If the Accept-Language header wasn't provided by the client, use the server's language preference in the LanguagePriority directive if one exists. If one variant has a higher language quality value than all the rest, it is chosen and sent to the client. If two or more variants tie, eliminate all other variants and continue.

6. Of the remaining variants, select the one that has the highest value for the content type. This value is available only if type maps are used; otherwise, the text/html content type is given a level of 2; all other media types are assigned a level of 0. If one variant has a higher value than all others, send it to the client. If two or more variants tie for the high level value, eliminate all other variants and continue.

7. From the variants remaining in our list (which should by now be growing quite short), select the variant with the highest character set priority, as determined from the `Accept-Charset` HTTP header provided by the client. If this header was not provided by the client, eliminate all variants that do not use the ISO-8859-1 character set (remembering that all `text/html` documents that are not specifically identified as using another character set are assumed to be in ISO-8859-1). If the list has now been reduced to a single variant, send it to the client. If the list still contains two or more variants, continue.

8. If the remaining list contains any variants that are *not* ISO-8859-1, we know that the client must have specified some other character set in its `Accept-Charset` header. So remove all ISO-8859-1 variants from the list and continue. If the list has only ISO-8859-1 variants, keep the list intact and continue.

9. Select the variants from the list that are specified in the client's `Accept-Encoding` HTTP header. If the client did not provide an `Accept-Encoding` header, and our list contains only variants that are encoded, or only variants that are *not* encoded, continue. If the list has a mixture of encoded and unencoded variants, discard all the encoded variants to reduce the list to unencoded variants only.

10. Of the variants remaining in the list, select the one that has the smallest content length and serve it to the client. If two or more tie for the distinction of being smallest, continue.

11. If you reach this point, and still have a list of at least two variants (seems unlikely, doesn't it?), select the first in the list. (That is, the first defined in the type map if it is used, or the first alphabetically if using Multiview.) Serve this file to the client.

In Sum

In closing this last chapter, it seems almost ironic to me that so little has been said about the information that Apache has the role of delivering to its clients. After all, the Web exists for the purpose of exchanging information. However, Web servers (like Apache) are only one component of the Web, and those servers are not responsible for the interpretation or rendering (display) of information. For that reason, there has been almost no discussion in this book of document-formatting standards like HTML. For the most part, the Apache server, and its administrator, require little knowledge of document content. The role of determining the content type of a document, deciding how to display it, or which external application to load to process the document could be left entirely up to the browser. Browsers could, for example, be instructed to interpret all files they receive with a filename extension `.html` as HTML-formatted text. That's a safe enough assumption. That's not how things work, however. Part of the role of the Web server is to provide its client with several important pieces of information about the document it is sending to that client.

Metainformation is information describing other information resources. Apache always sends several pieces of metainformation with the resources that it serves to clients. The metainformation is obtained from different sources and is often inferred from a disk file attribute (for example, the filename extension, or even the folder in which the file is located).

Apache deals with four basic pieces of information about files: 1) content type, 2) natural (human-readable) language, 3) character set, and 4) encoding. In its simplest configuration, Apache determines these information attributes about a resource and simply informs the client (with the pertinent HTTP headers) of this information about the file it is serving. That's the purpose of the module mod_mime, discussed first in this chapter.

HTTP/1.1 provides additional headers (both client-request and server-response headers) to support *content negotiation*, in which the client (generally from a browser configuration) identifies required or desired attributes for the files it requests, and the server, in turn, offers information about the different resource versions it offers. Content negotiation is used whenever multiple versions of resources are available. The most common application for this capability is when a server supports multiple language versions of resources it hosts (often in alternate character sets).

Appendices

Apache Directives

Table A.1 lists all the directives included in the standard Apache distribution as of version 1.3.12, subject to change. The columns represent the following information:

Directive   The name of the Apache directive.

Context   Indicates where in the server's configuration the directive may appear, which may be one of the following:

Server   The directive can occur only in one of Apache's configuration files (usually `httpd.conf`, but also `srm.conf` and `access.conf`, if either of these now-obsolete files is used).

Virtual Host   The directive can appear only inside a `<VirtualHost>` container directive, and it applies only to the relevant virtual host.

Container   The directive can appear only inside `<Directory>`, `<File>`, or `<Location>` containers, which restrict its applicability.

.htaccess   The directive can appear only inside a per-directory `.htaccess` file and applies only to files that reside in that directory (if no override is in effect for the directive).

Override   For directives that can appear in an `.htaccess` context, this column lists the value that will enable the associated directive. This value must appear in an `AllowOverride` directive (unless the default value `AllowOverride All` is in effect). For example, for the `Action` directive, the override value is `FileInfo`. Thus, the `Action` directive enabled is enabled in an `.htaccess` file only if an `AllowOverride`

FileInfo directive is already in effect. See "The AllowOverrides Directive" in Chapter 4.

Module   Lists the name of the module that must be loaded and enabled in Apache for the directive to be available for use.

Default   The default value for the directive, if any.

NOTE   A few of the modules in this table were not discussed in the book, as they are relevant only to Web page designers (content providers) and aren't related to Apache server administration.

Table A.1   Apache Directives

Directive	Context	Override	Module	Default
AccessConfig	Server, Virtual Host		Core	conf/access.conf
AccessFileName	Server, Virtual Host		Core	.htaccess
Action	Server, Virtual Host, Container, .htaccess	FileInfo	mod_actions	
AddAlt	Server, Virtual Host, Container, .htaccess	Indexes	mod_autoindex	
AddAltByEncoding	Server, Virtual Host, Container, .htaccess	Indexes	mod_autoindex	
AddAltByType	Server, Virtual Host, Container, .htaccess	Indexes	mod_autoindex	
AddCharset	Server, Virtual Host, Container, .htaccess	FileInfo	mod_mime	
AddDefaultCharset	Server, Virtual Host, Container, .htaccess		Core	Off
AddDescription	Server, Virtual Host, Container, .htaccess	Indexes	mod_autoindex	
AddEncoding	Server, Virtual Host, Container, .htaccess	FileInfo	mod_mime	

Table A.1   Apache Directives *(continued)*

Directive	Context	Override	Module	Default
AddHandler	Server, Virtual Host, Container, .htaccess	FileInfo	mod_mime	
AddIcon	Server, Virtual Host, Container, .htaccess	Indexes	mod_autoindex	
AddIconByEncoding	Server, Virtual Host, Container, .htaccess	Indexes	mod_autoindex	
AddIconByType	Server, Virtual Host, Container, .htaccess	Indexes	mod_autoindex	
AddLanguag	Server, Virtual Host, Container, .htaccess	FileInfo	mod_mime	
AddModule	Server		Core	
AddModuleInfo	Server, Virtual Host		mod_info	
AddType	Server, Virtual Host, Container, .htaccess	FileInfo	mod_mime	
AgentLog	Server, Virtual Host		mod_log_agent	logs/agent_log
Alias	Server, Virtual Host		mod_alias	
AliasMatch	Server, Virtual Host		mod_alias	
allow	Container, .htaccess	Limit	mod_access	
AllowCONNECT	Server, Virtual Host		mod_proxy	443 (https) 563 (snews)
AllowOverride	Container		Core	All
Anonymous	Container, .htaccess	AuthConfig	mod_auth_anon	
Anonymous_Authoritative	Container, .htaccess	AuthConfig	mod_auth_anon	Off
Anonymous_LogEmail	Container, .htaccess	AuthConfig	mod_auth_anon	On
Anonymous_MustGiveEmail	Container, .htaccess	AuthConfig	mod_auth_anon	On

Table A.1   Apache Directives *(continued)*

Directive	Context	Override	Module	Default
Anonymous_NoUserID	Container, .htaccess	AuthConfig	mod_auth_anon	Off
Anonymous_VerifyEmail	Container, .htaccess	AuthConfig	mod_auth_anon	Off
AuthAuthoritative	Container, .htaccess	AuthConfig	mod_auth	
AuthDBAuthoritative	Container, .htaccess	AuthConfig	mod_auth_db	On
AuthDBGroupFile	Container, .htaccess	AuthConfig	mod_auth_db	
AuthDBMAuthoritative	Container, .htaccess	AuthConfig	mod_auth_dbm	On
AuthDBMGroupFile	Container, .htaccess	AuthConfig	mod_auth_dbm	
AuthDBMUserFile	Container, .htaccess	AuthConfig	mod_auth_dbm	
AuthDBUserFile	Container, .htaccess	AuthConfig	mod_auth_db	
AuthDigestAlgorithm	Container, .htaccess	AuthConfig	mod_auth_digest	
AuthDigestDomain	Container, .htaccess	AuthConfig	mod_auth_digest	
AuthDigestFile	Container, .htaccess	AuthConfig	mod_digest or mod_auth_digest	AuthDigestFile
AuthDigestGroupFile	Container, .htaccess	AuthConfig	mod_auth_digest	
AuthDigestNonceLifetime	Container, .htaccess	AuthConfig	mod_auth_digest	300 (seconds)
AuthDigestQop	Container, .htaccess	AuthConfig	mod_auth_digest	
AuthGroupFile	Container, .htaccess	AuthConfig	mod_auth	
AuthName	Container, .htaccess	AuthConfig	Core	
AuthType	Container, .htaccess	AuthConfig	Core	
AuthUserFile	Container, .htaccess	AuthConfig	mod_auth	

Table A.1 Apache Directives *(continued)*

Directive	Context	Override	Module	Default
BindAddress	Server		Core	* (all interfaces)
BrowserMatch	Server		mod_browser	
BrowserMatchNoCase	Server		mod_browser	
CacheDefaultExpire	Server, Virtual Host		mod_proxy	1 (hour)
CacheDirLength	Server, Virtual Host		mod_proxy	1 (character)
CacheDirLevels	Server, Virtual Host		mod_proxy	3
CacheForceCompletion	Server, Virtual Host		mod_proxy	90 (percent)
CacheGcInterval	Server, Virtual Host		mod_proxy	
CacheLastModifiedFactor	Server, Virtual Host		mod_proxy	0.1
CacheMaxExpire	Server, Virtual Host		mod_proxy	24 (hours)
CacheNegotiatedDocs	Server		mod_ negotiation	
CacheRoot	Server, Virtual Host		mod_proxy	
CacheSize	Server, Virtual Host		mod_proxy	5 (KB)
CheckSpelling	Server, Virtual Host, Container, .htaccess	Options	mod_spelling	Off
ClearModuleList	Server		Core	
ContentDigest	Server, Virtual Host, Container, .htaccess	Options	Core	Off
CookieExpires	Server, Virtual Host		mod_usertrack	
CookieLog	Server, Virtual Host		mod_log_config	
CookieName	Server, Virtual Host, Container, .htaccess		mod_usertrack	
CookieTracking	Server, Virtual Host, Container, .htaccess	FileInfo	mod_usertrack	

Table A.1 Apache Directives *(continued)*

Directive	Context	Override	Module	Default
CoreDumpDirectory	Server		Core	Same as ServerRoot
CustomLog	Server, Virtual Host		mod_log_config	
DefaultIcon	Server, Virtual Host, Container, .htaccess	Indexes	mod_autoindex	
DefaultLanguage	Server, Virtual Host, Container, .htaccess	FileInfo	mod_mime	
DefaultType	Server, Virtual Host, Container, .htaccess	FileInfo	Core	text/html
deny	Container, .htaccess	Limit	mod_access	
<Directory>	Server, Virtual Host		Core	
DirectoryIndex	Server, Virtual Host, Container, .htaccess	Indexes	mod_dir	index.html
<DirectoryMatch>	Server, Virtual Host		Core	
DocumentRoot	Server, Virtual Host		Core	/usr/local/apache/htdocs
ErrorDocument	Server, Virtual Host, Container, .htaccess	FileInfo	Core	
ErrorLog	Server, Virtual Host		Core	logs/error_log
Example	Server, Virtual Host, Container, .htaccess	Options	mod_example	
ExpiresActive	Server, Virtual Host, Container, .htaccess	Indexes	mod_expires	
ExpiresByType	Server, Virtual Host, Container, .htaccess	Indexes	mod_expires	
ExpiresDefault	Server, Virtual Host, Container, .htaccess	Indexes	mod_expires	
ExtendedStatus	Server		mod_status	Off

Table A.1 Apache Directives *(continued)*

Directive	Context	Override	Module	Default
FancyIndexing	Server, Virtual Host, Container, .htaccess	Indexes	mod_autoindex	
<Files>	Server, Virtual Host, .htaccess		Core	
<FilesMacth>	Server, Virtual Host, .htaccess		Core	
ForceType	Container, .htaccess		mod_mime	
Group	Server, Virtual Host		Core	−1 (nobody)
Header	Server, Virtual Host, Container		mod_header	
HeaderName	Server, Virtual Host, Container, .htaccess	Indexes	mod_autoindex	
HostNameLookups			Core	Off
IdentityCheck	Server, Virtual Host, Container		Core	Off
<IfDefine>	Server, Virtual Host, Container, .htaccess		Core	
<IfModule>	Server, Virtual Host, Container, .htaccess		Core	
ImapBase	Server, Virtual Host, Container, .htaccess	Indexes	mod_imap	
ImapDefault	Server, Virtual Host, Container, .htaccess	Indexes	mod_imap	
ImapMenu	Server, Virtual Host, Container, .htaccess	Indexes	mod_imap	
Include	Server, Virtual Host, Container, .htaccess	Indexes	Core	
IndexIgnore	Server, Virtual Host, Container, .htaccess	Indexes	mod_autoindex	

Appendices

Table A.1 Apache Directives *(continued)*

Directive	Context	Override	Module	Default
IndexOptions	Server, Virtual Host, Container, .htaccess	Indexes	mod_autoindex	
IndexOrderDefault	Server, Virtual Host, Container, .htaccess	Indexes	mod_autoindex	
KeepAlive	Server		Core	On
KeepAliveTimeout	Server		Core	15 (sec)
LanguagePriority	Server, Virtual Host, Container, .htaccess	FileInfo	mod_negotiation	
<Limit>	Server, Virtual Host, Container, .htaccess		Core	
<LimitExcept>	Server, Virtual Host, Container, .htaccess		Core	
LimitRequestBody	Server, Virtual Host, Container, .htaccess		Core	0 (unlimited)
LimitRequestFields	Server		Core	100
LimitRequestFieldsize	Server		Core	8190 bytes
LimitRequestLine	Server		Core	8190 bytes
Listen	Server		Core	
ListenBacklog	Server		Core	511 (connections)
LoadFile	Server		mod_so	
LoadModule	Server		mod_so	
<Location>	Server, Virtual Host		Core	
<LocationMatch>	Server, Virtual Host		Core	
LockFile	Server		Core	logs/accept.lock
LogFormat	Server, Virtual Host		mod_log_config	

Table A.1 Apache Directives *(continued)*

Directive	Context	Override	Module	Default
LogLevel	Server, Virtual Host		Core	error
MaxClients	Server		Core	256
MaxKeepAliveRequests	Server		Core	100
MaxRequestsPerChild	Server		Core	0 (never expires)
MaxSpareServers	Server		Core	10
MetaDir	Container (1.3), Server only (pre-1.3)		mod_cern_meta	.web
MetaFiles	Container		mod_cern_meta	Off
MetaSuffix	Container (1.3), Server only (pre-1.3)		mod_cern_meta	.meta
MimeMagicFile	Server, Virtual Host		mod_mime_magic	
MinSpareServers	Server		Core	5
MMapFile	Server		mod_mmap.static	
NameVirtualHost	Server		Core	
NoCache	Server, Virtual Host		mod_proxy	
NoProxy	Server, Virtual Host		mod_proxy	
Options	Server, Virtual Host, Container, .htaccess	Options	Core	
order	Container, .htaccess	Limit	mod_access	
PassEnv	Server, Virtual Host		mod_env	
PidFile	Server		Core	logs/httpd.pid
Port	Server		Core	80
ProxyBlock	Server, Virtual Host		mod_proxy	
ProxyDomain	Server, Virtual Host		mod_proxy	

Table A.1 Apache Directives *(continued)*

Directive	Context	Override	Module	Default
ProxyPass	Server, Virtual Host		mod_proxy	
ProxyPassReverse	Server, Virtual Host		mod_proxy	
ProxyReceiveBufferSize	Server, Virtual Host		mod_proxy	
ProxyRemote	Server, Virtual Host		mod_proxy	
ProxyRequests	Server, Virtual Host		mod_proxy	Off
ProxyVia	Server, Virtual Host		mod_proxy	Off
ReadmeName	Server, Virtual Host, Container, .htaccess	Indexes	mod_autoindex	
Redirect	Server, Virtual Host, Container, .htaccess	FileInfo	mod_alias	
RedirectMatch	Server, Virtual Host, Container, .htaccess	FileInfo	mod_alias	
RedirectPermanent	Server, Virtual Host, Container, .htaccess	FileInfo	mod_alias	
RedirectTemp	Server, Virtual Host, Container, .htaccess	FileInfo	mod_alias	
RefererIgnore	Server, Virtual Host		mod_log_referer	
RefererLog	Server, Virtual Host		mod_log_referer	
RemoveHandler	Container, .htaccess		mod_mime	
require	Container, .htaccess	AuthConfig	Core	
ResourceConfig	Server, Virtual Host		Core	conf/srm.conf
RewriteBase	Container, .htaccess	FileInfo	mod_rewrite	
RewriteCond	Server, Virtual Host, Container, .htaccess	FileInfo	mod_rewrite	

Table A.1 Apache Directives *(continued)*

Directive	Context	Override	Module	Default
RewriteEngine	Server, Virtual Host, Container, .htaccess	FileInfo	mod_rewrite	Off
RewriteLock	Server		mod_rewrite	
RewriteLog	Server		mod_rewrite	
RewriteLogLevel	Server, Virtual Host		mod_rewrite	0 (no logging)
RewriteMap	Server, Virtual Host		mod_rewrite	
RewriteOptions	Server, Virtual Host, Container, .htaccess	FileInfo	mod_rewrite	
RewriteRule	Server, Virtual Host, Container, .htaccess	FileInfo	mod_rewrite	
RLimitCPU	Server, Virtual Host		Core	Not set (use Linux values)
RLimitMEM	Server, Virtual Host		Core	Not set (use Linux values)
RLimitNPROC	Server, Virtual Host		Core	Not set (use Linux values)
Satisfy	Container, .htaccess		Core	all
ScoreBoardFile	Server		Core	logs/apache_ status
Script	Server, Virtual Host, Container		mod_actions	
ScriptAlias	Server, Virtual Host		mod_alias	
ScriptAliasMatch	Server, Virtual Host		mod_alias	
ScriptInterpreterSource	Container, .htaccess		Core	script
ScriptLog	Server		mod_cgi	
ScriptLogBuffer	Server		mod_cgi	1024 (bytes)

Appendices

Table A.1   Apache Directives *(continued)*

Directive	Context	Override	Module	Default
ScriptLogLength	Server		mod_cgi	10385760 (bytes)
SendBufferSize	Server		Core	
ServerAdmin	Server, Virtual Host		Core	
ServerAlias	Virtual Host		Core	
ServerName	Server, Virtual Host		Core	
ServerPath	Virtual Host		Core	
ServerRoot	Server		Core	/usr/local/apache
ServerSignature	Server, Virtual Host, Container, .htaccess		Core	Off
ServerTokens	Server		Core	Full
ServerType	Server		Core	Standalone
SetEnv	Server, Virtual Host		mod_env	
SetEnvIf	Server		mod_setenvif	
SetEnvIfNoCase	Server		mod_setenvif	
SetHandler	Container, .htaccess		mod_mime	
StartServers	Server		Core	5
ThreadsPerChild	Server		Core	300
TimeOut	Server		Core	On
TransferLog	Server, Virtual Host		mod_log_config	
TypesConfig	Server		mod_mime	
UnsetEnv	Server, Virtual Host		mod_env	
UseCanonicalName	Server, Virtual Host	Options	Core	−1 (nobody)

Table A.1 Apache Directives *(continued)*

Directive	Context	Override	Module	Default
User	Server, Virtual Host		Core	
UserDir	Server, Virtual Host		mod_userdir	public_html
VirtualDocumentRoot	Server, Virtual Host		mod_vhost_alias	
VirtualDocumentRootIP	Server, Virtual Host		mod_vhost_alias	
<VirtualHost>	Server		Core	
VirtualScriptAlias	Server, Virtual Host		mod_vhost_alias	
VirtualScriptAliasIP	Server, Virtual Host		mod_vhost_alias	
XBitHack	Server, Virtual Host, Container, .htaccess	Options	mod_include	Off

B

Online References

This appendix lists the online sources of information (and in some cases, software) that I have found most useful as an Apache administrator. Along with many Web sites, you'll find some mailing lists and Usenet newsgroups. Entries are grouped into the following categories:

- Information about the Web and HTTP
- General Apache resources
- Information about Apache modules
- Information about Apache security
- General programming resources
- Information about PHP programming
- Information about Perl/CGI programming
- Information about Java programming

The URLs and addresses listed here were verified shortly before this book went to press, but all are subject to change.

WWW and HTTP Resources

Not surprisingly, the Web and its underlying protocol, HTTP, are among the most thoroughly documented subjects on the Internet.

HTTP: Hypertext Transfer Protocol

```
http://www.w3.org/Protocols
```

Everything you ever wanted to know about the HyperText Transfer Protocol (HTTP) protocol is at the World Wide Web Consortium's (W3C) site devoted to HTTP.

HTTP Made Really Easy

```
http://www.jmarshall.com/easy/http
```

Subtitled "A Practical Guide to Writing Clients and Servers," this is James Marshall's excellent simplification of the HTTP specification; what it is and how it works.

Hypertext Transfer Protocol — HTTP1.1

```
http://www.w3.org/Protocols/rfc2616/rfc2616.html
```

Request For Comments (RFC) 2616 is the specification that describes the latest version of the HyperText Transfer Protocol, version 1.1.

mnot: Web Caching

```
http://www.mnot.net
```

Mark Nottingham's web caching site contains a lot of information on Web caching, caching engines and proxy servers, and how to control Web caching from the server.

Mime-Types.com

```
http://www.mime-types.com
```

Billed as "your complete one-stop resource for Internet MIME-types," this is where you should go to find out what MIME content types are in standard use.

Persistent Client State HTTP Cookies (Netscape Cookies Specification)

```
http://www.netscape.com/newsref/std/cookie_spec.html
```

Netscape "invented" the Web cookie. This is where they specify how the technology should work.

W3C: The World Wide Web Consortium

`http://www.w3.org`

Created in 1994, the World Wide Web Consortium works to promote and standardize the Web and to provide information to its community of developers.

The Virtual Library of WWW Development

`http://wdvl.internet.com/Vlib`

One of the oldest bookmarks I have, the WWW Virtual Library is a source of links on a lot of topics. You are sure to find a few links of interest.

History of the Web

Learning about the Web's history may or may not make you a better Apache administrator, but it's interesting and fun. Whenever you want to know about where the Web came from, start with these sources.

Chapter 2: A History of HTML

`http://www.w3.org/People/Raggett/book4/ch02.html`

This chapter from *Raggett on HTML 4* (Dave Raggett, et al, Addison-Wesley Longman, 1998) provides a good historical look at the World Wide Web. It's got pictures, too!

Connected: An Internet Encyclopedia

`http://www.FreeSoft.org/CIE/index.htm`

A good searchable source for history and information of all kinds related to the Web.

Hobbes' Internet Timeline

`http://www.isoc.org/guest/zakon/Internet/History/HIT.html`

Considered the definitive Internet history, Hobbes' Timeline of the Internet has been around forever and continues to be updated with new developments.

General Apache Resources

These sites and mailing lists provide information about various aspects of Apache.

Apache HTTP Server Project

`http://www.apache.org`

Appendices

The home page of the Apache Software Foundation, this is the definitive site for all things Apache, and it is the most important URL in this appendix.

Mailing List To receive announcements of new Apache product releases and news, send a message with anything in the body of the message (or leave the body blank) to:

```
announce-subscribe@apache.org
```

Apache Directives

```
http://www.apache.org/docs/mod/directives.html
```

A list of the directives in all the standard Apache modules.

Apache Today

```
http://apachetoday.com
```

Excellent online publication filled with articles and links to all manner of Apache-related topics and news. Be sure to sign up for a free user account and their mailing list.

Mailing List To subscribe to a text or HTML newsletter from ApacheToday.com, link to the subscription form at

```
http://apachetoday.com/newsletter.php3
```

A User's Guide to URL Rewriting with the Apache Webserver

```
http://www.engelschall.com/pw/apache/rewriteguide
```

The best single piece of documentation available for mod_rewrite, by Ralf S. Engelschall, the module's author.

Apache Week

```
http://www.apacheweek.com
```

Another great publication, *Apache Week* is issued weekly. It's very newsy, with good feature articles, and it's a great way to keep up with Apache "happenings." Don't fail to be on their once-a-week mailing.

Mailing List To receive *Apache Week* via e-mail, send a message to:

```
majordomo@apacheweek.com
```

The body of the message should contain

```
subscribe apacheweek
```

for a text formatted mailing or

```
subscribe apacheweek-html
```

for HTML format.

kHTTPd: Linux HTTP Accelerator

```
http://www.fenrus.demon.nl
```

Discussed in Chapter 13, "Proxying and Performance Tuning," kHTTPd (a minimal but *very* fast HTTP server engine) is now a part of the Linux kernel. Here's its author's site, with all you need to know about kHTTPd.

Microsoft FrontPage 2000 Server Extensions Resource Kit

```
http://officeupdate.microsoft.com/frontpage/wpp/serk
```

The FrontPage 2000 Server Extensions for Unix/Linux are part of this resource kit, and this is the site for all things related to the FP Server Extensions.

Newsgroup Microsoft maintains this newsgroup for discussion of the FrontPage Extensions for Unix:

```
microsoft.public.frontpage.extensions.unix
```

O'Reilly Network's Apache DevCenter

```
http://oreilly.apacheweek.com
```

As the name would imply, this site is very oriented toward Web site developers. As part of the O'Reilly Network, it devotes considerable space to books published, and conferences organized, by O'Reilly.

Ready-to-Run Software (FrontPage Extensions)

```
http://www.rtr.com
```

The FrontPage 2000 Server Extensions for Unix/Linux were written by Ready-to-Run Software, Inc. This is an alternate site for the FP Extensions, and contains a FAQ and discussion group not available at the Microsoft site.

Appendices

RPM Repository

```
http://rufus.w3.org/linux/RPM
```

The best site for Linux RPM packages; it is mentioned as a source throughout this book.

The Web Robots Pages

```
http://info.webcrawler.com/mak/projects/robots/robots.html
```

The best site for information on Web robots: how they work, how to attract them to your site, and how to control the darned things when they do find you.

Web Server Comparisons

```
http://www.acme.com/software/thttpd/benchmarks.html
```

Although the information is somewhat dated, these are excellent comparisons of Web server performance in benchmark tests on various platforms. There's also good information here on how the different Web servers differ technically.

Web Techniques

```
http://www.webtechniques.com
```

The online version of the printed publication *Web Techniques*. There are a lot of good articles here that probably wouldn't appear in a print-only publication. Very developer-oriented.

WebReference.com: The Webmaster's Reference Library

```
http://www.webreference.com
```

Covering all aspects of Web development, this site is a free service of internet.com Corporation.

Mailing List Sign up at www.Webreference.com for weekday HTML mailings and/or a weekly text summary of articles on all manner of Web development topics. I recommend the weekly summary, as the daily mailings are large and repetitive.

Apache GUIs

```
http://gui.apache.org
```

A focus point to make sure that all Apache GUI projects are publicized.

Covalent Technologies

```
http://www.covalent.net/projects/comanche
```

Covalent Technology's site for the open-source Comanche Apache GUI configuration utility.

TkApache

```
http://www.eunuchs.org/linux/TkApache/
```

The official page for the TkApache GUI configuration utility.

Apache on Linux Newsgroup

```
comp.infosystems.www.servers.unix
```

A newsgroup for all things related to Web servers for Unix/Linux platforms. Most of the discussion is directly relevant to Apache.

Resources for Apache Modules

These sites provide information about Apache's standard modules, discussed in Chapter 5, or about specific third-party modules.

Apache Standard Modules

```
http://www.apache.org/docs/mod/index.html
```

Official documentation for all of the modules that are part of the Apache distribution.

Apache Module Registry

```
http://modules.apache.org
```

A registry service provided by the Apache Software Foundation for third-party modules, with a searchable database of links to sites where the modules can be obtained.

Apache::ASP Perl Module

```
http://www.nodeworks.com/asp
```

The official site for the commercially supported `Apache::ASP` module, which permits the use of Perl in Active Server Pages with Apache.

Mod_perl_faq

```
http://perl.apache.org/faq
```

A Frequently Asked Questions list for one of the most popular Apache modules.

The mod_mime_magic Module for Apache HTTPD

```
http://www.employees.org/~ikluft/apache/mod_mime_magic
```

Stored and documented in a nonstandard location, this is the documentation for the `mod_mime_magic` module discussed in Chapter 16.

Appendices

Apache Security Resources

These sites provide information about Apache tools for implementing security (discussed in Chapters 14 and 15) or about specific security issues.

Apache-SSL

```
http://www.apache-ssl.org
```

Everything you could ever want to know about Apache-SSL, as discussed in Chapter 15.

CERT/CC Understanding Malicious Content Mitigation

```
http://www.cert.org/tech_tips/malicious_code_mitigation.html
```

This page, published by the Computer Emergency Response Team (CERT) Coordination Center, describes a problem with malicious tags embedded in client HTTP requests.

mod_ssl: The Apache Interface to OpenSSL

```
http://www.modssl.org
```

The official page for the mod_ssl implementation of SSL for Apache.

Mailing Lists   You can join the following mailing lists at `http://www.modssl.org/support/`:

```
modssl-announce
modssl-users
```

OpenSSL: The Open Source Toolkit for SSL/TLS

```
http://www.openssl.org
```

Official page for the OpenSSL toolkit, which is used to provide a cryptography library for other applications (like SSL).

SSLeay and SSLapps FAQ

```
http://www2.psy.uq.edu.au/~ftp/Crypto
```

This FAQ, although it has not been updated in a few years, provides a lot of good information on the SSLeay cryptographic library on which OpenSSL is based. Much of the information here is still very useful.

General Programming Resources

These sites provide information about various programming topics that may be of interest to Apache administrators, as discussed in Chapters 8 and 9.

ASP Today

> http://www.asptoday.com

Full of articles of interest to Active Server Page programmers.

Developer Shed: The Open Source Web Development Site

> http://www.devshed.com

Covers all aspects of Web programming.

How-to on Scalability/Load-Balancing/Fault-Tolerance with Apache JServ

> http://java.apache.org/jserv/howto.load-balancing.html

A guide to installing multiple Apache JServ servers for redundancy and load balancing.

Web Application Benchmarks

> http://www.chamas.com/bench/

Joshua Chamas' site is oriented toward comparisons of programming methodologies, rather than hardware platforms. These benchmarks are current and constantly updated.

EmbPerl: Embed Perl in Your HTML Documents

> http://perl.apache.org/embperl

This is the site for EmbPerl, a set of Perl modules that implement embedded Perl code in HTML documents.

Mason HQ

> http://www.masonhq.com/

This is the site for Mason, a set of Perl modules that implement embedded Perl code in HTML documents.

MySQL

> http://mysql.com/

The source for all things related to the MySQL open-source relational database.

Appendices

Mailing List To subscribe to the main MySQL mailing list, send a message to the e-mail address:

```
mysql-subscribe@lists.mysql.com
```

Purple Servlet FAQ and Resources by Alex Chaffee

```
http://www.jguru.com/jguru/faq/faqpage.jsp?name=Servlets
```

Hosted by JGuru (Alex Chaffee), this is a very valuable list of Frequently Asked Questions (and answers) on Java servlets.

The Server Side Includes Tutorial

```
http://www.carleton.ca/~dmcfet/html/ssi.html
```

An excellent beginner's tutorial on implementing Server Side Includes (SSI).

BigNoseBird.Com's Server Side Include Page

```
http://bignosebird.com/ssi.shtml
```

Another good guide to SSI. You might want to check out some of the other resources on the BigNoseBird site, although most are oriented toward site design rather than programming or Apache.

Webmonkey

```
http://hotwired.lycos.com/webmonkey
```

HotWired's "Web Developer's Resource," this is probably one of the hottest Web developer's sites on the Internet.

PHP Programming Resources

These sites provide information about the PHP hypertext preprocessor, discussed in Chapter 9.

PHP Hypertext Preprocessor

```
http://www.php.net
```

The official PHP page, this is where to get PHP and where to learn about it. The online documentation is some of the best I've ever seen.

PHP: Links to Code Samples and Tutorials

http://www.php.net/links.php3

A page on the PHP site that contains links to a number of other sites offering instruction and useful sample code for PHP applications.

PHP: MySQL Tutorial

http://hotwired.lycos.com/webmonkey/databases/tutorials/tutorial4.html

This is a really super tutorial that shows how to use PHP as a front-end to a MySQL relational database.

PHPBuilder.com

http://phpbuilder.com/

A good resource site for PHP developers.

Perl-CGI Programming Resources

These sites and newsgroups provide information about Perl-CGI programming, as discussed in Chapter 8.

The Perl Language Home Page

http://www.perl.com/pub

Though commercially hosted, this site proclaims itself the official page of the Perl language.

Perlmonth, Online Perl Magazine

http://www.perlmonth.com

Great articles, posted monthly, with in-depth information on programming in Perl.

Apache/Perl Integration Project

http://perl.apache.org

Naturally very oriented toward the mod_perl module, this is the official site for Perl and Apache integration.

Mailing List   To subscribe to a mailing list for mod_perl, send an e-mail message to:

modperl-request@apache.org

Appendices

CGI.pm: a Perl5 CGI Library

http://stein.cshl.org/WWW/software/CGI/cgi_docs.html

Author Lincoln Stein's official site for the CGI.pm Perl module.

FastCGI Home

http://www.fastcgi.com

The official page for FastCGI as discussed in Chapter 8.

MM MySQL JDBC Drivers

http://www.worldserver.com/mm.mysql

The MM JDBC drivers are widely considered the best Java Database Connectivity drivers for MySQL, and the ones I use.

mod_perl Guide

http://perl.apache.org/guide

Actually far more than a "Guide," this is a very complete and indispensable set of documentation to the mod_perl module.

Getting Help and Further Learning

http://perl.apache.org/guide/help.html#Contacting_me

Actually part of the mod_perl Guide, this page lists a number of good links to other sites for information on mod_perl.

SymbolStone Perl Stuff (DBI-DBD)

http://forteviot.symbolstone.org/technology/perl/index.html

The best "jumping-off" site for learning all about DBI programming for Perl.

The Apache/Perl Module List

http://perl.apache.org/src/apache-modlist.html

Lists all the Perl modules that have been written to support Apache.

The CGI Resource Index

http://cgi-resources.com

This is quite an old site, and it hosts a tremendous number of CGI samples. Most are in Perl, of course, but there are examples in C, Unix shell, and others.

The CPAN Search Site

```
http://search.cpan.org
```

The official repository of registered, supported Perl modules, with mirror sites around the world, this is the site to search for Perl modules. The modules found here are retrievable by the CPAN.pm module on Linux systems.

Perl Newsgroups

These are three of the most valuable newsgroups for discussing Perl.

```
comp.lang.perl.misc
```

Newsgroup for all things related to Perl. I've read this one faithfully for years.

```
comp.lang.perl.announce
```

Stay up-to-date on the new product announcements for Perl.

```
comp.lang.perl.module
```

Newsgroup for questions and discussions relating to Perl modules, not directly related to the Perl language itself.

Java Programming Resources

These sites provide information about programming with Java and related tools, as discussed in Chapter 9.

Configuring and Using Apache JServ

```
http://www.magiccookie.com/computers/apache-jserv
```

I've seen this article by Ari Halberstadt reproduced, in one form or another, in several places. A must-read for anyone setting up Apache JServ.

Blackdown JDK for Linux

```
http://WWW.BLackdown.org
```

The most respected port of Sun Microsystem's Java Development Kit to Linux. Get your JDK for Linux and learn how to set it up here.

JavaServer Pages Developer's Guide

```
http://java.sun.com/products/jsp/docs.html
```

A super tutorial on JavaServer Pages by the writer of the JSP specification, Sun Microsystems.

Appendices

JavaServer Pages Technology

```
http://java.sun.com/products/jsp
```

The official JSP page from Sun Microsystems. Links here to JSP information of all kinds.

JavaServer Pages Technology: White Paper

```
http://java.sun.com/products/jsp/whitepaper.html
```

Good "executive overview" or white paper on Java Server Pages, also available in Adobe PDF format.

JDBC Basics

```
http://java.sun.com/docs/books/tutorial/jdbc/basics/index.html
```

Learn the very basic skills necessary to use Java Database Connectivity (JDBC) with Java programs.

JDBC Guide: Getting Started

```
http://java.sun.com/products/jdk/1.1/docs/guide/jdbc/getstart/
introTOC.doc.html
```

A good document from Sun that provides a very comprehensive look at JDBC programming.

Servlet Central

```
http://www.servletcentral.com
```

A good site for Java servlet sources.

Servlets

```
http://java.sun.com/docs/books/tutorial/servlets/TOC.html
```

Sun Microsystem's tutorial on Java servlets. A very good learning tutorial.

java.sun.com: The Source for Java Technology

```
http://www.javasoft.com
```

This is the pinnacle for all Java-programming-related pages on Sun Microsystems' site. From here, you should be able to find just about any Java specification or implementation.

The Java Tutorial

```
http://java.sun.com/docs/books/tutorial
```

Nearly all of these online tutorials are worth working through. Most are online reprints of material available as the printed book *The Java Tutorial*, by Mary Campione and Kathy Walrath (Addison-Wesley, 1998).

Writing Java Programs

```
http://java.sun.com/tutorial/java/index.html
```

A good tutorial for those just starting out with Java programming, this site also provides a good introduction to object-oriented programming, classes, and namespaces.

Resin

```
http://www.caucho.com/
```

Caucho technology provides this site for information about Resin. To subscribe to the Resin mailing list, send mail to

```
resin-interest-request@caucho.com
```

with a body containing the one word:

```
subscribe
```

Usenet Newsgroup Archives

```
http://www.deja.com/usenet
```

Deja.com maintains Deja News, the most extensive archive of Usenet discussion groups available, making it an invaluable resource for questions that have been asked and answered on Usenet newsgroups.

Appendices

Transferring Files
to Apache

This book is devoted to the Apache Web server on Linux. For that reason, very little has been said about the client side of any Web connection, the browser component. Although the use of Web browsers running in Linux desktop environments is rapidly increasing, the majority of Web browsers in use on the Internet are run on Windows-based PCs. The same is true of most Web application development and HTML editing systems; most are Windows products, and there are a surprising variety of them. I still use a couple of the older and more established HTML editing systems (HotDog and SoftQuad's HoTMetaL Pro).

The traditional Webmaster's role usually included a healthy amount of time spent creating Web pages. As the Internet becomes increasingly important in supporting business processes (especially in the areas of marketing, sales, and customer support), however, the tasks of site administration and page authoring are often separated. As an Apache administrator, you may have little need to know how to use HTML. For that reason, I've devoted little space to issues involving Web site authoring.

As an Apache administrator, even if you are only hosting pages composed by others, you need to provide some means by which the documents Apache delivers can be uploaded or moved to your Apache server. This is most commonly done using the ubiquitous File Transfer Protocol (FTP), and many Web authoring tools have strong built-in support for FTP. Most readers will already be aware of FTP, but I will mention a strong FTP client utility that I've used for years and recommend to anyone who needs such a tool. Most of this appendix is devoted to two Apache "add-ons" that support client file uploading (or *publishing*, if you prefer the term), mod_put and the FrontPage Extensions for Linux.

Using Samba

On a local area network, the easiest way to transfer files from a Windows-based Web authoring tool is to export directories using Samba, a suite of programs that is installed as an integral part of all major Linux distributions. Samba enables a Linux server to communicate with Windows systems (which must be running TCP/IP) using the Microsoft Server Message Block (SMB) networking protocol. In other words, Samba allows Linux to participate in a Windows network, as a file/print server or client. It even allows you to use the Microsoft user authentication schemes (MS-CHAP and NT domain authentication).

A complete description of Samba configuration is beyond the scope of this appendix. For more information on Samba I recommend reading David Wood's *SMB HOWTO*, available from the Linux Documentation Project (www.linuxdoc.org) or the book *Samba: Integrating UNIX and Windows* by John Blair, Specialized Systems Consultants, July 1999.

I will demonstrate how I shared my Apache DocumentRoot using Samba on my Linux server for access by Windows 98 and NT workstations on my local area network.

The first step is to create a password file for Samba. While it is possible to use Unix authentication with Windows 95 workstations, this will generally not work with Windows 2000 systems or NT systems that have recent service packs installed. These do *not* attempt to authenticate users across a network with a plain-text password (the older LAN Manager style of user authentication used by Windows 95). I included the following statements in the smb.conf file:

```
encrypt passwords = yes
smb passwd file = /etc/smbpasswd
```

To create the initial smbpasswd file, it is easiest (particularly if you have a large number of accounts to manage) to use the mksmbpasswd.sh utility provided with Samba. In the following command line, mksmbpasswd.sh takes the Linux /etc/passwd file as input, and the output is redirected into a new file, /etc/smbpasswd:

```
# /usr/bin/mksmbpasswd.sh < /etc/passwd > /etc/smbpasswd
```

Then, after creating the password file, I assigned a new password to each authorized user, beginning with myself:

```
# smbpasswd caulds newpass
Password changed for user caulds.
```

I added the following section to the smb.conf file to export my Apache DocumentRoot directory (which will be seen by Windows systems on the network as a share named WebStuff). Access is limited by setting public to no, which indicates that access to the file share will be granted only to the users on the valid users line. Both of these users must have a valid /etc/smbpasswd line. They both have write access to the share (writeable = yes).

```
[WebStuff]
comment = Apache DocumentRoot
path = /home/httpd/html
valid users = caulds csewell
public = no
writable = yes
```

Once I had Samba configured, the WebStuff folder on my Linux server was fully accessible from my NT workstation, as you can see in the view from Explorer illustrated in Figure C.1.

Figure C.1   Using Explorer to Access a Samba Share

Using FTP

The best way to upload files to a Linux server from a remote host is using the File Transfer Protocol (FTP). FTP is supported by nearly every Linux server, and many client application options exist, from simple command-line tools to sophisticated GUI tools that allow easy drag-and-drop or mark-and-copy capability. The ability to copy an entire directory tree with one operation makes publishing Web resources via FTP far easier than you may realize (especially if you have only used the command-line version).

While tools like Netscape Composer and FrontPage 2000 seek to simplify Web publishing directly from the authoring tool itself, they alleviate only a small part of the work required to develop and publish Web pages. These are fine tools, but a good FTP client is something every Web developer and administrator should possess.

Several years ago, it seemed that the trend in file-transfer utilities on PCs was to merge them with the Windows Explorer so that files could be moved to remote servers with Explorer drag-and-drop operations. While I applaud the developers' efforts to present the user with a single unified interface to file management, trying to deal with a number of files in different physical locations through a single hierarchical tree structure is inefficient and often confusing. I've often dropped files into the wrong location because it had the same folder and filenames as another drive. Fortunately, most FTP clients still support the two-pane window, where local and remote files are clearly differentiated. I highly recommend a shareware utility called WS_FTP (available from www.ipswitch.com), which I've used since I first began administering a Web server in 1994. Figure C.2 shows a typical WS_FTP session in which I'm about to transfer a whole tree of files from my local hard disk to my Apache server.

Using the `mod_put` Module

Another tool for file transfer takes advantage of the HTTP request method PUT, which was specified as optional in HTTP/1.0 but is standardized in HTTP/1.1. Clients use PUT to send a resource (usually a local disk file) to the server, by specifying a URL that identifies a location where the server should place the resource. In other words, PUT allows client uploading of files. While the POST method in HTTP/1.0 permitted clients to send resources, these were sent in a stream to the server. A server application (usually a CGI file that received the stream on its stdin file handle) had to parse this stream into its components, whether it consisted of form input or entire files. PUT is designed specifically for file uploads. It allows the HTTP client to say to the server, "Here's a file; store it in /home/caulds/stuff/MyLogo.jpg."

Figure C.2 Using WS_FTP to upload Web files

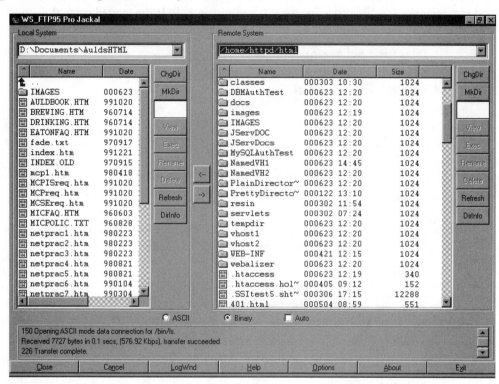

A small third-party module called mod_put implements both the HTTP/1.1 PUT and DELETE methods in Apache. Standard Apache, without this module, does not support those HTTP/1.1 methods. Although mod_put isn't a new module, it has never been one of the modules accepted as part of the standard Apache distribution. I believe this is because allowing Web clients to upload files to your server can be very risky, unless the administrator has given special attention to system security by allowing uploads only into directories designated for that purpose.

The mod_put module has been included with Red Hat's Apache distribution (it's installed by the Apache RPM on the Red Hat Linux distribution CD) and is loaded as a DSO module by Apache on Red Hat Linux systems.

If you're using a different Linux distribution, you can download mod_put from its author's site at www.ec-lyon.fr/~vincent/apache/mod_put.html or find a link to a source at

Appendices

`modules.apache.org`. The module is packaged a `.gz` archive (`mod_put.tar.gz`), which contains the C source code for the module and an HTML-formatted page of documentation. Download the file into any directory and extract its contents:

```
# ls -al mod_put_tar.gz
-rw-r--r--   1 caulds    caulds         5021 Jun 22 10:02 mod_put_tar.gz
# tar xvzf mod_put_tar.gz
mod_put-1.3/
mod_put-1.3/mod_put.html
mod_put-1.3/mod_put.c
```

Change into the newly created source directory for the module:

```
# cd mod_put-1.3
```

The archive actually contains only two files, the `.c` source file (which is the only necessary component) and a single HTML-formatted page of documentation:

```
# ls -al
total 18
drwx------  2 20       gopher 1024 May 11  1999 .
drwxr-xr-x 37 caulds   root   4096 Jun 22 10:03 ..
-rw-------  1 20       gopher 6892 May 11  1999 mod_put.c
-rw-------  1 20       gopher 5455 May 11  1999 mod_put.html
```

Installation of `mod_put`, including the necessary modifications to the `httpd.conf` file, is a simple single-step operation using the `apxs` utility. The following command line will compile the module as a DSO, place it into the `libexec` directory under the Apache installation, and make the necessary modifications to Apache's `httpd.conf` file to load and enable the module when the server is started:

```
# /usr/local/apache/bin/apxs -c -i -a mod_put.c
gcc -DLINUX=2 -DMOD_SSL=206104 -DUSE_HSREGEX -DEAPI -DUSE_EXPAT -I../lib/expat-l
ite -DUSE_RANDOM_SSI -DUSE_PARSE_FORM -fpic -DSHARED_MODULE -I/usr/local/apachel
_3_12/include  -c mod_put.c
gcc -shared -o mod_put.so mod_put.o
cp mod_put.so /usr/local/apache1_3_12/libexec/mod_put.so
chmod 755 /usr/local/apache1_3_12/libexec/mod_put.so
[activating module `put' in
```

```
/usr/local/apache1_3_12/conf/httpd.conf]
[root@jackal mod_put-1.3]# grep mod_put
/usr/local/apache1_3_12/conf/httpd.conf
LoadModule put_module          libexec/mod_put.so
AddModule mod_put.c
```

The most important mod_put directives, EnablePut and EnableDelete, enable or disable the HTTP/1.1 PUT and DELETE request methods for a single directory or for all resources accessed with a specific request URL. While mod_put directives are valid in <Directory> and <Location> containers, I find that it is always best to combine these directives with a user authentication and authorization scheme in .htaccess files. This ensures that only authorized users can use these methods to upload files into the affected directory or delete files from it.

WARNING Always ensure that write access to files using mod_put is limited to trusted users and the module is enabled only for specific directories that you keep a close eye on.

For example, the following .htaccess file uses basic file-based authentication to permit only two users (caulds and csewell) to upload files into my personal home directory (as described in Chapter 4), and also to prohibit both users from using the HTTP/1.1 DELETE method to remove files from it:

```
# /home/caulds/public_html/.htaccess
#
EnablePut On
EnableDelete Off
AuthType Basic
AuthName "CAulds personal Web"
AuthUserFile /usr/local/apache/auth/userfile
require user caulds csewell
```

mod_put provides one additional directive, umask. This directive is used like its Linux counterpart to set the new-file creation bitmask (expressed in octal). This bitmask is used to determine the file access permissions assigned to all new files created by mod_put. The default value of 0007 sets the permissions on newly created files to 770, which means that the file owner and group have read, write, and execute or full access and all others have no access. If I change the default bitmask, I usually include the following directive in my .htaccess file:

umask 0027

A file created with this umask in effect will have permissions set to 740 (or read/write/execute access for the file owner, read-only access for group members, and no access for all others). If you don't want to do the octal math yourself, Table C.1 is provided as a helpful aid in determining the bitmask value for each possible combination of access permissions. For example, the octal value of the bitmask used to grant read-only privileges is 3 (in octal); your umask command would contain a 3 in the second position to grant read-only access to the file owner, in the third position for the group, and in the last position for all users. A umask command that will cause new files to be created with full access assigned to the owner, read and execute for the group owner, and read-only access to all other users would look like this:

umask 0023

Table C.1   Numeric umask File Modes

	0	1	2	3	4	5	6	7
Read access	X	X	X	X				
Write access	X	X			X	X		
Execute access	X		X		X		X	

While mod_put can be used to upload files from any client application that can submit an HTTP/1.1 PUT command (usually a Web page in a browser), one of the most common uses of this module is to support the Composer component of Netscape Communicator. Although Netscape Composer is not the most full-featured Web authoring system available, I've been impressed with its ease of use and convenience. It's great for those with relatively light demands for HTML composition. Figure C.3 shows a typical use of Netscape Composer. Here I've opened an HTML page from my server in Composer (which also downloads all supporting files like embedded images). I used the Composer editor to modify the page and then used the Publish option to place it back on the server.

Figure C.3 Netscape Composer using the functionality provided by mod_put

FrontPage 2000 Extensions

FrontPage 2000 is, of course, Microsoft's HTML authoring application. If you don't already need to support Web developers working with it, you may soon. Included in the FrontPage CD is a suite of programs called the FrontPage Extensions for Unix, which makes it easy for users of Microsoft's FrontPage Web-authoring application to publish Web pages to an Apache server and manage the pages already there. Users of FrontPage access FrontPage webs (a "web" in FrontPage is essentially a collection of pages that functions as a single Web site and is equivalent to a virtual host or user directory on an Apache server) by URL. To access and manage the root FrontPage web on my server (which corresponds to my Apache DocumentRoot), you would enter the URL http:// jackal.hiwaay.net/ as the "location" of the published web. FrontPage webs, therefore, are already valid directories, virtual hosts, or user directories on the Apache server.

Installing the FrontPage Extensions

The first step is to download and install the FrontPage Extensions for Unix (the Linux version, of course). Keep in mind that, at this point, you are installing a Linux application that has nothing to do with Apache. In the "Patching Apache" section later in the chapter, I'll show how Apache can be modified (or *patched*) to support the creation of user webs directly from FrontPage 2000.

From either the Ready-to-Run Software or Microsoft site, make sure you download two files. The first is the installation script (`fp_install.sh`), which is used to install the second file, the FrontPage Extensions themselves. The version of this file for Linux is named `fp40.linux.tar.Z` if you download it from Microsoft or `fp40.linux.tar.gz` if you get it from `www.rtr.com`. The files are identical when uncompressed. Do not download a file named `change_server.sh`. This is a script to install a patched version of Apache's `httpd` daemon. You do not want to do this, because it will replace the Apache daemon that you custom configured and installed with a generic Apache `httpd` program of its own. Rather than install a prepatched binary, we'll patch our own Apache source and recompile Apache. The necessary patch is included as part of the FrontPage Extension distribution.

Place these two files somewhere on your Linux file system. The first step is to uncompress the FrontPage Extension archive. If you downloaded the Microsoft `.Z` archive, use:

```
# gunzip fp40.linux.tar.Z
```

If you downloaded Ready-to-Run Software's `.gz` archive, use this:

```
# gunzip fp40.linux.tar.gz
```

The `gunzip` utility can decompress either archive format and will leave you with a single file named `fp40.linux.tar`, which the installation script will expect to find in the current working directory. Now run `ft_install.sh`:

```
# ./fp_install.sh
```

The first prompt as the script runs is this:

```
Are you satisfied with your backup of the system (y/n) [N]?
```

If you have a current backup of Apache's configuration file (`httpd.conf`), answer this question Y; otherwise, simply hit Return and back up `httpd.conf` before starting again.

Next you'll see this prompt:

```
FrontPage Extensions directory [/usr/local/frontpage/]:
```

Always press Return at this prompt to install the extensions in /usr/local/frontpage; although it is possible to install them elsewhere, they must be accessible through that path (either directly or through a symbolic link). Unless you have a very strong reason for installing them elsewhere, put them in this, their proper place.

The script creates the necessary directories and expands the tar file there. It then asks:

```
Do you want to install a root web (y/n) [Y]?
```

You should always answer Y to this prompt, to create the root FrontPage web, which should match the DocumentRoot setting of your Apache server. (Remember that a "web" in FrontPage is a collection of pages that function as a single Web site and must correspond to a URL that is valid on the Apache server.) Since you may have multiple Apache servers, the next prompt asks you which configuration file describes the server you want to use with FrontPage:

```
Server config filename: /usr/local/apache/conf/httpd.conf
```

Enter the full path and filename of the httpd.conf file for your server.

You'll then be prompted for the FrontPage administrator's username:

```
FrontPage Administrator's user name:  www
```

Enter a name that is used by FrontPage clients to publish content to your Web server. This does *not* have to be the same as a Linux username, and I recommend avoiding duplicating a Linux user account.

The next prompts allow you to specify the account and group names under which Apache runs:

```
Unix user name of the owner of this new web:[nobody]
Unix group of this new web:[nobody]
```

If the default values of nobody apply to your server, simply press Return. If you are using an alternate account and/or group, provide these names.

You will then be prompted to identify the type of server:

```
    1.  ncsa
    2.  apache
    3.  apache-fp
    4.  netscape-fasttrack
    5.  netscape-enterprise
    6.  stronghold
What type of Server is this:  2
```

Always enter 2-apache for this prompt. Do *not* select 3-apache-fp. That option is for servers that are running a prepatched binary version of Apache that includes the FrontPage Extensions. While that binary works fine, it cannot be altered (by recompiling the Apache source). Instead of the **apache-fp** binary that is packaged with FrontPage, we will be using our own version of Apache, patching it ourselves to support the FrontPage Extensions, if we desire. You'll then be prompted for a password:

```
Password for user "www":
Confirm password:
```

Enter a password that matches the FrontPage Administrator's user name. Avoid using the password of a regular Linux user account. At this point, you should theoretically be finished:

```
Creating web http://jackal.hiwaay.net
Chowning Content in service root web
Chmoding Extensions in service root web
Install completed.
```

If you see those lines, congratulations. Your installation has succeeded. To install a FrontPage web successfully, however, the script needs to be able to edit all .htaccess files in all the directory trees beneath the document root. It is smart enough to recognize existing .htaccess files and will not touch them. If you have .htaccess files beneath the root FrontPage web you are trying to create (to protect the contents of subdirectories of the DocumentRoot), you'll see a message like this:

```
The access control file "/home/httpd/html/DBMAuthTest/.htaccess" was not created
by this client program and cannot be edited safely using this client program.
ERROR:  / installation failed.
Hit enter to continue

Exiting due to an error!  Please fix the error and try again.
```

If this occurs, you need to temporarily rename all existing .htaccess files in the root FrontPage web and restart the installation. Once it is successfully installed, you'll accept a couple of defaults.

```
1.   LATIN1 (ISO 8859-1)
2.   LATIN2 (ISO 8859-2)
3.   EUCJP  (Japanese EUC)
4.   EUCKR  (Korean EUC)
Which local character encoding does your system support: [1]
```

Most of us will accept Latin 1, which is the default character encoding Apache uses for all documents of content type `text/html`. Then select one of the language defaults here:

```
1.  English
2.  French
3.  German
4.  Italian
5.  Japanese
6.  Spanish
What should the default language be: [1]


Install new sub/per-user webs now (y/n) [Y]?  N
```

At this point, always answer N. In the last section, I'll show how to set up sub and per-user FrontPage webs, using the provided `fpsrvadm.exe` utility. You should learn to use this utility, since it is quite easy to write scripts to automate the use of the utility.

```
Installing Virtual Webs..
Do you want to install Virtual Webs (y/n) [Y]?  N
```

Again, answer N to this prompt. I'll show how to use `fpsrvadm.exe` to install virtual FrontPage webs (that is, FrontPage webs that match name- or IP-based virtual hosts defined for your server).

```
Installation completed!  Exiting...
```

That's what you wanted to see.

Adding FrontPage Webs

At this point, we have installed the FrontPage Extensions only for the root FrontPage web of our server (which maps to the location defined by Apache's `DocumentRoot` directive). In many cases, this is wholly sufficient. There are also two types of FrontPage web that serve files outside the scope of the root FrontPage web: any virtual hosts we have defined (either name- or IP-based), and user directories (accessed using a URL ending in ~username). These were discussed in Chapter 6, and they should be created on your server as outlined in that chapter before you attempt to create a FrontPage web for each of them. The creation of a FrontPage web only allows a FrontPage user to manage a virtual host or user directory that Apache already knows about.

A command-line utility called `fpsrvadm.exe` is provided with the FrontPage Extensions to create additional FrontPage webs. I'll demonstrate how it is used to create both virtual and subwebs in this section. The documentation for the utility is a bit difficult to locate, but you'll find it on the FrontPage 2000 Server Extensions Resource Kit Web site at officeupdate.microsoft.com/frontpage/wpp/serk/adfpsr.htm

If you patch your Apache server as discussed in the "Patching Apache" section below, it is possible for users to create their own subwebs using the FrontPage client application. Keep in mind that, even though fpsvradm.exe can always be used to do this if, for example, you'd prefer not to let users create their own subwebs.

Virtual Webs

For each virtual FrontPage web on your server for which you intend to support web publishing from FrontPage, you need to run fpsvradm.exe using the following syntax:

```
fpsrvadm.exe -o install -p 80 -m virtualWeb -u AdminName -pw AdminPassword
-t server_type -s httpd.conf  -xu UNIXUserName -xg UNIXGroupName
```

Where:

-o is the operation to be performed; use -o install to install a new FrontPage web for a virtual server.

-p gives the port number of the web.

-m is the domain name of the new virtual server.

-u is the username of the FrontPage web's administrator. This administrator can add authors using the FrontPage client.

-pw is the password of the FrontPage web's administrator.

-t is the server type. Use apache-fp if you've patched your Apache server to support FrontPage Extensions, or apache for an unpatched server.

-s specifies the full path to the server's configuration file.

-xu is the Linux user account that the FrontPage Server Extensions will use; files published by FrontPage will be given this account owner.

-xg is the Linux group account that the FrontPage Server Extensions will use; files published by FrontPage will be given this group account owner.

Here's the command I used to install FrontPage Extensions for a name-based virtual host on my system:

```
# fpsrvadm.exe -o install -t apache-fp -m vhost1.hiwaay.net -u caulds -pw
mysecret -s "/usr/local/apache/conf/httpd.conf" -xu nobody -xg nobody
Starting install, port: vhost1.hiwaay.net:80, web: "root web"

Creating web http://vhost1.hiwaay.net
Chowning Content in service root web
Chmoding Extensions in service root web
Install completed.
```

Adding Sub/User Webs

You use fpsvradm.exe to create a subweb or user web at a specified directory within an existing FrontPage web. Note that, instead of specifying the –o install command, this form of the command uses –o create. The syntax is:

```
fpsrvadm.exe -o create -p 80 -Web subwebname -xu unixuser -xg unixgroup -u
username -pw password
```

Where:

-o is the operation to be performed by fpsvradm.exe; use create to create a new subweb or user web.

-p 80 is the port number of the new subweb.

-xu is your Linux user account (which must exist in /etc/passwd).

-xg is your Linux group account (which must exist in /etc/groups).

-username is the FrontPage user ID (which does not need to match a Linux account).

-password is the FrontPage user password.

-t is the type of apache server (apache or apache-fp).

-s is the path to your httpd.conf file.

Here's an example of the command line I used to install a FrontPage subweb matching my user account:

```
# fpsrvadm.exe -o install -p 80 -w "~caulds" -xu "caulds" -xg "mypass" -u
"CharlesA" -p w "FPpasswd"
Starting create, port: 80, web: "~caulds"

Creating web http://jackal.hiwaay.net/~caulds
Chowning Content in service ~caulds
Chmoding Extensions in service /~caulds
Install completed.
```

Remember that, if your Apache has been patched as described in the next section, FrontPage users can create their own subwebs using the FrontPage client. If this fails to work, or if you choose not to patch your server to support this function, you can always use fpsrvadm.exe to create new user webs.

Patching Apache

The FrontPage Extensions package includes an optional patch for Apache that allows users of the FrontPage client to create FrontPage subwebs on the server. This patch essentially

Appendices

allows the FrontPage client to modify the Apache server configuration, something that Apache's normal security provisions would prohibit. Remember that the FrontPage Extensions do *not* require a patched Apache server, but on such servers, the only way to create new subwebs is with the `fpsrvadm.exe` utility as described above.

The instructions that follow are for the Apache server patch that is provided with the FrontPage Extensions. This patch has never worked with suEXEC, which is now a standard part of Apache. An alternative to this Apache patch is the `mod_frontpage` module, available from `ftp.vr.net/pub/apache`. It is supposed to be a full replacement for the FrontPage Extensions patch, offering better performance and a promise that it works with suEXEC. I have not tried this alternative patch, which was not available for Apache 1.3.12 at the time of writing. Note that this alternative patch is *not* a replacement for the FrontPage Server Extensions, which must be installed on your Apache server prior to applying the patch.

After installing the FrontPage Server Extensions, you'll find the Apache server patch on your Apache server as:

```
/usr/local/frontpage/version4.0/apache-fp/fp-patch-apache_1.3.12
```

Note that the downloadable version of the FrontPage Server Extensions includes a patch for the latest production release of Apache. If you aren't running this version of Apache, you will need to obtain an older version of the alternative patch from `ftp.vr.net`.

Copy this file into your Apache source directory, and make sure that this directory is the current working directory before proceeding:

```
# pwd
/usr/local/apache1_3_12
# cp /usr/local/frontpage/version4.0/apache-fp/fp-pat
ch-apache_1.3.12 .
```

Apply the patch as follows:

```
# patch -p0 < fp-patch-apache_1.3.12
patching file `./src/include/httpd.h'
Hunk #1 succeeded at 825 (offset 33 lines).
patching file `./src/main/util.c'
patching file `./src/main/http_request.c'
patching file `./mod_frontpage.c'
```

TIP To reverse all the changes made by applying a Linux source patch, add the -R argument to the same command line used to apply the patch. To remove the Apache FrontPage patch, for example, use **patch -p0 -R < fp-patch-apache_1.3.12**

Note that the patch makes modifications to two Apache source files (util.c and http_request.c) and actually creates a new module source file (mod_frontpage.c) in the Apache source directory, rather than in the standard location src/modules.

Run the configure utility, adding the line --add-module=frontpage.c. I did this by adding that line to my build.sh script, and then running that script:

```
# cat build.sh
SSL_BASE="/usr/local/src/openssl-0.9.5a" \
CFLAGS="-DUSE_RANDOM_SSI -DUSE_PARSE_FORM" \
./configure \
"--enable-rule=EAPI" \
"--with-layout=Apache" \
"--prefix=/usr/local/apache1_3_12" \
"--enable-module=most" \
"--enable-module=ssl" \
"--enable-shared=max" \
"--activate-module=src/modules/perl/libperl.a" \
"--add-module=frontpage.c" \
"$@"
# ./configure
-- Output not shown --
```

Run make to compile the patched server, and make install to install it:

```
# make
# make install
-- Output not shown --
```

That's it. After restarting the now-patched server, you'll find that you can now connect to the server with a FrontPage 2000 client and create new user FrontPage webs.

Appendices

Information about FrontPage Extensions

The FrontPage Extensions for Unix are developed for Microsoft by a company called Ready-to-Run Software (`www.rtr.com`) and are available from RtR's Web site or directly from Microsoft (`msdn.microsoft.com/workshop/languages/fp/2000/unixfpse.asp`).

Both sites contain a lot of good documentation. Most of the documentation I used to install and set up FrontPage on my Apache server was linked from Microsoft's FrontPage Server Extensions Resource Kit page (`officeupdate.microsoft.com/frontpage/wpp/serk`), but RtR's Web site contains a "must-see" FAQ and a discussion group that has answers and solutions to a large number of questions and problems. See `www.rtr.com/fpsupport/documentation.htm` for both of these online resources. Another source for information on the FrontPage Extensions is the Usenet newsgroup `microsoft.public.frontpage.extensions.unix`.

Using Apache Documentation Effectively

Because of the decentralized, modular approach by which it has been developed and extended, Apache is the work of a large number of developers, scattered all over the globe. It should come as no surprise, then, that the documentation for Apache is not all located in any one place but is also scattered across the Internet. In fact, many of the core developers of the Apache Software Foundation have provided valuable documentation on the use of their respective parts of Apache as articles you can find on the excellent Webzines like *Apache Today* and *Apache Week* (see Appendix B).

Many of the third-party add-on modules to Apache are documented by README files and HTML pages provided with the source files. Look for these whenever you download and install a new module that is not one of the Apache standard modules. The Web sites for these modules usually include good documentation, often supplemented with tutorials, FAQ lists, and online discussion forums. Always visit these sites when you install a new module and familiarize yourself with what's available there, especially if the module is extensive (like mod_ssl, for example).

Apache is documented very well (if not extensively), according to the loosely standardized documentation format used by the Apache Software Foundation. The Apache documentation is always available online at www.apache.org/docs. This same set of documentation (without the search features) is also provided with the source distribution of Apache.

Figure D.1 shows the main documentation page (also known as the *Apache 1.3 User's Guide*).

Figure D.1   Apache 1.3 online user's guide

From this page, you can directly access the two most important pages used to document the Apache server and the standard Apache modules distributed with it. These are accessed through the links "Run-time configuration directives" (Figure D.2) and "Modules" (Figure D.3). These pages are actually different indexes into the documentation pages for the Apache modules. Each Apache module is documented through a single Web page that provides examples and syntax for each directive supplied to Apache by the module.

Figure D.2   Documentation for Apache directives

Figure D.3   Documentation for Apache standard modules

Since either of the links mentioned leads directly to the documentation page for selected modules (or to the directive within that page, if you choose), the documentation pages are the same for both the modules and the Apache runtime directives used to control them. I'll describe a typical documentation page to help you understand the documentation for both Apache modules and directives.

Figure D.4 shows the documentation for the UseCanonicalName directive, part of the Core module and an integral part of the Apache server. Each page includes the following information:

> **Syntax**   Shows the format of the directive, as it should appear in the Apache configuration file. In the UseCanonicalName directive, you can see that the directive is used with one of three keywords (on, off, or DNS) appearing immediately behind it.

Figure D.4   Documentation for UseCanonicalName

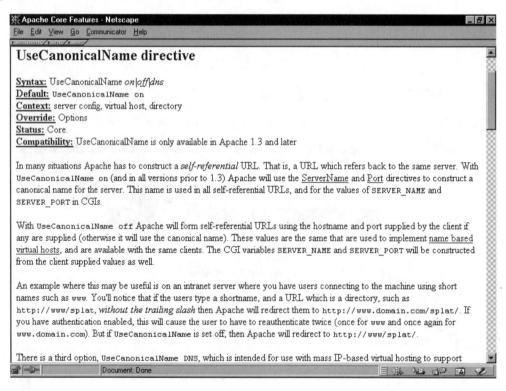

Default   Indicates default values for directives. If no default value for a directive has been defined, the value should be indicated as None. Otherwise, the default value is usually shown as a complete and valid use of the entire directive in an `httpd.conf` file. You will find that some of these defaults are actually placed in Apache's default `httpd.conf` file, even though their inclusion is unnecessary. This is done for clarity, so that the default behavior is made obvious and explicit. Default values are very important—possibly the most important thing to know about most directives—because they determine the behavior of Apache if the directive is omitted from the server configuration. In that sense, the behavior of an unmodified Apache server is almost completely defined by the default values of its core directives and of the directives supplied by all its active modules.

Context   Indicates the scope in which a directory is valid. The value can be any one (or more) of the following:

server config   The directive applies to the entire server configuration, but it may not appear in narrower scopes (such as a <VirtualHost> or <Directory> container). Most directives that are valid in the server config context are also valid in these containers, but this must be explicitly stated. A directive that operates only in the server config context (a good example is the Listen directive) must not appear in any other context.

virtual host   The directive may appear inside a <VirtualHost> container.

directory   The directive may appear inside <Directory>, <Files>, and <Location> containers.

.htaccess   The directive is valid when it appears inside an .htaccess file and has a per-directory scope.

Override   Indicates which configuration overrides must be in effect for the directive to be processed if it is found inside an .htaccess file. Unless the controlling override for a directive has been explicitly activated for a directory (by an AllowOverride directive set for that directory or one of its parent directories), the directive is ignored if found in an .htaccess file in that directory. For example, the controlling override for all directives supplied by authentication modules is AuthConfig. Unless the AuthConfig override has been activated for a directory, directives used to implement authentication schemes (for example, Require, AuthName, and AuthGroupFile) are ignored if found in an .htaccess file for that directory. The Override column in Appendix A indicates which overrides must be in effect before a directive can be used in an .htaccess context.

Appendices

Status   Specifies one of the following four values to indicate the degree to which the directive is integrated into the Apache server:

Core   The directive is a part of the Apache core and cannot be removed or disabled; it is always available for use.

Base   The directive is supplied by one of the standard Apache modules and is part of the base distribution. The module that supplies the directive is compiled into the standard Apache product; however, its use is optional and it can be removed.

Extension   The directive is supplied by one of the standard Apache modules and is part of the base distribution. The module that supplies the directive is not compiled into the standard Apache product, however; and it must be explicitly compiled and enabled before the directive can be used.

Experimental   Indicates that the directive is being supplied as part of a module that is not necessarily supported by the Apache development team. In other words, this is a directive to use at your own risk.

Module   Names the module that supplies the directive.

Compatibility   Contains information about which Apache versions support the directive. The `UseCanonicalName` directive shown in Figure D.4 above, for example, is only supplied with Apache versions 1.3 and higher. In other words, in the unlikely event that you are using Apache version 1.2.x, this directive is not available to you.

When Apache is installed, as part of the installation, it places a copy of the complete documentation for the installed Apache version under the directory defined by the `DocumentRoot` directive in the default `httpd.conf` file. This documentation is available from the default home page for the new server (Figure D.5).

The documentation pages are most quickly and conveniently accessed when they are maintained on your own server. If you modify the location of your Apache `DocumentRoot` directory (as I recommended in Chapter 3), this documentation will probably no longer be readable from a Web browser. To make the Apache documentation accessible from the new Web server, you can copy it to your new `DocumentRoot` directory (or create a symbolic link to it), but I find it more convenient to simply provide an alias to the documentation file. The following `Alias` directive will accomplish that:

```
Alias /ApacheDocs "/usr/local/apache/htdocs/manual"
```

Now, the docs can be accessed with the following URL:

```
http://jackal.hiwaay.net/ApacheDocs
```

Figure D.5   The default home page for a newly installed Apache server includes a link to the documentation.

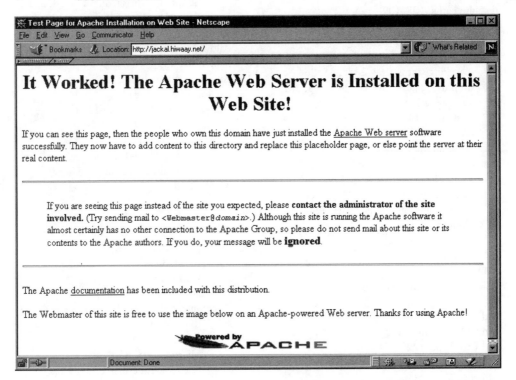

While the documentation pages provided with Apache are complete, viewing them from your own server (while convenient) is limited in two ways. First, the documentation will not be updated until you install a newer version of Apache, and second, you will not have the search capability of the Apache Web site (although you will have a link to the main Apache site for searches). For quick lookups of directive usage, though, you'll save time by referencing the documentation on your server. Consider creating a hyperlink to it on your home page.

Index

Note to reader: **Bold** page references indicate definitions. *Italicized* page references indicate illustrations.

Index

Praise for Craig Hunt

Readers and reviewers praise Craig Hunt's *Linux Network Servers 24seven* (Sybex, 1999):

> If I had to pick a reference book for a new Linux administrator or to have as a reference guide to Linux administration in the office, this would be it.
>
> *Alan Cox,* www.linux.org.uk

> *Linux Network Servers: 24 Seven* does an outstanding job of explaining how to turn a machine running Linux 2.2 …into a reliable, high-performance provider of network services. This book will help you build a fire-and-forget network server on the Linux platform.
>
> *Amazon.com Reader*

> To master Linux networking you have to understand how to use and configure a surprisingly large number of applications. Fortunately, Craig Hunt knows his subject. This is a valuable read …
>
> *Amazon.co.uk Reader*

> Free time is the one thing I don't have. That's why I love this book. It has the answers and they are easy to find. Everything about a Linux network server is in this book put together in a well-organized way without any unnecessary garbage. The book is also well indexed, which I think is important. People who say all books are a waste are full of it. I love books and this is a great one!
>
> *Amazon.com Reader*

> Researching the book I found that no less of an authority than Alan Cox, the guy that Linux Journal called "the Linux community's very own Mr. Wizard," said it was the system administration reference he would recommend. After all that, I had to give the book a try. I'm glad I did. This book has the details about everything I needed to get a Linux network server running.
>
> *Amazon.com Reader*

> I have several books on Linux but I found this one the most useful. It is so clearly written that it could make a beginner become an expert after finishing the whole book! Now, I placed it near my Linux server for my daily reference.
>
> *Amazon.com Reader*